HISTORICAL DICTIONARY

The historical dictionaries present essential information on a broad range of subjects, including American and world history, art, business, cities, countries, cultures, customs, film, global conflicts, international relations, literature, music, philosophy, religion, sports, and theater. Written by experts, all contain highly informative introductory essays of the topic and detailed chronologies that, in some cases, cover vast historical time periods but still manage to heavily feature more recent events.

Brief A–Z entries describe the main people, events, politics, social issues, institutions, and policies that make the topic unique, and entries are cross-referenced for ease of browsing. Extensive bibliographies are divided into several general subject areas, providing excellent access points for students, researchers, and anyone wanting to know more. Additionally, maps, photographs, and appendixes of supplemental information aid high school and college students doing term papers or introductory research projects. In short, the historical dictionaries are the perfect starting point for anyone looking to research in these fields.

HISTORICAL DICTIONARIES OF SPORTS
Jon Woronoff, Series Editor

Competitive Swimming, by John Lohn, 2010.
Basketball, by John Grasso, 2011.
Golf, by Bill Mallon and Randon Jerris, 2011.
Figure Skating, by James R. Hines, 2011.
The Olympic Movement, Fourth Edition, by Bill Mallon and Jeroen Heijmans, 2011.
Tennis, by John Grasso, 2011.

Historical Dictionary of Tennis

John Grasso

The Scarecrow Press, Inc.
Lanham • Toronto • Plymouth, UK
2011

Published by Scarecrow Press, Inc.
A wholly owned subsidiary of The Rowman & Littlefield Publishing Group, Inc.
4501 Forbes Boulevard, Suite 200, Lanham, Maryland 20706
http://www.scarecrowpress.com

Estover Road, Plymouth PL6 7PY, United Kingdom

Copyright © 2011 by John Grasso

All rights reserved. No part of this book may be reproduced in any form or by any electronic or mechanical means, including information storage and retrieval systems, without written permission from the publisher, except by a reviewer who may quote passages in a review.

British Library Cataloguing in Publication Information Available

Library of Congress Cataloging-in-Publication Data

Grasso, John.
  Historical dictionary of tennis / John Grasso.
    p. cm. — (Historical dictionaries of sports)
  Includes bibliographical references.
  ISBN 978-0-8108-7237-0 (cloth : alk. paper) — ISBN 978-0-8108-7490-9 (ebook)
  1. Tennis—History—Dictionaries. I. Title.
  GV990.G73 2011
  796.342—dc22
                                                              2011009577

∞™ The paper used in this publication meets the minimum requirements of American National Standard for Information Sciences—Permanence of Paper for Printed Library Materials, ANSI/NISO Z39.48-1992.

Printed in the United States of America

Contents

Editor's Foreword *Jon Woronoff*	vii
Preface	ix
Acronyms and Abbreviations	xi
Chronology	xv
Introduction	1
THE DICTIONARY	19
Appendixes	
A. International Tennis Hall of Fame Inductees	319
B. Wimbledon Champions	325
C. United States National/Open Champions	337
D. French National/Open Champions	351
E. Australian Championships/Open Champions	361
F. Davis Cup Champions	371
G. Wightman Cup Champions	375
H. Federation Cup Champions	377
I. Olympic Games Champions	379
Bibliography	391
About the Author	419

Editor's Foreword

Tennis has become one of the most popular sports around the world, to judge by the numbers of people playing it and also the sizes of audiences watching it on television. Yet, for the longest time, it was relatively marginal in the world of sports. That was partly due to a mindset that found it perhaps less sporting than other sports and partly because of disadvantages inflicted on it by purists, making it more complicated and inaccessible than necessary, and by the sports associations that were again more purist than in other fields and insisted that it remain an "amateur" sport when everything militated against that. Now that it has been given free reign, it is easier to see why tennis appeals to so many, whether they engage in it themselves or just watch. Thus, over the years, it has spawned numerous generations of top-seeded players, whose names are almost household words but who are surrounded by large numbers of less known but quite good players, men and women, of all races and, increasingly, all nationalities. And they have created records, repeatedly outdoing their predecessors, which makes this aspect of the sport almost a specialization in its own.

It is on this background that the *Historical Dictionary of Tennis* should meet with a warm welcome since it traces the history, reaching back to the oldest recorded predecessors and working its way gradually up to the present day. That is done, among other things, in the introduction, which provides a broad overview of the underlying progression and the issues it had to contend with, while passing in review some of the best tennis players. The chronology is no less important, tracing this evolution from year to year. And, to follow the sport, it does not hurt to have lists of the acronyms of the major tennis associations and the country codes. Nor can the appendixes be overlooked as they list the top players over the years. But obviously, the most important part is a fairly large dictionary section with fairly long entries that track, among other things, the careers of outstanding players and the relative standing of major countries while also informing us about the top championships, main organizations, and larger stadiums. Other entries provide simple definitions of basic terms and concepts, including the rules for scoring, among many other things.

The author of this volume, John Grasso, has a rather eclectic range of sports interests, all of which he has increasingly broadened and deepened and on which he has also written. His initial (and still active) interest was in boxing, on which he has written widely. Then comes basketball, which has already generated two books as well as the *Historical Dictionary of Basketball* in this series. Tennis only came later, but now he is also deeply involved, playing a bit of tennis himself, but especially compiling a huge library on the topic and researching it whenever and wherever possible. Certainly, just reading this volume will show the incredible number of facts and figures he has accumulated, which is actually the easy part, and how he managed to organize them coherently to present the careers of dozens and dozens of players, which is far harder. And even harder than that, although Grasso accomplishes it simply in passing, is to put all the pieces together so they form a coherent picture and give us a feeling for a sport that has come from behind but is now known to everyone everywhere, some just superficially, others quite passionately.

Jon Woronoff
Series Editor

Preface

It is impossible in a book of this size to cover all aspects of an activity that has been practiced worldwide for more than 100 years. I have tried to include a fair representation of both men and women from all eras and countries. The emphasis has been on their performance in Grand Slam events, the Olympic Games, and team events, such as the Davis Cup, Federation Cup, and Wightman Cup. As can be seen by the list of people inducted into the International Tennis Hall of Fame (appendix A), there have been many contributors to the sport that have had to be omitted from this volume. Space limitations have restricted entries to brief sketches, but readers interested in more details are advised to make use of the extensive bibliography at the end of this book. It is hoped that the information contained here will provide the neophyte reader with a general introduction to tennis and that some of the anecdotal details will be of interest to the reader with a broader background.

I would like to thank Dorothy A. Grasso, my first tennis partner, for putting up with my reclusive hobbies for more than 40 years; Steve Grasso, manufacturing engineer and Corvette and motocross racer (but nontennis player), and Laurel Zeisler, speech therapist and one-time number-one player on the Bainbridge-Guilford High School tennis team, for their encouragement and support; Doug Stark, Joanie Agler, and Troy Gowen of the International Tennis Hall of Fame and Museum for their assistance with this project; Dr. Bill Mallon, orthopedic surgeon and Olympic Games expert, for getting me involved with this project; and Jon Woronoff, series editor, Andrew Yoder, production editor, April Snider, acquisitions editor, and Melissa Lind, copyeditor, for helping to bring it to fruition.

This book is dedicated to Trooper Thorn whose appreciation of tennis consists of playing "catch," "fetch," and chewing on used tennis balls until they split. It is also dedicated to the memory of his predecessors Bravo, Samson, and Brandy.

Acronyms and Abbreviations

ORGANIZATIONS

AITA	All India Tennis Association
ATA	American Tennis Association
ATP	Association of Tennis Professionals
CAT	Confederation of African Tennis
ILTF	International Lawn Tennis Federation
IMG	International Management Group
IPA	Independent Players' Association
ITA	Intercollegiate Tennis Association
ITF	International Tennis Federation
LTA	Lawn Tennis Association
MIPTC	Men's International Professional Tennis Council
NAIA	National Association of Intercollegiate Athletics
NCAA	National Collegiate Athletic Association
NTL	National Tennis League
UCLA	University of California, Los Angeles
USLTA	United States Lawn Tennis Association
USPTA	United States Paddle Tennis Association
USTA	United States Tennis Association
WCT	World Championship Tennis
WIPTC	Women's International Professional Tennis Council
WTA	Women's Tennis Association
WTT	World Team Tennis

OTHER

VASSS	Van Alen Streamlined Scoring System

COUNTRIES

ALG	Algeria
ARG	Argentina
AUS	Australia
AUT	Austria
BAH	Bahamas
BEL	Belgium
BLR	Belarus
BOH	Bohemia
BRA	Brazil
BUL	Bulgaria
CAN	Canada
CHI	Chile
CHN	China (People's Republic of China)
COL	Colombia
CRO	Croatia
CYP	Cyprus
CZE	Czech Republic
DEN	Denmark
ECU	Ecuador
EGY	Egypt
ENG	England
ESP	Spain
EUN	Commonwealth of Independent States (Unified Team)
FRA	France
FRG	West Germany
GBR	Great Britain
GER	Germany
GRE	Greece
HUN	Hungary
IND	India
IRI	Iran
IRL	Ireland
ISR	Israel
ITA	Italy
JPN	Japan
KAZ	Kazakhstan
LAT	Latvia
LUX	Luxembourg
MEX	Mexico
NED	The Netherlands
NOR	Norway

NZL	New Zealand
PAK	Pakistan
PAR	Paraguay
PER	Peru
POL	Poland
PUR	Puerto Rico
RHO	Rhodesia
ROM	Romania
RSA	South Africa
RUS	Russia
SCG	Serbia and Montenegro
SLV	Slovenia
SRB	Serbia
SUI	Switzerland
SVK	Slovakia
SWE	Sweden
TCH	Czechoslovakia
TPE	Chinese Taipei (Republic of China)
TUN	Tunisia
UKR	Ukraine
URS	Union of Soviet Socialist Republics
URU	Uruguay
USA	United States of America
WAL	Wales
YUG	Yugoslavia
ZIM	Zimbabwe

Chronology

1874 England: Major Walter C. Wingfield patents a new game to be played outdoors on lawns and calls it *sphairistike*. The game quickly catches on with the upper class throughout England. **12 September:** An advertisement announcing the patent appears in a London newspaper for "W.C. Wingfield, Belgrave Road, Pimlico, London. A new and improved portable court for playing the ancient game of tennis—This is effected by means of an arrangement of oblong and triangular nets placed in certain positions to each other by means of standards and ropes driven and fixed to the ground."

1876 United States August: The first lawn tennis tournament in the United States is played in Nahant, Massachusetts, according to the recollection of Dr. James Dwight, the first president of the United States National Lawn Tennis Association.

1877 England 9–16 July: The inaugural English Championships are played at the All-England Croquet and Lawn Tennis Club in Wimbledon. Spencer Gore outlasts 21 others and defeats William Marshall for the Gentlemen's Singles Championship—the only event contested.

1881 United States 21 May: The United States National Lawn Tennis Association is organized in New York City. R. S. Oliver is named president and Clarence M. Clark, secretary. **31 August–3 September:** The inaugural United States Championships are played at the Newport Casino in Newport, Rhode Island. Richard Sears defeats William Glyn for the Men's Singles Championship. In men's doubles, the team of Clarence Clark and Frederick Winslow Taylor defeat Alexander Van Rensselaer and Arthur E. Newbold for the title.

1884 England 19 July: Women's Singles Championships are added at Wimbledon. Maud Watson, a vicar's daughter, defeats her older sister, Lillian Watson, for the title in a field of 13 entrants. Gentlemen's Doubles Championships are also added, and the Renshaw twins, William and Ernest, win the first of their five championships, defeating the team of E. W. Lewis and E. L. Williams.

1887 United States: The first United States National Ladies' Singles Championships are played at the Philadelphia Cricket Club in Chestnut Hill, Pennsylvania. Ellen Hansell defeats Laura Knight for the title.

1888 England 26 January: The Lawn Tennis Association is founded in London. The organization is still the governing body of British tennis.

1889 United States: United States National Ladies' Doubles Championships are contested at the Philadelphia Cricket Club for the first time. The team of Margarette Ballard and Bertha Townsend defeat Marion Wright and Laura Knight for the championship.

1891 France: The inaugural French Championships (Championnat de France International de Tennis) is played at the Stade Français in Paris. The one-day tournament, limited to players who are members of French clubs, is ironically won by an Englishman, H. Briggs.

1896 Greece 8–11 April: Tennis is one of the sports contested at the first modern Olympic Games. The men's singles event has 13 entrants from seven nations competing. The men's doubles event attracts five teams.

1900 France 6–11 July: At the second modern Olympic Games, held in Paris, tennis events are held for both men and women. Only four nations participate in the tournament. **United States 8–10 August:** The first International Lawn Tennis Challenge event (later renamed the Davis Cup) is held. The United States wins all three matches from the British Isles at the Longwood Cricket Club in Boston, Massachusetts, and wins the sterling silver cup donated by Dwight F. Davis, one of the American players.

1903 United States 4–8 August: The Doherty brothers, Reggie and Laurie, win four matches from the United States team at the Longwood Cricket Club in Boston, Massachusetts, to win the Davis Cup for the British Isles. The Brits retain the Cup until 1907, when they are defeated by Australasia.

1904 United States 29 August–3 September: At the Olympic Games in St. Louis, a tennis tournament is held. Only men's singles and doubles events are contested.

1905 Australia 25 November: The inaugural Australasian Championships are held at the Warehouseman's Cricket Ground in Melbourne.

1906 Greece 23–26 April: The Olympic Games in Athens hold tennis matches in four events—men's singles, men's doubles, women's singles, and mixed doubles.

1908   England 6–9 May: Covered court (or indoor tennis) is the first of three separate tennis tournaments to be played at the Olympic Games in London and is played at the Queen's Club in West Kensington. **18–28 May:** *Jeu de paume* (also known as real tennis or court tennis) is the second of the tennis events contested at the London Olympics and is also held at the Queen's Club. **6–11 July:** The outdoor lawn tennis events at the London Olympic Games are held at Wimbledon. The champions are all British even though players from nine nations enter.

1912   Sweden: 5–12 May: The Olympic Games are held in Stockholm. Covered court events take place at the Royal Tennis Pavilion. **28 June–12 July:** The Olympic outdoor lawn tennis competition is held at the Östermalm Idrottsplatts in Stockholm. The largest men's field in Olympic tennis history to that date, 49 entrants from 12 nations, take part in the men's singles.

1913   France: 1 March: In Paris, the International Lawn Tennis Federation is created by 12 national associations. **England:** Ladies' doubles and mixed doubles are added to the Wimbledon Championships program for the first time.

1915–19   Three of the four major tournaments and most other minor tournaments are not held due to World War I. The Australian is not contested from 1916 to 1918, the French from 1915 to 1919, and Wimbledon from 1915 to 1918. As the war is not fought on United States soil, its national championships continue to be held in each of these years.

1920   Belgium 16–24 August: The Olympic Games in Antwerp include tennis competition in all five events for the first time.

1922   Australia: Women's events and mixed doubles are added to the Australian Championships.

1923   United States 11–13 August: The United States defeats Great Britain, 7–0, in the inaugural Wightman Cup, played at the West Side Tennis Club in Forest Hills, New York.

1924   France 14–24 July: The Olympic Games, held in Paris, again includes tennis tournaments in all five events.

1926   France 16 February: In a highly anticipated match, 26-year-old Suzanne Lenglen defeats the 20-year-old Helen Wills. **United States 9 October:** At New York's Madison Square Garden, Suzanne Lenglen makes her professional debut as a member of promoter C. C. Pyle's troupe of touring professional players.

1927 England 2 July: Henri Cochet saves seven match points and comes from two sets down to defeat countryman Jean Borotra in the gentlemen's singles final at Wimbledon. **United States 8–10 September:** France wins the Davis Cup for the first time by defeating the United States, 3–2, on grass at the Germantown Cricket Club in Philadelphia, Pennsylvania. **The Netherlands 13 December:** The advisory committee of the International Lawn Tennis Federation votes three to two against having tennis in the 1928 Olympic Games.

1928 Netherlands 28 July–12 August: For the first time, tennis is not contested at the Olympic Games. It is not played as an Olympic medal sport until 1988. Concerns over amateurism in tennis lead to its exclusion from the Games.

1933 United States 28 January: In a mixed-sexes exhibition match in San Francisco, Helen Wills Moody defeats eighth-ranked Phil Neer, 6–3, 6–4. **United States 10 September:** Australian Jack Crawford, after winning the first three Grand Slam events and leading in the United States Open final round, two sets to one, falls victim to the heat and humidity and loses the final two sets to Englishman Fred Perry, 6–0, 6–1.

1937 England 20 July: American Don Budge, after losing the first two sets, defeats Baron Gottfried von Cramm of Germany in the fifth and deciding rubber of the Inter-Zone Davis Cup tie. The match is considered by many to be the "greatest tennis match of all time."

1938 United States 24 September: Don Budge wins the United States National Championship in four sets over Gene Mako and becomes the first winner of the Grand Slam.

1939 England 9 July: Americans Bobby Riggs and Alice Marble each win their respective singles and doubles championships at Wimbledon and then team to win the mixed doubles.

1940 United States 29 July: American Tennis Association champion Jimmy McDaniel, an African American, plays an exhibition with Grand Slam champion Don Budge at the Cosmopolitan Club in Harlem, New York City, which Budge easily wins 6–1, 6–2.

1939–45 With the outbreak of World War II, most of the major tennis tournaments are cancelled for the duration. The Championships at Wimbledon, the French National Championships, the Davis Cup, and the Wightman Cup are not held from 1940 to 1945. The Australian Championships are not held from 1941 to 1945, but the United States National Championships continue without interruption.

1947 United States 26 December: Despite the worst snowstorm (26.4 inches) in New York City history, 15,114 people come to Madison Square Garden to see Jack Kramer make his professional debut against Bobby Riggs. Riggs wins the match.

1948 United States 11 March: Dr. Reginald Weir wins his first round match at the United States National Indoor Tennis Championship held at the Seventh Regiment Armory in New York City. Dr. Weir becomes the first African American to play in a United States Lawn Tennis Association championship tournament.

1950 United States 3 February: Bill Tilden is named the Greatest Tennis Player of the first half-century in an Associated Press poll of sportswriters, despite "the personal tragedy which has befallen the great champion in recent years." **29–30 August:** Althea Gibson becomes the first African American to play in the United States National Championships at Forest Hills, New York.

1953 United States 1 February: Creation of a Tennis Hall of Fame to be located at Newport Casino in Newport, Rhode Island, is announced by James Van Alen.

1954 United States 20 July: French and Wimbledon champion Maureen Connolly suffers a crushed right leg when a truck hits the horse she was riding. Her tennis career is ended at age 19.

1956 France 26–27 May: Althea Gibson becomes the first African American to win a major tennis championship when she wins the French National women's singles title by defeating England's Angela Mortimer.

1963 England 17–20 June: The International Tennis Federation celebrates its 50th anniversary by creating the Federation Cup. A team tournament for women, similar to the Davis Cup, the inaugural event is played at the Queen's Club in London with 16 nations competing. **United States 8 September:** Ken Fletcher and Margaret Smith win the United States National Mixed Doubles Championship for their fourth Grand Slam mixed doubles title this year.

1967 Luxembourg 12 July: The International Lawn Tennis Federation (ILTF) votes 139–83 against letting professional tennis players play in the major events. **United States 17–18 August:** At the Newport Invitational tournament in Newport, Rhode Island, the doubles team of Dick Leach and Dick Dell defeat Len Schloss and Tom Mozur, 3–6, 49–47, 22–20. The 147-game set is the longest in tennis history and is not topped until 2010. **England 14 December:** The Lawn Tennis Association of Britain votes nearly unanimously to abolish the distinction between amateur and professional players starting 22 April 1968.

1968 **France 30 March:** At a special meeting, the ILTF votes unanimously to allow open tennis tournaments. **England 22 April:** The first open tennis tournament is the British Hard Court (clay court) Championships, where Owen Davidson defeats John Clifton at the West Hants Lawn Tennis Club at Bournemouth. **England 24 June:** The Championships at Wimbledon become an open tournament, and professional and amateur players both compete. It is the first of the major tournaments to become open. **United States 9 September:** The United States National Championships become the United States Open as professionals are allowed to enter along with amateurs. Amateur Arthur Ashe becomes the first black male to win the United States National Championships, but runner-up Tom Okker, technically an amateur but listed as a "registered player," receives the $14,000 first-prize money. **Mexico 14–26 October:** The Olympic Games in Mexico City revives tennis with demonstration and exhibition tournaments held at Guadalajara, Mexico.

1969 **England 25 June:** In a first-round match, 41-year-old Pancho Gonzáles defeats the 25-year-old Charlie Pasarell, 22–24, 1–6, 16–14, 6–3, 11–9, a total of 112 games that take 5 hours and 12 minutes in the longest match in Wimbledon history. The record stands until 2010 when John Isner and Nicolas Mahut play a much-longer marathon.

1971 England June 22: In response to the Gonzales–Pasarell marathon match of 1969 Wimbledon introduces a tiebreak set to be played once the score of any set except the final set reaches 8 games all. With players alternating serves, the first player to win seven points with a margin of two wins the set.

1973 **United States 27 April:** World Team Tennis, a creation of Billie Jean and Larry King, is founded by Larry King, Dennis Murphy, Fred Barman, and Jordan Kaiser. **13 May:** Bobby Riggs defeats Margaret Smith Court, 6–2, 6–1, on Mother's Day in a "battle of the sexes" match in Romana, California, before a capacity crowd of 3,500 people. **19 June:** The Association of Tennis Professionals votes to boycott the upcoming Wimbledon tournament scheduled to start on 25 June. The boycott is in response to the banning of Yugoslavian Niki Pilić, who was banned from playing at Wimbledon by the International Lawn Tennis Federation after he failed to appear for a Davis Cup match. **England 8 July:** Czech Jan Kodeš wins the boycotted Wimbledon singles, defeating Alex Metreveli of the Soviet Union. **United States 20 September:** Bobby Riggs is defeated by 29-year-old Billie Jean King at the Houston Astrodome in a $100,000 winner-take-all match, amid a circus-like atmosphere in front of 30,492 people—the largest paid-attendance in history for a tennis match.

1974 United States 6 May: World Team Tennis begins as the Philadelphia Freedoms defeat the Pittsburgh Triangles, 31–25. **26 August:** Denver Racquets defeat the Philadelphia Freedoms, 28–24, in the second match of the best two-of-three match championships and win the first World Team Tennis Championship. **South Africa 7 November:** India refuses to travel to South Africa to play the Davis Cup final in protest of South Africa's apartheid policies, and South Africa wins the Davis Cup by default. This is the first time that the United States, Great Britain, Australia, or France has not been Davis Cup champion.

1977 West Germany 6 July: The International Lawn Tennis Federation drops the word "lawn" from its name and becomes simply the International Tennis Federation.

1978 West Germany 8–15 May: The inaugural Nations Cup tournament (later renamed the World Team Cup) is played on clay courts in Dusseldorf. **United States 29 August:** The United States Open is begun at the new National Tennis Center at Flushing Meadows, New York.

1980 England 6 July: Björn Borg defends his Wimbledon singles title by defeating John McEnroe, 1–6, 7–5, 6–3, 6–7(18), 8–6, in 3 hours and 53 minutes, in a match cited by some as the "greatest match in tennis history."

1982 England 4 July: At Wimbledon, due to rain throughout the tournament, Anne Smith and Kevin Curren play four mixed doubles matches in one day—a total of 96 games. **United States 11 July:** In the fifth and deciding rubber of a Davis Cup World Group quarterfinal tie, John McEnroe of the United States defeats Mats Wilander of Sweden, 9–7, 6–2, 15–17, 3–6, 8–6. The match takes 6 hours and 22 minutes and is the longest in Davis Cup history.

1984 United States 6–11 August: The Olympic Games in Los Angeles includes demonstration men's and women's singles tournaments for players 21 years of age or younger. Stefan Edberg and Steffi Graf win. **24 September:** In a first round Women's Tennis Association match in Richmond, Virginia, Vicki Nelson-Dunbar defeats Jean Hepner in straight sets, 6–4, 7–6 (13), in a match that takes 6 hours and 31 minutes, which includes a 643-shot rally that lasts 29 minutes.

1985 England 6 July: The record 109-match doubles winning streak of Martina Navratilova and Pam Shriver is ended in the Wimbledon final by Kathy Jordan and Elizabeth Smylie, 5–7, 6–3, 6–4. **United States 23 August:** Vitas Gerulaitis teams with 67-year-old Bobby Riggs and loses in a challenge of sexes match against Martina Navratilova and Pam Shriver in Atlantic City. **27 August:** Mary Joe Fernández, a 14-year-old, defeats Sara Gomer in the first round of the United States Open, becoming the youngest player to win a match in that tournament.

1987 Turkey 11 May: The International Olympic Committee votes to include tennis as a medal sport in the 1988 Olympic Games in Seoul, and professional players will be allowed to compete.

1988 Korea 20 September–1 October: The Olympic Games in Seoul includes tennis as a medal sport for the first time since 1924.

1988–89 Australia 28 December 1988–1 January 1989: The inaugural Hopman Cup is played and won by the Czechoslovakian team of Miloslav Mečíř and Helena Suková at the Burswood Entertainment Complex in Perth.

1989 France 5 June: Michael Chang, age 17, overcomes leg cramps and, using unorthodox tactics, comes from two sets down to defeat world number-one–ranked Ivan Lendl in 4 hours and 37 minutes in a memorable fourth round match at the French Open. Chang goes on to win the title and becomes the youngest male Grand Slam singles winner.

1990 United States 20 February: The United States Tennis Association and the Lawn Tennis Association, the governing body of tennis in Great Britain, jointly announce the indefinite suspension of the Wightman Cup due to lack of interest caused by years of American domination of the event.

1992 Spain 28 July–9 August: The Olympic Games are held in Barcelona. Men's and women's singles and doubles are contested.

1993 Germany 30 April: Monica Seles is stabbed in the back by a crazed fan during a quarterfinal match at a tournament in Hamburg. **United States 11 September:** At the United States Open, Sande French becomes the first African American, male or female, to be the chair umpire for a Grand Slam championship match.

1994 United States 17 September: A malfunction in a heating system causes carbon monoxide to enter the guesthouse in Southampton, Long Island, where Vitas Gerulaitis is sleeping, and he dies of carbon monoxide poisoning at the age of 40.

1995 England 28 June: At Wimbledon, Englishman Tim Henman becomes the first player in the modern era to be disqualified from the Wimbledon championships.

1996 United States 23 July–3 August: The Olympic Games are held in Atlanta, Georgia.

2000 Australia 19–28 September: The Olympic Games are held in Sydney.

2003 United States: The Tennis Channel, a 24-hour a day, 7-day a week television station devoted exclusively to tennis is launched in Santa Monica, California.

2004 France 25 May: Fabrice Santoro wins the longest match in history (by time) by defeating Arnaud Clément in a first round French Open match in 6 hours and 33 minutes, 6–4, 5–3, 6–7 (5), 3–6, 16–14. The record is broken six years later by John Isner and Nicolas Mahut. **Greece 15–22 August:** The Olympic Games are held in Athens. **United States 24 September:** In a Davis Cup semifinal match, one of Andy Roddick's serves is measured at 155 miles per hour. This is the fastest recorded serve in tennis history.

2008 England 6 July: Rafael Nadal defeats Roger Federer in the gentlemen's singles final at Wimbledon in a match that some say is the greatest tennis match of all time. **China 10–17 August:** The Olympic Games are held in Beijing.

2009 England 5 July: In the men's singles final at Wimbledon, Roger Federer defeats Andy Roddick, 5–7, 7–6, 7–6, 3–6, 16–14, in a match that sees Roddick lose serve only once, in the 77th and final game. **United States 13 September:** Unseeded wild card, Kim Clijsters, in just her third tournament, easily defeats Caroline Wozniacki for the championship and becomes the first mother to win a Grand Slam singles title since Evonne Goolagong Cawley won the Australian Open in 1980.

2010 United States 5 May 2010: Colleen Hanzes, a 50-year-old business major at Broome Community College in Binghamton, New York, wins the National Junior College Athletic Association's Division III National Championship. **England 22–24 June:** John Isner defeats Nicolas Mahut in a first round match at Wimbledon, 6–4, 3–6, 6–7 (7), 7–6 (3), 70–68, in 11 hours and 5 minutes over 3 days—the longest match in history by far. **Belgium 8 July 2010:** Kim Clijsters defeats Serena Williams at King Baudouin Stadium in Brussels before 35,681 fans, the largest live attendance for a tennis match. **Serbia 3-5 December:** Novak Djoković wins two singles matches and helps Serbia defeat France to win the Davis Cup.

2011 Belgium 26 January: Justine Henin announces her retirement from tennis after an elbow injury sustained during her comeback fails to heal sufficiently. **Croatia 5 March:** Ivo Karlović sets the record for fastest serve with one measured at 156 miles per hour (251 km/h) in the fourth set of a Davis Cup doubles match in Zagreb. **Italy 15 May:** Novak Djoković defeats Rafael Nadal to win the Rome Masters championship. This is Djoković's

39th consecutive victory and the seventh title he has won in 2011 including the Australian Open. **France 3 June:** Roger Federer defeats Djoković in the semi-finals of the French Open ending Djoković's winning streak at 43. 5 June: Rafael Nadal defeats Federer to win his sixth French Open championship tying him with Bjorn Börg for most French Open singles titles.

Introduction

The sport of tennis has been played in one form or another for more than 800 years. It can trace its roots to games played by monks in the 12th century. Through the years, the game has evolved from one in which the ball was struck with the hands to the modern game in which rackets are used to propel the ball in excess of 100 miles per hour, with extremes of over 150 miles per hour being achieved.

The game has evolved from one played by monks to one played by the general populace to one played by the nobility and upper-class to one played by all. It also has survived being classified as a "sissy," nonmanly sport to one where a champion's stamina will rival that of a champion distance runner or prizefighter.

THE BEGINNINGS OF TENNIS

While the game cannot be attributed to a single creator, as in the case of basketball (Dr. James Naismith) or volleyball (William G. Morgan), its origin cannot even be pointed to a specific century. There are literary references as early as the mid-14th century to a game called "tenes." United States National tennis champion from 1898 to 1900, Malcolm D. Whitman, did extensive research on the origins of the game, and in his 1932 book, *Tennis: Origins and Mysteries*, provides details and theories on the sports origins and the history of some of its peculiar terminology. Some of Whitman's findings are challenged, though, by Dr. Heiner Gillmeister in his 1997 scholarly work, *Tennis: A Cultural History*.

The early game, first played in France with the hands and called *jeu de paume* (game of the palm), evolved from the use of an open hand to strike the ball to a glove (12th century), to a thong binding over the hand (13th century), to a type of racket with a solid face or battoir (14th century), to racquets with stringed faces (16th century), and to various other forms of racquets. The balls used were usually made of cloth. One theory as to the origin of the name of the sport is that an Egyptian city called Tennis was, in fact, known for its production of cloth. The word "racquet" is said to be derived from the

Arabic *rahat*, meaning "palm." As the use of a racquet replaced the use of the palm, the instrument took on that name. Another theory as to the origin of the game's name is that when the players were about to begin, they would call out "tenez" or "tenetz," which meant, in effect, "play ball."

Although the earliest forms of the game consisted of hitting a ball against the wall of a monastery, during the 14th century, closed courts were built in France. The sport, played indoors, evolved into the game that today is known as "court tennis," "real tennis," or *jeu de paume* and is still played, although its rules are complex, and very few people understand or follow the sport. Tennis writer, Allison Danzig, in his 1930 book *The Racquet Game*, wrote of court tennis, "It is a game that is less read about than any other of the red-blooded sports. It is a game about the nature of which not one person in ten thousand in the United States has the slightest inkling. Of the 120,000,000 people who populate the country, not more than five thousandths of a per cent have seen it played, and less than half that number have a thorough understanding of it." There are less than 50 courts remaining in 2010. The one at the Newport Casino, in Newport, Rhode Island, site of the International Tennis Hall of Fame and Museum, is open to the public.

MAJOR WINGFIELD AND "SPHAIRISTIKE"

If there is an "inventor" of the sport of lawn tennis, it would have to be Major Walter Clopton Wingfield. Major Wingfield was educated at Rossall School in Lancashire, England, and was a member of the Royal Guard and was a captain in the 1st Dragoon Guards. In 1874, he patented a new game to be played outdoors on lawns to which he gave the Greek name *sphairistike*. He packaged the equipment for the game and sold more than 1,000 sets in 1874–75. The game caught on among the upper class, but it soon began to be called "lawn tennis." He also published two books on the new game, *The Book of the Game* and *The Major's Game of Lawn Tennis*. His game featured an hourglass-shaped court, which gradually became the rectangular one known today. Miss Mary Ewing Outerbridge of New York discovered the game being played by British officers in Bermuda and brought the game back with her. She convinced her brother, A. Emilius Outerbridge, an active cricket player, to set up a net and mark off a court on the grounds of his cricket club in Staten Island, New York. The game spread, and in 1874, a lawn tennis court was set up in Nahant, Massachusetts, a seaside resort near Boston.

EARLY TOURNAMENT PLAY

In Whitman's book, he quotes Dr. James Dwight, one of the earliest lawn tennis champions, from an 1891 magazine article: "The first set of lawn tennis in New England—indeed, I fancy, in the country—was played at Mr. William Appleton's place at Nahant. In the summer of 1875 a set of pharistiké [sic], or lawn tennis, was brought out from England, where the game was just coming into fashion. . . . Mr. F. R. Sears, the elder brother of the champion, and I put up the net and tried the game . . . . That is the first tennis that I know of that was played in New England, and for two years we played incessantly. At the end of our second Summer, in August, 1876, we held our first tournament."

In England, the new pastime's popularity led to the establishment of lawn tennis courts at the All-England Croquet Club in Wimbledon, a London suburb. From 9 July to 16 July 1877, the club hosted a gentlemen's lawn tennis tournament, in which 22 men took part. Spencer Gore defeated William Marshall in three straight sets to win the championship. Gore did not think too highly of the game and later wrote (as quoted by Bud Collins in his encyclopedia): "That anyone who has really played well at cricket, tennis, or even rackets, will ever seriously give his attention to lawn tennis, beyond showing himself to be a promising player, is extremely doubtful; for in all probability the monotony of the game as compared with the others would choke him off before he had time to excel at it." Fortunately, his view was not shared by most, and the game continued to draw new enthusiasts.

In 1881, the United States National Lawn Tennis Association was created and conducted a national tournament at the Newport Casino in Newport, Rhode Island, from 31 August to 3 September. Again, only men contested the tournament, but unlike the tournament in Wimbledon, both men's singles and doubles events were held. Richard Sears defeated William Glyn in singles, and the team of Clarence Clark and Frederick Winslow Taylor defeated Alexander Van Rensselaer and Arthur E. Newbold in doubles. Taylor, a mechanical engineer, later became an efficiency expert and is best remembered as the "father of scientific management," rather than as a tennis champion.

In 1884, the Championships at Wimbledon were opened to ladies, and Maud Watson defeated her sister, Lillian, to win the initial ladies' championship. Gentlemen's doubles were also contested there for the first time, and the Renshaw twins, Willie and Ernest, exhibited their mastery of the sport by winning their first of five Wimbledon men's doubles titles.

A United States national ladies' singles tournament was first held in 1887 at the Philadelphia Cricket Club in Chestnut Hill, Pennsylvania. Ellen Hansell defeated Laura Knight in straight sets to win the first title. Two years later, a national ladies' doubles tournament was contested there, and the team of Margarette Ballard and Bertha Townsend defeated Marion Wright and Laura Knight for the championship.

In 1891, the inaugural French Championships (Championnat de France International de Tennis) was played at the Stade Français in Paris. The one-day tournament, which was limited to players who were members of French clubs, was, ironically, won by an Englishman, H. Briggs. Women's singles were not played there until 1897, when Adine Masson won the first of her five French National Championships.

At the revival of the Olympic Games in Athens in 1896, lawn tennis was one of the sports contested. Athletes from 10 nations took part in 43 events in 9 sports. Lawn tennis was one of those nine sports. The tennis tournament was put together on short notice, and most of the world's better players were not in Athens. The only tennis players there were seven Greeks and a Frenchman. Athletes from other sports were recruited to play and fill out the draw. Among the 13 contestants from 7 nations who comprised the final field were Momcsilló Tapavicza, a wrestler and weightlifter from Hungary (described as "a player who had only the most rudimentary notion of playing"—yet he won his first match and finished tied for third); Friedrich "Fritz" Traun, a 100- and 800-meter runner from Germany; George Robertson, British hammer thrower who finished fourth in the discus as the hammer throw was not one of the Athens events; Australian Teddy Flack, 800- and 1500-meter Olympic running champion and marathon contestant; and John Pius Boland, a tourist from Ireland, who won both the singles and doubles events.

In 1905, a national tournament was held in Melbourne, Australia. It was known as the Australasian Championships as New Zealanders were also included. Rodney Heath defeated Arthur Curtis to win the men's championship, and the team of Randolph Lycett and Tom Tachell defeated E. T. Barnard and E. Spence to win the doubles. The tournament was not opened to women until 1922.

THE DAVIS CUP

Dwight Davis and his fellow Harvard classmate, Holcombe Ward, were finalists at the United States National Doubles Championships for five consecutive years, 1898–1902, and won the title in 1899, 1900, and 1901. The Davises were wealthy St. Louis merchants and sent Dwight to study at Harvard University. While there, he took up tennis, devoted more time to the game than to his studies, and was intercollegiate champion in 1899. As Davis enjoyed team competition, he commissioned a silver bowl from a Boston silversmith, costing about $1,000, and offered it as the prize to the winning team in an international lawn tennis competition. A challenge was made to a team from the British Isles, and the event, called the International Lawn Tennis Challenge, took place at the Longwood Cricket Club in Boston, Massachusetts, on 8–10 August 1900. The format was best of five sets with two singles contests on the first day, a doubles contest the second day, and two more singles on the third day, with the opponents switching. The Americans, led by Davis and Malcolm Whitman playing singles and Davis and Ward playing doubles, won the first three matches. The fourth match was halted in the second set, and the fifth was not played. The tournament became an annual one, and with only few exceptions, has been played each year since. It was renamed "the Davis Cup" after Dwight's death in 1945 and has grown from its initial contest of just two teams to its present-day nearly year-long tournament with more than 100 nations taking part. The Davis Cup is the most prestigious international men's team tennis competition and has spawned the Federation Cup, a similar team tennis event for women.

THE IMPACT OF WORLD WAR I

During the early years of the 20th century, lawn tennis was an established sport with annual tournaments and international team play in the Davis Cup. It still was primarily a sport played by the upper class. When World War I began in 1914, a halt was called to the major tournaments. The Championships at Wimbledon were not contested from 1915 to 1918, the French Championships were not held from 1915 to 1919, the Davis Cup was not played from 1915 to 1918, and the Australian Championships were not played from 1916 to 1918. Quite a few of the top players enlisted in military service for their countries, and sadly, there were several casualties. The most famous casualty was New Zealander Tony Wilding, an Olympic medalist and Wimbledon and Davis Cup champion. Captain Wilding was killed in action at the battle of Aubers Ridge in France in May 1915. Other players of note who did not return from the war were J. J. Addison, Arthur O'Hara Wood, Ernest Parker, Kenneth Powell, Robert Powell, and Arthur Wear. Hope Crisp, winner of the first Wimbledon mixed doubles in 1913, lost his right leg in service but, upon his return, continued to play tennis on his artificial leg.

THE GOLDEN AGE OF SPORTS

The decade of the 1920s has been called by some writers "the Golden Age of Sports." Most of the major American sports had one or two players whose charisma and sporting accomplishments received much public acclaim.

Baseball had George Herman "Babe" Ruth, boxing had Jack Dempsey, football had Harold "Red" Grange, and tennis had Suzanne Lenglen and Bill Tilden.

Both were extremely talented, arrogant, and charismatic. They were usually the center of attention and gloried in that role. They both had long winning streaks and achieved popularity previously unknown to the sport. They helped to increase public attention to an activity formerly limited to upper-class society and were supplemented during this era by a supporting cast consisting of Molla Bjurstedt Mallory, Mary K. Browne, Kitty McKane Godfree, Helen Hull Jacobs, and Helen Wills, among the women, and Bill Johnston, Vinnie Richards, Gerald Patterson, and R. Norris Williams, among the men.

During this decade, the idea of a team competition for women was initiated by Hazel Hotchkiss Wightman, herself an accomplished tennis player. As was the case with the Davis Cup, she personally donated a sterling vase as the prize for the event and set up a challenge match between a ladies' team from the United States and one from Great Britain. This tournament, begun in 1923, was initially known as the Ladies International Tennis Challenge. It was played annually (except during World War II), and the site alternated between Great Britain and the United States. It was terminated in 1990 due to the U.S. dominance of the event.

Midway through the decade, the rise of the Four Musketeers also contributed to the public's interest in the sport. Frenchmen Jacques "Toto" Brugnon, Jean Borotra, Henri Cochet, and René Lacoste each had different styles and personalities, and all four won more than their share of Grand Slam championships. Borotra won 19 (5 singles, 9 doubles, 5 mixed doubles), Brugnon, a doubles specialist, won 13 (11 doubles, 2 mixed doubles), Cochet won 16 (8 singles, 5 doubles, 3 mixed doubles), and Lacoste won 10 (7 singles, 3 doubles). More importantly, all four played in the Davis Cup for France, enabling that country to win it for the first time in 1927 and retain it annually through 1932. Their 1927 victory over the United States was remarkable in that it was achieved by playing on grass (their least favorite surface), in the United States, and with very few fans in attendance supporting them.

In 1933, it became Great Britain's turn to dominate the sport. By then, Tilden had been playing professionally, and ineligible for the Davis Cup, Lacoste had retired; the other three Musketeers were all in their 30s, and England's Fred Perry and Henry "Bunny" Austin were in their prime. Great Britain defeated France for the Cup in 1933 and retained possession until defeated in 1937 by the United States, led by Don Budge. By that year, Perry had become a professional and, thus, did not play in the Davis Cup for Great Britain.

THE GREATEST MATCH EVER PLAYED—FIRST NOMINEE

1937 was a good year for Budge as he defeated Germany's Baron Gottfried von Cramm for the Wimbledon championship and also won the Wimbledon men's doubles and mixed doubles. After defeating Japan and Australia in preliminary Davis Cup ties, the United States was matched with Germany in the Inter-Zonal or semifinal round. Since defending champion Great Britain no longer had Perry, the winner of the semifinal round was favored to win the Cup. Von Cramm easily defeated American Bryan "Bitsy" Grant in the first rubber of the tie. Budge defeated Henner Henkel to even the score after the first day's play. On the second day, in doubles, Budge and partner Gene Mako defeated von Cramm and Henkel in four sets. The final day saw Henkel defeat Grant in the first rubber. The fifth and deciding rubber was between Budge and von Cramm. It turned out to be one of the greatest matches in tennis history. After losing the first two sets, Budge came back to win, 8–6, in the final set. As was expected, the United States easily defeated Britain the following week to win the Cup. Budge capped off his year by winning the United States National Men's Singles Championship, again defeating von Cramm. Budge also won the National mixed doubles, but he and Mako were upset by von Cramm and Henkel in the U.S. National men's doubles.

THE GRAND SLAM

The following year, Budge had the most extraordinary year of any tennis player to that date. After winning the Australian Championships in January, he decided to attempt to win the four major national championships—the Australian, French, British (Wimbledon), and the American. He was successful in his quest and became the first person to win all four—dubbed the "Grand Slam" by sportswriter Allison Danzig. After reaching his goal, Budge then signed a professional contract and spent the next decade as a touring professional.

His feat, of winning all four major tournaments in one year, had nearly been accomplished five years earlier, in 1933, as Australian Jack Crawford won the first three major tournaments and was leading in the fourth, the U.S. Nationals, two sets to one, when he was overcome by the heat and humidity and lost to Fred Perry in five sets. Since then, only Rod Laver (in 1962 and 1969) has won the men's Grand Slam, and only Maureen Connolly (1953), Margaret Smith Court (1970), and Steffi Graf (1988) have won the women's Grand Slam. Graf also won the Olympic women's singles that year—the only person to win all five major tournaments in a single year.

THE IMPACT OF WORLD WAR II

With the outbreak of World War II, most of the major tennis tournaments were cancelled for the duration. The Championships at Wimbledon, the French National Championships, the Davis Cup, and the Wightman Cup were not held from 1940 to 1945. The Australian Championships were not held from 1941 to 1945, but the United States National Championships continued without interruption. Among the war's casualties were Henner Henkel, 1937 French National singles champion and German Davis Cup player, who was killed in action at the Battle of Stalingrad, and Joe Hunt, 1943 U.S. National singles champion, who died on 2 February 1945 during a U.S. Navy training flight.

Tennis did continue in the United States during the war, although tournaments were fewer and entry lists not as all-inclusive. One oddity occurred in a tournament in Cincinnati. Due to the lack of available competition, Sarah Palfrey Cooke was allowed to enter the men's doubles at the Tri-State Championships as the partner of her husband, Elwood Cooke. Surprisingly, the pair reached the final round. Also during the war years, Ecuador native Francisco "Pancho" Segura, a student at the University of Miami, won the National Collegiate Athletic Association Men's Singles Championship, three consecutive years from 1943 to 1945. This feat of winning three consecutive national collegiate titles had been accomplished only once before (by Malcolm Chace of Yale in the 1890s) and has not been duplicated since.

INTEGRATION AND POSTWAR PLAY

The major event in the history of lawn tennis in the postwar period was the integration of the sport. Since tennis had evolved as a class-oriented activity, most of the game was played in private country clubs with restricted membership. Virtually all sport in America for the first half of the 20th century was played under segregated conditions. Although there were a few instances of integration in football and basketball, boxing was the only sport in which more than a few black athletes took part in integrated competition. After World War II, most sports began to integrate, albeit in small steps. Tennis was no exception.

The American Tennis Association (ATA), a black organization, was organized in 1916 and had been conducting annual national championships since 1917. Its leaders had been unsuccessful in convincing the United States Lawn Tennis Association (USLTA) to allow black players to enter the USLTA sponsored tournaments. A breakthrough of sorts occurred in 1940 when the Wilson Sporting Goods Company promoted an exhibition between former

U.S. National champion Don Budge and ATA champion Jimmy McDaniel on 29 July at the Cosmopolitan Club in Harlem, New York City. The two-set exhibition ended with Budge easily winning, 6–1, 6–2, but the match was played on clay, and McDaniel was used to the faster hard-court surfaces of California. Budge, though, was quite complimentary about McDaniel's abilities and said "Jimmy is a very good player. I'd say he'd rank with the first 10 of our white players. And with some more practice against players like me, maybe he could some day beat all of them." (That was not to be the case, as the sport was not integrated during McDaniel's prime playing years.)

Alice Marble was another champion who played an integrated exhibition match. In 1944, she and Mary Hartwig played a mixed doubles exhibition with ATA champions Bob Ryland and Dr. Reginald Weir. It was after this match that she became aware of another ATA player, Althea Gibson. Alice stood up for Althea and wrote an open letter that was published in *American Lawn Tennis Magazine*. The letter helped paved the way, and Althea Gibson was allowed to play in the U.S. National tournament at Forest Hills in August 1950, becoming the first African American to play in that tournament. By 1956, she would reach the finals and the following year win the championship. Miss Gibson was also able to break similar barriers at Wimbledon, winning the ladies' singles there in 1957 and 1958. She was followed by several others. Indeed, the two best female players in the early 21st century, the Williams sisters, are black.

Ironically, although the color barrier was broken, there would be very few black players in major tennis competition. Arthur Ashe became the first black man to achieve major success, and he, too, won both the U.S. Open men's singles and Wimbledon men's singles, but he has not been joined by any other black American males. Although there does not appear to be any overt prejudice, and there are black coaches, linesmen, and umpires, the tennis hierarchy still retains some of its original upper-class strains, and it may be another century before the percentage of blacks involved with the sport equals the percentage of blacks in American society.

Other major league sports, such as football and basketball, which also had been integrated in the 1950s, progressed from a minority black participation to one in which, by the 21st century, the overwhelmingly majority of professional players are black.

THE "SHAMATEURS"

Although tennis made some racial progress in the 1950s, one area in which its leaders clung to the past was in amateurism. The independently wealthy leisure class participated in 19th-century sport, and the concept of the amateur sportsman was the norm. A player who derived a living from the pursuit of sport was looked down upon, and the true "amateur" sportsman did not want to sully his reputation by participating in a contest with a "professional." Consequently, when the Olympic Games were revived in 1896, only amateur contestants were allowed to participate. Lawn tennis tournaments were also only open to amateur entrants. By the middle of the 20th century, this antiquated concept was still being enforced in the Olympic Games and the major tennis tournaments as well. Despite the fact that admission was charged for spectators to witness championships contested by amateurs, only the tournament promoters reaped any gains from the events. The players still only received trophies and expenses. As top players gradually became professional and were banned from the major tournaments, promoters began to increase the "expense money" paid to "amateur" players to entice them to enter their tournaments. As a result, many so-called amateur players during the 1950s and 1960s were able to make a good living by playing "amateur" tennis. This was also true of some of the established stars of the 1920s, and players like Bill Tilden were able to have first-class accommodations as inducements for their tournament participation.

OPEN TENNIS

Jack Kramer, who headed professional tennis tours during the 1950s and 1960s, was an outspoken advocate for "open" tennis, in which both amateurs and professionals would take part. At the 12 July 1967 meeting of the International Lawn Tennis Federation (ILTF), representatives from Great Britain introduced a proposal to allow professional players to play in the major events. The proposal, seconded by Australia and supported by the United States, was voted down, 139–83, primarily by representatives from smaller nations and the Iron Curtain countries. On 14 December, the Lawn Tennis Association (LTA), the British governing body, in defiance of the ILTF, passed a resolution that tournaments in Britain, effective 22 April 1968, would be open. Then, at its meeting in France on 30 March 1968, the ILTF voted unanimously to allow open tennis tournaments, in effect rubber stamping the decision made by the LTA. In a compromise decision, the vote was in favor of "retention of the notion of amateurism in the rules of the ILTF, as its removal would indisputably weaken the ideals which the ILTF have the duty to protect and develop." It then decided to limit the number of open tournaments to 12 in 1968 and allowed each of its 65 member nations to decide for itself whether to differentiate between amateurs and professionals. The ILTF established four categories of players:

1. Amateurs—those who play for fun and prizes
2. Registered players—top stars who will be allowed to receive big expenses and make profit from the game without making it their profession
3. Contracted professionals—those who compete in touring groups and operate under their own control
4. Other professionals, including coaches, who still come under the authority of their national associations

Davis Cup play, which did not come under the ILTF jurisdiction at that time, was still restricted to amateur players.

The net effect of this decision was to create some silly and downright ludicrous situations over the next few years. The first open tournament was held in Bournemouth, England, beginning on 22 April 1968. Many of the top players did not enter as some were doubtful about the legality of playing for money, some amateurs were afraid that they were not skilled enough to compete against professionals, and some felt they could make more money playing for "expenses" than for what the tournament had to offer.

The first United States Open, in 1968, was won by Arthur Ashe, at that time a lieutenant in the U.S. Army and member of the Davis Cup team. To retain his Davis Cup status, Ashe was an amateur. As such, he received about $25 per day for expenses, even though he won the championship. Tom Okker, the runner-up, was a "registered player" and was awarded the $14,000 first prize. Margaret Smith Court won prize money in open tournaments in Great Britain but was still eligible to play in the United States Amateur Championship, receiving only expense money.

THE 1970S' TENNIS BOOM

As the bugs began to be ironed out in open tennis, political battles began among the various organizations attempting to gain control of the sport. In an era reminiscent of 21st-century professional boxing's "alphabet soup" regime, the ILTF, USLTA, WCT, and NTL did battle, and the WTA and ATP emerged.

World Championship Tennis (WCT) was an organization founded by Texas oilman Lamar Hunt, who was one of the founders of the American

Football League in 1959 and the North American Soccer League in 1967. He formed the WCT in 1967 and immediately signed eight of the top men's tennis players to contracts. The players, known as the Handsome Eight, were John Newcombe, Tony Roche, Niki Pilić, Roger Taylor, Dennis Ralston, Cliff Drysdale, Earl "Butch" Buchholz, and Pierre Barthès. A rival professional organization was formed by former U.S. Davis Cup captain George MacCall, and it was called the National Tennis League (NTL). It had some of the players who had previously been professional players, such as Rod Laver, Ken Rosewall, Pancho Gonzáles, and Andrés Gimeno. The NTL also signed former amateurs Roy Emerson, Owen Davidson, and Fred Stolle.

In 1970, the ILTF organized a point system based on performance in various tournaments under its auspices and called it the Grand Prix. The intent of this system was to compete directly with the WCT and NTL. Over the next few years, the prize money kept increasing, but the confusion as to who could play where did also. During the 1980s, the confusion began to be sorted out, and the present-day Association of Tennis Professionals (ATP), the men's organization, and the Women's Tennis Association (WTA) emerged.

BILLIE JEAN AND EQUALITY

Women wanted their fair share of the prize money, and led by Billie Jean King and Gladys Heldman, founder of World Tennis magazine, they formed a women's professional tour in 1970. They were backed by Joe Cullman, an executive at the Philip Morris Company, and were sponsored by Virginia Slims cigarettes. Nine of the leading female players signed token one-dollar contracts with Heldman and begin their own series of tournaments. The nine were Billie Jean King, Rosie Casals, Kristy Pigeon, Jane "Peaches" Bartkowicz, Judy Dalton, Val Ziegenfuss, Kerry Melville, Julie Heldman (Gladys's daughter), and Nancy Richey.

Another milestone in the 1970s was two exhibition matches between former Wimbledon champion Bobby Riggs and the two leading female players, Margaret Smith Court and Billie Jean King. The 55-year-old Riggs challenged Court (who had won 89 of her last 92 matches on the women's tour) to a "battle of the sexes" match played on 13 May 1973 (Mother's Day) in Romana, California, to prove that women's tennis, in his words, "stinks." Ironically, Riggs, at five feet eight inches tall, was two inches shorter than Smith and played a baseline game more typical of women's tennis. The five-foot ten-inch Court, known for her powerful serve, lost a battle of nerves and played poorly. The nationally televised match was won easily by Riggs,

6–2, 6–1, in 57 minutes. Riggs then challenged Billie Jean King. That match received much more publicity and was held at the Astrodome in Houston, Texas. The $100,000, winner-take-all match, held 20 September 1973, was played before 30,492 fans in a circus-like atmosphere, and Riggs was trounced by Billie Jean, 6–4, 6–3, 6–3. That match did wonders for women's tennis and helped to establish the fact that the leading women players were quite talented.

Billie Jean and her husband, Larry King, also came up with the idea for team tennis competition, and the innovative World Team Tennis was born in 1974. Teams of two men and two women (with substitutes) played contests that consisted of five one-set matches—one each of men's and women's singles and doubles and mixed doubles. Sets were played to five games, and each game won counted in the overall scoring. The team winning the most games won the contest. No-ad scoring was used, and fans were encouraged to cheer for their favorites—unlike traditional tennis that insisted on silence for much of the match. A 16-team league began in 1974, playing a 44-game schedule in 16 cities throughout the United States. Because of the uniqueness of the league and the influence of Billie Jean King, it was able to attract many of the top professionals. The league flourished from 1974 to 1978 but then fell by the wayside. It resurfaced and was still active in 2010, although with a more limited schedule.

All of these factors helped the sport to boom during the 1970s. Two other major stars during this decade were Jimmy Connors and Chris Evert. They began the decade as teenagers (Chris just 16 at her debut in the 1971 U.S. Open and Jimmy, 17 at his U.S. Open the previous year). Both rapidly reached championship caliber and also became engaged and were known as "America's Sweethearts." Although their marriage plans did not work out, their play continued to excel, and they also helped increase interest in the sport.

During the 1980s, Connors was challenged by Björn Borg, John McEnroe, Ivan Lendl, Stefan Edberg, and Mats Wilander. Evert's main rivals were Martina Navratilova, Tracy Austin, and Steffi Graf. Women's tennis also saw a rise in the number of extremely young players, and soon 13- and 14-year-olds were becoming professionals and winning. Tennis schools, such as Nick Bollettieri's Tennis Academy in Florida, were one reason, and the amount of money that the sport was paying to its champions was another.

In the 1990s, Pete Sampras, Andre Agassi, Michael Chang, and Jim Courier, all four Americans, were among the world's best. Steffi Graf, Monica Seles, Arantxa Sánchez Vicario, and Martina Hingis were the top women players.

RETURN TO THE OLYMPIC GAMES

After the 1924 Olympic Games, tennis was dropped from the Olympic program. It did not return until the 1968 Games in Mexico City, when both a demonstration tennis tournament and an exhibition tennis tournament were held in Guadalajara, Mexico. Both men's and women's singles and doubles and mixed doubles were contested. Although both tournaments had extensive participation, tennis remained out of the Olympics until 1984. In that year, men's singles and women's singles demonstration tournaments were held. Participants had to be 21 years of age or younger, ostensibly, to retain the amateur status of contestants.

In 1988, the sport returned as a full-fledged medal in the Seoul Olympic Games, with no restrictions on the status of entrants. Men's and women's singles and doubles events were held. Most of the top players entered, but the results were somewhat surprising. Miloslav Mečíř defeated Stefan Edberg in the semifinal round and won the gold medal by defeating Tim Mayotte. Steffi Graf capped an outstanding year in which she won all four Grand Slam events by also winning the Olympic gold medal. In subsequent Olympic Games, the tennis community sent its best players, although the number of entrants per country was limited to ensure adequate international representation.

Many of the world's top-rated players struggled in Olympic play and among the nonmedalists in 1992 were Australian and French Open champion Jim Courier, U.S. Open champion Stefan Edberg, and U.S. Open runner-up Pete Sampras, as well as Boris Becker, Michael Chang, and Michael Stich. In later years, Roger Federer failed three times in singles, although he did win the 2008 doubles.

THE INTERNATIONAL GAME

The sport of tennis is played in nearly every country in the world. Davis Cup participation has grown from only two countries participating in its early years to 24 countries in the 1920s to more than 50 in the 1970s to its present-day total of over 125 countries. Fed Cup participation has experienced similar growth from its initial total of 16 teams in 1963 to its present total of 80 teams. Olympic tennis also has a large number of participating nations.

Not only is tennis played worldwide, but also many countries have outstanding world-class players. The sport, which was dominated by the United States, Australia, Great Britain, and France for its first 100 years, has grown internationally, and its elite players now come from more than 50 nations. The 2010 United States Open included representatives from 63 different nations. Unlike Davis Cup and Fed Cup competition, which is open to teams from every tennis-playing country, the U.S. Open is limited to the top 128 male and 128 female players in both singles and doubles.

An example of the international quality of professional tennis can be seen by examining the nationality of the ATP's top 50 players. Ranked in the first 10 on 1 November 2010 are citizens of Spain (three players), Switzerland, Serbia, Great Britain, Sweden, the Czech Republic, the United States, and Russia. Austria, France, Croatia, and Cyprus have representatives in the next 10. Argentina, Latvia, and Brazil have players ranked between 21 and 30. Chinese Taipei, Germany, and Kazakhstan have players ranked between 31 and 40. Finland, Uzbekistan, the Netherlands, the Ukraine, and Italy have players ranked between 41 and 50. A total of 23 different nations are represented by the top 50 male players. The second 50 players include an additional 11 nations. The Women's Tennis Association has a similarly diverse makeup.

Although the four major tournaments—Wimbledon, the United States Open, the French Open, and Australian Open—have continued to be the major events for nearly 100 years, other professional tournaments are played worldwide and draw international entry lists. Both the ATP and WTA routinely play tournaments on all six continents and draw large and often sellout crowds worldwide.

One interesting aspect of the international quality of the sport is the fact that most of its top players are bilingual as a minimum and often multilingual. Serbian Novak Djoković, for example, upon winning a tournament in Italy, addressed the crowd in fluent Italian and then switched to near-perfect English for a television interview. Djoković, in addition to his native Serbian, is also fluent in German and Croatian. In fact, virtually the only players who are not multilingual are the American and British native-English speakers.

TWENTY-FIRST-CENTURY TENNIS

Tennis has thrived in the 21st century. Several innovations have helped it to become a fan favorite. The Tennis Channel, a cable channel begun in 2003, broadcasts 24 hours, 7 days a week. As its viewership has grown, the station has expanded its coverage and now has telecast rights to the four major Grand Slam tournaments as well as Davis Cup, Fed Cup, Association of Tennis Professionals tournaments and Women's Tennis Association tournaments. It also sponsored its own tournament from 2006 to 2008 in Las Vegas, Nevada, and has many features on tennis players and tennis instruction. To fill additional time, it will often replay classic matches of the past. It also has a website filled with articles, tennis news, and video snippets and has become an essential station for the tennis fanatic.

A second innovation that has impacted upon the sport is the development of the Hawk-Eye challenge system. It was developed by engineers in Great Britain in 2001 and subsequently patented. It was first used for tennis matches in 2006 and now is used by virtually all major tournaments on matches played on their center courts. Through a combination of video recording and computer simulation, each point played is recorded. A player may challenge a line call, and the computer video simulation is then used to determine whether the call was correct. If the call was incorrect, the point is either replayed or awarded to the challenging player, depending on the circumstances. Players are generally allowed three incorrect challenges per set, with an additional challenge should the set require a tiebreaker. It has greatly eliminated the incessant arguing that was characteristic of the sport during the prior three decades.

In the late 1990s and first few years of the 21st century, Pete Sampras and Andre Agassi were the dominant male players. Beginning in 2004, Roger Federer exerted an influence unmatched in the open era. An extremely capable player who has won 16 Grand Slam singles championships, more than any other male player, he has also reached at least the semifinal round of 23 consecutive Grand Slam singles tournaments and has been called by many "the greatest tennis player in history." On top of his many achievements, he has an extremely pleasant personality and is well liked by his fellow players as well as the fans.

Rafael Nadal, a few years younger than Federer, has proven to be Federer's nemesis, defeating him in 17 of the 25 matches they have played through the 2011 French Open. Nadal also has a pleasing personality and is also extremely popular with players and fans. The Bryan twins, Mike and Bob, have played as doubles specialists during this decade and have won more than 70 events as partners.

The most impressive female tennis players of the decade are the Williams sisters, Serena and Venus. They are the two most accomplished African American tennis players in history and, through 2010, have won a combined 48 Grand Slam championships, including 12 women's doubles in which they were partners. On eight occasions, the two met in the finals of a Grand Slam event. Other top females in the decade were two Belgians, Justine Henin and Kim Clijsters, and several Eastern European players, including Maria Sharapova, Svetlana Kuznetsova, and Jelena Janković.

THE GREATEST MATCH EVER PLAYED—THREE MORE NOMINEES

Tennis in recent years has been blessed by three extraordinary matches. The 2008 Wimbledon gentlemen's singles final between Roger Federer and

Rafael Nadal is another nominee for "the greatest tennis match ever played." Federer was going for a modern record sixth consecutive Wimbledon championship, and Nadal, who had been defeated by Federer the previous two years at Wimbledon, was seeking his first. Nadal won the first two sets, 6–4, 6–4, but Federer came back to win the third and fourth sets, both in tiebreakers, 7–6 (5) and 7–6 (8). In the fourth set, Federer saved two championship points to enable the match to continue to a fifth set. According to Wimbledon rules, that set could not end in a tiebreak but had to be played to a conclusion. It finally ended with Nadal winning, 9–7. The match was interrupted by rain, and when it ended, darkness was falling, and, most likely, play would have been suspended had not Nadal ended it when he did. The match required 4 hours and 48 minutes but ended, due to the delays, 7 hours and 15 minutes after its scheduled start. Former Wimbledon champion, John McEnroe, who was broadcasting the match, called it the greatest match he had ever seen (and he, himself, had taken part in a Wimbledon final in 1980 that had previously received that accolade).

In 2009, Federer met Andy Roddick in the Wimbledon final in a match that was nearly as good as the previous year's final with Nadal. That match also would be on some lists as "the greatest match ever played." Federer was attempting to win his 15th Grand Slam singles championship. He was tied with Pete Sampras at 14. The final score was 5–7, 7–6 (8), 7–6 (7), 3–6, 16–14. Roddick did not lose his serve until the 77th and final game. After 4 hours and 16 minutes of play, Federer was victorious and won his 15th Grand Slam singles title in the longest fifth set in Wimbledon finals history.

A third outstanding match took place at Wimbledon in 2010. Although it was only a first round match, it became one for the ages. John Isner, 6 feet 9 inches, 245 pounds, and seeded 23rd, played Nicolas Mahut, a qualifier. The marathon match required 3 days to complete and took 11 hours and 5 minutes of elapsed time and 183 games. The final score was 6–4, 3–6, 6–7 (7), 7–6 (3), 70–68. Isner, known for his powerful serve, recorded a record 112 aces in the match, and Mahut had 103. Three epic battles at Wimbledon in three years: no wonder that the popularity of tennis is as great as it is.

From the sport of the elite to the sport played by elite athletes, the sport of lawn tennis has grown immensely in the past 135 years, and it remains one of the few sporting pastimes that is played extensively by people of all ages and all nationalities and enjoyed by all.

ACE. An ace is the tennis term used for a **serve** that is not returned or touched by an opponent's **racket**. It usually is recorded on the first serve by a player with a powerful serve but may occasionally be scored on the second serve. From time to time, a player with a weaker serve may score one, usually by placing it where the opponent does not expect it. In recent years, as tennis **statistics** have been kept in more detail, the number of aces scored by each player in a **match** has been recorded. Aces are more prevalent on faster **surfaces** such as **hard court** or **grass**.

ADVANTAGE. In tennis **scoring**, after the score has been tied at 40–40, also known as **deuce**, two consecutive **points** must then be won to win the **game**. The first point won after the score of deuce is termed *advantage*. If the **server** wins the point, the score is advantage (ad in), and if the receiver wins the point, the score is advantage (ad out).

AFRICAN AMERICAN PLAYERS. Until the late 1940s, in the **United States**, most sports were not integrated. **Lawn tennis** was no exception. Black players were banned from white **tournaments** and took part in events run by the **American Tennis Association**, a black organization. **Ora Mae Washington** was the best black female player of her era but never had the chance to play a white opponent. Jimmie McDaniel was one of the best in the 1930s and even played an exhibition with **Don Budge** in 1940. Dr. Reginald Weir became the first African American to play in a **United States Lawn Tennis Association** championship tournament when he won his first round **match** at the United States National Indoor Tennis Championship held at the Seventh Regiment Armory in New York City on 11 March 1948. In 1952, he became the first black male to play in the **United States National Championships** at **Forest Hills**.

    Althea Gibson was the first American black player, male or female, to achieve fame in integrated tennis in the 1950s, and she first played in the United States National Championships on 29 August 1950. She later achieved many other notable firsts, including the first **Grand Slam** championship (1956 **French Nationals**) and first **Wimbledon** championship (1957).

But she was not followed by any other notable players until **Arthur Ashe** in the mid-1960s. Since then, there have been several outstanding black American players, including **James Blake, Zina Garrison**, Lori McNeil, Chanda Rubin, MaliVai Washington, and **Serena** and **Venus Williams**. Other black American professional players who have not achieved that level include Katrina Adams, Leslie Allen, Thomas Blake, Rene Blount, Marcus Fugate, Angela Haynes, Chip Hooper, Scoville Jenkins, Raquel Kops-Jones, **John Lucas**, Shenay Perry, Bryan Shelton, Phillip Simmonds, Sloane Stephens, Blake Strode, Alexandra Stevenson (daughter of basketball star Julius Erving), Mashona Washington, and Donald Young.

Foreign black players of note include Frenchmen **Yannick Noah, Gaël Monfils**, and **Jo-Wilfried Tsonga**. Other foreign black players, not quite as accomplished as the three Frenchmen, include Ronald Agenor of Haiti, Dustin Brown of Jamaica, Jeff Coetzee of **South Africa**, Gianni Mina and Josselin Ouanna of France, and Roger Smith of the Bahamas. Although the sport has become fully integrated, the preponderance of players, officials, and spectators is still white. *See also* JOHNSON, ROBERT WALTER "WHIRLWIND"; SAITCH, EYRE.

AFRICAN TENNIS. Although there have been many great sportsmen from the continent of Africa in athletics, basketball, boxing, and football (soccer), the sport of **lawn tennis** is not widely played there. The Confederation of African Tennis is the governing organization. Egypt, Morocco, Zimbabwe, and **South Africa** are the only African countries to have produced top-flight tennis players. Egypt has competed in the **Davis Cup** since 1929, with a 58–71 record in 129 ties over 67 **tournaments**. Its best finish was in reaching its zone semifinals twice. Among Egypt's top players are Ismail El Shafei and Karim Maamoun. Madagascar has had the Randriantefy sisters, Dally and Natacha, enter the **Olympic Games**, although they never advanced past the first round. In 1992, they both played **singles** and **doubles**. They played Olympic doubles again in 1996, and Dally also played singles in 1996 and 2004. They competed on the **Women's Tennis Association** tour, where Dally achieved a high **ranking** of 44th in the world. Côte d'Ivoire (Ivory Coast), Benin, Kenya, Nigeria, and Togo have all entered male players in Olympic competition. The N'Goran brothers, Claude and Clement, from Côte d'Ivoire, won their first round match in 1996 Olympic doubles, and Tony Mmoh of Nigeria reached the second round in 1988 Olympic singles. Clement N'Goran competed on the **Association of Tennis Professionals** tour and in all four major tournaments, with a high ranking of 150.

Although most African nations have competed in the Davis Cup, only South Africa has won the Cup. In 1974, South Africans were Cup champions when **India** refused to play them in the final round. Top South African players include **Hall of Famers Bob Hewitt, Johan Kriek**, and **Frew McMillan**. Other players of note from South Africa are David Adams, Pieter Aldrich, John-Laffnie de Jager, **Cliff Drysdale**, Ellis Ferreira, **Wayne Ferreira**, Wesley Moodie, Brian Norton, Piet Norval, Abe Siegal, Eric Sturgess, Christo Van Rensburg, and Danie Visser. The best South African female players include Linky Boshoff, Irene Bowder, Amanda Coetzer, Marian de Swardt, Rosalyn Fairbank, Tanya Harford, Ilana Kloss, Sandra Reynolds, Renee Schuurman, Greer Stevens, and Patricia Walkden.

Morocco, which first played Davis Cup tennis in 1961, reached the World Group three times (2001, 2002, 2004) but lost in the first round all three times. Its best players include Karim Alami, Hichan Arazi, and Younes El Aynaoui. Zimbabwe reached the quarterfinals of the Davis Cup World Group in 1998. Its best players include Kevin Ulyett and the Black family—brothers Byron and Wayne and their sister, Cara. All four have won multiple **Grand Slam** doubles championships, with Cara's 10 titles leading the group.

AGASSI, ANDRE KIRK. B. 29 April 1970, Las Vegas, Nevada. Andre Agassi is the son of Emmanuel "Mike" Agassi, an Iranian who competed in the 1948 and 1952 **Olympic** boxing **tournaments** and later immigrated to the United States. Mike was Andre's first **coach** and was a severe taskmaster. Andre began his **professional** tennis career in 1986 at the age of 16 and is one of only three people to win all four **Grand Slam** championships plus the Olympic gold medal—the others are his wife **Steffi Graf** and **Rafael Nadal**. From 1990 to 2005, Agassi won eight Slam **singles** titles and was runner-up seven times. He won the **Australian Open** in 1995, 2000, 2001, and 2003. The 5-foot 11-inch right-hander won the **French Open** in 1999 and was runner-up in 1990 and 1991. He won **Wimbledon** in 1992 and was runner-up in 1999. At the **United States Open**, he won in 1994 and 1999, was runner-up three times to **Pete Sampras** in 1990, 1995, and 2002, and, at the age of 35, won three five-**set matches** to reach the final against 24-year old **Roger Federer** in 2005 but lost in four sets. Agassi competed in the 1996 Olympic Games and won the singles event but lost in the second round of the **doubles** with partner MaliVai Washington. In **Davis Cup** play for the United States, in 11 years and 22 **ties**, from 1988 to 2005, Andre had a record of 30–6 in singles competition and did not play doubles. He helped his country win the Cup in 1990 and 1992 and played in the quarterfinals and semifinals for the 1995 team, which also won the Cup.

In 1997, Agassi married actress Brooke Shields, but they divorced in 1999. In 2001, he married former tennis professional Steffi Graf. He retired in 2006, due to a series of injuries, but continues to occasionally play **World**

Team Tennis and charitable events. In retirement, he has devoted his energy to the Andre Agassi Foundation, which sponsors various children's projects, including the Andre Agassi College Preparatory Academy. He was inducted into the **International Tennis Hall of Fame** in 2011.

AKHURST COZENS, DAPHNE JESSIE. B. 22 April 1903, Ashfield, Sydney, New South Wales, **Australia**. D. 9 January 1933, Sydney, New South Wales, Australia. Daphne Akhurst attended Miss E. Tildesley's Normanhurst School in Ashfield (a Sydney suburb) and then the Sydney Conservatorium of Music, where she studied to be a music teacher. Her tennis career was relatively brief, but she was one of the dominant players in Australian women's tennis during the 1920s. She won 14 **Australian Championships** from 1924 to 1931—the fourth most of any player in history. She won five **singles**, five **doubles**, and four **mixed doubles**. In 1925, 1928, and 1929, she won all three titles in each of those years. She also won the singles and was runner-up in doubles and mixed doubles in 1926. Her doubles partners were Sylvia Lance, Esna Boyd, Louie Bickerton, and Marjorie Cox. Her mixed doubles were won with three different partners—John Willard, **Jean Borotra**, and Gar Moon. She was also the runner-up in the 1928 mixed doubles at **Wimbledon** with partner **Jack Crawford**. In 1925, she, Esna Boyd, and Sylvia Lance Harper were the first Australian women tennis players to travel abroad. She reached the quarterfinals at Wimbledon that year. In 1928, she was **ranked** third worldwide—her highest ranking. Her best performance at Wimbledon was in 1928, when she reached the semifinals of both the singles and doubles. That same year she also reached the quarterfinal round at the **French National Championships**.

On 26 February 1930, in Sydney, she married Royston Stuckey Cozens, a tobacco manufacturer. The couple resided in Strathfield (a Sydney suburb) and had one son. She died following an ectopic pregnancy at the age of 29. Since 1934, the Women's singles champion at the Australian Open is presented with the Daphne Akhurst Memorial Cup. She was inducted into the Australian Tennis Hall of Fame in 2006 but has not yet been enshrined in the **International Tennis Hall of Fame**.

ALL. In tennis, the word "all" is used to denote an even score, as in "30-all" or "two **games** all" or "two **sets** all."

ALL-COMERS. In the early years of the Championships at **Wimbledon** and also in the **United States National Championships**, the event was open to "all-comers" (providing, of course, that they were **amateur** and white). The winner of the all-comers **tournament** would then play the previous year's champion in the **challenge round** to determine the tournament champion.

ALL-ENGLAND LAWN TENNIS AND CROQUET CLUB. Located in **Wimbledon**, England, on the outskirts of London, the All-England Lawn Tennis and Croquet Club is the sponsoring organization for the major **tournament** officially called "the Championships, Wimbledon" but usually referred to simply as "Wimbledon." It is a private club and was founded in 1868 as the All-England Croquet Club. In 1877, the first **lawn tennis** championships for men were held, and the club's name was changed to the All-England Croquet and Lawn Tennis Club. In 1889, as lawn tennis had superseded croquet as the more popular sport, by far, the present name was adopted. The tennis **courts** used for championship **matches** are **grass**, although the club also has several **clay** courts and indoor courts for members' use. Queen Elizabeth II is the patron of the club, and the club's president is the Duke of Kent. The Championships are often attended by members of the royal family. The Wimbledon Lawn Tennis Museum, open to the public, is also located on the grounds.

ALLEY. The alley on a **lawn tennis court** refers to the area (4.5 feet) on each side of the court that extends the inbounds area for **doubles** play. The court is thus widened from 27 feet to 36 feet.

AMATEUR. An amateur tennis player is one who does not receive money for playing or teaching the sport. Amateurs are only permitted to receive reimbursement for expenses incurred in playing **tournaments**. Until the late 1960s, most major tournaments were limited to amateur players. In 1968, tournaments began to offer prize money and accept **professional** players. Tournaments were classified as "**open**," and both amateurs and professionals were allowed to compete. Amateurs, even if they won the tournaments, were not allowed to accept prize money. In recent times, most tournaments are open tournaments.

AMBIDEXTROUS PLAYERS. There have been several **lawn tennis** players who have developed the ability to play equally well with either hand. Among them have been Beverly Baker Fleitz, **John Bromwich**, Giorgio di Stefani, Juan-Manuel Elizondo, Jarmila Groth, Pavel Hutka, Luke Jensen, Yevgeniya Kulikovskaya, Lita Liem, Evan Noel, Guillermo Olaso, and Marijke Schaar. Liem actually faced Schaar at **Wimbledon** in 1972 and defeated her. Some of these players would **serve** with either hand, and others would switch the **racket** hand so as not to hit a **backhand** shot. *See also* CONVERTED PLAYERS; LEFT-HANDED PLAYERS.

AMERICAN TENNIS ASSOCIATION (ATA). The American Tennis Association was founded in 1916 as an alternative to the **United States Lawn**

Tennis Association, which, until the 1950s, was a segregated organization that did not allow black players to participate in its events. The ATA's first **tournaments** were held in 1917. The organization is still in existence in 2010 and still conducts annual regional and national championships while promoting tennis in the black community. *See also* AFRICAN AMERICAN PLAYERS; GIBSON (DARBEN) (LLEWELLYN), ALTHEA; JOHNSON, ROBERT WALTER "WHIRLWIND."

AMRITRAJ FAMILY. The Amritraj family of Madras (now known as Chennai), **India**, is the leading Indian **lawn tennis** family. Brothers Vijay (born 14 December 1953), Anand (born 20 March 1952), and Ashok (born 22 February 1957) all had substantial **professional** careers. Vijay's son Prakash (born 2 October 1983 in Los Angeles, California) became a professional tennis player in 2003. Anand's son Stephen (born 28 March 1984 in Los Angeles) is also a professional tennis player. Vijay competed in the 1988 **Olympic Games** but lost in the first round. With partner Anand, they reached the second round of **doubles**. From 1968 to 1988, Anand played in 39 **ties** in 19 years for India in the **Davis Cup**, had a record of 11–16 in **singles** and 21–14 in doubles (26 of the **matches** with Vijay as partner), and helped India to reach the final tie in 1974, where India defaulted to **South Africa**, and in 1987, when India was defeated by **Sweden**. Vijay's Davis Cup record from 1970 to 1988 was 27–18 in singles and 18–10 in doubles in 32 ties over 17 years. Prakash, although born in the **United States**, played in the Davis Cup for India for five years, from 2003 to 2008, appearing in 10 ties, playing singles only, with a record of 7–11. He attended the University of Southern California, where he was a member of the 2002 **National Collegiate Athletic Association** championship team.

Ashok has become a much more successful film producer than tennis player and has produced more than 100 films and also acted in a few. Vijay, after retiring from active play, still occasionally plays in **seniors'** events and has appeared in several television series and motion pictures, with a regular role in the television comedy *What a Country* in 1986–87. He also created the Vijay Amritraj Foundation, which aids charitable organizations in India.

ANDERSON, MALCOLM JAMES "MAL," "COWBOY." B. 3 March 1935, Theodore, Queensland, **Australia**. Mal Anderson was raised on a 6,000-acre ranch in rural Queensland and was nicknamed Cowboy by his fellow players. He should not be confused with Mal Anderson, a contemporary **table tennis** champion from Wisconsin, who is a member of the USA Table Tennis Hall of Fame. Cowboy Anderson's first appearance in a major **tournament** was in 1954 at the **Australian Championships**, where he won his first two **matches** before being defeated in the third round. In 1957, he had his greatest victory when he won the **United States National Singles Championship** at **Forest Hills** even though he was **unseeded**. The following year, he reached the finals of the Australian Championships and United States National Championships and was a quarterfinalist at **Wimbledon**. He won the Australian **Mixed Doubles** Championship in 1957 with Fay Muller and was the men's **doubles** finalist that year with **Ashley Cooper**. At **Roland Garros** that year, Anderson and Cooper won the men's doubles. By December 1957, Anderson was the second-**ranked** singles player in the world. He played for Australia in the **challenge round** of the **Davis Cup** in 1957 and 1958 and helped win the Cup in 1957, before becoming a **professional** and ineligible for Cup competition in 1959. In his first year as a professional, the six-foot one-inch right-hander won the highly regarded London Indoor Pro Championships at Wembley.

When Davis Cup eligibility rules were changed to allow professionals to compete, he again played in 1972 and 1973. His overall Davis Cup record was 11–3 in singles and 2–3 in doubles in eight **ties** in the four years he competed. He also was allowed to play in the Australian Championships when it became an open event in 1968 and reached the finals again in 1972, at the age of 36, 14 years after his first Australian Championship finals. He won the doubles in 1973 with **John Newcombe** as partner. Mal married Daphne Emerson, sister of tennis star **Roy Emerson**. After retiring from competitive tennis, Mal and Daphne ran a tennis and **squash** facility in Queensland. Mal was inducted into the **International Tennis Hall of Fame** in 2000 and the Australian Tennis Hall of Fame in 2001.

ARGENTINA. The governing organization for **lawn tennis** in Argentina is the Argentine Tennis Association (Asociación Argentina de Tenis), founded in 1921. Although Argentina competed in the 1924 **Olympic** tennis events and participated in **Davis Cup** play from 1921, tennis did not really become popular there until the 1970s, when **Guillermo Vilas** became a world-class competitor. Since then, Argentina has been among the leading countries in international tennis. From 1923 through 2011, Argentina has competed in 57 Davis Cup **tournaments**, with a record of 75–58 in 133 **ties**. The country has competed 19 times in the World Group since its formation in 1981 and was losing finalist in 1981, 2006, and 2008. Argentina's top Davis Cup players have been Guillermo Vilas, **David Nalbandian**, and José-Luis Clerc. Vilas, inducted into the **International Tennis of Hall of Fame** in 1991, won four **Grand Slam** titles in his career and was a losing finalist on four other occasions. **Juan Martín del Potro** defeated **Roger Federer** to become the 2009 **United States Open** champion. Gastón Gaudio was the 2004 **French Open**

champion when he defeated fellow Argentine Guillermo Coria. In 1996, Argentines Javier Frana and Patricia Tarabini won the French Open **mixed doubles** title.

Among the best male tennis players have been Guillermo Vilas, José Acasuso, Pablo Albano, Agustín Calleri, Guillermo Cañas, Héctor Cattaruzza, Juan Ignacio Chela, José Luis Clerc, Guillermo Coria, Juan Martín del Potro, Javier Frana, Gastón Gaudio, Cristian Miniussi, Enrique Morea, and David Nalbandian, who was the **Wimbledon** finalist in 2002 and, later, reached a world **ranking** of three. The best female tennis players include **Gabriela Sabatini**, Norma Baylon, Gisela Dulko, Inés Gorrochategui, Ivanna Madruga, Mercedes Paz, Paola Suárez, Patricia Tarabini, and Adriana Villagran. Suárez won eight Grand Slam **doubles** championships and was runner-up in eight others. Sabatini was the United States Open champion in 1990 and Wimbledon doubles champion in 1988, as well as runner-up in five other Grand Slam events. In **Federation Cup** competition, from 1964 to 2011, Argentina has competed 43 years, 33 years in World Group, played ties with a record of 70–52, and reached the semifinals in 1986 and 1993. Its best Olympic showing was Sabatini's silver medal in 1988. The team of Suárez and Tarabini won bronze in 2004, and Miniussi and Frana won bronze in the 1992 men's doubles.

ARIAS, JAMES "JIMMY." B. 16 August 1964, Buffalo, New York. Jimmy Arias became a **professional lawn tennis** player at the age of 16 in 1980, reaching the second round of the **United States Open** that year. His best years were his first few years, and he reached his highest **singles ranking** of five in 1984. His only **Grand Slam** title was in 1981 at **Roland Garros** when he and **Andrea Jaeger**, each only 16 years old, won the **mixed doubles**. He won five professional singles titles, all on **clay** and all in 1982 or 1983. He also was voted the **Association of Tennis Professionals** (ATP) Most Improved Player in 1983 and reached the United States Open men's singles semifinal round that year. In 1984, he reached the fourth round of the **French Open** and **Wimbledon**. He competed in the demonstration tennis tournament in the 1984 **Olympic Games** and lost in the semifinal round to **Stefan Edberg**, the eventual tournament winner. Arias was on the **United States Davis Cup** team in 1984, 1986, and 1987, with a record of one win and four losses in three **ties**. He lost in a **dead rubber** in the final round in 1984, in his first Cup appearance. His career went downhill rapidly, and although he continued on the ATP Tour until 1994, the 5-foot 9-inch, 155-pound right-hander did not win another championship. After retiring with a career singles record of 286–223, he became a commentator for the **Tennis Channel** and occasionally plays on the **Champions Series**.

ARTHUR ASHE STADIUM. Arthur Ashe Stadium, opened in 1997, is the main stadium at the **USTA Billie Jean King National Tennis Center** in **Flushing Meadows,** New York. Named for the **Hall of Fame** tennis champion, **Arthur Ashe,** it has a seating capacity of 22,547 and has 90 luxury suites in addition. It is, by far, the largest tennis-only stadium in the world.

ASHE, ARTHUR ROBERT, JR. B. 10 July 1943, Richmond, Virginia. D. 6 February 1993, New York, New York. Arthur Ashe was the first prominent male **African American lawn tennis** player to play in integrated **tournaments.** He was mentored by **Dr. Walter Johnson** who saw Ashe's potential and had him transfer to the integrated Sumner High School in St. Louis, Missouri. From there, Ashe received a scholarship to the University of California, Los Angeles (UCLA), where he won the **National Collegiate Athletic Association** national **singles** title in 1965 and helped UCLA to win the team championship. He made his first appearance at the **United States National Championships** in 1959, at the age of 16, and progressed to the semifinal round there in 1965. Still an **amateur**, in 1968, he won the first United States Open tournament.

The 6-foot 1-inch, slim (155 pounds) right-hander became a **professional** in 1969 and was the runner-up at the 1972 U.S. Open. He won **Wimbledon** in 1975. He was a finalist at the **Australian Championships** in 1966 and 1967, won it in 1970 and again lost in the finals in 1971. His best result at **Roland Garros** was the quarterfinals in 1971. In **doubles** competition, he and **Tony Roche** won the 1977 Australian Open, and Ashe and Marty Riessen won the 1971 **French Open.** In 1971, Ashe and **Dennis Ralston** were finalists at Wimbledon, and in 1968, Ashe and **Andrés Gimeno** were finalists in the U.S. Open Doubles Championships at **Forest Hills.** Ashe served in the U.S. Army from 1966 to 1968 and reached the rank of first lieutenant. After being refused a visa to play tennis in **South Africa** in 1968, Ashe became an active opponent of South Africa's apartheid position. He was finally granted a visa in 1973 and that year won the South African Open Doubles Championship and lost the **singles** championship to **Jimmy Connors.** Later, after apartheid was overturned, Ashe met with President Nelson Mandela. Ashe played for the **United States** in **Davis Cup** competition from 1963 to 1978 and helped win the Cup in 1968, 1969, and 1970. He played only in preliminary round competition on the Cup-winning teams of 1963 and 1978. His overall record was 27–5 in singles and 1–1 in doubles in 18 **ties** in 10 years.

His playing career ended in 1979 after he suffered a heart attack requiring a quadruple bypass heart operation. As nonplaying team captain from 1981 to 1985, he led the United States to the Davis Cup championship in 1981 and 1982. He was inducted into the **International Tennis Hall of Fame** in 1985.

He later required a second heart operation in 1983, and as the result of a blood transfusion during that surgery, contracted Human Immunodeficiency Virus. That condition was not diagnosed until 1988, and Ashe was able to conceal it from the public until 1992. During the last year of his life, he worked to call attention to the disease and founded the Arthur Ashe Institute for Urban Health. During that time, he also cowrote *Days of Grace: A Memoir*, which was published posthumously. During the 1980s, he spent much of his time writing the three-volume *A Hard Road to Glory: A History of the African-American Athlete*, which also saw posthumous publication. In 1993, he was posthumously awarded the Presidential Medal of Freedom by President Bill Clinton. The **Arthur Ashe Stadium** at the **USTA Billie Jean King National Tennis Center** in **Flushing Meadows**, New York, opened in 1997, four years after his death. In 2005, a United States commemorative stamp was

Arthur Ashe was a champion tennis player and civil rights activist who died prematurely in 1993 at 49 years of age. (courtesy of the International Tennis Hall of Fame and Museum, Edward Fernberger Collection)

issued honoring Ashe. As of 2010, Ashe and Frenchman **Yannick Noah** are the only two men of black African heritage to win a **Grand Slam** singles championship.

ASSOCIATION OF TENNIS PROFESSIONALS (ATP). The Association of Tennis Professionals was organized in 1972. It governs male **professionals** only and controls player **rankings** and **tournaments**. In 1990, it took over the operation of tournaments, which were then known as the ATP Tour (renamed in 2009 as the ATP World Tour). It has various levels of tournaments ranging from Futures and **Challenger** tournaments at the lowest level to ATP World Tour Masters 1000 series events, in which the top-ranked professionals are required to compete. Player ranking points are won by the player's performance in these events. These points are used to determine eligibility and **seeding** for upcoming tournaments.

ATKINSON BUXTON, JULIETTE PAXTON. B. 15 April 1873, Rahway, New Jersey. D. 2 January 1944, Lawrenceville, Illinois. Juliette Atkinson was the daughter of a Brooklyn, New York, physician and was an all-around athlete. During the 1890s, she was America's best female tennis player. She played at a time when women's championship tennis matches were contested in a best-of-five **sets** format, and several of her victories went the full five sets. (The **United States Lawn Tennis Association** only changed to a three-set format in 1902). Although only five feet tall, Juliette Atkinson won 13 **United States National Championships** from 1894 to 1902. Each year, from 1895 to 1899, she was either the **singles** champion or runner-up, winning the title in 1895, 1897, and 1898. In 1895 and again in 1897, she had to defeat her sister, Kathleen, in the semifinal round on her way to the championship. From 1894 to 1898, she won five straight **doubles** championships and won two more in 1901 and 1902. Her doubles partners were Helen Hellwig (twice), Elisabeth Moore, Juliette's sister, Kathleen (twice), Myrtle McActeer, and Marion Jones. She also won the **mixed doubles** with Edwin Fischer each year from 1894 to 1896. She was inducted into the **International Tennis Hall of Fame** in 1974. She married George B. Buxton in 1918 and had no children.

AUSTIN, HENRY WILFRED "BUNNY." B. 26 August 1906, London, England. D 26 August 2000, Couldson, South London, England. Bunny Austin is best known as the man who first wore shorts at **Wimbledon**. As a schoolboy soccer player, he wore shorts and could not see why, as a practical matter, **lawn tennis** players should not do likewise. So at **Forest Hills** in 1932, for the **United States National Championships**, he did so. The following year he wore them at Wimbledon. Austin attended Repton School in

Derbyshire and Cambridge University. While at Cambridge, he reached the Wimbledon semifinals in 1926. In 1932 and 1938, he reached the finals at Wimbledon and, as of 2010, is the last British man to reach the Wimbledon **singles** final. He also lost at the **Roland Garros** finals in 1937. He was a finalist in **mixed doubles** at Roland Garros in 1931 and Wimbledon in 1934, both with Dorothy Shepherd Barron, and at **Forest Hills** in 1929, with Phyllis Howkins Covell. A five-foot nine-inch right-hander, he played **Davis Cup** tennis for **Great Britain** each year from 1929 to 1937 and helped win the Cup in 1933, 1934, 1935, and 1936. His Davis Cup record was 36–12 in 24 **ties**, all **matches** played in **singles** competition.

His older sister, Joan, was a Wimbledon **doubles** finalist in 1923. Henry was married to British actress Phyllis Konstam from 1931 until her death in 1976. In 1940, they moved to the **United States** to help promote world peace through sports. While there, he was subject to the draft and served in the U.S. Army Air Corps. He was inducted into the **International Tennis Hall of Fame** in 1997 and died in a nursing home on his 84th birthday in 2000.

AUSTIN (HOLT), TRACY ANN. B. 12 December 1962, Palos Verdes, California. Tracy Austin is the daughter of Jeanne and George Austin. Her father was a nuclear physicist. Her mother enjoyed playing tennis and worked in the pro shop of the **Jack Kramer** Tennis Club in Rolling Hills, California. Tracy would accompany her mother to work and began playing tennis at age three. Her formal tennis instruction began with **coach** Vic Braden before she was in kindergarten. Robert Lansdorp replaced Braden as coach when Tracy was seven years old and remained as her coach throughout most of her career. At just 15 years of age, she became a **professional** tennis player while still attending Rolling Hills High School. Her four siblings—brothers Doug, John, and Jeff and sister Pam—all played professional tennis.

The diminutive (5 feet 3 inches, 110 pounds) Tracy had the honor of playing on the opening night of the new **USTA National Tennis Center** at **Flushing Meadows** in the **United States Open**, 29 August 1978, and easily won her **match** that night against Pat Bostrom, 6–0, 6–1. She reached the quarterfinals of the U.S. Open that year, where she was defeated by **Chris Evert**. Tracy reached the semifinals at **Wimbledon** and then won the U.S. Open **Singles** Championship in 1979, at the age of 16, the youngest player ever to win that title. She played singles on the **United States Federation Cup** team in 1978, 1979, and 1980 and won 13 of 14 matches, helping the United States to win the Cup each year. She was a member of the United States **Wightman Cup** team in 1978, 1979, and 1981 and had a record of 6–2 in three events. In 1980, she reached the semifinals of both Wimbledon and the U.S. Open. In 1981, she again won the U.S. Open title. She and her brother John won the Wimbledon **mixed doubles** in 1980 (the only sister-brother pair ever to win that title) and were runners-up in 1981. She competed only twice in the **Australian Open** and was a quarterfinalist in 1981.

By 1981, back injuries curtailed her career, and she began limiting her schedule and won her last championship in 1982. She continued playing but with much less success. In the **French Open**, in three appearances, she reached the quarterfinals in 1982 and 1983. In 1988, she attempted a comeback, restricting her play to **doubles**. A car accident nearly ended her life on 3 August 1989. She made one final comeback attempt in 1993 but retired permanently in July 1994. During her relatively brief professional tennis career, Tracy won 30 singles championships and 5 doubles championships. She was the youngest player ever inducted into the **International Tennis Hall of Fame** when she was so honored in 1992, at just 29 years of age. She married real estate entrepreneur Scott Holt on 17 August 1993, and they are the parents of three sons. Since retiring from active play, she has worked in television as a commentator.

AUSTRALASIA. From 1905 to 1922, the countries of **Australia** and New Zealand entered a combined team in **Davis Cup** competition under the name "Australasia." Of the 13 **tournaments** that were held in those years, Australasia won the event six times—1907, 1908, 1909, 1911, 1914, and 1919. Among the players on those teams were Australians James Anderson, **Norman Brookes**, **Jack Crawford**, Jack Hawkes, Rod Heath, Pat O'Hara Wood, and **Gerald Patterson** and New Zealanders Alfred Dunlop and **Tony Wilding**.

AUSTRALASIAN CHAMPIONSHIPS. *See* AUSTRALIAN OPEN.

AUSTRALIA. Lawn tennis has long been one of the most popular sports in Australia. For a large portion of the 20th century, Australia along with the **United States** were the dominant nations in the sport. Australia has competed in 47 **Davis Cup** final rounds, with a record of 28–19. From 1938 through 1968, Australians either won the Cup or finished second each year that it was contested. And from 1950 to 1967, the team won it in 15 of the 18 years. From 1905 through May 2011, Australia has competed in 91 Davis Cup tournaments, with a record of 175–63 in 238 **ties**. From 1905 to 1922, Australia competed with New Zealand players as **Australasia**. Australia has reached the World Group 26 times since its formation in 1981 and has won the Cup 28 times, second only to the United States. Australia's top Davis Cup players have been **Lleyton Hewitt**, **Adrian Quist**, and **the Woodies**, **Mark Woodforde** and **Todd Woodbridge**. The **Australian Championships**

(known since 1969 as the **Australian Open**) is one of the four major annual tennis tournaments.

Among the best Australian male tennis players have been **Hall of Famers Mal Anderson, John Bromwich, Norman Brookes, Ashley Cooper, Jack Crawford,** Owen Davidson, **Roy Emerson, Neale Fraser, Lew Hoad, Harry Hopman, Rod Laver,** Ken McGregor, **John Newcombe, Gerald Patterson,** Adrian Quist, **Pat Rafter, Tony Roche, Merv Rose, Ken Rosewall, Frank Sedgman, Fred Stolle,** Todd Woodbridge, and Mark Woodforde. Other players of note include John Alexander, James Anderson, Bill Bowrey, Darren Cahill, Don Candy, Ross Case, **Pat Cash, Phil Dent,** Mark Edmondson, **Ken Fletcher,** Rex Hartwig, John Hawkes, Lleyton Hewitt, Bob Howe, Colin Long, Randolph Lycett, Bob Mark, Geoff Masters, Vivian McGrath, the **doubles** team of **Peter McNamara** and Paul McNamee, Gar Moon, Patrick O'Hara Wood, **Mark Philippoussis,** Horace Rice, and Ray Ruffels.

The best Australian female tennis players include Hall of Famers **Evonne Goolagong Cawley, Margaret Smith Court, Lesley Turner Bowrey, Wendy Turnbull,** and **Nancye Wynne Bolton.** Other female Australian tennis champions include **Daphne Akhurst Cozens,** Mary Bevis Hawton, Esna Boyd Robertson, Mary Carter Reitano, Lorraine Coghlan Robinson, Marjorie Cox Crawford, **Thelma Coyne Long,** Jelena Dokić, Robyn Ebbern, Joyce Fitch Rymer, Helen Gourlay Cawley, Elizabeth Hall Hopman, Joan Hartigan Bathurst, Emily Hood Westacott, Sylvia Lance Harper, Jan Lehane O'Neill, Rachel McQuillan, Kerry Melville Reid, Margaret Molesworth, Alicia Molik, Beryl Penrose Collier, Nicole Pratt, Nicole Provis Bradtke, Elizabeth Sayers Smylie, **Samantha Stosur,** Rennae Stubbs, and **Judy Tegart Dalton.** In **Federation Cup** competition, from 1963 to May 2011, Australia has entered all 49 years, 38 years in World Group, played 166 ties with a record of 120–46, and won the Cup seven times—in 1964, 1965, 1968, 1970, 1971, 1973, and 1974—the second most of any nation.

Tennis was not an **Olympic** sport when Australian tennis was at its peak in the midcentury, and its Olympic triumphs are few. Sayers Smylie and Turnbull, in 1988, and McQuillan and Provis, in 1992, won bronze medals in women's doubles, and Alicia Molik, in 2004, won women's singles. The Woodies, Todd Woodbridge and Mark Woodforde, won the 1996 Olympic doubles and were silver medalists in 2000. In 1896, Australian Edwin Flack teamed with Englishman George Robinson to finish third in the Olympic doubles competition, although only five teams entered that year.

AUSTRALIAN CHAMPIONSHIPS. See AUSTRALIAN OPEN.

AUSTRALIAN OPEN. The Australian Open is one of the four major (**Grand Slam**) tennis **tournaments**. It began in 1905 with **singles** and **doubles** events for men only. In 1922, ladies' singles, doubles, and **mixed doubles** were added. It was originally called the **Australasian** Championships. In 1927, the name was changed to the Australian Championships, and in 1969, the tournament became **open** to both **amateur** and **professional** players, and the name was changed to the Australian Open. The tournament is run by Tennis **Australia**, an organization formerly known as the **Lawn Tennis** Association of Australia. The tournament has been held in Melbourne, Sydney, Adelaide, and Brisbane and, in its early years, Perth, Australia (three times), and Christchurch and Hastings, New Zealand (once each). Since 1972, Melbourne has been its permanent home. The tournament is played in the Australian summer in January. In 1977, the date was changed from January to December, and thus, two tournaments took place that year. In 1986, it was changed back to January, and there was no tournament in 1986. During the early years, as travel to Australia was very time consuming, there were few foreign entrants. In recent years, it has become well attended by players worldwide. *See also* APPENDIX E (for a list of champions).

B

BACKHAND. A backhand is a shot hit with the back of the hand facing the **net**. A right-handed player will hit returns on his or her left-hand side using a backhand and vice versa for **left-handed** players. Many female players and some male players employ two hands when hitting a backhand shot. It is generally a more difficult shot to master than a **forehand**. Among the players known for having the best backhand are **Don Budge**, **Jimmy Connors**, and **Ken Rosewall**. **Steffi Graf**, **Justine Henin**, and **Jelena Janković** are among the women with the best backhand stroke.

BADMINTON. Badminton is a game similar to tennis but played on a smaller **court** using lighter **rackets** and with a feathered device known as a shuttlecock or birdie, rather than a **ball**, as the object to hit over the **net**. The shuttlecock is not allowed to touch the ground. Neurosurgeon Dr. David Guthrie Freeman was one of the world's greatest badminton players but also an accomplished **lawn tennis** player and was the finalist in the **United States National** Men's **Doubles** Championships in 1943. Freeman was inducted into the U.S. and also the World Badminton Hall of Fame. **Kathleen "Kitty" McKane** was also an international badminton champion, as well as a **Wimbledon lawn tennis** champion. Since 1992, badminton has been included in the summer **Olympic Games**.

BAGEL. A bagel in tennis terminology is a **set** with a shutout score, 6–0, in which one player fails to win a **game**. A double bagel is two straight sets by that score, 6–0, 6–0. A triple bagel is three straight sets where one player fails to win a game, 6–0, 6–0, 6–0.

BAGHDATIS, MARCOS. B. 17 June 1985, Limassol, Cyprus. Marcos Baghdatis is Cyprus's greatest tennis player. At the age of 13, he went to Paris, **France**, to study at the Mouratoglou Tennis Academy. In January 2000, he made his **Davis Cup** debut while still only 14 years old and won his **doubles match**. After being named the World's **Junior Tennis** Champion by the **International Tennis Federation** in 2003, he became a **professional** and reached the second round of the **United States Open** in 2004. The 6-foot tall, 180-pound right-hander competed in the 2004 **Olympic singles** event but lost in the second round. His most successful year was 2006. He was **unseeded** at the **Australian Open** but defeated **Andy Roddick**, Ivan Ljubičić, and **David Nalbandian** to reach the finals, where he lost to **Roger Federer** after winning the first **set**. Later that year, he reached the semifinals at **Wimbledon** but was defeated by **Rafael Nadal** and reached a career-high ranking of eight in August. In 2008, he played a memorable match at the Australian Open that started at 11:52 p.m. and ended at 4:34 a.m., losing to **Lleyton Hewitt** in five sets.

Injuries in 2008 and 2009 hampered his play, and by mid-2009, he was playing at the **Challenger** level and won an event in Vancouver. He recovered from his injuries and, in 2010, played a full schedule in the **Association of Tennis Professionals** tour, winning an event in Sydney, Australia, in January and defeating Roger Federer at **Indian Wells** in March. Baghdatis's Davis Cup record is outstanding, and from 2000 to 2010, he has played in 67 matches, with a record of 38–3 in singles and 16–10 in doubles. Marcos's brothers Marinos and Petros have also played Davis Cup tennis for Cyprus.

BALL. *See* TENNIS BALL.

BALL BOY. A ball boy is a person (male or female) who retrieves the **tennis balls** for players during **matches**. Other tasks include providing players with balls to **serve**, providing players with towels between **points**, and holding umbrellas over players to provide shade during rest periods. Several ball boys are stationed behind each end of the **court** and one at each end of the **net**. Ball boys (and girls) usually range in age from eight years to mid-teens.

BASELINE. The baseline is the line at each end of the **court**. Players **serving** must stand behind it. During play, the **ball** must strike the court on or between the baselines.

BEACH TENNIS. Beach tennis is a relatively new game. It originated in Aruba around 2000. The game is a combination of tennis and beach volleyball. It is played on the sand using a beach volleyball **court** (30 feet by 60 feet). A standard tennis **racket** and slightly depressurized **tennis ball** are used. Tennis **scoring** is used, but the ball is played as a **volley** (since the ball will not bounce on the sand).

BECKER, BORIS FRANZ. B. 22 November 1967, Leimen, **Germany**. Boris Becker began playing competitive tennis in 1983, at the age of 15. By

1985, age 17 and **unseeded**, he became the youngest men's **Wimbledon singles** champion. From 1985 to 1991, he reached the finals at Wimbledon six of the seven years, winning the **tournament** in 1985, 1986, and 1989 and being runner-up in 1988, 1990, and 1991. He was also a Wimbledon finalist in 1995. He won the **United States Open** in 1989, the **Australian Open** in 1991 and 1996, and was a three-time semifinalist at the **French Open**. His career record for **Grand Slam** events is 163–40, a winning percentage of over 80 percent. Becker was known for his powerful **serve** and was a far better player on fast **surfaces**, such as **grass**, than he was on **clay**. The 6-foot 3-inch, 180-pound, right-handed redhead competed in the 1992 **Olympic Games** and lost in the third round of the singles but, with partner **Michael Stich**, won the **doubles** event. Becker played **Davis Cup** tennis for West Germany from 1985 to 1989, leading the team to the final in 1985 and championship in 1988 and 1989. He represented Germany from 1991 to 1999 but did not play for them in 1993 when Germany won the Cup. His overall Davis Cup record is 38–3 in singles and 16–9 in doubles in 28 **ties** in 12 years. In 1987, he defeated **John McEnroe** in a Davis Cup match that lasted over six hours—one of the longest in Cup history. He won the **Hopman Cup** in 1995 with partner Anke Huber. Becker is one of only two players to win the Wimbledon, the Olympic Games, Davis Cup, **World Team Cup**, and Hopman Cup.

When Becker retired from competitive play in 1999, he had compiled a career record of 49 singles and 15 doubles titles and had reached world **rankings** of one in singles in 1991 and six in doubles in 1986. He was inducted into the **International Tennis Hall of Fame** in 2003. In retirement, he has been the owner of a tennis **racket** and clothing manufacturer. *See also* LONGEST MATCH IN TENNIS HISTORY; STATISTICS.

BEHR, KARL HOWELL. B. 30 May 1885, Brooklyn, New York. D. 15 October 1949, New York, New York. Karl Behr was educated at Lawrenceville School and Yale University, where he obtained a law degree. In 1904, he won the **intercollegiate doubles** championship while at Yale. In 1905, the 5-foot 9-inch, 155-pound right-hander won both the **singles** and doubles championships of New Jersey. In 1907, he and partner Beals Wright reached the men's doubles final at **Wimbledon**, where they were defeated by Australian **Norman Brookes** and New Zealander **Tony Wilding**. Shortly afterward, Behr and Wright played for the **United States** against **Australasia** in the **Davis Cup** and defeated Brookes and Wilding. Behr lost both Davis Cup singles matches, and the American team lost the **tie**. Australasia then defeated the **British Isles** team in the **challenge round**. Behr achieved a **ranking** of 3 in the United States in 1907 and was ranked in the top 10 in six other years.

In 1912, he booked first class passage on the *Titanic* in pursuit of a friend of his sister, Helen Newsom, who he was attempting to court. When the ship hit an iceberg, Behr, Newsom, and members of her family managed to obtain a place in a lifeboat and were saved. Behr allegedly proposed to her in the lifeboat, and they were married in March 1913. Although Behr was admitted to the bar in 1910, he did not practice law but went into banking. He became a vice president of Dillon, Read and Company and later sat on the board on several major corporations. Behr's brother, Max H. Behr, became a well-known golfer. Karl Behr was inducted into the **International Tennis Hall of Fame** in 1969. *See also* WILLIAMS, RICHARD NORRIS, II "DICK."

BELGIUM. The Royal Belgian Tennis Federation administers tennis competition in Belgium. In 1904, Belgium was one of three countries to compete in the fourth edition of the **International Lawn Tennis Challenge** (currently known as the **Davis Cup**). Belgium defeated **France** in the preliminary round but was defeated by the **British Isles** in the **challenge round**. Through May 2011, Belgium has competed in 89 total Davis Cup **tournaments** with a record of 85–87 in 172 **ties**. Since the formation of Davis Cup World Group competition in 1981, Belgium has competed 14 times and reached the semifinal round once, in 1999.

Among the best Belgian male tennis players have been Jacques Brichant, Paul de Borman, Steve Darcis, William le Maire de Warzée, Xavier Malisse, the Rochus brothers (Olivier and Christophe), and Philippe Washer. The best female tennis players include Sabine Appelmans, Els Callens, **Kim Clijsters**, Laurence Courtois, Ann Devries, Kirsten Flipkens, Michele Gurdal, **Justine Henin**, Monique van Haver, Dominique van Roost-Monami, Sandra Wasserman, and Yanina Wickmayer. In **Federation Cup** competition, from 1963 to May 2011, Belgium has competed 47 years, 41 in World Group, played 130 ties with a record of 67–63, won the Cup in 2001, and was runner-up in 2006. Tennis was contested in the 1920 **Olympic Games** held in Antwerp, Belgium, and the Belgian team of Marie Storms and Fernande Arendt finished in fourth place in the women's doubles competition. Justine Henin-Hardenne (in 2004) is the only Belgian to win an Olympic tennis championship.

BETZ ADDIE, PAULINE MAY "BOBBIE." B. 6 August 1919, Dayton, Ohio. D. 31 May 2011, Washington, DC. Pauline Betz was raised in Southern California and attended Los Angeles High School and Los Angeles City College. In 1940, she was awarded a full scholarship to play tennis on the men's team at Rollins College in Florida, which she did, and graduated in 1943. Although she won five major **singles** titles, had she played in a different era, she undoubtedly would have won more as most of the major international tournaments were not held during the World War II years. From 1941 to 1946, she reached the finals of the **United States National Championships** women's singles, winning the event in 1942, 1943, 1944, and 1946 and losing to **Sarah Palfrey Cooke** in 1941 and 1945. Betz also won the **Wimbledon** ladies' singles championship in 1946 and was runner-up in the **French National Championships** that year, her only appearance in both of those **tournaments**. In **doubles** competition, she and **Doris Hart** were runners-up in the 1946 French championships and 1946 Wimbledon. At the United States championships, Betz lost in the finals five straight years, from 1941 to 1945—the first with partner Dorothy Bundy and the next four years with partner Hart. She was defeated by **Margaret Osborne** and Sarah Cooke in 1941 and by Osborne and **Louise Brough** the next four years. In **mixed doubles**, she and **Budge Patty** won the 1946 French mixed doubles title, and she and **Bobby Riggs** in 1941 and **Pancho Segura** in 1943 lost in the finals of the United States championships. She never competed in the **Australian Championships**. In 1946, as a member of the **Wightman Cup** team, she helped the **United States** to a 7–0 victory with two singles wins and one doubles win.

Her tennis career was effectively curtailed by the **United States Tennis Association** in 1947, which ruled that she was a **professional** and ineligible for their events. Her "crime" was that she was asked to participate in a professional tour with Sarah Palfrey Cooke, and she was ruled ineligible even though she had not accepted. After being banned, she then was, in effect, forced to become a professional tennis player. She toured with Cooke in 1947 and with **Gussie Moran** in 1951. She was inducted into the **International Tennis Hall of Fame** in 1965. She married sportswriter Bob Addie in 1949. They had five children, one daughter and four sons. She was widowed in 1982. She wrote an autobiography, *Wings on My Tennis Shoes*, in 1949 and two instructional books, *Tennis for Teenagers* (1966) and *Tennis for Everyone* (1974). In 2008, the Pauline Betz Addie Tennis Center in Potomac, Maryland, was renamed in her honor.

BHUPATHI, MAHESH SHRINIVAS. B. 7 June 1974, Madras (Chennai), **India**. Mahesh Bhupathi, from the mid-1990s through the first decade of the 21st century, has been one of the world's best **doubles** players. He attended the University of Mississippi and played tennis there in 1994 and 1995, winning the 1995 **National Collegiate Athletic Association** doubles title. His father, C. G. K. Bhupathi, a former top-ranked player in India, built the Nike-Bhupathi Tennis Village in Bangalore, India, in 1995, to train young tennis players. He is the first player born in India to win a **Grand Slam tournament**. In 1997, teaming with Rika Hiraki, he won the **French Open mixed doubles**. He subsequently won the mixed doubles at the other three

Grand Slam tournaments and has won the men's doubles at all of them except the **Australian Open**. The 6-foot 1-inch, 200-pound, right-handed player has won a total of four major men's doubles titles and seven major mixed doubles titles. He was also runner-up six times in men's doubles and three times in mixed doubles. He reached the number-one doubles **ranking** for the first time in 1999.

With **Leander Paes** as doubles partner, he reached the finals of all four Grand Slam men's doubles in 1999, winning the French Open and **Wimbledon**. In 2001, they again won the French Open. With Max Mirnyi Bhupathi, he won the 2002 United States Open and was runner-up in 2003 at Wimbledon. In 2009, with **Mark Knowles** as his partner, he was runner-up at both the Australian and United States Open tournaments. His winning partners in Grand Slam mixed doubles have been Rika Hiraki, Ai Sugiyama, Elena Likhovtseva, **Mary Pierce**, Daniela Hantuchová, **Martina Hingis**, and Sania Mirza. Through May 2011, he has won a total of 48 doubles titles. He has competed in four **Olympic** doubles tournaments for India with Paes, from 1996 to 2008. They finished in fourth place in 2004 and were quarterfinalists in 2008. Bhupathi has represented India in **Davis Cup** competition every year except 2007 from 1995 to 2010 and, through 2010, has a record of 8–14 in singles and 26–6 in doubles in 34 **ties** over 15 years.

BILLIE JEAN KING NATIONAL TENNIS CENTER. *See* USTA BILLIE JEAN KING NATIONAL TENNIS CENTER.

BJÖRKMAN, JONAS LARS. B. 23 March 1972, Alvesta, **Sweden**. The 6-foot tall, 180-pound Jonas Björkman began his **professional** tennis career in 1991. Although an effective **singles** player who reached a **ranking** of fourth in the world in 1997, he has been an outstanding **doubles** player who has won nine major doubles events and been runner-up eight times. He won a doubles championship at all four major **tournaments**. He won the **Australian Open** doubles title in 1998, 1999, and 2001; the **French Open** doubles title in 2005 and 2006; **Wimbledon** doubles in 2002, 2003, and 2004; and the **United States Open** doubles in 2003. He was the French Open doubles finalist in 1994 and Wimbledon doubles finalist in 2008, a remarkable stretch of 15 years in which he was one of the world's best doubles players. He also was a United States Open doubles finalist in 1997, 2005, and 2006 and Australian Open doubles finalist in 2007. In **mixed doubles**, he reached the finals at Wimbledon in 1999 and 2007.

As a singles player, Björkman reached the semifinals of the United States Open in 1997 and Wimbledon in 2006. He has won six singles titles and 54 doubles titles overall in his outstanding career. He competed in both singles and doubles in the 1996, 2004, and 2008 **Olympic Games** but was defeated in the first round in each of his six matches. His major tournament doubles partners have included Jacco Eltingh, **Patrick Rafter**, **Todd Woodbridge**, and Max Mirnyi in **Australia**; Jan Apell and Mirnyi in **France**; Woodbridge and Kevin Ulyett in Wimbledon; Woodbridge, Mirnyi, and Nicolas Kulti at the U.S. Open; and **Anna Kournikova** and Alicia Molik in mixed doubles at Wimbledon. In **Davis Cup** competition, he played for Sweden in 36 **ties** in 14 years, from 1994 to 2008, and had a record of 18–11 in singles and 21–14 in doubles, leading Sweden to the championship in 1994, 1997, and 1998 and runner-up position in 1996. He retired from active competition in 2008.

BJURSTEDT MALLORY, ANNA MARGARETHE "MOLLA." B. 6 March 1884, Mosvik, Noord-Trondelag, Norway. D. 22 November 1959, Stockholm, **Sweden**. Molla Bjurstedt was a relatively unknown player when she came to the **United States** in 1915 to work as a masseuse. She then established one of the most outstanding records at the **United States National Championships**, although she was past 30 years of age when she did so, concluding her career in 1929, at the age of 45. In the 15 years from 1915 to 1929, she was the champion eight times, losing finalist twice, semifinalist four times, and quarterfinalist once. From 1915 to 1922, she won the title in seven of the eight years. She also won the women's **doubles** in 1916 and 1917 with Eleonora Sears as partner and was runner-up in 1918 and 1922 with two other partners. In **mixed doubles**, she reached the finals 8 times in 10 years, from 1915 to 1924, winning the title in 1917 with partner Irving Wright and in 1922 and 1923 with partner **Bill Tilden**. In 1922, she also reached the finals at **Wimbledon** but was defeated by **Suzanne Lenglen**, whom she had defeated in a preliminary round the previous year at **Forest Hills**. Molla competed in both the **singles** and mixed doubles in both the 1912 and 1924 **Olympic Games** and won the bronze medal in the 1912 women's singles event.

She was the coauthor of *Tennis for Women*, an instructional book published in 1916. On 18 September 1920, she married Franklin Mallory. She played in the inaugural **Wightman Cup** in 1923 and in Wightman Cups in 1924, 1925, 1927, and 1928, with a 6–6 record in those matches. In 1958, she was inducted into the **International Tennis Hall of Fame**.

BLAKE, JAMES RILEY. B. 28 December 1979, Yonkers, New York. When James Blake was 13 years old, he was diagnosed with severe scoliosis and was required to wear a full-length back brace for 18 hours a day, although he was allowed to remove it to play tennis. He graduated Fairfield High School in Fairfield, Connecticut, and attended Harvard University for two years, leaving college to pursue his **professional** tennis career in 1999. He made a remarkable comeback in 2005 after breaking a bone in his neck, suffering from a virus that paralyzed part of his face, and losing his father in 2004. This story is well told in his 2007 autobiography, *Breaking Back: How I Lost Everything and Won Back My Life*.

Blake reached a career-high world **ranking** of four in 2006 and was the highest-ranked **African American** since **Arthur Ashe**. Blake has never fared very well in **Grand Slam** tournaments and has only reached the quarterfinals of the **Australian Open** once (in 2008) and twice at the **United States Open** (2005, 2006). His best at **Wimbledon** was the third round in 2006 and 2007 and the third round at **Roland Garros** in 2006. The 6-foot 1-inch, 180-pound right-hander competed in both **singles** and **doubles** in the 2008 **Olympic Games**. He defeated **Roger Federer** in the quarterfinals but lost his semifinal **match** to Fernando González, even though Blake had a triple **match point** in the final **set**. He then was defeated by **Novak Djoković** in the bronze medal match. In the doubles, he lost in the first round with partner **Sam Querrey**. Blake has played **Davis Cup** tennis for the **United States** from 2001 to 2003 and 2005 to 2009. His record in 17 **ties** is 18–11 in singles and 3–1 in doubles, and he helped win the Cup in 2007. He is the only player to win the **Hopman Cup** in consecutive years—in 2003 with **Serena Williams** and in 2004 with **Lindsay Davenport**. Through May 2011, Blake's career record is 10 singles and 5 doubles titles. Blake's brother, Thomas, was also a professional tennis player and **coach**.

BOLLETTIERI, NICHOLAS JAMES "NICK." B. 31 July 1931, Pelham, New York. Although not a champion tennis player himself, Nick Bollettieri has made a substantial impact on the sport. After graduating from Spring Hill College and serving in the U.S. Army, he began teaching tennis to help put himself through law school. While doing so, he met football **coach** Vince Lombardi and Australian tennis coach **Harry Hopman**. After one year at the University of Miami Law School, he realized that his future would be in tennis, not law, and he dropped out of school to devote full time to his tennis activities. From 1959 to 1978, Bollettieri was the tennis director at the Dorado Beach Hotel in Puerto Rico.

In 1972, with help from Lombardi, Nick established a tennis camp in Beaver Dam, Wisconsin. With Harry Hopman, he then created a tennis camp at Amherst, Massachusetts. In 1981, he established the Nick Bollettieri Tennis Academy in Bradenton, Florida. The academy was the first of its kind to include a boarding school for elite athletes. Among his star pupils were **Andre Agassi**, **Boris Becker**, **Jim Courier**, **Martina Hingis**, Marcelo Ríos, and **Monica Seles**. Others that he coached include **Jimmy Arias**, Carling Bassett, Rodney Harmon, and **Aaron Krickstein**. By 1986, his influence was so widespread that the **main draw** of the **United States Open** included 26 of his former students.

In 1987, he sold the academy to the International Management Group but continues to play an active role in the organization. In 2008, **Jelena Janković** reached a world **ranking** of number one—Bollettieri's 10th former pupil to be so ranked.

BOLTON, NANCYE. *See* WYNNE BOLTON, NANCYE HAZEL MEREDITH.

BORG, BJÖRN RUNE. B. 6 June 1956, Sodertalje, **Sweden**. Björn Borg became a tennis **professional** while still a teenager and, in 1974, became the youngest male to win the **French Open** (a record later broken by **Mats Wilander** and then by **Michael Chang**). From 1974 to 1981, Borg was nearly unbeatable at the two European **Grand Slam** championships. He won the French Open in 1974 and 1975 and then again each year from 1978 to 1981. He won the **Wimbledon singles** each year from 1976 to 1980 and was a losing finalist in 1981. His 1980 Wimbledon final with **John McEnroe** has been cited by some as the "**greatest match of all-time**." The five-**set match** included a fourth set **tiebreaker** that was won by McEnroe, 18–16, in which McEnroe saved five **match points** and Borg saved six **set points**. He competed only once in **Australia**, reaching the third round in 1974. He reached the finals of the **United States Open** four times but lost each time—in 1976 and 1978 to **Jimmy Connors** and 1980 and 1981 to John McEnroe. A 5-foot 11-inch, 160-pound right-hander, he played basically from the **baseline** and used a two-handed **backhand** with much **topspin** on both **forehand** and backhand shots. He played ice hockey as a youth and developed his two-handed backhand tennis stroke from the ice hockey slap shot.

By 1982, he was burned out and basically retired, playing only one tournament that year. In January 1983, he officially announced his retirement from tennis, although he was just 26 years of age. He was inducted into the **International Tennis Hall of Fame** in 1987. He attempted a comeback in 1991 and from 1991 to 1993 lost in the first round 12 consecutive times in **Association of Tennis Professionals** events. In **Davis Cup** play for Sweden from 1972 to 1975 and 1978 to 1980, he won 37 of 40 singles matches but only split 16 **doubles** matches in 21 **ties**. He led Sweden to the Davis Cup championship in 1975. He won his first Davis Cup match on 5 May 1972, when he was only 15 years old. In his career, he won 77 singles and four doubles championships, was the world's number-one–**ranked** player, and set quite a few records as the youngest player to win various championships. In

Björn Borg became the youngest male to win the French Open in 1974, and his 1980 Wimbledon final with John McEnroe has been cited by some as the "greatest match of all time." (courtesy of the International Tennis Hall of Fame and Museum)

2010, at the age of 53, he returned to senior play in the **Champions Series** of tournaments.

BOROTRA, JEAN ROBERT. B. 13 August 1898, Arbonne, **France**. D. 17 June 1994. One of the **Four Musketeers**, Jean Borotra began his tennis career in 1922. A tall, slender (six feet one inch, 160 pounds) right-hander, he was known for wearing a blue beret while playing. He won 19 **Grand Slam** championships from 1924 to 1936. In 1928, he won all three championships—men's **singles**, **doubles**, and **mixed doubles**—at the **Australian Championships**. The **United States Nationals** were the only major **tournament** in which he failed to win a singles title, although he lost in the finals in 1926 to countryman **René Lacoste** but won the mixed doubles that year with **Elizabeth "Bunny" Ryan**. At **Wimbledon**, he was the singles finalist in 1924 thru 1927 and 1929, winning in 1924 and 1926 and losing to René Lacoste in 1925 and **Henri Cochet** in 1927 and 1929. He was Wimbledon men's doubles champion in 1925 with Lacoste and in 1932 and 1933 with **Jacques Brugnon**. Borotra and Brugnon also were losing finalists in 1934. In 1925, he won the Wimbledon mixed doubles with **Suzanne Lenglen**. At **Roland Garros**, Borotra won nine titles and was runner-up five times. He won the singles in 1924 and 1931 and was runner-up to Lacoste in 1925 and 1929. In men's doubles, Borotra won in 1925, 1928, 1929, 1934, and 1936 and was runner-up in 1927 and 1939. He won mixed doubles in 1927 and 1934 and was runner-up in 1926. He entered all three events in the 1924 **Olympic Games** in Paris and won the men's doubles bronze medal with partner René Lacoste, was defeated by **Italy's** Umberto de Morpurgo in the bronze medal men's singles match, and lost in the first round of the mixed doubles with partner Marguerite Broquedis-Billout.

He played every year for France in the **Davis Cup** from 1922 to 1937 and then played once more at age 48, after the war in 1947. His record was 19–12 in singles and 17–6 in doubles. He played 17 years in 32 **ties** and helped lead France to the Cup finals in 9 straight years, from 1925 to 1933, where France won six consecutive times from 1927 to 1932. From 1940 to 1942, he was the first general commissioner of sports in the Vichy government in France. He was arrested by the Germans and was interred in a concentration camp from November 1942 until May 1945. In 1963, he founded the Comité International pour le Fair Play, a nonprofit organization, to promote sportsmanship in international competition and recognize sportsmanship by presenting annual awards. He was inducted into the **International Tennis Hall of Fame** in 1976, along with the other three Musketeers.

BOYS' TOURNAMENTS. *See* JUNIOR TENNIS.

BRAZIL. The South American country of Brazil has a long tradition as a sports-loving nation, although tennis has never been one of the most popular sports. From 1932 through May 2011, Brazil has competed in 62 **Davis Cup tournaments**, with a record of 81–63 in 144 **ties**. Brazil has competed 11 times in the World Group since its formation in 1981. In 1992 and 2000, Brazil reached the semifinals. The country's top Davis Cup players have been Thomaz Koch and José-Edison Mandarino. Among the best male tennis players have been Ricardo Acioly, Thomaz Bellucci, Marcos Daniel, Ricardo Hocevar, **Gustavo Kuerten**, Luiz Mattar, Fernando Meligeni, Marcelo Melo, Cassio Motta, Jaime Oncins, André Sá, Flávio Saretta, and Bruno Soares. The best female tennis player was **Hall of Famer Maria Bueno**. Other top Brazilian female players include Silvana Campos, Claudia Chabalgoity, Joana Cortez, Miriam D'Agostini, Patricia Medrado, Vanessa Menga, Gisele Miro, Claudia Monteiro, Suzana Petersen, and Andrea Vieira. In **Olympic** competition, Brazil's best finish was fourth place in the 1996 men's singles by Meligeni. In 1968 Olympic **exhibition** competition, Petersen was a semifinalist in both **singles** and **mixed doubles**. In **Federation Cup** competition, from 1965 to May 2011, Brazil has competed 37 years (19 years in World Group), played 132 ties with a record of 69–63, were quarterfinalists in 1965 and 1982, and reached the World Group playoffs in 2003 and 2005.

BREAK POINT. A break **point** occurs when a player is **serving** and the next point if won by the opponent will give the opponent the **game**. If the score is 15–40, it is considered a double break point; 0–40 is triple break point.

BRITISH ISLES. From 1900 to 1922, players from England and Ireland competed in **Davis Cup** competition as the British Isles. Of the 17 **tournaments** contested in those years, the British Isles team won five times—1903 through 1906 and 1912. Among the players on those teams were Englishmen Alfred Beamish, Ernest Black, Charles Dixon, the **Doherty** brothers—**Hugh** and **Reggie**—Arthur Gore, Algernon Kingscote, Arthur Lowe, Frank Riseley, Herbert Roper-Barrett, and Sydney Smith and Irishmen James Cecil Parke and Joshua Pim. *See also* GREAT BRITAIN.

BROMWICH, JOHN EDWARD. B. 14 November 1918, Kogarah, New South Wales, **Australia**. D. 21 October 1999, Geelong, Victoria, Australia. John Bromwich was one of the rare **ambidextrous** players in tennis history. Although he was a natural **left-hander**, he **served** right-handed, used a two-handed **forehand**, and used his left-hand singly instead of a **backhand**. He reached the finals on 23 occasions in the **Australian Championships**—7 times in **singles**, 10 in **doubles**, and 6 in **mixed doubles** and won 11. He won the singles in 1939 and 1946 and was runner-up in 1937, 1938, 1947, 1948, and 1949. The 6-foot tall 150-pounder was the men's doubles finalist in 1937 with Jack Harper, losing to the team of **Adrian Quist** and Don Turnbull. The following year, he became Quist's partner, and the two won the doubles for the next eight **tournaments**. At **Wimbledon**, Bromwich reached the men's singles finals in 1948 and had **match point** against Bob Falkenburg at 5–3 in the fifth **set** but lost that **point** and the next four **games**. Bromwich did win the men's doubles (with **Frank Sedgman**) and mixed doubles (with **Louise Brough**) that year. He and Brough also won the mixed doubles in 1947 and were runners-up in 1949.

In 1950, Bromwich and Quist won the Wimbledon doubles. At **Forest Hills**, in 1936 and again in 1938, the team of Bromwich and Quist were runners-up in men's doubles. In 1939, they won the event. Ten years later, Bromwich repeated with Bill Sidwell as partner and the following year won again with Sedgman as partner. In mixed doubles, at Forest Hills, Bromwich and **Thelma Coyne Long** were losing finalists in 1938, and Bromwich and Brough won the tournament in 1947. In **Davis Cup** play for Australia, he competed in 23 **ties** in seven years from 1937 to 1950, had a record of 19–11 in singles and 20–1 in doubles, and helped Australia win the Cup in 1939 and 1950. In 1939, Australia lost the first two matches and won the final three to win the Cup, with Bromwich winning the final match over **Frank Parker**. Bromwich was inducted into the **International Tennis Hall of Fame** in 1984.

BROOKES, SIR NORMAN EVERARD "THE WIZARD." B. 14 November 1877, Melbourne, Victoria, **Australia**. D. 28 September 1968, Melbourne, Victoria, Australia. Norman Brookes was one of the first great Australian tennis players. The son of a wealthy gold miner, he was educated at Melbourne Grammar School and learned the game of tennis at his family's private **court**. He was also quite athletic and was an accomplished cricket player and Australian rules footballer. After graduating school in 1895, he became a junior clerk at the Australian Paper Mills Company, where his father was managing director. By 1904, Brookes had worked his way up to being a member of the board of directors.

His first major **tournament** appearance was at **Wimbledon** in 1905, and he won the **all-comers** tournament but lost to incumbent champion **Laurie Doherty** in the **challenge round**. Two years later, he again won the all-comers tournament. This time, Doherty did not compete in the challenge round, and Brookes was named Wimbledon champion. He and **Tony Wilding** also won Wimbledon **doubles** in 1907. Brookes did not return to defend his title in 1908. His next appearance at Wimbledon was in 1914, when he again won the all-comers tournament and defeated Tony Wilding in the challenge round and teamed with Wilding to again win the doubles. World War I suspended the tournament. Wilding was killed in action during the war, and Brookes, who was ineligible for the armed services due to stomach ulcers, served as commissioner of the Australian branch of the British Red Cross in Egypt from 1915 to 1916. In 1917, he became commissioner for the British Red Cross in Mesopotamia and was then appointed assistant director of local resources for the British Expeditionary Force, with a rank of lieutenant colonel.

In 1919, the championships at Wimbledon resumed, and Brookes, aged 41, returned to defend his championship but was defeated by fellow Aussie **Gerald Patterson** in the challenge round. He teamed with Patterson to defeat **Bill Tilden** and **Vinnie Richards** at the **United States National Championships** that year. Brookes competed once more at Wimbledon in 1924, at age 46, and reached the fourth round. Brookes only played **singles** once in the Australian Championships. He won the 1911 tournament and was runner-up in doubles that year. In 1924, at the age of 46, he and James Anderson won the Australian men's doubles. In **Davis Cup** competition, the 5-foot 11-inch, **left-handed** Brookes played for the **Australasian** team from 1905 to 1920. In seven years and 14 **ties**, he had a record of 18–7 in singles and 10–4 in doubles and helped to lead the team to the Cup championships in 1907, 1908, 1909, and 1914. He did not play on the championship teams of 1911 and 1919. In 1926, he became the first president of the **Lawn Tennis** Association of Australia and served in that capacity until 1955. He helped to develop **Kooyong** as a major tennis center.

He was knighted on 8 June 1939, "in recognition of service to public service." The men's singles championship at the Australian Open is now the Norman Brookes Challenge Cup. He was inducted into the **International Tennis Hall of Fame** in 1977. In 1981, the Australia Post honored him, and he became one of the few tennis players to be pictured on a commemorative postage stamp.

BROUGH (CLAPP), ALTHEA LOUISE. B. 11 May 1923, Oklahoma City, Oklahoma. Louise Brough (pronounced "bruff") learned her tennis on the public **courts** in California and played her first major **tournament** in 1939, as a 16-year old, at the **United States National Championships**. She played competitive tennis until 1957 and reached the finals in 53 **Grand Slam** tournaments, winning 35 Grand Slam championships—the fifth most of all players, male or female, in both categories. She won **doubles** championships at all four Grand Slam venues and was a **singles** champion at all except

Roland Garros. At the United States National Championships, she won 17 titles—1 singles, 12 women's doubles, and 4 **mixed doubles**. She competed at the **Australian Championships** only in 1950 and won the singles and women's doubles, with partner **Doris Hart**. At Roland Garros, she competed four times and reached the singles semifinals three of those times. She and **Margaret Osborne duPont** won the women's doubles there in 1946, 1947, and 1949 and were runners-up in 1950. At **Wimbledon**, Louise won the ladies' singles in 1948, 1949, 1950, and 1955, defeating her doubles partner Osborne duPont in 1949 and 1950. Louise was also runner-up in 1946, 1952, and 1954. In women's doubles at Wimbledon, Brough and Osborne duPont won five times (1946, 1948, 1949, 1950, 1954) and were runners-up twice (1947, 1951). Louise also paired with **Maureen Connolly** in 1952 and was runner-up. In 1946 through 1950 and 1955, Louise Brough was the Wimbledon mixed doubles finalist, winning it in 1946 with Tom Brown, 1947 and 1948 with **John Bromwich**, and 1950 with Eric Sturgess.

Her most impressive accomplishments were in the United States National Championships. She won the women's singles in 1947, defeating Osborne duPont, and was a five-time runner-up (losing to **Pauline Betz** in 1942 and 1943, Osborne duPont in 1948, Doris Hart in 1954, and **Althea Gibson** in 1957.) From 1942 to 1950, for nine straight years, the team of Brough and Osborne were undefeated at the United States Nationals—the most consecutive wins by a team at any Grand Slam event in history. They won again three more times from 1955 to 1957 and were runners-up in 1953 and 1954. In 1952, teaming with Maureen Connolly, Brough was also the runner-up. Brough was U.S. National women's doubles finalist 15 times in the 16 years from 1942 to 1957. The Brough–Osborne duPont partnership had a record of 58–2 in their 14 U.S. National tournaments and lost only five **sets**. She also won the U.S. National mixed doubles four times, with four different partners, from 1942 to 1949, and was runner-up once with a fifth different partner. She had a perfect record in **Wightman Cup** play, winning all 12 singles **matches** and all 10 doubles matches, from 1946 to 1957, as the **United States** easily defeated **Great Britain** in 12 straight years.

Louise married Dr. Alan Townsend Clapp on 9 August 1958 and remained married to him until his death 24 November 1999. She retired from competition after her marriage but continued teaching tennis. She was inducted into the **International Tennis Hall of Fame** in 1967.

BROWNE SMITH, MARY KENDALL "BROWNIE." B. 3 June 1891, Ventura, California. D. 19 August 1971, Laguna Hills, California. From 1912 to 1914, Mary K. Browne was the best women's tennis player in the **United States**. The five-foot two-inch right-hander won all three **United States Na-**

tional **Championships** (**singles**, **doubles**, and **mixed doubles**) in each of those years—a feat accomplished only by **Hazel Hotchkiss Wightman** in 1909 through 1911 and **Alice Marble** in 1938 through 1940. In February 1918, she retired from competitive play to become a teller at a Southern California bank. She returned to the game three years later and, in 1921, was runner-up in the singles and won both women's and mixed doubles events at the U.S. National Championships. In 1926, she was the runner-up there in women's doubles, won the **Wimbledon** ladies' doubles, and was runner-up in the mixed doubles. She played on the **Wightman Cup** team in 1925 and 1926 and had a record of 1–3. In 1926, she was offered a **professional** contract by promoter C. C. Pyle to tour with **Suzanne Lenglen**, who had recently defeated her in the finals of the **French National Championships**. The 38-**match** tour ended in February, and at its end, Browne had not won a single match.

"Brownie" later became a close friend and mentor of Alice Marble. Browne was inducted into the **International Tennis Hall of Fame** in 1957. She married Dr. Kenneth Smith in 1958, but they later divorced. She also played golf at a high level, and in 1924, she was the runner-up in the United States National Amateur Championships.

BRUGNON, JACQUES "TOTO." B. 11 May 1895, Paris, **France**. D. 20 March 1978. Jacques Brugnon was one of France's **Four Musketeers**. Of the four, he had the least success in **singles** events and was primarily a **doubles** specialist, although he competed in singles at **Wimbledon** in 1920 and in 1922 through 1939 and at **Roland Garros** and **Forest Hills** nearly every year in that period as well. In 1926, at Wimbledon, he reached the semifinals and had five **match points** in a losing effort. The diminutive (5 feet 6 inches, 140 pounds) right-hander won 12 **Grand Slam** doubles events and was a losing finalist in 7 others. In 1928, he and **Jean Borotra** traveled to **Australia** and won the men's doubles at the **Australian Championships**. Brugnon and **Henri Cochet** won Wimbledon in 1926 and 1928 and lost in the finals in 1927 and 1931. Brugnon and **René Lacoste** won in 1933 and lost in the 1934 finals. At the **French National Championships**, Brugnon reached the men's doubles finals each year from 1925 to 1930 and again in 1932, 1934, and 1939. His partner was Henri Cochet in 1925 through 1928, 1930, and 1932 and Jean Borotra in the other years. Brugnon won five of the nine French doubles finals (1927, 1928, 1930, 1932, 1934). He teamed with **Suzanne Lenglen** to win the first two French National **mixed doubles** titles in 1925 and 1926.

Brugnon entered the 1920 **Olympic Games** in Antwerp, reached the third round of the men's singles, and finished in fourth place in men's doubles with partner François Blanchy. In the 1924 Olympic Games in Paris, he won the silver medal in the men's doubles event, with partner Henri Cochet. Brugnon played **Davis Cup** tennis for France from 1921 to 1934 and appeared in 31 **ties** in 11 years with a record of 4–2 in singles and 22–9 in doubles. He helped lead France to the Cup championship in finals in 1927, 1930, 1931, and 1932 but did not play on France's championship teams of 1928 and 1929.

After retiring from competitive play, he was a teaching professional in California for a while. He was inducted into the **International Tennis Hall of Fame** in 1976 with the other three Musketeers.

BRYAN, MICHAEL CARL "MIKE." *See* BRYAN TWINS.

BRYAN, ROBERT CHARLES "BOB." *See* BRYAN TWINS.

BRYAN TWINS. The Bryan **twins**, Robert Charles and Michael Carl, were born 29 April 1978 in Camarillo, California. They attended Rio Mesa High School in Oxnard, California, and spent two years at Stanford University before leaving school to play **professional** tennis. Their father, Wayne Bryan, is a tennis instructor and a **coach** in **World Team Tennis**. Their mother, Kathy Blake Bryan, also a tennis instructor, was a former world-class player and **Wimbledon** contestant.

As junior players, the Bryan brothers won tournaments at 14-, 16-, and 18-year-old levels. In 1998, Bob won the **National Collegiate Athletic Association singles** and **doubles** (with Mike) and was a member of the championship team. Although the twins are both 6 feet 3 inches tall and 200 pounds, Bob is **left-handed** while Mike is right-handed. Known for their chest bump celebrations after successful play, they have become one of the greatest doubles combinations of all time. In February 2010, they won their 600th match and, in July 2010, passed **the Woodies'** record for most career doubles victories when they won their 62nd doubles championship. They won twice more after that and, through July 2011, had a total of 73 doubles titles. In 2005 and 2006, they reached the finals of seven consecutive **Grand Slam** events and won three. Their eleven slam titles are a record shared by the Woodies.

At the **Australian Open**, they were runners-up in 2004 and 2005 and won the championship in 2006, 2007, 2009, 2010, and 2011. At the **French Open**, they won the tournament in 2003 and were runners-up in 2005 and 2006. Mike won the 2003 **mixed doubles** at **Roland Garros** with Lisa Raymond and Bob won it in 2008 with Victoria Azarenka and in 2009 with Liezel Huber. The twins won Wimbledon in 2006 and 2011 and were runners-up in 2005, 2007, and 2009. In mixed doubles, at Wimbledon, Bob won in 2008 with Samantha Stosur and was runner-up in 2006 with Venus Williams. Mike was twice runner-up with Liezel Huber in 2001 and with Katarina Srebotnik in 2008. At the

United States Open, the Bryans won in 2005, 2008, and 2010 and were runners-up in 2003. In mixed doubles, Mike and **Lisa Raymond** defeated Bob and Katarina Srebotnik in 2003 to win the championship, and Bob and Srebotnik won in 2004. Bob also won the mixed doubles in 2004 with Vera Zvonareva and in 2006 with the 49-year-old **Martina Navratilova**, her 59th and final Grand Slam title. In 2010, Bob and Liezel Huber won the U.S. Open mixed doubles.

The brothers entered both the 2004 and 2008 **Olympic Games** and won the bronze medal in 2008 and were quarterfinalists in 2004. They played **Davis Cup** tennis for the **United States** every year from 2003 to July 2011 and were members of the 2007 championship team. Bob's record in 21 **ties** is 4–2 in singles (all in **dead rubbers**) and 19–2 in doubles (with brother Mike as partner for all except one **match** when injuries caused **John Isner** to replace Mike.) Mike's record from 2003 to 2011 in 21 ties is 0–1 in singles and 19–2 in doubles with Mardy Fish replacing brother Bob in one match.

One of their hobbies is music, with Bob playing keyboard, Mike playing drums and guitar, and father Wayne on guitar in the Bryan brothers' band.

BUCHHOLZ, EARL HENRY "BUTCH," JR. B. 16 September 1940, St. Louis, Missouri. Earl Buchholz was an accomplished tennis player who contributed much to the sport after retiring from active play. As a **junior tennis** player, he won **Wimbledon** and **Roland Garros** boys' titles in 1958 and the Australian junior championships in 1959. In 1959, he and **Alex Olmedo** were runners-up in the men's **doubles** at the **United States National Championships**. The six-foot two-inch, right-handed Buchholz was a member of the **United States Davis Cup** team in 1959 and 1960. He competed in six **ties** and had a record of 3–1 in **singles** and 3–2 in doubles. He was the fifth-ranked **amateur** player in the world in 1960 and became a **professional** in 1961.

He played on the professional tour from 1961 to 1967 and won the **U.S. Pro Championships** in 1962. In 1968, he was one of the eight players (dubbed the Handsome Eight by sportswriters) signed by promoter Lamar Hunt to begin the **World Championship Tennis** tour. After retiring from active play, he became an executive and was **World Team Tennis** commissioner from 1977 to 1978 and executive director of the **Association of Tennis Professionals** from 1981 to 1982.

In 1985, he founded the Lipton International Players Championships, an annual **tournament** played in South Florida that has become one of the more prestigious tournaments. He also developed Altenis, a company that oversees tennis tournaments in Latin America. He was inducted into the **International**

Tennis Hall of Fame in 2005 as a contributor. His brother, Clifford, was also a top-ranked player who worked with him at the Lipton tournament.

BUDGE, JOHN DONALD "DON." B. 13 June 1915, Oakland, California. D. 26 January 2000, Scranton, Pennsylvania. Don Budge is considered by many to be among the top five male players of all time and was **Jack Kramer's** choice as number one. The son of Jack Budge, a Scottish soccer player, who, after a football accident, contracted respiratory problems and immigrated to California for his health, Don attended University High School in Oakland, California, and spent some time at the University of California in Berkeley. He played all sports as a youth and was on his high school basketball team. He was **ambidextrous** and played baseball and football **left-handed** but tennis right-handed. He was taught tennis by his older brother, Lloyd, who was a good college player and later became a teaching **professional** and author of instructional books on tennis. Lloyd goaded Don into entering the California state 15-and-under championship in 1930, which Don won.

That spurred his interest in the sport, and by 1934, he was good enough to enter the **United States National Championships** at **Forest Hills**. The following year, the six-foot one-inch redhead entered **Wimbledon** for the first time and reached the semifinals there. He was a semifinalist there again in 1936 and finalist at Forest Hills, losing to **Fred Perry** in five **sets**, with the final set score being 10–8. In 1937, Budge defeated **Gottfried von Cramm** to win Wimbledon and repeated his performance again, defeating Von Cramm to win the U.S. National Championships. In 1938, Budge decided to try to win all four major titles in one year—a feat that had not previously been accomplished, although **Jack Crawford** came very close in 1933, winning the first three events and losing the fourth in a fifth set match. Budge concentrated on only those four events and traveled to **Australia** in January for his only appearance in that **tournament**. After winning that, he went to **France** and won his only attempt at the **French National Championships**. He then won Wimbledon and the U.S. Nationals and became the first person to win all four events in one year, an accomplishment dubbed the **Grand Slam** by sportswriters. The feat has since only been duplicated by **Rod Laver** (twice), **Maureen Connolly**, **Margaret Smith Court**, and **Steffi Graf**.

As a **doubles** player, he won the Wimbledon men's doubles in 1937 and 1938, with Gene Mako. Budge was a Wimbledon **mixed doubles** finalist in 1936, with **Sarah Palfrey**, and won it in 1937 and 1938, with **Alice Marble**. Budge and Mako were also doubles finalists in 1938 at the French Nationals. The pair reached the U.S. National doubles finals in four straight years (1935–38), winning in the even numbered years. Budge and Sarah Palfrey

Don Budge in 1938 was the first person to win all four major singles championships in the same year. *(courtesy of the International Tennis Hall of Fame and Museum)*

were U.S. mixed doubles losing finalists in 1936 and winners in 1937. In 1938, Budge teamed with Alice Marble to again win the title.

After his sensational year in 1938, he was offered a **professional** contract, which he accepted. He toured with Fred Perry, **Ellsworth Vines**, and **Bill Tilden** and defeated Vines 21 matches to 18, Perry 18–11, and the 47-year-old Tilden, 51–7. Budge won the **U.S. Pro Championships** in 1940 and 1942 and then joined the U.S. Army Air Force. While serving in the military, he suffered a shoulder injury that effectively diminished the quality of his tennis for the rest of his life. After being discharged, he continued playing professional tennis and reached the finals of the U.S. Pro Championships in 1946, 1947, 1949, and 1953 but lost each time. He was a member of the **United States Davis Cup** team in 1935, 1936, 1937, and 1938. In the 1937 Inter-Zonal final against **Germany**, the fifth round deciding **match** against Baron Gottfried von Cramm, where Budge came from two sets down to defeat Von Cramm, 6–8, 5–7, 6–4, 6–4, 8–6, has been called the "**greatest match of all time**." Budge's Davis Cup record in 11 **ties** in the four years is 19–2 in singles and 6–2 in doubles. He led the United States to the Cup championship in 1937 and 1938.

After retiring from competitive play, he owned a laundry in New York, with former tennis star, Sidney Wood, and a bar in Oakland. He also gave youth tennis lessons. He was inducted into the **International Tennis Hall of Fame** in 1964. In 1969, his autobiography, *Don Budge: A Tennis Memoir*, was published.

BUENO, MARIA ESTHER ANDION. B. 11 October 1939, São Paulo, **Brazil**. Maria Bueno was a talented **junior** player who competed in the 1955 Pan American Games, at the age of 15, and won the **Orange Bowl** in 1957. Her older brother, Pedro, was also quite talented and won the National Association of Intercollegiate Athletics (NAIA) **doubles** championship in 1955, 1956, and 1957 and the NAIA **singles** title in 1958, at Lamar State College in Texas. Maria Bueno played her first **Grand Slam** tournament, the **French National Championships**, in 1957, at the age of 17, and was defeated in the first round. Her next 26 appearances in Grand Slam singles events from 1958 to 1967 saw her reach at least the quarterfinal round each time, one of the most remarkable streaks of all time. In her career, she appeared in the finals of 35 Grand Slam events, winning 19. In 1959, still only 19 years old, she won **Wimbledon** and the **United States National Championships**. In 1960, she played in the **Australian Championships** and reached the quarterfinals. She was a semifinalist at Roland Garros, won Wimbledon, and lost in the finals of the U.S. Nationals to **Darlene Hard**. Bueno was a finalist at the Australian in 1965 (in her only other appearance there), finalist at **Roland Garros**

in 1964, Wimbledon champion for the third time in 1964, and champion at **Forest Hills** again in 1963, 1964, and 1966. She reached a world number-one singles **ranking** in 1959.

The 5-foot 7-inch, 125-pound right-hander was also quite formidable in doubles play. In 1960, she won all four Grand Slam women's doubles events—in Australia with Christine Truman and the other three with Darlene Hard. Bueno was women's doubles champion at the Australian in 1960; six-time Wimbledon women's doubles finalist (1958, 1960, 1963, 1965, 1966, 1967, winning all but 1967); three-time Wimbledon **mixed doubles** finalist (1959, 1960, 1967, losing all three times); French National women's doubles champion in 1960 and losing finalist in 1961; French National mixed doubles champion in 1960 and losing finalist in 1965; United States National women's doubles champion in 1960, 1962, 1966, and 1968 and losing finalist in 1958, 1959, and 1963; and losing U.S. mixed doubles finalist in 1958 and 1960.

She retired from **amateur** play in 1969 but returned as a **professional** in 1974 and played on the women's tour through 1977. She was on the Brazilian **Federation Cup** team in 1965 as an amateur and again in 1976 and 1977 as a professional. In five **ties**, her record was 2–2 in singles and 1–1 in doubles. She was inducted into the **International Tennis Hall of Fame** in 1978.

BYE. A bye occurs when the number of players in a **draw** will not allow each player to play a **match** in every round, and a player receives a free pass into the next **tournament** round. In a tournament in which 48 players are entered, 32 players will be matched in the first round, while the remaining 16 players will receive a bye into the second round.

CANADA. In Canada, tennis is not one of the major sports. Through 2011, Canada has competed in 82 total **Davis Cup tournaments**, with a record of 55–81 in 137 **ties**. Since the formation of Davis Cup World Group competition in 1981, Canada has competed three times. In 1913, the team reached the final round of the preliminary tournament—its best result. One of the best male tennis players representing Canada is Yugoslavian-born Daniel Nestor, winner of the men's **doubles** at each one of the four major tournaments and 2000 **Olympic Games**, **Australian Open mixed doubles** winner, and losing doubles and mixed doubles finalist 11 times in the four majors. Canadian-born **Greg Rusedski** reached the finals of the 1997 **United States Open singles** but was representing England at that time. Sebastian Lareau won the 1999 United States Open doubles title and 2000 Olympic doubles. Grant Connell reached the doubles finals at **Wimbledon** three times and once at the Australian Open. Other top Canadian male players include Frank Dancevic, Glenn Michibata, Frederic Niemeyer, and Milos Raonic.

The best female tennis players include Olympians Carling Bassett, Rene Collins, Marianne Groat, Sonya Jeyaseelan, Helen Kelesi, Jana Nejedly, and Vanessa Webb. Jill Hetherington reached the finals of the Australian and U.S. Open women's doubles events and **French Open** mixed doubles. Lois Moyes Bickle was a finalist in the U.S. Open women's doubles. Aleksandra Wozniak has been ranked among the top 25 singles players. In **Federation Cup** competition, from 1963 to May 2011, Canada has competed 48 of the 49 years, 31 years in World Group, played 148 ties with a record of 86–62, and was quarterfinalist four times.

CAPRIATI, JENNIFER MARIE. B. 29 March 1976, New York, New York. Jennifer Capriati began her **professional** tennis career in 1990, a few days shy of her 14th birthday, although she had played at age 13, in 1989, in the last **Wightman Cup** event, defeating Clare Wood, 6–0, 6–0. By 1993, Capriati, at the age of just 17, was burned out and required two years' respite from tennis. The 5-foot 7-inch, 135-pound right-hander won the 1992 **Olympic** women's **singles** gold medal in Barcelona. In 1996, after playing very few competitive **matches** in the previous two years, she returned to the tour and worked her way back to the top 25 in the **rankings** and was named the **Women's Tennis Association (WTA)** Comeback Player of the Year. In 2001, she had the best year of her career when she won the **Australian** and **French Open** singles championships, was ranked number one in the world, and won the WTA Player of the Year award. She again won the Australian Open in 2002, but this was to be her last **Grand Slam** championship. She played on the **United States Federation Cup** team in 1990, 1991, 1996, 2000, and 2002. Her record in 14 **ties** was 10–3 in singles and 1–1 in **doubles**. She helped the United States win the Cup in 1990 and 2000 and was on the losing team in the 1991 final. She played in a quarterfinal tie in 1996 but did not play in the final round that was won by the United States. After a series of injuries, she effectively retired from tennis in 2004, although she never officially announced her retirement. In her career, she won 14 singles titles and 1 doubles title.

CASALS, ROSEMARY "ROSIE." B. 16 September 1948, San Francisco, California. Although only 5 feet 2 inches tall and 117 pounds, Rosie Casals was one of the best players in her era and was known for her distinctive headband. Although primarily a **doubles** player (27 of her 29 **Grand Slam** finals appearances were in doubles), she still did well in **singles** (**ranked** number three in the world in 1970) and reached the **United States Open** singles finals in 1970 and 1971, where she was defeated by two of the greatest women's players of all time—**Margaret Smith Court** and **Billie Jean King**. She lost to Court in three sets and to King, her doubles partner, in a second set **tiebreaker**. Casals's 12 Slam championships include five **Wimbledon** women's doubles with Billie Jean King (1967, 1968, 1970, 1971, 1973), two **mixed doubles** with **Ilie Năstase** (1970, 1972), one mixed doubles with Dick Stockton (1975), and four United States Open women's doubles (1967 with King, 1971 with **Judy Tegart**, 1974 with King, 1982 with **Wendy Turnbull**). She also was a losing doubles finalist with King in 1969 at the **Australian Open**, at Wimbledon with Turnbull in 1980 and 1983, at **Roland Garros** with King in 1968 and 1970, and with Turnbull in 1982 and six times at the United States Open (1966, 1968, 1973, 1975 with King; 1970 with **Virginia Wade**; 1981 with Turnbull). She lost in mixed doubles at Wimbledon in 1976 with Stockton and at the U.S. Open in 1967 with **Stan Smith** and in 1972 with Năstase.

She played on the **United States Federation Cup** team as an **amateur** in 1967 and again as a **professional** from 1976 to 1981. Her record in 29 **ties** was 8–1 in singles and an outstanding 26–1 in doubles, her only doubles loss occurring in a **dead rubber** in the 1977 final. The United States won the Cup in each of the seven years that she was a team member, and she played in the final round every year except 1978. She played on the **Wightman Cup** team in seven years, from 1967 to 1982, and had a 7–4 record (6–1 in doubles). Casals and with Billie Jean King were the players most responsible for the rise of women's professional tennis, the start of the **Virginia Slims** tour, and the founders of the **Women's Tennis Association** Tour Players Association. In the first full year of the Virginia Slims tour, 1971, Casals played in 32 tournaments in singles, 31 in doubles, and a total of 205 matches. In her career, which ended in 1991, she played in a total of 685 singles and doubles tournaments, winning 112 doubles titles. She was inducted into the **International Tennis Hall of Fame** in 1996.

CASH, PATRICK HART "PAT." B. 27 May 1965, Melbourne, Victoria, **Australia**. Pat Cash had an exceptional **junior** career, winning both the **Wimbledon** and **United States** junior championships. He turned **professional** in 1982. He competed in the 1984 **Olympic** demonstration tournament but was defeated in his first match by Paolo Cane of **Italy**. In 1984, and again in 1985, he reached the men's **doubles** finals at Wimbledon. His best year was 1987, when he reached the finals of the **Australian Open** and won the Wimbledon **singles** championship—his only **Grand Slam** title. In 1988, he again lost in the finals of the Australian Open. Cash played **Davis Cup** tennis for Australia every year from 1983 to 1990 and had a record of 23–7 in singles and 8–3 in doubles in 19 **ties** in the eight years, leading Australia to the Cup in 1983 and 1986 and to the finals in 1990. In his first Davis Cup, in 1983, he became the youngest player ever to appear in a Davis Cup final. A series of injuries caused a decline in his play throughout the 1990s and led to his retirement. The six-foot tall right-hander won 7 singles and 12 doubles titles in his career.

After leaving the tour, he **coach**ed **Mark Philipoussis** and **Greg Rusedski** and opened a tennis academy in Australia. He still plays occasionally on the **Champions Tour** and in **senior** Slam events, and in 2010, he and **Todd Woodbridge** won the over 45s Wimbledon legends' doubles event, making him the first player to win junior, senior, and legends events at Wimbledon.

CAWLEY, EVONNE GOOLAGONG. *See* GOOLAGONG CAWLEY, EVONNE FAY.

CENTRE COURT. Centre Court is the main **court** at the **All-England Lawn Tennis and Croquet Club** in **Wimbledon**. In 2009, a retractable roof was added so that matches may be played in inclement weather. Above the players' entrance way to the court is a quotation from the poem "If—" by Rudyard Kipling: "If you can meet with Triumph and Disaster, and treat those two impostors just the same." The phrase "center court" is also often used generically to mean the main court at other tennis venues.

CHAIR UMPIRE. The chair umpire is the person who is in charge of keeping score during a **match** and can overrule a **linesperson's** call of in or out. The chair umpire usually sits in a chair raised about 10 feet off the ground on the side of the **net**. The umpire will introduce the players, supervise a coin toss or **racket** spin for choice of first **serve**, and announce the score prior to each **point** played. The umpire is also responsible to ensure that the rules of tennis are properly followed and may penalize a player for failure to do so. Both males and females have umpired matches of the opposite sex. Tennis officiating was originally an unpaid job, but in recent years, a level of **professionalism** has been sought, and umpires are paid. The **United States Tennis Association** certifies tennis officials. *See also* REFEREE.

CHALLENGE. At some venues, in recent years, an electronic system (known as Hawk-Eye) records each **point** played. A player may challenge a line call, and a computer video simulation is then used to determine whether the call was correct. Players are generally allowed three incorrect challenges per **set**, with an additional challenge should the set require a **tiebreaker**.

CHALLENGE ROUND. In some **tournaments**, such as **Wimbledon** and **Davis Cup**, the previous year's winner was exempt from competing in the preliminary tournament rounds and would face the winner in a challenge round for the championship. Wimbledon used this system through 1921 and Davis Cup through 1971.

CHALLENGER TOUR. The Challenger Tour is a lower-level series of **tournaments** sponsored by the **United States Tennis Association**. Prize money is usually quite modest. Players on the tour are generally ones that have not recorded much success on the regular tour and are either new to the game or veterans attempting to come back from injury. Venues are generally low key, often just public parks, and admission prices are also quite inexpensive. They generally provide the greatest bargain in tennis as a fan can see top-quality tennis with excellent seats at minimal cost. An example is the annual Challenger event played in Binghamton, New York, the second week of August since 1994. Tickets are free for the two days of **qualifying**, just $3 per day for the first four days of the tournament and just $6 per day for the quarterfinals, semifinals, and finals. Players who have participated in recent years have included **Andy Murray**, **James Blake**, **Mark Philippoussis**, and **Ivo Karlović**.

CHAMPIONSHIP POINT. *See* MATCH POINT.

CHAMPIONS SERIES. The Champions Series (also known as the Champions' Tour) is a series of men's **tournaments** featuring a select group of semiretired players with a minimum age of 30 but usually in their late 30s and early 40s. Tournaments are usually run with eight players divided into two groups playing a round-robin format. The two group winners then compete for the tournament championship, while the two runners-up compete for third place. One concession to the players' age is that although matches are best two of three **sets**, the third set, if necessary, is played as a "Champions' tiebreak"—the player to first reach 10 **points** with a 2-point margin wins the set. To qualify for the tour, a player must have either been ranked among the top five players worldwide, been a **Grand Slam** finalist, or a **singles** player on a championship **Davis Cup** team. Each tournament is also allowed one **wild-card** entry who would not otherwise qualify. The quality of tennis can be quite good at times, although the players on the tour do not have quite the same physical abilities that they once had. Former **professional** tennis player **Jim Courier** organized InsideOut Sports & Entertainment in 2004, which is the promoter of the Champions Series. In 2011, the structure was changed to a series of 12 one-night tournaments, each in a different city, from 22 September through 22 October. Each night's event will consist of two semi-final matches with the winners playing an eight-game pro set final. The three top finishers at the end of the season will share a one million dollar bonus.

CHANG, MICHAEL TE-PEI. B. 22 February 1972, Hoboken, New Jersey. A **Chinese** American, Michael Chang was raised in California and began his **professional** tennis career in 1987, at the age of 15. That year, he became the youngest male to win a **match** in the **main draw** at the United States Open when he defeated Paul McNamee in the first round before losing in five **sets** to Nduka Odizor in the second round. At the age of 17, he became the youngest male to win a **Grand Slam** title when he won the **French Open** in 1989. His fourth round victory in that **tournament** was a memorable one as he came from two sets down to defeat the world number-one–**ranked Ivan Lendl**. During the fourth and fifth sets, Chang suffered from leg cramps and used unorthodox tactics (such as serving underhanded and standing well inside the **baseline** to receive **serve**) to disrupt Lendl. Unfortunately, Chang was never able to win another Slam title, although he reached the final of the French Open in 1995 and the **Australian Open** and **United States Open** in 1996. His best showing at **Wimbledon** was in 1994 when he reached the quarterfinal round. The 5-foot 9-inch, 160 pound Chang was known for his defensive abilities and speed on **court** and, in 1992, at the U.S. Open, lost in the semifinals to eventual champion **Stefan Edberg** in five sets in five hours and 26 minutes, the longest match in U.S. Open history. In 1996, Chang reached his highest ranking of second in the world. His entourage usually included his brother and **coach**, Carl, and was referred to by tennis writer and commentator **Bud Collins** as the "Chang Gang."

Michael competed in both the 1992 and 2000 **Olympic Games** without much success, losing in the second round in 1992 and first round in 2000. Chang was on the **United States Davis Cup** team in 1989, 1990, 1996, and 1997. Playing only singles, his record was 8–4 in six **ties**. He was on the victorious Cup team in 1990. He was also a member of the United States team that won the **World Team Cup** in 1993. When he retired from tour play in 2003, he had won 34 singles titles. He now competes in the **Champions Series**.

The year 2008 was a memorable one for Michael Chang: he was inducted into the **International Tennis Hall of Fame**; known in China as Zhang Depei, he opened a tennis academy in Shenzhen, China, to help improve the skills of Chinese players, and on 18 October, he married Amber Liu, a former Stanford University **collegiate** tennis champion and professional tennis player.

CHATRIER, PHILIPPE GEORGES YVES. B. 2 February 1928, Créteil, France. D. 23 June 2000, Dinard, France. Although a pretty good tennis player (1945 French **junior** singles and doubles champion), Philippe Chatrier's major contribution to tennis was as an international administrator. A journalist who founded one of the leading tennis magazines, *Tennis de France*, he was president of the Fédération Française de Tennis (French Tennis Federation) from 1972 to 1992 and the **International Tennis Federation** from 1977 to 1991. He helped build the **French Open** into a true major tournament and was instrumental in the updating of Stade **Roland Garros**. He was also a major factor in the return of tennis to the **Olympic Games** as a medal sport. He became a member of the International Olympic Committee in 1988 and was inducted into the **International Tennis Hall of Fame** as a contributor in 1992. After his death, in 2000, the main **court** at Stade Roland Garros was renamed the Court Philippe Chatrier. His son, Jean-Philippe Chatrier, was a movie and television actor until his death on 6 July 2010.

CHILE. For a country with a population of only 16 million people, Chile has done quite well in tennis. Chile was a finalist in the **Davis Cup** and has produced **Olympic singles** and **doubles** champions and **Australian, French,** and **United States National** champions as well as both a male and female player **ranked** number one in the world. The central organization that administers the sport is the Federación de Tenis de Chile. Among the best male Chilean tennis players have been Ricardo Acuña, Jorge Aguilar, Luis Ayala, Paul Capdeville, Patricio Cornejo, Horacio de la Peña, Jaime Fillol, Hans Gildemeister, Fernando González, Nicolás Massú, Belus Prajoux, Marcelo Ríos (world number one in 1998), and the Torralva brothers—Domingo and Luis.

The best female tennis players include Paula Cabezas, Barbara Castro, Valentina Castro, Anita Lizana, and Paulina Sepulveda. Lizana was ranked number one worldwide after she won the United States National Championships in 1937 over **Jadwiga Jędrzejowska** in the first U.S. final between two foreign-born players. In **Federation Cup** competition, from 1968 to May 2011, Chile has competed 29 years, nine years in World Group, played 103 **ties** with a record of 54–52, and reached the World Group playoffs in 1996.

From 1928 through May 2011, Chile has competed in 64 Davis Cup tournaments with a record of 74–63 in 137 ties. Chile has competed nine times in the World Group since its formation in 1981. In 1976, Chile was the tournament runner-up, losing to **Italy** in the final. In 1973, Cornejo and Fillol played the longest **set** in Davis Cup history, winning the second set 39–97 but losing the match in five sets to Americans Erik Van Dillen and **Stan Smith**. The match also required 122 **games** and holds the Davis Cup record for most games in a **rubber**. Chile's top Davis Cup players have been Ayala, Cornejo, Gildemeister, González, and Massú. Chile competed in the 1924 Olympic tennis events and in each one from 1992 to 2008. They have won four Olympic tennis medals—Massú won both **singles** and **doubles** in 2004; his doubles partner, González, won the 2004 doubles gold medal and 2008 singles silver medal.

CHINA. China has had tennis competition since the early 20th century. The China Tennis Association, founded in 1953, is the governing body. One of the more prestigious events, the Tennis Masters Cup, was held in Shanghai in 2002 and from 2005 to 2008. From 1924 through May 2011, China has competed in 36 **Davis Cup tournaments** with a record of 36–41 in 77 **ties**. China has yet to compete in the World Group since its formation in 1981. The Republic of China competed from 1924 to 1946, and from 1983 to 2010, the People's Republic of China competed. The Chinese were Eastern Zone finalists in 1987. Top Davis Cup players have been Jia-Ping Xia, Shao-Xuan Zeng, and Bing Pan. China has competed in each **Olympic** tennis competition from 1984 to 2008. Li Ting and Sun Tian-Tian won the women's 2004 **doubles** event. Zheng Jie and Yan Zi won the bronze medal in that event in 2008. In 2008, in Beijing, **Li Na** finished fourth in women's **singles**. In **Federation Cup** competition, from 1981 to May 2011, China has competed 31 years, 16 years in World Group, played 112 ties with a record of 69–43, and was a semifinalist in 2008. The best female tennis players include Yan

Zi and Zheng Jie, **Australian Open** and **Wimbledon** doubles champions in 2006; Sun Tian Tian, 2008 Australian Open **mixed doubles** champion (with Serbian partner Nenad Zimonjić); and Li Na, **ranked** 5th in the world in May 2011. She followed that triumph by winning the 2011 Australian Open singles title. Hu Na defected from China in 1982 to the United States and competed on the **Women's Tennis Association** tour until 1991 with reasonable success, reaching a high ranking of 48th in the world and the third round at Wimbledon. China has yet to produce any strong men's tennis players, although this may change soon as Chinese American **Michael Chang** (known in China as Zhang Depei) opened a tennis academy in Shenzhen in 2008.

ČILIĆ, MARIN. B. 28 September 1988, Medjugorje, Bosnia, **Yugoslavia**. One of tennis's tallest players (six feet six inches), at the age of 15, Čilić moved to San Remo, Italy, upon the recommendation of **Goran Ivanišević**, to be **coached** by Bob Brett, Ivanišević's former coach. Čilić began playing **professionally** in 2005 and won the Boys' **Singles** Championship at the **French Open**. Čilić lost in the second round of the 2008 **Olympic** men's singles. He has played for the **Croatian Davis Cup** team from 2006 to 2011 with a record of 9–6 in singles and 3–4 in **doubles**. His Davis Cup victories include two in 2009 that helped Croatia defeat the **United States**, 3–2. His first **Association of Tennis Professionals** victory was in New Haven, Connecticut, in August 2008. He won twice in 2009 and was finalist in two other **tournaments**. He won another two events in 2010. His most impressive accomplishment occurred at the 2010 **Australian Open**. After winning three five-**set matches** (including a 4-hour 38-minute victory over reigning **United States Open** champion **Juan Martín Del Potro**), Čilić reached the semifinals, where he lost to **Andy Murray**. His highest **ranking** as of May 2011 is ninth.

CLAY. Clay is one of the four main tennis **court surfaces**. Clay courts are made of crushed shale, stone, or brick and come in two types—red clay and Har-Tru or American green clay. Clay courts are much more common in Europe and Latin America than they are in the **United States**. The surface plays slower than any of the other surfaces, and consequently, **rallies** are longer. Because of this some players, play much better on clay courts than on other surfaces. The **French Open** at **Roland Garros** is presently the only major **tournament** played on clay, although for a brief period of time (1975–77), the **United States Open** also was played on clay courts.

CLIJSTERS (LYNCH), KIM ANTONIE LODE. B. 8 June 1983, Bilzen, **Belgium**. Kim Clijsters was born a natural athlete. Her father, Lei Clijsters, was a soccer player, and her mother, Els Vandecaetsbeek, was a national gymnastics champion. Kim's younger sister, Elke, also played **professional** tennis, from 2002 to 2004, before injuries ended her career.

As a **junior tennis** player, Kim was the runner-up at **Wimbledon** in the 1998 girls' **singles** tournament and won the 1998 **French Open** and **United States Open** girls' **doubles** tournaments. She began playing professionally in 1999. In 2003, she was **ranked** number one in both singles and doubles—one of only five women to ever accomplish this feat. She and Ai Sugayama won both the French Open and Wimbledon women's doubles in 2003 and were runners-up there in 2001. Clijsters won her first **Grand Slam** singles championship in 2005, when she defeated **Mary Pierce** to win the U.S. Open. Kim was the women's singles runner-up four times at Slam events—three times to countrywoman **Justine Henin-Hardenne** and once to **Jennifer Capriati**. She played on the Belgian **Fed Cup** team from 2000 to 2006 and again in 2010 and 2011. Her Fed Cup record in 17 **ties** is 21–3 in singles and 3–1 in doubles. In 2001, she helped lead Belgium to the Cup championship. She retired from professional tennis in 2007 to marry and raise a family, wedding American basketball player Brian Lynch. After their daughter, Jada, was born in 2008, Kim decided to return to tennis and made a comeback in August 2009. She, surprisingly, won the United States Open in September as an **unseeded wild-card** entrant. On 8 July 2010, she played **Serena Williams** in an **exhibition** match, **umpired** by **Martina Navratilova**, at King Baudouin Stadium in Brussels, Belgium, before 35,681 people, the largest attendance for a tennis match. She repeated her U.S. Open singles triumph in 2010, winning it for the third time. On 5–6 November 2011, the Czech Republic and Russia play for the 2011 Fed Cup championship.

Kim is one of the most popular players on the **Women's Tennis Association (WTA)** tour and has won the Karen Krantzcke Sportsmanship award seven times (2001–4, 2006–7, 2010). Clijsters was also the recipient of the WTA Most Impressive Newcomer in 1999, the WTA Player of the Year in 2005, 2006, and 2011, the WTA Comeback Player of the Year in 2006 and 2010, and the WTA Humanitarian of the Year in 2006. Through May 2011, she has won 41 WTA singles titles and 11 doubles titles.

COACHES. Tennis is one of the few sports in which coaching is not permitted during play, although in recent times, a few **tournaments** and **World Team Tennis** have experimented with allowing coaching during breaks in play. When tennis first started, most players did not have coaches, but in recent times, nearly every player employs one or more, often changing coaches when the player's game is not successful. Many retired players become tennis instructors at clubs, and some continue coaching players on the **Association of Tennis Professionals** and **Women's Tennis Association** tours. Coaches are sometimes players' **relatives**, such as **Rafael Nadal's** uncle,

Toni; Li Na's husband, Jiang Shan; or Marion Bartoli's father, Walter, who gave up a career as a physician to mentor his daughter. *See also* BOLLETTIERI, NICHOLAS JAMES "NICK"; GILBERT, BRADLEY N. "BRAD"; HIGUERAS, JOSÉ; HOPMAN, HENRY CHRISTIAN "HARRY"; ROCHE, ANTHONY DALTON "TONY"; SEGURA CANO, FRANCISCO OLEGARIO "PANCHO," "SEGOO."

COCHET, HENRI JEAN. B. 14 December 1901, Villeurbanne, **France**. D. 1 April 1987, Saint Germain-en-Laye, France. Henri Cochet began playing tennis in Lyon, where his father was the secretary of a tennis club and Henri was a **ball boy**. Only 5 feet 6 inches and 145 pounds, he became one of France's top players during the 1920s and was dubbed one of the **Four Musketeers**. During his career, he won eight **Grand Slam singles** championships, winning **Wimbledon** twice (1927, 1929), **Roland Garros** five times (1922, 1926, 1928, 1930, 1932), and **Forest Hills** once (1928). He also lost in the final round once in each of those three **tournaments** (1928 at Wimbledon, 1932 at Forest Hills, 1933 at Roland Garros). His 1927 victory at Wimbledon was remarkable in that he came from two **sets** down in each of his last three **matches** to defeat Frank Hunter in the quarterfinals, **Bill Tilden** in the semifinals, and **Jean Borotra** in the finals, saving seven **match points** against Borotra. As of 2010, Cochet is the last man to win Wimbledon after losing the first two sets of the final. (Although **Roger Federer** nearly accomplished this feat in 2008.)

Cochet was an excellent **doubles** player and reached the finals of the men's doubles at Wimbledon four times with partner **Jacques Brugnon** (1926–28, 1931), winning in 1926 and 1928. He won the 1927 United States **mixed doubles** with partner Eileen Bennett. At Roland Garros, he reached the finals of the men's doubles seven times (1925–30, 1932) and the finals of the mixed doubles four times (1925–28, 1930). He won the men's doubles there in 1927, 1930, and 1932 with Brugnon and won the mixed doubles in 1928 and 1929 with Bennett. His 17 finals appearances at Roland Garros and 10 championships are the most for any man there. He competed in the 1924 **Olympic Games** in Paris and won silver medals in both men's singles and doubles events. He was on the French **Davis Cup** team from 1922 to 1924 and 1926 to 1933. In that time, he played 26 **ties**, had a record of 34–8 in singles and 10–6 in doubles, and helped France win the Cup six consecutive times from 1927 to 1932. In 1933, he became a **professional** player. He was inducted into the **International Tennis Hall of Fame** in 1976, along with the three other Musketeers.

COLLEGIATE TENNIS. In the **United States**, **lawn tennis** is one of the intercollegiate sports overseen by the National Collegiate Athletic Association (NCAA). Colleges play **matches** against one another during the season, and an annual national **tournament**, featuring both individual and team championships, is held. Quite a few of the individual winners of the national collegiate championships have later become successful players on the tour. Collegiate tennis remains limited to **amateur** players. The most successful schools include the University of Southern California, Stanford University, the University of Georgia, and the University of Southern California in Los Angeles (UCLA). Some of the individual champions who won the tournament more than once include Matias Boeker, Somdev Devvarman, **Alex Olmedo**, Mikael Pernfors, **Dennis Ralston**, Ham Richardson, and **Francisco "Pancho" Segura**. **Hall of Famers** who won NCAA championships once include **Arthur Ashe**, **Jimmy Connors**, **John McEnroe**, **Rafael Osuna**, and **Tony Trabert**.

COLLINS, ARTHUR WORTH "BUD," JR. B. 17 June 1929, Lima, Ohio. Bud Collins graduated from Berea High School in Ohio and Baldwin-Wallace College. He served in the U.S. Army and, after his discharge, attended Boston University Graduate School. He began writing for the *Boston Herald* and, a few years later, moved to the *Boston Globe*. As a newspaperman, he covered boxing, tennis, and other sports. He also covered politics and, in 1967, was a candidate for mayor of Boston. He was also a pretty good tennis player and won the U.S. Indoor **mixed doubles** in 1961 and reached the finals of the **French senior doubles** in 1975. He was tennis **coach** at Brandeis University from 1959 to 1963. In 1963, he began doing television commentary. Since then, he has worked almost continuously reporting tennis on television and in print.

Collins is, by far, the best known tennis writer and broadcaster. His colorful way with words has led him to apply nicknames to virtually every player he has seen. He matches that with his colorful apparel—bow ties and loud pants. He is the author of several books, including his memoirs, *My Life with the Pros*, biographies of **Rod Laver** and **Evonne Goolagong**, and the most comprehensive tennis encyclopedia. Updated every few years, it has appeared under several names, the *Modern Encyclopedia of Tennis*, *Bud Collins' Tennis Encyclopedia*, and *Bud Collins' Total Tennis: The Ultimate Tennis Encyclopedia*. He was inducted into the **International Tennis Hall of Fame** as a contributor in 1994. In 1999, he received the prestigious Red Smith Award from the Associated Press.

CONNOLLY (BRINKER), MAUREEN CATHERINE "LITTLE MO." B. 17 September 1934, San Diego, California. D. 21 June 1969, Dallas, Texas. Maureen Connolly began playing tennis at age 10 and at age 14 won 56 consecutive **matches**. The following year, she won the **United States National** Girls' **Junior** Championships. In 1951, at age 16, she became the youngest to win the United States National Championships at **Forest Hills**. In 1952, she won **Wimbledon** as well as the U.S. title. In 1953, Little Mo, a 5-foot 4-inch, 120-pound right-hander, matched **Don Budge's** achievement and won all four **Grand Slam** championships, becoming the first woman to do so. She did not compete in the 1954 **Australian tournament** but won the **French** and Wimbledon.

Her career was abruptly ended on 20 July 1954, when the horse she was riding was hit by a truck, and Maureen suffered a crushed right leg. In her brief career, she won 9 of the 11 Grand Slam **singles** tournaments that she entered, losing only the United States Nationals in 1949 and 1950, when she was just 14 and 15 years old. She also did well in the Grand Slam **doubles** events, winning the women's doubles in Australia in 1953 and both the women's and **mixed doubles** at **Roland Garros** in 1954. She was runner-up in women's doubles in 1952 at Wimbledon and Forest Hills and in 1953 at Roland Garros and Wimbledon. In 1953, she was runner-up in the mixed doubles at Australia and Roland Garros. On the **Wightman Cup** team, from 1951 to 1954, she won all her matches—seven singles and two doubles—as the United States only lost one **rubber** to **Great Britain** in those four years.

She married Norman E. Brinker in June 1955. He was a member of the 1952 **United States Olympic** equestrian team. He later became prominent in the restaurant business and founded the Steak and Ale chain. Following its sale to Pillsbury, he became president of restaurant operations. The couple had two daughters. Although she was unable to play competitive tennis, she still spent time as an instructor and worked with the British Wightman Cup team when the team visited the United States. She was stricken with stomach cancer in 1966 and died three years later at the age of 34. She was inducted into the **International Tennis Hall of Fame** in 1968.

CONNORS, JAMES SCOTT "JIMMY," "JIMBO." B. 2 September 1952, Belleville, Illinois. Jimmy Connors was taught the game of tennis by his mother, Gloria Thompson Connors, a teaching **professional**, and played in the **United States** boys' 11-and-under **tournament** at the age of 8. When he was 16, Jimmy moved to California with his mother and began taking lessons from **Pancho Segura** at the Beverly Hills Tennis Club. Jimmy graduated from Rexford High School, a private school in Beverly Hills. He attended the University of California, Los Angeles (UCLA) for one year, won the **National Collegiate Athletic Association** National **Singles** Championship in 1971, and was a member of the national champion UCLA team. He dropped out of school to pursue a professional tennis career that lasted until the 1990s. He was known for his feisty, aggressive manner, and though only 5 feet 10 inches tall and 150 pounds, without a powerful **serve**, the **left-hander** had one of the best returns of serve. His competitive spirit enabled him to reach the world number-one **ranking** in July 1974 and remain on top for 160 consecutive weeks. His breakthrough year was 1974 as he won the **Australian, Wimbledon**, and United States singles championships and was prevented from playing in the **French** championships because he had signed to play **World Team Tennis (WTT)** and the French Tennis Federation opposed WTT since it scheduled matches opposite the **French Open** tournament. When he finally did play at **Roland Garros**, he reached the semifinal round in 1979, 1980, 1984, and 1985 but could never win the tournament. His only other appearance at the Australian Open resulted in a loss in the finals in 1975 to **John Newcombe**. Connors's best Grand Slam performances were at Wimbledon and the **United States Open**.

He won the Wimbledon singles in 1974 (over **Ken Rosewall**) and 1982 (over **John McEnroe** in five **sets**) and was the losing finalist in 1975 (to **Arthur Ashe**), 1977 and 1978 (to **Björn Borg**), and 1984 (to McEnroe). Connors also reached the semifinals on five other occasions. Connors's tennis home was the United States Open, where vociferous crowds cheered him on to championships in 1974, 1976, 1978, 1982, and 1983. Connors was also a losing finalist there in 1975 and 1977. In one of his more remarkable accomplishments, he was entered in the 1991 U.S. Open as a **wild card**. In his fourth round match in that event, on his 39th birthday, he defeated **Aaron Krickstein** in five sets in 4 hours and 41 minutes. Connors won his quarterfinal match but was defeated by **Jim Courier** in the semifinals. Connors was not nearly as good a **doubles** player, but with **Ilie Năstase** as partner, he still won the Wimbledon doubles in 1973 and the U.S. Open doubles in 1975 and reached the 1973 French Open finals.

In 1974, with then fiancée **Chris Evert**, he reached the U.S. Open **mixed doubles** finals. Jimmy later married former Playboy playmate Patti McGuire in 1979. Connors played singles for the **United States Davis Cup** team in 1975, 1981, and 1984. In seven **ties**, he had a record of 10–3. He was inducted into the **International Tennis Hall of Fame** in 1998. After retiring from competitive tennis, he has done television work and was a **coach** for **Andy Roddick**.

CONVERTED PLAYERS. There have been several accomplished top-level tennis players who were naturally **left-handed** but were taught to play right-handed. Among these are: José Acasuso, **Maureen Connolly, Carlos Moyá, Ken Rosewall**, and **Maria Sharapova**. A few naturally right-handed players were taught to play left-handed. The most noted of these are Jürgen Melzer and **Rafael Nadal**. *See also* AMBIDEXTROUS PLAYERS.

COOPER, ASHLEY JOHN. B. 15 September 1936, Melbourne, Victoria, **Australia**. In his relatively brief career as an **amateur** tennis player, the 5-foot 10-inch, right-handed Ashley Cooper won eight major championships and was runner-up in five others. He and **Lew Hoad** were **doubles** finalists at **Roland Garros** in 1956. Cooper had two more outstanding years, 1957 and 1958, before becoming a **professional** in 1959. In 1957, he won the **Australian** men's **singles**, was runner-up at **Wimbledon** and **Forest Hills**, and was a semifinalist at the **French National Championships**. In doubles, in 1957, he and **Mal Anderson** won the French championships and were runners-up in the Australian, and he and **Neale Fraser** won the **United States National Championships**. In 1958, Cooper won the Australian, Wimbledon, and United States championships and was a semifinalist in the French. In doubles, in 1958, he and Fraser won the Australian and French championships and were runners-up at Wimbledon. Cooper was **ranked** first in the world in 1957. In **Davis Cup** play, in 1957 and 1958, he split his two **matches** each year, but his win over **Vic Seixas** helped Australia win the Cup in 1957. Following his retirement from active play, he was the tennis player development administrator for Tennis Queensland and was a member of the board of directors for Tennis Australia. He was inducted into the **International Tennis Hall of Fame** in 1991. In 2007, he was appointed an Officer of the Order of Australia.

COURIER, JAMES SPENCER "JIM," JR. B. 17 August 1970, Sanford, Florida. Jim Courier was an excellent **junior tennis** player who attended the **Nick Bollettieri** Tennis Academy, won the **Orange Bowl** in 1986 and 1987, and won the **French Open** Junior **Singles** Championship in 1987. He became a **professional** in 1988. In his career, he reached a world number-one singles **ranking** in 1992 and was a seven-time finalist in **Grand Slam** singles championships, winning the French Open in 1991 and 1992 and the **Australian Open** in 1992 and 1993. He was the runner-up at the 1991 **United States Open**, the 1993 French Open, and 1993 **Wimbledon**. The 6-foot 1-inch, 180-pound right-hander competed in the 1992 **Olympic Games** in Barcelona, reaching the third round of the men's singles and second round of the men's **doubles**. He played on the **United States Davis Cup** team from 1991 to 1999. In 14 **ties** in seven years, he had a record of 16–10 in singles and 1–0 in doubles and was on the winning Cup team in 1992 and 1995. When he retired in 2000, he had won 23 singles titles and 6 doubles titles. He was inducted into the **International Tennis Hall of Fame** in 2005. After retiring from tennis in 2004, he founded InsideOut Sports & Entertainment, a sports promotion company that created the **Champions Series** with retired tennis stars playing periodic tournaments. Courier also plays in that series and, through July 2010, has won four of its tournaments. On 27 October 2010, he was named captain of the United States Davis Cup team.

COURT. The game of **lawn tennis** is played on a tennis court. Although the court **surface** can be composed of **clay**, **grass**, asphalt, concrete, or a synthetic material, the dimensions of the court are uniform: 78 feet long, divided in the middle by a **net**, and 27 feet wide for **singles matches** or 36 feet wide for **doubles** matches. Additional space around the court is also required, and a total of 60 feet wide and 120 feet long is recommended, but that space can vary. The length of each of two **service** boxes on each side of the net is 21 feet from the net. The net is 3 feet 6 inches at each side and droops to 3 feet in the center. Courts can be constructed indoors or outdoors.

COURT, MARGARET SMITH. *See* SMITH COURT, MARGARET.

COURT TENNIS. Court tennis, also known as real tennis, *jeu de paume*, or simply tennis, is an ancient game and is the forerunner of **lawn tennis**. The game dates back to the 16th century, although similar games using the hand instead of a **racket** go back to the 12th century. Henry VIII of England was one of the advocates of the game and had a court built at Hampton Palace. The scoring is similar to lawn tennis in that **points** are scored 15-30-40-game, but six **games** wins a **set** even if the opponent has won five games. **Matches** are generally best three of five sets. The **ball** is cork based and similar to the balls originally used. The balls are heavier and have less bounce than **lawn tennis balls**. Wooden rackets, 27 inches long, tightly strung with a slight curve are used.

The court is enclosed on four sides with an arched roof on three sides. **Service** is always made from the same side, and the **serve** must hit the penthouse (sloped ceiling to the left of the server) and land in a designated area. The game is much more complicated than lawn tennis, and if a ball bounces twice on the server's end, the point is not lost. A "chase" is called, and later in the game, the server can play off the chase by striking the ball so that its second bounce is further from the **net** than the chase. Service only changes after a chase has been called and can change mid-game, unlike lawn tennis where the server continues for an entire game. Window-like openings in the penthouse also provide targets for players to win a point by hitting the ball into the opening. Strategies for play are thus much more complex than lawn tennis.

There are less than 50 courts remaining in the world in which the sport is played. Some of the more noteworthy ones are the Royal Tennis Court at Hampton Court in England; Falkland Palace in Fife, Scotland (the oldest in the world, dating to 1539); the Racquet and Tennis Club in New York City; and the **Newport Casino** in Newport, Rhode Island, which houses the **International Tennis Hall of Fame** and includes a court open to the public. Some of the game's best players include **Pierre Etchebaster**, Jay Gould II, Eustace Miles, Tom Pettitt, and **Richard D. Sears**. Former New York Knickerbocker professional basketball player John "Bud" Palmer was also quite adept at court tennis.

COYNE LONG, THELMA DOROTHY. B. 14 August 1918, Sydney, New South Wales, **Australia**. Although Thelma Coyne won 18 **Australian Championships** and a **French National mixed doubles** title, she undoubtedly would have won quite a few more had not World War II interrupted her career. On 30 January 1941, she married Maurice Newton Long of Melbourne. They divorced several years later, but she retained his name. During the war, she joined the Red Cross in May 1941. In February 1942, she joined the Australian Women's Army Service and rose to the rank of captain by 1944.

She won the Australian National women's **singles** in 1952 and 1954 and was the losing finalist in 1940, 1951, 1955, and 1956. Her **doubles** record was outstanding, and she won 12 Australian women's doubles titles and was twice runner-up. From 1936 to 1940, she and **Nancye Wynne** were doubles champions. War interrupted the **tournament**, and when it resumed in 1946, they were runners-up. From 1947 to 1949, they were again champions. They were runners-up in 1950 and won again in 1951 and 1952. After Nancye Wynne retired, Thelma teamed with Mary Bevis Hawton and won twice more in 1956 and 1958. In 1957, the pair reached the finals at **Wimbledon** and, in 1958 (when Thelma was 39 years old), the finals at **Roland Garros**. In 1951, 1952, 1954, and 1955, Thelma also won the Australian **mixed doubles** title, three times with George Worthington and once with Rex Hartwig. She and Bill Sidwell were also runners-up in 1948. Although she only entered the other **Grand Slam** tournaments outside of Australia a few times, she reached the singles quarterfinals of the **French Nationals** in 1951 and of Wimbledon and the **United States** in 1952. In 1952, at Wimbledon, she and Enrique Morea were mixed doubles finalists. In 1956, she and Luis Ayala won the French mixed doubles, and in 1951, she and **Merv Rose** were runners-up there. She was twice a finalist at the United States National mixed doubles— in 1938 with **John Bromwich** and 14 years later, in 1952, with **Lew Hoad**. In 1952, she reached a world **ranking** of seven.

After retiring from active play, from a career that saw championships 22 years apart, she became a teaching **professional**. She was nominated for 2011 induction to the **International Tennis Hall of Fame** but was not elected.

CRAWFORD, JOHN HERBERT "JACK." B. 22 March 1908, Urangeline, New South Wales, **Australia**. D. 10 September 1991, Sydney, New South Wales, Australia. **Adrian Quist** is the only man who has won more **Australian Championships** than Jack Crawford. Quist had 13 and Crawford, 11, the same number as **John Bromwich**. Crawford was also an Australian finalist 20 times and is second among men to Bromwich's 23. In addition, Crawford won three **Wimbledon** titles and three **French National** titles and was runner-up twice in the **United States National Championships**. His total of 17 **Grand Slam** championships and 32 Grand Slam finals appearances is topped by only nine other men. He is one of only nine men to win **singles**, **doubles**, and **mixed doubles** in the Australian Championships. Crawford and **Jean Borotra** are the only two men, and **Doris Hart**, **Margaret Smith Court**, and **Martina Navratilova** are the only three women to win all three events at each of the Australian, British, and French championships. In 1933, Crawford nearly became the first player to win all four Grand Slam titles in one year. He won the Australian, French, and British and reached the finals of the United States National Championships, where he faced **Fred Perry** on a hot, muggy day. Crawford was leading, 3–6, 13–11, 6–4, but ran out of energy and lost the last two **sets**, 0–6, 1–6. He was an asthmatic, which probably contributed to his lack of stamina.

Crawford was the Australian singles finalist each year from 1931 to 1936, losing only in 1934 and 1936. He won the doubles there in 1929, 1930, 1932, and 1935 and was the losing finalist in 1931, 1933, 1936, and 1940. With Marjorie Cox, he lost in the finals in mixed doubles in 1929 and 1930, but after they married, they won the mixed doubles the next three years. At Wimbledon, Jack won the men's singles in 1933 and was runner-up in 1934 and won the doubles in 1935 with Adrian Quist. In Wimbledon mixed doubles, Crawford was a losing finalist in 1928 with **Daphne Akhurst** as partner and won it in 1930 with **Elizabeth "Bunny" Ryan** as partner. In 1939, he and **Harry Hopman** reached the finals of the United States National Championships but were defeated by Quist and Bromwich. Crawford was a member of the Australian **Davis Cup** team from 1928 to 1937. In that time, he played in 22 **ties** in eight years and had a record of 23–16 in singles and 13–5 in doubles. He was inducted into the **International Tennis Hall of Fame** in 1979.

CROATIA. Tennis has a long history in Croatia. In 1922, the Croatian Tennis Association (Hrvatski Teniski Savez) was founded one month before the Yugoslav Tennis Association (Teniski Savez Jugoslavije). Until 1992, Croatian players represented **Yugoslavia** in international competition. From 1993 through May 2011, Croatia as an independent nation has competed in all 19 **Davis Cup tournaments** with a record of 24–17 in 41 **ties**. Croatia has competed 10 times in the World Group. In 2005, Croatia was the tournament champion, defeating **Slovakia** in the final. Croatian top Davis Cup players have been Ivan Ljubičić, Mario Ančić, and **Goran Ivanišević**. Croatia competed in **Olympic** tennis from 1992 to 2008. In 1992, Goran Ivanišević was the bronze medalist in the men's **singles** and, with partner Goran Prpić, was the bronze medalist in the men's **doubles**. In 2004, Mario Ančić and Ivan Ljubičić were also bronze medalists in men's doubles. Other top male tennis players include **Marin Čilić**, Ivan Dodig, **Ivo Karlović**, Nikola Mektic, and Antonio Veić. Among the best Croatian-born players who competed for Yugoslavia were Željko Franulović, Boro Jovanović, and **Niki Pilić**.

The best female tennis players include Mirjana Lučić, Iva Majoli, and Karolina Šprem. Sabrina Goleš was born in Croatia but represented Yugoslavia. In **Federation Cup** competition, from 1992 to May 2011, Croatia has competed 20 years, 7 years in World Group, played 57 **ties** with a record of 30–27, and was a quarterfinalist in 2002.

CROSSCOURT. A crosscourt shot in tennis is one hit diagonally, over the **net**, from the right side to the left or vice versa.

CZECHOSLOVAKIA. The former country of Czechoslovakia has a long tradition as a sports-loving nation. After its dissolution in 1992, the separate nations of the **Czech Republic** and **Slovakia** have competed individually. From 1921 through 1992, Czechoslovakia competed in 59 Davis Cup **tournaments** with a record of 92–57 in 149 **ties**. Czechoslovakia competed 12 times in the World Group since its formation in 1981. In 1975, the team lost to **Sweden** in the final round, but in 1980, Czechoslovakia was the tournament champion, defeating **Italy** in the final. Top **Davis Cup** players have been Vladimir Cernik, **Jaroslav Drobný**, **Jan Kodeš**, and Rodrich Menzel.

Czechoslovakia entered **Olympic** tennis in 1920 and 1924 and again in 1988 and 1992. In the Olympic Games prior to 1920, Czechoslovakian players represented Bohemia. In 1920, Milayda Skrbková and **Ladislaw Žemla** won the bronze medal in **mixed doubles**. Žemla also competed in the 1906, 1908, and 1912 Olympic Games as a representative of Bohemia, won the bronze medal in men's **doubles** in 1906, with his brother, Zdeněk, and finished fourth in both men's **singles** and doubles in 1912. In 1988, Miloslav Mečíř won the gold medal in men's singles and, with partner Milan Šrejber, won the bronze in men's doubles.

Among the best Czechoslovakian male tennis players not previously mentioned have been Stanislav Birner, Jiri Javorsky, Jan and Karel Koželuh, **Ivan Lendl**, Karel Nováček, Pavel Složil, and Tomáš Šmíd. The best female tennis players include **Hana Mandlíková**, Regina Maršíková, **Martina Navratilova, Jana Novotná, Helena Suková**, Věra Suková, and Renáta Tomanová. In **Federation Cup** competition, from 1963 to 1992, Czechoslovakia competed 22 years, played 79 ties with a record of 62–17, and was the champion in 1975, 1983, 1984, 1985, and 1988 and runner-up in 1986.

CZECH REPUBLIC. The Czech Republic was created in 1993 after the dissolution of **Czechoslovakia**. Tennis is administered there by the Czech Tennis Federation with its headquarters in Prague. Prior to 1993, the Czech Republic competed as Czechoslovakia. From 1993 through May 2011, the Czech Republic has competed in all 19 **Davis Cup tournaments** with a record of 24–18 in 42 **ties**. This country has competed 17 times in the World Group. Top Davis Cup players for the Czech Republic have been Tomáš Berdych, Lukáš Dlouhý, and Radek Štěpánek. As an independent country, the Czech Republic competed in the **Olympic Games** from 1996 to 2008. In 1996, **Jana Novotná** won the bronze medal in women's **singles**. She and **Helena Suková** won the silver medal in women's **doubles**. They had previously won the silver medal in the 1988 Olympic Games as representatives of Czechoslovakia. Among the best male tennis players have been Martin Damm, Jan Hernych, **Petr Korda**, Ivo Minář, Cyril Suk, Daniel Vacek, and Pavel Vizner, in addition to the three players mentioned above.

The best female tennis players include Iveta Benešová, Lucie Hradecká, Petra Kvitová (2011 Wimbledon singles winner), Květa Peschke (2011 Wimbledon doubles winner), Lucie Šafářová, Nicole Vaidišová, and Klára Zakopalová. In **Federation Cup** competition, from 1993 to May 2011, the Czech Republic has competed 19 years, 18 years in World Group, played 44 ties with a record of 26–18, and was a losing semifinalist in 1997. In 2009, the Czech Republic was the tournament runner-up, losing to **Spain** in the final. On 5–6 November 2011, the Czech Republic and Russia play for the 2011 Fed Cup championship.

D

DANZIG, ALLISON. B. 27 February 1898, Waco, Texas. D. 27 January 1987, Ridgewood, New Jersey. Allison Danzig was the most prolific tennis writer of his time. Raised in Albany, New York, he served in the U.S. Army during World War I as an infantry lieutenant at Camp Grant in Rockford, Illinois. Although only 5 feet 6 inches tall and 125 pounds, he was a member of the Cornell University football team but saw limited action. After graduating in 1921, he began his sportswriting career at the *Brooklyn Eagle* and moved to the *New York Times* in 1923, remaining there until his retirement in 1968—the same year that he was the first journalist inducted into the **International Tennis Hall of Fame.** He also covered college football, **squash**, rowing, and the **Olympic Games** and was one of the few writers to be knowledgeable about **court tennis.** He is credited with originating the term "**Grand Slam**" to denote the four major tennis **tournaments.** Among the books he wrote are *The Racquet Game* (a book on all **racquet** sports), *The Fireside Book of Tennis* (an anthology), and *Oh, How They Played the Game* (a history of early college football). He has been honored by Columbia University, which established the Allison Danzig Cup, awarded to the winner of the annual Columbia-Cornell tennis matches; the **Longwood Cricket Club,** which presents an annual Allison Danzig award for distinguished tennis writing; and by the Nassau Country Club, which established the Danzig Award for Sportsmanship.

DAVENPORT, LINDSAY. B. 8 June 1976, Palos Verdes, California. Lindsay Davenport is the daughter of Winthrop "Wink" Davenport, a member of the 1968 **United States** men's **Olympic** volleyball team. She attended Chadwick School in Palos Verdes Peninsula, California, and then transferred to Murrieta Valley High School in Murrieta, California. One of the tallest female tennis players of all time at six feet two inches tall, she began playing **professionally** in 1993, at the age of 16. She has won titles at each of the four **Grand Slam** events and has reached 20 Grand Slam finals, although she only won six. She was the **Australian Open** women's **singles** champion in 2000 and lost in the finals there in 2005. She reached the women's **doubles** finals in **Australia** each year from 1996 to 1999 and also in 2001 and 2005 but came up short each time. At the **French Open**, she won the 1996 women's doubles title with **Mary Joe Fernández** and was runner-up in 1994 and 1998 with other partners. Davenport was the **Wimbledon** singles champion in 1999 and runner-up to **Venus Williams** in 2000 and 2005. In 1999, she was also doubles champion with **Corina Morariu** and runner-up in 1998 with **Natasha Zvereva**. In 1998, at the United States Open, Lindsay won the women's singles. In 2000, she was again defeated by Venus Williams there. Davenport and **Jana Novotná** won the **U.S. Open** women's doubles in 1997, and Davenport and Zvereva were runners-up there in 1998.

In 2006, Davenport retired from the tour to raise a family, but after her son was born, on 10 June 2007, she announced that she would return to the tour. She continued to play but took time off in 2009 to give birth to a daughter on 30 June. She again returned to competition in 2010. Through May 2011, she has won 55 singles and 38 doubles titles and has been **ranked** number one in both singles and doubles. She won the Olympic women's singles gold medal in 1996 in Atlanta and returned to the Olympic Games 12 years later in Beijing in the doubles competition, reaching the quarterfinal round with partner Liezel Huber. In 2003, she married Jon Leach, an investment banker, former All-American tennis player at the University of Southern California, and brother of **Rick Leach**. She was a member of the United States **Fed Cup** team from 1993 to 2000, 2002, 2005, and 2008. She helped the United States win the Cup in 1996, 1999, and 2000. In 20 **ties**, her record was 26–3 in singles and 7–0 in doubles. She won the **Hopman Cup** in 2004 with partner **James Blake**.

DAVIS, DWIGHT FILLEY. B. 5 July 1879, St. Louis, Missouri. D. 28 November 1945, Washington DC. Although Dwight Davis was a champion tennis player and three-time **United States National doubles** champion, he is best known for originating the tournament that today bears his name. The Davises were wealthy St. Louis merchants and sent him to study at Harvard University. While there, he took up tennis and devoted more time to the game than to his studies. In 1898, he was the runner-up to Malcolm Whitman at the United States National Championships **singles** competition. In 1899, Davis won the **intercollegiate** singles championship as a representative of Harvard. He and his fellow Harvard classmate, Holcombe Ward, were finalists at the United States National Doubles Championships for five consecutive years, 1898–1902, and won the title in 1899, 1900, and 1901.

Davis originated the **International Lawn Tennis Challenge** tournament in 1900 and donated a silver bowl to the **United States National Lawn Tennis Association** to be awarded to the winner of a match between a team from the **British Isles** and a team from the **United States**. The tournament became extremely successful and was renamed the **Davis Cup** after his death in 1945. He played for the United States in the first two tournaments. In 1900, he won a singles and a doubles match to give the United States a 3–0 lead. In the fourth match of the event, he won the first set from Arthur Gore, but the second set was discontinued after the players were at 9-**all**. In 1902, he played doubles, but he and Holcombe Ward were defeated by the **Doherty brothers**. The **left-handed** Davis competed in the 1904 **Olympic Games** in St. Louis and reached the third round of the men's singles and quarterfinals of the men's doubles with partner Ralph McKittrick.

Davis graduated Washington University (St. Louis) Law School, and although he was not a practicing attorney, entered politics as a member of the Republican Party. He was the Commissioner of Public Parks in St. Louis from 1911 to 1915. Under his jurisdiction, the first municipal tennis courts in the United States were created. He served in the U.S. Army during the First World War with the rank of major and received the Distinguished Service Cross for "extraordinary heroism in action" in France 29–30 September 1918. He was discharged as a lieutenant colonel. In 1920, he lost a race for the Senate. In 1923, he became the president of the United States Lawn Tennis Association. From 1923 to 1925, he was the assistant secretary of war under Calvin Coolidge and served as secretary of war from 1925 to 1929. From 1929 to 1932, he was governor general of the Philippines. He later became chairman of the board of the Brookings Institution, a nonprofit public policy institute in Washington DC. He was inducted into the **International Tennis Hall of Fame** in 1957. He is interred in the Arlington National Cemetery.

DAVIS CUP. The Davis Cup is the most important **lawn tennis** team competition for men. It was originated in 1900 by **Dwight Davis**, who had competed in **intercollegiate** tennis as a member of the Harvard University team and enjoyed team competition. He commissioned a silver bowl from a Boston silversmith, costing about $1,000, and offered it as the prize to the winning team in an international competition. A challenge was made to a team from the **British Isles**, and the event, called the **International Lawn Tennis Challenge**, took place at the **Longwood Cricket Club** in Boston, Massachusetts, from 8 August to 10 August. The format was best of five **sets** with two **singles** contests on the first day, a **doubles** contest the second day, and two more singles on the third day, with the opponents switching. The Americans, led by Davis and Malcolm Whitman playing singles and Davis and Holcombe Ward playing doubles, won the first three matches. The fourth match was halted in the second set, and the fifth was not played. The challenge proved successful, and another was scheduled for the following year. In 1901, the

British were unable to field a team, and no matches were held. In 1902, the **Doherty brothers** came to the **United States** to represent the British Isles, and the second series of matches were held.

Since then, the event, more popularly known as the Davis Cup, has been held annually with the exception of 1910 and the two World War periods. Other countries joined the challenge and preliminary rounds were scheduled with the winner to play the current cup holder in a **challenge round** for the cup. By 1925, there were 26 countries involved, and by 1960, there were 40, although the United States, **Australia**, **Great Britain**, and **France** had been the only winners. In 1972, the concept of a challenge round was abolished, and all competing countries engaged in the **tournament** with the two survivors meeting for the cup. Since then, there have been nine other Cup-winning nations.

In 1981, a tiered elimination system was introduced, with the top 16 teams competing in a World Group and lesser countries involved in regional competition. In a system similar to the European league system of relegation, the four worst countries are dropped from the World Group each year, and the four best countries from regional groups replace them. Through 2010, the United States has won the Cup 32 times, Australia 28 times, Great Britain and France 9 each, **Sweden** 7, **Spain** 4, **Germany** and **West Germany** 3, **Russia** 2, and **Italy**, **Czechoslovakia**, **South Africa**, **Croatia**, and **Serbia** once each. *See also* APPENDIX F (for a list of champions).

DAVYDENKO, NIKOLAY VLADIMIROVICH. B. 2 June 1981, Severodonezk, Ukraine, **Union of Soviet Socialist Republics**. Nikolay Davydenko played **junior tennis** in Germany before moving to **Russia** as a teenager and becoming a Russian citizen. The prematurely bald Davydenko has always appeared to be much older than his opponents. He began playing **professional** tennis in 1999. He competed in the 2004 and 2008 **Olympic Games** in both **singles** and **doubles**. Of the four events, his best showing was the quarterfinals in the 2008 doubles tournament. He played in the **Davis Cup** for Russia each year from 2003 to 2008 and again in 2010. In that time, his record was 14–9 in singles and 2–2 in doubles in 16 **ties**, and he helped Russia win the Cup in 2006 and reach the finals the next year. The 5-foot 10-inch, 150-pound right-hander reached the **French Open** (2005, 2007) and **United States Open** (2006, 2007) semifinal rounds twice each and was a four-time quarterfinalist at the **Australian Open**. His best showing at **Wimbledon** has only been the fourth round in 2007. In August 2007, he was involved in some controversy. In a match with Martín Vassalo Argüello, in a relatively unimportant tournament in Sopot, **Poland**, there was an exceptionally high amount of betting on Arguello after Davydenko had won the first **set** of the best-of-three-sets match. Davydenko withdrew during the third set, claiming a foot injury. The British gambling company Betfair notified the **Association of Tennis Professionals (ATP)** and voided all bets on the match. After a one-year investigation, both players were exonerated. In 2009, Davydenko won the year-end ATP World Tour Finals, beating both **Rafael Nadal** and **Roger Federer** to win the championship. Through May 2011, Davydenko has won 21 singles titles and 1 doubles title and was **ranked** number three in the world in singles in 2006.

DEAD RUBBER. *See* RUBBER.

DELL, DONALD. B. 17 June 1938, Bethesda, Maryland. Donald Dell was a good tennis player who made his greatest contribution to tennis after he retired from active play. Dell played **collegiate** tennis at Yale University, where he was an All-American in 1958, 1959, and 1960. He was a National Collegiate Athletic Association singles finalist in 1959 and semifinalist in 1960. In 1961, he reached the quarterfinals of the **United States National Singles Championships** at **Forest Hills**. He played on the **United States Davis Cup** team in 1961 and 1963, appearing in three **ties** with a 1–0 record in singles and a 2–1 record in **doubles**. In 1968 and 1969, he was Davis Cup team captain and led the **United States** to the Cup in both years. He received a law degree from the University of Virginia in 1964. In 1970, he founded ProServ, one of the first sports management firms. As one of the first sports agents, his clients included **Arthur Ashe**, **Jimmy Connors**, and **Stan Smith**. Dell was also one of the founders of the **Association of Tennis Professionals** and the Legg Mason Tennis Classic and is the vice chairman of the **International Tennis Hall of Fame**. He was inducted into the International Tennis Hall of Fame in 2009 as a contributor.

DEL POTRO, JUAN MARTÍN. B. 23 September 1988, Tandil, **Argentina**. Juan Martín del Potro began playing tennis at age seven. In 2002, he won the **Orange Bowl** 14s title. He became a **professional player** in 2005. He entered the **French Open**, his first **Grand Slam** event, in 2006 but lost in the first round. Three years later, he was a semifinalist there, was a quarterfinalist in the **Australian Open**, and, in a major upset, won the 2009 **United States Open** Men's **Singles** Championship by defeating four-time champion **Roger Federer**, after losing the first **set**. An injured wrist in 2010 has limited play that year and caused his ranking to drop to 485. He played well in the first five months of 2011, winning two tournaments, and was able to improve his ranking to 26th by 23 May 2011. The six-foot six-inch Del Potro is one of the tallest players on the men's pro tennis tour. He appeared in five **Davis Cup ties** for Argentina, from 2007 to 2009, and had a record of 6–2 in singles. He played in the Cup finals in 2008, in which Argentina was defeated by **Spain**.

Through May 2011, he has won nine singles and one doubles title in his relatively brief career and has reached a high **ranking** of four in 2009.

DEMENTIEVA, ELENA VIATCHESLAVOVNA. B. 15 October 1981, Moscow, **Russia**, **Union of Soviet Socialist Republics**. Elena Dementieva began playing tennis at the age of seven at the Spartak Tennis Club. One of her first **coaches** was Rauza Islanova, the mother of **Marat Safin** and **Dinara Safina**, both also future tennis **professionals**. She then transferred to the Central Red Army Club when she was 11 years old. In 1998, she began her professional tennis career. She injured a shoulder early in her career and had to alter her **service** motion to accommodate the injury. After it healed, the awkward motion often resulted in her inability to **serve** properly, and she committed as many as 19 **double faults** in a match. Nonetheless, she managed to overcome this handicap and still be **ranked** among the top 10 in the world. The 5-foot 11-inch right-hander had one of her best years in 2004, when she reached the finals of both the **French Open** and **United States Open**, where she was defeated by a countrywoman each time—Anastasia Myskina at the French Open and **Svetlana Kuznetsova** at the U.S. Open. She also twice reached the women's **doubles** finals of the U.S. Open—in 2002 with partner Janette Husárová and in 2005 with partner Flavia Pennetta. Elena did well at all four **Grand Slam** events, although she did not win one. She reached the **singles** semifinals at the 2008 and 2009 **Wimbledon** and 2009 **Australian Open**.

Elena competed in three **Olympic Games**—2000, 2004, and 2008. She won the women's singles gold medal in 2008 and won the silver medal in 2000, joining **Steffi Graf** as the only women to win gold and silver medals in Olympic women's singles. In 2004, she lost in the first round of both the singles and doubles events. She played on the Russian **Fed Cup** team from 1999 to 2010. Her record in 18 **ties** in eight years is 22–5 in singles and 4–4 in doubles. She helped lead Russia to the Cup in 2005 and was on the losing finals team in 1999 and 2001. She announced her retirement on 29 October 2010. In her career, she won 19 singles and 9 doubles titles and had a world **ranking** of 3 in singles (2009) and 5 (2003) in doubles.

DENT, PHILLIP "PHIL." B. 14 February 1950, Sydney, New South Wales, **Australia**. Phil Dent won the **junior tournaments** in 1968 in both the **Australian** and **French Championships**. As a **professional**, the 6-foot tall, 175-pound right-hander reached the men's **singles** finals of the **Australian Open** in 1974, where he was defeated by **Jimmy Connors** in four **sets**. In 1975, he and John Alexander won the Australian Open men's **doubles**. He and Alexander also reached that tournament's finals in 1970, 1973, and 1977 and lost in the **Wimbledon** finals in 1977 and in the **French Open** finals in 1975. With partner Ross Case, Dent lost in the French Open finals in 1979. Dent and **Billie Jean King** won the **United States Open mixed doubles** in 1976. He played **Davis Cup** tennis for Australia from 1969 to 1982, and in 1977, he was a member of the Davis Cup champion Australian team. In 13 Cup **ties**, his record was 6–2 in singles and 7–4 in doubles over eight years. In his first Davis Cup appearance (against **Mexico** in 1969), he and partner John Alexander lost in straight sets in one of the longest three-set Davis Cup matches, 16–18, 10–12, 4–6. Dent's career record was 352–306 in singles competition and 406–253 in doubles. His highest singles **ranking** was 19 in singles in 1978 and 51 in doubles in 1983. He retired to Southern California. He married (but later divorced) tennis professional Betty Ann Grubb, and their son, **Taylor Dent**, was a professional tennis player also.

DENT, TAYLOR PHILLIP. B. 24 April 1981, Newport Beach, California. Taylor Dent is the son of **Phil Dent**, **Australian** tennis champion, and Betty Ann Grubb, American tennis champion. He began his **professional** tennis career in 1998, after graduating from Corona del Mar High School in Newport Beach. The 6-foot 2-inch 195-pounder was known for his powerful **serve** and was one of the few players in the 21st century to use a **serve-and-volley** style of play. In the 2004 **Olympic Games**, he placed fourth in men's **singles**, losing the bronze medal match to Fernando González, 4–6, 6–2, 14–16. The final **set** was the longest in Olympic history to decide a medal. (In that same Olympic Games, the men's **doubles** bronze medal was also decided by a 16–14 final set.)

Dent played one match for the **United States** in the 2003 **Davis Cup**, losing in a **dead rubber** to Mario Ančić of **Croatia**. One of his biggest victories occurred in 2006 when he won the **Hopman Cup** with partner **Lisa Raymond**. On 8 December 2006, he married tennis professional Jennifer Hopkins. His career record is 148–137 in singles. His highest **ranking** was 21 in 2005, and he won four singles tournaments. He reached the fourth round at the **United States Open** in 2003 and in **Wimbledon** in 2005. He missed most of 2006 and 2007 due to injuries and, in March 2007, underwent back surgery. While sidelined, he worked for the **Tennis Channel** as a color commentator. His stepbrother Brett Hansen-Dent played professional tennis briefly, and his cousin Misty May-Treanor was a beach volleyball gold medalist in the 2004 and 2008 Olympic Games. On 8 November 2010, Taylor announced his retirement after a brief comeback from injuries.

DEUCE. Deuce is the score when each player (or team) has won four **points** in a **game**. The score after the next point is called "**advantage**." If the player at advantage wins the next point, he or she wins the game. If he or she loses the next point, the score reverts to deuce. In recent years, some **doubles** events (as well as **World Team Tennis**) have changed their rules to "**no-ad**" **scoring**, whereby when the score reaches deuce, the winner of the next point wins the game. *See also* SCORING.

DIBBS, EDDIE. B. 23 February 1951, Brooklyn, New York. As a **professional** tennis player from 1971 to 1984, the diminutive Eddie Dibbs was known for his patience and perseverance. Only 5 feet 7 inches tall and 160 pounds, he was an effective **baseline** player who would often engage in extremely long **rallies** and played his best on **clay courts**. Although he reached a world **ranking** of six in 1977, he never played in **Davis Cup** competition, and he played **Wimbledon** only once but reached the semifinals at **Roland Garros** in 1975 and 1976 and the quarterfinals of the **United States Open** three times. He won 22 **tournaments** and was runner-up in 20 others. His career record was 362–165, with a clay court record of 256–87. After retiring from the tour, he had hip replacement surgery and returned to play briefly in the **Association of Tennis Professionals senior** tour.

DJOKOVIĆ, NOVAK "NOLE." B. 22 May 1987, Belgrade, **Serbia**, Yugoslavia. Novak Djoković began playing tennis at an early age and, when he was 12 years old, was sent to study at **Niki Pilić**'s tennis academy in Munich, **Germany**. Novak became a **professional** at the age of 16, in 2003, and has rapidly progressed. Through July 2011, his **tournament** wins include 26 **singles** and 1 **doubles**. He probably would have even more tournament victories had he not been a contemporary of **Roger Federer** and **Rafael Nadal**, two of the greatest players of all time. Novak won the 2008 and 2011 **Australian Open** singles title—and the 2011 Wimbledon title. The win in Australia in 2011 began a five-month undefeated string which reached 41 consecutive victories over seven tournaments (plus two more victories in the 2010 Davis Cup) that ended when he was defeated by Federer in a very competitive match in the French Open semi-finals. One of the highlights of his career occurred in August 2007, at the Rogers Cup tournament in Montreal, when he defeated the world number-three player, **Andy Roddick**, in the quarterfinal round, the world number-two player, Rafael Nadal, in the semifinal round, and the world number-one player, Roger Federer, in the final round. The following month, Novak lost to Federer in the finals of the 2007 **United States Open**.

Djoković's record in Grand Slam tournaments is outstanding. From 2005 through the 2011 Wimbledon Open, he entered every one of the four major singles events. His **match** record in those events is 92–23, and he has reached the semifinals of all four events. He has won 80% of his matches in those events and has a match record of 96–24. In 2010, he reached the rank of number two and in September, defeated Roger Federer in the U.S. Open semifinal round, after saving two **match points**, but lost to Rafael Nadal in the final. Djoković, a 6-foot 2-inch, 175-pound right-hander, won the bronze medal in the 2008 **Olympic** men's singles event but lost in the first round of the doubles in that year's tournament. He represented his native country each year from 2004 to 2010 in **Davis Cup** play. In 15 **ties**, his record is 19–6 in singles and 2–1 in doubles. In December 2010, he won two matches to help Serbia win the Davis Cup final over France. He has an excellent personality and sense of humor and has, on more than one occasion, entertained the crowd following his match by doing impersonations of other well-known tennis players. In July 2011, he became the 25th man to achieve the number one ranking.

DOD, CHARLOTTE "LOTTIE." B. 24 September 1871, Lower Bebington, Cheshire, England. D. 27 June 1960, Sway, Hampshire, England. Lottie Dod was one of the most versatile sportswomen in history. Coming from a wealthy family, she was able to devote all her time and energy to various sports. Her two brothers and sister were also avid sports people. Lottie began playing the relatively new sport of **lawn tennis** when she was just 9 years old and, by the age of 11, was playing in local **tournaments** with her sister, Annie. In 1885, Lottie won **singles**, **doubles**, and **mixed doubles** in the Waterloo tournament. Two years later, in 1887, she won the **Wimbledon** ladies' singles, at the age of 15, by defeating the reigning champion, Blanche Bingley Hillyard. Dod is still the youngest female to win the Wimbledon singles. Lottie retained her Wimbledon title in 1888 but did not defend it in 1889 and lost the **challenge round** to Hillyard in a **walkover**. Dod did not enter Wimbledon in 1890. She returned the following year and again defeated Hillyard for the title. Lottie won it for the fourth and fifth times in 1892 and 1893 but did not defend in 1894 and again lost in a walkover.

She then turned her attention to other sports. She helped to establish a ladies' golf club in Moreton, England, in 1894 and began competing in championship tournaments, twice reaching the semifinal round of the British National Championships. In 1904, she won the National Championships and is the only woman ever to win British national titles in both tennis and golf. In 1897, she helped to found a field hockey club and, by 1899, was playing for the English national field hockey team. She became interested in archery in 1905, competed in the 1908 **Olympic Games** in London, and won a silver medal in the women's double national round event. Her brother, Willie, won the Olympic gold medal in the men's double York round event that year. During World War I, she served as a Red Cross nurse in England. She never married. In 1983, she was inducted into the **International Tennis Hall of Fame**.

DOHERTY, HUGH LAURENCE "LAURIE." B. 8 October 1875, London, England. D. 21 August 1919, Broadstairs, England. Laurie Doherty attended Cambridge University and played on the **lawn tennis** team there. Along with his brother, **Reggie**, they dominated play at **Wimbledon** around the turn of the 20th century. In 1898, Laurie won the Wimbledon **all-comers tournament** and met his brother, Reggie, in the **challenge round**. Reggie won in five **sets**. From 1902 to 1906, Laurie was Wimbledon **singles** champion each year. In **doubles**, the pair was nearly unbeatable, winning at Wimbledon annually from 1897 to 1901, losing in five sets in 1902, and winning from 1903 to 1905 before again losing in five sets in 1906. They played in the **United States National Championships** in 1902 and 1903, winning the doubles both years. Laurie forfeited to his brother in the 1902 singles quarterfinals, and his brother reciprocated in the 1903 singles quarterfinals. Laurie, the shorter (at 5 feet 10 inches) and younger (known as Little Do), went on to win the tournament that year and became the first non-American to win the U.S. National title.

He competed in the 1900 **Olympic Games** in Paris and medaled in all three events. After brother Reggie refused to play him in the semifinal round and conceded the match, Laurie won the men's singles by defeating Harold Mahony; he and Reggie won the men's doubles, and he and partner Marion Jones, lost to Reggie and his partner, Charlotte Cooper, in the semifinals of the **mixed doubles**. He is one of the few players to be undefeated in **Davis Cup** competition, leading the **British Isles** to the Cup in 1903, 1904, 1905, and 1906. He also played in the 1902 Cup, in which the **United States** defeated the British Isles. Doherty's record was 7–0 in singles and 5–0 in doubles. Laurie, like his brother, suffered from respiratory problems throughout his life and died at an early age (as did his brother) after a prolonged illness. He and his brother were both inducted into the **International Tennis Hall of Fame** in 1980.

DOHERTY, REGINALD FRANK "REGGIE." B. 14 October 1872, London, England. D. 29 December 1910, Kensington, England. Reggie Doherty attended Cambridge University and played on the **lawn tennis** team there. He was the **Wimbledon singles** champion each year from 1897 to 1900 and lost in the 1901 **challenge round** to Arthur Gore. In 1896, Reggie teamed with Harold Nisbet and lost in the Wimbledon **doubles** finals. Reggie then played doubles with his brother, **Laurie**, and they were virtually unbeatable. They were the Wimbledon doubles champions each year from 1897 to 1901. They were defeated 11–9 in the fifth **set** in 1902, and then won the championship from 1903 to 1905, before again losing in five sets in 1906. In 1902, Reggie and Laurie competed in the **United States National Championships**. They reached the quarterfinals and were matched against each other. Laurie conceded the match to his brother, and Reggie went on to win the **all-comers** event but lost to champion Bill Larned in the **challenge round**. They returned to the **United States** in 1903, and this time Reggie conceded his quarterfinal match to his brother, who went on to become the champion. In doubles, the brothers won the United States championships in 1902 and 1903.

The 6-foot 1-inch, slender (140 pounds), right-handed Reggie competed in the 1900 **Olympic Games** in Paris and duplicated his brother's feat of three medals in three events. Reggie won the men's doubles with his brother, conceded to him in the semifinals of the men's singles, still won the bronze medal in that event, and won the **mixed doubles** with partner Charlotte Cooper after defeating Laurie and his partner, Marion Jones, in the semifinals. Reggie also entered the men's doubles in the 1908 Olympic Games in London and won it with partner George Hillyard. In **Davis Cup** play for the **British Isles** from 1902 to 1906, he had a near perfect record, 2–1 in singles and 5–0 in doubles, his only loss coming in the deciding match in 1902, where he lost to Malcolm Whitman of the United States. In the other four years, his effort helped the British Isles to win the Cup each year. Reggie, who suffered from respiratory problems much of his life, died at the age of 38 after having been "in ill health for some time," according to his *New York Times* obituary. The Doherty brothers were both inducted into the **International Tennis Hall of Fame** in 1980.

DOUBLE FAULT. A double fault occurs when the **server** hits two consecutive **balls** that do not land in the opponent's **service** box. The penalty is the loss of a **point**.

DOUBLES. Tennis matches may be contested between two players or between teams of two players a side. When two players comprise a team, the game is called doubles, and the **court** is widened by four and one-half feet on each side. This extra width is referred to as the doubles **alley**. Doubles events are held for teams of two men, two women, or one man and one woman (called **mixed doubles**). *See also* SINGLES.

DOUGLASS LAMBERT CHAMBERS, DOROTHEA KATHERINE. B. 3 September 1878, Ealing, England. D. 7 January 1960, Kensington, England. Dorothea Douglass was one of the best female **lawn tennis** players at the beginning of the 20th century. She was **Wimbledon singles** champion seven times and earned it by winning the **all-comers** event five times. She entered her first Wimbledon tournament in 1900 and reached the quarterfinal round. In 1902, she was a semifinalist. She won the tournament in 1903 and successfully defended her title in 1904. In 1905, she lost in the **challenge round** to May Sutton and alternated winning the title with her in 1906 and

1907. Dorothea won again in 1910, defended successfully in 1911, did not defend in 1912, won the all-comers in 1913, and successfully defended in 1914. World War I interrupted the Wimbledon tournament from 1915 to 1918. In 1919, she was defeated by **Suzanne Lenglen** in the longest Wimbledon final to that date, 10–8, 4–6, 9–7. In 1920, at the age of 41, she won the all-comers only to lose the challenge round to Lenglen. Dorothea continued playing doubles until 1927. With partner Charlotte Cooper Sterry, she was a Wimbledon ladies **doubles** runner-up in 1913, the first year that event was held, and, with Ethel Thomson Larcombe as partner, was runner-up again in 1919 and 1920, losing to Lenglen and **Elizabeth "Bunny" Ryan** both those years. She also reached the finals of the **mixed doubles** in 1919.

She was a **Wightman Cup** team member in 1925 and 1926. In 1925, at the age of 46, she won a singles and doubles match to help **Great Britain** win the Wightman Cup. She lost her doubles match in 1926. She then became a **professional** tennis instructor. She also won the women's singles at the 1908 **Olympic Games** in London.

In 1907, she married Robert Lambert Chambers and used her married name in tournaments from then on. In 1910, she wrote one of the first tennis books aimed at female players, *Tennis for Ladies*. She was inducted into the **International Tennis Hall of Fame** in 1981.

DRAW. In tennis **tournaments**, a blind draw is held to determine opponents for the tournament. The best players are usually **seeded** and spaced throughout the draw so that they will not play each other in early rounds.

DROBNÝ, JAROSLAV. B. 12 October 1921, Prague, **Czechoslovakia**. D. 13 September 2001, London, England. Jaroslav Drobný was both an ice hockey player and tennis player. He entered his first **Wimbledon tournament** in 1938. In 1946, he was a finalist at the **French National Championships**, losing to Marcel Bernard after winning the first two sets. Drobný played center in the Czechoslovakian ice hockey league from 1938 to 1949 and also in the 1947 World Ice Hockey Championships for the winning Czechoslovakian team. In the 1948 Winter **Olympic Games**, he won a silver medal with Czechoslovakia as well. In 1949, the Boston Bruins of the National Hockey League in the United States offered Drobný $20,000 to play for the team, but Drobný did not want to forfeit his **amateur** standing and chance to play tennis. Although a hockey injury affected his eyesight, Drobný wore prescription sunglasses while playing tennis and was able to play well. At **Roland Garros**, in 1948, Drobný again reached the finals but lost to **Frank Parker**.

While at a tennis tournament in Gstaad, **Switzerland**, in July 1949, he received a message from Prague telling him to withdraw from the tournament and return home. He later was told that in person as two members of the Czech foreign ministry met him in Switzerland. Fearing that he might not be allowed ever to leave the country to play tennis again, Drobný defected. He stayed in Switzerland for two years and was then invited by Egyptian King Farouk to become an Egyptian citizen. In 1959, Drobný became a British citizen. He was a **French National Championship** finalist once more in 1950 but lost to **Budge Patty** in five sets. In 1951, the **left-handed** Drobný finally won the French tournament and, in 1952, won it for a second time. He was the French men's **doubles** and **mixed doubles** champion in 1948 and runner-up in men's doubles in 1950. At Wimbledon, he was a losing finalist in 1949 and 1952, before finally winning it in 1954. He also reached the men's doubles finals there in 1951 but was defeated. He reached the semifinals of the **United States Nationals** twice, in 1947 and 1948, and only competed in **Australia** once, in 1950, when he reached the fourth round but was a losing men's doubles finalist. In 1954, he was the world number-one–**ranked singles** player.

He played **Davis Cup** tennis for Czechoslovakia from 1946 to 1949. In those four years, he appeared in 15 **ties** and had a record of 24–4 in singles and 13–2 in doubles. He had an exceptionally long career, beginning at Wimbledon in 1938 and concluding at Roland Garros in 1965. He was inducted into the **International Tennis Hall of Fame** in 1983 and, in 1997, was inducted into the International Ice Hockey Federation Hall of Fame.

DROP SHOT. A drop shot is a shot that is played to just clear the **net** in order to make it difficult for the opponent to reach it. It is usually hit with a lot of backspin so that is does not carry toward the opponent.

DRYSDALE, ERIC CLIFFORD "CLIFF." B. 26 May 1941, Nelspruit, South Africa. Cliff Drysdale began playing major **tournaments** in 1962. His best year was 1965, when he was a semifinalist at **Roland Garros** and **Wimbledon** and reached the finals at **Forest Hills**, losing to **Manuel Santana**, and had a career-high world **ranking** of four. Drysdale's only other **Grand Slam** final appearance occurred in 1972, when he and Roger Taylor won the **United States Open** men's **doubles** title. The 6-foot 2-inch, 170-pound right-hander was unusual in that he had a two-handed **backhand** when players of his era usually only used one hand. He was one of the eight initial players (nicknamed the Handsome Eight) signed by Lamar Hunt for the **professional World Championship Tennis** tour in 1968. Drysdale played on the South African **Davis Cup** team from 1962 to 1967 and 1973 to 1974 and was a member of the championship team that won by default from **India** in 1974. His record in 24 **ties** over eight years was 32–12 in **singles** and 3–2 in doubles. Since retiring from active play following the 1980 season, he has become a popular television broadcaster in the **United States**. He became an American citizen and founded Cliff Drysdale Tennis, a resort, hotel, and club tennis management company.

DUPONT, MARGARET OSBORNE. *See* OSBORNE DUPONT, MARGARET.

DURR BROWNING, FRANÇOISE "FRANKIE." B. 25 December 1942, Algiers, Algeria. Françoise Durr was born in Algeria as her father was in the **French** Air Force and was stationed there at the time. She was known for her unorthodox array of shots, using a limp wrist **backhand**, as well as her unorthodox behavior. The 5-foot 4-inch, 120-pound right-hander reached 27 **Grand Slam** finals during her career, winning 12. Her only Grand Slam **singles** final was the 1967 **French National Championships**. She reached the quarterfinals twice at **Australia** (1965, 1967), semifinals in 1970 at **Wimbledon**, and semifinals in 1967 at the **United States Nationals**. She achieved a world **ranking** of three in 1967. In **doubles**, she fared much better and won the French women's doubles five consecutive years (1967–71) and was runner-up three additional times (1965, 1973, 1979). She also reached the finals of the French **mixed doubles** six consecutive years (1968–73) with Jean Claude Barclay, winning in 1968, 1971, and 1973 and runner-up in 1969, 1970, and 1972. At Wimbledon, she was a losing women's doubles finalist six times (1965, 1968, 1970, 1972, 1973, 1975). She and **Tony Roche** won Wimbledon mixed doubles in 1976. She twice won the United States National women's doubles (1969, 1972) and was runner-up in 1971 and 1974. She also was the runner-up in the United States National mixed doubles in 1969 with **Dennis Ralston**. In her career, from 1960 to 1979, she won 26 singles and 60 doubles titles.

During the 1970s, on the **Virginia Slims** tour, she was accompanied onto the **court** by her dog, named **Topspin**, who carried her **racket**. In 1975, she married Boyd Browning, an American tennis player, who did promotional work for the women's tour. They lived in Phoenix, Arizona, for about 10 years and then moved to France. She played on the French **Federation Cup** team from 1963 to 1979 and had a record of 16–8 in singles and 15–9 in doubles in 27 **ties** over 10 years. In 1993, she was appointed the technical director of women's tennis for the French Tennis Federation and was the Fed Cup nonplaying captain from 1993 to 1997. She was inducted into the **International Tennis Hall of Fame** in 2003.

DWIGHT, JAMES. B. 14 July 1852, Paris, **France**. D. 13 May 1917, Mattapoisett, Massachusetts. James Dwight was one of the first players of **lawn**

tennis in the **United States**. He was a graduate of Harvard University and Harvard Medical School and was a physician. After his graduation, in 1874, he traveled in Europe and saw lawn tennis being played. He returned and persuaded his uncle to lay out a **court** on his property in Nahant, Massachusetts. He played the game with his cousin Fred Sears in 1874 and organized and won a **tournament** in 1876 at Nahant, giving rise to his appellation as the "father of American lawn tennis." He helped create the **United States National Lawn Tennis Association** in 1882 and was its first president. He served in that capacity from 1882 to 1884 and again from 1894 to 1911. He also helped bring about the first **Davis Cup** match in 1900 at the **Longwood Cricket Club**.

He was an accomplished player and was the **United States National doubles** champion each year from 1882 to 1887 with his partner and cousin, **Dick Sears**. In 1883, he was the United States National **singles** finalist but was defeated by his doubles partner, Sears. Dwight traveled to **Wimbledon** in 1884 and became one of the first Americans to compete there, although he only won one match. He and Sears did reach the Wimbledon doubles semifinals but were defeated by the **Renshaw twins**. He returned to Wimbledon in 1885 and reached the singles semifinals. In 1886, he wrote one of the first books on tennis, entitled simply *Lawn Tennis*. His son, Richard Dwight, also a physician, was an avid tennis player who competed in **senior** and super-senior events until his death. James Dwight was inducted into the **International Tennis Hall of Fame** in the inaugural class of 1955.

E

ECUADOR. Ecuador, although a small nation with a population of only about 13 million people, has made its mark in the tennis world. From 1961 through May 2011, Ecuador has competed in 45 **Davis Cup tournaments** with a record of 51–46 in 97 **ties**. Ecuador has competed five times in the World Group since its formation in 1981. In 1985, Ecuador was a quarterfinalist and, in 1967, won the American Zone (including a defeat of the **United States**) but lost in the Inter-Zonal semifinals. The United States team in 1967 had **Arthur Ashe**, **Clark Graebner**, Cliff Richey, and Marty Riessen; Ecuador had Francisco "Pancho" Guzman and Miguel Olvera. Ecuador's top Davis Cup players have been Andrés Gómez, Nicolás LaPentti, and Ricardo Ycaza. Ecuador had representatives in both the **exhibition** and demonstration tennis events at the **Olympic Games** in **Mexico** in 1968. Ecuador's Davis Cup team of Olvera and Guzman finished fourth in the demonstration **doubles** event, and Guzman and **Soviet Union** player Teimuraz Kakulia finished third in the exhibition doubles. Maria-Eugenia Guzman finished third in the exhibition women's **singles**. Ecuador has also competed in the 1996, 2004, and 2008 Olympic Games.

In **Federation Cup** competition, from 1972 to May 2011, Ecuador competed 17 years, only once in World Group, and played 68 **ties** with a record of 38–30. The country's best performance was in 1972, when it reached the round of 16. The Federación Ecuatoriana de Tenis (Ecuador Tennis Federation) is the national organization that administers the sport. **Hall of Famer Francisco "Pancho" Segura** was one of the best tennis players in the world during the 1940s and 1950s, both as an **amateur** and a **professional**, winning the **National Collegiate Athletic Association** National Championship three consecutive years while at the University of Miami and winning the **U.S. Pro Championships** three consecutive years from 1950 to 1952. The **left-handed** Andrés Gómez achieved a **ranking** of fourth in singles in 1990 and first in doubles in 1986. He won 21 singles and 33 doubles titles, including the **United States Open** doubles in 1986, **French Open** doubles in 1988, and French Open singles in 1990. Other top Ecuadorian tennis players have been Pablo Campana, Luis Morejón, Maria-Dolores Campana, and Nuria Niemes.

EDBERG, STEFAN BENGT. B. 19 January 1966, Vastervik, **Sweden**. In 1983, Stefan Edberg had one of the best years ever as a **junior** player, winning all four **Grand Slam** junior **singles** championships, the only player ever to do so. He became a **professional** player later than year. In 1985, he won his first **main draw** Grand Slam event—the **Australian Open**. He repeated in **Australia** in 1987 and that year also won the men's **doubles** event with Anders Järryd as his partner. Edberg also reached the men's singles final there in 1990, 1992, and 1993 but was defeated each time. The official logo for that **tournament** is based on Edberg's distinctive service motion. In 1996, he won his last Grand Slam title at the Australian as he and **Petr Korda** won the men's doubles. At **Wimbledon**, Edberg met **Boris Becker** three straight years, 1988 to 1990, in the men's singles final. The pair alternated championships with Edberg, winning in four **sets** in 1988 and five sets in 1990. Edberg's best effort at the **French Open** occurred in 1989, when he was defeated by the 17-year-old **Michael Chang** in five sets in the final. Edberg and Järryd were also losing doubles finalists at **Roland Garros** in 1986. At the **United States Open**, Edberg was singles champion in 1991 and 1992 and, with Järryd, doubles runner-up in 1984 and champion in 1987.

Edberg, a 6-foot 2-inch, 170-pound right-hander, played **serve-and-volley** style with a strong **serve**. His serve actually caused the death of a **linesman** at the U.S. Open in 1983. During the boys' junior tournament, an errant serve by Edberg struck linesman Dick Wertheim, knocking him from his chair. Wertheim landed on his head, incurring a fatal skull fracture. Edberg competed in the 1984, 1988, and 1992 **Olympic Games** and won the bronze medal in both singles and doubles in 1988. The 1984 Olympic Games were a demonstration event, and Edberg won the singles in that tournament.

He played **Davis Cup** tennis for Sweden each year from 1984 to 1996. His record of 35–15 in singles and 12–8 in doubles in 35 **ties** during those 13 years helped lead Sweden to 6 consecutive finals appearances, from 1984 to 1989, and the Cup championship in 1984, 1985, 1987, and 1994. In 1985, he defeated Michael Westphal of West **Germany** in the fifth and deciding **rubber**. Edberg retired in 1996, with career totals of 42 singles and 18 doubles titles, and was one of only two men (**John McEnroe** is the other) to be **ranked** by the **Association of Tennis Professionals** world number one in both singles and doubles. He was inducted into the **International Tennis Hall of Fame** in 2004.

EMERSON, ROY STANLEY "EMMO." B. 3 November 1936, Blackbutt, Queensland, **Australia**. Roy Emerson was raised on a farm in rural Queensland. Once he demonstrated a talent for the sport of tennis, his family moved to Brisbane so that he could receive the proper **coaching**. He has won more **Grand Slam** championships than any other male (28) and has reached more Grand Slam finals than any other male (45). He won two or more **singles** and two or more **doubles** titles at each of the four major venues, again a feat not matched by any other male. He competed at each of the four major tournaments for the first time in 1954, but it wasn't until 1961 that he won his first Grand Slam singles title. From 1961 to 1967, he won 12 of a possible 28 Grand Slam titles, was runner-up three times, semifinalist twice, quarterfinalist eight times, and reached the fourth round the other three times.

Although his feats are unmatched, critics claim that in that era of **amateur** play, once a player had proved himself, he became **professional** and, consequently, could not compete in these events. Emerson's competition, therefore, was not truly the best players but simply the best players who chose to remain amateur. **Jack Kramer** was one of those critics, and in 1979, in his book, listed his choice for the top 21 players of all time and omitted Emerson, although he rated Emerson as one of the best doubles players. Emerson was also an excellent doubles player, winning 16 Grand Slam men's doubles titles from 1959 to 1971—three of eight men's doubles finals in Australia, three of five at **Wimbledon**, six of ten at **Roland Garros**, and four of five at the **United States Nationals**. He also was a losing **mixed doubles** finalist once each at Australia and Roland Garros. He won 7 of his 16 doubles titles with **Neale Fraser**, 4 with **Fred Stolle**, 3 with **Rod Laver**, and 1 each with **Manuel Santana** and **Ken Fletcher**.

Nicknamed Emmo, the 6-foot tall, 175-pound right-hander represented Australia in **Davis Cup** competition each year from 1959 to 1967. In those nine years, Australia won the Cup each year except 1963, an unprecedented accomplishment in Davis Cup history. Emerson's record in 18 **ties** was 21–2 in singles and 13–2 in doubles. He basically retired in 1973, with an unofficial total of 106 amateur and professional singles championships, although he continued to play an occasional tournament as late as 1983. His son, Antony, was an All-American tennis player at the University of Southern California and briefly played on the pro tour. Roy and his son won the United States **Hard Court** Father-and-Son Championship in 1978. Roy, a resident of California and Gstaad, **Switzerland**, was inducted into the **International Tennis Hall of Fame** in 1982.

ENGLAND. *See* GREAT BRITAIN.

ETCHEBASTER, PIERRE. B. 8 December 1893, St. Jean de Luz, **France**. D. 24 March 1980, St. Jean de Luz, France. Pierre Etchebaster was the greatest **court tennis** player of all time. After serving in the French army during World War I, he was introduced to the game of "real tennis" or court tennis.

His previous experience playing several Basque **racket** games proved useful, and he quickly learned the sport. In 1928, he became world champion. In 1930, he moved to New York City and became the head professional at the **Racquet** and Tennis Club there. Until recent years, the sport of court tennis did not have a regular **tournament**; rather, the champion would accept periodic challenges for the world title in a manner similar to 19th century prizefighting. From 1928 until his retirement at age 60 in 1954, Etchebaster withstood all challenges and was undefeated, although in that time, he was challenged only seven times. In 1955, he was awarded the Legion of Honor— the highest French honor. He is the author of *Pierre's Book*, an instructional book on court tennis, published in 1971, and was inducted into the **International Tennis Hall of Fame** in 1978.

EVERT LLOYD, CHRISTINE MARIE "CHRIS." B. 21 December 1954, Fort Lauderdale, Florida. Chris Evert is the son of Jimmy Evert, a tennis **professional** in Florida. Both her sister Jeannie and brother John were accomplished tennis players. Chris began playing at an early age and by age 14 was the number-one–**ranked** player in her age group in the **United States**. In 1969, still only 14, she entered a **senior**-level **tournament** in Fort Lauderdale and reached the semifinals. In 1970, in a minor tournament, she defeated **Margaret Smith Court**, who that year had won all four **Grand Slam singles** championships. The precocious teenager played her first **United States Open** tournament in 1971, at the age of 16. Her very first **match** in that tournament was played on Thursday, 2 September, and it was on **center court**. She easily defeated the 35-year-old Edda Buding, 6–1, 6–0. While she was playing on the main stadium court, **Jimmy Connors** was making his second U.S. Open appearance and was celebrating his 19th birthday by coming from two **sets** down to defeat the 35-year-old **Alex Olmedo** in five sets on the grandstand court. Connors lost in the second round, while Evert reached the semifinals after winning her second-round match by saving six **match points**. The two would later become "America's Sweethearts" and eventually engaged.

From 1971 to 1986, Evert reached at least the semifinal round of the U.S. Open each year, a most outstanding record. She competed at the U.S. Open from 1987 to 1989 and reached the quarterfinals twice and semifinals once in that span. Her record at **Wimbledon** was nearly as remarkable. From 1972 to 1989, she competed in the women's singles each year and reached at least the semifinals each year, with the exception of 1983, when she lost in the third round. She competed six times in women's singles at the **Australian Open**, between 1974 and 1988, and reached the finals all six times, winning twice. At **Roland Garros**, on **clay** (her best **surface**), she entered 13 times between 1973 and 1988 and was also at least a semifinalist each time, except in 1988, when she was defeated in the third round. Her career record in singles at Grand Slam events from 1971 to 1989 was 56 tournaments entered, 18 championships, 16 losses in the finals, 18 losses in the semifinals, 2 quarterfinal losses, and 2 third-round losses. She won at least one Grand Slam singles title each year for 13 straight years, from 1974 to 1986. She also won the **French Open** women's **doubles** title in 1974 with Olga Morozova, the following year with **Martina Navratilova**, and the 1976 Wimbledon ladies' doubles title with Martina. Evert was the losing women's doubles finalist in 1988 at the Australian Open with **Wendy Turnbull** as partner, and in 1974, she and then fiancé Jimmy Connors reached the U.S. Open **mixed doubles** finals.

The 5-foot 6-inch, 125-pound right-hander competed in the 1988 **Olympic Games** and reached the third round. She played on the **United States Federation Cup** team from 1977 to 1982, 1986 to 1987, and 1989. Her Cup record was 40–2 in singles and 17–2 in doubles. She won 34 consecutive Cup matches from 1978 to 1986. She lost two matches in 1987 to **Steffi Graf** in singles and with **Pam Shriver** to Graf and Claudia Kohde-Kilsch in doubles. She lost the third to Italian Sandra Cecchini in 1986 and the fourth in a doubles **dead rubber** with partner **Rosie Casals** to Australians Wendy Turnbull and Kerry Reid in 1977. She played more **Wightman Cup** matches than any

Chris Evert, "America's sweetheart," played her first Grand Slam tournament at age 16 and won 18 Grand Slam singles championships in her career. (courtesy of the International Tennis Hall of Fame and Museum, Edward Fernberger Collection)

other American and was undefeated in singles in 13 years of Cup play. Her overall Wightman Cup record was 26–0 in singles and 8–4 in doubles from 1971 to 1985. When she finally retired in 1989, she had won 157 professional singles championships and 32 doubles championships and had a singles match won-lost record of 1,309–146, a 90 percent success record. She was inducted into the **International Tennis Hall of Fame** in 1995.

She later married **British** tennis professional **John Lloyd** in 1979. They divorced in 1987. She married Olympic skier Andy Mill in 1988, and they had three sons. They were divorced in 2006. She then married professional golfer Greg Norman on 28 June 2008, but they divorced on 8 December 2009. After retiring from competitive tennis, Chris opened a tennis academy in Boca Raton, Florida.

EXHIBITION MATCH. Exhibition matches are those played outside of **tournaments**. Tennis players often compete in them to display their skills and earn extra money. Usually, they feature players who do not ordinarily play against each other in tournaments. Some famous exhibitions include **Bobby Riggs** vs. **Margaret Court** and Riggs vs. **Billie Jean King** in "battles of the sexes" in 1973; **Pete Sampras** vs. **Roger Federer** in several matches in 2008; and **Don Budge** vs. **American Tennis Association** champion Jimmie McDaniel in the first major interracial tennis **match**.

FAULT. A fault is a **serve** that does not land in the opponent's service box. A second serve is then taken. If that also is a fault, a **double fault** is called, and the **point** is lost. A foot fault occurs when the server steps on or over the **baseline** before the **ball** is struck.

FEDERATION CUP. The Federation Cup (name shortened in 1995 to Fed Cup) is an international **tournament** for women's teams similar to the **Davis Cup** for men. It was created by the **International Tennis Federation** in 1963 to mark its 50th anniversary. The first year's competition had 16 teams competing. The tournament has grown considerably, and by 2010, there were 80 teams divided into zonal play with the top eight competing in the World Group. Since 1995, **ties** consist of five **rubbers**. Prior to 1995, only three rubbers were played. The **United States** has won the most tournaments, with 17 victories, and **Australia** has won the second most, with 7. *See also* APPENDIX H (for a list of champions).

FEDERER, ROGER. B. 8 August 1981, Basel, **Switzerland**. Roger Federer is arguably the greatest male tennis player of all time and will definitely be inducted into the **International Tennis Hall of Fame** once he has retired from active play. He had an outstanding **junior** career, winning the **Wimbledon** boys' title in 1998 and losing the **United States Open** boys' championship final to **David Nalbandian** that year. He became a **professional** player in 1998, but it wasn't until 2003 that he won his first **Grand Slam singles** championship. Since then, he has been nearly unbeatable in Grand Slam tournaments, with a total of 16 singles championships from 2003 to May 2011. Along with those championships, he was also a losing Grand Slam finalist seven times. He won the **Australian Open** in 2004, 2006, 2007, and 2010 and lost in the final to **Rafael Nadal** in 2009. He won **Wimbledon** five consecutive years from 2003 to 2007, lost the final to Nadal in 2008, and won again in 2009. He won the **United States Open** five consecutive years from 2004 to 2008 but lost the final to **Juan Martín Del Potro** in 2009. The **French Open**, played on **clay**, presented the most problems for Roger as he lost to Nadal, one of the best clay **court** players in history, in the finals from 2006 to 2008 and again in 2011. In 2009, Nadal was upset in a fourth round match by **Robin Söderling**, and Federer defeated Söderling in the finals to win his only French Open title. Federer's friendly rivalry with Nadal has produced some remarkable matches with the 2008 Wimbledon championship that Nadal won named by some as the "**greatest match of all time**." Probably Federer's most remarkable achievement was reaching the semifinal round in 23 consecutive Grand Slam events from 2003 to 2010. No other player in history is even close to that feat. In that time, he reached 10 consecutive Grand Slam finals and 18 of 19 finals from 2005 to 2010.

The 6-foot 1-inch, 185-pound right-hander has a complete game—excellent **serve**, excellent **forehand**, excellent **backhand**—and has a likeable disposition that has made him quite popular among his opponents as well. He competed in three **Olympic Games**—2000, 2004, and 2008. He finished fourth in the 2000 singles event, losing to **Tommy Haas** in the semifinals and Arnaud Di Pasquale in the bronze medal match. In 2004, he lost in the second round in both singles and doubles. In 2008, he lost in the quarterfinals of the men's singles, but he and Swiss partner Stanislaus Wawrinka won the doubles gold medal. Federer played **Davis Cup** tennis for Switzerland each year from 1999 to 2009. His record in that time is 27–6 in singles and 10–5 in doubles in 18 **ties**. He won the **Hopman Cup** in 2001 with partner **Martina Hingis**.

He married Mirka Vavrinec, a former professional tennis player, who retired from the pro tour following an injury to become Roger's business manager. The couple became parents of **twin** girls in 2009. Through May 2011, Federer has won 64 singles and 8 doubles tournaments and was **ranked** as the world number-one player for 285 weeks (237 consecutive) throughout his career, which most likely has several more years until his retirement.

FERNÁNDEZ, BEATRIZ "GIGI." B. 22 February 1964, San Juan, Puerto Rico. Gigi Fernández is Puerto Rico's greatest tennis player and was the first female representing Puerto Rico to win an **Olympic** medal. In 1982 and 1983, she attended Clemson University, was named All-American, and reached the National Collegiate Athletic Association singles final. She competed in **singles** in the 1984 Olympic demonstration event but was defeated in her first round **match**. In 1992 and 1996, she, with partner **Mary Joe Fernández** (no relation), won the Olympic gold medal in the women's **doubles**. She played on the **United States Federation Cup** team in 1988, 1990 to 1992, and 1994 to 1997. Her Cup record was 3–1 in singles and 20–2 in doubles in 25 **ties** over eight years. She played for the 1990 Cup championship team in the finals and for the Cup runner-up team in the 1991, 1994, and 1995 finals. The

5-foot 7-inch, 145-pound right-hander was on the **Wightman Cup** team in 1987 and 1988 and won her doubles match each year.

As a doubles specialist, she won 17 **Grand Slam** women's doubles titles from 1988 to 1997—the **United States Open** in 1988, 1990, 1992, 1995, 1996; the **French Open,** five consecutive years from 1991 to 1995 and 1997; **Wimbledon,** 1992–94 and 1997; and the **Australian Open** in 1993 and 1994. She partnered with **Natalia Zvereva** for 14 of the championships. She was also runner-up six times in women's doubles Slam events and three times in **mixed doubles** Slam events. When she retired in 1997, she had compiled 69 doubles titles and 2 singles titles, had a record of 664–184 in doubles, and had reached a world number-one **ranking** in doubles in 1991 and world 17 ranking in singles that same year. In 1999, she was named Puerto Rico's Female Athlete of the Century.

After retiring from tennis, she returned to school and received a bachelor's degree from the University of South Florida in 2003 and a master's degree in business administration from Rollins College. She is the mother of **twins** and started a company called Baby Goes Pro, which produces DVDs that introduce children to sports. She also **coaches** at the University of South Florida and the Puerto Rican national team. She was inducted into the **International Tennis Hall of Fame** in 2010, along with her doubles partner, Natalia Zvereva.

FERNÁNDEZ GODSICK, MARIA JOSÉ (MARY JOE). B. 19 August 1971, Lugar de Nacimiento, Dominican Republic. Although born in the Dominican Republic of a Spanish father and Cuban mother, Mary Joe Fernández was raised in Miami, Florida. She won the **Orange Bowl junior** title in 1983, and in 1985, just eight days after her 14th birthday, she became the youngest player to win a **main draw match** at the **United States Open**. The 5-foot 8-inch, 120-pound right-hander won the **Australian Open Doubles** Championship in 1991 with partner Patty Fendick. In 1996, Fernández and **Lindsay Davenport** won the **French Open** doubles title. In 1990 and 1992, she reached the finals of the Australian Open **singles tournament** and, in 1993, was the finalist at the French Open singles. She was also a losing finalist in women's doubles in 1990, 1992, and 1996 at the Australian Open, the French Open in 1997, and the United States Open in 1989.

In 1992 and 1996, she, with partner **Beatriz "Gigi" Fernández** (no relation), won the **Olympic** gold medal in the women's doubles. In addition, Mary Joe won a bronze medal in the 1992 women's singles and finished fourth in that event in 1996. She was a member of the **United States Federation Cup** team in 1991 and from 1994 to 1998. Her record in 18 **ties** was 12–8 in singles and 4–2 in doubles. She played in the final round in 1991,

1994, 1995, and 1996, but the United States only won the Cup in 1996, losing to **Spain** the other three years. She later was the nonplaying team captain of the American Fed Cup team in 2009 and 2010. She won all three of her matches, two singles and one doubles, for the **United States** 1989 **Wightman Cup** team—the last year that the event was contested. She retired from the **Women's Tennis Association** tour in 2000 with a record of 437–203 in singles and 344–141 in doubles, 7 singles titles, 19 doubles titles, and career-high **ranking** of 4 in singles in 1990 and 4 in doubles in 1991.

On 8 April 2000, in Miami, she married Tony Godsick, a sports agent with the International Management Group. They have two children. In retirement from playing, Mary Joe Fernández has become one of the most popular television tennis announcers.

FERREIRA, WAYNE RICHARD. B. 15 September 1971, Johannesburg, South Africa. Wayne Ferreira had an excellent **junior tennis** career and was **ranked** number one in **doubles** in 1989, after winning the **United States Open** junior doubles title that year. He began his **professional** career that year. The 6-foot 1-inch, 185-pound right-hander competed in both **singles** and doubles in the 1992 and 1996 **Olympic Games**. In singles, he lost in the second round in 1992 and quarterfinal round in 1996. In doubles, he and partner Piet Norval won the silver medal in 1992. Teaming with Ellis Ferreira (no relation), in 1996, they reached the quarterfinals. Wayne played **Davis Cup** tennis for South Africa from 1992 to 2005 each year except 2002, appearing in 25 **ties** with a record of 30–14 in singles and 11–4 in doubles in 13 years of competition. He won the **Hopman Cup** in 2000 with partner Amanda Coetzer. Although he set a **Grand Slam** record (since broken) by participating in 56 consecutive Slam events from 1991 to 2004, his best result was only reaching the semifinal round of the 1992 and 2003 **Australian Open**. He was a quarterfinalist in **Flushing Meadows** in 1992 and at **Wimbledon** in 1994 and reached the fourth round at **Roland Garros** in 1996. During his career, he reached a **ranking** of 6 in singles in 1985 and 11 in doubles in 2001 and won 15 singles and 11 doubles titles. He retired from the **Association of Tennis Professionals** tour in 2005 but still plays in the **Champions Series** and is an assistant **coach** at the University of California, Berkeley. He is president and chief executive officer of EcoloBlue Life and Energy, an environmental and renewable resources firm.

FIBAK, WOJCIECH (WOJTEK). B. 30 August 1952, Poznań, **Poland**. Wojtek Fibak is Poland's greatest male tennis player. He played in **Davis Cup** competition for Poland from 1972 to 1979 and again in 1984, 1990, and 1992. In that time, he appeared in 17 **ties** in 11 years and had a record of 19–5 in **singles** and 9–7 in **doubles**. He also played tennis with and gave tennis lessons to Karol Wojtyła, the future Pope John Paul II. Fibak, a 6-foot tall, 160 pound right-hander, won 15 singles and 52 doubles championships, including the **Australian Open** Doubles Championship in 1978 with partner Kim Warwick. Fibak was also a semifinalist at the other three major tournaments. He and **Jan Kodeš** were the runners-up in the 1977 **French Open** men's doubles. Fibak reached a doubles ranking of world number three in 1979 and a singles ranking of 10 in 1977. In his career, he won 514 matches and lost 306. In retirement from active play, he founded the Polish Tennis Club in Southern California. He was a **coach** for **Ivan Lendl** and an entrepreneur who owned newspapers and real estate.

FLETCHER, KENNETH NORMAN "KEN." B. 15 June 1940, Brisbane, Queensland, **Australia**. D. 11 February 2006. Brisbane, Australia. A graduate of St. Laurence's College in Brisbane, Ken Fletcher played at the same time as many of Australia's greatest players and, consequently, never appeared in a **Davis Cup** match for Australia nor achieved the fame of his compatriots. His **forehand** stroke was acclaimed by Australian tennis **coach Harry Hopman** as the "best forehand in the world." Fletcher and **Margaret Smith Court** are the only couple to win a calendar year **Grand Slam** in **mixed doubles**, which they accomplished in 1963. They also won the **Australian** mixed doubles in 1964, the **French National** mixed doubles in 1964 and 1965, and **Wimbledon** mixed doubles in 1965, 1966, and 1968. In 1964, he and **Roy Emerson** were the French National men's **doubles** champions, and in 1966, he and **John Newcombe** were the Wimbledon men's doubles champions. He was also a losing finalist seven times in men's doubles and twice in mixed doubles at Slam events. Although more adept at doubles, he did reach the men's **singles** final at the 1963 Australian Championships. He was described as a "larrikin"—an irreverent type who lived life one day at a time. He spent much of his time in Hong Kong. A friend of billionaire Chuck Feeney, he helped Feeney with his philanthropic efforts. Australian author Hugh Lunn wrote several books that featured Fletcher's exploits. He also wrote a biography of Fletcher in 2008, entitled The Great Fletch. Ken Fletcher died of prostate cancer at the age of 65.

FLUSHING MEADOWS. Flushing Meadows is a section in the borough of Queens in New York City. It was the site of the World's Fairs of 1939–40 and 1964–65. During the 1970s, one structure that remained from the World's Fair of 1964–65, Singer Bowl, was converted to be used as a tennis stadium. A tennis complex with multiple **courts** was also created there, and the **United States National Championships** (**U.S. Open**) was moved there in 1978.

See also ARTHUR ASHE STADIUM; LOUIS ARMSTRONG STADIUM; USTA BILLIE JEAN KING NATIONAL TENNIS CENTER.

FOOT FAULT. *See* FAULT.

FOREHAND. A forehand is a type of tennis stroke made with the palm of the hand facing forward. It is the most natural stroke and the easiest one to master. A right-handed player hitting a forehand shot would contact the **ball** on the right side of his body. *See also* BACKHAND.

FOREST HILLS. Forest Hills is a section in the borough of Queens in New York City that contains the **West Side Tennis Club**. The Forest Hills Stadium was the site of the **United States National Championships** from 1915 until 1977. The championships were often referred to simply as "Forest Hills."

FORGET, GUY. B. 4 January 1965, Casablanca, Morocco. Guy Forget's (pronounced ghee for-zhay) first major accomplishment in the tennis world was winning the **French Open Junior Singles** Championship in 1982. He became a **professional** player later that year but never quite lived up to that potential, although he had a solid professional career and was **ranked** third in the world in **doubles** in 1986 and fourth world wide in **singles** in 1991. His best finish in the four major **Grand Slam tournaments** was only the quarterfinals, which he achieved five times—three times at **Wimbledon** and twice at the **Australian Open**. He also reached the fourth round at **Roland Garros** and the **United States Open**, twice each. In his career, he won 11 singles tournaments and 28 doubles tournaments and twice reached the finals (1987, 1996) of the French Open doubles. The **left-handed** Forget represented **France** in international competition at the 1984, 1988, and 1992 **Olympic Games**, reaching the singles quarterfinals in 1984 and doubles quarterfinals in 1988. He played **Davis Cup** tennis for France from 1984 to 1997 and was a member of the Cup championship team in 1991 and 1996. In 26 **ties**, his record was 17–7 in singles and 21–4 in doubles in 12 years. In retirement from active play, he has captained the French Davis Cup team and also France's **Fed Cup** team.

FOUR MUSKETEERS. During the 1920s, **France** had four extremely capable **lawn tennis** players: **Jean Borotra, Jacques "Toto" Brugnon, Henri Cochet**, and **René Lacoste**. In some years, in the late 1920s, all 4 were **ranked** in the world top 10. They led France to the **Davis Cup** finals each year from 1925 to 1933 and to six consecutive championships from 1927 to

1932. All four were inducted into the **International Tennis Hall of Fame** in 1976.

FRANCE. Tennis in France is under the auspices of the Fédération Française de Tennis. The organization was created in 1888 by the l'Union des Sociétés Françaises des Sports Athlétiques (Union of French Societies of Athletic Sports) as the Commission de **Lawn Tennis** Club. In 1920, it was renamed the Fédération Française de Lawn Tennis, and in 1976, the word "lawn" was dropped, and it received its present name. The president since 2009 is Jean Gachassin. The golden age of French tennis occurred when France had **Suzanne Lenglen**, the top female player, and four of the top male players, **Jean Borotra, Jacques "Toto" Brugnon, Henri Cochet**, and **René Lacoste**, who were dubbed the **Four Musketeers** by American sportswriters. Stade **Roland Garros** in Paris, France, is also the site of one of the four major **tournaments**, known collectively as the "**Grand Slam**."

France was the first nation besides the **United States** and **Great Britain** to compete for the **Davis Cup**. From 1904 through May 2011, France has competed in 92 Davis Cup tournaments with a record of 153–82 in 235 **ties**. France has competed in the World Group every year except 1986, a total of 29 times since its formation in 1981. France has won the Cup nine times through 2009, most recently in 2001, and has been runner-up seven times. In 2010, Serbia defeated France in the Cup final. Top Davis Cup players include Jean Borotra, Jacques "Toto" Brugnon, Henri Cochet, Pierre Darmon, **Guy Forget**, François Jauffret, René Lacoste, and **Henri Leconte**.

France has had entrants in tennis in every **Olympic Games** from 1896 to 2008 with the exception of 1904. French Olympic medalists in tennis in 1900 were: Max Decugis, silver medal, men's **doubles** (his partner was an American, Spalding de Garmendia); André Prévost and Georges de la Chapelle, bronze medal men's doubles; and Hélène Prévost (André's wife), silver medal women's **singles** and also silver medal **mixed doubles** (with British partner Harold Mahony). In 1906, Decugis won the gold medal in men's singles, doubles (with Maurice Germot), and mixed doubles (with his wife, Marie). Germot also won the silver medal in men's singles, and Marie Decugis lost in the quarterfinals of the women's singles. In 1912, André Gobert won the gold medal in the covered **court** men's singles and, with partner Germot, won the gold medal in covered court men's doubles. In the outdoor events, Albert Canet and Edouard Mény de Marangue won the bronze in men's doubles and Canet and Marguerite Broquedis-Billout, the bronze in mixed doubles. Broquedis-Billout also won the women's singles. The 1920 Olympic Games were Suzanne Lenglen's time to shine. She won the women's singles, mixed doubles (with Max Decugis), and the bronze medal in women's doubles with Elisabeth d'Ayen. Decugis and Pierre Albarran won the bronze in men's doubles. In the Games in Paris in 1924, Henri Cochet won silver in men's singles and the Four Musketeers won silver and bronze in men's doubles—Cochet and Jacques Brugnon, silver and René Lacoste and Jean Borotra, bronze. Julie "Didi" Vlasto won silver in women's singles. In Mexico, in 1968, Pierre Darmon, with Mexican partner Joaquin Loyo-Mayo, was third in the demonstration men's doubles and second in the **exhibition** tournament. Pierre's wife, Rosa Maria Reyes Darmon, and American partner, Julie Heldman, were second in the demonstration tournament and won the exhibition. The Darmons finished fourth in the demonstration mixed doubles and third in the exhibition event. In the 1984 demonstration Olympic tennis tournament, Catherine Tanvier finished third in women's singles. France's next Olympic medalist was not until 2000 in Sydney, when Arnaud Di Pasquale won the bronze in men's singles. Amélie Mauresmo won the silver medal in women's singles in 2004.

Among the best French male **lawn tennis** players not mentioned above are Jean-Claude Barclay, Pierre Barthès, Julien Benneteau, Marcel Bernard, Jérémy Chardy, Arnaud Clément, Richard Gasquet, Sébastien Grosjean, Michaël Llodra, Nicolas Mahut, Paul-Henri Mathieu, **Gaël Monfils**, **Yannick Noah**, Yvon Petra, Cédric Pioline, **Fabrice Santoro**, Gilles Simon, **Jo-Wilfried Tsonga**, and André Vacherot. In addition, Pierre Etchebaster was arguably the best **court tennis** player in history. The best female tennis players include Marion Bartoli, **Françoise Durr**, Tatiana Golovin, Sylvie Jung Henrotin, Françoise Masson, **Simone Passemard Mathieu**, **Mary Pierce**, and Nathalie Tauziat, in addition to the players named above. In **Federation Cup** competition from 1963 to May 2011, France has competed all 49 years, 49 years in World Group, played 135 ties with a record of 82–53, won the championship in 1997 and 2003, and was runner-up in 2004 and 2005.

FRASER, NEALE ANDREW. B. 3 October 1933, Melbourne, Victoria, **Australia**. Neale Fraser was educated at St. Kevin's College, Toorak, Victoria. He competed in his first major **tournament**, the **Australian Championships**, in 1952 and his last in 1975, also the Australian. His best years as a tennis player were from 1956 to 1962. In that time, he won the **United States National singles** in 1959 and 1960 and **Wimbledon** singles in 1960. He was also a three-time losing finalist at the Australian Championships and once at Wimbledon. The six-foot one-inch left-hander was an excellent **doubles** player and won the men's doubles at each one of the four **Grand Slam** events. He reached the finals at the Australian Championships five times with four different partners, winning it in 1957 with **Lew Hoad**, 1958 with **Ashley Cooper**, and 1962 with **Roy Emerson** and losing in 1956 with Clive

Wilderspin and 1960 with Emerson. He was also Australian **mixed doubles** champion in 1956 with Beryl Penrose. At **Roland Garros**, Fraser and Emerson won in 1960 and 1962 and were runners-up in 1959. Fraser and Cooper won at Roland Garros in 1958. Fraser's best record was at the United States Nationals, where he reached eight finals and was undefeated in them—he won singles in 1959 and 1960, men's doubles in 1957 with Cooper and 1959 and 1960 with Emerson, and mixed doubles in 1958, 1959, and 1960 with **Margaret Osborne duPont**. His feat of winning men's singles, doubles, and mixed doubles in one year at the U.S. Nationals has not been matched since 1960.

His record at Wimbledon was not quite as good, although he reached nine doubles finals, he only won three. Fraser and Emerson won men's doubles in 1959 and 1961, and Fraser lost in 1955 with **Ken Rosewall**, 1957 with Hoad, 1958 with Ashley Cooper, and 1973, at the age of 39, with Cooper's brother, John. In Wimbledon mixed doubles, Fraser and duPont won in 1962, and he lost in the finals with **Althea Gibson** in 1957 and **Maria Bueno** in 1959. He played **Davis Cup** tennis for Australia each year from 1958 to 1963 and helped that team win four consecutive Cups from 1959 to 1962, losing in the finals to the United States in the other two years. In 11 **ties** during those six years, his record was 11–1 in singles and 7–2 in doubles. From 1970 to 1993, Fraser was Australian Davis Cup team captain.

In 1974, Neale Fraser was honored with the Most Excellent Order of the British Empire (MBE). An equivalent Australian honor, the Order of Australia (AO), was bestowed upon him in 1988. He was inducted into the **International Tennis Hall of Fame** in 1984. In 2001, the International Tennis Hall of Fame and the **International Tennis Federation** created the Davis Cup Award of Excellence, which is presented annually to "a past or present Davis Cup player from the country or region where the final is being held, who represents the ideals and spirit of the competition." Neale Fraser was the first recipient of that award. In 2008, he was honored by the International Tennis Federation with its highest honor, the **Philippe Chatrier** Award for outstanding achievements in tennis.

FRENCH NATIONALS. *See* FRENCH OPEN.

FRENCH OPEN. The French Open is one of the four major **Grand Slam** tennis **tournaments**. It is usually held in late May and early June over a two-week period, and since 2006, it begins on Sunday, the only one of the four majors to do so. It originated in 1891 as the French National Championships and was only open to **amateur** members of French tennis clubs. Ironically, the first men's **singles** competition was won by an Englishman, H. Briggs, who was residing in France and was a member of a French tennis club. Women's singles competition began in 1897. In 1925, the tournament was opened to all amateur players, regardless of club membership. The tournament was held at various venues prior to 1928, but since then, it has been held at the Stade **Roland Garros** in Paris and is known officially as Les Internationaux de France de Roland Garros. It is also popularly known simply as "Roland Garros." It is currently the only one of the four major tournaments played on a **clay surface** and the only one to begin tournament play on a Sunday. In 1968, the tournament, previously limited to amateur players, became open to **professionals**. *See also* APPENDIX D (for a list of champions).

FROMHOLTZ BALESTRAT, DIANNE LEE. B. 10 August 1956, Albury, New South Wales, **Australia**. The five-foot five-inch Dianne Fromholtz began playing **professional** tennis in the **Women's Tennis Association** tour in 1973. She was a finalist at the **Australian Championships** in January 1977, where she was defeated in the women's **singles** by Kerry Melville Reid. In that same tournament, she and Helen Gourlay Cawley won the **women's doubles** title. Her only other final in a **Grand Slam** event was in the 1980 **Wimbledon mixed doubles**, where she and Mark Edmondson lost to the brother and sister pair of John and **Tracy Austin**. The **left-handed** Fromholtz reached the semifinals of the **United States Open** in 1976, the semifinals of the **French Open** in 1979 and 1980, and the quarterfinals at Wimbledon in 1979 and 1987. She was a member of the Australian **Federation Cup** team each year from 1974 to 1983. Her record in 37 **ties** was 24–9 in singles and 11–2 in doubles. She played in the finals in 1974, 1975, 1977, 1979, and 1980 but was on the Cup championship team only in 1974. In her career, she won six singles and two doubles titles and reached a singles world **ranking** of four in 1979. She married **French** businessman Claude Balestrat in 1983.

FRY-IRVIN, SHIRLEY JUNE. B 30 June 1927, Akron, Ohio. Shirley Fry is one of only six players (**Doris Hart, Margaret Smith Court, Martina Navratilova, Serena Williams,** and **Roy Emerson** are the others) to have won all four **Grand Slam singles** and **doubles** championships in her career. She won 17 Slam titles overall, was runner-up an additional 15 times, and was **ranked** number one in 1956. She began playing at a young age and reached the quarterfinals of the **United States National Championships** in 1942, at the age of 15, after having played in that tournament the previous year, aged 14. She graduated from Rollins College in 1949. The 5-foot 5-inch, 120-pound right-hander won the **French National Championships** in 1951, **Wimbledon** and United States championships in 1956, and the **Australian Championships** in 1957. She was also the runner-up at the French

Championships in 1948 and 1952 and at Wimbledon and the United States Championships in 1951. In addition, she was an outstanding doubles player and won the women's doubles at all four major tournaments. With Doris Hart as partner, she won the French National Championships each year from 1950 to 1953, Wimbledon in 1951, 1952, and 1953, and the United States National Championship each year from 1951 to 1954. In 1956, she and **Vic Seixas** won the Wimbledon **mixed doubles** title. Fry won the Australian women's doubles title in 1957.

She remained in **Australia**, and the following month married Karl E. Irvin, Jr., an American advertising executive and tennis **umpire**, on 15 February 1957, at Rose Bay Methodist Church in Rose Bay, New South Wales, Australia. They had four children. She played on the **United States Wightman Cup** team in 1949 and 1951 to 1956 and had a record of 10–2 as her team won the Cup each year. In 1970, she was inducted into the **International Tennis Hall of Fame**. She continued playing in **senior** events and won the United States **Grass Court** Championships in 1967 (women's 40 doubles), 1976 (women's 40 singles), 1978 and 1979 (women's 50 doubles), and 1983 (women's 55 doubles). She also won the 1985 United States Women's 55 Singles **Clay Court** Championship.

GAME. In **lawn tennis scoring**, four **points** constitutes a game, although if the score is tied at three points each (known as 40–40 or **deuce**), a player must then win the next two points to win the game.

GARRISON JACKSON, ZINA LYNNA. B. 16 November 1963, Houston, Texas. Zina Garrison was one of the first black female tennis players to achieve fame and the first **African American** female since **Althea Gibson** to reach the finals of a major **tournament**. She began playing tennis at age 10 in Houston and was an accomplished **junior** player, winning the **United States National** Girls' 18s Championship when she was only 14. As a high school junior, she won the **Wimbledon** and United States junior **singles** titles and was the world's number-one–**ranked** junior player. She graduated from Sterling High School in Houston in 1982 and became a **professional** tennis player. In her career, which lasted until 1997, she reached the finals of nine **Grand Slam** tournaments. She and Lori McNeil became the first black **doubles** partnership to reach the finals of a Grand Slam tournament, in 1987, at the **Australian Open**. Garrison and **Mary Joe Fernández** also reached the finals there in 1992. In 1987, Garrison and Sherwood Stewart won the Australian **mixed doubles**. She also was a losing mixed doubles finalist in Australia in 1989, 1990, and 1993. She was Wimbledon mixed doubles champion in 1988 and 1990, and in 1990, she lost to **Martina Navratilova** in the Wimbledon singles final. In other Grand Slam singles competition, she was a semifinalist twice at the **United States Open** (1988, 1989), once at the Australian Open (1983), and a quarterfinalist in 1982 at the **French Open**.

She competed in the 1988 and 1992 **Olympic Games** and became the first black athlete (male or female) to win an Olympic tennis medal. She won the bronze medal in the 1988 singles event and, teaming with **Pam Shriver**, won the gold medal in the 1988 doubles. She married Willard Jackson, president of a hazardous waste disposal company, in September 1989, but they divorced in 1997. She played on the **United States Federation Cup** team in 1984 to 1987, 1989 to 1991, and 1994. Her Cup record was 7–4 in singles and 15–1 in doubles in 23 **ties**. She played in the finals for the Cup championship team in 1989 and 1990 and in 1991 for the runner-up team. From 2004 to 2008, she was the nonplaying team captain of the United States Fed Cup team. On the **Wightman Cup** team in 1987 and 1988, her record was 4–2. In her career, she won 14 singles and 20 doubles titles and was ranked four in singles in 1989 and five in doubles in 1988.

In addition to overcoming the pressures associated with being one of the few **African American** professional tennis players, Garrison also battled bulimia throughout much of her early pro career. In retirement, she was a nonplaying captain of the Fed Cup team, was a coach of the 2008 U.S. Olympic tennis team, has done television work, and has devoted her energies to two foundations that she sponsors.

GAY PLAYERS. Although during its early years tennis was thought of by some people as a "sissy game," it was primarily due to its emphasis on sportsmanship and etiquette. Anyone who has seen two top players slug it out over five **sets** can liken the sport more to a championship boxing match than any other sport. Nonetheless, during its nearly 150 years, the sport of lawn tennis has had several champions who were admittedly gay. **Bill Tilden**, arguably the greatest of all players, was a homosexual who was arrested in 1946 for "contributing to the delinquency of a minor" and served seven and one-half months of a one-year prison sentence. In 1949, he was again arrested on a morals charge, although the judge convicted him only on a parole violation rather than the felony with which he was charged. This time, he served 10 months of a 1-year sentence.

In Nazi Germany, **Baron Gottfried von Cramm** also was arrested for the "crime" of homosexuality in 1938 and served six months of a one-year sentence; although, in his case, the arrest was probably due more to his anti-Nazi stance.

In recent years, as the gay movement has gained public acceptance, several top female players have acknowledged their same-sex preferences, among them **Billie Jean King**, **Martina Navratilova**, **Lisa Raymond**, Rennae Stubbs, and **Amélie Mauresmo**.

GERMANY. Tennis in Germany is administered by the Deutscher Tennis Bund, which was founded in 1902 and is one of the oldest sports federations in the world. From 1913 through May 2011, Germany has competed in 76 **Davis Cup tournaments** with a record of 137–72 in 209 **ties**, although this includes West Germany from 1963 to 1989. Germany has competed 28 times in the World Group since its formation in 1981, has won the Cup three times (1988, 1989, 1993), and was runner-up twice (1970 and 1985). From 1961 to 1989, German players competed as the Federal Republic of Germany (West Germany). The German Democratic Republic (East Germany) did not enter teams in Davis Cup competition. Germany's top Davis Cup players have included Wilhelm Bungert, Jürgen Fassbender, Hans-Jürgen Pohmann, and **Baron Gottfried von Cramm**.

Germany competed in tennis at the **Olympic Games** in 1896. Fritz Traun teamed with Irishman John Pius Boland to win the men's **doubles**. Germany did not have any entrants in Paris in 1900 but was the only foreign nation to send an entrant to the Olympic tournament in St. Louis in 1904. Hugo Hardy reached the third round of the **singles** and, with an American partner, lost in the first round of the doubles. Germany had no entrants in 1906, but in 1908, Otto Froitzheim won the silver medal in the outdoor men's singles. Oscar Kreuzer won the bronze medal in outdoor men's singles in 1912. Dora Köring won silver in outdoor women's singles and the gold medal in **mixed doubles** with Heinrich Schomburgk. Germany was banned from the Olympic Games in 1920 and 1924. In 1968, Helga Niessen, Jürgen Fassbender, and siblings Ingo and Edda Buding all represented West Germany in the demonstration and **exhibition** tournaments in **Mexico**. In the demonstration events, Niessen won women's singles, Niessen and Edda Buding won women's doubles, and Niessen and Fassbender were second in mixed doubles. Ingo Buding was second in exhibition men's singles, and he and American Jane Bartkowicz were second in exhibition mixed doubles. In the women's singles demonstration, in 1984, 15-year-old **Steffi Graf** was the winner. She won again in 1988, and she and Claudia Kohde-Kilsch won the bronze in the 1988 women's doubles as representatives of West Germany. In 1992, Germany was again unified, and Graf won the silver medal in women's singles and **Boris Becker** and Michael Stich the gold medal in men's doubles. In 1996, David Prinosil and Marc-Kevin Goellner won the bronze medal in men's doubles. **Tommy Haas** won the silver medal in men's singles in 2000. Nicolas Kiefer and Rainier Schüttler won the doubles in 2004.

Other of the best German male tennis players have been Henner Henkel, Heinrich Kleinschroth, Philipp Kohlschreiber, Florian Mayer, Hans Nüsslein, Philipp Petzschner, and Daniel Prenn. The best female tennis players include Cilly Aussem, Bettina Bunge, Anna-Lena Grönefeld, Sylvia Hanika, Marie Luise Horn, Anke Huber, Hilde Krahwinkel, and Helga Schultze, in addition to the ones named above. In **Federation Cup** competition from 1963 to May 2011, Germany has competed 47 years, played 133 ties, 42 years in World Group, with a record of 86–47, won the championship in 1987 and 1992, and was runner-up four times—in 1966, 1970, 1982, and 1983.

GERULAITIS, VYTAUTAS KEVIN "VITAS." B. 26 July 1954, Brooklyn, New York. D. 17 September 1994, Southampton, New York. Vitas Gerulaitis was raised in Howard Beach, Queens, New York, attended Archbishop Molloy High School, and spent one year at Columbia University. He, and his sister, Ruta (who also became a tennis **professional**), were taught by their father, Vitas Sr, a Lithuanian immigrant who had been a champion in his native country and who became a tennis pro at the **United States** Tennis Center in **Flushing Meadows**. Gerulaitis furthered his tennis education at the Port Washington Tennis Academy in Long Island, New York, and became a professional tennis player in 1971. Although he won the **Australian Open** in December 1977, was a semifinalist at **Wimbledon** in 1977 and 1978, and was a finalist at the **United States Open** in 1979 and at the **French Open** in 1980, he was always thought of as a player who did not fulfill expectations. In 1975, he won the men's **doubles** title at Wimbledon with **Gene Mayer** as partner, and in 1977, Gerulaitis and **Billie Jean King** reached the **mixed doubles** finals of the United States Open. He reached a world **ranking** of number three in 1978. A 6-foot tall, 155-pound right-hander, with long, flowing blond hair, he played on the **United States Davis Cup** team in 1976 and 1978 to 1980. In seven **ties** during those four years, playing only **singles**, his record was 11–3. The United States won the Cup in 1978 and 1979. Gerulaitis did not play in the final tie in 1978 but helped his team defeat **Italy** by winning two matches in the 1979 final.

Gerulaitis drove a yellow Rolls-Royce, was a heavy partier, and was a regular at Studio 54, a well-known discotheque in New York City. In 1983, he was named in a federal grand jury investigation into an alleged conspiracy to purchase cocaine. Although he was not indicted, his image suffered. He retired from the tennis tour in 1986 and had compiled 25 singles and 8 doubles titles. He successfully completed a rehabilitation program run by former basketball and tennis professional **John Lucas**, himself a former drug addict. In 1994, a malfunction in a heating system caused carbon monoxide to enter the guesthouse where Gerulaitis was sleeping, and he died of carbon monoxide poisoning at the age of 40. Although there was some speculation of foul play, his death was found to be the result of an accident. The Vitas Gerulaitis Memorial Tennis Centre now exists in Vilnius, Lithuania.

GET. In **lawn tennis**, a "get" is the successful return of an opponent's shot. The word is used more often when a player has had to run to retrieve the **ball**.

GIBSON (DARBEN) (LLEWELLYN), ALTHEA. B. 25 August 1927, Silver, South Carolina. D. 28 September 2003, East Orange, New Jersey. Althea Gibson was, in some ways, the Jackie Robinson of tennis. She was the first black tennis player to be successful in major **tournaments**. In a pairing of outcasts, she later teamed with the Jewish Angela Buxton (who would become one of Gibson's closest friends) to win the **Wimbledon doubles** in 1956. Gibson was born in South Carolina but raised in Harlem in New York

City. **Dr. Walter Johnson** found out about Gibson's athletic ability and helped improve her game. He enabled her (with backing from **Alice Marble**) as the **American Tennis Association's (ATA)** champion to enter the **United States National Championships** at **Forest Hills** in 1950. Gibson reached the second round that year. She continued winning the ATA championship (a record 10 consecutive years, 1947–56) and continued playing at Forest Hills, reaching the quarterfinals in 1953.

In 1956, she went to Europe and won the **French National Championships,** becoming the first black winner of a **Grand Slam** tournament. She and Buxton also won the 1956 French doubles title. That year, Gibson reached the quarterfinals at Wimbledon and was the runner-up at Forest Hills, losing to **Shirley Fry** in the final. In 1957, Gibson again lost to Fry in the finals of the **Australian Open** but teamed with her to win the women's doubles. Gibson also won Wimbledon and the United States Nationals in 1957. In 1958, she repeated her triumphs at Wimbledon and Forest Hills. She also won the Wimbledon women's doubles in 1957 with **Darlene Hard** and in 1958 with **Maria Bueno**. Although she won the Wimbledon women's doubles each year from 1956 to 1958, she was a losing **mixed doubles** finalist there in each of those years with different partners each year. At Forest Hills, she was the women's doubles runner-up in 1957 with Fry and in 1958 with Bueno and the 1957 mixed doubles champion with Kurt Nielsen. She was the world number-one singles player in 1957.

After retiring from **amateur** tennis in 1958, she toured as a **professional** tennis player, playing matches with Karol Fageros, prior to the Harlem Globetrotters' basketball games, and dominated the series, winning 114 of 118 matches. In 1959, she also recorded a record album, wrote her autobiography, and appeared in the John Wayne Hollywood film *The Horse Soldiers.* In 1963, she became the first black member of the Ladies Professional Golf Association and played pro golf through 1978. Her best finish on the golf tour was a tie for second in a 1970 tournament. In 1976, she competed in the Women's Superstars event (a made-for-television competition) and, although then nearly 50 years old, finished in second place in the bowling and basketball events and was ninth overall. Also in that 12-woman competition was **Martina Navratilova**, who finished 11th. The 2004 book *The Match: Althea Gibson and Angela Buxton,* by Brian Schoenfeld, provides a moving history of the Buxton-Gibson story.

She married William Darben on 17 October 1965. They were divorced in 1976. On 11 April 1983, she married Sidney Llewellyn, and they divorced in 1988. She had a 5–1 record on the **United States Wightman Cup** team in 1957 and 1958 and was inducted into the **International Tennis Hall of Fame** in 1971.

GILBERT, BRADLEY N. "BRAD." B. 9 August 1961, Oakland, California. Brad Gilbert attended Foothills Junior College and Pepperdine University. In 1982, he was a finalist at the **National Collegiate Athletic Association** National Tennis Championships but lost to **unseeded** Mike Leach. Gilbert became a **professional** in 1982. In his career, he won 20 **singles** and 3 **doubles** titles and, in 1990, was **ranked** four in the world in singles. He did not do particularly well at **Grand Slam** events, and his best showing was as a quarterfinalist at **Wimbledon** (1990) and the **United States Open** (1987), the fourth round of the **Australian Open** (1984), and third round of the **French Open** (1993). He did not have a strong **serve** or any other strong strokes but used his guile and ability to keep the **ball** in play to win his **matches**. Brad won the bronze medal in the men's singles event in the 1988 **Olympic Games** in Seoul, Korea. He played **Davis Cup** tennis for the **United States** from 1986 to 1993. In eight **ties**, playing only singles, his record was 10–5 in five years of competition. The United States won the Cup in 1990 and was a finalist in 1991, but Gilbert did not play in either final, although he played in preliminary round ties each year.

After retiring from active play in 1994, he wrote a book entitled *Winning Ugly: Mental Warfare in Tennis—Tales from the Tour and Lessons from a Master*, which gave tips on defeating better opponents and became a best-selling instructional book. Gilbert has become quite successful as a **coach** and television commentator. Among his pupils have been **Andre Agassi**, **Andy Roddick**, **Andy Murray**, and Alex Bogdanovic.

GIMELSTOB, JUSTIN JEREMY. B. 27 January 1977, Livingston, New Jersey. Justin Gimelstob had an exceptional record as a **junior** but never quite lived up to his potential as he got older. He was **ranked** number one in 1991 in the **United States Tennis Association (USTA)** boys' 14 age group and, two years later, was again number one in the 16-year old group. In 1995, he won the USTA boys' 18-year-old championship. As a high school sophomore, in 1993, he led Newark Academy of Livingston, New Jersey, to an undefeated record and the state championship. He attended the University of California, Los Angeles (UCLA), for two years, before leaving school to become a **professional** tennis player. As a college sophomore, he won the **National Collegiate Athletic Association Doubles** Championship and helped lead UCLA to the runner-up position in the national tournament. He won the **Hopman Cup** in 1997 with partner Chanda Rubin. Gimelstob teamed with **Venus Williams** to win the **Australian Open** and **French Open** **mixed doubles** events in 1998.

Gimelstob, a six-foot five-inch right-hander, played in three **Davis Cup** matches for the **United States** in 1998 and 2001 and lost all three, one

singles match and two doubles matches in two **ties**. Although he never won any **Association of Tennis Professionals (ATP)** tour singles events, he was a finalist at the 2006 Newport Hall of Fame Championships and did win nine ATP **Challenger** singles titles. He did better as a doubles player, winning 13 doubles titles and reaching a doubles ranking of 18 in 2000. His best results in **Grand Slam** events were the third round, which he reached three times at Wimbledon and twice at the **United States Open**. After retiring from competition in 2007, following back surgery in 2006, he has become a successful television announcer. In 2008, he came out of retirement to play **World Team Tennis** for the Washington Kastles. On 7 November 2010, Gimelstob completed the New York City Marathon in 4:09:58 in his first attempt at marathon running. In doing so, he won a $10,000 bet from **Andy Roddick** for his Justin Gimelstob's Children's Fund for pediatric cancer.

GIMENO TOLAGUERA, ANDRÉS. B. 3 August 1937, Barcelona, **Spain**. Andrés Gimeno first played major tennis events in 1956. He reached the third round at **Wimbledon** in 1956 and 1959, the third round at **Roland Garros** in 1957 and 1958, and the quarterfinals at the **Australian Championships** in 1959. At Roland Garros, he and partner José-Luis Arilla were men's **doubles** finalists in 1960. The slender, six-foot two-inch right-hander played **Davis Cup** tennis as an **amateur** for Spain in 1958, 1959, and 1960, before becoming a **professional** in 1960. When the eligibility rules were changed to allow professionals to compete, he again represented Spain in 1972 and 1973. In his five years of Cup play, his record was 18–5 in singles and 5–5 in doubles in 13 **ties**. He also played in the **Grand Slam** events again from 1968 to 1973, after they became **open tournaments**. He was a semifinalist at the **French Open** in 1968, finalist at the **Australian Open** in 1969, reached the fourth round at the **United States Open** in 1969, was a semifinalist at Wimbledon in 1970, and won the French Open in 1972 at the age of 34. In 1968, Gimeno and **Arthur Ashe** were runners-up in the United States Open men's doubles. When Gimeno retired in 1974, he had won seven **singles** and four doubles titles as a professional. He was inducted into the **International Tennis Hall of Fame** in 2009.

GIRLS' TOURNAMENTS. *See* JUNIOR TENNIS.

GODFREE, KATHLEEN MCKANE "KITTY." *See* MCKANE GODFREE, KATHLEEN "KITTY."

GOLDEN SLAM. When **Steffi Graf** won the four major **singles** tournaments, the **Australian Open, French Open, Wimbledon**, and the **United**

States Open in 1988 and topped it off by winning the gold medal at the Olympic Games in Seoul, sportswriters referred to this feat as the "Golden Slam." It has never been accomplished by any other player in one year. See also GRAND SLAM.

GONZÁLEZ, RICARDO ALONZO "PANCHO," "GORGO." B. 9 May 1928, Los Angeles, California. D. 3 July 1995, Las Vegas, Nevada. When Ricardo González began playing tennis, his name was mistakenly spelled with a final *s* instead of the correct *z*. It was not until he was retired from the sport that he insisted on the correct spelling. The son of Mexican immigrants, he had a middle-class upbringing, although he faced the prejudice that was common to Mexican Americans of that era. Even his nickname of Pancho was somewhat of an ethnic slur as it is normally given to Hispanics named Francisco. As a result, he played with a perpetual chip on his shoulder and was one of the most competitive players of all time. González learned to play tennis on the public courts of Los Angeles. After serving in the U.S. Navy for two years following World War II, he turned his attention to tennis and played in the United States National tournament for the first time in 1947, losing in five sets in the second round to Gardnar Mulloy. González returned to Forest Hills in 1948 and won the tournament. He played at Roland Garros and Wimbledon in 1949, reaching the semifinals in France and the fourth round at Wimbledon but won the men's doubles with Frank Parker at both venues. He played Davis Cup tennis in 1949 for the United States and won both of his singles matches to help the United States defeat Australia and win the Cup.

He then won the United States National singles title again and was signed by Jack Kramer to play on the professional tennis tour. He was considered by many to be the top player in the world during the 1950s and won the U.S. Pro Championships each year from 1953 to 1959 and again in 1961. He was also runner-up in that tournament in 1951, 1952, and 1964. In the one-night-stand tours against individual players, González was defeated by Jack Kramer, 96–27, in 1949–50 but defeated Frank Sedgman and Pancho Segura in 1954, Tony Trabert in 1955 and 1956, Ken Rosewall in 1957, Lew Hoad in 1958, and Hoad, Mal Anderson, and Ashley Cooper in a round-robin in 1959. The 6-foot 2-inch, 180-pound right-hander had one of the hardest serves of his era. After a sportswriter referred to him as a "cheese champion" when he did not do well in a tournament, his doubles partner Frank Parker began calling him "Gorgonzales." The nickname was shortened to "Gorgo" and was used affectionately by his fellow competitors.

When the Grand Slam tournaments became open to professionals in 1968, he entered them for a number of years even though by then he was in his 40s.

He reached the semifinals at Roland Garros and quarterfinals at Forest Hills that year. In 1969, at Wimbledon, he played the longest match in the history of that tournament, a record that was not broken until the Isner-Mahut marathon in 2010. On 25 June, in a first round match, the 41-year-old González defeated the 25-year-old Charlie Pasarell, 22–24, 1–6, 16–14, 6–3, 11–9, a total of 112 games that took 5 hours and 12 minutes. He was inducted into the **International Tennis Hall of Fame** in 1968. After retiring from active play, he was a tennis instructor at Caesars Palace in Las Vegas. He was married six times, the last time to Rita Agassi, sister of **Andre Agassi**. González died of cancer at the age of 67 in 1995. *See also* LONGEST MATCH IN TENNIS HISTORY.

GOOLAGONG CAWLEY, EVONNE FAY. B. 31 July 1951, Griffith, New South Wales, **Australia**. Evonne Goolagong was one of the few **professional** tennis players of Aboriginal heritage and the only one to become a **Grand Slam** champion. She was raised in a small country town in New South Wales. In 1967, the proprietor of a tennis school in Sydney learned of her talent and invited her to move to Sydney to further her tennis education. She played in her first **Australian Championship tournament** that year and reached the third round. By 1971, her game had improved, and she reached the finals of the **Australian Open**, losing to **Margaret Smith Court**, 7–5, in the third **set**. That year, she won the **French Open** and defeated Court in the **Wimbledon** final and was **ranked** number one in the world in December. From 1971 to 1980, each year she reached at least the semifinal round in a Grand Slam tournament. In 1972, she was the runner-up at three of the four Grand Slam tournaments and reached the third round at the **U.S. Open**. The following year, she was losing finalist at Australia and **Forest Hills** and losing semifinalist at the French Open and Wimbledon. She won the Australian Open four consecutive years, from 1974 to 1977, although she did not compete in the January 1977 event but won the one held in December of that year. At Wimbledon, she was losing finalist in 1975 and 1976, and at Forest Hills, she reached the finals four consecutive years, from 1973 to 1976, but failed to win any of those matches. Her final Grand Slam **singles** win was in 1980 at Wimbledon.

The 5-foot 6-inch, 130-pound right-hander was known for her graceful style and cheerful disposition. She was a five-time women's **doubles** champion at the Australian Open, Wimbledon women's doubles and mixed doubles champion, and French Open **mixed doubles** champion. She married British tennis player Roger Cawley in 1975 and was known professionally as Evonne Goolagong Cawley from that **point** on. They lived in Florida for eight years, had two children, and then moved to Queensland, Australia. She played on the Australian **Federation Cup** team in 1970, 1972 to 1976, and 1982. Her record was 22–3 in singles and 13–2 in doubles in 26 **ties** in 7 years. She was a member of the Cup championship team in 1970, 1973, and 1974 and runner-up team in 1975 and 1976. In 2002, she was named captain of the Australian Fed Cup team. She was inducted into the **International Tennis Hall of Fame** in 1988. In retirement, she worked for the Hilton Head Racquet Club in South Carolina, was a member of the Board of the Australian Sports Commission, and is the Australian Sports Ambassador to the Aboriginal and Torres Strait Islander communities.

GOTTFRIED, BRIAN EDWARD. B. 27 January 1952, Baltimore, Maryland. Brian Gottfried had a stellar **junior tennis** career. The winner of 14 national junior titles, he enrolled at Trinity University in Texas in 1970 and helped lead that team to the **National Collegiate Athletic Association (NCAA)** National Championship in 1972. An All-American in 1971 and 1972, he was the NCAA National runner-up in both **singles** and **doubles** in 1972. He became a **professional** later that year. The 6-foot tall, 165-pound right-hander had his best years as a pro in 1977 and 1978. He was the **French Open** men's singles finalist in 1977, losing to **Guillermo Vilas**. He reached the **U.S. Open** quarterfinals in both 1977 and 1978 and the **Wimbledon** quarterfinals in 1978. In 1980, he was a Wimbledon singles semifinalist. His only appearance at the **Australian Open** was in 1980, when he reached the third round. In doubles, he won the 1976 Wimbledon men's doubles with **Raúl Ramírez** as partner, and the pair were finalists there in 1979. At **Roland Garros**, Gottfried and Ramírez were 1975 and 1977 champions and 1976 and 1980 runners-up. In 1977, they were U.S. Open runners-up.

Gottfried played for the **United States Davis Cup** team in five years from 1975 to 1982. He had a record of 6–7 in singles and 1–0 in doubles in seven **ties** and helped the United States win the Cup in 1978. The United States also won the Cup in 1982, but Gottfried only played in a preliminary round that year. When Gottfried retired from active play, after the 1984 season, he had recorded 25 singles and 54 doubles titles to his credit. He has **coached** at the **Harold Solomon** Tennis Institute and also at the **Nick Bollettieri** Tennis Academy.

GRAEBNER, CLARK EDWARD. B. 4 November 1943, Cleveland, Ohio. The six-foot two-inch, bespectacled Graebner was considered a dead ringer for Clark Kent, Superman's alter ego. But the mild-mannered Graebner had one of the most powerful **serves** in tennis in his era. Graebner was raised in Lakewood, Ohio, and attended Lakewood High School. He was the Ohio state high school champion three times. His father, Paul Graebner, also was raised in Lakewood, attended Lakewood High School, and was the state high school tennis champion. Paul graduated Western Reserve University dental school and went into dental practice with his father, Clark's grandfather. He gave up his own tennis playing to teach his son Clark the sport. In his teens, Clark was found to have osteochondrosis, a problem with his spinal column that caused him to wear a back brace for 14 months but did not pose a problem to his tennis activity, but as a result, Clark's posture was exceptionally upright, and his walk was almost a strut. Clark graduated from Northwestern University.

In 1966, he won his only **Grand Slam** title when he and **Dennis Ralston** defeated **Ion Țiriac** and **Ilie Năstase** to win the **French Open** men's **doubles**. Graebner and Ralston were also runners-up at the **United States Nationals**. Graebner also reached the **mixed doubles** finals at **Roland Garros** with partner **Ann Haydon Jones**. In 1967, he reached the finals of the United States National Championships but was defeated by **John Newcombe**. In 1968, Graebner was a semifinalist at both **Wimbledon** and the U.S. Open. Graebner played on the **United States Davis Cup** team each year from 1965 to 1968 and helped to win the Cup in 1968 by winning both his **singles** matches. His overall Cup record is 11–2 in singles and 5–2 in doubles.

He married tennis star Carol Caldwell in 1964. They had two children and separated in 1975 but never divorced. She died from cancer in 2008. In 1973, the Graebners authored *Mixed Doubles Tennis*.

GRAF, STEFANIE MARIA "STEFFI." B. 14 June 1969, Mannheim, West **Germany**. Steffi Graf began playing **professional** tennis in 1982, when she was only 13 years of age. From 1987 to 1996, she was nearly unbeatable in **Grand Slam tournaments**. In that 10-year span, she played in 36 Grand Slam **singles** tournaments and won 21 of them. She was also runner-up eight times and semifinalist four times. The 5-foot 9-inch, 130-pound Graf reached the quarterfinals of two others and, in 1994, at **Wimbledon**, was defeated in the first round by Lori McNeil. In 1988, Steffi won the Grand Slam—all four major tournaments in one calendar year. She also won the **Olympic** gold medal that year, a feat sometimes referred to as a **"Golden Slam,"** and is the only player male or female to win all five singles events in the same year. That year she also won her only major **doubles** title, Wimbledon, with **Gabriela Sabatini**. The pair also was three-time runner-up at the **French Open**, in 1986, 1987, and 1989.

Steffi has one of the most outstanding records in Olympic competition— she won the 1984 demonstration singles event, the 1988 singles gold medal, the 1988 doubles bronze medal (with partner Claudia Kohde-Kilsch), the 1992 singles silver medal, and she reached the second round of the 1992 doubles (with partner Anke Huber). She was a member of the West German **Federation Cup** team in 1986, 1987, and 1989 and of the German team in 1991 to 1993 and 1996. Her Cup record is 20–2 in singles and 8–2 in doubles in 20 **ties** over 7 years. She played on the Cup championship team in 1987 and 1992. She won the **Hopman Cup** in 1993 with partner **Michael Stich**. She was inducted into the **International Tennis Hall of Fame** in 2004. She married **Andre Agassi** in October 2001. They have two children.

GRAND SLAM. Winning the four major tournaments—**Wimbledon** and the **French, Australian,** and **United States National Championships**—is known as a "Grand Slam." The term was coined during the 1930s by tennis writer **Allison Danzig** and derives from the contract bridge term of winning all 13 tricks in one hand. **Don Budge**, in 1938, was the first player to win all four **singles** events in one year. Since then, **Rod Laver** is the only other male to do so—in 1962, as an **amateur**, and again in 1969, as a **professional**. Among females, only **Maureen Connolly** in 1953, **Margaret Smith Court** in 1970, and **Steffi Graf** in 1988 have accomplished this feat.

Frank Sedgman and Ken McGregor, in 1951, won the men's **doubles** Grand Slam, and **Martina Navratilova** and **Pam Shriver** won the women's doubles Grand Slam in 1984. The Australian Open was changed from a December event to a January one in 1985–87 and was played in December 1985 and next played in January 1987. Martina Navratilova won both of those doubles tournaments as well as the other three major tournaments in 1986. Her partner was Pam Shriver for the two Australian titles, Wimbledon, and the United States Open and Andrea Temesvári for the French Open. **Maria Bueno** won all four doubles events in 1960 by winning the Australian title with Christine Truman as partner and the remaining three events with **Darlene Hard** as partner. **Martina Hingis**, in 1998, won the Australian Open with Mirjana Lučić and the remaining three tournaments with **Jana Novotná**.

Margaret Smith Court and **Ken Fletcher** won a **mixed doubles** Grand Slam in 1963. Court again won all four mixed doubles in 1965, with **John Newcombe**, in Australia (cochampions as the final was not played), Fletcher in France and Wimbledon, and **Fred Stolle** at the United States Championships. Owen Davidson and **Lesley Turner** won the Australian mixed doubles in 1967, and Davidson and **Billie Jean King** won the other three tournaments that year. In 1983, Stefan Edberg won all four major **junior** tournaments and is the only player to win a junior Grand Slam. The four major tournaments are also occasionally referred to as "Slam" tournaments. *See also* GOLDEN SLAM.

GRASS. Lawn tennis began as a game played on a grass lawn. For much of the game's history, the best tennis clubs had lawn tennis courts, and major championships were conducted almost exclusively on grass. **Clay** courts were developed, and over the past half-century, **hard courts** of various compositions have been created. Today, only **Wimbledon**, of the major tournaments, is conducted on grass. The **Newport Casino**, site of the **International Tennis Hall of Fame and Museum**, still maintains grass courts, conducts an annual **tournament**, and makes the courts open to the public. Of the present-day **surfaces**, grass is probably the most challenging, since the bounce of the **ball** can be unpredictable. It is also a "fast" surface, and a player's reaction time has to be quite fast to be able to compete successfully on a grass court.

GREAT BRITAIN. England can rightly be deemed the birthplace of **lawn tennis**. Major **Walter Wingfield's** *sphairistike* was patented there in 1874, and the country embraced the sport from the start. The Lawn Tennis Association, founded in 1888, administers tennis in Great Britain. From 1900 through May 2011, Great Britain is the only nation to compete in all 100 **Davis Cup** tournaments. The country's record is 139–92 in 231 **ties**. Great Britain has competed 12 times in the World Group since its formation in 1981 and was Davis Cup champion nine times, from 1903 to 1906, 1912, and 1933 to 1936. Great Britain was runner-up eight times, the most recent being in 1978. The team lost to the **United States** in the first Davis Cup in 1900. From 1900 until 1912, the team competed as the **British Isles** and included Irish players. Top Davis Cup players have been **Henry "Bunny" Austin**, Patrick Hughes, **Fred Perry**, **Greg Rusedski**, Mike Sangster, and Bobby Wilson.

Great Britain has competed in tennis in every **Olympic Games** in which tennis was a medal sport, with the exception of 1904 and 1906. Most of Great Britain's Olympic tennis success occurred in the earliest Games. Irishman John Pius Boland won both the **singles** and **doubles** in the first Modern Olympic Games in 1896. The 1900 men's singles semifinals was contested among four Englishmen, with **Hugh Doherty** winning the title. Doherty and his brother, **Reggie**, won the 1900 doubles. Charlotte Cooper won the women's singles in 1900, and she and Reggie Doherty won the 1900 **mixed doubles**. Great Britain had no entrants in either the 1904 or 1906 Games but dominated the entries in 1908, when the Games were held in London. In that year, three tennis tournaments were held—covered **court** lawn tennis, outdoor lawn tennis, and *jeu de paume* or real tennis. The three covered court events and the three outdoor lawn tennis events—men's singles and doubles and women's singles—were all won by players from Great Britain. The *jeu de paume* event was won by an American, but in second, third, and fourth place were Englishmen. In 1912 covered court events, Charles Dixon was second in singles and third in doubles with Alfred Beamish. Edith Hannam won women's singles, and Hannam and Dixon won mixed doubles. The outdoor events were held at the same time as Wimbledon, and consequently, there were no British entries. In 1920, only outdoor events were scheduled. Noel Turnbull finished fourth in men's singles but won the men's doubles with **Max Woosnam**. Dorothy Holman finished second in women's singles. In the women's doubles competition, held for the first time in the Olympic Games, the four finalists were all representatives of Great Britain. Winnie McNair and **Kitty McKane** defeated Holman and Geraldine Beamish. McKane and Woosnam also finished second in mixed doubles. In 1924, McKane won the bronze medal in women's singles, the team of McKane and Phyllis Covell won the silver medal in women's doubles, and Dorothy Shepherd-Barron and Evelyn Colyer won the bronze medal in women's doubles. McKane and Brian Gilbert finished fourth in mixed doubles. Great Britain had no entrants in the **exhibition** and demonstration tennis events in 1968 in **Mexico**. Great Britain competed in tennis in every Olympic Games from 1984 to 2008 but only won one medal—a silver in 1996 men's doubles by Neil Broad and **Tim Henman**.

Among the best British male tennis players not mentioned above have been the Baddeley **twins** (Herbert and Wilfred), Herbert Roper Barrett, Andrew Castle, Hope Crisp, Arthur Gore, George Hughes, Algernon Kingscote, Herbert Lawford, E. W. Lewis, **John Lloyd**, Buster Mottram, **Andy Murray** and his brother Jamie Murray, James Parke, Joshua Pim, the **Renshaw twins** (Willie and Ernest), Frank Riseley, Sydney Smith, and Roger Taylor. The best female tennis players include Eileen Bennett Whittingstall, Blanche Bingley Hillyard, Shirley Bloomer, Angela Buxton, Charlotte Cooper, **Lottie Dod**, **Dorothea Douglass Lambert Chambers**, **Ann Haydon-Jones**, Angela Mortimer, **Betty Nuthall Shoemaker**, **Dorothy Round Little**, May Sutton, Christine Truman, **Virginia Wade**, and Billie Yorke. In **Federation Cup** competition from 1963 to May 2011, Great Britain has competed all 49 years, 31 years in World Group, played 175 **ties** with a record of 111–64, and was runner-up four times—in 1967, 1971, 1972, and 1981. In **Wightman Cup** competition against the United States, from 1923 to 1989, Great Britain only won 10 of 61 ties.

GREATEST MATCH OF ALL TIME. There have been quite a few **matches** that have been called the "greatest match of all time." There are at least two books with that as part of the title. The **Don Budge–Gottfried von Cramm** match in the **Davis Cup** Inter-Zone finals in 1937 was one match described that way in Marshall Jon Fisher's *A Terrible Splendor*, and the more recent **Roger Federer–Rafael Nadal Wimbledon** championship match in 2008, as reported by L. Jon Wertheim in *Strokes of Genius*, is the other. Among other matches given that distinction are: **Ken Rosewall–Rod Laver**, 1972 **World Championship Tennis** final; **Björn Borg–John McEnroe**, 1980 Wimbledon final, which included a 18–16 **tiebreak set**, in which McEnroe saved five **match points**; the **Roger Federer–Andy Roddick** Wimbledon championship in 2009, which concluded with a 16–14 fifth set; and the **John Isner**–Nicolas Mahut 11-hour five-minute marathon 2010 Wimbledon match.

GRIP. Grip in tennis refers to the rubberized substance around the base of the handle of the tennis **racket**. It also refers to the method in which a player holds the racquet. Since the racket handle is octagonal in shape, it can be held in various manners. The most common grips are the Continental, Eastern, and Western, with variations of each. Players often change their grip depending on whether they are serving, hitting **forehands**, or hitting **backhands**. One of the most unusual grips was that of Alberto Berasategui, who hit both backhands and forehands with the same racket surface.

GROUND STROKE. A ground stroke is a shot made after the **ball** bounces, in contrast to a **volley** or an **overhead**, which are hit while the ball is still in the air.

GUNTER, NANCY RICHEY. *See* RICHEY GUNTER, NANCY ANNE.

HAAS, TOMMY formerly **THOMAS MARIO "TOMMY."** B. 3 April 1978, Hamburg, West **Germany**. Tommy Haas began playing tennis at a very early age and actually won a **tournament** when he was just five years old, but his **professional** tennis career has been plagued by misfortune. As a **junior** player, he was quite talented and won a full scholarship to the **Nick Bollettieri** Tennis Academy in Florida. But in December 1995, he broke his right ankle, and after that healed, broke the left ankle in December 1996. In 2000, he had a bulging disk in his back. His worst setback occurred on 8 June 2002, when his parents were seriously injured in a motorcycle accident in Sarasota, Florida. His father, Peter, a former European judo champion and schoolmate of bodybuilder and California governor Arnold Schwarzenegger, was in a coma for three weeks, and Haas spent time away from tennis assisting his parents. In 2003, Haas required shoulder surgery and missed the entire year. In 2007, he had to withdraw from **Wimbledon** after reaching the fourth round when he tore an abdominal muscle. In 2010, he had hip surgery.

Despite all these setbacks, the 6-foot 2-inch, 195-pound right-hander still has managed some impressive results. In 1999, 2002, and 2007, he reached the semifinals of the **Australian Open**. He was a semifinalist at Wimbledon in 2009 and quarterfinalist at the **United States Open** in 2004, 2006, and 2007. In 2002 and 2009, he reached the fourth round at **Roland Garros**. Haas won the silver medal in the 2000 men's **singles Olympic** event, was a quarterfinalist in the 2000 **doubles**, and reached the second round of the 2004 Olympic men's singles. He played Davis Cup tennis for Germany each year from 1998 to 2007, except for 2003. In those nine years, his record was 19–7 in singles and 3–1 in doubles in 16 **ties**. Through May 2011, he has won 12 singles championships and 1 doubles championship and has been runner-up in 9 other singles events.

On 27 January 2010, Haas became a citizen of the **United States**. In 2010, he also changed his name legally from Thomas Mario Haas to just Tommy Haas.

HALF-VOLLEY. A half-volley is a tennis shot taken after a short bounce. It is usually made with the **racket** near the ground and is one of the more difficult shots to master.

HALL OF FAME. See **INTERNATIONAL TENNIS HALL OF FAME AND MUSEUM**.

HARD (WAGGONER), DARLENE RUTH. B. 6 January 1936, Los Angeles, California. Darlene Hard should not be confused with **Doris Hart**. Both women were among the world's best tennis players during the 1950s, and both won a large number of major **doubles** titles. Hard reached the finals of 35 **Grand Slam** events, winning 22. Most of her titles were in doubles, but she was **French National** champion in 1960, **United States National** champion in 1960 and 1961 and runner-up in 1958 and 1962, and **Wimbledon** runner-up in 1957 and 1959. She was already an international tennis champion when she enrolled at Pomona College in 1957, and in 1958, won the first national **intercollegiate** tennis championship for women. In 1957, she was the second **ranked** women's **singles** player in the world.

At 5 feet 6 inches and 145 pounds, she was known for her powerful right-handed **serve** and excellent **volleying**. In doubles, she was a losing finalist in both the women's doubles and **mixed doubles** in **Australia** in 1962. At **Roland Garros**, she won the women's doubles three times with three different partners (1955, 1957, 1960) and was twice runner-up (1956, 1961). She was also mixed doubles champion there in 1955 and 1961. She was a four-time women's doubles champion at Wimbledon (1957, 1959, 1960, 1963) and three-time mixed doubles champion (1957, 1959, 1960) and, in 1963, mixed doubles runner-up there. At the United States National Championships, she was the women's doubles finalist in seven consecutive years, from 1957 to 1963, winning five straight (1958–62). She came out of semiretirement in 1969 to partner **Françoise Durr** and win a sixth U.S. National doubles title. She was also a three-time U.S. National mixed doubles finalist (1956, 1957, 1961).

At the 1963 Pan American Games in São Paulo, Brazil, she was also a medalist, winning the doubles and placing third in the singles. She married Richard Waggoner, but they later divorced. She played on the United States **Wightman Cup** in five years, from 1957 to 1963, and had a record of 10–4. She was also a member of the inaugural **Federation Cup** team in 1963 and helped the **United States** win the Cup by winning six of her seven matches in four **ties** (3–1 in singles, 3–0 in doubles). After retiring from tennis, she worked in the office of the University of Southern California and owned two tennis stores in the Los Angeles area. She was inducted into the **International Tennis Hall of Fame** in 1973.

HARD COURT. Hard court is a type of tennis **surface** that is neither **grass** nor **clay**. It is usually made of asphalt, but synthetic surfaces are also used. The **ball** will bounce faster and truer on a hard court surface than on other types of surface.

HART, DORIS JANE. B. 20 June 1925, St. Louis, Missouri. When Doris Hart was just 15 months old, she incurred a knee infection. Her family physician was unavailable, and the substitute mistreated it. There was fear of gangrene, and amputation of the leg was recommended. Fortunately, her regular physician returned and was able to operate on the knee and save it, although the leg remained weak. Her father's business caused the family to move to Miami, Florida, when she was four years old. Being able to play and swim in the salt water daily helped restore the leg. At the age of nine, she developed a bilateral hernia that was successfully operated on but required a four-week stay in the hospital to convalesce. Her hospital room overlooked tennis courts at a park, and watching them daily created an interest in the sport. She began playing with her older brothers and soon progressed to being an effective **tournament** player. By 1940, she was the Florida State Girls' High School Champion. She competed in her first **United States National** tournament later that year, reaching the second round. In 1942, she was a quarterfinalist, in 1943 a semifinalist, and in 1946, a finalist.

When she retired from competitive play, in 1955, she had reached 68 **Grand Slam** finals and won 35 of them. This was more Grand Slam finals and more Grand Slam championships than any player, male or female, had recorded to that point. Since then, only **Margaret Smith Court**, with 64 wins in 87 finals appearances, and **Martina Navratilova**, with 59 wins in 85 finals appearances, have exceeded Hart's finals total. **Billie Jean King**, with 39 championships, and **Margaret Osborne duPont**, with 37 championships, are the only other players to exceed Hart's championship totals. She attended Barry College for Women in Florida from 1943 to 1945 and then resumed her education at the University of Miami in 1947.

Her tennis résumé:

Australian Championships

- **Singles** champion in 1949, runner-up in 1950
- Women's **doubles** runner-up in 1949 with Marie Toomey, champion in 1950 with **Louise Brough**
- **Mixed doubles** champion in 1949 and 1950 with **Frank Sedgman**

French Nationals

- Singles champion in 1950 and 1952, runner-up in 1947, 1951, and 1953
- Women's doubles champion in 1948 with Pat Canning Todd, in 1950 through 1953 with **Shirley Fry**, runner-up in 1946 with **Pauline Betz**, in 1947 with Todd
- Mixed doubles champion in 1951 and 1952 with **Frank Sedgman**, in 1953 with **Vic Seixas**, runner-up in 1948 with Sedgman, in 1956 with Bob Howe

Wimbledon

- Singles champion in 1951, runner-up in 1947, 1948 and 1953
- Women's doubles champion in 1947 with Todd, in 1951 through 1953 with Fry, runner-up in 1946 with Betz, in 1948 with Todd, in 1950 and 1954 with Fry
- Mixed doubles champion in 1951 and 1952 with Sedgman, in 1953 through 1955 with Seixas, runner-up in 1948 with Sedgman

United States Nationals

- Singles champion in 1954 and 1955, runner-up in 1946, 1949, 1950, 1952, and 1953
- Women's doubles champion in 1951 through 1954 with Shirley Fry, runner-up in 1942 through 1945 with Betz, in 1947 and 1948 with Todd, in 1949, 1950, and 1955 with Fry
- Mixed doubles champion in 1951 and 1952 with Sedgman, in 1953 through 1955 with Seixas, runner-up in 1945 with Bob Falkenburg, in 1950 with Sedgman

A member of the outstanding **United States Wightman Cup** teams from 1946 to 1955, in 10 years of competition, her record was 14–1 in singles and 8–1 in doubles as the United States won the Cup each of those 10 years, losing only three **ties**. Her 1955 autobiography, *Tennis with Hart*, provides a good discussion of her life and women's tennis in the post–World War II era. She was inducted into the **International Tennis Hall of Fame** in 1969.

HAWK-EYE. *See* CHALLENGE.

HAYDON-JONES, ADRIENNE SHIRLEY "ANN." B. 7 October 1938, Birmingham, England. Ann Haydon was the daughter of two champion **table tennis** players. Her father, Adrian Haydon, was the number-one–**ranked** British table tennis player. She began playing table tennis as a youth and competed in five world championships during the 1950s. She also played **lawn tennis** and won the 1956 **Wimbledon girls' singles** championship. In 1967, she was runner-up to **Billie Jean King** for the Wimbledon ladies' singles championship and, two years later, defeated Billie Jean to become Wimbledon champion—the first **left-handed** female to win that title. The 1969 **match** was voted as one of the top 10 Wimbledon finals of all time by a London newspaper in 2009. Billie Jean had won Wimbledon the previous three years and was a huge favorite to do so again, but after losing the first set, Ann rallied to take the next two. At **Roland Garros**, she reached the women's singles final five times, winning in 1961 and 1966 and being the runner-up in 1963, 1968, and 1969. She also was a **United States National** singles finalist in 1961 and 1967. She reached the singles semifinals in 1969 at the **Australian Open**, and she and **Fred Stolle** were declared **mixed doubles** cochampions with the team of **Margaret Smith Court** and Marty Riessen as the final match was not played. At Wimbledon, in ladies' **doubles**, she and **Françoise Durr** lost to King and **Rosie Casals** in 1968. The 5-foot 7-inch, 135-pound Haydon-Jones was also mixed doubles runner-up in 1962 and mixed doubles champion there in 1969. She was a four-time women's doubles finalist at Roland Garros, losing in 1960 and winning in 1963, 1968, and 1969, and three-time mixed doubles finalist there, losing in 1960, 1966, and 1967.

She married P. F. Jones in 1962 and afterward was known as Ann Haydon-Jones. She played on the **Great Britain Federation Cup** team from 1963 to 1967 and 1970 and had a record of 10–7 in singles and 11–5 in doubles in 18 **ties**. She was a member of the runner-up team in 1967. She played on the British **Wightman Cup** team 13 years, from 1957 to 1975, and had a record of 16–17 in that time. In her career, from 1957 to 1970, she was ranked second in the world in 1967. In 1968, she became a member of one of the first female **professional** tours, along with Billie Jean King. In retirement, she worked for the British Broadcasting Corporation as an announcer, was the chairman of the International Women's Tennis Council, and was a member of Wimbledon's Committee of Management. She was inducted into the **International Tennis Hall of Fame** in 1985.

HELDMAN WEISS, JULIE MEDALIE. B. 8 December 1945, Berkeley, California. Julie Heldman is the daughter of Julius and Gladys Heldman.

Julius was a **ranked** tennis player in the 1930s and 1940s, and Gladys was the founder and publisher of *World Tennis* magazine. Julie won several national **junior** championships and enrolled at Stanford University. As a member of the Stanford tennis team, she reached the finals of the **intercollegiate singles** and **doubles** national championships in 1964. She played as an **amateur** until 1969, when she became a **professional** as most tournaments then became **open** ones. That year, she had her highest world singles ranking of five as she reached the quarterfinals of the three **Grand Slam** tournaments that she entered—all but **Australia**. She also competed at the Maccabiah Games in **Israel** and won all three events—singles, doubles, and **mixed doubles**. In 1970, she was a semifinalist at **Roland Garros**, and in 1974, she reached the **United States Open** semifinals. In her only appearance at the **Australian Open**, she was also a semifinalist in 1974.

She was one of the nine original members of the **Virginia Slims** women's professional tour, which her mother helped to sponsor. She competed in all three events in both the demonstration and **exhibition** tennis events in the 1968 **Olympic Games** in **Mexico** and won the exhibition women's doubles and demonstration mixed doubles, was the runner-up in exhibition singles and demonstration women's doubles, was third in demonstration singles, and reached the quarterfinals in exhibition mixed doubles. The 5-foot 7-inch, 120-pound right-hander was a member of the **United States Federation Cup** team in 1966, 1969, 1970, 1974, and 1975. Her record was 13–6 in singles and 8–3 in doubles in 19 **ties**. She played for the Cup championship team in 1966 and 1969 and for the runner-up team in 1974. In **Wightman Cup** play, from 1969 to 1971 and 1974, her record was 5–4. In 1975, she retired from professional tennis and returned to school, enrolling at the University of California, Los Angeles (UCLA) and earning a JD from UCLA law school in 1981. She married Bernard Weiss in 1981. In 1985, she became the president and cochairman of Signature Eyewear. She also did television tennis commentary and wrote for her mother's tennis magazine.

HENIN (-HARDENNE), JUSTINE. B. 1 June 1982, Liege, **Belgium**. Justine Henin, although only 5 feet 6 inches and 125 pounds, had one of the hardest **serves** in women's tennis. She is also one of the sport's fiercest competitors. In 1995, she came under the tutelage of **coach** Carlos Rodriguez and won the 1997 **French Open junior singles**. She became a **professional** player in 1999 and won her first professional **Women's Tennis Association tournament** in Antwerp. In 2001, she reached the ladies' singles finals at **Wimbledon** but was defeated by **Venus Williams** in three sets. Justine then defeated countrywoman **Kim Clijsters** to win the 2003 French Open and defeated her again at the 2003 **United States Open**. Justine won the 2004

Australian Open and the gold medal in the 2004 **Olympic** women's singles competition. In 2006, Justine faced **Amélie Mauresmo** in the Australian Open finals but retired in the second set with a stomach injury. She reached the finals of the other three **Grand Slam** tournaments that year but was only able to win the French Open, losing to Mauresmo in three **sets** at Wimbledon and **Maria Sharapova** at the U.S. Open. She won the French Open for a fourth straight time in 2007 and also won the U.S. Open. In 2008, a loss in the quarterfinals at the Australian Open ended a 32-match winning streak.

Over the next few months, her play was mediocre, and fatigue and injuries played a factor. On 14 May 2008, shortly before the start of the French Open, a tournament in which she was still favored to win, she announced her retirement, citing mental and physical fatigue. She devoted her energies to her tennis academy, Justine N1 (pronounced in French similar to Henin). After seeing **Roger Federer** finally win the French Open in 2009, her tennis enthusiasm was renewed, and she announced a comeback on 22 September. She returned in January for a tournament in Brisbane and reached the final, losing to Clijsters. Justine then reached the final of the Australian Open but was defeated by **Serena Williams** in three sets. At the French Open, in a third round match, she lost the second set to Sharapova, although she won the match. This ended her streak at **Roland Garros** of 40 consecutive sets won, tying **Helen Wills** for the all-time record. In the fourth round, she was defeated by **Samantha Stosur**, Justine's first loss at Roland Garros since 2004. Justine was defeated by Kim Clijsters in the fourth round at Wimbledon in 2010 but injured her elbow while doing so. As a result, she was sidelined for the remainder of the year and on 26 January 2011 announced her permanent retirement from the sport.

She married Pierre-Yves Hardenne on 16 November 2002 and used the hyphenated Henin-Hardenne name until their separation in 2007. She then assumed her maiden name for competition. They divorced in 2008. She played for Belgium in **Federation Cup** tennis from 1999 to 2003, 2006, and 2010. Her record through 2010 is 15–2 in singles and 0–2 in doubles. She was a member of the Cup championship team in 2001. In 2006, she won her two singles matches in the Cup final in Charleroi in her native Belgium but was forced to retire due to a knee injury during the deciding doubles match, allowing Italy to win the Cup. She won 43 singles and 2 **doubles** titles in her career and was the world number-one–**ranked** player for more than 100 weeks total, first reaching that height in 2003.

HENMAN, TIMOTHY HENRY "TIM." B. 6 September 1974, Oxford, England. Tim Henman comes from a sporting family with several ancestors who competed at **Wimbledon**. His great-grandfather, great-grandmother, grandfather, grandmother, and mother all played there. He attended the

Dragon School, Oxford and Reed's School, Cobham. In 1992, he won the English National **junior singles** and **doubles** titles and became a **professional** tennis player in 1993. In an unfortunate incident in 1995, he became the first player in the modern era to be disqualified from the Wimbledon championships when, in frustration after losing a **point**, he hit a **ball** toward the **net**, and the ball unfortunately hit a **ball girl**, who was only a few feet away, in the side of the head. Although she was not badly hurt, Henman's actions caused **umpire** Wayne McKewen and tournament **referee** Alan Mills to disqualify Henman. In 1996, Tim was named the **Association of Tennis Professionals** Most Improved Player. He was a four-time semifinalist at Wimbledon in men's singles (1998, 1999, 2001, 2002) but, to the disappointment of his country, could never reach the final round. In 2004, he reached the semifinals at the **French Open** and **United States Open**. His best performance at the **Australian Open** was the fourth round, which he reached in 2000, 2001, and 2002. He competed in the 1996 and 2004 **Olympic Games** and won the silver medal in the 1996 men's doubles event with partner Neil Broad. Henman played **Davis Cup** tennis for **Great Britain** each year from 1994 to 2004 and again in 2007. In 21 **ties** in 12 years of Cup competition, his record was 29–8 in singles and 11–6 in doubles. He retired in 2007 with a career record of 11 singles and 4 doubles titles. In retirement, he has worked as a television commentator for the Wimbledon championships.

HEWITT, LLEYTON GLYNN. B. 24 February 1981, Adelaide, South Australia, **Australia**. Lleyton Hewitt's parents were both professional athletes. His father, Glynn, was an Australian rules football player, and his mother, Cherilyn, played professional netball (a women's game similar to basketball, played primarily in countries in the former British Empire). Lleyton attended Immanuel College, a private school in Adelaide. He became a **professional** tennis player in 1998 and won his first **Association of Tennis Professionals** tournament in Adelaide in January, while still only 16 years old, defeating **Andre Agassi** in the semifinal round. By 2000, age 19, Hewitt reached the semifinals of the **United States Open singles** and, with Max Mirnyi, was the **doubles** champion. That year, he also was a finalist in the **mixed doubles** at **Wimbledon** with then girlfriend, **Kim Clijsters**. In 2001, he won the U.S. Open singles title, and in 2002, he won Wimbledon. His best performance at the **Australian Open** occurred in 2005, when he reached the finals but was defeated by **Marat Safin**. At the **French Open**, Hewitt's best result was the quarterfinals in 2001 and 2004. In 2004 and 2005, Hewitt lost to the eventual champion in seven consecutive **Grand Slam** tournaments. Included in that streak was the 2004 U.S. Open final, which he lost to **Roger Federer**. Hewitt was known as an excellent returner and for his ability to keep the **ball** in play.

He competed in the 2000 and 2008 **Olympic Games** and lost in the singles first round in 2000 and the second round in 2008 and reached the 2008 men's doubles quarterfinals with partner Chris Guccione. The 5-foot 11-inch, 170-pound right-handed Hewitt played for Australia in **Davis Cup** competition each year from 1999 to 2010 and helped lead that team to the final in 1999, 2000, 2001, and 2003. Australia won the Cup in 1999 and 2003. His Davis Cup record in 29 **ties** during those 12 years was 36–9 in singles and 8–3 in doubles. Although a hip injury that necessitated surgery slowed him in 2008 and 2009, he has continued to compete. Through May 2011, he has won 29 singles and 2 doubles titles and was the world number-one–**ranked** singles player in 2001.

HEWITT, ROBERT ANTHONY JOHN "BOB." B. 12 January 1940, Dubbo, New South Wales, **Australia**. Bob Hewitt is one of only seven players to have won men's **doubles** and **mixed doubles** championships at all four **Grand Slam** events. The others are **Frank Sedgman, Mark Woodforde, Todd Woodbridge, Doris Hart, Margaret Smith Court,** and **Martina Navratilova**. In his career, he reached 20 Grand Slam doubles finals and won 15 of them. As a **singles** player, he reached the semifinals of the **Australian Championships** three times and the quarterfinals of **Wimbledon** three times, but it was as a doubles player that he starred. In his long career (1958–80), he won 7 singles titles and 65 doubles titles and was known for his fiery personality on the court. The 6-foot 3-inch, 205-pound right-hander won his first five Grand Slam titles as a representative of Australia. With **Fred Stolle** as partner, he won the Australian Championships in 1963 and 1964 and was runner-up in 1962. They won Wimbledon in 1962 and 1964 and were runners-up in 1961. In 1965, Hewitt and **Ken Fletcher** were Wimbledon and **French** runners-up. In mixed doubles, Hewitt and Australian Jan Lehane won the Australian Championship in 1961. Hewitt and American **Darlene Hard** were Wimbledon runners-up in 1963.

Hewitt married **South African** model Delaille Nicholas and moved to South Africa in 1964. For the greater part of his tennis career, he represented South Africa in competition. With South African **Frew McMillan**, Hewitt won Wimbledon in 1967, 1972, and 1978, the **French Open** in 1972, and the **United States Open** in 1978. In mixed doubles, Hewitt teamed with South African Greer Stevens to win Wimbledon in 1977 and Wimbledon and the U.S. Open in 1979. At the French Open, representing South Africa, Hewitt won two mixed doubles titles, teaming with American **Billie Jean King** in 1970 and Australian **Wendy Turnbull** in 1979. He played **Davis Cup** tennis for South Africa from 1967 to 1978. His record was 22–3 in singles and 16–1 in doubles in 17 **ties** over 7 years. In 1974, he helped South Africa reach the final round, where it won the Cup by default from **India**. He was inducted into the **International Tennis Hall of Fame** in 1992, along with his doubles partner McMillan. In retirement, he has worked as a television commentator, owned citrus groves, and was involved in property development in Addo, South Africa, where he resides.

HIGUERAS, JOSÉ. B.1 March 1953, Diezma, Granada, **Spain**. Although José Higueras was a top 10 player during the 1970s, he has made more of a name for himself as a **coach**. He played **professionally** from 1974 to 1986 and won 16 **singles** and 3 **doubles** titles. He was also runner-up 12 times in singles and twice in doubles. He was a member of the Spanish team that won the inaugural **World Team Cup tournament** in 1978. He played **Davis Cup** tennis from 1973 to 1975 and 1977 to 1980. In those 7 years, he played in 17 **ties** and had a record of 15–15 in singles and 6–3 in doubles. A **clay court** specialist, he was a semifinalist at **Roland Garros** in 1982 and 1983 and was **ranked** seventh in the world in 1983. He only entered **Wimbledon** twice and reached the second round each time; he played in the **United States Open** four times, reaching the fourth round in 1977, and he never competed in the **Australian Open** in his 14-year pro career. He has been the coach of **Michael Chang**, **Jim Courier**, **Pete Sampras**, and Robby Ginepri, among others and, in 2008, was hired by **Roger Federer** for help with the clay court season. Higueras runs the José Higueras Tennis Training Center in Palm Springs, California. In 2008, he was hired by the **United States Tennis Association** as its director of coaching for elite player development.

HINGIS, MARTINA. B. 30 September 1980, Košice, **Czechoslovakia**. Martina Hingis was named for tennis great **Martina Navratilova** and had a **professional** tennis career that was almost as great. The daughter of two former top-20 Czechoslovakian tennis players, she began playing at age two and entered her first **tournament** at age four. Her parents divorced when she was just six, and she moved with her mother to **Switzerland**. Throughout her life, she has set records for youngest champion. She won the 1993 **girls'** (18 and under) **singles** title at **Roland Garros** when she was just 12—the youngest ever to win a **junior Grand Slam** title. The following year, she again won the Junior **French Open** singles title, also won the **Wimbledon** junior singles, and was the **United States Open** junior runner-up. In October of that year, she became a professional player, shortly after she celebrated her 14th birthday. In January 1995, she won her first round **match** in the **main draw** of the **Australian Open** and was the youngest player to win a Grand Slam main draw contest. In 1996, she won the Wimbledon women's doubles title with **Helena Suková**, while still only 15 years old—again, the youngest to win a

Grand Slam title. She competed in the 1996 **Olympic Games** and reached the singles second round and **doubles** quarterfinal round. Her best year was 1997, when she won the Australian Open (and became the youngest Grand Slam singles winner in the 20th century), Wimbledon, and the United States Open and was the runner-up at the French Open, losing to Iva Majoli, who won her only Grand Slam title of her career. Martina achieved the world number-one **ranking** in March 1997 and was the youngest player in history to be ranked number one. Martina again won the Australian Open in 1998 and 1999 and was runner-up there in 2000, 2001, and 2002. She was the runner-up at the 1998 and 1999 United States Open and 1999 French Open.

The 5-foot 7-inch, 130-pound right-hander also was a good doubles player and was ranked number one in the world in doubles in 1998. At the Australian Open, she won the women's doubles in 1997, 1998, 1999, and 2002 and was runner-up in 2000, playing with different partners in four of the five years. At Wimbledon, she won women's doubles titles in 1996 and 1998. At Roland Garros, she won doubles titles in 1998 and 2000 and was runner-up in 1999. She was United States Open women's doubles champion in 1998. In 1998, she won the women's doubles title at all four Grand Slam events—with Mirjana Lučić in Australia and with **Jana Novotná** at the other three. Hingis represented Switzerland in **Federation Cup** play from 1995 to 1998 and had a record of 18–2 in singles and 8–2 in doubles in 14 **ties**. In 1998, she was a member of the runner-up team. She won the **Hopman Cup** in 2001 with partner **Roger Federer**. In 2001, she began having physical problems and had ankle surgery in October.

A series of injuries caused her to announce her retirement in February 2003, at the age of just 22. She attempted a comeback in 2005 and played reasonably well, winning the Australian mixed doubles with **Mahesh Bhupathi** in 2006. Injuries continued to plague her in 2007, and in November, it was announced that she was suspended for two years by the **International Tennis Federation** for testing positive for cocaine. In 2010, she played some **exhibition** matches and also played in **World Team Tennis** but did not attempt to rejoin the **Women's Tennis Association**.

HOAD, LEWIS ALAN "LEW." B. 23 November 1934, Glebe, New South Wales, **Australia**. D. 3 July 1994, Fuengirola, **Spain**. From 1953 to 1957, the stocky (5 feet 8 inches tall, 175 pounds) but strong Lew Hoad was one of the world's best tennis players. In that brief period, he won 13 **Grand Slam** events and was runner-up 10 times. In 1956, he was **ranked** number one in the world after he won the men's **singles** in Australia, **France**, and **Wimbledon** and was defeated in the finals at **Forest Hills** by his **doubles** partner, **Ken Rosewall**. That year, he and Rosewall won the doubles in Australia,

Wimbledon, and Forest Hills, and Hoad and **Darlene Hard** were **mixed doubles** finalists at Forest Hills. Hoad played **Davis Cup** tennis for Australia for four years, from 1953 to 1956, before becoming a **professional** and ineligible for further competition. He helped lead Australia to the championship in 1953, 1955, and 1956. His **match** against Tony Trabert in 1953, when Hoad was only 19 years old, was his most memorable. Australia trailed in the **challenge round**, two **rubbers** to one, when they met. Hoad won the first two **sets**, 13–11 and 6–3. Trabert won the next two 3–6, 2–6, but Hoad pulled out the final set, 7–5, to level the **tie** at two rubbers all. The next day, Ken Rosewall defeated **Vic Seixas** and Australia retained the Davis Cup. Hoad's record in nine ties was 10–2 in singles and 7–2 in doubles. He became a professional after winning Wimbledon in 1957 and played a series of matches with **Pancho Gonzáles** in 1958. Sporadic back troubles hampered his play during the next few years, although when the major tournaments became open ones, he played at Wimbledon and **Roland Garros** in 1968, 1970, and 1972, with his best result being the fourth round at Roland Garros in 1970.

After he retired from competition, he relocated to Fuengirola, Spain, and ran a tennis resort with his wife, the former Jenny Staley. Staley had been a world-class player who was a women's singles finalist at the Australian Championships in 1954 and mixed doubles finalist there in 1955 with Hoad as her partner. While suffering from leukemia and awaiting a bone marrow donor, he died of a heart attack at the age of 59. He was inducted into the **International Tennis Hall of Fame** in 1980.

HOPMAN, HENRY CHRISTIAN "HARRY." B. 12 August 1906, Glebe, New South Wales, **Australia**. D. 27 December 1985, Largo, Florida, **United States**. Harry Hopman is one of those tennis players who is better known for his **coaching** abilities, although he was also a champion player. He attended Rosehill Public School and Parramatta High School in the Sydney suburbs. In his tennis career, he reached the finals of 18 **Grand Slam** events, winning 7 **doubles** titles. Although only 5 feet 7 inches tall and 135 pounds, he was the runner-up in the **Australian** men's **singles** in 1930, 1931, and 1932. He won the Australian men's doubles in 1929 and 1930 with **Jack Crawford** as partner, and the pair lost in the finals in 1931. Hopman and **Gerald Patterson** lost in the 1932 finals to Crawford and Gar Moon. In Australian **mixed doubles**, Hopman and Eleanor Mary "Nell" Hall won in 1930. Hopman and Hall married in 1934, and they won again in 1936, 1937, and 1939 and were runners-up in 1940. In 1939, at the **United States National Championships**, Hopman was the men's doubles runner-up with Crawford and won the mixed doubles with **Alice Marble**. Hopman lost in the 1932 Wimbledon mixed doubles with Josane Sigart and the 1935 tournament with his wife. Hopman and

Jim Willard were runners-up at Roland Garros in 1930, and 18 years later, at the age of 41, he again reached the finals there with **Frank Sedgman** in 1948.

Hopman played on the Australian **Davis Cup** team in 1928, 1930, and 1931. In seven **ties**, he had a record of 4–5 in singles and 4–3 in doubles. He also coached the team in 1938 and 1939. He had been working for the *Melbourne Herald* as a sportswriter, and after World War II, he dropped his tennis activities to concentrate on his work as a journalist. He was enticed to return as Davis Cup coach after the United States began to dominate that competition. He returned in 1950 and remained as coach through 1969. He helped lead Australia to 16 Davis Cup championships in 22 attempts.

After the death of his wife in 1968, he moved to the United States in 1969 and became associated with the Port Washington Tennis Academy on Long Island in New York. The academy was where future professionals, such as **Vitas Gerulaitis** and **John McEnroe**, had their early training. He also joined with **Nick Bollettieri** in a tennis camp in Amherst, Massachusetts, and later opened the Hopman Tennis Academy in Largo, Florida. On 2 February 1971, Hopman married Lucy Pope Fox in Port Washington. He was inducted into the **International Tennis Hall of Fame** in 1978.

HOPMAN CUP. The Hopman Cup is an international tournament held in Perth, **Australia**, prior to the **Australian Open**, with teams consisting of one man and one woman playing **ties** consisting of a men's **singles**, women's singles, and **mixed doubles**. It was the creation of former Australian professional tennis players Paul McNamee and Charlie Fancutt and is named in honor of **Hall of Fame** Australian tennis **coach Harry Hopman**. It began in 1989 and has usually attracted some of the best players. The **United States** has won the event six times, and 11 other countries have won it at least once, with 7 other countries reaching the finals but losing. There have been five players who have won the event twice: **Arantxa Sánchez Vicario** (1990, 2002), Tommy Robredo (2002, 2010), **James Blake** (2003, 2004), **Serena Williams** (2003, 2008), and Dominik Hrbatý (2005, 2009).

HOTCHKISS WIGHTMAN, HAZEL VIRGINIA. B. 20 December 1886, Healdsburg, California. D. 5 December 1974, Chestnut Hill, Massachusetts. Hazel Hotchkiss Wightman, although only about five feet tall, was the premiere female American tennis player in the early years of the 20th century. In a 1910 tournament in Seattle, Washington, she defeated one opponent in straight sets without the loss of a **point**, winning 48 consecutive points. A 1911 graduate of the University of California, Berkeley, she won the **United States National singles, doubles**, and **mixed doubles** three consecutive years from 1909 to 1911, a feat only accomplished two other times (by **Mary**

K. Browne** in 1912 to 1914 and **Alice Marble** in 1938 to 1940) and never accomplished at any of the other **Grand Slam** tournaments. All told, Wightman won four U.S. singles and was runner-up once, won six U.S. women's doubles and was runner-up twice, and won six U.S. mixed doubles and was runner-up twice. She also won the **Wimbledon** women's doubles in 1924 with **Helen Wills**. Wightman's other U.S. singles title was in 1919, and she was runner-up to **Molla Mallory** in 1915. Her U.S. women's doubles championships in 1909 and 1910 were with partner Edith Rotch and in 1911 with Eleonora Sears. She won again with Sears in 1915 and with Helen Wills in 1924 and 1928—the latter title at age 41. Sears and Wightman were runners-up in 1919, and Wightman and Eleanor Goss were runners-up in 1923. Her U.S. mixed doubles triumphs occurred in 1909, 1911, and 1920 with Wallace Johnson, in 1910 with Joseph Carpenter, in 1915 with Harry Johnson, and in 1918 with Irving Wright. She and **René Lacoste** were runners-up in 1926 and 1927. She won the gold medal in the women's doubles (with partner Helen Wills) and mixed doubles (with partner **Richard Norris Williams**) in the 1924 **Olympic Games**.

In 1912, she married lawyer George William Wightman, a member of a prominent Boston family and Harvard tennis player, and settled in Massachusetts. They had five children and were divorced in 1940.

One of her major contributions to tennis was the creation of the Ladies' International Tennis Challenge event in 1923. This was an annual competition between the **United States** and **Great Britain** along the lines of the Davis Cup. Wightman donated the trophy, later popularly known as the **Wightman Cup**. She was also one of the team members in the early years of the event. She played in a doubles match for the American team in 1923, 1924, 1927, 1929, and 1931, winning the first three times and losing the last two, when she was past 40 years of age. She was also the Wightman Cup team captain 13 times between 1923 and 1948. She enjoyed teaching young players and would open her home near Boston to them. "Mrs. Wightie," as they referred to her, was instrumental in the careers of many young players. Her last championship occurred in 1943, when she, aged 56, and **Pauline Betz** won the U.S. Indoor Women's Doubles Championship. She was inducted into the **International Tennis Hall of Fame** in 1957.

HUNGARY. Tennis in Hungary began quite early with the first **court** built in 1881. In 1894, the Hungarian National Tennis Championships were first held, making Hungary one of only four countries to have national tennis championships at that time, the others being **Great Britain**, the **United States**, and New Zealand. The Hungary Tennis Association is the national administrator and was founded in 1907. Hungary's best result in **Olympic** tennis occurred in the very first Modern Olympic Games in 1896, when Momcsilló Tapavicza finished third in men's **singles**. He also entered the weightlifting and wrestling events that year. Hungary had entrants in tennis in 1906, 1908, 1912, 1924, and 1988 through 2008, but none was a medalist.

From 1924 through May 2011, Hungary competed in 77 **Davis Cup** tournaments with a record of 72–78 in 150 **ties**. Hungary has competed twice in the World Group since its formation in 1981. Its best results were in 1976 and 1978, when the team reached the final round of the Europe Zone, and in 1994 and 1996, when Hungary competed in the first round of the World Group. Top Davis Cup players have been Balázs Taróczy, Peter Szoke, and István Gulyás. Among the best male tennis players have been Béla von Kehrling, József Asbóth (**French** champion in 1947), and István Gulyás (1966 **French Open** runner-up). Taróczy won **Wimbledon doubles** in 1985, French Open doubles in 1981, and reached a high singles ranking of 13 in 1982.

The most successful female tennis player was Andrea Temesvári, daughter of Olympic basketball player Otto Temesvári. She was ranked seventh in 1984 in singles and won five singles and six doubles titles, including the 1986 French Open Doubles Championship. Other top Hungarian female tennis players include Zsuzsa "Suzi" Körmöczi (French Open champion in 1958 and runner-up in 1959), Ágnes Szávay, and Melinda Czink. In **Federation Cup** competition, from 1963 to May 2011, Hungary has competed 36 years, 18 years in World Group, played 118 ties with a record of 60–58, and was a quarterfinalist in 1963 and 1985.

I FORMATION. The I formation is used in **doubles** when the **server's** partner lines up at the **net** almost directly in front of the server in the middle of the **court**. This gives the net player the option of **poaching** on either side of the court.

INDIA. Tennis has been played in India since the 1880s as **British** Army officers introduced the game there. The All India Tennis Association (AITA), formed in 1920, is its governing body. In **Federation Cup** competition, from 1991 to May 2011, India has competed 20 years, none in World Group, played 77 **ties** with a record of 39–38. India's best result was in 2006, when it was the runner-up in Asia/Oceania Group I. The best Indian female players include Olympians Manisha Malhotra, Sania Mirza, N. Polley, Sunitha Rao, and Nirupama Sanjeev. In 2009, Mirza and **Mahesh Bhupathi** won the **Australian Open mixed doubles** after being runners-up in that **tournament** the previous year.

From 1921 through May 2011, India has competed in 75 **Davis Cup** tournaments with a record of 109–72 in 181 ties. The team has competed 13 times in the World Group since its formation in 1981. In 1966, 1974, and 1987 India was the tournament runner-up. In 1974, India forfeited to **South Africa** in the final in protest against South Africa's apartheid policy. India's top Davis Cup players have been Mahesh Bhupathi, **Ramanathan Krishnan**, and **Leander Paes**. India first competed in **Olympic** tennis in 1924 and has had tennis players in each Olympics from 1984 to 2008. Leander Paes won the men's **singles** bronze medal in 1996, and the **doubles** team of Bhupathi and Paes finished fourth in 2004. In addition to the players named above, other top male Indian players include the **Amritraj family** (brothers Anand, Ashok, and Vijay and Vijay's son Prakash), **Ramesh Krishnan** (Ramanathan's son), Somdev Devvarman, and Lewis Deane, who was a finalist in mixed doubles at Wimbledon in 1923.

INDIAN WELLS. Indian Wells is a city in Southern California that is the site of one of the more prestigious tennis **tournaments** for both men and women. The Indian Wells Tennis Garden, constructed in 2000, is the facility for the tournament. Its main stadium, one of the largest tennis stadiums in the world, has a seating capacity of 16,100. The tournament, known by the name of its sponsor, began as the Pacific Life tournament but in 2010 was known as the BNP Paribas Open.

INTERCOLLEGIATE TENNIS ASSOCIATION (ITA). The Intercollegiate Tennis Association is the governing body of college tennis. It oversees men's and women's tennis at all collegiate levels, including institutions in all three divisions of the National Collegiate Athletic Association, in the National Association of Intercollegiate Athletics, and in junior and community colleges. It administers various collegiate **tournaments** and individual and team **rankings**. Organized as a collegiate **coaches** organization in 1956, it was known as the Intercollegiate Tennis Coaches Organization from 1958 to 1992. It maintains an ITA Men's Hall of Fame at the University of Georgia in Athens, Georgia, and an ITA Women's Hall of Fame at the College of William and Mary in Williamsburg, Virginia. Since 2000, its main offices have been located in Skillman, New Jersey, near Princeton University. By 2010, it had over 1,500 coaches and 15,000 players in 1,000 colleges and universities. *See also* COLLEGIATE TENNIS.

INTERNATIONAL LAWN TENNIS CHALLENGE. *See* DAVIS CUP.

INTERNATIONAL LAWN TENNIS FEDERATION. *See* INTERNATIONAL TENNIS FEDERATION.

INTERNATIONAL TENNIS FEDERATION (ITF). The International Tennis Federation is the governing body of international tennis. It is made up of national tennis federations. It was created on 1 March 1913 in Paris, **France**, by 12 national tennis associations as the International Lawn Tennis Federation (ILTF). As less and less tennis was played on **grass courts**, the organization, in 1977, changed its name to the International Tennis Federation. Its headquarters were originally in France, but during World War II, they were moved to England, where they remain. The ITF runs the major team tennis events: the **Davis Cup, Fed Cup,** and **Hopman Cup** and sanctions the four major tournaments, **Australian Open, French Open, Wimbledon,** and **United States Open.**

INTERNATIONAL TENNIS HALL OF FAME AND MUSEUM. The International Tennis Hall of Fame and Museum is located in Newport, Rhode Island, on the grounds of the **Newport Casino.** The Casino, built in 1880, was the site of the first **United States National Championships** in 1881. The Tennis Hall of Fame was created in 1954 by **James Van Alen**. In addition to the museum, the Casino has an indoor **court tennis** facility, 13 **grass courts**, one red **clay** court, and three indoor **hard courts**, all open to the public. The Hall of Fame also hosts an annual **Association of Tennis Professionals** grass tournament during its induction week. Through 2010, there have been 218 players and contributors inducted in the Hall of Fame. The facility also houses a substantial Information Research Center containing photo and document collections, a library, and an audio, film, and video collection. *See also* APPENDIX A (for a list of inductees).

ISNER, JOHN ROBERT. B. 26 April 1985, Greensboro, North Carolina. The six-foot nine-inch John Isner is one of the tallest men ever to play **professional** tennis. His height helps him have one of the most difficult **serves** to return, and he accumulates many **aces** in most of his matches. A graduate of Walter Hines Page Senior High School in Greensboro, he played **collegiate** tennis at the University of Georgia. He was defeated by Somdev Devvarman in the 2007 **National Collegiate Athletic Association (NCAA)** final, but Georgia won the NCAA team championship. Upon graduating college in 2007, with a degree in speech communication, he became a professional tennis player. After winning a Futures and a **Challenger** tournament, he was given a last-minute **wild-card** entry to the **Association of Tennis Professionals (ATP)** Legg Mason Tennis Classic in Washington DC. He defeated five **ranked** players in five consecutive days, all in third-**set tie breakers**, and reached the final, where he lost to **Andy Roddick**. Isner raised his ranking from 839, when he began as a professional, to 193 after just six weeks. In the **United States Open** later that summer, he won his first two **matches** but lost his third-round match in four sets to the eventual champion, **Roger Federer**. Isner was one of only two players to win a set from Federer in that tournament and had 66 total aces in his three matches.

In 2008, at the **Australian Open**, he teamed with the tallest player in tennis, 6-foot 10-inch **Ivo Karlović**, to become the tallest **doubles** team in tennis history but lost in the first round. After recovering from mononucleosis in 2009, Isner played another memorable match in the United States Open. In the first round, against Victor Hănescu, Isner won in straight sets, and he won the second set tiebreak by a 16–14 score and saved 10 **set points** in doing so. In the third round of that tournament, he defeated the fifth-ranked Andy Roddick but lost in the next round to Fernando Verdasco in four sets. Isner received the ATP Most Improved Player award in 2009. His first appearance on the United States **Davis Cup** team was in March 2010, when he was defeated in two **singles** matches but won the doubles match with **Bob Bryan** as a substitute for Bob's injured brother, **Mike**. Isner reached a world ranking of 18 in July 2010 but most likely will rise even higher as he makes his mark in the tennis world.

On 24 June 2010, John Isner defeated Nicolas Mahut in the most incredible match in tennis history. The first round match at **Wimbledon**, which required three days to complete, took 11 hours and 5 minutes of elapsed time and 183 games. The fifth set required 138 games and took 8 hours and 11 minutes. The score was 6–4, 3–6, 6–7 (7), 7–6 (3), 70–68. Isner served 112 aces to Mahut's 103, both numbers easily breaking the previous record of 78. *See also* LONGEST MATCH IN TENNIS HISTORY.

In 2011, he teamed with Bethanie Mattek-Sands to win the **Hopman Cup** in January. Isner and partner **Sam Querrey** were runners-up at a doubles tournament in April and won a doubles championship in May. At the 2011 **French Open**, he won two of the first three sets from **Rafael Nadal** before losing in five sets. This was the first time that Nadal was required to play five sets at **Roland Garros**. Through July 2011, Isner has won two singles and three doubles championships but will undoubtedly win more before his tennis career is over.

ISRAEL. The Israel Tennis Association, founded in 1950, is the governing body for tennis in Israel. The Israel Tennis Center, a separate not-for-profit organization, founded in 1976, runs 14 tennis facilities throughout the country to promote physical education among Israel's youth. From 1949 through May 2011, Israel has entered 58 **Davis Cup tournaments**, has a record of 43–57 in 100 **ties**, and has competed nine times in the World Group since its formation in 1981. In 2009, Israel was a tournament semifinalist. Top Davis Cup players have been Shlomo Glickstein, Andy Ram, Jonathan Ehrlich, and Eleazar Davidman.

Israel had entrants in **Olympic** tennis in 1984, 1988, 1992, 2004, and 2008. The best result was in 2004 when Jonathan Erlich and Andy Ram reached the quarterfinals in men's doubles. Other top male players include Noam Behr, Gilad Bloom, Harel Levy, Amos Mansdorf, Noam Okun, Shahar Perkiss, and Dudi Sela. The best female tennis players are Shahar Pe'er, Ilana Berger, Tzipora Obziler, Hila Rosen, and Anna Smashnova. In **Federation Cup** competition, from 1972 to May 2011, Israel has competed 38 years, 19 years in World Group, and played 127 ties with a record of 66–61. Israel's best result was in 2008, when it reached the World Group, losing in the first round.

There have been some political interventions with Israeli players. The 2009 Davis Cup match with **Sweden** in Malmo, Sweden, was held behind closed doors without spectators due to potential protests. Israel defeated Sweden and later defeated **Russia** in an upset to reach the semifinals. Shahar Pe'er was denied a visa to play in Dubai in 2009, but other players supported her, and the following year, she was allowed to play there. One of the best examples of sport transcending politics is the **doubles** team of Israeli Amir Hadad and Muslim Pakistani Aisam-Ul-Haq Qureshi, who reached the third round at **Wimbledon** in 2002. The following year, the teammates received the **Arthur Ashe** Humanitarian award from the **Association of Tennis Professionals** for their efforts.

ITALY. Tennis in Italy is administered by the Federazione Italiana Tennis founded in 1910. One of the most prestigious tournaments for both men and women is the Internazionale d'Italia played at the Foro Italico in Rome. Italy first competed in **Olympic** tennis in 1920. Since then, Italy has entered contestants in each Olympic Games in which tennis was played. In 1924, Count Umberto de Morpurgo won the bronze medal in men's **singles**. In 1968, **Nicola Pietrangeli** finished third in the men's singles **exhibition**. In 1984, Paolo Cane, in men's singles, and Raffaella Reggi, in women's singles, each finished third in the demonstration tournaments. Since then, there have been no other Italian tennis medalists.

From 1922 through May 2011, Italy has competed in 80 **Davis Cup** tournaments with a record of 153–80 in 233 **ties**. Italy competed 20 times in the World Group since its formation in 1981, won the Cup in 1976, and has been runner-up six times, most recently in 1998. Top Davis Cup players have been Nicola Pietrangeli and Orlando Sirola. Pietrangeli, with an overall record of 120–44, 78–32 in singles and 42–12 in **doubles**, holds the Davis Cup records for most **rubbers** (164), most singles wins, and most doubles wins. He and Sirola hold the record for most successful doubles partnership with a record of 34–8. Other top Italian men's players include Corrado Barrazutti, Paolo Bertulucci, Giorgio di Stefani, Fabio Fognini, Potito Starace, Filippo Volandri, and Tonino Zugarelli.

The best Italian female players include Maria Elena Camarin, Sara Errani, Silvia Farina Elia, Tathiana Garbin, Flavia Pennetta, Raffaella Reggi, **Francesca Schiavone**, Mara Santangelo, and Roberta Vinci. In **Federation Cup** competition, from 1963 to May 2011, Italy has competed all 49 years, 43 years in World Group, played 120 ties with a record of 67–53, and was the champion in 2006, 2009, and 2010 and runner-up in 2007.

IVANIŠEVIĆ, GORAN SIMUN. B. 13 September 1971, Split, **Croatia**, **Yugoslavia**. The 6-foot 4-inch, 180-pound Goran Ivanišević played professionally from 1988 until 2005 and was known for his powerful **left-handed serve**. He reached the finals at **Wimbledon** in 1992, 1994, and 1998 but, despite recording 39 **aces**, lost to **Andre Agassi** in five **sets** in 1992, Pete

Sampras in three sets in 1994, and Sampras in five sets in 1998. In 1992, he totaled more than 200 aces in 7 **matches** at Wimbledon. He competed in four **Olympic Games**, from 1988 to 2000, and won bronze medals in both **singles** and **doubles** (with Goran Prpić) in 1992. In 1990 (with **Petr Korda**) and again in 1999 (with Jeff Tarango), he reached the doubles finals at the French Open. From 1999 to 2001, he suffered from a shoulder injury, and his performance and rankings fell. In 2001, he was only ranked 125, but due to his previous successes at Wimbledon, he was given a **wild-card** entry into the **main draw**. He then won seven consecutive matches and the Wimbledon championship. His seven victims were **qualifier** Fredrik Jonsson, **Carlos Moyá**, **Andy Roddick**, **Greg Rusedski**, **Marat Safin**, **Tim Henman**, and **Pat Rafter**. His semifinal and final match both required five sets, and he became the only wild card and lowest ranked player to win Wimbledon. He played **Davis Cup** for Yugoslavia from 1988 to 1991.

After Croatia became an independent nation, Ivanišević played for the country from 1993 to 2005. He was a member of the 2005 Davis Cup championship team, although he did not see any action that year. His combined Cup record was 28–9 in singles and 20–6 in doubles in 26 ties over 13 years. He was a member of the Yugoslavian **World Team Cup** championship team in 1990. He won the **Hopman Cup** in 1996 with partner Iva Majoli. In his career, Ivanišević won 22 singles titles and 9 doubles titles and had an **Association of Tennis Professionals (ATP)** career match record of 599–333. Although retired from the main tour, he continues to play in the ATP **Champions Tour**.

J

JACOBS, HELEN HULL. B. 8 August 1908, Globe, Arizona. D. 2 June 1997. Helen Jacobs was raised in Berkeley, California, and learned her tennis at the Berkeley Tennis Club. She graduated from the University of California and was one of the world's best female tennis players from 1927 to 1941 and was **ranked** number one in the world in 1936. A 5-foot 6-inch, 145-pound right-hander, she was a contemporary of several of the other great female tennis players, and thus her record, while outstanding, was not quite as spectacular as it could have been had she played in a different era. Of the 27 **Grand Slam** finals she reached, she only won 9. Although she won the **Wimbledon** ladies' **singles** in 1936, the **United States National** women's singles four consecutive years from 1932 to 1935, the U.S. National women's **doubles** with **Sarah Palfrey** in 1932, 1934, and 1935, and U.S. National **mixed doubles** with **George Lott** in 1934, she lost in the finals at Grand Slam tournaments 11 times in singles, 6 times in women's doubles, and once in mixed doubles.

Her nemesis was usually **Helen Wills**, who defeated her in 1929, 1932, 1935, and 1938 at Wimbledon, in 1930 at **Roland Garros**, and in 1928 at the U.S. Nationals, or **Alice Marble**, who defeated her in 1936, 1939, and 1940 at the U.S. Nationals. Jacobs also lost to **Dorothy Round** at Wimbledon in 1934 and to Margaret Scriven at Roland Garros in 1934. Jacobs lost in women's doubles at Wimbledon in 1932 with **Elizabeth "Bunny" Ryan**, 1936 with Sarah Palfrey, and 1939 with Billie Yorke. Ironically, each of her three Wimbledon partners won doubles there with different partners. Jacobs lost the 1934 **French National** women's doubles with Sarah Palfrey and the U.S. Nationals in 1936 with her; Jacobs also lost in 1931 with Dorothy Round and mixed doubles in 1932 with **Ellsworth Vines**. She played on the **United States Wightman Cup** team from 1927 to 1937 and 1939. Her record for those events was 14–8 in singles and 5–3 in doubles.

Jacobs served in U.S. Navy intelligence during the World War II and reached the rank of commander, one of only five women to do so. The author of 19 books, including some fiction, in 1943, when still a lieutenant (junior grade) in the Naval Reserve, she authored a book about her life in the military service, *"By Your Leave, Sir": The Story of a WAVE.* She was inducted into the **International Tennis Hall of Fame** in 1962. She never married, and her lifelong companion, Virginia Gurnee, survived her.

JAEGER, ANDREA. B. 4 June 1965, Chicago, Illinois. Andrea Jaeger was a top tennis player before she graduated Chicago's Stevenson High School. She won the **Orange Bowl** tournament in 1979 and turned **professional** that year. In 1980, shortly after her 15th birthday, she became the youngest player to be **seeded** in the **main draw** at **Wimbledon**—a record later broken by **Jennifer Capriati.** That year, she reached the quarterfinals at Wimbledon and the semifinals at the **United States Open.** In 1981, she and 16-year-old **Jimmy Arias** won the **French Open mixed doubles**, the youngest pair ever to win a **Grand Slam** mixed doubles. She had her best year in 1982 as she was a semifinalist at the **Australian Open**, finalist at the French Open (losing to **Martina Navratilova**), reached the fourth round at Wimbledon, and reached the semifinals at the United States Open. In 1983, she did not play in Australia but was a semifinalist at the French Open, finalist at Wimbledon (again losing to Navratilova), and a quarterfinalist at the United States Open. She played singles for the **United States Federation Cup** team in 1981 and 1983, had a record of 8–1, and was on the Cup championship team in 1981. She played on the United States **Wightman Cup** team in 1980 and 1981 and had a record of 3–1. She competed in the 1984 **Olympic** demonstration tournament but lost in the second round.

In 1985, Andrea suffered a severe shoulder injury, and her career was effectively ended, although she did continue playing some until 1987. She returned to college and studied theology. She devoted her life to philanthropy by establishing a foundation in Aspen, Colorado, to work with children who are cancer patients. On 16 September 2006, she became an Anglican Dominican nun and is now known as Sister Andrea.

JANKOVIĆ, JELENA. B. 28 February 1985, Belgrade, **Serbia**, **Yugoslavia.** Jelena Janković began playing tennis as a nine-year-old in Serbia and was a member of the Red Star Tennis Club in Belgrade. She later trained at the **Nick Bollettieri** Academy in Florida. She became a **professional** in 2000, and in 2001, she won the **Australian Open Junior** Championship. She reached the singles finals of the **United States Open** in 2008, losing to **Serena Williams.** Janković was a semifinalist at the Australian Open in 2008 and the **French Open** in 2007, 2008, and 2010 and reached the fourth round at **Wimbledon** four times. She has won 1 **doubles** and 13 **singles** titles. In 2008, she reached a world number-one **ranking.** The 5-foot 10-inch, 130-pound right-hander won the 2007 Wimbledon **mixed doubles** with partner Jamie Murray. She is extremely personable and is an excellent retriever, able to slide on all **surfaces**. She competed in singles in both the 2004 and 2008 **Olympic Games** and reached the quarterfinals in 2008. She played in the **Federation Cup** from 2001 to 2005 and 2007 to 2010, representing Yugoslavia in 2001 to 2003, Serbia and Montenegro in 2004 and 2005, and Serbia from 2007 to 2011. Through May 2011, her record was 24–7 in singles and 7–5 in doubles in 27 **ties**.

JAPAN. The Japan Tennis Association administers the sport in Japan. Since 1920, Japan has competed in **Olympic** tennis and has not missed an Olympic tennis competition. Japan's best showing was in 1920 when Ichiya Kumagae won the silver medal in men's **singles** and Kumagae and Seiichiro Kashio won the silver medal in men's **doubles**. In 2004, the team of Ai Sugiyama and Shinobu Asagoe finished fourth in women's doubles. Sugiyama, in 2001, achieved a number-one **ranking** in doubles, the first Asian to do so. She also won doubles championships at three of the four major **tournaments** in her career and was runner-up seven times. From 1921 through May 2011, Japan has competed in 77 **Davis Cup** tournaments with a record of 97–77 in 174 **ties**, competing twice in the World Group since its formation in 1981. In 1921, in Japan's first Davis Cup tournament, the team was the runner-up, losing to the **United States** in the final. Top Davis Cup players have been Tsuyoshi Fukui, Satoshi Iwabuchi, and Takao Suzuki. Among the best male tennis players have been Kosei Kamo, Shuzo Matsuoka, Ryuki Miki, Atsushi Miyagi, Kei Nishikori, Ryosuke Nunoi, Jiro Sato, and Zenzo Shimizu. Sato, a **Wimbledon** doubles finalist in 1933, with a 22–6 record in Davis Cup play, achieved a world ranking of three in 1933 by reaching the semifinals at **Roland Garros** and Wimbledon but committed suicide on 5 April 1934 by jumping from a ship in the Strait of Malacca. The best female tennis players include Shinobu Asagoe, Kimiko Date-Krumm, Rika Hiraki, Ayumi Morita, Kyoko Nagatsuka, Naoko Sato, Kazuku Sawamatsu, Naoko Sawamatsu, and Ai Sugiyama. In **Federation Cup** competition, from 1964 to May 2011, Japan has competed 44 years, 32 in World Group, played 133 ties with a record of 78–55. Japan's best result was reaching the semifinals in 1996.

JĘDRZEJOWSKA (GALLERT), JADWIGA "JA-JA." B. 15 October 1912, Kraków, **Poland**. D. 28 February 1980, Katowice, Poland. Jadwiga Jędrzejowska was Poland's best female tennis player. She entered her first **Wimbledon singles tournament** in 1931 and was still competing in major tournament **doubles** in 1957 when she reached the quarterfinals of the **French Nationals**. In 1936, she was a finalist in women's doubles at **Roland Garros** with partner Susan Noel. She reached the women's **singles** final at

Wimbledon in 1937 but was defeated by **Dorothy Round**. Jędrzejowska reached her highest world ranking of three that year as she also was a finalist at **Forest Hills** but was defeated by the tiny Anita Lizana. In a preliminary **match** during that tournament, on 6 September, she defeated Edna Smith in just 18 minutes, 6–1, 6–1. In 1938, she and **Simone Mathieu** reached the women's doubles finals at Forest Hills. At Roland Garros, in 1939, Jadwiga was defeated by Mathieu for the women's singles title but then teamed with her to win the doubles for Jadwiga's only major title. After World War II, she was **mixed doubles** finalist at Roland Garros in 1947. She won 65 national titles, the last one in 1966 (women's doubles), when she was 52 years old. Had her career not been interrupted by World War II, she undoubtedly would have won more championships.

JEU DE PAUME. See COURT TENNIS.

JOHNSON, ROBERT WALTER "WHIRLWIND." B. 16 April 1899, Norfolk, Virginia. D. 1 June 1971, Lynchburg, Virginia. Robert W. Johnson was born to Jerry John Johnson and Nancy Scott Johnson on Jerry's 25th birthday. Jerry was a logging contractor, and the family lived a middle-class existence, despite the fact that they were **African Americans** living in the southern United States during the early 20th century. Robert enrolled at historically black Shaw University and played football there but was asked to leave due to his constant rule breaking in the pursuit of enjoyment. He then entered Virginia Union but, again, couldn't last more than one year. His final stop was Lincoln University in Pennsylvania. At Lincoln, his football prowess became legendary, and he was named to the Negro All-America team. After his graduation, he worked as a railroad porter and then football **coach** at Virginia Seminary College, Morris Brown College, and Atlanta University. He entered Meharry Medical College, and while interning at Prairie View Hospital in Texas, he discovered tennis.

He began his medical practice in Lynchburg, Virginia, and as it grew rapidly, he was able to move into a large house in a predominantly white neighborhood with an adjoining piece of land. He built a tennis **court** on that land and would play tennis there in his spare time with other local black professionals. He and his friend, Dr. Hubert Eaton, became aware of **Althea Gibson** and would invite her to live in Lynchburg with their families in the summers. Dr. Johnson became her mentor and taught her the proper rules of etiquette on and off the court. He also played **mixed doubles** with her in the American Tennis Association (ATA) and won its national title seven years from 1948 to 1955, missing out only in 1951. With help from such established stars as

Alice Marble, Althea was finally able to crack the color line and, in a few years, was **Wimbledon** and **United States National** champion.

Dr. Johnson continued his summertime backyard junior tennis training program with other black players, teaching them technique, discipline, and good nutritional habits. His next major accomplishment was in directing **Arthur Ashe**, who also became a Wimbledon and U.S. National champion. Dr. Johnson continued supporting players throughout his life, although at times, he became involved in political conflicts with the leaders of the ATA. His story is told in *Whirlwind: The Godfather of Black Tennis*, a 2004 book by Doug Smith. Johnson was inducted into the **International Tennis Hall of Fame** in 2009.

JOHNSTON, WILLIAM M. "BILL," "LITTLE BILL." B. 2 November 1894, San Francisco, California. D. 1 May 1946, San Francisco, California. Bill Johnston was known as "Little Bill" throughout much of his tennis playing career to distinguish him from his teammate and rival, **William "Big Bill" Tilden**. Johnston learned his game on the public parks' courts of San Francisco and was a graduate of Lowell High School. At 5 feet 8 inches tall and 120 pounds, the right-handed Johnston had a powerful **forehand** that was considered to be the best in his era. He played at **Wimbledon** only twice, 1920 and 1923, and was the men's **singles** champion in 1923. In 1915, he won the **United States National** men's singles, defeating **Maurice McLoughlin**. The following year, Johnston was defeated by **Richard Norris Williams** in the final. Johnston then served in the U.S. Navy during World War I. From 1919 to 1925, Little Bill Johnston met Big Bill Tilden in the U.S. National singles each year. Johnston won the first meeting in 1919 but then lost to Tilden six times in six years. They met in the finals in each year except 1921. That year, Tilden defeated Johnston in a preliminary round, and because of this, **seeding** was instituted in the tournament in subsequent years.

Johnston won the U.S. National men's **doubles** three times with Clarence Griffin (1915, 1916, 1920) and lost in the finals in 1927 with Williams as his partner. In 1921, he and **Mary K. Browne** defeated Tilden and **Molla Mallory** for the U.S. National **mixed doubles**. He played **Davis Cup** tennis for the United States each year from 1920 to 1927, compiling a record of 14–3 in singles and 4–0 in doubles with Bill Tilden, while helping to lead the team to the Cup seven consecutive years from 1920 to 1926. In 1927, he lost the fifth and deciding **rubber** to **Henri Cochet** to give **France** its first Cup victory and retired from competition shortly afterward. He died of tuberculosis in 1946, at the age of 51, and was inducted into the **International Tennis Hall of Fame** in 1958.

JUNIOR TENNIS. Junior tennis consists of **tournaments** for players less than 18 years of age. Tournaments are sponsored by the **International Tennis Federation** and are generally limited to players of a certain age or under. Tournaments are held for players 12 years old and under, 14 and under, 16 and under, and 18 and under. Particularly talented junior players have often played (and won) in regular tournaments without regard to age. In the major tournaments, such as **Wimbledon** or **United States Open**, the junior event designation is boys' or girls' to distinguish it from the men's and women's events.

KAFELNIKOV, YEVGENY ALEKSANDROVICH. B. 18 February 1974, Sochi, **Russia**, Union of Soviet Socialist Republics. Yevgeny Kafelnikov began his **professional** tennis career in 1992, at the age of 18. In 1994, he was voted the **Association of Tennis Professionals (ATP)** Most Improved Player. By 1995, he was **ranked** in the top 10 of the world, and in 1999, he reached a ranking of number one. In 1996, he became the first Russian to win a **Grand Slam singles** title when he won the **French Open**. He won his second major singles title in 1999 at the **Australian Open** and was a finalist there in 2000. In his career, he reached the semifinals of the **United States Open** twice and was a quarterfinalist at **Wimbledon**. In **doubles**, he won the **French Open** three times (1996, 1997, 2002) and United States Open in 1997. The 6-foot 3-inch, 185-pound right-hander also won the 2000 **Olympic** men's singles event. He competed in doubles as well but was defeated in the second round. He played **Davis Cup** tennis for Russia each year from 1993 to 2003, had a record of 31–16 in singles and 13–12 in doubles, and helped Russia reach the finals in 1994 and 1995 and win the Cup in 2002. One of his major accomplishments was defeating **Roger Federer** in four of six matches, one of very few players to hold an edge over Federer. Kafelnikov had a career record of 609–306 in singles and 358–213 in doubles and won 26 singles and 27 doubles titles. Since retiring from the ATP tour in 2004, he has played on the European Professional Golf Association tour, competed in the 2005 World Series of Poker, competed in the ATP **Champions Tour**, and done television commentary for Russian television.

KARLOVIĆ, IVO "DR. IVO." B. 28 February 1979, Zagreb, **Croatia**, Yugoslavia. Ivo Karlović is the tallest person to ever play **professional** tennis. At 6 feet 10 inches tall, he towers over most of his opponents. His **serve** is one of the best in the game, and he has set many **tournament** records for **aces**. On 5 March 2011, he set the world's record for fastest serve when one of his serves was measured at 156 miles per hour (251 km/h) during a Davis Cup doubles match against Germany in Zagreb, Croatia. Despite his height, he is fairly agile and moves well. He began his professional tennis career in 2000. One of his most notable victories came in his first **Grand Slam match**.

Karlović, ranked 203, first had to **qualify** to reach the **main draw** at **Wimbledon** in 2003. In the first round of the main draw, he defeated the first **seed** and defending champion, **Lleyton Hewitt**, 1–6, 7–6, 6–3, 6–4. Karlović reached the third round that year before losing to Max Mirnyi in four sets. In 2009, Ivo reached the quarterfinals at Wimbledon, his best showing at a slam event. He reached the third round of the men's singles at the 2004 **Olympic Games**.

He played **Davis Cup** tennis for Croatia from 2000 to 2011 and appeared in 12 ties over 8 years with a record of 7–7 in **singles** and 3–3 in **doubles**. Although Croatia won the Cup in 2005, he only played one match in a **dead rubber** in the semifinal round. In a Davis Cup match against Radek Stepanek in 2009, Karlović served a record 78 aces but lost 7–6, 6–7, 6–7, 7–6, 14–16 in 5 hours and 59 minutes. There were only three **service** breaks in the entire match. In 2008, Karlović teamed with six-foot nine-inch **John Isner** at the **Australian Open** to form the world's tallest doubles team, but they were defeated in the first round. Isner, in a marathon singles match at Wimbledon in June 2010, surpassed Karlović's match record for aces. Through May 2011, Karlović has four **Association of Tennis Professionals (ATP)** tournament singles victories and three second place finishes. He also won one doubles event (with Chris Haggard) and finished second once. His highest ATP ranking has been 14 in singles in 2008.

KING, BILLIE JEAN MOFFITT. B. 22 November 1943, Long Beach, California. Billie Jean King has done more for the sport of **lawn tennis** and women's equality in sport than anyone else. In her long career, from 1959 to 1983, she reached the finals of 65 **Grand Slam** events, winning 39 of them; 53 of the 65 finals were at **Wimbledon** (28) and the **United States Nationals** (25), and 33 of her 39 championships were at those two venues. From 1966 to 1975, she was the Wimbledon **singles** finalist in 8 of the 10 years, winning in 1966, 1967, 1968, 1972, 1973, and 1975 and finishing second in 1969 and 1970. She was also an excellent **doubles** player, winning Wimbledon 10 times and finishing second twice. She won in 1961 and 1962 with Karen Hantze, 1965 with **Maria Bueno**, 1967, 1968, 1970, 1971, and 1973 with **Rosie Casals**, 1972 with **Betty Stove**, and 1979 with **Martina Navratilova**. She is 1 of only 15 players (6 women and 9 men) to win **mixed doubles** at all four Grand Slam tournaments, winning four times each at Wimbledon and the U.S. Nationals, twice at **Roland Garros**, and once in Australia. She won 8 of the 11 mixed doubles titles with Owen Davidson and once each with Dick Crealy, **Bob Hewitt**, and **Phil Dent**. Only **Margaret Smith Court**, Martina Navratilova, and **Doris Hart** appeared in more Grand Slam finals, and only Court and Navratilova won more Grand Slam titles.

In one of the most publicized (and significant) **matches** in tennis history, former Wimbledon champion 55-year-old **Bobby Riggs** challenged

Billie Jean King, finalist in 65 Grand Slam events and winner of 39 of them, did more for women's equality in sport than anyone else. (courtesy of the International Tennis Hall of Fame and Museum, Edward Fernberger collection)

the 29-year-old Billie Jean King to a $100,000 winner-take-all "battle of the sexes" match that was held at the Astrodome in Houston, Texas, on 20 September 1973. Riggs had previously defeated Margaret Smith Court earlier that year. Played before 30,492 fans in a circus-like atmosphere, Riggs was trounced by King, 6–4, 6–3, 6–3. That match helped to give women's tennis a large boost in popularity. Riggs remained friends with King until his death in 1995.

She was raised in Southern California and attended Long Beach Polytechnic High School and California State University, Los Angeles, and learned to play tennis on the public courts in Long Beach. A **serve-and-volley** player, although only 5 feet 4 inches and 130 pounds, her greatest strengths were her quickness and strong competitive spirit. Her first major victory was at Wimbledon in 1961, when she and partner Karen Hantze, both only 18 years old, became the youngest pair to win the ladies' doubles there. Billie Jean won singles championships at all four major venues—six at Wimbledon, four at the United States Nationals, and one each at **Roland Garros** and the **Australian Championships**. She was also the losing singles finalist three times at Wimbledon, twice at the U.S. Nationals, and once at the Australian. Her younger brother, Randy Moffitt, was a major league baseball relief pitcher for 12 years with the San Francisco Giants, Houston Astros, and Toronto Blue Jays.

She married Lawrence King on 17 September 1965. They were childless and divorced in 1987. She and he created **World Team Tennis** in 1973. She has been a player, **coach**, and administrator in that organization since that time and is still active in promoting it. She played on the **United States Federation Cup** team from 1963 to 1967 as an **amateur** and 1976 to 1979 as a **professional**. In 36 **ties**, her record was 26–3 in singles and 26–1 in doubles. In each one of the eight years she competed in the Federation Cup, her team reached the final round. She was a member of the Cup championship team in 1963, 1966, 1967, 1976, 1977, 1978, and 1979 and was on the runner-up team in 1964 and 1965. She played on the United States **Wightman Cup** team 10 years, from 1961 to 1978, and had a record of 14–2 in singles and 7–3 in doubles. She was inducted into the **International Tennis Hall of Fame** in 1987. On 12 August 2009, she was awarded the Presidential Medal of Freedom and is one of only two tennis players to receive that honor. (The other was **Arthur Ashe**, posthumously.)

KNOWLES, MARK SAMUEL. B. 4 September 1971, Nassau, Bahamas. Mark Knowles is the Bahamas' greatest tennis player. The son of Nassau tennis **professionals**, he trained at the **Nick Bollettieri** Tennis Academy. He won the **United States** Indoor **Junior Singles** Championship at the age of 15.

He attended the University of California in Los Angeles and was selected as an All-American. The six-foot three-inch right-hander became a professional player in 1991 and was still playing in 2011. As a **singles** player, he never passed the second round of a **Grand Slam** tournament, and his highest **ranking** was 96 in 1996. He became a **doubles** specialist and reached the world number-one ranking in 2002. Playing with partner Daniel Nestor, they won the **Australian Open** in 2002, the **French Open** in 2004, and the **United States Open** in 2007. He and Nestor were also finalists twice each in Australia and once each at **Wimbledon** and the United States Open. Their partnership ended in 2007, and Knowles then teamed with **Mahesh Bhupathi** and reached the finals in Australia and the U.S. Open in 2009. Knowles also won the French Open **mixed doubles** in 2002 with Elena Bovina and Wimbledon mixed doubles in 2009 with Anna-Lena Grönefeld.

Knowles held the record for the longest **match** at Wimbledon—singles or doubles—until **John Isner** and Nicolas Mahut surpassed it in 2010. On 5 July 2006, he and Nestor defeated Simon Aspelin and Todd Perry in six hours and nine minutes over two days by a score of 5–7, 6–3, 6–7, 6–3, 23–21. The fifth **set** lasted more than three hours, and they saved five **match points** to win. Interestingly, the team that set the previous Wimbledon doubles record for longest match, 21 years earlier, Heinz Günthardt and Balázs Taróczy, happened to be playing in an over-45 doubles match while the Nestor–Knowles/Aspelin–Perry match was taking place.

Knowles is one of only four players (**Ladislav Žemla, Arantxa Sánchez Vicario, Leander Paes**) to compete in tennis in five **Olympic Games**, but despite being one of the most successful doubles players of his era, he only managed to reach the Olympic quarterfinals once. He also competed in the 1996 Olympic singles event but lost in the first round. He has played **Davis Cup** tennis for the Bahamas from 1989 to 2008. His Cup record is 23–25 in singles and 18–7 in doubles in 29 **ties** over 14 years. In his long career, through May 2011, Knowles has won 53 doubles championships and been runner-up 45 times. Knowles has hosted an annual celebrity charity tennis tournament in the Bahamas since 2001. *See also* LONGEST MATCH IN TENNIS HISTORY.

KODEŠ, JAN. B. 1 March 1946, Prague, **Czechoslovakia**. Jan Kodeš was best known as a **clay court** player and was the **French Open singles** champion in 1970 and 1971. Only five feet nine inches tall, he also won **Wimbledon** in 1973 on a **grass** court, although the championship was somewhat tainted since 13 of the top 16 men's players boycotted the **tournament** that year. He was runner-up at the **United States Open** in 1971 and 1973, when that tournament was played on grass and a full roster of top players competed.

In 1971, as an **unseeded** player, his first round victory was over the number-one seed, **John Newcombe**. In 1973, he achieved his highest world **ranking** at number five and lost in the finals of the United States Open in five sets to Newcombe. He also graduated from the University of Economics in Prague that year.

He played **Davis Cup** tennis for Czechoslovakia every year from 1966 to 1980 and holds the Czechoslovakian Davis Cup records for most years played, **ties** played, total wins, and singles wins. His record in 39 ties over 15 years is 39–19 in **singles** and 21–15 in **doubles**. He played in the final round in 1975 when Czechoslovakia was defeated by **Sweden**, 3–2, and was on the team for a preliminary round tie in 1980 but did not play in the final when Czechoslovakia won the Cup. He captained the Czech Davis Cup team from 1982 to 1987. In his career, he won 8 tournaments (including 3 Grand Slam events) and was runner-up 18 times. He was inducted into the **International Tennis Hall of Fame** in 1990. From 1994 to 1998, he was the president of the Czech Tennis Association. He was also the tournament director of the **Association of Tennis Professionals** Czech Open from 1987 to 1998. He has also been a partner in Hugo Boss men's and women's luxury clothing stores.

KOOYONG STADIUM. Kooyong Stadium is a **grass court lawn tennis** facility in Melbourne, **Australia**, built in 1927 and was the site of the **Australian Championships** until 1988. Its seating capacity is 8,500.

KORDA, PETR. B. 23 January 1968, Prague, **Czechoslovakia**. Petr Korda did well as a **junior** player winning the **French Open boys' doubles** title in 1985 and earning a junior **ranking** of number one. He became a **professional** tennis player in 1987. The 6-foot 3-inch, 160-pound left-hander played **Davis Cup** tennis for Czechoslovakia each year from 1988 to 1992 and for the Czech Republic each year from 1993 to 1997. In 10 years of Cup play, his record was 18–9 in **singles** and 11–4 in doubles in 18 **ties**. He won the **Hopman Cup** in 1994 with partner **Jana Novotná**. His biggest victory as a professional was in **Australia** in 1998, when he defeated Marcelo Ríos to win the **Australian Open** singles title. In 1996, he teamed with **Stefan Edberg** to win the Australian Open Doubles Championship. He also was a finalist in the French Open doubles in 1990 and singles in 1992. In 1997, he defeated defending champion **Pete Sampras** in the fourth round of the **United States Open** to reach the quarterfinals. He was also a quarterfinalist at **Wimbledon** in 1998. Korda retired from tennis in 1999 after testing positive for a banned substance and incurring a one-year suspension.

He is married to Regina Rajchrtová, a professional tennis player who competed in the 1988 **Olympic Games**. The oldest of their three children, Jessica

Korda, is a golfer who finished 19th in the 2008 United States Women's Open as a 15-year old **amateur** (with her father as caddy). In his tennis career, Korda won 10 singles and 10 doubles championships and had 17 singles and 14 doubles second-place finishes.

KOURNIKOVA, ANNA SERGEYEVNA. B. 7 June 1981, Moscow, **Russia**, Union of Soviet Socialist Republics. Anna Kournikova is the daughter of Dr. Sergei Kournikov, a former Greco-Roman wrestling champion and professor at the University of Physical Culture and Sport. Anna's mother, Alla, had also been an athlete, competing in 400-meter track events. Anna's tennis development began when she was quite young, and by age 10, she was a student at the **Nick Bollettieri** Tennis Academy. She began playing **professional** tennis at the age of 14, in 1995. In 1996, aged 15, she reached the fourth round of the **United States Open** and the following year was a semifinalist at **Wimbledon**. She entered both the **singles** and **doubles** events in the 1996 **Olympic Games**, at the age of 15, but lost both first round **matches**.

She played for the Russian **Fed Cup** team in 1996, 1997, and 2000. In 12 **ties**, her record was 2–5 in singles and 10–2 in doubles. She never quite lived up to her potential, and by 2001, injuries restricted her play and caused her to retire from competitive tennis in 2003, at the age of 22. Although she reached a high singles **ranking** of eight in 2000, she never won a **Women's Tennis Association (WTA)** singles tournament. Her doubles career was more successful as she achieved a ranking of number one in 1999. She and **Martina Hingis** won the **Australian Open** doubles in 1999 and 2002 and were finalists at the **French Open** in 1999. She was 1999 Wimbledon **mixed doubles** finalist with **Jonas Björkman** and United States Open mixed doubles finalist in 2000 with Max Mirnyi. Kournikova had much more success as a model beginning in the mid-1990s. Since retiring from the WTA tour, she has played at numerous charity **exhibition** matches and also in **World Team Tennis**.

KRAJICEK, RICHARD PETER STANISLAV. B. 6 December 1971, Rotterdam, **the Netherlands**. Richard Krajicek became a **professional** tennis player in 1989 after having won several Dutch **junior** championships. In 1992, he reached the semifinals at the **Australian Open** but was forced to withdraw due to a shoulder injury. The following year, the six-foot five-inch right-hander was a semifinalist at the **French Open**. The highlight of his career occurred in 1996 when he won the **Wimbledon** men's **singles** championship after defeating defending champion **Pete Sampras** in the quarterfinals. This was Sampras' only Wimbledon defeat in the eight years from 1993 to 2000. Krajicek's best performance at the **United States Open** was the quarterfinals, which he reached three times. In his 1999 quarterfinal-round five-set loss to **Yevgeny Kafelnikov** there, Krajicek set a record (since surpassed) for most **aces** in an **Association of Tennis Professionals (ATP)** match with 49. In 1999, Krajicek was **ranked** fourth worldwide, his best career singles ranking. He played **Davis Cup** tennis for the Netherlands from 1991 to 1996 and 1999 to 2000. In nine **ties**, his record was 6–8 in **singles** and 1–0 in **doubles** in eight years.

In 1999, he married actress-model Daphne Deckers. The couple has two children. In 2000, he received the ATP **Arthur Ashe** Humanitarian of the Year award and, in 2002, was named the ATP Comeback Player of the year. He retired in 2003 with a career record of 17 singles tournament victories, 9 singles runner-up finishes, and 3 doubles victories. His half-sister, Michaella Krajicek, who is younger by 17 years, is also a professional tennis player. In retirement from tennis, he runs the Richard Krajicek Foundation, which builds sports facilities for underprivileged Dutch children, is tournament director for an ATP event in Rotterdam, and has written several books.

KRAMER, JOHN ALBERT "JACK," "JAKE." B. 1 August 1921, Las Vegas, Nevada. D. 12 September 2009, Bel Air, California. Jack Kramer was raised in Southern California and was guided in his development by Perry Jones at the Los Angeles Tennis Club. There, as a **junior**, he played against some of the top players of the day, such as **Ellsworth Vines**, **Bobby Riggs**, and **Bill Tilden**. As a student at Montebello High School, Kramer won the **United States National** Boys' Championship in 1936 and National Junior Interscholastic tournament in 1938. He attended Rollins College and played tennis there in 1941 and 1942. During World War II, he was a member of the U.S. Coast Guard. As the war suspended the major tournaments, he did not get to play at **Wimbledon** until 1946 and was the Wimbledon men's **singles** champion in 1947 and men's **doubles** champion in 1946 and 1947. The **U.S. National Championships** were not suspended for the duration, and Kramer was a finalist in 1943 and champion in 1946 and 1947. He was United States men's doubles champion in 1940, 1941, 1943, and 1947 and **mixed doubles** finalist in 1940 and champion in 1941. Military service precluded him from playing in that tournament in 1942, 1944, and 1945. Tall for his era, at six feet two inches, he was a powerful **serve and volleyer**. He was on the **United States Davis Cup** team in 1939, 1946, and 1947 and was undefeated in singles with a 6–0 record but was just 1–2 in doubles. The United States won the Cup in 1946 and 1947 and lost to **Australia** in the 1939 **challenge round**.

In 1947, after a successful **amateur** career, he became a **professional**. On 26 December 1947, for his professional debut against Bobby Riggs, 15,114 people came to Madison Square Garden despite the worst snowstorm (26.4 inches) in New York City history. Riggs won that match, but Kramer defeated him in that tour, 69 matches to 20. Kramer's next tour opponent was **Pancho Gonzáles**, and Kramer defeated him 96–27. Kramer defeated **Pancho Segura**, 64–28, and **Frank Sedgman**, 54–41, in subsequent tours before retiring in 1954 from competitive play due to a back ailment, although he continued as tour promoter. When **open** tennis arrived in 1968, Kramer helped develop the Grand Prix series of tournaments. He was inducted into the **International Tennis Hall of Fame** in 1968. In 1972, he helped found the **Association of Tennis Professionals** and became its first executive director. He was also one of the main television analysts, both in the United States and England. A successful businessman, the Jack Kramer model tennis **racket** produced by the **Wilson Sporting Goods** company was the most popular racket ever sold, and Kramer's percentage of sales had him earning more money than the president of Wilson. He owned the Jack Kramer Tennis Club in Rolling Hills, California, and later owned the Los Serranos Country Club (golf club) and was an owner of thoroughbred race horses.

KRICKSTEIN, AARON. B. 2 August 1967, Ann Arbor, Michigan. Aaron Krickstein attended the University Liggett School in Grosse Point Woods, Michigan. At the age of 16, he became a **professional** tennis player and became the youngest male to win an **Association of Tennis Professionals (ATP) tournament** when he won in Tel Aviv, **Israel**, just two months after his 16th birthday. Although never winning a **Grand Slam** event, he reached a career-high world **singles ranking** of six in 1990. He did reach the **United States Open** semifinals in 1989 and **Australian Open** semifinals in 1995. His was troubled by injuries throughout his career. His tennis strength was his ability to come from behind, and he won 10 5-**set matches** after losing the first two sets. The 6-foot tall, 160-pound right-hander was on the **United States Davis Cup** team in 1985, 1986, 1987, and 1990. In 1990, although the United States won the Cup, Krickstein only played in the quarterfinal round. His overall Cup record for five **ties** in four years was 6–4 in singles. He did not play **doubles**. He retired from the ATP tour in 1996 with a total of nine singles tournament victories but continues to play in **Champions Tour** events.

KRIEK, JOHAN CHRISTIAN. B. 5 April 1958, Pongola, **South Africa**. Although born in South Africa, Kriek moved to the **United States** in 1978 to begin his **professional** tennis career. His biggest victories were the 1981 and 1982 **Australian Open singles** titles. He also reached the semifinals there in 1984. A **grass-court** player, he only entered the **clay** court **French Open** tournament three times but surprisingly reached the semifinals there in 1986. His best performance at the **United States Open** was the semifinals in 1980 and at **Wimbledon**, the quarterfinals in 1981 and 1982. In 1982, he became an American citizen. He did not play **Davis Cup** tennis for either South Africa or the United States. In his career, he won 14 singles titles and was runner-up 13 times and won 8 **doubles** titles and was runner-up 7 times. He retired from competitive tennis in 1992 and has since devoted his efforts to the Global Water Foundation and his tennis academy in Lakewood Ranch, Florida.

KRISHNAN, RAMANATHAN. See KRISHNAN FAMILY.

KRISHNAN, RAMESH. See KRISHNAN FAMILY.

KRISHNAN FAMILY. Ramanathan Krishnan was born 11 April 1937 in Madras, **India**. His son, Ramesh, was born 5 June 1961, also in Madras (now known as Chennai). The Krishnan family played a vital role in India's **Davis Cup** history, and in 29 years, either father or son was a member of the Indian Davis Cup team. Ramanathan's father, T. K. Ramanathan, was also one of India's top players. In 1954, Ramanathan Krishnan won the **Wimbledon boys' singles** championship. In 1960 and 1961, he again reached the Wimbledon gentlemen's singles semifinals but both times was defeated by the eventual champion—**Neale Fraser** in 1960 and **Rod Laver** in 1961. Krishnan also reached the **French National** Championships quarterfinals in 1962. Ramanathan Krishnan played on the Indian Davis Cup team from 1953 to 1963, 1965 to 1969, and again in 1975, at the age of 43. He helped India reach the final in 1966. His record was 50–19 in singles and 19–9 in **doubles** in 43 **ties** in 16 years. His highest world **ranking** was six in 1961. In retirement, he managed a gas distribution agency.

In 1979, Ramesh Krishnan won both the Wimbledon and **French Open** boys' titles. He played Davis Cup tennis for India from 1977 to 1993. In 24 ties, played in 13 years, his record was 23–19 in singles and 6–2 in doubles. He led India to the final round in 1987, where the team was defeated by **Sweden**. Ramesh competed in the 1992 **Olympic Games** in both singles and doubles and reached the quarterfinal round in the doubles event. Ramesh reached the quarterfinals at Wimbledon and the **United States Open** and won eight **Association of Tennis Professionals** singles titles and one doubles title in his career, which ended in 1993. His highest ranking was 23 in 1985. In retirement, he runs a tennis academy in Chennai and has captained India's Davis Cup team. Father and son have also authored a book about their tennis lives, entitled *A Touch of Tennis: The Story of a Tennis Family.*

KUERTEN, GUSTAVO "GUGA." B. 10 September 1976, Florianópolis, **Brazil**. Gustavo Kuerten began playing tennis at the age of six. His father,

Aldo, was an **amateur** tennis player and tennis official, who died of a heart attack while **umpiring** a tennis match when Gustavo was just eight years old. At the age of 14, Gustavo was mentored by Larri Passos, who helped develop his game and **coached** him for the next 15 years. Gustavo became a **professional** tennis player in 1995 and, two years later, won the **French Open Singles** Championship. He also won the French Open in 2000 and 2001. His best result in the **United States Open** and **Wimbledon** was the quarterfinals. He finished the 2000 season **ranked** number one in the world as a result of his victory at the year-end Tennis Masters Cup tournament. The 6-foot 3-inch, 165 pound right-hander competed in the 2000 and 2004 **Olympic Games**. In 2000, he reached the quarterfinals in the singles event but lost in the **doubles** first round. In 2004, he lost in the first round of the singles. He was a member of the Brazilian **Davis Cup** team each year from 1996 to 2007 except for 2004. In 23 **ties**, his record was 21–11 in singles and 13–7 in doubles. In a Davis Cup **match** in 2003, Kuerten had 47 **aces**, at that time the second highest recorded total in tennis history. In 2000, Brazil reached the Davis Cup semifinals with defeats of **France** and **Slovakia** before losing to **Australia**. Kuerten retired in 2008 following several years of subpar play due to injuries. His **Association of Tennis Professionals** totals include 20 singles and 8 doubles victories.

KUZNETSOVA, SVETLANA ALEKSANDROVNA "SVETA." B. 27 June 1985, Leningrad (now St. Petersburg), **Russia**, Union of Soviet Socialist Republics. Svetlana Kuznetsova comes from an accomplished sporting family. Her father, Aleksandr Kuznetsov, is a cycling **coach** with five **Olympic** champions to his credit. Her mother, the former Galina Tsareva, was a world-champion cyclist. Svetlana's brother, Nikolay, was an Olympic champion cyclist in 1996. Svetlana tried cycling but did not like the sport and played tennis instead. At the age of 13, she went to **Spain** to train at the Sánchez-Casal Academy. In 2000, at the age of 15, she became a **professional** tennis player. By 2004, she won the **United States Open Singles** Championship and five years later won the **French Open singles** title. In 2006, she was runner-up at the French Open to **Justine Henin**, and in 2007, she was runner-up to Henin at the United States Open. The five-foot nine-inch Sveta reached the singles quarterfinals three times at **Wimbledon** and twice at the **Australian Open**. In 2007, she was the second-**ranked** women's singles player in the world. She is also an accomplished **doubles** player, ranked third in 2004, and has won the Australian Open in 2005 and been a losing doubles finalist in all four **Grand Slam** events (Australian Open in 2004, United States Open in 2003 and 2004, French Open in 2004, and Wimbledon in 2005). She competed in both singles and doubles in the 2004 and 2008 Olympic Games and was a singles quarterfinalist in 2004 and doubles quarterfinalist in 2008. She was a member of the Russian **Fed Cup** team in 2004 and 2007 to 2011. Through May 2011, her record was 15–6 in singles and 6–1 in doubles in 13 **ties**. She played for the Cup championship team in 2004, 2007, and 2008 and on 5–6 November 2011 she will play for Russia in the Fed Cup final against the Czech Republic. Through May 2011, still only 25 years old, has won 13 singles championships and was runner-up 19 times.

L

LACOSTE, JEAN RENÉ "THE CROCODILE." B. 2 July 1904, Paris, France. D. 12 October 1996, France. Along with **Jacques "Toto" Brugnon, Jean Borotra,** and **Henri Cochet,** René Lacoste was one of the **Four Musketeers** of tennis. The son of a wealthy automobile manufacturer, he promised his father he would become world champion in five years or abandon the sport for a business career. Nicknamed "the Crocodile" (although reasons for the name are unclear), he reached the finals of the **French National Championships** each year from 1924 to 1929, winning in odd-numbered alternate years. He was also **Wimbledon** champion in 1925 and 1928 and runner-up in 1924 and **United States National** champion in 1926 and 1927. He and Borotra were 1925 Wimbledon men's **doubles** champions, French doubles champions in 1925 and 1929, and French losing finalists in 1927. He and **Hazel Wightman** reached the United States **mixed doubles** finals in 1926 and 1927. He was a student of the game and analyzed his play more than his contemporaries, which resulted in a world number-one **ranking** for him in 1926. He competed in the 1924 **Olympic Games** in Paris and was a quarterfinalist in **singles** and won the bronze medal in the doubles event with partner Jean Borotra. He was a member of the French **Davis Cup** team each year from 1923 to 1928 and helped France win the Cup in 1927 and 1928. He became the nonplaying captain of the team in 1931. His playing record for 26 **ties** was 32–8 in singles and 8–3 in doubles. In 1929, he married French golf star Simone Thion de la Chaume. The couple had four children.

In 1933, he and André Gillier founded the Société Chemise Lacoste, a French apparel company that made a tennis shirt with an alligator (or crocodile) embroidered on the chest. The Lacoste brand of clothing has become one of the largest worldwide. In 1963, his company introduced a new type of tennis **racket** with a frame made of tubular steel, rather than the traditional wood. It was marketed in America by **Wilson Sporting Goods** company and became quite popular. The company has remained in the Lacoste family, with René's son Bernard becoming the manager in 1963 and his brother, Michel, in 2005. René Lacoste was inducted into the **International Tennis Hall of Fame** in 1976, along with the other three Musketeers.

LADIES' INTERNATIONAL TENNIS CHALLENGE. *See* **WIGHTMAN CUP.**

LARSEN, ARTHUR DAVID "ART," "TAPPY." B. 17 April 1925, Hayward, California. After serving in the U.S. Armed Forces during the Second World War, where he spent quite a bit of time on the front lines, Art Larsen turned to tennis to help him forget his wartime experiences, although he continued to have problems with his nerves. A 5-foot 10-inch, 150-pound **left-handed** player, he was known as "Tappy" by his fellow players for his variety of eccentricities, including touching things for good luck. He attended the University of San Francisco and was a member of the 1949 **National Collegiate Athletic Association** national championship team. The next year, he won the **United States National** Men's **Singles** Championship and was the top-**ranked** player in the country and third-ranked in the world. In 1951, he was a semifinalist at the **Australian Championships** and United States National Championships and quarterfinalist at **Wimbledon**. He won the United States **Clay Court** Championships and **Hard Court** Championships in 1952 and Indoor Championships in 1953, becoming the first man to win championships on all four **surfaces** as the 1950 U.S. National Championships, which he won, was played on **grass** at **Forest Hills**. He played singles on the United States **Davis Cup** team in three **ties** in 1951 and 1952 and won all four of his **matches**. In 1954, he was defeated by **Tony Trabert** in the finals of the **French National** Championship men's singles. In 1955, he was the gold medalist at the Pan American Games. His career was cut short by a motor scooter accident on 10 November 1956, where he lost the sight of an eye and was partially paralyzed. He was inducted into the **International Tennis Hall of Fame** in 1969.

LAVER, RODNEY GEORGE "ROD." B. 9 August 1938, Rockhampton, Queensland, **Australia**. Rod Laver is one of the players always mentioned in a discussion of the greatest tennis players of all time. Only 5 feet 8 inches tall and 145 pounds, the redheaded **left-hander** had a powerful **serve** and was one of the first players to employ a lot of **topspin**. He was nicknamed "Rocket" as a teenager by Australian tennis **coach** and **Davis Cup** captain **Harry Hopman**. He is the only man in addition to **Don Budge** to win all four major tennis tournaments in one calendar year—the **Grand Slam**—which he did as an **amateur** in 1962. After doing so, he became a **professional** and was ineligible for those tournaments. When the rules were changed and tournaments became **open** to amateurs and professionals, he won the Grand Slam a second time in 1969. That year, he won 17 singles **tournaments** of 32 played and had a 106–16 **match** record against both amateur and professional opponents. His 1962 season was nearly as good, with 19 of 34 and 134–15 match record against strictly amateur competition. In his career, he won 20 Grand Slam tournament events and was runner-up in 14 others. He was unable to play in them from 1963 to 1968, the height of his career; otherwise, the totals would have been much higher. He was **Australian** champion in 1960, 1962, and 1969 and runner-up in 1961. He was **French National** champion in 1962 and 1969 and runner-up in 1968. He was **Wimbledon** champion in 1961, 1962, 1968, and 1969 and runner-up in 1959 and 1960. He was **United States National** runner-up in 1960 and 1961, in addition to his championships in 1962 and 1969.

He also did well in **doubles**, winning the Australian four times—1959 to 1961 with Bob Mark and 1969 with **Roy Emerson**. He was Wimbledon men's doubles runner-up with Mark in 1959 and champion in 1971 with Emerson. He won the French with Emerson in 1961 and the pair was runner-up there in 1968 and 1969. At the United States Nationals, he was runner-up in 1960 with Mark, in 1970 with Emerson ,and in 1973 with **Ken Rosewall**. In **mixed doubles**, he and **Darlene Hard** won Wimbledon in 1959 and 1960 and the French in 1961, and he and Renee Schuurman were the Australian and French runners-up in 1959. During the years as a professional, he was the finalist at the **U.S. Pro Championships** each year from 1963 to 1970, winning in 1964 and 1966 to 1969. He was a member of the Australian Davis Cup team from 1959 to 1962, but after he became a professional, he was ineligible for further Cup play. After the eligibility rules were changed, he again played for Australia in 1973. Australia won the Cup in each of the five years that he played for that team. His record was 16–4 in singles and 4–0 in doubles in 11 **ties**. He was inducted into the **International Tennis Hall of Fame** in 1981.

In 1998, he suffered a stroke while being interviewed on television but was able to make a complete recovery. In 2000, the **centre court** at Melbourne Park, site of the Australian Open, was renamed the Rod Laver Arena. In 2003, he was honored by the Australia Post with a commemorative postage stamp bearing his portrait.

LAWN TENNIS. "Lawn tennis" is the term given to the game more popularly known as tennis. The game was originally meant to be played outdoors on **grass**, but in the 20th century, other **surfaces**, such as **clay** and asphalt, have been used, and the game is also played indoors. It was originally called lawn tennis to differentiate it from **court tennis** (or real tennis, or *jeu de paume*), an indoor game that is significantly different.

LAWN TENNIS SCORING. *See* SCORING.

LEACH, RICK. B. 28 December 1964, Arcadia, California. Rick Leach is the son of the University of Southern California (USC) tennis **coach**, Dick Leach. Rick played for his father at USC from 1984 to 1987 and was a four-time All-American and the **National Collegiate Athletic Association doubles** champion in 1986 and 1987. The six-foot, two-inch left-hander became a **professional** in 1987. A doubles specialist, his highest **ranking** as a **singles player** was 110 in 1987. He became the world number-one–ranked doubles player in 1990. He won 46 doubles titles in his career and did not win any singles titles. He won 10 **Grand Slam** doubles titles and was a losing finalist 11 other times. At the **Australian Open**, he and Jim Pugh won the men's doubles in 1988 and 1989, and Leach and Ellis Ferreira won in 2000. Leach and Kelly Jones lost to **the Woodies** in Australia in 1992. At **Wimbledon**, he and Pugh won in 1990 after being runners-up in 1989. Leach and Scott Melville also reached the finals in 1995 but were again defeated by the Woodies. He and Pugh lost at **Roland Garros** in 1991, and in the **United States Open**, Leach and Ken Flach won in 1993. Leach also reached the U.S. Open doubles finals in 1988 with Jim Pugh, 1992 with Kelly Jones, and 2000 with Ellis Ferreira but was defeated each time. In Grand Slam **mixed doubles**, Leach and **Zina Garrison** were twice losing finalists at the Australian Open (1990, 1993). He won it in 1995 with **Natasha Zvereva** and again in 1997 with Manon Bollegraf. He and Garrison won Wimbledon in 1990. He and **Larisa Savchenko Neiland** were **French Open** finalists in 1999. In 1997, he and Manon Bollegraf won the United States Open. He lost in 1989 with Meredith McGrath and in 1996 with Bollegraf.

He played **Davis Cup** tennis for the **United States** from 1990 to 1992 and again in 1997 and 2000. His record was 7–3 in doubles and 0–1 in singles in 10 **ties** during those five years. He helped lead the United States to the Cup in 1990 and was a member of the 1992 Cup-winning team, although he did not play in the finals that year. Rick's brother, Jon Leach, was also an All-American tennis player at Stanford and, in 2003, married tennis champion **Lindsay Davenport**. After retiring from active play, Rick Leach became an assistant coach to his father at USC.

LECONTE, HENRI. B. 4 July 1963, Lilliers, **France**. Henri Leconte made his first mark in tennis by winning the **French Open junior singles** title in 1981. He turned **professional** following that victory and, in 1984, won the **French Open** Men's **Doubles** Championship with partner **Yannick Noah**. The following year, the pair reached the finals of the **United States Open** doubles but was defeated by Americans Ken Flach and Robert Seguso. In 1986, Leconte achieved his highest world **ranking** of five in singles and six in doubles as a result of his performances at **Wimbledon**, where he reached the **singles** semifinals, and the United States Open, where he reached the singles quarterfinals. He was also a member of the French **World Team Cup** squad that won the event that year. In 1988, Leconte was defeated in the men's singles final at the French Open by **Mats Wilander**.

The 6-foot 1-inch, 175-pound, **left-handed** Leconte competed in both singles and doubles in the 1988 and 1992 **Olympic Games** and lost in the second round of each event in all but 1988 doubles, where he reached the quarterfinals. He played on the French **Davis Cup** team each year from 1982 to 1994 and was a member of the 1991 Cup championship team and 1982 runner-up team. His Cup record was 24–20 in singles and 17–5 in doubles in 28 ties during those 13 years. He retired in 1996 with a total of 10 singles and 9 doubles championships. He continues to play in **senior**-level tournaments, is manager of a **Belgian** event company, and has done television tennis commentary in English for **Australian** television and in French for French television.

LEFT-HANDED PLAYERS. Lawn tennis is one sport in which left-handed players can have an advantage. One reason is that most players' **forehands** are better than their **backhands** and a left-hander's forehand will then be played **crosscourt** to the right-hander's backhand. Another advantage is that right-handed players do not often play left-handers since only about 10 percent of the population is left-handed, and thus, the righty is not used to the spin or angles that the lefty plays. Doubles teams often employ one left-handed and one right-handed player, for example, **Bob Bryan–Mike Bryan**, **Mark Woodforde–Todd Woodbridge**, **Martina Navratilova–Pam Shriver**, Daniel Nestor–**Mark Knowles**, and **John McEnroe**–Peter Fleming. Some of the most successful players who played left-handed (even though a few were natural right-handers) include: **Norman Brookes**, Bob Bryan, Mary Carillo, **Jimmy Connors**, Owen Davidson, **Dwight Davis**, John Doeg, **Jaroslav Drobný**, Guy Forget, Andrés Gómez, Tom Gullikson, Sylvia Hanika, **Goran Ivanišević**, Petr Korda, **Art Larsen**, **Rod Laver**, **Henri LeConte**, John McEnroe, Jürgen Melzer, Thomas Muster, **Rafael Nadal**, Martina Navratilova, Daniel Nestor, **Manuel Orantes**, **Nikki Pilić**, Marcelo Ríos, **Mervyn Rose**, **Greg Rusedski**, Patty Schnyder, Monica Seles, **Roscoe Tanner**, Roger Taylor, **Torben Ulrich**, Fernando Verdasco, **Guillermo Vilas**, Mark Woodforde, and Beals Wright. *See also* AMBIDEXTROUS PLAYERS; CONVERTED PLAYERS.

LENDL, IVAN. B. 7 March 1960, Ostrava, **Czechoslovakia**. Ivan Lendl is the son of Jiri Lendl and Olga Lendlova. Jiri was a lawyer, chess master, and top-15-**ranked** player in Czechoslovakia. In 1990, he became the president of the Czech tennis federation. Olga was the second-ranked Czechoslovakian female tennis player. Ivan began playing tennis at a young age and was both the **French** and **Wimbledon boys'** champion in 1978. A 6-foot, 2-inch, 175-pound right-hander, he reached the finals of 19 **main draw Grand Slam** men's singles events in 11 consecutive years (1981–91), winning championships at all except Wimbledon. He won the **Australian Open** in 1989 and 1990 and was runner-up in 1983. He won the French Open in 1984, 1986, and 1987 and was runner-up in 1981. At Wimbledon, he was a losing semifinalist five times and runner-up in 1986 and 1987. From 1982 to 1989, eight consecutive years, he was a finalist at the **United States Open** and won it in 1985 through 1987. He did not often play **doubles** but won six doubles titles in his career and reached a world doubles' ranking of 20 in 1986. In **singles**, he was ranked number one in the world for 270 weeks throughout his career.

He moved to the **United States**, lived with **Wojtek Fibak** at first, and then purchased a house in Connecticut. Although he did not defect, per se, he pursued United States citizenship, which he achieved in 1992. He was a member of the Czechoslovakian **Davis Cup** team each year from 1978 to 1985. In those eight years, his record was 18–11 in singles and 4–4 in doubles in 17 ties, and he was a member of the 1980 Cup championship team. He announced his retirement in 1994 due to chronic back problems and was credited with 144 singles championships. He has since become an excellent golfer, with a zero handicap, and has won four titles on the Celebrity Golf Tour. Four of his five daughters have also done well in that sport and daughter Isabelle has played on the Junior Ryder Cup team. He has sponsored an annual Ivan Lendl Golf Classic and has created the Ivan Lendl Champions' Academy to provide instruction in both golf and tennis to juniors. He was inducted into the International Tennis Hall of Fame in 2001.

LENGLEN, SUZANNE RACHEL FLORE. B. 24 May 1899, Compiègne, France. D. 4 July 1938, France. Suzanne Lenglen was a rather delicate child and had various health issues, including chronic asthma, which plagued her throughout her life. Her parents thought that competing in tennis would help to build up her strength and encouraged her to play on the family court. Her father, Charles Lenglen, **coached** her and was so successful that she competed in the 1914 **French National tournament** at the age of 14. She won the tournament but was defeated in the **challenge round** by the reigning champion Marguerite Broquedis. This would be the last **Grand Slam** tournament where she reached the final **match** and did not win. World War I suspended play in the major tournaments, and when they resumed in 1919, she won the French **singles** championships in six of the next seven years, missing only in 1924, when her health failed her. She also won the **Wimbledon** ladies'

The flamboyant Suzanne Lenglen was the first female player to headline a professional tennis tour. (courtesy of the International Tennis Hall of Fame and Museum)

singles and **doubles** (with **Elizabeth "Bunny" Ryan**) each year from 1919 to 1925, again failing only in 1924. She was also a three-time Wimbledon **mixed doubles** champion—in 1920 with **Gerald Patterson**, 1922 with Pat O'Hara Wood, and 1925 with **Jean Borotra**. In her first championship at Wimbledon, in 1919, the 20-year-old Lenglen defeated the seven-time champion, **Dorothea Douglass Chambers**, in three **sets**, 10–8, 4–6, 9–7 and saved two **match points** in the process.

Lenglen was known for her flamboyant, emotional manner and her tennis outfits with bare forearms and calf-length dresses that were considered revealing for her day. She was also known to sip brandy between sets of her matches. She brought an interest in women's tennis that was previously unknown.

She competed in all three events in the 1920 **Olympic Games** and won the women's singles and mixed doubles (with Max Decugis) and was the bronze medalist in the women's doubles (with Elisabeth d'Ayen). Doubles began at the French tournament in 1925, and she won both the women's doubles with Didi Vlasto and the mixed doubles with **Jacques Brugnon** in 1925 and 1926. Altogether she reached the finals of 26 Grand Slam events and won 25 of them. After her successful year in 1925, she was offered $50,000 by promoter C. C. Pyle to compete as a **professional** in a tour with **Mary K. Browne**, the 1926 French Nationals losing finalist. They toured in 1926 with Lenglen, defeating the 35-year-old Browne in every one of their 38 matches. Exhausted from the tour, Lenglen stopped playing competitive tennis and opened a tennis school in Paris.

Lenglen was diagnosed with leukemia in June 1938 and died shortly afterward from "pernicious anemia" at the age of 39. In her career, she was credited with 81 singles titles, 73 doubles titles, and 8 mixed doubles titles. She was inducted into the **International Tennis Hall of Fame** in 1978. In 1997, the second **court** at Stade **Roland Garros** was renamed Court Suzanne Lenglen.

LET. A let is a replay of a **point**. It can occur when a **serve** touches the **net** but lands in the proper **service** box or it can be called by the **umpire** if there is a distraction during the point. In "New Yorkese," it is a "do-over."

LI, NA. B. 26 February 1982, Wuhan, Hubei, China. Li Na (family name Li, given name Na) is the greatest female Chinese tennis player in history. She began playing **badminton**, emulating her father, Li Shengpeng, himself a champion badminton player, but was switched to tennis at the age of nine. She became a member of the Chinese national team when she was 15 and became a professional at the age of 17. She is a graduate of Huazhong University of Science and Technology with a degree in journalism. In 2006 she married Jiang Shan, a former national teammate who then became her coach.

From 1999 to 2008 she appeared in 28 **Fed Cup ties** for China with a record of 24-4 in **singles** and 8-6 in **doubles**. She played both singles and doubles in the 2000 **Olympic Games** but lost in the first round of both. In the 2008 Olympic Games in Beijing, she reached the semi-finals where she lost to Dinara Safina. In the third-place playoff, she lost to Vera Zvonareva. Through May, 2011 Li has won four **Women's Tennis Association** singles titles and two doubles titles, 19 **International Tennis Federation** singles and 16 doubles titles. A quarter-finalist at **Wimbledon** in 2006 and 2010 and at **the U.S. Open** in 2009, she was a losing finalist at the 2011 **Australian Open**, the first Asian woman to reach a **Grand Slam** singles final and winner at the 2011 **French Open**. She reached a number five ranking following that **tournament**. She has an excellent sense of humor and her television interviews are always fun to watch.

LINESPERSON. A linesperson (also referred to as a line **umpire**) is a **match** official responsible for determining whether a **ball** lands within the **court** boundaries. Most important matches will employ at least four, two at each end of the court. Until recent times, these officials have usually served unpaid.

LLOYD, CHRIS EVERT. *See* EVERT LLOYD, CHRISTINE MARIE "CHRIS."

LLOYD, JOHN. B. 27 August 1954, Leigh-on-Sea, England. John Lloyd was one of three brothers (older brother, David, younger brother, Tony) who became tennis **professionals**. John turned professional in 1973 and reached the third round of the men's **singles** at **Wimbledon** that year. Unfortunately for the British tennis fans, this would be his best singles result there in 14 attempts. He did reach the quarterfinals at the **United States Open** and, in December 1977, the finals of the **Australian Open**, where he was defeated by **Vitas Gerulaitis**. He was more successful in **mixed doubles**. Although he married tennis star **Chris Evert** in 1979, he played mixed doubles with Australian **Wendy Turnbull**. In 1982, Lloyd and Turnbull won the **French Open** mixed doubles. They reached the finals of the Wimbledon mixed doubles in 1982 and won Wimbledon in 1983 and 1984. He played **Davis Cup** tennis for Great Britain from 1974 to 1986, playing every year except 1981 and 1982. His Cup record was 16–19 in singles and 11–5 in **doubles** in 23 ties in 11 years. In 1978, the British team reached the finals, where the team was defeated by the **United States**.

After his playing career concluded, he was nonplaying captain of the British Davis Cup team from 2006 to 2010. He has also worked for British television as a tennis commentator. In his career, Lloyd reached a high **ranking** of 21 in singles in 1978 and 34 in doubles in 1986 and won one singles title and two other doubles titles, one with his younger brother, David. John Lloyd and Chris Evert cowrote a book with Carol Thatcher (daughter of British Prime Minister Margaret Thatcher), published in 1985, entitled *Lloyd on Lloyd*, about their tennis careers. They divorced in 1987,

LOB. A lob is a tennis stroke in which the **ball** is hit high over the **net** and aimed to land just inside the **baseline**. It can be used offensively to hit the ball out of the reach of the opponent when the opponent is at the net. It is also used defensively when the player hitting the lob needs time to recover his position. *See also* MOONBALL.

LONGEST MATCH IN TENNIS HISTORY. On 24 June 2010, **John Isner** defeated Nicolas Mahut in the most incredible **match** in tennis history. The first round match at **Wimbledon**, which required three days to complete, took 11 hours and 5 minutes of elapsed time and 183 **games**. They played 980 **points**, Mahut won 502 to Isner's 478, the fifth **set** required 711, and again Mahut outscored Isner, 365–346. But the only statistic that counted was that Isner won 70 games in the fifth set, and Mahut only won 68. The players held **serve** for 168 games from the second set until the last game of the final set. The final score was 6–4, 3–6, 6–7 (7), 7–6 (3), 70–68. In the fifth set, Mahut saved four **match points** to enable him to prolong the match. The 6-foot, 9-inch, 245-pound, right-handed Isner, an American who was seeded 23rd in the tournament, is known for his powerful serve, and he recorded a record 112 **aces** in the match. The six-foot three-inch Frenchman, Mahut, who had to win three **qualifying** matches just to enter the **main draw** and is known as a **serve and volleyer** with a good serve, recorded 103 aces.

The match was begun at 6:09 p.m. on Tuesday, 22 June, and suspended due to darkness after playing the first four sets in 2 hours and 54 minutes. They resumed play on Wednesday, 23 June, at 2:05 p.m., and the match was suspended at 9:11 p.m. due to darkness after 7 hours and 6 minutes, with the score tied, 59–59, in the fifth set. The **chair umpire** was Mohamed Lahyani. In a qualifying match earlier in the tournament, Mahut played a four-hour match that ended with a 24–22 set. In Isner's next match the following day, he was so exhausted that he did not record one ace and lost in 1 hour and 14 minutes to Thiemo de Bakker, 6–0, 6–3, 6–2.

Previous records for longest tennis match by time:

6:33, 25 May 2004, French Open, **Fabrice Santoro** d. Arnaud Clément, 6–4, 6–3, 6–7 (7), 3–6, 16–14

6:33, 24 September 1984, Richmond, Virginia, Vicki Nelson-Dunbar d. Jean Hepner, 6-4, 7–6 (13), in a match that included a 643-shot **rally** that lasted 29 minutes
6:22, 11 July 1982, Davis Cup, **John McEnroe** d. **Mats Wilander**, 9–7, 6–2, 15–17, 3–6, 8–6
6:20, 21 September 2002, Davis Cup, Lucas Arnold–**David Nalbandian** d. Yevgeny Kafelnikov–**Marat Safin**, 6–4, 6–4, 5–7, 3–6, 19–17
6:20, 24 July 1987, Davis Cup, **Boris Becker** d. John McEnroe, 4–6, 15–13, 8–10, 6–2, 6–2

Previous records for longest tennis match by number of games:

147, 17–18 August 1967, Newport Invitational, Dick Leach–Dick Dell d. Len Schloss–Tom Mozur, 3–6, 49–47, 22–20 (Schloss and Mozur played a 106-game set the previous week)
144, 1968, U.S. Indoor, Salisbury, Maryland, Bobby Wilson–Mark Cox d. Ron Holmberg–Charlie Pasarell, 26–24, 17–19, 30–28
135, 15 May 1949, Southern California Championships, Los Angeles, Ted Schroeder–Bob Falkenburg d. **Pancho González**–Hugh Stewart, 36–34, 2–6, 4–6, 6–4, 19–17
126, 1966, Kings Cup, Warsaw, Poland, Roger Taylor d. Wiesław Gasiorek, 27–29, 31–29, 6–4
122, 4 August 1973, Davis Cup, **Stan Smith**–Erik Van Dillen d. Patricio Cornejo–Jaime Fillol, 7–9, 37–39, 8–6, 6–1, 6–3
112, 25 June 1969, Wimbledon, Pancho González d. Charlie Pasarell, 22–24, 1–6, 16–14, 6–3, 11–9

LONGWOOD CRICKET CLUB. The Longwood Cricket Club is located in Chestnut Hill, Massachusetts, a western suburb of Boston. Founded in 1877, **lawn tennis** was introduced to the club in 1878, with the first **tournament** held in 1882. The first International Lawn Tennis Challenge (now the **Davis Cup**) was held at the club in 1900. Longwood was also the site of the **United States National Doubles** Championships from 1917 to 1967, except for 1934 and 1942 through 1945. Longwood also hosted the United States National **mixed doubles** at various times, and in 1968, the **United States Lawn Tennis Association** held two **singles** championships for men—one open to all players at **Forest Hills** and one restricted to **amateurs** held at Longwood. From 1964 to 1994 and 1997 to 1999, another tournament called the **U.S. Pro Championships** was held at Longwood. The club is still in operation as a tennis club with over 900 members who use the club's 44 **courts**—25 **grass** and 19 **clay**.

LOTT, GEORGE MARTIN, JR. B. 16 October 1906, Springfield, Illinois. D. 2 December 1991, Chicago, Illinois. George Lott was a graduate of the University of Chicago High School and the University of Chicago. The 6-foot tall, 160-pound right-hander played on the **United States Davis Cup** team each year from 1928 to 1934 except 1932. In his very first Cup appearance on 25 May 1928, he defeated Paul Kong of **China**, 6–0, 6–0, 6–0 in a second round Davis Cup **match** in Kansas City, Missouri, to become the first American player in Davis Cup history to win a match without losing a single **game**. He again won a Davis Cup shutout two years later against Ignacio de la Borbolla of **Mexico**. Lott's overall Davis Cup record in 18 **ties** in 6 years was 7–4 in **singles** and 11–0 in **doubles**. While he was a member of the team, the United States reached the **challenge round** four times but was defeated each time. Lott was better known as a doubles player than a singles player. His best year was 1931, when he won the men's doubles and **mixed doubles** at **Wimbledon** and the men's doubles at **Roland Garros**, was a singles runner-up at the **United States Nationals**, and won the United States National mixed doubles. At **Forest Hills**, he was also mixed doubles champion in 1929 and 1934 and runner-up in 1933 and men's doubles champion in 1928, 1929, 1930, 1933, and 1934. He also won the Wimbledon men's doubles in 1934 and was a losing men's doubles finalist in 1930.

In 1934, he became a touring **professional** tennis player and was no longer eligible for the **Grand Slam** tournaments. In 1935 and 1937, he won the professional doubles championships. He was inducted into the **International Tennis Hall of Fame** in 1964. He became tennis **coach** at DePaul University in 1969 and, at 85, was the oldest college tennis coach in the country at the time of his death in 1991.

LOUIE HARPER, MAREEN "PEANUT." B. 16 December 1960, San Francisco, California. Mareen Louie was never one of tennis's greatest stars, but she had one of the all-time greatest nicknames—"Peanut" Louie—which sounded like the name of the mascot for the Planters Peanuts company. She was called "Peanut" by her father because she was the youngest of five children, not because of her height, which was a respectable five feet five inches. A **Chinese** American, she began playing at a young age and won 14 national **junior** titles and was the number-one–**ranked** American 16-year-old in 1976. At **Wimbledon**, she reached the junior **singles** finals in 1977 and junior semifinals in 1978. She played **professionally** until 1995 but never quite achieved the same success that she had as a junior. She won four singles titles and had a career-high ranking of 19 in 1985. She married Tim Harper in 1986. They have two children. After retiring from active play, she authored children's books and runs a graphic design firm in San Francisco, California. Her sister Marcie was also a professional tennis player.

LOUIS ARMSTRONG STADIUM. Louis Armstrong Stadium is one of the two large arenas at the **Billie Jean King National Tennis Center** at **Flushing Meadows**, New York. It was originally built for the New York World's Fair of 1964 and was then known as the Singer Bowl. When the **United States Open** tournament was moved from **Forest Hills** to the former World's Fair area in Flushing Meadows, the stadium was renovated and renamed after the jazz musician who had lived in nearby Corona. The adjacent Grandstand Stadium was also constructed. Louis Armstrong Stadium had a seating capacity of 18,000, with an additional 6,000 seats for the Grandstand. In 1997, **Arthur Ashe Stadium** was built and replaced Louis Armstrong Stadium as the facility's main stadium. Louis Armstrong Stadium was again renovated, and its capacity reduced to around 10,000.

LOVE. "Love" is the tennis term for zero in English. A score of 40–0 will be announced as forty-love. Its origin is unknown, although it is said it derives from the French term *l'oeuf*, meaning egg. It is also thought to be an Old English word meaning nothing. In most other languages, the word for zero is used, for example, *cero* in Spanish, *null* in German, *nul* in Dutch, and so forth. *See also* SCORING.

LUCAS, JOHN HARDING, JR. B. 31 October 1953, Durham, North Carolina. John Lucas attended Hillside High School in Durham and the University of Maryland. In 1966, at the age of 12, he won the **American Tennis Association** boys' 12-and-under singles and also the boys' 16-and-under singles championships. He was an All-American basketball player and also an All-American tennis player in college, twice winning the Atlantic Coast Conference **singles** championship. He was the first overall selection in the 1976 National Basketball Association (NBA) draft and played 14 years of **professional** basketball and holds the NBA record for most assists in one quarter. From 1977–79, he also played **World Team Tennis (WTT)** and partnered **Renée Richards** in **mixed doubles**—one of the more unusual pairings—a 6'3" black basketball player and a 6'1" white transsexual, both left-handed. In 2005, he returned to WTT as the **coach** of the Houston Wranglers. He played in the junior division of the **U.S. Open** and was also a member of the U.S. Junior **Davis Cup** team. His son, John III, also played in the NBA and was also a nationally ranked **junior tennis** player.

LUTZ, ROBERT CHARLES "BOB." B. 29 August 1947, Lancaster, Pennsylvania. Bob Lutz played tennis for the University of Southern California and won the **National Collegiate Athletic Association singles** title in 1967 and, with partner **Stan Smith**, won the **doubles** in 1967 and 1968.

After graduation, he was a member of the **United States Davis Cup** team from 1968 to 1981. His record was 1–0 in singles and 14–2 in doubles in 16 **ties** in 9 years. His doubles partner was Stan Smith for 14 of his 16 matches. He was a member of the 1968, 1969, 1970, 1978, and 1979 Cup championship teams. On the **professional** tour, he won 9 singles titles, was a singles finalist 15 other times, won 43 doubles titles (usually with Smith), and was runner-up 30 other times. The 5-foot 11-inch, 180-pound Lutz with partner Smith won the **United States National** Championship men's doubles in 1968 (twice), 1974, 1978, and 1980 and the **Australian Open** men's doubles in 1970. In 1968, the United States National Championships held both **amateur** and **open** tournaments, and Lutz and Smith won both. They were also losing doubles finalists three times at **Wimbledon** and once each at **Roland Garros** and the United States Open. Lutz's best performance in **Grand Slam** singles competition was the semifinals of the 1971 Australian Open. He reached the quarterfinals of Wimbledon in 1969, the fourth round at Roland Garros in 1971, and the fourth round of the United States Open on five occasions.

He retired in 1985, after 20 years of competitive tennis. He helped to found the Rancho San Clemente Tennis and Fitness Club in California and is part-owner and tennis instructor there. He was nominated to the **International Tennis Hall of Fame** in 2010 but was not elected.

MAIN DRAW. At major tournaments that have competition for **junior** players less than 18 years of age as well as competition for players over 18, the phrase "main draw" is used to designate the most important events that are open to players of all ages and also to distinguish them from the **qualifying** rounds that precede it.

MALEEVA (-FRAGNIÈRE), MANUELA GEORGIEVA. *See* MALEEVA SISTERS.

MALEEVA (NOKOV), MAGDALENA GEORGIEVA. *See* MALEEVA SISTERS.

MALEEVA (STOIMENOV), KATERINA GEORGIEVA. *See* MALEEVA SISTERS.

MALEEVA SISTERS. Katerina, Magdalena, and Manuela Maleeva, all born in Sofia, Bulgaria, played **professional** tennis in the 1980s to the first decade of the 21st century. Katerina was born on 7 May 1969, Magdalena on 1 April 1975, and Manuela on 14 February 1967. Manuela won the 1984 **United States Open mixed doubles** title with Tom Gullickson—the only one of the three to win a **Grand Slam** championship. In 1994, Katerina reached the finals of the United States Open women's **doubles** with Robin White. Magdalena never was a finalist in a Grand Slam event. Manuela reached the quarterfinals of all four Grand Slam singles events and was a semifinalist at the United States Open in 1992 and 1993. She had a career-high **singles ranking** of 3 in 1985 and 11 in doubles in 1993. In her career, which spanned from 1982 to 1994, the 5-foot 8-inch, 125-pound right-hander won 19 singles and 4 doubles titles.

Katerina, who played from 1984 to 1996, was a 5-foot 6-inch, 120-pound right-hander who reached the singles quarterfinals of all four Grand Slam events, won 11 singles and 2 doubles titles in her career and reached a high singles ranking of six in 1990.

Magdalena, the youngest, also a 5-foot 6-inch, 120-pound right-hander, played professional tennis from 1989 to 2005. She reached the fourth round of all four Grand Slam singles events and, in 1992, was a quarterfinalist at the United States Open. She won 11 singles and 6 doubles titles and had a high ranking of 4 in singles in 1996 and 13 in doubles in 2004. On 1 October 2010, she came out of retirement at the age of 35 and won the Bulgarian National Championship.

All three sisters competed in the 1992 **Olympic Games** in both singles and doubles—the only instance of three sisters playing in the same Olympic tennis tournament. In addition, Katerina and Manuela played in both singles and doubles in 1988; Katerina played doubles in the 1996 Games, and Magdalena played singles and doubles in 1996 and singles in 2004. Katerina's best Olympic performance was third round in 1988 singles, Magdalena's best was third round in both 1992 and 1996 singles, and Manuela was the bronze medalist in 1988 singles and quarterfinalist in 1992 singles.

Manuela was married in 28 November 1987 to Swiss tennis player François Fragnière. They have three children. Magdalena married Lubomir Nokov in 2004. They have two children. Katerina married Georgi Stoimenov in 1994. They also have two children. In the **Federation Cup**, Katerina played for Bulgaria from 1984 to 1987, 1989, and 1991 to 1995 and had a record of 20–9 in singles and 9–13 in doubles in 28 **ties** in 10 years. Magdalena played for Bulgaria from 1991 to 1995, 1998, 2002, 2003, and 2005. In 24 ties over 9 years, her record was 18–8 in singles and 6–9 in doubles. Manuela played for Bulgaria from 1983 to 1987 and 1989 and for **Switzerland** in 1991 and 1992. Her record in 26 ties was 21–5 in singles and 7–10 in doubles in 8 years. Manuela won the **Hopman Cup** in 1992 with partner Jakob Hlasek. In retirement, the sisters and their mother, Julia Berberian-Maleeva, are partners in the Maleeva Tennis Club in Sofia.

MALLORY, MOLLA. *See* BJURSTEDT MALLORY, ANNE MARGARETHE "MOLLA."

MANDLIKOVÁ, HANA. B. 19 February 1962, Prague, **Czechoslovakia**. Hana Mandlikova is the daughter of Vilém Mandlik, a sprinter for Czechoslovakia in the 1956 **Olympic Games**. As a **junior** player in 1978, she was **ranked** number one in the world. She became a **professional** tennis player in 1978. She reached the finals of each of the four **Grand Slam tournaments** and won the **Australian Open** in 1980 and 1987, the **French Open** in 1981, and the **United States Open** in 1985. She was also runner-up at **Wimbledon** in 1981 and 1986 and the U.S. Open in 1982 and 1985. She won the U.S. Open women's **doubles** in 1989 with **Martina Navratilova** and was the women's doubles runner-up in 1984 at the French Open and in 1986 at both Wimbledon and the U.S. Open. Mandlíková was a member of the Czechoslovakian **Federation Cup** team each year from 1978 to 1987. Her record in 45 **ties** in those 10 years was 34–6 in singles and 15–6 in doubles. She was a member of the Cup championship team in 1983, 1984, and 1985 and runner-up team in 1986. She retired from active play in 1990 with 27 singles and 19 doubles titles to her credit and a high world ranking of three in singles and seven in doubles. She has since become a successful tennis **coach** with **Jana Novotná** among her pupils. Mandlíková was inducted into the **International Tennis Hall of Fame** in 1994. In 1986, she married restaurateur Jan Sedlak of Sydney, **Australia**, and became an Australian citizen. They divorced two years later.

MARBLE (CROWLEY), ALICE. B. 28 September 1913, Beckwith, California. D. 13 December 1990, Palm Springs, California. Alice Marble's life story should have been made into a Hollywood film. As a young teenager, she played baseball with major league players Joe DiMaggio and Lefty O'Doul. She was befriended by William Randolph Hearst and was a frequent house guest at Hearst Castle where she was a dinner partner of George Bernard Shaw and recreational tennis partner of many Hollywood film stars such as Charlie Chaplin. At the age of 18, she was runner-up at the **United States National** women's **doubles** in 1932. The following year, she played on the **United States Wightman Cup** team and lost a doubles **dead rubber**. In 1934, she collapsed on the **court** at the **French National Championships** from an attack that was first diagnosed as pleurisy but was later diagnosed as tuberculosis. She took a year off from tennis to recuperate and, while doing so, became good friends with actress Carole Lombard. Marble recovered fully and won the U.S. National women's **singles** in 1936. In 1937, she won **Wimbledon mixed doubles** with **Don Budge** and the U.S. National doubles with **Sarah Palfrey Fabyan**. That year, she also won two singles and one doubles match to lead the **United States** to a 6–1 victory in the Wightman Cup. She won Wimbledon women's and mixed doubles again in 1938 with the same partners, won all three events at the United States Nationals with Fabyan and Budge, and split two singles matches and won a doubles match in another Wightman Cup victory. In 1939, she won all three events at Wimbledon in 1939, this time with **Bobby Riggs** as mixed doubles partner, won all three events at the U.S. Nationals with **Harry Hopman** as mixed doubles partner, and won both singles and a doubles match in another U.S. Wightman Cup victory. With Riggs again as mixed doubles partner and Fabyan as women's doubles partner, Marble won all three U.S. National events in 1940.

She attempted to enlist in the U.S. military and was rejected but was offered a position by President Franklin Delano Roosevelt as cochairman of a physical fitness program for the Office of Civilian Defense, along with oarsman Jack Kelly (father of Grace Kelly). She spent some time as a **professional** nightclub singer and later signed a professional tennis contract in 1940 and played on the pro tour in a preliminary match to the Don Budge–**Bill Tilden** main event. In 1943, she married Army Air Force Captain Joe Crowley. In 1944, she was in an auto accident on Long Island and suffered a miscarriage as a result and shortly afterward lost her husband on Christmas Eve when his plane was shot down over **Germany**. Due to her photographic memory, she was recruited by Army intelligence to reunite with a former lover, a **Swiss** banker, to steal records of Nazis who invested in his bank. She successfully carried out her mission in 1945 but was shot in the back while escaping.

In 1950, she helped **Althea Gibson** break the color line by writing an eloquent open letter to the **United States Lawn Tennis Association**, which was published in *World Tennis* magazine. Alice later coached **Darlene Hard** and **Billie Jean Moffitt (King)**. In 1964, Alice Marble was inducted into the **International Tennis Hall of Fame**. After surviving colon cancer in 1981, she died of pernicious anemia in 1990. Her fascinating life story is well chronicled in *Courting Danger*, an autobiography published posthumously in 1991.

MARTIN, TODD CHRISTOPHER. B. 8 July 1970, Hinsdale, Illinois. Todd Martin was raised in Lansing, Michigan, and attended East Lansing High School. He continued his education at Northwestern University and played on the tennis team there. In 1990, he dropped out of school to become a **professional** tennis player. In 1993, he was named the **Association of Tennis Professionals (ATP)** Most Improved Player as his **ranking** rose from 87 to 13. The following year, he had a record of 18–4 at the four major **tournaments**. He reached the finals of the **Australian Open** but was defeated by **Pete Sampras**, reached the third round at the **French Open**, lost to eventual champion Sampras in the semifinals at **Wimbledon**, and lost to eventual champion **Andre Agassi** in the semifinals at the **United States Open**. He had another excellent year in 1999, reaching the quarterfinals at the Australian Open and Wimbledon, losing to Agassi in the finals of the United States Open, and reaching a career-high ranking of four.

The 6-foot 6-inch, 205-pound Martin, one of the tallest players of his era, competed in the 2000 **Olympic Games** in Sydney, **Australia**, but lost in the first round of the **singles** event. He was a member of the **United States Davis Cup** team each year from 1994 to 2002 and helped the United States win the Cup in 1995 over **Russia**, 3–2, with his **doubles** victory with Pete Sampras. Martin also played on the 1997 team that lost in the finals to **Sweden**. His

Davis Cup record for 18 **ties** in 9 years is 11–8 in singles and 5–6 in doubles. In his career, he won eight ATP championships and reached the finals in 12 other ATP events. From 1995 to 1997 and again from 1998 to 1999, he was president of the ATP Player Council. Although he retired from the ATP tour in 2004, he continues to play and win on the **Champions Tour** and was the **coach** of **Novak Djoković**, briefly.

MARTÍNEZ BERNAT, IMMACULADA CONCEPCIÓN "CONCHITA." B. 16 April 1972, Monzón, Spain. Conchita Martínez became a **professional** tennis player in 1988, at the age of 16. In 1994, she defeated **Martina Navratilova** at **Wimbledon** to win her only **Grand Slam** title. In 1998, she was defeated by **Martina Hingis** in the final of the **Australian Open**, and in 2000, **Mary Pierce** defeated Martínez in the finals at **Roland Garros**. She reached the finals in two Grand Slam events, both at Roland Garros—the 1992 women's **doubles** with **Arantxa Sánchez Vicario** as partner and the 2001 women's doubles with Jelena Dokić as partner. The 5-foot 7-inch, 130-pound, right-handed Martínez competed in four **Olympic** tennis **tournaments**—one of only sixteen people to do so. In the 1992 Games, in her native country, she won the silver medal in doubles with partner Arantxa Sánchez Vicario and was a quarterfinalist in singles. In 1996, she and Arantxa won the bronze medal in doubles, and Martínez again reached the singles quarterfinals. She entered only doubles in 2000 and lost in the second round. In 2004, she again won the bronze medal in doubles (with **Virginia Ruano Pascual** as partner) but lost her first round singles match. She is one of only nineteen competitors to win three Olympic tennis medals. She played on the Spanish **Federation Cup** team from 1988 to 1996, 1998, and 2000 to 2004 and had a record of 47–18 in singles and 21–5 in doubles in 53 **ties** over 17 years. She played in the finals for the Cup championship team in 1991, 1993, 1994, 1995, and 1998 and runner-up team in 1989, 1992, 1996, 2000, and 2002. She retired in April 2006 with 33 singles and 13 doubles titles to her credit and high **rankings** of two in the world in singles in 1995 and seven in doubles in 1993.

MATCH. A **lawn tennis** match generally consists of two out of three **sets** for men and women, **singles** and **doubles**. Some of the major men's **tournaments** are played best three out of five sets. In the early days of lawn tennis (c. 1890s), women occasionally also played best three out of five sets. *See also* SCORING.

MATCH POINT. Match point in **lawn tennis** occurs when the score is such that the winner of that **point** wins the **match**. In **tournament** play, match point in the tournament final match is also referred to as championship point. It is not uncommon for a player to save one or more match points against himself or herself and then go on to win the match.

MATHIEU, SIMONE PASSEMARD. *See* PASSEMARD MATHIEU, SIMONE.

MAURESMO, AMÉLIE SIMONE. B. 5 July 1979, St. Germain en Laye, France. Amélie Mauresmo began playing tennis at the age of four after seeing Frenchman **Yannick Noah** win the **French Open** in 1983. In 1996, she was the **junior** French Open champion and was selected by the **International Tennis Federation** as the junior world Champion for that year. In 1999, she reached the finals of the **Australian Open** but was defeated by **Martina Hingis**. In 2006, Mauresmo was again a finalist and won the **tournament** when **Justine Henin-Hardenne** became ill during the final **match** and retired. Mauresmo also defeated Henin at **Wimbledon** that year for her second **Grand Slam** title and became the first Frenchwoman since **Suzanne Lenglen** in 1925 to win the Wimbledon championship. In 2005, at Wimbledon, Mauresmo and **Svetlana Kuznetsova** reached the finals of the women's **doubles** but lost to doubles specialists Cara Black and Liezel Huber. In 2004, Mauresmo reached the **singles ranking** of world number one; although, to that point, she had not won a major Grand Slam tournament. She is one of a small number of players to do so.

The 5-foot 9-inch, 140-pound right-hander competed in both **singles** and doubles in the 2000 and 2004 **Olympic Games**. She reached the quarterfinals in 2000 in doubles and won a silver medal in 2004 in singles. She was a member of the French **Federation Cup** team from 1998 to 1999 and 2001 to 2009. In 21 **ties** over 11 years, her record was 30–9 in singles and 2–2 in doubles. She played for the Cup championship team in 2003 and runner-up team in 2005. She announced her retirement from tennis on 3 December 2009. In her career, she won 25 singles and 3 doubles titles. She spent part of 2010 as an advisor to Michaël Llodra and also ran and finished the New York City Marathon in a very good time of 3:40:20.

MAYER, EUGENE "GENE." B. 11 April 1956, Flushing, New York. Although born in New York, Gene Mayer was raised in New Jersey, where he attended Wayne Valley High School and was undefeated on its tennis team. He attended Stanford University, graduating in just three years, with a degree in political science and as an All-American on the tennis team. He and his brother Sandy were both **coached** by their father, Alex Mayer Sr. Gene began his **professional** tennis career in 1973 and, in 1975, partnered **Vitas Gerulai-**

tis to the **Wimbledon** men's **doubles** championship. Mayer and Hank Pfister won the 1978 **French Open** doubles title, and the following year, Mayer again won it with his brother Sandy as partner. In 1980, Gene reached a world **singles ranking** of four. A 6-foot tall, 150-pound right-hander, Gene reached the singles quarterfinals twice at Wimbledon and twice at the **United States Open**, reached the fourth round at the French Open, and never played the **Australian Open**. He played singles only in three **ties** on the 1982 and 1983 **United States Davis Cup** team and helped win the 1982 Cup. He won four of his six **matches** as a team member. He retired from active play in 1986, after having won 14 singles and 15 doubles titles. He **coached Leander Paes** and **Fabrice Santoro**, among others. In 2005, he opened the Gene Mayer International Tennis Academy on Long Island, but the project was short lived and the organization terminated in 2007.

MAYOTTE, TIMOTHY "TIM." B. 3 August 1960, Springfield, Massachusetts. Tim Mayotte attended Stanford University and won the **National Collegiate Athletic Association Singles** Championship in 1981. He became a **professional** tennis player in 1981. He reached the semifinals at **Wimbledon** in 1982, semifinals at the **Australian Open** in 1983, second round at the **French Open** in 1988 and 1989, and quarterfinals at the **United States Open** in 1989. The six-foot three-inch right-hander won the men's singles silver medal in the 1988 **Olympic Games**. He played singles only in three **ties** for the **United States Davis Cup** team in 1986 and 1987. His record was one win and four losses and one unfinished **match**. He retired from competitive tennis in 1992 with a lifetime record of 12 singles victories, 11 singles runner-up finishes, and a career-high **ranking** of seven in 1988. His older brother Chris played professional tennis briefly and won one doubles tournament with Tim. In 2009, Mayotte was hired by the **United States Tennis Association** as a national **coach**.

MCENROE, JOHN PATRICK, JR. B. 16 February 1959, Wiesbaden, Germany. John McEnroe was born in Germany while his father was serving in the U.S. Air Force. John was raised in New York City in the Douglaston section of the borough of Queens. He began playing at the Douglaston Tennis Club and, at age 12, continued his training at the Port Washington Tennis Academy, run by **Australian** tennis **coach Harry Hopman**. McEnroe graduated Trinity School, a private school in New York City, in 1977, and went to Stanford University for one year, winning the 1978 **National Collegiate Athletic Association** national **singles** title and helping his team win the national championship. He joined the **professional** tour in 1978 and played on it through 1992, reaching 24 **Grand Slam** finals and winning 17

Grand Slam championships. The 6-foot tall, 170-pound **left-hander** was one of the best **doubles** players in history and won nine Grand Slam doubles titles. He won the **United States Open** Singles Championship in 1979, 1980, 1981, and 1984 and was runner-up to **Ivan Lendl** in 1985. He reached the **Wimbledon** men's singles final each year from 1980 to 1984, winning it in 1981, 1983, and 1984. In 1984, he lost in the finals of the **French Open**. His best effort in singles at the **Australian Open** was 1983, when he reached the semifinals. In doubles, at Wimbledon, he reached the finals seven times between 1978 and 1992. He and partner Peter Fleming were champions there in 1979, 1981, 1983, and 1984 and runners-up in 1978 and 1982. In 1992, McEnroe and **Michael Stich** also won at Wimbledon. The Fleming–McEnroe team won the U.S. Open in 1979, 1981, and 1983 and was runner-up in 1980. McEnroe also won the U.S. Open with **Mark Woodforde** as partner in 1989. McEnroe's one championship at **Roland Garros** occurred in 1977, when he and his Douglaston neighbor and friend Mary Carillo won the **mixed doubles**.

Johnny Mac, as he is popularly known, is remembered for his temper and tirades on the **court**. He was suspended and fined often and was ejected from the 1990 Australian Open for swearing at the **umpire, linesman,** and **referee**. John McEnroe had one of the best **Davis Cup** records for the **United States**. A member of the team from 1978 to 1984, 1987 to 1989, 1991, and 1992, he played in 30 **ties** and had a record of 41–8 in singles and 18–2 in doubles. He was a member of the Cup championship team in 1978, 1979, 1981, 1982, and 1992. He appeared in 6 final ties and had a record of 12 wins and only 2 defeats in them, losing both **matches** in 1984 when Sweden won the Cup. McEnroe played and won the longest match in Davis Cup history. On 11 July 1982, he defeated **Mats Wilander** of **Sweden** in a match lasting 6 hours and 22 minutes in the final match of the quarterfinals by a score of 9–7, 6–2, 15–17, 3–6, and 8–6 to enable the United States to win the tie and advance in the competition. His younger brother **Patrick McEnroe** was also a professional tennis player and Davis Cup captain.

John McEnroe was inducted into the **International Tennis Hall of Fame** in 1999. Although he retired from the **Association of Tennis Professionals** tour in 1992, he has continued to play in the **Champions Tour** and **World Team Tennis** and still is able to compete against players 10 or more years younger. He has been a television tennis analyst for several networks and is one of the best with an extremely pleasant (in contrast to his playing persona) and knowledgeable style. In 2010, he opened the John McEnroe Tennis Academy on Randalls Island in New York City. *See also* LONGEST MATCHES IN TENNIS HISTORY.

The fiery John McEnroe won 59 of 69 Davis Cup matches for the United States, including two that each lasted more than six hours. (courtesy of the International Tennis Hall of Fame and Museum, Edward Fernberger Collection)

MCENROE, PATRICK JOHN. B. 1 July 1966, Manhasset, New York. Patrick McEnroe is **John McEnroe's** younger brother and has made a name for himself as a **professional** tennis player, **coach**, and television commentator. In 1987, he won the men's **doubles** at the Pan American Games with partner Luke Jensen. Jensen and McEnroe had previously won the 1984 **French Open junior** doubles. A 1988 graduate of Stanford University, with a degree in political science, Patrick was a member of Stanford's tennis team and helped the team win the 1986 and 1988 National **Collegiate** Athletic Association team championships. The 6-foot tall, 160-pound right-hander reached a high world **ranking** of 3 in doubles in 1993 and 28 in singles in 1995 in his professional career, which lasted from 1988 to 1998. He won 16 doubles championships (only one, in 1984, with his brother John as partner) and 1 **singles** title, in 1995, in Sydney, **Australia**. McEnroe and Jim Grabb won the 1989 French Open men's doubles, and McEnroe and David Wheaton were 1991 **Australian Open** men's doubles runners-up. He appeared in four ties for the **United States** in the **Davis Cup** in 1993, 1994, and 1996 and won three of his four singles **matches**. In 2000, he became the United States Davis Cup captain and led the team to the championship in 2007. He retired as Davis Cup captain after the final match in 2010. In 2004, he was the nonplaying captain of the United States men's **Olympic** tennis team. He has also worked as an analyst for several television networks for the major tennis tournaments.

MCKANE GODFREE, KATHLEEN "KITTY." B. 7 May 1896, London, England. D. 19 June 1992, London, England. In her first attempt at **Wimbledon**, Kitty McKane reached the quarterfinals in 1919. She reached the finals in 1923 and was the ladies' **singles** champion in 1924 and 1926, sending **Helen Wills** to her only Wimbledon defeat in 1924. From 1927 to 1938, Wills would win eight singles titles there. McKane also reached the women's **doubles** finals at Wimbledon in 1922, 1924, and 1926 but lost each time—in 1922 with her sister Margaret as partner, in 1924 with Phyllis Howkins Covell, and in 1926 with Evelyn Colyer. In 1924, she and Brian Gilbert won the Wimbledon **mixed doubles**. She married tennis player Leslie Allison Godfree in January 1926. They were mixed doubles champions at Wimbledon in 1926 and runners-up in 1927 and were the only married couple ever to win that championship. McKane reached the **French National** finals in 1925 but was defeated by **Suzanne Lenglen**, and McKane and Colyer were defeated by Lenglen and Didi Vlasto in the 1925 and 1926 women's doubles there. She competed at the **United States Nationals** most years from 1921 to 1927 and reached the women's singles final in 1925, where she was defeated by Helen Wills. McKane and Covell won the U.S. National women's doubles in

1923, and McKane and Ermyntrude Harvey won it in 1927. McKane and Jack Hawkes were U.S. mixed doubles runners-up in 1923 and champions in 1925.

She entered all three events in both the 1920 and 1924 **Olympic Games** with much success. In 1920, she won the bronze medal in women's singles, gold medal in women's doubles (with Winnie McNair), and silver medal in mixed doubles (with **Max Woosnam**). In 1924, she again won bronze in singles and silver in doubles (with Covell) and was fourth in mixed doubles (with John Gilbert). She has won more Olympic tennis medals than any other female competitor and is second only to Max Decugis, who won six. She was also an international **badminton** champion and winner of the All-England Open Badminton Championships singles in 1920 through 1922 and 1924, women's doubles in 1921 and 1924, and mixed doubles in 1924 through 1925. She played on the British **Wightman Cup** team from 1923 to 1927 and again in 1930 and 1934. Her record in those events was 5–5 in singles and 2–5 in doubles. She was inducted into the **International Tennis Hall of Fame** in 1978.

MCKINLEY, CHARLES ROBERT, "CHUCK," JR. B. 5 January 1941, St. Louis, Missouri. D. 10 August 1986, Dallas, Texas. Chuck McKinley came from a blue-collar, working-class family in St. Louis, Missouri, and learned tennis on the public **courts**. He attended Trinity University in Texas and was a member of its tennis team. Although only 5 feet 8 inches tall and 155 pounds, he was quite athletic and had a powerful **serve**. In 1961, he reached the finals at **Wimbledon** but lost to **Rod Laver**. Two years later, after Laver had become a **professional** (and ineligible to compete at Wimbledon), McKinley became Wimbledon men's **singles** champion with a victory over **Fred Stolle** in the finals. That year, McKinley (**seeded** fourth) won all seven **matches** at Wimbledon without losing a **set**, although he did not have to play any other seeded players en route to the title. From 1961 to 1964, McKinley and partner **Dennis Ralston** reached the finals of the **United States National Doubles** Championships. In 1961, 1962, and 1963, the pair faced **Mexicans** Antonio Palafox and **Rafael Osuna** in the finals and defeated them in the odd-numbered years. In 1964, McKinley and Ralston won their third United States doubles title by defeating British players Graham Stilwell and Mike Sangster in the final round.

McKinley was a member of the **United States Davis Cup** team each year from 1960 to 1965. In his six years of Davis Cup play, his record was 16–6 in singles and 13–3 in doubles in 16 **ties**. In 1963, after losing the first set, he defeated **John Newcombe** of Australia in the fifth and deciding match of the **challenge round** to enable the United States to win the Cup, 3–2. The following year, the situation was reversed as **Roy Emerson** of **Australia** defeated McKinley in the fifth and deciding match after McKinley won the first set. McKinley did not become a professional player but worked as a stockbroker in New York. In his relatively brief **amateur** career, he competed at Wimbledon only four times, reaching the second round in 1962 and semi-finals in 1964, in addition to his two finals appearances. He never entered the **Australian** or **French National** Championships, and he reached a world ranking of two in 1963. He was inducted into the **International Tennis Hall of Fame** in 1986 and died shortly afterward, at the age of 45, from a brain tumor.

MCLOUGHLIN, MAURICE EVANS "MAC," "MAURY," "RED." B. 7 January 1890, Carson City, Nevada. D. 10 December 1957, Hermosa Beach, California. Maurice McLoughlin was raised in northern California and attended Lowell High School in San Francisco. Contrary to most of the tennis players of his era, he learned the game at the public parks' **courts**. He was one of the first players to use a powerful **serve-and-volley** technique. His time in the tennis limelight was relatively brief as he served in the U.S. Army during World War I and never regained his form after his discharge from the service. From 1911 to 1915, he played in the finals of the **United States National Championships**, winning the **tournament** in 1912 and 1913. The **challenge round** was abolished in 1912, so unlike previous U.S. champions, he had to earn his way to the finals each year. He also was a U.S. National **doubles** finalist in 1909 and 1912 to 1916, winning the title with partner Tom Bundy in 1912, 1913, and 1914. In 1913, he competed at **Wimbledon** as a prelude to the **Davis Cup** and won the **all-comers** tournament but was defeated by reigning champion **Tony Wilding** in the **challenge round**. McLoughlin played on the United States Davis Cup team in 1909 and 1911 to 1914 (there was no tournament in 1910). In eight **ties** in the five years, his record was 9–4 in singles and 3–4 in doubles. In 1913, he helped the **United States** defeat **Great Britain** to win the Cup.

In 1915, *Tennis as I Play It*, an instructional book by Maurice E. McLoughlin, was published. Although he was credited as author, it is claimed that it was, in fact, ghost-written by Sinclair Lewis, who had yet to become the Nobel-Prize winning author. McLoughlin was inducted into the **International Tennis Hall of Fame** in 1957, shortly before his death later that year.

MCMILLAN, FREW DONALD. B. 20 May 1942, Springs, **South Africa**. Frew McMillan was unique in that he used a two-handed **forehand** and two-handed **backhand**. No other world-class player in his era played in that manner. A **doubles** specialist, who usually wore a white cap, he won 63 doubles titles and only two **singles** titles in his career, which lasted until 1981, and was ranked number one in the world in doubles in 1977. He began his **professional** tennis career in 1969 after playing as an **amateur** from 1962. Although he entered the **Wimbledon** singles 17 consecutive years from 1962 to 1978, he only reached the third round twice. The slim (155 pounds), six-foot right-hander reached the third round twice in singles at the **French Nationals** and was a quarterfinalist in the 1972 **United States Open** singles tournament.

It was in doubles in which he shone, and he was the Wimbledon men's doubles champion in 1967, 1972, and 1978 with partner **Bob Hewitt**. The pair also won the **French Open** doubles in 1972 and United States Open doubles in 1977. McMillan and **Betty Stove** reached the **mixed doubles** final at Wimbledon four times, winning in 1978 and 1981 and losing in 1977 and 1979. From 1976 to 1980, the couple were United States Open mixed doubles finalists each year, winning in 1977 and 1978. He and **Judy Tegart Dalton** also reached the United States Open mixed doubles final in 1970 but lost. He and Annette Van Zyl were French National champions in 1966. He was on the South African **Davis Cup** team from 1965 to 1969 and 1973 to 1978. He appeared in 28 **ties** and had a record of 2–0 in singles and 23–5 in doubles during those 11 years and was a member of the 1974 team that won the Cup by default over **India**. He was inducted into the **International Tennis Hall of Fame** in 1992. In retirement, he has been a television commentator for European television.

MCNAMARA, PETER. B. 5 July 1955, Melbourne, Victoria, **Australia**. Peter McNamara was one of the top **doubles** players of his era. He and partner Paul McNamee won the **Australian Open** doubles in 1979 and were runners-up in 1980. They also won the **Wimbledon** doubles title in 1980 and 1982. In 1981, McNamara and Heinz Günthardt were losing finalists at the **United States Open**. In 1982, McNamara was selected by the **Association of Tennis Professionals** as the Most Improved Player. The 6-foot 1-inch, 165-pound right-hander was a member of the Australian **Davis Cup** team from 1980 to 1982 and 1985 to 1986. He played in 10 **ties** with a record of 9–7 in **singles** and 1–4 in doubles. His losing Davis Cup record in doubles is surprising since he and Paul McNamee were among the top **ranked** doubles team at one time. Although Australia won the Cup in 1986, McNamara only played in one preliminary round tie that year. In his career, he won 5 singles and 19 doubles titles and reached high rankings of seven in singles in 1983 and three in doubles in 1982. His career was relatively brief as a severe knee injury caused a nearly two-year hiatus in his activity. After retiring from tennis, he turned to **coaching** with **Mark Philippoussis** as one of his star pupils and has taught at the Mouratoglou Tennis Academy in Paris, **France**.

MERION CRICKET CLUB. The Merion Cricket Club is located in Haverford, Pennsylvania, a Philadelphia suburb. It was founded in 1865, and **lawn tennis** was first played there in 1879. It has been the site of the National **Intercollegiate Tournament** as well as the **Davis Cup**.

MEXICO. Although not the favorite sport in Mexico, tennis is still played by many Mexicans, and they have achieved notable success. The Federación Mexicana de Tenis is the organization that administers the sport there. One of the **Association of Tennis Professionals** tour events is held in Acapulco, Mexico. From 1924 through May 2011, Mexico has competed in 80 **Davis Cup tournaments** with a record of 76–82 in 158 **ties**. Mexico has played 10 times in the World Group since its formation in 1981. In 1962, Mexico was the tournament runner-up, losing to **Australia** in the final. Top Davis Cup players have been Alejandro Hernández, Leonardo Lavalle, Jorge Lozano, **Rafael Osuna**, and Antonio Palafox.

From 1924 to 2000, Mexico had entrants in the **Olympic** tennis competition. In 1968, during the Olympic Games in Mexico City, there were demonstration and **exhibition** tennis tournaments held in Guadalajara, Mexico. Rafael Osuna and Vicente Zarazua won both the demonstration and exhibition men's **doubles**, Osuna won the exhibition **singles** and was fourth in the demonstration singles, and Joaquin Loyo-Mayo partnered Frenchman Pierre Darmon and finished third in demonstration doubles and second in exhibition doubles. Lourdes Gongora was fourth in demonstration women's singles, and she and Patricia Montano were third in demonstration women's doubles. Cecilia Rosado of Mexico and Zaiga Yansone of the **Soviet Union** finished third in exhibition women's doubles. In 1984, Francisco Maciel finished second in the demonstration men's singles tournament. In 1992, Leonardo Lavalle reached the quarterfinals of men's singles. The best male tennis player was Hall of Famer Osuna. In addition to the players named above, other top male players include Marcello Lara and **Raúl Ramírez**.

The best female tennis players include Yola Ramírez, Rosa Reyes Darmon, and Xóchitl Escobedo. In **Federation Cup** competition, from 1964 to May 2011, Mexico has competed 41 years, 18 years in World Group and played 137 ties with a record of 64–73. Mexico reached the round of 16 five times prior to 1995, when the new format was instituted. Since then, the team's best showing was as runner-up in the Americas I group in 1995.

MIXED DOUBLES. Mixed Doubles is a tennis **match** between teams consisting of one male and one female player. It is one of the most common forms of matches in recreational tennis and is the least popular in championship **tournaments**. *See also* DOUBLES; SINGLES.

MOFFITT KING, BILLIE JEAN. *See* KING, BILLIE JEAN MOFFITT.

MONFILS, GAËL SÉBASTIEN. B. 1 September 1986, Paris, **France**. Gaël Monfils is of Caribbean heritage. His father is from Guadeloupe, and his mother from Martinique. Monfils had an exceptional **junior** career and reached a **ranking** of number-one junior in 2004 after winning the **Australian, French**, and **Wimbledon** junior championships. As a **professional**, he is an exciting player to watch as his speed enables him to retrieve **balls** that would be **winners** against lesser opponents. His professional career has been somewhat disappointing though. Through May 2011, he has reached a ranking of nine in 2009 and has only managed to win three **singles** tournaments and was the losing finalist on 10 other occasions. His best performance in a **Grand Slam** event was in 2008 when he reached the semifinals at **Roland Garros**. He has reached the third round at Wimbledon three times, the fourth round at the Australian, and quarterfinals at the United States Open. He competed in the 2008 **Olympic Games** and reached the quarterfinals in singles but lost in the first round of **doubles**. As of May 2011, Monfils had played for France in one **Davis Cup tie** in 2009 and four ties in 2010, winning four of six singles matches and was a member of the Cup runner-up team in 2010. He also won a tournament in **paddle tennis** in 2006.

MOONBALL. A moonball is a tennis shot that is hit high and deep, usually with a lot of spin. It is used during a **baseline rally** for a change of **pace**. It became popular during the 1970s. Two of the better "moonballers" were **Eddie Dibbs** and **Harold Solomon**. *See also* LOB.

MORAN, GERTRUDE AGUSTA "GUSSIE." B. 8 September 1923, Santa Monica, California. Although Gussie Moran was an accomplished tennis player who was a finalist in **mixed doubles** at the **United States National tournament** in 1947 (with **Pancho Segura**), winner of the 1948 United States **Hard-court singles** and **doubles** championships, member of the 1949 **United States Wightman Cup** team (winning her doubles match), and runner-up at the 1949 **Wimbledon** women's doubles (with Pat Canning Todd), she achieved more fame for her tennis apparel than for her tennis ability. For her debut at Wimbledon in 1949, she wore a tennis outfit that had lace-trimmed panties (knickers) under her skirt. The costume drew an excessive amount of attention and was considered scandalous. The designer, **Ted Tinling**, who had been an official host at Wimbledon for more than 20 years, was banned from the **All-England Lawn Tennis and Croquet Club** and did not return for 33 years. Sportswriters nicknamed her "Gorgeous Gussie." This was her only appearance there in that costume, and subsequently, she wore a more conservative shorts outfit. This one incident brought her extensive publicity though.

After her 1950 Wimbledon tournament, she became a **professional** tennis player, touring with **Pauline Betz**. Moran had a role in the Kathryn Hepburn–Spencer Tracy film, *Pat and Mike*, was featured on the cover of several national magazines, and even had a thoroughbred race horse named after her. She was a television sportscaster in the 1950s and did a pregame show for the Brooklyn Dodgers, among other assignments. She continued playing tennis until the early 1970s, and when the United States National tournament became open to professionals, she played in the 1971 women's singles at the age of 47.

MORARIU (TURCINOVICH), CORINA MARIE. B. 26 January 1978, Detroit, Michigan. Corina Morariu is the daughter of two **Romanian** doctors. Her father, Albin, immigrated to the United States in 1972. He taught Corina his favorite game, tennis, when she was just two years old. The family relocated to Boca Raton, Florida, where her game developed. She became a **professional** tennis player in 1994. A five-foot eight-inch right-hander, she was an adequate **singles** player (winning one championship and reaching three other finals) but made her mark in **doubles**. She won the **Australian Open** Doubles Championship with **Lindsay Davenport** in 1999. In 2000, she reached the **ranking** of number-one women's doubles player.

After winning the Australian Open **mixed doubles** with Ellis Ferreira in 2001, she became ill and was diagnosed with acute promyelocytic leukemia (APL). She was fortunate in that there are eight forms of acute myelogenous leukemia, a form of cancer that affects the blood and bone marrow, and the APL subtype has the highest survival rate. After successfully undergoing chemotherapy in 2001, she returned to play **World Team Tennis** in July 2002. After playing several **tournaments** in July and August, she entered the **U.S. Open**, where she was matched against eventual champion, **Serena Williams** in the opening round and, although she played competitively, was defeated 6–3, 6–2. Corina also entered doubles, where she and Kim Po-Messerli reached the quarterfinals, and the mixed doubles, reaching the semifinals with **Justin Gimelstob**. The Women's Tennis Association recognized her performance by instituting a Corina Morariu Courage Award in 2002 and making her the first recipient. The following year, she received the Comeback Player of the Year award. Shoulder surgery in 2002 and 2004 limited her singles play, but in 2005, Corina again reached the finals of the Australian Open doubles with Davenport. She was a member of the **United States Fed Cup** team in 1998 but did not see any action. In 2005, she again was named to the Fed Cup team and had a 1–1 record, playing doubles with Davenport. In

2007, she retired from competition and has since worked successfully as an announcer for the **Tennis Channel**. Her autobiography, *Living through the Racket,* was published in 2010.

MOYÁ LLOMPART, CARLOS. B. 27 August 1976, Palma de Mallorca, **Spain**. Carlos Moyá is one of the few players to achieve a world number-one **ranking**. He accomplished this in 1999 after winning the **French Open** in 1998 and reaching the **United States Open** semifinals in 1998. He was also the runner-up at the **Australian Open** in 1997. He competed in the 2004 **Olympic Games** in both **singles** and **doubles** and reached the quarterfinal round in singles but lost in the first round of the doubles. From 1996 to 2004, the muscular, 6-foot 3-inch 190-pounder played for Spain in **Davis Cup** competition and had a record of 20–7, all in singles competition in 15 ties. He was not on the team in 2000, when Spain won the Cup for the first time, but did play in the finals in 2003, when **Australia** defeated Spain for the Cup. In 2004, Moyá played a vital role by winning both matches to give Spain the Cup over the **United States** by a 3–2 score. In 2004, he reached the fourth round at **Wimbledon**, his best result in that tournament. A natural **left-hander**, he played tennis with his right hand, the opposite of his good friend, **Rafael Nadal**, a fellow Majorcan. On 17 November 2010, Moyá announced his retirement due to a foot injury that did not heal properly. In his career, he won 20 singles titles. In his career, he won 20 singles titles and was runner-up 24 times but did not win a doubles championship.

MULLOY, GARDNAR PUTNAM. B. 22 November 1913, Washington DC. Gardnar Mulloy has never stopped playing tennis. He attended the University of Miami on a football scholarship but, when he did not receive much playing time, started a college tennis team. He graduated with a law degree in 1938. He also won age-division championships as late as 1996 and was still playing and winning matches in the 21st century. Service in the U.S. Navy during World War II interrupted his career, which saw him win five **Grand Slam** championships and finish second 12 other times.

Most of his success was as a **doubles** player, although he did reach the **United States National singles** final in 1952 and was **ranked** seven in the world that year. With partner **Bill Talbert**, he won the United States National Doubles Championships four times—in 1942, 1945, 1946, and 1948. Nine years later, at the age of 43, he and **Budge Patty** won the **Wimbledon** doubles championship. He was also runner-up for the United States doubles title five times between 1940 and 1957, runner-up for the **French National** doubles in 1951 and 1952, and runner-up for Wimbledon doubles in 1948 and 1949. In 1955, he was the United States National **mixed doubles** finalist and, in 1956, the Wimbledon mixed doubles finalist.

He was on the **United States Davis Cup** team in 1946, 1948 through 1950, 1952, 1953, and 1957. The United States played in the **challenge round** each of those years, and Mulloy only played in that round from 1946 to 1950. In 12 **ties**, his record was 3–0 in singles and 8–3 in doubles. In 1957, Mulloy, then 44 years old, had a 1–1 record in Davis Cup doubles in Inter-Zonal competition. He was inducted into the **International Tennis Hall of Fame** in 1972. In 1996, he donated a trophy (the Gardnar Mulloy Cup) for an annual international team competition for men 80 years of age and older, under the auspices of the **International Tennis Federation**. As of 2009, he had won 127 United States National Championships in various age categories. He also authored three books, *The Will to Win*, *Advantage Striker*, and *As It Was*.

MURRAY, ANDREW "ANDY." B. 5 May 1987, Glasgow, Scotland. Andy Murray was raised in Dunblane, Scotland, and began playing tennis when he was five years old. On 13 March 1996, an armed man entered Murray's school, the Dunblane Primary School, and killed 16 children and 1 teacher. Murray was not harmed but remembers being told to hide under a table in his classroom. Murray later attended Dunblane High School, and at the age of 15, went to Barcelona, **Spain**, to study at the Sánchez-Casal Tennis Academy while attending the Schiller International School.

Murray began playing **professional** tennis at the **Challenger** and Futures levels in 2003. In 2004, he won the **boys' singles** at the **United States Open** and reached the semifinals of the boys' **doubles** with his brother, Jamie, as partner. He competed in the 2008 **Olympic Games** but lost in the first round of the singles and second round of the doubles (with brother Jamie as partner). In 2008, he reached the finals of the United States Open but lost to **Roger Federer**. In 2009, he reached the quarterfinals at the **French Open** and semifinals at **Wimbledon** and achieved a career-high **ranking** of second in the world. In 2010, he again lost to Federer at the finals of the **Australian Open**. In 2011, he repeated as losing finalist at the Australian Open, losing to Novak Djokovic and reached the semi-finals at the French Open, where he was defeated by Rafael Nadal. He was on the **Great Britain Davis Cup** team each year from 2005 to 2009 and had a record of 10–1 in singles and 1–5 in doubles in nine **ties**. In his career, through May 2011, Murray has reached the finals of 25 **Association of Tennis Professionals** tournaments and won 16 of them.

N

NA, LI. *See* LI, NA.

NADAL PARERA, RAFAEL "RAFA." B. 3 June 1986, Manacor, Majorca, **Spain**. Rafael Nadal was raised on the island of Majorca. He played both tennis and soccer as a youth and was **coached** in tennis by his uncle, Toni Nadal. Uncle Toni has remained with Rafael as his coach throughout his career. Toni changed the right-handed Rafa to play tennis **left-handed** as he thought it would give him an edge over his right-handed opponents. Rafa became a **professional** in 2001 and quickly established himself as a strong competitor who played every **point** as though it was the most important point of the **match**.

He played his first match at **Wimbledon** in 2003 and reached the third round. In 2005, he entered the **French Open** for the first time and won the event. He proved his dominance on the **clay surface** and was French Open champion again in 2006, 2007, 2008, 2010, and 2011, winning 81 consecutive matches on clay from 11 April 2005 to 20 May 2007. He was finally defeated on clay by **Roger Federer** in a tournament at Hamburg, **Germany**. The 6-foot 1-inch, 190-pound, **converted** left-hander was one of the very few players able to dominate Federer in head-to-head competition, with 17 victories in their 25 matches (through the 2011 French Open). Of the 17 wins, 12 have come on clay **courts**. On **grass** and **hard court surfaces**, Federer has a six to five advantage. One of Nadal's greatest victories came in the 2008 Wimbledon final against Federer. The five-**set** match has been called, by some, the **greatest tennis match** ever played and enabled Nadal to be **ranked** number one in the world for the first time in his career. This was Rafa's first **Grand Slam** title in an event other than the French Open. He followed that up with a victory over Federer in the finals of the 2009 **Australian Open**. Nadal won Wimbledon for the second time in 2010, when Federer was defeated by Tomáš Berdych in a quarterfinal match and Nadal defeated Berdych in the final. Nadal's also won the **United States Open** in 2010 and completed a career Grand Slam. He became only the third person (**Andre Agassi** and **Steffi Graf** are the others) to win all four Grand Slam singles championships and the **Olympic singles** title.

He competed in the 2004 and 2008 Olympic Games and won the men's singles event in 2008. He was a member of the Spanish **Davis Cup** team in 2004 through 2006, 2008, 2009, and 2011. His record through May 2011 was 16–1 in singles and 2–4 in doubles in 12 **ties**. He helped lead Spain to the Cup in 2004, 2008, and 2009, although in 2008, he was injured and unable to play in the championship final. From 2005 to 2009, he won 11 straight Cup matches, 10 in singles. In his career, through May 2011, he has won 46 singles and 7 doubles titles.

NALBANDIAN, DAVID PABLO. B. 1 January 1982, Córdoba, **Argentina**. David Nalbandian began his **professional** tennis career in 2000. Only two years later, he reached the final at **Wimbledon** but lost to **Lleyton Hewitt**. Since that time, he has reached a high world **singles ranking** of three in 2006 and has reached the semifinals of the **Australian Open** in 2006, the **French Open** in 2004 and 2006, and **United States Open** in 2003. The 5-foot 11-inch, 170 pound right-hander is one of only five players active in 2011 to have reached at least the semifinal round of all four **Grand Slam** singles events—the others being **Roger Federer**, **Rafael Nadal**, **Novak Djoković**, and **Andy Murray**, all except Murray won a Slam championship.

David competed in the 2008 **Olympic Games** in both singles and **doubles** and reached the third round of the singles. His was on the Argentinean **Davis Cup** team each year from 2002 to 2011, except for 2009 when he was injured. His record is 21–5 in singles and 11–5 in doubles in 20 **ties**, and he helped Argentina reach the Cup final in 2006 and 2008. In 2006, although Argentina was defeated by **Russia**, 3-2, Nalbandian won both his matches. A series of injuries have hampered Nalbandian since 2007. Through May 2011, he has won 11 singles and no doubles title in his career.

NĂSTASE, ILIE "NASTY." B. 19 July 1946, Bucharest, **Romania**. Ilie Năstase was one of the most colorful players on the **professional** tennis tour. His **court** antics and arguing with **umpires** was primarily gamesmanship, and despite his nickname of "Nasty," he was anything but. His **Association of Tennis Professionals** biography states, "Though he provoked controversy, and his career was marred by fines, disqualifications, and suspensions, Năstase was good-natured, likeable and friendly off-court. He had a sense of humor in his on-court shenanigans, but frequently did not know when to stop and lost control of himself. 'I am a little crazy,' he said, 'but I try to be a good boy.'" Năstase won seven **Grand Slam** titles and was runner-up six times. He was the 1972 **United States Open** and 1973 **French Open singles** champion and singles runner-up at the 1971 French Open and 1972 and 1976 **Wimbledon** tournaments.

In doubles, he and **Ion Țiriac** were runners-up in the 1966 French Nationals and 1970 French Open champions. Teaming with **Jimmy Connors**, Năstase was runner-up at the 1973 French Open and was 1973 Wimbledon and 1976 U.S. Open champion. Năstase also teamed with **Rosie Casals** to win Wimbledon **mixed doubles** in 1970 and 1972, and they were runners-up in 1972 at the U.S. Open. He was on the Romanian **Davis Cup** team from 1966 to 1977, 1979, 1980, and 1982 to 1985. In 18 years of Cup competition, his record is 74–22 in singles and 35–15 in doubles in 52 **ties**. In 1969, 1971, and 1972, he helped lead Romania to the Cup final, but the team was defeated by the **United States** each time. In both 1969 and 1971, Romania had to win six ties to reach the final round. In 1971, Năstase's Davis Cup record was 18–2 with 15 consecutive victories. In his long career, from 1966 to 1985, he won 87 singles and 45 doubles titles and was **ranked** world number one in singles in 1973 and world number ten in doubles in 1977. After retiring, he wrote some tennis novels in French and English and made an unsuccessful bid for mayor of Bucharest in 1996. He was inducted into the **International Tennis Hall of Fame** in 1991.

NATIONAL COLLEGIATE ATHLETIC ASSOCIATION. *See* COLLEGIATE TENNIS.

NAVRATILOVA (SUBERTOVA), MARTINA. B. 18 October 1956, Prague, **Czechoslovakia**. Martina Navratilova is one of the players to be included in a discussion of the greatest female tennis player of all time. When she finally retired on 9 September 2006, at age 49, after winning the **United States Open mixed doubles** with **Bob Bryan** for her 59th **Grand Slam** title, **Billie Jean King** said of her "She's the greatest **singles**, **doubles**, and mixed doubles player who's ever lived." She was born Martina Subertova, but after her parents divorced when she was three years old, her mother remarried, and Martina took the name of her stepfather, Miroslav Navratil. He also became her first tennis **coach**. She won the Czechoslovakia National Championship at age 15 in 1972 and came to the **United States** the following year. Over the next 33 years, she reached the finals of 85 Grand Slam events, winning 59 of them, and is second only to **Margaret Smith Court's** 64 titles in 87 finals. Navratilova won 18 of 32 Grand Slam singles (winning six consecutive in 1983 and 1984), 31 of 37 women's doubles (from 1975 to 1990, including all four in 1984), and 10 of 16 mixed doubles championships (her first in 1974 and last in 2006). She won singles, women's doubles, and mixed doubles at each of the four Grand Slam venues, a feat accomplished by only **Doris Hart** and Margaret Smith Court. Navratilova won a record total of 167 singles and 177 doubles titles. She had winning streaks of 74 singles matches and 109

Martina Navratilova won her first Grand Slam title in 1975 at age 18 and her last one in 2006, one month shy of her 50th birthday. (courtesy of the International Tennis Hall of Fame and Museum, Edward Fernberger Collection)

doubles matches with partner **Pam Shriver**. Martina reached the **Wimbledon** ladies' singles finals nine consecutive years, from 1982 to 1990, and won nine Wimbledon singles titles from 1978 to 1990. The nine Wimbledon singles titles are more than any other individual, man or woman.

In 1975, she asked for political asylum in the United States and became a United States citizen in 1981. In 2004, at the age of 47, she competed in the **Olympic** doubles event with 30-year-old partner **Lisa Raymond** and reached the quarterfinal round. She played in the **Federation Cup** for her native Czechoslovakia in 1975 and led the team to the championship. In 1982, 1986, 1989, 1995, 2003, and 2004, she played on the United States Fed Cup team. She won 40 consecutive Fed Cup matches in 25 **ties**. She was undefeated in singles with a 20–0 record, and her only Fed Cup loss came in her final match in a **dead rubber** doubles in 2004 at age 47. In 1982, 1986, and 1989, she led the United States to the Cup championship, and in 2003, she was on the runner-up team. She played on the United States **Wightman Cup** team in 1983, winning all three of her matches—two singles and one doubles. She was inducted into the **International Tennis Hall of Fame** in 2000. She has been a television analyst, written several books, played **World Team Tennis** until 2009, and been outspoken on a number of issues, including animal rights, underprivileged children, and **gay** rights. In 2010, she was diagnosed with breast cancer but has apparently overcome the affliction.

NET. A net is strung across the middle of the **court** to separate each player's half of the court. The net is attached to metal posts that are three feet six inches high on each side of the court, three feet from the sidelines. The net drops from three feet six inches at the ends to just three feet in the middle of the court and is held there by a two-inch wide strap. Players traditionally meet at the net with the **umpire** before play starts to decide who will **serve** first and which sides they will begin play on. At the end of the match, they also traditionally meet at the net for a handshake.

NET CORD. The **net** cord is the top cord or wire cable that supports the net. A shot that makes contact with it is also referred to as a net cord. The **ball** remains in play for all strokes, other than the **serve**, that make contact with the net cord. Serves that touch the net but land in the proper **service** box are called "**lets**" and must be replayed without penalty.

NETHERLANDS, THE. Tennis in the Netherlands is administered by the Koninklijke Nederlandse **Lawn Tennis** Bond (Royal Dutch Lawn Tennis Association), founded on 5 June 1899. From 1920 through May 2011, the Netherlands has competed in 84 **Davis Cup tournaments** with a record of 65–82 in 147 **ties**. The country has competed 17 years in the World Group since its formation in 1981. In 2001, the Netherlands reached the semifinals, its best effort. Top Davis Cup players have been Jacco Eltingh, Paul Haarhuis, Ivo Rinkel, Hendrik Timmer, and A. C. Van Swol. The Netherlands competed in **Olympic Games** tennis in 1906, 1908, 1912, 1924, and each year from 1984 to 2000. In 1906, Guus Kessler finished fourth in men's **singles**. Kessler had a remarkable tournament—his first three matches were won by default. In his semifinal match, he was shut out, 6–0, 6–0. He thus finished in fourth place without winning one game. In 1924, Kea Bouman and Henk Timmer won the bronze medal in **mixed doubles**. In 1996, both Dutch **doubles** teams finished fourth—Jacco Eltingh and Paul Haarhuis in men's and Manon Bollegraf and Brenda Schultz-McCarthy in women's. In 2000, the team of Kristie Boogert and Miriam Oremans won the silver medal in women's doubles.

Among the best Dutch male tennis players have been Thiemo de Bakker, **Richard Krajicek**, Tom Nijssen, **Tom Okker**, Menno Oosting, Michiel Shapers, and Martin Verkerk. The best female tennis players include Marijke Jensen, Michaella Krajicek, Marcella Mesker, **Betty Stove**, and Caroline Vis. The Netherlands also is the birthplace of the greatest **wheelchair tennis** player of all time, **Esther Vergeer**, several other of the best female wheelchair players, Jiske Griffioen, Korie Homan, Sharon Walraven, and two of the top male wheelchair players, Robin Ammerlaan and Maikel Scheffers. In **Federation Cup** competition, from 1963 to May 2011, the Netherlands has competed 48 years, played 159 ties, 33 years in World Group, with a record of 93–63. The country's best result was in 1968 and 1997, when it was runner-up.

NET JUDGE. Until recent times, a **net** judge was often assigned for important matches. He or she was positioned usually below the **umpire's** chair and sat with one hand on the **net cord** to determine whether a **serve** hit the net. If it did, and the serve had landed in the proper service **court**, a **let** would be called and the serve replayed. In recent years, electronic technology has been used for this function.

NEW BALLS. Since a **tennis ball** loses its bounce fairly quickly after the pressurized can of tennis balls is opened, **tournament** play usually requires new cans of tennis balls to be opened after the first seven games and then after every nine games, for the rest of the match. The reasoning behind using new balls after the first seven games is that new balls are used for the warm-ups and that is figured as roughly two games worth of use. It is the responsibility of the **chair umpire** to request new balls at the appropriate intervals. When a player is first serving with new balls, the custom is to raise one above his or her head to indicate that fact to his or her opponent.

NEWCOMBE, JOHN DAVID "NEWK." B. 23 May 1944, Sydney, New South Wales, **Australia**. John Newcombe was the Australian **junior** champion in 1961, 1962, and 1963. In 1966, he was the singles finalist at the **United States Nationals**, losing to countryman **Fred Stolle** in four sets. The following year, Newcombe won both the **Wimbledon** and U.S. National singles titles. He became a **professional** in 1968. In his career, as both an **amateur** and professional, he reached the finals of 34 **Grand Slam** events and won 26 of them. Only **Roy Emerson**, with 28 Grand Slam championships, won more than Newcombe, and only Emerson, Stolle, **John Bromwich**, and **Ken Rosewall** played in more Grand Slam finals. The 6-foot tall, 170-pound, right-handed Newcombe was **ranked** first in the world in 1967. He won **singles** titles at Australia in 1973 and 1975 and was runner-up in 1976. He was Wimbledon singles champion in 1967, 1970, and 1971 and was runner-up in 1969. His best singles performance at **Roland Garros** was in 1965 and 1969, when he reached the quarterfinal round. At the **United States Open**, he was men's singles champion in 1967 and 1973 and was runner-up in 1966.

Newcombe also excelled in **doubles** and won 17 Grand Slam men's doubles and two **mixed doubles** championships. He was five-time men's doubles champion at the Australian Championships (1965, 1967, 1971, 1976 with **Tony Roche**, and 1973 with **Mal Anderson**) and runner-up in 1963 with **Ken Fletcher** and in 1966 with Roche. At Wimbledon, Newcombe and Roche won in 1965, 1968, 1969, 1970, and 1974, and Newcombe and Fletcher won in 1966. At Roland Garros, Newcombe and Roche won in 1967 and 1969 and were runners-up in 1964. Newcombe and **Tom Okker** also won the event in 1973. Newcombe and Roche won the United States Nationals in 1967; with partner Owen Davidson, Newcombe was runner-up in 1972 and champion in 1973; and with Roger Taylor, Newcombe was 1971 champion. Newcombe's first Grand Slam title was the 1964 United States mixed doubles, which he won with **Margaret Smith**. Newcombe and Smith were also cochampions at the 1965 Australian Championships when the final **match** was unable to be played. In 1965, Newcombe and **Maria Bueno** were finalists at Roland Garros.

Newk played **Davis Cup** tennis for Australia from 1963 to 1967, but after becoming a professional, he was ineligible for Cup play. After the eligibility rules were changed, he again played in 1973, 1975, and 1976. His record was 16–7 in singles and 9–2 in doubles in 15 **ties** in 8 years. He played on the Cup-winning team in 1964, 1965, 1966, 1967, and 1973, although he played only in preliminary round matches in 1964. He also served as nonplaying Davis Cup captain in 1995. He was inducted into the **International Tennis Hall of Fame** in 1986. After retiring from the tour, he has done television work and runs the John Newcombe Tennis Ranch & Tennis Academy in New Braunfels, Texas. One of its protégés is Ryan Harrison, who, in his first United States Open **main draw** in 2010, successfully **qualified** for the tournament and defeated Ivan Ljubičić, seeded 15, in his first round match.

NEWPORT CASINO. The Newport Casino is located on Bellevue Avenue in Newport, Rhode Island. It was built in 1880 by famed architect Stanford White and was the site of the first **United States National Lawn Tennis** Championships, which were held there annually until 1914. The grounds are also the home of the **International Tennis Hall of Fame and Museum**. In 1987, it was designated as a National Historic Landmark. By the 1950s, the facility had deteriorated, and **James Van Alen** had it restored and established the Hall of Fame there. The facility includes the Casino building (which houses the Hall of Fame), a Horseshoe Piazza, the **Bill Talbert** Stadium (where an annual **Association of Tennis Professionals** tournament is held), a **court tennis** building, a theater, several **grass** tennis **courts**, and indoor tennis courts. The courts are open to the public. Although it is called "casino," it was never a gambling establishment as are modern-day casinos. The 19th-century use of the word was a group of buildings for social activities.

NO-AD SCORING. No-ad scoring is a method for shortening the duration of tennis **matches**. It is employed by **World Team Tennis** and, in recent years, has been used in **Association of Tennis Professionals** and **Women's Tennis Association** doubles matches. When the score reaches 40–40, or **deuce,** the winner of the next **point** wins the game. The **server's** opponent has the choice of which **court** in which to receive **serve.** *See also* ADVANTAGE; SCORING.

NOAH, YANNICK SIMONE CAMILLE. B. 18 May 1960, Sedan, France. Yannick Noah is the son of a French mother and a Cameroonian father, Zacharie Noah, a former member of the 1961 Coupe de France champion soccer team in France. After Zacharie ended his career due to injury, the family moved to the Cameroon, where Yannick was raised. As an 11-year old in Yaounde, Cameroon, and playing with makeshift equipment, Noah was discovered by **Arthur Ashe,** who was then on a goodwill tour of Africa. Ashe convinced **Philippe Chatrier,** president of the French Tennis Federation, to send Noah to a tennis academy in Nice, France, to help develop his skills.

Noah won the 1977 French **Junior** Singles Championship and was runner-up to **Ivan Lendl** at the **Orange Bowl** tournament. Noah quit high school in his junior year in 1977 to become a **professional** tennis player. In 1983, the 6-foot 4-inch, 190-pound, dreadlock-wearing right-hander recorded the most important victory in his career when he won the **French Open** men's **singles**. As of 2010, he is the last Frenchman to win that tournament. (**Mary Pierce,** representing France but a native of **Canada** and resident of the **United States,** won it in 2000.) Noah also won the French Open **doubles** with **Henri Leconte** in 1984 and was runner-up there in 1987 with **Guy Forget.** Leconte and Noah were also **United States Open** runners-up in 1985. He played **Davis Cup** tennis for France from 1978 to 1985 and 1988 to 1990. In 22 **ties,** his record was 26–15 in singles and 13–7 in doubles for those 11 years. In 1982, France was defeated by the United States in the Cup finals. Noah retired from active play in 1996, and in his career, was credited with 23 singles and 16 doubles titles and reached a high world **ranking** of three in singles and one in doubles, both in 1986.

After retiring, he has become a successful popular singer, who has recorded several albums, and is a restaurant owner on the island of St. Barthelemy (St. Barts) in the West Indies. He was also the captain of the French women's **Fed Cup** team in 1997 and helped lead the team to the championship. He was inducted into the **International Tennis Hall of Fame** in 2005. His 6-foot 11-

inch son, Joakim, was a member of the 2006 and 2007 **National Collegiate Athletic Association** national champion basketball team and has played professional basketball with the Chicago Bulls in the NBA since 2007. In 2010, Noah, aged 50, entered and completed the New York City Marathon in the excellent time of 4:01:38.

NORMAN, LEIF MAGNUS. B. 30 May 1976, Filipstad, **Sweden**. The 6-foot 2-inch, 205-pound Magnus Norman began playing **professional** tennis in 1992. In 1998, he had corrective surgery for a heart valve condition. The highlight of his career occurred in 2000, when he was a semifinalist in the **Australian Open**, reached the finals of the **French Open**, won the Masters tournament in Rome, and was **ranked** second in the world. He competed in the **singles** event in the 2000 **Olympic Games** and reached the third round. He won 12 titles in his career and had a record of 244–177. A member of the Swedish **Davis Cup** team from 1998 to 2003, he played each year except 2000. In seven **ties**, playing singles only, his record was 7–6. He played for Sweden in the 1998 Cup final when the team defeated Italy to become Cup champions. His career ended prematurely in 2004 due to various injuries. In retirement, he has been the **coach** of **Robin Söderling**.

NOVOTNÁ, JANA. B. 2 October 1968, Brno, **Czechoslovakia**. Jana Novotná became a **professional** tennis player in 1986 and retired in 1999. During those 14 years, she won 100 titles (24 **singles** and 76 **doubles**), was **ranked** second in the world in singles (1997) and first in doubles (first time in 1990), won women's doubles championships at all four **Grand Slam** events, won **mixed doubles** championships at three of the four Grand Slam events, won the **Fed Cup** with Czechoslovakia in 1988, won three **Olympic** medals, and was the 1998 **Wimbledon** singles champion. Yet despite all her accomplishments, the 5-foot 9-inch, 140-pound right-hander is not usually remembered in the same way as some of her contemporaries, such as **Lindsay Davenport**, **Steffi Graf**, **Martina Hingis**, or **Monica Seles**. Novotná was a finalist in 32 Grand Slam events and won 17 of them. In singles play, she lost in three sets at the **Australian Open** in 1991 and at Wimbledon in 1993 and 1997, before defeating Nathalie Tauziat in straight sets to win the 1998 Wimbledon title. For 10 years, from 1989 to 1998, Novotná was a finalist every year in at least one of the Grand Slam doubles events, and in 1990 and 1991, she was a finalist in all of them each year. In women's doubles, she won Wimbledon in 1989 with **Helena Suková**. In 1990, they won the first three Slam events and were runners-up at the **United States Open**. In 1991, she and **Gigi Fernández** won the **French Open** and were runners-up at the Australian and Wimbledon. Changing partners to **Larisa Savchenko Neiland**, she was runner-up at the

United States Open. With Neiland, in 1992, she was runner-up at Wimbledon and the U.S. Open. In 1993, the pair was runner-up at the French Open and Wimbledon. In 1994, **Arantxa Sánchez Vicario** became her partner; after being runners-up at Wimbledon, they won the U.S. Open. In 1995, they won the Australian and Wimbledon and were runners-up at the French Open. In 1996, they were runners-up at the U.S. Open. In 1997, Novotná and Lindsay Davenport won the U.S. Open. In 1998, Novotná and Martina Hingis won the French Open, Wimbledon, and the U.S. Open. In mixed doubles, Novotná and Jim Pugh won the Australian Open in 1988 and 1989, the U.S. Open in 1988, and Wimbledon in 1989, and she and Todd Woodbridge were runners-up at the 1994 U.S. Open.

Novotná competed in three Olympic Games from 1988 to 1996. In 1988, she was the silver medalist in women's doubles with partner Helena Suková, representing Czechoslovakia. In 1992, she and partner Andrea Strnadová reached the quarterfinals. In 1996, Novotná won the bronze medal in the singles event and, with partner Suková, won the silver medal in the doubles, this time representing the new Czech Republic. Novotná was a member of the Czechoslovakian Federation Cup team from 1987 to 1992. In 1993 and 1995 to 1998, she played for the Czech Republic. Her record was 22–7 in singles and 11–5 in doubles in 33 **ties** over 10 years. She was a member of the Federation Cup championship team in 1988. She won the **Hopman Cup** in 1992 with partner **Petr Korda**. After retiring, she was the **coach** of Carly Gullickson. Novotná was inducted into the **International Tennis Hall of Fame** in 2005.

NUTHALL SHOEMAKER, BETTY KAY. B. 23 May 1911, Surbiton, Surrey, England. D. 8 November 1983, New York, New York. Although British-born Betty Nuthall never passed the quarterfinal round at **Wimbledon**, she did reach the finals of the **United States National Championships** in her first attempt. In 1927, at the age of 16, she became the youngest female player to be a finalist at **Forest Hills**. Three years later, she won the **tournament**. In 1931, at **Roland Garros**, she reached the women's **singles** finals and won the women's **doubles** and **mixed doubles**. In 1932, she again won the **French National** mixed doubles and was runner-up in the women's doubles. In 1933, she was runner-up in mixed doubles. She was a three-time winner of the United States National women's doubles (1930, 1931, 1933) and a losing finalist once (1927), with a different partner each time. She also won the U.S. National mixed doubles twice. In 1929, she was ranked fourth in the world. She played on the British **Wightman Cup** team in seven years, from 1927 to 1939, and had a record of 6–7. She was inducted into the **International Tennis Hall of Fame** in 1977.

OKKER, TOM SAMUEL. B. 22 February 1944, Amsterdam, **the Netherlands**. The slightly-built Dutchman, Tom Okker, although only 5-feet 9-inches and 145 pounds, was one of the world's best players during the advent of the **Open** era in the late 1960s. Arguably the best male Dutch player in history, he played on the Netherlands **Davis Cup** team from 1964 to 1981. In 13 **ties** over 11 years, his record was 10–13 in **singles** and 5–7 in **doubles**. In **Grand Slam** events, his best performance was in the first Open **United States National Championships** in 1968 when, although finishing second to **amateur Arthur Ashe** (who received $20 per day in expenses), he won the first prize of $14,000. He also reached the semifinal round at each of the other major tournaments—**Roland Garros** in 1969, **Wimbledon** in 1978, and the **Australian Open** in 1971. Despite his singles success, he was best known as a doubles player, winning 78 doubles events in his career. He won the **French Open** in 1973 with **John Newcombe** and the **United States Open** in 1976 with Marty Riessen. With Riessen, he reached the Wimbledon finals in 1969, Australian Open finals in 1971, and United States Open finals in 1975. Okker was ranked number one in the world in doubles in 1969 and number three in singles in 1974.

One of the best Jewish players in tennis history, Okker won the 1965 Maccabiah Games singles and **mixed doubles** and, in 2003, was inducted into the International Jewish Sports Hall of Fame on the campus of Wingate Institute in Netanya, **Israel**. He is one of only 12 tennis players to be so honored. After retiring from tennis in 1981 (although continuing to play occasionally in **senior** events), he was a partner in the Jaski Art Gallery in Amsterdam. In 2005, he opened his own gallery—Tom Okker Art—in Hazerswoude-Dorp.

OLMEDO, LUIS ALEJANDRO "ALEX," "CHIEF." B. 24 March 1936, Arequipa, **Peru**. Alex Olmedo came to the **United States** in 1954 to study business at the University of Southern California. The 6-foot 1-inch, 168-pound right-hander played on the tennis team there and was the **National Collegiate Athletic Association singles** and **doubles** champion in 1956 and

1958. In 1959, he achieved a world **ranking** of two as he won the **Australian National** Singles Championships and **Wimbledon** singles and was the losing finalist at **Forest Hills**. He won the men's doubles there in 1958 and was a losing **mixed doubles** finalist in 1958 and men's doubles finalist in 1959. Although a Peruvian citizen, he was eligible as a student in the United States to play **Davis Cup** tennis for the United States in 1958 and 1959. His three victories in the 1958 semifinal against **Italy** and three more in the final against **Australia** won the Cup for the United States, 3–2. In 1959, he again played in the final but lost two of three matches as Australia won the Cup. His overall record for the three **ties** was 5–1 in singles and 2–1 in doubles. In 1960, he became a **professional** and joined the tour.

In 1965, he retired from the pro tour and became a teaching professional at the Beverly Hills Hotel, where his clients included actors Katherine Hepburn and Robert Duvall and comedian Chevy Chase. He remained there for more than 30 years. When the major tournaments became open tournaments, he resumed his playing career and played selected events through 1977. He was inducted into the **International Tennis Hall of Fame** in 1987. In 1999, he became a United States citizen.

OLYMPIC GAMES. The first modern Olympic Games in Athens in 1896 included **lawn tennis** among the sports contested. The sport was included in each subsequent Olympic Games through 1924 in Paris. It was then removed from the Olympic program (probably due to conflicts over the definition of **amateurism**) until 1988, although the 1968 Games in **Mexico** included both **exhibition** and demonstration tennis **tournaments**, and 1984 had a demonstration tennis tournament limited to players 21 years of age or younger.

In 1896, only men's **singles** and men's **doubles** events were held, and while 13 men took part, several of them were recruited from other sports to fill out the field. In 1900, women's singles and **mixed doubles** were also included. In 1904, only men's events were held. The 1906 Games in Athens (treated as an unofficial Olympics by some, although most Olympic historians consider it to be "official") had competition in men's singles and doubles, women's singles, and mixed doubles. The 1908 Games in London included three types of tennis events—outdoor lawn tennis, "covered lawn tennis" (played indoors), and *jeu de paume* (**court tennis** or real tennis). This was the only time in history that *jeu de paume* was played at the Olympic Games. Men's singles and doubles and women's singles were contested in the lawn tennis events, but only men's singles were played in court tennis. In 1912 in Stockholm, both indoor and outdoor lawn tennis events were held. All events, save women's doubles, were played both indoors and outdoors. World War I caused the 1916 Olympic Games to be cancelled. In 1920, at Antwerp, Belgium, all five events—men's and women's singles and doubles and mixed doubles—were held at the Olympic Games for the first time. The number of contestants was also the largest to that date—41 men and 18 women entered the singles competition, and many of them also played doubles and/or mixed doubles. In Paris in 1924, the largest field for Olympic tennis entered—82 men in singles, 39 men's teams in doubles, 31 women in singles, 11 women's teams in doubles, and 16 teams in mixed doubles. (When Olympic tennis was resumed in 1988 as a medal sport, the field was limited to 64 men in singles and 32 teams in doubles.)

In 1968, both exhibition and demonstration tournaments were held in Guadalajara during the Mexico City Olympics, and in 1984, a demonstration tournament limited to players 21 years of age and younger was held. Since 1988, men's and women's singles and doubles have been held at each Olympic Games. **Professional** players have been allowed to enter, and most of the top players have appeared, although not always with satisfactory results. For example, the 1992 Olympic tournament was won by Marc Rosset of **Switzerland** over Jordi Arrese of **Spain** with **Goran Ivanišević** and Andrei Chersakov finishing in third place. Among the nonmedalists that year in singles were **Boris Becker**, **Michael Chang**, **Jim Courier**, **Stefan Edberg**, **Guy Forget**, **Henri Leconte**, Thomas Muster, **Pete Sampras**, and **Michael Stich**—all top-rated players. The Olympic tennis tournament has now become respected by the professional players and is treated as a fifth major tournament. The 2012 Olympic Games scheduled for London will also include a mixed doubles event for the first time since 1924. *See also* APPENDIX I (for a list of champions).

OPEN. An open **tournament** is one in which both **amateur** and **professional** players may enter. Until 1968, the major tournaments were restricted to amateur players only. In 1968, **Wimbledon** broke tradition and became an open tournament, and the other major tournaments followed shortly afterward.

ORANGE BOWL. The Orange Bowl is a **Junior Tennis tournament** under the auspices of the **International Tennis Federation**. Held annually in December, since 1962, in South Florida, it consists of boys' and girls' (since 1980) tournaments for ages 12 and under and 14 and under. The tournament, one of the most prestigious, includes among its winners and runners-up many players who later had successful professional careers, such as **Jimmy Connors**, **Roger Federer**, **Tommy Haas**, **Juan Martín del Potro**, **Mary Joe Fernández**, **Justine Henin**, **Amélie Mauresmo**, **Monica Seles**, and Andrea Temesvári.

ORANTES CORRAL, MANUEL "MANOLO." B. 6 February 1949, Granada, **Spain**. Manuel Orantes played tennis from 1967 to 1984. A **clay court** specialist, his biggest victory was in 1975 when he won the **United States Open Singles** Championship by defeating **Jimmy Connors** in straight sets on clay. He also reached the finals of the **French Open** in 1974, where he lost to the 18-year-old **Björn Borg** in five sets after winning the first two sets. In his career, Orantes, a five-foot ten-inch **left-hander**, won 33 singles and 22 **doubles** titles. He reached the singles semifinals at both **Roland Garros** and **Wimbledon** in 1972. In his only entry in the **Australian Open**, he reached the quarterfinals in 1968. He was second-**ranked** in singles in 1973. He and **José Higueras** were finalists in the 1978 French Open doubles.

Orantes competed in the 1968 demonstration tennis tournament in the **Olympic Games** in **Mexico** and was the runner-up in men's singles and quarterfinalist in men's doubles. He played **Davis Cup** tennis each year for Spain from 1967 to 1980 and had a record of 39–19 in singles and 21–8 in doubles in 38 **ties** over 14 years. He helped Spain reach the Cup finals in 1967 but lost all three of his matches that year against **Australia**. In 1978, he was a member of the Spanish team that won the inaugural **World Team Cup**. After retiring from active play in 1984, he was the nonplaying captain of Spain's Davis Cup team from 1985 to 1992 and, since 2003, owns and operates the Manuel Orantes Future Pros Tennis School in Barcelona, Spain.

OSBORNE DUPONT, MARGARET EVELYN. B. 4 March 1918, Joseph, Oregon. Margaret Osborne duPont won more **United States National Championships** than anyone else by far. From 1941 to 1962, she won 25 titles at **Forest Hills**. Margaret Smith Court, with 18, is in second place in that category. Osborne duPont won 37 **Grand Slam** titles (fourth best of all time) and never played in the **Australian National tournament**. She also was the runner-up 14 times in Slam events. Had World War II not suspended play in three of the four major tournaments, her total might have even been greater. At **Wimbledon**, she won the 1947 ladies' **singles** title and was runner-up to her **doubles** partner, **Louise Brough**, in 1949 and 1950. The 1949 final was one of Wimbledon's classic matches, 10–8, 1–6, 10–8. She won the **French National** singles in 1946 and 1949 and the **United States National** singles in 1948, 1949, and 1950 after being runner-up in 1944 and 1947. The 1948 final was another classic match, 4–6, 6–4, 15–13, the longest women's final at Forest Hills.

Osborne duPont was an excellent doubles player and won 31 of her 37 Grand Slam titles in doubles and **mixed doubles**. She and Brough won the Wimbledon doubles in 1946, 1948, 1949, 1950, and 1954 and were runners-up in 1947 and 1951. In 1958, after Brough retired, Osborne duPont partnered with Margaret Varner and, at the age of 40, reached the finals there once more. One of Margaret Osborne duPont's more remarkable victories was in 1962 when, at the age of 44, she won the mixed doubles at Wimbledon with **Neale Fraser**, 15 years her junior. She had reached the Wimbledon mixed doubles final only once before, in 1954 with **Ken Rosewall**. At the French Nationals, she and Brough reached the finals in 1946, 1946, 1949, and 1950, winning in all but 1950. Perhaps her greatest accomplishment was in winning the United States National Women's Doubles Championship in 10 consecutive years from 1941 to 1950. She also won it from 1955 to 1957 and was runner-up in 1953 and 1954. Her partner was Louise Brough for all except the 1941 title, when **Sarah Palfrey Fabyan** was her partner.

A 5-foot 5-inch, 145-pound right-hander, Osborne duPont also won the U.S. National mixed doubles nine times and was runner-up three times from 1943 to 1960. Her partners were **Bill Talbert** (1943–49), Ken McGregor (1950), Ken Rosewall (1954–56), and Neale Fraser (1958–60). She was undefeated in **Wightman Cup** play in 10 years, from 1946 to 1962, winning 10 singles matches and 9 doubles matches. She also served as Wightman Cup team captain for most of the years between 1953 and 1965.

In 1947, she married William duPont Jr., a member of the prominent duPont family of Delaware and owner of a large thoroughbred racing farm, and they divorced in 1964. She interrupted her tennis career to give birth to their son, William duPont III, on 22 July 1952. She was inducted into the **International Tennis Hall of Fame** in 1967.

OSUNA, RAFAEL HERRERA "RAFE." B. 15 September 1938, Mexico City, **Mexico**. D. 4 June 1969, Monterrey, Mexico. The 5-foot 10-inch Rafael Osuna won the **United States Open Singles** Championship in 1963 and was **ranked** number one in the world that year. From 1961 to 1963, he and Antonio Palafox reached the United States Open **doubles** finals, winning the event in 1962. At **Wimbledon**, Osuna and **Dennis Ralston** won the men's doubles in 1960, and Osuna and Palafox won in 1963. At the 1968 **Olympic Games** in Mexico, Osuna competed in both the **exhibition** and demonstration tennis **tournaments** and won both doubles tournaments with partner Vicente Zarazua. Osuna also won the exhibition men's singles and was fourth in the demonstration men's singles. From 1958 until his death in 1969, he was a member of the Mexican **Davis Cup** team, playing each year except 1959. His record was 25–15 in singles and 17–8 in doubles in 25 **ties**. He helped Mexico reached the Cup final in 1962, for the only time in Mexico's history, but lost all three of his matches as **Australia** defeated Mexico to win the Cup for the fourth consecutive year. He died in an airplane crash while flying from

Mexico City to Monterrey in June 1969. Ten years later, he was inducted into the **International Tennis Hall of Fame**.

OUDIN, MELANIE. B. 23 September 1991, Marietta, Georgia. Melanie Oudin is one of the future stars of American tennis. As a **junior**, she was **ranked** second in the world. She became a **professional** tennis player in 2008. Although only five feet six inches tall, she reached the fourth round at **Wimbledon** in 2009 and was a quarterfinalist at the **United States Open** with upset come-from-behind victories over **Elena Dementieva, Maria Sharapova**, and Nadia Petrova. In each of those three matches, she lost the first **set**. She was a member of the **United States Fed Cup** team from 2009 to 2011 and played singles in seven **ties**. Through May 2011, her record was 5–8. In April 2010, she was ranked number 31, but that ranking will undoubtedly climb in the future.

OVERHEAD. An "overhead" in tennis is a shot taken when the **ball** is on its downward flight and the ball is hit with the **racket** extended over the head. If hit with exceptional force, it is called a **smash**.

P

PACE. "Pace" is the tennis term that denotes speed. It can refer to the speed of the **ball** or the speed of play.

PADDLE TENNIS. Paddle tennis is a sport similar to **lawn tennis** but played with a smaller **court** (50 feet by 20 feet) with no **doubles alleys**, a lower **net** (31 inches), a solid paddle instead of a strung **racket**, a depressurized **tennis ball**, and only one **serve** permitted, which must be underhand. Scoring is the same as in lawn tennis. It was created around 1915 in New York City by an Episcopal minister, Frank Peer Beal. The United States Paddle Tennis Association administers the sport in the **United States**. **Gaël Monfils**, a top-rated lawn tennis player, has also excelled in paddle tennis.

PAES, LEANDER ADRIAN. B. 17 June 1973, Calcutta (now Kolkata), **India**. Leander Paes is the son of two former athletes. His father, Vece Paes, was a member of the 1972 Indian **Olympic** field hockey team, and his mother, Jennifer, was the captain of the 1980 Asian Games champion basketball team. His great-grandfather, Michael Mahusudan Dutt, was a famous Bengali poet. Leander attended La Martiniere Calcutta (high school) and the University of Calcutta. He began playing tennis at the Britannia **Amritraj** Tennis Academy in Madras in 1985. After winning the **Junior United States Open** and junior **Wimbledon** championships, he became a **professional** in 1991. An excellent **doubles** player, the 5-foot 10-inch, 170-pound right-hander has reached the finals of both the men's doubles and **mixed doubles** of all four **Grand Slam tournaments** and, through May 2011, has won 12 of 24 Slam doubles finals. In 2003, Paes's tennis career and life was nearly ended as he was hospitalized for a suspected brain tumor that turned out to be a parasitic brain infection. Fortunately, he recovered and only missed a few months of activity. In 1999, with **Mahesh Bhupathi** as partner, they reached the finals of all four Grand Slam events, winning the **French Open** and Wimbledon. They also won the 2001 French Open. In 2004, Paes and David Rikl were runners-up at the United States Open. In 2006, with Martin Damm as partner, Paes was runner-up at the **Australian Open** and won the U.S. Open. Lukáš Dlouhý was Paes partner from 2008 to 2010, and they won the U.S. Open in 2008 and 2009 and were runners-up at the French Open in 2009 and 2010. Paes and Bhupathi were reunited in 2011. Known as "the Indian Express" they were runners-up at the 2011 Australian Open. In mixed doubles, Paes and **Lisa Raymond** won Wimbledon in 1999. Paes and the 46-year-old **Martina Navratilova** won the Australian and Wimbledon in 2003 and were runners-up at the 2004 Australian and 2005 French Open. In 2007, Paes and Meghan Shaughnessy were runners-up at the U.S. Open. Cara Black then became Paes' partner, and they won the 2008 U.S. Open, 2010 Australian, and 2010 Wimbledon and were runners-up at the 2009 Wimbledon and U.S. Open.

Paes is one of only four people to compete in five Olympic tennis tournaments. From 1992 to 2008, he entered the doubles each year with partners **Ramesh Krishnan** in 1992 and Mahesh Bhupathi from 1996 to 2008. Leander also entered the **singles** in 1992 and 1996. Although a doubles specialist, he did not win any Olympic medals in doubles but did win the singles bronze medal in 1996. In 2004, he and Bhupathi lost the bronze medal doubles match by a score of 6–7 (5), 6–4, 14–16. He has played for India in the **Davis Cup** each year from 1990 to 2010. His record through 2010 is 48–22 in singles and 38–9 in doubles in 47 ties in 21 years.

PALFREY FABYAN COOKE DANZIG, SARAH. B. 18 September 1912, Sharon, Massachusetts. D. 27 February 1996, New York, New York. Sarah Palfrey was a member of a prominent Boston family and was the great-granddaughter of Theodore Roosevelt. She and her four sisters were all accomplished tennis players and winners of **junior** titles. From 1928 to 1945, Palfrey was one of the world's best and, in 1934, had a world **ranking** of four. She won 18 **Grand Slam** titles and was a finalist 29 times total. In 1934 and 1935, she was runner-up to **Helen Jacobs** for the **United States National** women's **singles** title. In 1941 and 1945, Palfrey defeated **Pauline Betz** to win that title. The 5-foot 4-inch, 115-pound, right-handed Palfrey won the first of nine United States National **doubles** titles in 1930 with **Betty Nuthall** as partner. She won again in 1932 with Helen Jacobs. From 1934 to 1941, Palfrey was the women's doubles finalist eight consecutive years, winning each year except for 1936. Her partners were Helen Jacobs from 1934 to 1936, **Alice Marble** from 1937 to 1940, and **Margaret Osborne** in 1941. She also won the United States National **mixed doubles** title in 1932, 1935, 1937, and 1941 and was runner-up in 1933, 1936, and 1939. Her mixed doubles partners were **Fred Perry** (1932), **George Lott** (1933), Enrique Maier (1935), **Don Budge** (1936–37), Elwood Cooke (1939), and **Jack Kramer** (1941). At **Wimbledon**, she was a women's doubles finalist in 1930 with Edith Cross and in 1936 with Helen Jacobs and won the championship twice with Alice Marble in 1938 and 1939. She also reached the mixed doubles final there twice—with Don Budge in 1936 and Henner Henkel in 1938. In 1934, she and Helen Jacobs were finalists at Roland Garros, and in 1939, she and her future husband, Elwood Cooke, won the mixed doubles there.

Palfrey also recorded a somewhat unique distinction in 1945. Due to the lack of available competition during World War II, she was allowed to enter the men's doubles at the Tri-State Championships in Cincinnati with her then husband, Elwood Cooke. Surprisingly, the pair reached the final round. In 1947, she became a **professional** and toured against **Pauline Betz Addie**. Palfrey and Alice Marble were also instrumental in helping **Althea Gibson** break the color barrier as the pair successfully lobbied the **United States Lawn Tennis Association** for Gibson's inclusion in major tournaments.

Palfrey married socialite Boston architect Marshall Fabyan Jr. in 1934. They divorced in 1940, and she married tennis player T. Elwood Cooke on 5 October 1940. They were a successful mixed doubles team during the 1940s. They divorced, and she married radio broadcaster Jerome Alan Danzig in 1951. They remained married until her death from lung cancer in 1996. She and Cooke had a daughter, and she and Danzig had a son. In **Wightman Cup** play each year from 1930 to 1939, her record was 7–4 in singles and 7–3 in doubles. She and Marty Glickman were the radio broadcast team for the New York Knickerbockers first home basketball game in 1946. She was inducted into the **International Tennis Hall of Fame** in 1963.

PANATTA, ADRIANO. B. 9 July 1950, Rome, **Italy**. Adriano Panatta was the son of the caretaker at the most important tennis club in Rome, Parioli, and began playing tennis at an early age. He was enrolled in tennis camp and became a member of the Italian **junior** team under **coach** Mario Belardinelli. In 1969, Adriano began his **professional** career. His most memorable year was 1976. He won the **French Open singles** title (his only **Grand Slam** title), won the Italian Open title (after saving 11 **match points** in his opening round **match**), and helped lead Italy to its first and (as of 2010) only **Davis Cup** Championship. The six-foot tall right-hander's best performance at **Wimbledon** was the quarterfinals in 1979. He reached the fourth round at the **United States Open** in 1978. He entered the **Australian Championships** once, in 1969, and lost his only match.

Adriano was a member of the Italian Davis Cup team each year from 1970 to 1983. Italy reached the final round in 1976, 1977, 1979, and 1980 and won the Cup in 1976, when Panatta won all three of his matches. His overall Cup record for 14 years was 37–26 in singles and 27–10 in **doubles** in 38 **ties**. His younger brother, Claudio, also played professional tennis and was a member of the Italian Davis Cup team. Adriano retired from tennis in 1983 with 9 singles and 17 doubles titles to his credit and a high world **ranking** of four in 1976. After retiring from tennis, Adriano has been Italian Davis Cup captain, Italian Tennis Federation national coach, tournament director of the Rome Masters tournament, and publisher of an Italian tennis magazine. He also became involved in professional offshore power boat racing, was a member of the team that won the 2004 world championship, and is holder of two world speedboat records.

PARKER, FRANK ANDREW (FRANCISZEK ANDRZEJ PAJKOWSKI). B. 31 January 1916, Milwaukee, Wisconsin. D. 24 July 1997, San Diego, California. Frank Parker was one of the few tennis players of his generation from a working-class background. The son of Polish immigrant parents, he was discovered by tennis **coach** Mercer Beasley. Beasley took him under his wing and enrolled Pajkowski at Lawrenceville Academy, where Beasley was a coach. Beasley also had Franciszek change his name to the more "American" and more easily pronounceable Frank Parker. Parker later went to Princeton University. He became a top **amateur** player at the age of 16, winning the national **junior singles** championship and reaching the third round of the **main draw** of the **United States National** Singles Championship in 1932.

In a story worthy of a soap opera, Beasley's wife, Audrey, divorced him in 1938 and married Parker who was 20 years younger than her. Parker competed in the United States national **tournament** as an amateur until 1949, winning it in 1944 and 1945 (while a sergeant in the U.S. Army Air Force) and losing in the finals to Ted Schroeder in 1942 and **Jack Kramer** in 1947. At the age of 52, he returned to **Forest Hills** in 1968 and played in the first **United States Open**, losing his first match to eventual champion **Arthur Ashe**. The 5-foot 8-inch, 145-pound, right-handed Parker won the **French National** singles championship in 1948 and 1949. In **doubles**, he won championships at three of the four **Grand Slam** tournaments, not competing in **Australia**. He was runner-up for the United States National doubles title with **Frank Shields** in 1933 and with Ted Schroeder in 1948. Parker and Jack Kramer won the United States National doubles title in 1943. Parker and **Pancho González** won the French National and **Wimbledon** doubles in 1949. In 1948, he was the world's number-one–**ranked** tennis player. He played on the **United States Davis Cup** team in 1937, 1939, 1946, and 1948. Playing only singles, he compiled a record of 12–2 in seven **ties** in four years. He was on the Cup championship team in 1937, 1946, and 1948 but did not play in the 1946 **challenge round**. In 1949, he became a touring **professional** briefly and then was the sales manager for a paper products company in Chicago. He was inducted into the **International Tennis Hall of Fame** in 1966.

PASSEMARD MATHIEU, SIMONE. B. 11 January 1908, Neuilly-sur-Seine, **France**. D. 7 January 1980, Paris, France. Simone Passemard Mathieu was the best French female tennis player during the 1930s and reached the finals of 26 **Grand Slam** events, winning 13 titles. She married René Mathieu in 1925 and, for most of her tennis career, used both her maiden name and married name. She reached the finals at **Roland Garros** 19 times—more than any other player, male or female. Her 10 French championships are third behind **Margaret Smith Court's** 13 and **Martina Navratilova's** 11. Her nine French runner-up finishes are also more than anyone else. She won the **French National Singles** Championships in 1938 and 1939 after reaching the finals unsuccessfully six times previously (1929, 1932, 1933, 1935–37). She was more successful there in **doubles**, winning the women's doubles six times (1933, 1934, 1936–39) and being runner-up twice (1930, 1945). She also won the French **mixed doubles** in 1937 and 1938 and was runner-up in 1939. Her accomplishments weren't only confined to France as she was a three-time women's doubles champion at **Wimbledon** (1933, 1934, 1937) and twice runner-up (1935, 1938). She was also Wimbledon mixed doubles runner-up in 1937. She also reached the Wimbledon singles semifinals four times and United States National singles quarterfinals once. In 1938, she was runner-up at the **United States National** Women's Doubles Championships. During the Second World War, she was the head of the Corps Féminin Français, a branch of the Free French Forces. She was inducted into the **International Tennis Hall of Fame** in 2006.

PATTERSON, GERALD LEIGHTON. B. 17 December 1895, Melbourne, Victoria, **Australia**. D. 13 June 1967, Melbourne, Victoria, Australia. Gerald Patterson was the nephew of famed Australian opera singer Dame Nellie Melba. He was educated at Scotch College in Melbourne. In 1914, he reached the men's **singles** finals of the **Australian Championships** but was defeated by Arthur O'Hara Wood. Patterson served as an officer in the Australian army during World War I and received the Military Cross for bravery in 1917. The six-foot tall right-hander was nicknamed "the human catapult" for his powerful **serve** that led him to the finals of the Australian Championships three more times—in 1922, 1925, and 1927, when he finally won the title. He also reached the finals at **Wimbledon** three times, winning in 1919 and 1922 and being defeated by **Bill Tilden** in 1920. As a **doubles** player, he was five-time Australian champion (1914, 1922, 1925–27) and runner-up in 1924 and 1932. In 1922 and 1928, he was a losing men's doubles finalist at Wimbledon, but in 1920, he teamed with **Suzanne Lenglen** to win the Wimbledon **mixed doubles**. In 1919, he won the United States men's doubles title and was a losing finalist in 1922, 1924, 1925, and 1928.

Patterson played on the Australia **Davis Cup** team from 1920 to 1928, appearing in 16 **ties** in five years. His record was 21–10 in singles and 11–4 in doubles. He played in the **challenge round** three times but was on the losing side each time. The son of a wealthy family, he was managing director of the A. G. Spalding sporting goods company and chairman and director of several other businesses. He was the father of Australian Grand Prix champion race car driver, Bill Patterson. Gerald Patterson was inducted into the **International Tennis Hall of Fame** in 1989.

PATTY, JOHN EDWARD "BUDGE." B. 11 February 1924, Fort Smith, Arkansas. Budge Patty, although born in Arkansas, was raised in Los Angeles, California. The six-foot one-inch right-hander in 1950 became one of the few men to win the **Wimbledon** and **French National Singles** Championships in the same year. He was also the losing finalist in 1949, reached the quarterfinals three times and semifinals twice at the French championships. At Wimbledon, he was a semifinalist in 1947, 1954, and 1955. A resident of Europe, he competed in the French championships 15 times, at Wimbledon 14 times, but only eight times in the **United States National Championships**, where his best showing was twice reaching the quarterfinal round. He never entered the **Australian Championships**. He played one of the longest matches at Wimbledon, losing in the third round in 1953 to **Jaroslav Drobný** in 5 **sets** and 93 games over 4 hours and 20 minutes. In 1950, he was **ranked** number one in the world. In 1957, the 33-year-old Patty and his 43-year old partner, **Gardnar Mulloy**, won the Wimbledon **doubles** title and were runners-up at **Forest Hills**. In 1946, he and **Pauline Betz** were the French **mixed doubles** champions. Patty is the author of *Tennis My Way*, published in 1951. He played in only one **Davis Cup tie** for the **United States** in 1951 and won a singles and doubles match. He was inducted into the **International Tennis Hall of Fame** in 1977.

PERRY, FREDERICK JOHN "FRED." B. 18 May 1909, Stockport, Cheshire, England. D. 2 February 1995, Melbourne, Victoria, **Australia**. Fred Perry was the son of Samuel Perry, a member of the British House of Commons. Fred was educated at Ealing Green Grammar School for Boys. He was more interested in **table tennis** than **lawn tennis** and was world table tennis champion in 1929. He took up lawn tennis and became one of the world's best players, achieving the **ranking** of number one in 1934. He was the first person to win all four **Grand Slam singles** championships but not in the same year. He won the **Australian Championships** in 1934 and was runner-up in 1935. He won **Wimbledon** in 1934, 1935, and 1936. He won the

French Nationals in 1935 and was runner-up in 1936. He won the **United States National Championships** in 1933, 1934, and 1936.

In **doubles**, he and Pat Hughes were French champions in 1933 and Australian champions in 1934 and runners-up in 1935. Perry and **Dorothy Round** won Wimbledon **mixed doubles** in 1935 and 1936. He and **Betty Nuthall** were French mixed doubles champions in 1932 and runners-up in 1933. In 1932, he and **Sarah Palfrey** won the United States mixed doubles title. He was a member of the **Great Britain Davis Cup** team each year from 1931 to 1936 and led the team to the Cup championship in 1933, 1934, 1935, and 1936, winning all eight of his singles matches. In 1931, he was defeated by **Henri Cochet** in the fifth and deciding **rubber** of the **challenge round** to enable France to win the Cup. Perry's overall record in 20 **ties** in six years was 34–4 in singles and 11–3 in doubles. In 1937, Perry became a **professional** and toured with **Ellsworth Vines**. Perry lost to Vines, 32–29, in 1937 and, 49–35, in 1938.

Perry moved to the **United States**, became a part owner of the Beverly Hills Tennis Club, and became an American citizen in 1938. During World War II, he served in the U.S. Air Force. In the 1940s, Perry invented the wrist sweatband for tennis players. He also developed the Fred Perry polo shirt and became involved with the manufacture of tennis apparel. The Fred Perry brand is still one of the leading brands for tennis wear. He also wrote for a London newspaper and was involved with radio and television tennis broadcasting. A statue of Fred Perry was erected in 1984 on the grounds of the **All-England Lawn Tennis and Croquet Club** in Wimbledon to commemorate the 50th anniversary of his Wimbledon triumph. Its replica can be found at the **Newport Casino** in the United States. He was inducted into the **International Tennis Hall of Fame** in 1975.

PERU. Tennis in Peru is under the jurisdiction of the Federación Deportiva Peruana de Tenis. From 1968 through May 2011, Peru has competed in 38 **Davis Cup tournaments** with a record of 30–41 in 71 **ties**. The country competed only once in the World Group (in 2008) since its formation in 1981, its best effort. Peruvian **Alejandro "Alex" Olmedo**, while a student at the University of Southern California, was a member of the winning **United States** Davis Cup team in 1958 and the runner-up team in 1959. In 1959, Olmedo won the **Australian** Championship and **Wimbledon** and was the runner-up at the **United States National Championships**. Peru's top Davis Cup players have been Carlos Di Laura, Luis Horna, Ivan Miranda, and Jaime Yzaga.

Peru has had entrants in 1984, 1992, and 2004 **Olympic** tennis competition. The best result was in men's singles, where Carlos DiLaura reached the second round in the 1984 demonstration tournament and Jaime Yzaga also reached the second round in 1992. In 2008, Horna won the **French Open** Men's **Doubles** Championship with his Argentinean partner Pablo Cuevas. Other top Peruvian tennis players include Pablo Arraya and his sister Laura Arraya, Bianco Botto, Mauricio Echazú, Laura Gildemeister, Ivan Miranda, Carla Rodriguez, and Pilar Vasquez. Hans Gildemeister, born in Peru, has represented **Chile** in international competition. In **Federation Cup** competition from 1982 to May 2011, Peru has competed 48 years, five in World Group, and played 61 ties with a record of 31–28. Peru's best result was in 1982, when the team reached the round of 16.

PHILADELPHIA CRICKET CLUB. The Philadelphia Cricket Club was founded in the Chestnut Hill section of Philadelphia, Pennsylvania, in 1854. The club, which offered other sports besides cricket, was one of the founding members of the **United States Tennis Association** in 1881. In 1887, the **United States** Women's **Singles** Championships were held there. The United States Women's National **Doubles** Championships began there in 1889 and the United States **Mixed Doubles** Championship in 1892. The Club was the site of those **tournaments** until 1921, after which they were moved to **Forest Hills**, New York. One of the oldest country clubs in the United States, it celebrated its sesquicentennial in 2004.

PHILIPPOUSSIS, MARK ANTHONY. B. 7 November 1976, Melbourne, Victoria, **Australia**. Mark Philippoussis is an Australian of Greek ancestry. He attended Wesley College, a private school in Melbourne. The 6-foot 5-inch, 225-pound, right-handed player was known for his powerful **serve**, which earned him the nickname "Scud." He became a **professional** in 1994 and, the following year, was the youngest player **ranked** in the top 50. He worked his way up to a high ranking of eight in 1999, the year in which he and Jelena Dokić won the **Hopman Cup**. From 1995 to 2006, he was a member of the Australian **Davis Cup** team and was on its Cup championship team in 1999 and 2003. His Davis Cup record for eight years in 13 **ties**, playing only **singles**, was 13–10. In 1998, he was defeated by countryman, **Pat Rafter**, in the **United States Open** finals, and in 2003, he was defeated by **Roger Federer** in the finals at **Wimbledon**. In his career, at the **French Open** and the **Australian** Open, his best result was in reaching the fourth round on several occasions. He competed in the 1996 and 2004 **Olympic** singles, reaching the third round in 1996 and losing in the first round in 2004. After a series of injuries, his career went downhill sharply, and by 2007, he was playing in **Challenger** level tournaments. The handsome, 30-year-old bachelor was also featured in a television reality series, *Age of Love*, that year.

PIERCE, MARY CAROLINE. B. 15 January 1975, Montreal, Quebec, Canada. Mary Pierce is one of the few people in the world with citizenship in three countries. She was born in Canada to a French mother and American father and was raised in Florida but has represented **France** in international competition. She was taught tennis by her father, Jim Pierce, and won the **United States** 12-and-under **junior** championship. She became the youngest American **professional** player when she turned pro at the age of 14 in March 1989—a record later broken by **Jennifer Capriati** in 1990. Mary was **coached** by **Nick Bollettieri** and by her brother, David. In 1994, she reached the finals of the **French Open** but was defeated by **Arantxa Sánchez Vicario** in straight sets. She avenged that loss the following year in the finals of the **Australian Open** by defeating Sánchez Vicario in straight sets. Pierce also won the 2000 French Open and was runner-up in the 1997 Australian Open and the 2005 French Open and **United States Open**. Her best **singles** performance at Wimbledon was in 1996 and again in 2005, when she was a quarterfinalist. In 2000, playing **doubles** with **Martina Hingis**, she was runner-up at the Australian Open and won the French Open. Pierce also won the Wimbledon **mixed doubles** in 2005.

A 5-foot 10-inch, 150-pound right-hander, Pierce competed in the 1992, 1996, and 2004 **Olympic Games** as a representative of France. She was also named to the 2008 team but withdrew due to injury. In 1992, she only entered the singles but the other two years entered both singles and doubles. Her best finish for the five events was reaching the 2004 singles quarterfinal round. She played on the French **Federation Cup** team from 1990 to 1992, 1994 to 1997, and 2003 to 2005. Her record for 10 years was 16–10 in singles and 2–4 in doubles in 22 **ties**. She played in the finals for the Cup-winning team in 1997 and 2003 and for the runner-up team in 2005. A severe knee injury in 2006 may have ended her playing career, although she has made no official announcement as of May 2011. She has won 20 singles titles and 10 doubles titles to this point.

PIETRANGELI, NICOLA "NIKKI." B. 11 September 1933, Tunis, Tunisia. Nicola Pietrangeli is arguably the greatest **Italian** tennis player in history. A 5-foot 11-inch right-hander, he played his best on **clay** and made his debut at the **French National tournament** in Stade **Roland Garros** in 1954. For the next 20 years, he played annually in that tournament, winning the **singles** championship in 1959 and 1960 and finishing as runner-up to **Manuel Santana** in 1961 and 1964. Pietrangeli and Orlando Sirola were losing men's **doubles** finalists there in 1955 and won the 1959 men's doubles. They were also losing men's doubles finalists at **Wimbledon** in 1956. Pietrangeli teamed with Shirley Bloomer in 1958 to win the French **mixed doubles**.

He competed in singles at Wimbledon 15 times but only reached the fourth round once. He did reach the quarterfinals at the **United States Open** singles tournament and played the **Australian National** singles tournament just three times, reaching the third round twice. He competed in both **exhibition** and demonstration tournaments in the 1968 **Mexico Olympic Games** and was a semifinalist in the singles exhibition tournament.

Pietrangeli was a member of the Italian **Davis Cup** team from 1954 to 1972, playing each year except 1970. His record was 78–32 in singles and 42–12 in doubles in 66 **ties** in 18 years. In 1960 and 1961, he led Italy to the **challenge round**, where the team was defeated by Australia each time. As Italian Davis Cup nonplaying captain, he led Italy to its first (and only through 2010) Davis Cup championship in 1976. He holds Davis Cup records for most **rubbers** played, 164; most rubbers won, 120; most singles rubbers won, 78; most doubles rubbers won, 42; and (with Orlando Sirola) most rubbers won by a doubles team, 34. He was inducted into the **International Tennis Hall of Fame** in 1986. In 2006, the tennis stadium at the Foro Italico in Rome was renamed the Nicola Pietrangeli Stadium—an honor rarely given to living persons.

PILIĆ, NIKOLA "NIKI." B. 27 August 1939, Split, **Croatia, Yugoslavia**. Niki Pilić began playing major **tournament** tennis in 1960. The 6-foot 3-inch, 180-pound **left-hander** only won one **Grand Slam** tournament in his career—the 1970 **United States Open doubles** title with partner Pierre Barthès. He was also a doubles finalist in 1962 at Wimbledon with Boro Jovanović. Pilić's best finish in **singles** at the **Australian Open** was the third round, at **Wimbledon** he reached the fourth round, and at the **United States Open** he was a quarterfinalist once. He reached the 1973 **French Open** singles final but lost in straight sets to **Ilie Năstase**.

That year, he was the central figure in the Wimbledon boycott. The Yugoslav Tennis Federation suspended Pilić, claiming that he refused to play **Davis Cup** for Yugoslavia—a charge which Pilić denied. As a result, the **International Lawn Tennis Federation** upheld the suspension and did not allow Pilić to play at major tournaments, including Wimbledon. Of his fellow professionals, 70 (including 13 of the top 16 seeds at Wimbledon) sided with Pilić and withdrew from the tournament. He played **Davis Cup** tennis for Yugoslavia from 1961 to 1967 as an **amateur** and from 1974 to 1977 as a professional. In 23 **ties** over 11 years, his record was 27–12 in singles and 11–12 in doubles. He later was the Davis Cup captain for **Germany**, leading the team to the Davis Cup in 1988, 1989, and 1993. When Croatia began playing as a separate county in Davis Cup, he became the **coach** and led the team to the Cup in 2005, becoming the first man to captain two different nations to the Davis Cup championship. He was named the Croatian Sportsman of the Year three times—1962, 1964, and 1967. After retiring from active play in 1979, with three singles titles and six doubles titles to his credit and a high world ranking of seven reached in 1967, he became a coach and the head of the Niki Pilić Tennis Academy in Munich, Germany. Among his students have been Ernests Gulbis, **Novak Djoković**, and Ana Ivanović.

PING-PONG. *See* TABLE TENNIS.

PLACEMENT. Placement in tennis refers to the ability to place a shot in a specific area of the **court**. Proper placement will often win a **point** even in the stroke does not have much **pace**.

POACHING. In doubles play, a player at the **net** will occasionally move across the **court** to take a **volley** intended for his or her partner. Usually, he or she will hit a **winner** by doing so. This is referred to as poaching.

POINT. A point is the basic unit of scoring in **lawn tennis**. It is won by a player whose opponent cannot successfully return the **ball** within the **court** boundaries. *See also* SCORING.

POLAND. Tennis in Poland is administered by the *Polski Związek Tenisowy* (Polish Tennis Federation). From 1925 through May 2011, Poland has competed in 73 **Davis Cup** tournaments with a record of 68–72 in 140 **ties**. Poland has not yet competed in the World Group since its formation in 1981. Its best performance has been in reaching the Europe/Africa group's second round on six occasions. Top Davis Cup players have been Bartlomiej Dabrowski, Mariusz Fyrstenberg, Marcin Matkowski, and Tadeusz Nowicki. Poland has had entrants in 1988, 1992, 1996, 2004, and 2008 **Olympic** tennis events. Its best showing was in 2008, when Mariusz Fyrstenberg and Marcin Matkowski were quarterfinalists in men's doubles.

The best male tennis player from Poland has been **Wojtek Fibak**. Other top Polish male players include Tomasz Bednarek, Marcin Gawron, Jerzy Janowicz, Mateusz Kowalczyk, Wojciech Kowalski, Łukasz Kubot, Dawid Olejniczak, Grzegorz Panfil, Michał Przysiężny, and Adam Stepien. The best female tennis player was **Jadwiga Jędrzejowska**, who won the **French National** women's **doubles** and was a finalist in the **Wimbledon singles**. Other top Polish female players include the Radwańska sisters (Agnieszka and Urszula), Marta Domachowska, Magdalena Feistel, Magdalena Grzybowska, Klaudia Jans, Paula Kania, Katarzyna Nowak, Aleksandra Olsza, Alicja Rosolska, Katarina Teodorowicz, and Sandra Zaniewska. In **Federation Cup** competition, from 1966 to May 2011, Poland has competed 30 years, 13 years in World Group, and played 98 ties with a record of 48–50. Poland's best result was in 1992, when it was a quarterfinalist.

PRESSURE POINT. Pressure Point was a made-for-television **tournament** held in 1975 that was contested among the top-16-**ranked** women **professional** players. The tournament consisted of abbreviated **tiebreaker**-type matches of only 13 **points**, with the first player to reach 7 points winning the match. If the match was tied at 6 points **all**, the next point was known as a double **match point**—a match point for both players. The tournament was contested in one day, 14 January 1975, on a **clay court** in Palmas del Mar resort in Humacao, Puerto Rico. Announcers were Phyllis George, **Tony Trabert**, and **Rod Laver**. First prize was $12,000, and total prize money was $42,500. The matches (which lasted less than 10 minutes) were taped and shown on consecutive weeks during the men's tennis coverage on the Columbia Broadcasting System network.

The results:

First round

- Valerie Ziegenfuss d. Kathy Kuykendall, 7–6
- **Rosemary Casals** d. **Virginia Wade**, 7–1
- **Chris Evert** d. Wendy Overton, 7–2
- **Françoise Durr** d. **Martina Navratilova**, 7–2
- **Betty Stove** (replacement for **Billie Jean King**) d. Helen Gourley, 7–5
- **Nancy Gunter** d. Kerry Melville, 7–2
- Kristien Kemmer Shaw d. Lesley Hunt, 7–1
- Pam Teeguarden d. Jeanne Evert, 7–5

Quarterfinals

- Casals d. Ziegenfuss, 7–6
- Evert d. Durr, 7–4
- Stove d. Kemmer Shaw, 7–0
- Gunter d. Teeguarden, 7–5

Semifinals

- Evert d. Casals, 7–5
- Stove d. Gunter, 7–6

Finals

- Evert d. Stove, 7–6

PROFESSIONAL. A professional in **lawn tennis** is a player who receives money for playing or **coaching** the sport. During the early years of the 20th century, some organizations, such as the **United States Lawn Tennis Association**, held that being paid to write about the sport also made an individual a professional. As a result, **Bill Tilden**, who was also a journalist, was harassed by that organization at times. Until the late 1960s, most **tournaments** were closed to professional players. Since 1970, nearly all major tournaments have been **open** to both **amateur** and professional players.

QUALIFIER. Many modern **lawn tennis tournaments** have preliminary rounds known as qualifying rounds. Players who are otherwise not eligible for the tournament play a mini-tournament in which the best players in that event are allowed to play in the main tournament. These qualifying tournaments are sometimes referred to as "qualies" by the players. Admission to the qualifying tournament is often free, and the prize money, if any, is minimal.

QUERREY, SAM AUSTIN. B. 7 October 1987, San Francisco, California. Sam Querrey was raised in Thousand Oaks, California. He turned down a tennis scholarship to the University of Southern California to become a **professional** player in 2006, and in his first **tournament** as a professional, won the Yuba City **Challenger** event in June. The 6-foot 6-inch, 200-pound right-hander is known for his powerful **serve**, which registered a record 10 consecutive **aces** in a quarterfinal match at the Indianapolis **Association of Tennis Professionals (ATP)** tournament in 2007 against **James Blake**. He has been part of one of the tallest **doubles** teams in tennis history when he has played with the six-foot nine-inch **John Isner**. Querrey entered both **singles** and doubles in the 2008 **Olympic Games** but was defeated in both first-round matches. In **Davis Cup** competition, he played in 2008 and 2010 and has a singles record of 1–3 for the United States in two **ties**. In his young career, through May 2011, his highest singles **ranking** has been 17. In 2008 and 2010, he reached the fourth round of the **United States Open**, his best performance in a major tournament. He has won six ATP singles events, runner-up five times, and has won three ATP doubles events, runner-up twice.

QUIST, ADRIAN KARL. B. 14 August 1913, Medindie, South Australia, **Australia**. D. 17 November 1991, Sydney, New South Wales, Australia. Had not World War II cancelled most of the four major tennis **tournaments** from 1941 to 1945, Adrian Quist's record would have been even more outstanding than 24 major tournament finals and 17 major championships. His 13 total **Australian Championships** are more than any other male tennis player. Although the five-foot seven-inch Quist won three Australian **Singles** Championships (1936, 1940, 1948) and was runner-up in 1948, he was better known for his **doubles** play. He won 10 Australian doubles titles and was a doubles winner at **Roland Garros, Wimbledon,** and **Forest Hills,** as well. He was Australian doubles champion in every year from 1936 to 1950. In 1936 and 1937, Don Turnbull was his partner, and in 1938 to 1940 and 1946 to 1950, **John Bromwich** was his partner. Quist was also doubles runner-up in 1934 with Turnbull and in 1951 with Bromwich. At Roland Garros, he was men's doubles finalist with Vivian McGrath in 1933, mixed doubles finalist with **Elizabeth "Bunny" Ryan** in 1934, and men's doubles champion in 1935 with **Jack Crawford**. At Wimbledon, Quist won doubles with Crawford in 1935 and with Bromwich in 1950. At Forest Hills, he and Bromwich were doubles finalists in 1936 and 1938 and doubles champion in 1939.

Quist had an outstanding **Davis Cup** record for Australia from 1933 to 1948, with records of 24–10 in singles and 19–3 in doubles in 28 **ties** in nine years and the Cup in 1939. His highest world **ranking** was three in 1939. After retiring from active play, he was general manager of the Dunlop sporting goods company and occasional newspaper columnist for Sydney newspapers. He was inducted into the **International Tennis Hall of Fame** in 1984 and died of cancer in 1991.

RACKET. A tennis racket (or racquet) is the implement used to strike the **tennis ball**. A modern racket usually varies between 21 and 29 inches in length and weighs between 8 and 12.5 ounces unstrung. The **United States Tennis Association** rules specify "the frame shall not exceed 29.0 inches in overall length including the handle . . . and shall not exceed 12.5 inches in overall width. . . . The hitting surface shall not exceed 15.5 inches in overall length and 11.5 inches in overall width." The head size usually varies between 88 and 127 square inches. Up to the 1960s, rackets were generally smaller (65-square-inch heads) and were made of laminated wood. Since then, steel, aluminum, and graphite have been the main construction material. The major racket manufacturers are **Wilson**, Head, Prince, and Babolat. A recent innovation in tennis rackets is a two-handled one that the Battistone brothers, Dann and Brian, use. It has been approved by the **International Tennis Federation**, and the brothers claim it enables them to have more power with their strokes, using two-handed **forehands** and **backhands**. As of May 2011, they are the only **professionals** using this racket, and they have yet to reach the top 100 in **rankings**.

RACKETS. Rackets (or racquets) is an indoor sport played with a **ball** and a **racket**. The game originated in the 18th century in **English** prisons. The enclosed **court** is 30 by 60 feet with a ceiling of at least 30 feet high. The ball must hit the front wall above a line 26.5 inches above the ground and may strike the side walls before hitting the front wall. Games are played to 15 **points**, with points awarded only when serving. **Squash** racquets is an offshoot of this game, with slightly different rules.

RACQUET. *See* RACKET.

RACQUETS. *See* RACKETS.

RAFTER, PATRICK MICHAEL "PAT." B. 28 December 1972, Mount Isa, Queensland, **Australia**. Pat Rafter began his **professional** tennis career in 1991. Before it ended, 10 years later, he would win the **United States Open Singles** Championship twice and be twice runner-up at **Wimbledon**. In 1997 and 1998, he won the U.S. Open and, in 2000 and 2001, was runner-up at Wimbledon, losing in the fifth set, 9–7 to **Goran Ivanišević** in 2001. Rafter also reached the semifinal round of the **French Open** in 1997 and **Australian Open** in 2001. The 6-foot 2-inch, 190-pound right-hander was the world number-one–**ranked** singles player in 1999 and the sixth-ranked **doubles** player that same year. In 1999, and again in 2001, he was a member of the Australian **World Team Cup** championship team. In the 2000 **Olympic Games** in Sydney, he lost in the second round of the men's singles event. He played on the Australian **Davis Cup** team each year from 1994 to 2001. In eight years and 18 **ties**, his record was 18–10 in singles and 3–1 in doubles. He helped lead Australia to the Cup championship in 1999, although he did not play in the final round. In 2000 and 2001, he played in the final round, but Australia was defeated each time. When he retired from active play in 2001, he had compiled a career record of 11 singles and 10 doubles championships. He was inducted into the **International Tennis Hall of Fame** in 2006. In 2008, **centre court** at the new Queensland Tennis Centre in Brisbane, Australia, was named the Pat Rafter Arena.

RALLY. A rally in tennis consists of the strokes played between the **service** and the conclusion of a **point**. Rallies between two **baseline** players can occasionally extend to 30 or more strokes, although most rallies consist of fewer than 10 strokes.

RALSTON, ROBERT DENNIS "DENNY." B. 27 July 1942, Bakersfield, California. Dennis Ralston attended the University of Southern California (USC), where he won the **National Collegiate Athletic Association** National Tennis Championship in 1963 and 1964 and helped lead USC to the national team championship in 1962, 1963, and 1964. The 6-foot 2-inch, 170-pound right-hander was a member of the **United States Davis Cup** team each year from 1960 to 1966 and had a record of 14–5 in **singles** and 11–4 in **doubles** in 15 **ties** in seven years. He helped lead the United States to the Cup championship in 1963. He was a **coach** for the Davis Cup team from 1968 to 1971 and was the team captain from 1972 to 1975. He won five **Grand Slam** doubles titles (1960 **Wimbledon** as a 17-year-old with **Rafael Osuna**; 1961, 1963, 1964 United States with **Chuck McKinley**; 1966 French with **Clark Graebner**) and was runner-up eight other times (U.S. men's doubles three times, Wimbledon men's doubles once, U.S. and Wimbledon **mixed doubles** twice each). In 1966, he reached his only Slam singles final and was defeated by **Manuel Santana** at Wimbledon but achieved his career-high **ranking** of first in the United States and fifth in the world. He was a singles semifinalist at the **Australian Open** in 1970, reached the fourth round in singles at Roland Garros in 1966, and reached the singles quarterfinals at **Forest Hills** on five occasions. He was inducted into the **International Tennis Hall of Fame** in 1987. After retiring from the **professional** tour, he was a tennis coach at Southern Methodist University for 12 years, was **Chris Evert's** coach from 1982 to 1989, and was the director of tennis at the Broadmoor Hotel in Colorado Springs, Colorado.

RAMÍREZ, RAÚL CARLOS. B. 20 June 1953, Ensenada, **Mexico**. Raúl Ramírez attended the University of Southern California and played tennis there. He played **professional** tennis from 1971 to 1985 and, in that time, won 19 **singles** and 60 **doubles** titles. In 1976, the six-foot tall, right-hander was the number-one–**ranked** doubles player in the world and number four singles player as well. That year, he and **Brian Gottfried** won the **Wimbledon** doubles championship. They were also runners-up at Wimbledon in 1979. The Gottfried-Ramírez team won the **French Open** in 1975 and 1977 and was runner-up in 1976 and 1980. They were runners-up in the **United States Open** in 1977. In 1973, Ramírez and Janet Newberry were Wimbledon **mixed doubles** runners-up. As a singles player, Ramírez reached the semifinal round at **Roland Garros** in 1976 and 1977 and at Wimbledon in 1977 and the quarterfinal round at the United States Open in 1978. He was a member of the Mexican **Davis Cup** team from 1971 to 1985 and played in 20 **ties** with a record of 22–8 in singles and 14–5 in doubles in 12 years. His Davis Cup victory over his doubles partner, Gottfried, helped Mexico defeat the **United States** in a 1975 quarterfinal round tie. In 1981, he married the former Miss Universe, Maritza Sayalero.

RANKINGS. Rankings in recent years have been administered by the two main administrative organizations, the **Association of Tennis Professionals** and the **Women's Tennis Association**. Rankings are determined by a player's performance. **Tournaments** are assigned different rankings points depending upon the tournament's importance, and the points are earned by players depending on their final standing in the tournament. A player's ranking is used to determine eligibility for entry in tournaments. In earlier days of tennis, rankings were often arbitrarily assigned by tennis journalists.

RASKIND, RICHARD. *See* RICHARDS, RENÉE.

RAYMOND, LISA. B. 10 August 1973, Norristown, Pennsylvania. Lisa Raymond received a scholarship to the University of Florida and won the

1992 and 1993 **National Collegiate Athletic Association** National **Singles** Championship and helped Florida win the national team championship in 1992. She is one of the top **doubles** players of her era and, through May 2011, has reached the finals of 20 **Grand Slam** doubles **tournaments**, winning 9 of them. The 5-foot 5-inch, 120-pound right-hander is one of the few players who has won doubles titles at each of the four Slam tournaments. At the **Australian Open**, she won the 2000 women's doubles with Rennae Stubbs and was runner-up in 1997 with **Lindsay Davenport** and in 2006 with **Samantha Stosur**. At **Wimbledon**, Raymond and Stubbs were champions in 2001, and Raymond and Stosur were runners-up in 2008. Raymond and **Leander Paes** were Wimbledon **mixed doubles** champions in 1999, and she and Wesley Moodie were runners-up in 2010. At **Roland Garros**, she won with Stosur in 2006, with Davenport in 1994, and with **Mary Joe Fernández** in 1997, and with Stubbs in 2002, she was runner-up. Raymond and **Mike Bryan** won the 2003 mixed doubles at Roland Garros, and Raymond and Patrick Galbraith were runners-up there in 1997. At the **United States Open**, Raymond and Stubbs won in 2001, and Raymond and Stosur won in 2005 and were runners-up in 2008. In mixed doubles there in 1996, Raymond won with Galbraith and in 2002 with Bryan. She was runner-up with Galbraith in 1998 and with Paes in 2001.

In the 2004 **Olympic Games**, she reached the third round of the singles and the quarterfinal round of the doubles. She played for the **United States Fed Cup** team from 1997 to 2008. In 15 **ties** over eight years, her record was 3–6 in singles and 11–3 in doubles. She played in the finals for the Fed Cup championship team in 2000 and runner-up team in 2003. She won **the Hopman Cup** in 2006 with partner **Taylor Dent**. In her career, through May 2011, she has won 4 singles titles and had a world singles ranking of 15 in 1997 and won 71 doubles titles and was the world number-one doubles player for the first time in 2000.

REAL TENNIS. *See* COURT TENNIS.

REFEREE. A referee in tennis, unlike many other sports, is not the person who is in charge of a **match**. That person is termed the umpire (or **chair umpire**). The referee is the person in charge of the entire **tournament** and is involved with **seedings**, the **draw**, and the order of play. He or she may be called upon by the umpire during a match to adjudicate a situation or interpret a point of tennis rules. He or she also may be asked whether or not to suspend play due to darkness or weather. The referee can also penalize a player for misbehavior.

RELATIVES. Since tennis is a sport played by both men and women of all ages, it has been a family sport, and in its history, there have been many players whose ancestors, siblings, spouses, and descendents have also been successful. Among the best tennis-playing brothers have been: José and Manuel Alonso; **Anand**, **Ashok**, and **Vijay Amritraj**; **James** and Thomas **Blake**; Clarence and Joseph Clark; **Laurence** and **Reggie Doherty**; Luke and Murphy Jensen; Dimitrios and Xenophon Kasdaglis; Howard and Robert Kinsey; Giovanni, Leonardo, and Nicolás Lapentti; David, **John**, and Tony **Lloyd**; Arthur and Gordon Lowe; **Gene** and Sandy **Mayer**; **John** and **Patrick McEnroe**; **Andy** and Jamie **Murray**; Arthur and Pat O'Hara Wood; **Adriano** and Claudio **Panatta**; Christophe and Olivier Rochus; **Bill** and Herbert **Tilden**; Jørgen and **Torben Ulrich**; Aubrey and Jim Willard; and Bob and George Wrenn. **Twin** brothers include the Baddeleys—Herbert and Wilfred; the **Bryans**—**Bob and Mike**; the Gullicksons—Tim and Tom; and the **Renshaws**—**Ernest and William**. Brother-sister combinations include: Ivica, Mario, and Sanja Ančić; **Bunny** and Joan **Austin**; Pam, **Tracy**, Jeff, and John **Austin**; Byron, Cara, and Wayne Black; Edda and Ingo Buding; **Richard** and Michaella **Krajicek** (half-brother and sister); Buster and Linda Mottram; Cliff and **Nancy Richey**; **Marat Safin** and **Dinara Safina**; and Cyril Suk and **Helena Suková**. Tennis-playing sisters include **Juliette** and Katherine **Atkinson**; **Chris** and Jeanne **Evert**; Carly and Chelsey Gullickson; Georgina and Marion Jones; Barbara and Kathy Jordan; **Katerina**, **Magdalena**, and **Manuela Maleeva**; Lee, Mianne, Polly, and **Sarah Palfrey**; Agnieszka and Urszula Radwańska; Dally and Natacha Randriantefy; and **Serena** and **Venus Williams**. Second generation families include fathers and sons: Anand and **Stephen Amritraj**, Vijay and **Prakash Amritraj**, Syd and Carsten Ball, **Phil** and **Taylor Dent**, Sammy Giammalva Sr. and Jr., and **Fred** and Sandon **Stolle**. Quite a few tennis players married other tennis players. Among those who teamed in **mixed doubles** are Eleanor Hall and **Harry Hopman**, Marjorie Cox and **Jack Crawford**, **Thelma Coyne** and Colin Long, **Kitty McKane** and Leslie Godfree, Max and Marie Decugis, and Pierre Darmon and Rosa Reyes.

RENSHAW, JAMES ERNEST. *See* RENSHAW TWINS.

RENSHAW, WILLIAM CHARLES "WILLIE." *See* RENSHAW TWINS.

RENSHAW TWINS. The Renshaw twins, William "Willie" Charles and James Ernest, were born 3 January 1861, in Leamington Spa, England. Willie Renshaw was the greatest tennis player of his time, and his twin brother,

Ernest, was a close second. Willie won the **Wimbledon singles** championship seven times—six consecutive years from 1881 to 1886 and again in 1889. He did not defend his title in 1887 due to an elbow injury. He was also runner-up in 1890. His brother, Ernest, won Wimbledon in 1888 and was runner-up to his brother in 1882, 1883, and 1889. The brothers won the Wimbledon **doubles** championship in 1884, 1885, 1886, 1888, and 1889. Their feat was made easier since, in that era, the defending champion did not play in the **all-comers** (preliminary) rounds but only faced the all-comers winner in a **challenge round**. Ernest died 2 September 1899 in Waltham St. Lawrence, England, and William died 12 August 1904 in Swanage, England. Their tennis careers were ended before the **Davis Cup** competition began in 1900. They were both inducted into the **International Tennis Hall of Fame** in 1983.

RICHARDS, RENÉE (RICHARD RASKIND). B. 19 August 1934, New York, New York. Renée Richards is unique among **professional** athletes. Richard Raskind attended the Horace Mann School in New York, played on the tennis team, and won the Eastern Private Schools Interscholastic Singles Championship. He attended Yale University and was captain of its tennis team in 1954. He then studied at the University of Rochester medical school and became an eye surgeon. He competed in the **United States National Championships** in men's **singles** in 1953, 1955 through 1957, and 1960 and twice reached the second round. In 1970, he married and became the father of a son. Raskind reached the finals of the men's 35-and-over national championships in 1972. In 1973, he became the **coach** of the **United States** team in the Maccabiah Games and helped lead the team to the silver medal, after failing in a tryout to make the team as a 38-year-old player.

In 1975, he underwent surgery and became a woman as Renée Richards. She attempted to enter the 1976 **United States Open** tournament but was barred by the **United States Lawn Tennis Association**. Richards successfully sued the organization and, in 1977, entered the United States Open women's singles and **doubles**. She played there from 1977 to 1981 and reached the third round in 1979. In the women's doubles in 1977, Richards, aged 43, and Betty Ann Grubb Stuart reached the finals, losing 6–1, 7–6 to **Martina Navratilova** and **Betty Stove**. She also entered the **mixed doubles** in 1978, 1979, and 1980 with **Ilie Năstase** and reached the semifinal round in 1979. In 1979, she was ranked 20th in the world. She won the women's 35-and-over national championships in 1979. She also played mixed doubles with **John Lucas** in **World Team Tennis**. She retired from tennis in 1981, at the age of 47, and returned to her medical practice. The 1983 book *Second Serve: The Renée Richards Story*, by Renée Richards and John Ames, provides a fascinating look into the life of an accomplished but troubled individual.

RICHARDS, VINCENT "VINNIE." B. 20 March 1903, Yonkers, New York. D. 28 September 1959, New York, New York. Vincent Richards attended Fordham Prep, Fordham University, and the Columbia University School of Journalism. In 1918, at the age of 15, he was **Bill Tilden's** partner and won the **United States National Doubles** Championships. He is the youngest male player to win a **Grand Slam** championship event. The following year, he and Tilden were runners-up in that event, and they won it again in 1921 and 1922. Richards won it twice more in 1925 and 1926 with **Dick Williams** as his partner. Richards won the United States National **mixed doubles** in 1919 and 1924 and was runner-up in 1925—each time with a different partner. He also won the **Wimbledon** men's doubles in 1924 with Frank Hunter and was runner-up in 1926 with Howard Kinsey. He and Kinsey won the **French National** doubles title in 1926.

Richards competed in all three tennis events at the 1924 **Olympic Games** in Paris and won the gold medal in both men's **singles** and men's doubles (partner Frank Hunter) and won the silver medal in mixed doubles (partner Marion Jessup). He is the only American to win three Olympic tennis medals in one tournament and one of only three Americans to win a total of three Olympic tennis medals—the others are **Mary Joe Fernández** and **Venus Williams**. He was a member of the **United States Davis Cup** team in 1922, 1924, 1925, and 1926 and played in the **challenge round** in each of those years. His record of 2–0 in singles and 2–1 in doubles in the four **ties** helped enable the United States to win the Cup in each of those four years.

In 1927, he became one of the first top players to become a **professional** tennis player. As a professional, he toured with the Czechoslovakian Karel Koželuh but lost the majority of his matches to him. Richards did win the **U.S. Pro Championships** in 1927, 1928, 1930, and 1933 and was runner-up in that event in 1929 and 1931. In 1945, he and Tilden, then aged 52, won the U.S. Pro doubles title. Richards was a vice president of the sports division of the Dunlop Tire and Rubber Company for 20 years prior to his death from a heart attack in 1959, just a short time after he had been inducted into the **International Tennis Hall of Fame**.

RICHEY GUNTER, NANCY ANNE. B. 23 August 1942, San Angelo, Texas. Nancy Richey and her brother Cliff began playing tennis under the guidance of their father, George, a teaching **professional** in Texas. Both brother and sister eventually were **ranked** number one in the **United States**—the only American brother-sister pair to reach those heights. Nancy began playing in major **tournaments** at the age of 17 in 1959. Her continued improvement resulted in reaching the **United States National** women's **singles** quarterfinals in 1963, semifinals in 1964 and 1965, and finals in 1966. Her first major title was won in 1965, when she won the United States National women's **doubles** with Carol Caldwell Graebner. In 1966, Nancy achieved her best results as she was also a finalist at the **Australian** and **French** championships and was a quarterfinalist at **Wimbledon**. She also won three of the four women's doubles major titles that year—all except the French Championships. In 1967, she won the Australian Championships and was runner-up in the Wimbledon doubles and, in 1968, won the French Championships. In 1969, she was the losing finalist at the French Championships. In 1969, she was also the losing finalist at the United States Championships but reached her career-high world ranking of second that year.

She married Kenneth S. Gunter, a San Angelo, Texas, television executive, on 15 December 1970, but they divorced in 1976. While married, she played as Nancy Gunter. She was a member of the United States **Federation Cup** team in 1964, 1968, and 1969. Her record in 11 **ties** was 10–1 in singles and 5–1 in doubles. She was a member of the Cup championship team in 1969 and runner-up team in 1964. She played for the United States each year from 1962 to 1970 in the **Wightman Cup** and had a record of 9–7 in singles and 3–2 in doubles. In 1970, she was one of the nine players, led by **Billie Jean King**, who formed the women's professional tour initially sponsored by **Virginia Slims** cigarettes. In her career, which lasted through 1978, she won 69 singles titles, including the United States **Clay Court** Championships a record six consecutive times from 1963 to 1968. She was inducted into the **International Tennis Hall of Fame** in 2003.

RIGGS, ROBERT LARIMORE "BOBBY." B. 25 February 1918, Los Angeles, California. D. 10 October 1995, Encinitas, California. Bobby Riggs began playing tennis at age 11 in Los Angeles and was taught by Dr. Esther Bartosh, one of the top local players at that time, who had seen him playing on public **courts** and took him under her wing. Although slight of stature, he used his wiles to outthink his opponents. By the time he was 18, he won the men's Southern California Championship. He played in his first **United States National tournament** at **Forest Hills** in 1936 and reached the fourth round. The following year, he reached the semifinals. In 1939, he traveled to **Roland Garros** for his only appearance in that **tournament** and was the tournament runner-up. He then played at **Wimbledon** and won the men's **singles**, teamed with Elwood Cooke to win the men's **doubles**, and partnered with **Alice Marble** to win the **mixed doubles**. A notorious hustler and gambler, he later wrote in his 1949 autobiography that he had bet $500 on himself to win the singles, parlayed his winnings on the doubles, and parlayed those winnings on the mixed doubles, walking away with over $100,000. (He actually did not walk away with the money since he later claimed that, due to the war, he was not allowed to take the money out of the country, which he was finally able to do in 1946.) He then won the United States National singles in 1939, was runner-up in 1940, and won again in 1941. He was U.S. mixed doubles champion in 1940 with Alice Marble and runner-up in 1941 with **Pauline Betz**. He played on the **United States Davis Cup** team in 1938 and 1939 in the **challenge round** and had a record of 2–2 in singles, winning and losing one match each year. In 1938, he was a member of the Cup championship team.

He became a **professional** in 1942 and reached the finals of the **U.S. Pro Championships**, where he was defeated by **Don Budge**. After serving in the U.S. military in World War II, he resumed his pro career in 1946 and reached the U.S. Pro Championships finals each year from 1946 to 1949, losing only in 1948 to **Jack Kramer**. On the pro tour, he defeated Don Budge in a series in 1946 through 1947, 23 matches to 21, but on the 1947–48 tour, Riggs was defeated by Jack Kramer, 69–20. During the 1950s, he concentrated more on promoting pro tennis than on playing on the tour. He then faded from the limelight for the next 20 years but resurfaced in 1973 to take part in one of the most highly promoted tennis events of all time and one that set an attendance record that was not broken for three decades.

The 55-year-old Riggs challenged **Margaret Smith Court** (who had won 89 of her last 92 **matches** on the women's tour) to a "battle of the sexes" match, played on 13 May (Mother's Day), in Romana, California, to prove that women's tennis, in his words, "stinks." Ironically, Riggs, at five feet eight inches tall, was two inches shorter than Smith Court and played a **baseline** game more typical of women's tennis. The 5-foot 10-inch Smith Court, known for her powerful **serve**, lost a battle of nerves and played poorly. The nationally televised match was won easily by Riggs, 6–2, 6–1, in 57 minutes. Riggs then challenged **Billie Jean King**. That match received much more publicity and was held at the Astrodome in Houston, Texas. The $100,000 winner-take-all match, held 20 September, was played before 30,492 fans in a circus-like atmosphere, and Riggs was trounced by Billie Jean, 6–4, 6–3, 6–3. That match helped to give women's tennis a large boost in popularity. He remained friends with Billie Jean until his death from prostate cancer in 1995. He was inducted into the **International Tennis Hall of Fame** in 1967.

ROCHE, ANTHONY DALTON "TONY." B. 17 May 1945, Tarcutta, New South Wales, **Australia**. Tony Roche learned his tennis from **Harry Hopman**, Australia's most famous **coach**. Roche made his first appearance at the major **tournaments** in 1963. From 1965 to 1970, he reached the finals of one **Grand Slam** tournament each year but was only victorious in 1966, at **Roland Garros**. He lost at Roland Garros in 1965 and 1967, at **Wimbledon** in 1968, and at **Forest Hills** in 1969 and 1970. He was an excellent **doubles** player, and with **John Newcombe** as a partner, the 5-foot, 10-inch, 175-pound, **left-handed** Roche won 12 Grand Slam titles and was runner-up twice. The pair won championships at each of the four major tournaments—Australia 1965, 1967, 1971, and 1976; Roland Garros 1967 and 1969; Wimbledon 1965, 1968–70, and 1974; and **United States** 1967. They were runners-up in 1964 at Roland Garros and 1966 at the Australian. Roche teamed with **Arthur Ashe** to also win the **Australian Open** in January 1977. Roche also won the **mixed doubles** title with **Judy Tegart** in 1966 in Australia, and the pair was runner-up there in 1967 and also at Wimbledon in 1965 and 1969. He won his last Grand Slam title in 1976 with **Françoise Durr** at Wimbledon.

In 1968, Roche was one of the eight players who signed **professional** contracts with **World Championship Tennis**. In 1970, he defeated **Rod Laver** to win the **U.S. Pro Championships**. Roche was a member of the Australian **Davis Cup** team as an **amateur** from 1964 to 1967 and as a professional from 1974 to 1978. In nine years of **Davis Cup** competition, his record was 7–3 in **singles** and 7–2 in doubles in 12 **ties**. Australia won the Cup each year from 1964 to 1967 and again in 1977, and Roche played in the final in each of those years except 1964. His career ended due to shoulder and elbow injuries. In retirement, he has become one of the most sought-after coaches and, at various times, he has coached **Ivan Lendl**, **Patrick Rafter**, **Roger Federer**, and **Lleyton Hewitt**. He was inducted into the **International Tennis Hall of Fame** in 1986, along with his doubles partner and good friend, John Newcombe.

RODDICK, ANDREW STEPHEN "ANDY." B. 30 August 1982, Omaha, Nebraska. Although born in Nebraska, Andy Roddick was raised in Texas. At the age of 11, he accompanied his brother to Boca Raton, Florida, to further his brother's tennis education. Roddick attended Boca Prep International (high school), where he was on the basketball team with future pro tennis player Mardy Fish. Roddick then transferred to Highlands Christian Academy, from which he graduated in 2000. He was the world number-one **junior** player in 2000, after winning the **Australian Open** and **United States Open** junior **singles** titles. By 2003, he achieved the men's world number-one singles **ranking** and won the U.S. Open men's singles title after saving a **match point** in the semifinals. As of May 2011, this is his only **Grand Slam**

title; although, he was a singles finalist at **Wimbledon** in 2004, 2005, and 2009 and at the U.S. Open in 2006, losing to **Roger Federer** all four times.

Roddick, a 6-foot, 2-inch, 195-pound right-hander has one of the hardest **serves** in the history of tennis and held the world record for fastest recorded serve at 155 miles per hour, which he set in a **Davis Cup** match 2004. This record was broken by **Ivo Karlovic's** 156 miles per hour serve in 2011, also in a Davis Cup match. Roddick competed in the 2004 **Olympic Games** and reached the third round of the men's singles but lost in the first round of the men's **doubles**. He was a member of the **United States** Davis Cup team in each year from 2001 to 2009, and again in 2001. He helped the team win the Cup championship in 2007. In 25 **ties** in ten years, his Cup record is 33–12, with all matches being singles matches. Through May 2011, Roddick has recorded 30 singles and 4 doubles titles in his career.

ROLAND GARROS. B. 6 October 1888, D. 5 October 1918. Roland Garros was a **French** aviator and fighter pilot during the First World War. He became a prisoner of war in 1915, escaped from a prisoner-of-war camp in February 1918, and returned to action. He was shot down and killed in October 1918. In the 1920s, a tennis center that he had frequented was renamed Stade de Roland Garros. This stadium became the site of the French National Championships in 1928. The **French National** Championships, later known as the **French Open**, one of the four major international tennis **tournaments** (**Grand Slam** tournaments), is also referred to simply as Roland Garros, although its official title is *Les Internationaux de France de Roland Garros*.

ROMANIA. Tennis in Romania is under the auspices of the Federatia Romana de Tenis (Romanian Tennis Federation), founded in 1912. From 1922 through May 2011, Romania has competed in 68 **Davis Cup tournaments** with a record of 71–66 in 137 **ties**. The country has competed 14 times in the World Group since its formation in 1981 and was the tournament runner-up three times, 1969, 1971, and 1972, losing to the **United States** in the final each time. Top Davis Cup players have been **Ilie Năstase** and **Ion Ţiriac**. Romania competed in the 1924 **Olympic** tennis tournament and has also entered each one from 1992 to 2008. Its best result was in 1992, when the men's **doubles** team of Gheorghe Cosac and Dino-Mihai Pescariu reached the quarterfinal round. The best Romanian male tennis players, by far, were Năstase and Ţiriac. Other good ones include Christian Caralulis, Andrei Dirzu, Victor Hănescu, Dumitru Hărădău, Nicolae Mişu, Andrei Pavel, and Horia Tecău. The best female tennis players include Sorana Cîrstea, Cătălina Cristea, Florenţa Mihai, sisters Gabriela and Monica Niculescu, **Virginia Ruzici**, Mariana Simionescu, and Irina Spîrlea. In **Federation Cup** competition, from 1973 to May 2011, Romania has competed 31 years, 12 years in World Group, and played 112 ties with a record of 64–48. Romania was a quarterfinalist five times between 1973 and 1981.

ROSE, MERVYN GORDON "MERV." B. 23 January 1930, Coffs Harbour, New South Wales, **Australia**. Merv Rose reached the finals of 19 **Grand Slam** events—16 in **doubles**—and won 7 of them. He lost to **Ken Rosewall** in the **Australian singles** final in 1953 and then won the championship in 1954 by defeating Rex Hartwig. Rose also was the **French National** singles champion in 1958. He won the Australian doubles title with Rex Hartwig as partner in 1954 and was a three-time runner-up for that title with Don Candy (1952, 1953, 1956). Rose and Hartwig also won the **Wimbledon** doubles in 1954 and were runners-up in 1953. Rose was twice runner-up for the French doubles—in 1953 with Clive Wilderspin and in 1957 with Candy. At the **United States Nationals**, Rose reached the doubles final in three consecutive years with three different partners. He lost in 1951 with Candy, won in 1952 with **Vic Seixas**, and won again in 1953 with Hartwig. In **mixed doubles**, Rose and **Darlene Hard** won Wimbledon in 1957, and Rose and **Nancye Wynne Bolton** were runners-up there in 1951. He was twice runner-up at the French Nationals—in 1951 with **Thelma Coyne Long** and in 1953 with **Maureen Connolly**. In 1951, Rose and **Shirley Fry** were finalists at the United States Nationals. The six-foot tall **left-hander** only played three matches in two **ties** for Australia in **Davis Cup** competition, losing both singles matches in 1951 and winning the doubles match in 1957, but both appearances were in the **challenge round** when Australia won the Cup.

He became a **professional** in 1959, joined Jack Kramer's tour, and, in Rose's words, "learned more about tennis from **Pancho González**, **Lew Hoad**, Ken Rosewall and the rest than I'd ever known." He turned to **coaching** shortly afterward, and among his pupils were **Billie Jean King**, **Margaret Smith Court**, **Arantxa Sánchez Vicario**, and Nadia Petrova. After the Australian Championships became an **open** tournament, he made two final appearances there in 1971 and 1972, winning one **match** at the age of 41. He was inducted into the **International Tennis Hall of Fame** in 2001 and was presented with the Order of Australia Medal in 2006.

ROSEWALL, KENNETH ROBERT "KEN," "MUSCLES." B. 2 November 1934, Sydney, New South Wales, **Australia**. Ken Rosewall learned to play tennis on his family's own tennis **courts**. A natural **left-hander**, he was **converted** to playing right-handed by his father. Rosewall had one of the longest tennis careers, playing his first **Australian** Championships in 1951 and his last in 1978. He won eight **Grand Slam singles** championships and was runner-up in eight others. He undoubtedly would have won many more had he not become a **professional** in 1957 and was precluded from playing in them for 11 years, until they became **open tournaments**. His total of appearing in 36 Grand Slam finals is second of all time among men to **Roy Emerson** and shared with **John Bromwich** and **Fred Stolle**.

The 5-foot 7-inch, 135-pound Rosewall, sarcastically nicknamed "Muscles" by his fellow players, won the **Australian Open** in 1953 and 1955 as an **amateur** and again in 1971 and 1972 as a professional. He was also runner-up there in 1956. He won the **French Nationals** in 1953 and the **French Open** in 1968 and was runner-up in 1969. **Wimbledon** was the only major tournament at which he was unable to win a singles championship, reaching the finals in 1954, 1956, 1960, and 1974 (at the age of 39). He won the **United States Nationals** in 1956 and the **U.S. Open** in 1970 and was a runner-up in that tournament in 1955 and 1974. In **doubles** play, he won the Australian Championships in 1953 and 1956 with **Lew Hoad** and 1972 with Owen Davidson and was runner-up in 1955 with Hoad and in 1969 with Stolle. Rosewall and Hoad won Wimbledon in 1953 and 1956. Rosewall and **Neale Fraser** were Wimbledon doubles runners-up in 1955, and Rosewall and Stolle were runners-up in 1968 and 1970. Rosewall and Hoad won the French Nationals in 1953 and were runners-up the following year and Rosewall and Stolle won it in 1968. Rosewall-Hoad won the United States Nationals in 1956 after being runners-up in 1954, and Rosewall-Stolle won it in 1969. Rosewall teamed with **Rod Laver** in 1973 at **Forest Hills** and was runner-up.

During his professional years, Rosewall won the **U.S. Pro Championships** in 1963, 1965, and 1971 and lost to Laver in the 1966 finals. As an amateur, he played on the Australian **Davis Cup** team from 1953 to 1956 and as a professional in 1973 and 1975. His overall Cup record was 17–2 in singles and 2–1 in doubles in 11 **ties** in 6 years. He played for the Cup championship team in the challenge round in 1953, 1955, and 1956. In 1977, Rosewall won his last tournament at the age of 43 but continued playing occasionally until 1982. He was inducted into the **International Tennis Hall of Fame** in 1980.

ROUND LITTLE, DOROTHY EDITH. B. 13 July 1909, Dudley, England. D. 12 November 1982, Kidderminster, England. As the top British female tennis player during the 1930s, Dorothy Round's first success at a major championship occurred in 1931 as she and **Helen Jacobs** reached the finals of the **United States National** women's **doubles tournament**. In 1933, Round reached the women's **singles** semifinals there and the finals of the singles at **Wimbledon** but was defeated in the finals by **Helen Wills Moody**, who won her sixth Wimbledon title. In 1934, Moody did not compete at Wimbledon, and Round defeated her former doubles partner, Helen Jacobs, to win the title. As the ladies' singles champion at Wimbledon in 1934, she traveled to **Australia** in 1935 and became the first non-Australian woman to win the national championships there. This was her only appearance in those championships. In 1937, she again won the Wimbledon singles. She was also an excellent **mixed doubles** player and won the Wimbledon mixed doubles in three consecutive years, from 1934 to 1936. In 1934, she teamed with her mentor, Ryuki Miki (the first **Japanese** to win a Wimbledon title), and in 1935 and 1936, **Fred Perry** was her partner. She played on the British **Wightman Cup** team each year from 1931 to 1936 and had a record of 4–7 in singles and 0–2 in doubles.

A devout Christian and a Methodist Sunday School teacher, she refused to play on Sundays. She married Dr. Douglas Little in 1938 and ended her serious tennis play. She remained as a **coach** and journalist and was president of the Worcestershire **Lawn Tennis** Association. She was the author of two instructional books, *Modern Lawn Tennis* and *Tennis for Girls*, both published at the height of her career. She was inducted into the **International Tennis Hall of Fame** in 1986.

RUANO PASCUAL, VIRGINIA. B. 21 September 1973, Madrid, **Spain**. A **doubles** specialist, Virginia Ruano Pascual, reached the finals of 17 **Grand Slam** doubles events and won 11 of them, through July 2010. She won the **French Open** women's doubles six times (2001, 2002, 2004 and 2005 with Paola Suárez and 2008 and 2009 with Anabel Medina Garrigues), the **United States Open** women's doubles three times (2002, 2003, and 2004 with Suárez), the **Australian Open** women's doubles once (2004 with Suárez), and the French **mixed doubles** once (with Tomás Carbonell in 2001, defeating her doubles partner Suárez and Jaime Oncins). She and Suárez were runners-up at **Wimbledon** in 2002, 2003, and 2006; at the Australian Open in 2003; and at the French Open in 2003.

As a **singles** player, her record was not nearly as stellar, although she was **ranked** number 28 in the world in 1999 and won seven singles titles in her career. In doubles, she won 53 titles and was the world number-one–ranked player in 2003. The 5-foot 7-inch, 130-pound right-hander competed in three **Olympic Games**—1996, 2004, and 2008. In 1996, she lost in the second round of the singles event, but in 2004 with **Conchita Martínez** and again in 2008 with Anabel Medina Garrigues, she was the silver medalist in the women's doubles competition. From 1992 to 1997, 1999 to 2004, and 2006 to 2007, she played on the Spanish **Fed Cup** team. Her record for 31 **ties** was 0–4 in singles and 15–13 in doubles over 14 years. She played in the finals for the championship team in 1995 and for the runner-up team in 1996, 2000, and 2002. In 1993 and 1994, she helped Spain win the Cup, although she did not play in any final round **rubbers**. Ruano Pascual turned **professional** in 1992 and was still playing in 2010, at age 36, winning a **Women's Tennis Association** doubles title in Poland on 22 May with partner Meghann Shaughnessy. Virginia retired following the 2010 season.

RUBBER. A rubber is an individual **match** in a team event, such as **Davis Cup** or **Fed Cup**. The series of matches in those events are called **ties**. A **dead rubber** occurs when a team has established a winning advantage in the tie by winning three rubbers, but one or two rubbers remain to be played. Dead rubbers in Davis Cup are usually shortened to best of three **sets**.

RUSEDSKI, GREGORY "GREG." B. 6 September 1973, Montreal, Quebec, **Canada**. Greg Rusedski was raised in Canada by a **British**-born mother and **German**-born father. In 1991, he won the **Wimbledon boys' doubles** title with partner Karim Alami. Rusedski became a **professional** tennis player later that year. His early tennis career was as a Canadian, but in 1995, he decided to become a British citizen and represent **Great Britain** in international play. The 6-foot 4-inch, 190-pound **left-hander** competed in the 1996 **Olympic Games** for Great Britain and reached the third round of the men's **singles**. The highlight of his career occurred in 1997, when he reached the finals of the **United States Open**, where he lost to **Pat Rafter** in four **sets** and achieved a career-high **ranking** of world number four. That year, he also reached the quarterfinals at Wimbledon for his best performance there. His best showing at the **Australian Open** and the **French Open** was in reaching the fourth round in each of those **tournaments** once. He played on the Great Britain **Davis Cup** team each year from 1995 to 2007. In 20 **ties**, his record was 20–10 in singles and 10–3 in doubles over the 13 years. He retired from tennis in 2007 and compiled 15 singles and 3 doubles victories in his career. Since retiring, he has written a newspaper column, done television work, and appeared as an actor in an episode of a British television show.

RUSSIA. The Russian Tennis Federation is the administering organization for Russian tennis. Russian players competed for the Union of Soviet Socialist Republics (USSR) from 1962 through 1991, for the Commonwealth of Independent States in 1992, and for Russia since then. From 1962 through May 2011, Russia has competed in 47 **Davis Cup tournaments** with a record of 79–43 in 122 **ties**. The team has competed 24 times in the World Group since its formation in 1981. In 2002 and 2006, Russia won the Cup, and in 1994, 1995, and 2007, the team was the tournament runner-up. Top Davis Cup players have been Alex Metraveli and Sergei Likhatchev. Russia sent two entrants to the 1912 **Olympic Games**, and Mikhail Sumarakhov-Elston and Aleksandr Alenitsyn reached the quarterfinals of the men's doubles.

In 1968, the Soviet Union sent five players to compete in the **exhibition** and demonstration tennis events in **Mexico**. In 1992, competing as the Commonwealth of Independent States (also known as the Unified Team), Andrey Cherkasov won the bronze medal in men's **singles**, and **Natasha Zvereva** and Leila Meshki won the bronze medal in **doubles**. As an independent country, Russia's next appearance in Olympic tennis was in 1996. In 2000, **Yevgeny Kafelnikov** won the gold medal in men's singles, and **Elena Dementieva** won the silver medal in women's singles. Anastasiya Myskina was fourth in women's singles in 2004, and in 2008, Russia won all three medals in women's singles—Dementieva won the gold, **Dinara Safina**, the silver, and Vera Zvonareva, the bronze. The two women's doubles teams—**Svetlana Kuznetsova** and Safina, Zvonareva and Elena Vesnina—both reached the quarterfinal round.

Among the best Russian male tennis players have been Igor Andreev, **Nikolay Davydenko**, Igor Kunitsyn, **Marat Safin**, Dmitry Tursonov, and Mikhail Youzhny. The best female tennis players include **Anna Kournikova**, Elena Likhovtseva, Anastasia Pavlyuchenkova, **Maria Sharapova**, Elena Vesnina, and Vera Zvonareva. In **Federation Cup** competition from 1968 to May 2011, Russia has competed 35 years, 29 years in World Group, and played 118 ties with a record of 84–34. Russia was the champion four times—in 2004, 2005, 2007, and 2008. The country was runner-up in 1988, 1990, 1999, and 2001. On 5–6 November 2011, Russia and the Czech Republic play for the 2011 Fed Cup championship.

RUZICI, VIRGINIA. B. 31 January 1955, Cimpa-Turzil, **Romania**. Virginia Ruzici was a member of the Romanian **Federation Cup** team from 1973 to 1983. The five-foot eight-inch, right-handed player's record for eight years and 24 **ties** was 14–7 in **singles** and 11–6 in **doubles**. In 1973, she helped Romania reach the semifinal round. She became a **professional** tennis player in 1975 and played until 1987. During her career, she had her best success at the **French Open**, where she won the women's singles title in 1978, was runner-up in 1980, won the doubles with Mima Jaušovec in 1978, and was runner-up in the **mixed doubles** in 1978 and 1979. She and Jaušovec were also runners-up at Wimbledon in 1978. Her best singles performance at the other three majors was the quarterfinal round, which she reached several times. In Ruzici's career, she recorded a high world singles **ranking** of eighth in 1978 and won 11 singles and 15 doubles titles.

RYAN, ELIZABETH MONTAGUE "BUNNY." B. 5 February 1892, Santa Monica, California. D. 6 July 1979, London, England. Bunny Ryan established a record that many thought would never be broken—until **Billie**

Jean King arrived. Miss Ryan won 19 **Wimbledon** championships and was a finalist there 25 times. She also reached the finals of the **French National** Championships six times, winning four, and reached the finals of the **United States National Championships** seven times with three victories. Her total of 38 **Grand Slam** finals played and 26 championships won is 10th on the all-time list of champions. These records are all the more remarkable when one realizes that she never won a Grand Slam **singles** final (although she played in three of them), never played in the **Australian Championships**, and only played in the United States National Championships four times. She was born in the **United States** but spent most of her life in England and played on the British **Wightman Cup** team in 1926, with a record of 2–1, splitting her singles matches and winning the **doubles**. In Grand Slam singles competition, her finals losses were all to future Hall of Famers—**Suzanne Lenglen** at Wimbledon in 1921, **Molla Bjurstedt Mallory** at **Forest Hills** in 1926 (losing 9–7 in the third set), and **Helen Wills Moody** at Wimbledon in 1930. Her totals would have been even greater had World War I not caused Wimbledon to suspend play for three years from 1915 to 1917.

Her first Wimbledon ladies' doubles was won in 1914 and her last in 1934. She won 12 titles and was runner-up once with partners Agnes Morton (1914), Suzanne Lenglen (1919–23, 1925), **Mary K. Browne** (1926), Helen Wills (1927, 1930), **Helen Jacobs** (1932 runner-up), and **Simone Passemard Mathieu** (1933–34). In **mixed doubles** at Wimbledon, she won 7 of 10 finals with partners Randolph Lycett (1919, 1921, 1923 won; 1920, 1922 runner-up), Umberto de Morpurgo (1925 runner-up), Frank Hunter (1927), Pat Spence (1928), **Jack Crawford** (1930), and Enrique Maier (1932). She only competed at the United States Nationals four times—1925 (singles quarterfinalist, women's doubles finalist), 1926 (singles finalist, doubles champion with Eleanor Goss, mixed doubles champion with **Jean Borotra**), 1933 (doubles finalist with Helen Wills Moody, mixed doubles champion with **Ellsworth Vines**), 1934 (singles quarterfinalist, mixed doubles finalist with Lester Stoefen).

At **Roland Garros**, she was the women's doubles finalist five consecutive years, 1930 to 1934, winning all but 1931 with partners Helen Wills Moody (1930, 1932), Cilly Aussem (1931), and Simone Passemard Mathieu (1933, 1934). She was also runner-up in mixed doubles there in 1934 with **Adrian Quist**. She was inducted into the **International Tennis Hall of Fame** in 1972. She cherished her records and reportedly did not want to meet Billie Jean King. Ryan died at the age of 87 on the grounds of the **All-England Lawn Tennis and Croquet Club** at Wimbledon on the day before Billie Jean King broke Ryan's Wimbledon record for most championships.

S

SABATINI, GABRIELA BEATRIZ. B. 16 May 1970, Buenos Aires, **Argentina**. In 1983, at the age of 13, Gabriela Sabatini won the **Orange Bowl tournament** in Florida. The following year, she won the **French Open Girls' Singles** Championship. In January 1985, at the age of 14, she became a **professional** tennis player and, in May, became the youngest player ever to reach the semifinals of the French Open **main draw**. In 1988, she teamed with **Steffi Graf** to win the women's **doubles** title at **Wimbledon**. Sabatini then reached the finals of the **United States Open**, where she was defeated by Graf. In 1989, she achieved her career-high world **ranking** of three. In 1990, she won the United States Open by defeating Graf and, in 1991, again lost to Graf at the Wimbledon finals. In her career, the 5-foot 9-inch, 130-pound, right-handed Sabatini reached the singles semifinals at the **Australian Open** four times and French Open five times. She and Graf reached the women's doubles finals at the French Open in 1986, 1987, and 1989 but were defeated each time.

Gabriela competed in singles and doubles in the 1988 and 1996 **Olympic Games** and was the silver medalist in the 1988 women's singles, losing to Graf in the finals. In addition, she was the Argentine flag bearer during the Opening Ceremonies in 1988. She played on the Argentine team in the **Federation Cup** in 1984 to 1987 and 1995. In 15 **ties**, her record was 13–3 in singles and 11–3 in doubles. When she retired in 1996, at the age of 26, she had won 27 singles and 14 doubles titles. She was inducted into the **International Tennis Hall of Fame** in 2006.

SAFIN, MARAT MIKHAILOVICH. B. 27 January 1980, Moscow, **Russia**, Union of Soviet Socialist Republics. Both Marat Safin's parents are tennis **professionals**. His mother is a tennis **coach**, and his father is the director of the Spartak Moscow tennis club. When Marat was a teenager, he moved to Valencia, **Spain**, to train on **clay courts**, feeling that they were better for his knees. He began his professional tennis career in 1997, and by November 2000, he was **ranked** number one in the world. He defeated **Pete Sampras** to win the **United States Open** men's **singles** in 2000. Safin was runner-up at the **Australian Open** in 2002 and 2004 and won it in 2005. He was also a semifinalist at the **French Open** in 2002 and at **Wimbledon** in 2008. The 6-foot 4-inch, 195-pound, right-handed Safin was a colorful player, whose emotions often got the better of him, and he smashed hundreds of **rackets** in frustration throughout his career.

Safin competed in the singles and **doubles** events in both the 2000 and 2004 **Olympic Games**. His best result was reaching the second round in the 2000 doubles and 2004 singles. He played on the Russian **Davis Cup** team from 1998 to 2009, each year except for 2003. In 23 **ties**, his record was 21–15 in singles and 10–6 in doubles. He helped Russia win the Cup in 2002 and 2006. His sister, **Dinara Safina**, is also one of the top female tennis players and also reached a world number-one singles ranking in her career. When Safin retired from tennis on 11 November 2009, he had won 15 singles and 2 doubles titles.

SAFINA, DINARA MIKHAILOVNA. B. 27 April 1986, Moscow, **Russia**, Union of Soviet Socialist Republics. Dinara Safina is the younger sister of **Australian** and **United States Open** champion **Marat Safin**. Their mother is a tennis **coach**, and their father is the director of the Spartak Moscow tennis club. She began playing **professional** tennis in 2001, one year after her world number-one–**ranked** brother won the U.S. Open. Dinara, a 6-foot tall, 150-pound right-hander, is nearly as tall as her brother and also has a powerful **serve**, as he does. She has reached the women's finals of the **French Open** in 2008 and 2009 and the Australian Open in 2009. She was a semifinalist at the United States Open in 2008 and at **Wimbledon** in 2009. She reached a world number-one ranking in 2009. This marked the first time that a brother and sister both were world number-one–ranked tennis players. (**Nancy** and Cliff **Richey** both were United States number one but never world number one.) In 2006, Safina and Katarina Srebotnik were United States Open women's **doubles** finalists. The following year, Safina teamed with Nathalie Dechy and won the title.

Safina won the silver medal in the 2008 **Olympic** women's **singles** and reached the quarterfinals in the doubles. She played in five **ties** in the **Fed Cup** for Russia in 2005, 2006, and 2008. She lost both singles matches but won all five doubles matches. With partner **Elena Dementieva**, she won the fifth and deciding match over France in 2005 to enable Russia to win the Cup. Safina, through May 2011, has won 16 singles and 12 doubles titles.

SAITCH, EYRE. B. 20 February 1905, New York, NY. D. November 1985, Englewood, NJ. Eyre Saitch was a champion tennis player who did not get the chance to fully display his abilities as he played during a time of segregated competition. He attended DeWitt Clinton High School in the Bronx, New York. An **African American** who played tennis during the 1920s and 1930s, he won the 1926 **American Tennis Association** National **Singles** Championships and 1926, 1928, and 1929 National **doubles** championships. He was better known in the white community as a member of the New York Renaissance basketball team that won 88 consecutive games in the 1930s and was later inducted as a team into the Naismith Memorial Basketball Hall of Fame.

SAMPRAS, PETROS "PETE." B. 12 August 1971, Washington DC. Although born in Washington DC, Pete Sampras was raised in Southern California from the age of seven. His family joined the **Jack Kramer** Club, and Sampras was discovered by Dr. Peter Fischer, who became his **coach**. Sampras became a **professional** player in 1988 and retired in 2003. In that time, he won a men's record 14 individual **Grand Slam** championships and was runner-up 4 times. His record was surpassed by **Roger Federer** in 2009. Sampras was the **Australian Open** champion in 1994 and 1997 and was runner-up to **Andre Agassi** in 1995. He won **Wimbledon** each year from 1993 to 2000, with the exception of 1996, when he was defeated in the quarterfinals by eventual champion **Richard Krajicek**. His Wimbledon record of seven championships is more than anyone else except 19th-century champion **Willie Renshaw**. Renshaw also won seven championships, but as he played during the **challenge round** era, he only had to win one match to defend his title in five of those years. From 1990 to 2002, Sampras was the men's finalist at the **United States Open** eight times, winning in 1990, 1993, 1995, 1996, and 2002 and losing the final in 1992, 2000, and 2001. The 6-foot 1-inch, 175-pound right-hander was a **serve-and-volley** player known for his powerful **serve**. Consequently, he did not do nearly as well at the **French Open**, where the slower **clay courts** helped to neutralize his serve. He did, however, reach the semifinal in 1996, where he lost to eventual champion **Yevgeny Kafelnikov**.

Sampras entered both **singles** and **doubles** in the 1992 Barcelona **Olympic Games** and reached the third round in singles and second round in doubles. He played on the **United States Davis Cup** team from 1991 to 2002. In 16 **ties** over eight years, his record was 15–8 in singles and 4–1 in doubles. He led the United States to the 1995 Cup championship by winning all three of his matches in the final round and won the doubles match in 1992 to help win the Cup that year as well. In 1991 and 1997, he played on the losing side in the Cup final. When he retired in 2003, at the age of 32, he said he would not make a comeback on the **Association of Tennis Professionals** tour, but in 2006, he resumed playing **exhibitions** and played a series with Roger Federer in 2007 and 2008. He also played in the **Champions Series** and **World**

Team Tennis. He was inducted into the **International Tennis Hall of Fame** in 2007.

SÁNCHEZ VICARIO, ARÁNZAZU ISABEL MARIA "ARANTXA."
B. 18 December 1971, Barcelona, **Spain**. Arantxa Sánchez Vicario followed her brothers, Emilio and Javier, and also became a **professional** tennis player. Her career results were quite a bit better than theirs, although Emilio did win five **Grand Slam doubles** events. All three siblings played in the **Olympic Games** in 1988, but Arantxa is the only one to win an Olympic medal. Sánchez Vicario is the only woman and one of only four people to compete in the tennis tournament in five different Olympic Games. She competed in the 1988, 1992, and 1996 **singles** events and won the bronze medal in 1992 and silver medal in 1996. She entered the doubles in 1992, 1996, 2000, and 2004, and with partner **Conchita Martínez**, won the silver medal in 1992 and bronze in 1996. Sánchez Vicario's professional tennis career lasted from 1985 to 2004. In that time, she won 29 singles and 69 doubles championships and reached the finals of 31 Grand Slam events, winning 14. The 5-foot 7-inch, 125-pound right-hander won the 1989, 1994, and 1998 **French Open** singles titles and the 1994 **United States Open** singles. She lost to **Monica Seles** in the finals of the 1991 French Open and 1992 U.S. Open. She lost to **Mary Pierce** in the finals of the 1995 **Australian Open**, but her nemesis was **Steffi Graf**, who defeated her in five Grand Slam finals—the 1994 Australian and the 1995 and 1996 French Open and **Wimbledon**. In 1995, Sánchez Vicario reached a world number-one singles **ranking**.

She was also quite talented as a doubles player, ranked world number one in 1992, and reached 11 Grand Slam women's doubles finals, winning 6, and 8 **mixed doubles** finals, winning 4. She won the 1992 Australian and the 1993 United States Open with **Helena Suková**, the 1994 U.S. Open and the 1995 Australian and Wimbledon with **Jana Novotná**, and the 1996 Australian with Chanda Rubin. In mixed doubles, she won the 1990 French Open with Jorge Lozano, the 1992 French Open with **Mark Woodforde**, the 1993 Australian with Woodforde's usual doubles partner, **Todd Woodbridge**, and the 2000 U.S. Open with Jared Palmer. She was mixed doubles runner-up in 1989 with Horacio de la Peña at **Roland Garros**, in 1991 at the U.S. Open with her brother Emilio, and in 1992 and 2000 at the Australian with Woodbridge. From 1986 to 2002, she played for Spain in the Federation Cup every year except for 1999. She holds the **Fed Cup** record for most **ties** played and most total **matches** won. Her record in 58 ties was 50–22 in singles and 22–6 in doubles. She was on the Cup-winning team in 1991, 1993, 1994, 1995, and 1998 and the Cup runner-up team in 1989, 1992, 1996, 2000, and 2002. She won the **Hopman Cup** in 1990 with her brother Emilio as partner. She won it again in 2002 with Tommy Robredo.

She married sportswriter Juan Vehils on 21 July 2000. They divorced in 2001. Her second marriage was to businessman José Santacana in 2008. They have one daughter, also named Arantxa. Sánchez Vicario was inducted into the **International Tennis Hall of Fame** in 2007.

SANTANA MARTÍNEZ, MANUEL "MANOLO." B. 10 May 1938, Madrid, **Spain**. Manuel Santana is the only 20th century player to win five **Grand Slam** finals without losing any. (**Dick Sears** won all 13 of his **United States Nationals** finals appearances, but he played during the **challenge round** era and did not have to play any matches in the **tournament** prior to the final **match**.) Santana won the **French National singles** in 1961, overcoming a two-**sets**-to-one deficit to defeat **Nicola Pietrangeli** in five sets. He defeated Pietrangeli in four sets to again win the French title in 1964. In 1965, the 5-foot 11-inch, right-handed Santana won the United States Nationals, and in 1966, he won **Wimbledon** and was ranked number one in the world. In 1963, he and **Roy Emerson** were the French National **doubles** champions.

Santana competed in the demonstration tennis events at the 1968 **Olympic Games** in Mexico and won the singles and was runner-up in the doubles. He was a member of the Spanish **Davis Cup** team each year from 1958 to 1970 and again in 1973 and holds the Spanish Davis Cup record for most years played, most **ties** played, most total victories, most singles victories, and most doubles victories. In 14 years of Cup competition, his record was 69–17 in singles and 23–11 in doubles in 46 ties. In 1965 and 1967, he helped lead Spain to the challenge round, where the team was defeated by **Australia** each time. He also captained the Spanish Davis Cup team. When he concluded his playing career in 1978, he had 72 singles titles to his credit. He was inducted into the **International Tennis Hall of Fame** in 1985. In 1997, he opened the Manolo Santana Racquets Club in Marbella, Spain.

SANTORO, FABRICE VEDEA. B. 9 December 1972, Tahiti, French Polynesia. Fabrice Santoro is the best tennis player in history to be born in Tahiti. He was raised in southern **France** and began playing tennis when he could barely hold a **racket**. Consequently, he used both hands for **forehand** and **backhand** strokes. The 5-foot 10-inch, 160-pound right-hander is a fan favorite, best known for his variety of shots and ability to retrieve. He reached his highest **singles** ranking of 17 in the world in 2001 and, in 1999, was sixth in the world in **doubles**. In his long professional career, from 1989 to January 2010, he had a record of 470 wins and 444 losses in **Association of Tennis**

Professionals competition. He holds the record for most **Grand Slam** singles events entered in a career with 70, but he never advanced past the third round at the **United States Open** or **Wimbledon**, only reached the fourth round at the **French Open** twice, and was a quarterfinalist at the **Australian Open** once, in 2006. He played his last Grand Slam singles in 2010 and became the only male to compete in Grand Slam singles competition in each of four decades.

He was more successful in Grand Slam doubles and reached the finals of the Australian Open in 2002, 2003, and 2004 with partner Michaël Llodra, winning the latter two years. They were also losing finalists in 2004 at the French Open. Santoro and Nenad Zimonjić were finalists at Wimbledon in 2006. In 2005, Santoro and Daniela Hantuchová won the **mixed doubles** at the French Open. At the French Open in 2004, he won the longest match (by time) in tennis history (to that date) by defeating Arnaud Clément in 6 hours and 33 minutes, 6–4, 5–3, 6–7 (5), 3–6, 16–14. That record was eclipsed in 2010 by the 11-hour **John Isner**–Nicolas Mahud marathon match. Santoro competed in three **Olympic Games**—1992, 2000, and 2004 and was a quarterfinalist in the 1992 singles and 2004 doubles events. He was a member of the French **Davis Cup** team from 1991 to 2004. In 17 **ties**, his record was 6–6 in singles and 9–5 in doubles. He was a member of the Cup championship team in 2001 and played on the losing side in the Cup finals in 1999 and 2002. He won 6 singles and 24 doubles titles in his career. *See also* LONGEST MATCH IN TENNIS HISTORY.

SAVCHENKO NEILAND, LARISA. B. 21 July 1966, Lvov, **Russia**, Union of Soviet Socialist Republics. Larisa Savchenko was best known as a **doubles** specialist, although she did reach a world **ranking** of 13 in **singles** in 1988. In 1989, she married Alex Neiland and competed afterward as Larisa Savchenko Neiland. In doubles, she first reached the world number-one **ranking** in 1992. She was a doubles finalist at all four **Grand Slam** events. At the **Australian Open**, she won the **mixed doubles** in 1994 and 1996 and was the losing finalist in 1997. At **Wimbledon**, she won the mixed doubles in 1992 and lost in the finals in 1996 and 1997. At **Roland Garros**, she won the 1995 mixed doubles and lost in 1994 and 1999. In women's doubles, she reached Grand Slam finals six times at Wimbledon, four times at Roland Garros, and twice at the **United States Open** but was able to win only 2 of her 12 finals—at Roland Garros in 1989 and Wimbledon in 1991, with **Natasha Zvereva** as partner.

The five-foot six-inch, right-handed Savchenko competed in both singles and doubles in the 1988 and 1992 **Olympic Games**; she reached the quarterfinals of both events in 1988 but lost in the first round of both events in

1992. She played for the Soviet Union **Federation Cup** team every year from 1983 to 1991 and for Latvia from 1992 to 1997, 1999, 2000, and 2003. Her record in 57 **ties** over 18 years is 29–15 in singles and 38–7 in doubles. In 1988 and 1990, she played in the final round on the runner-up team. In her career, from 1983 to 1999, she won 2 singles titles and 65 doubles titles. In retirement, she has been the **coach** of **Svetlana Kuznetsova** and of the Russian Fed Cup team.

SCHIAVONE, FRANCESCA. B. 23 June 1980, Milan, Italy. Francesca Schiavone became a **professional tennis** player in 1996 at the age of 16. Although she was a competent player for her first 12 years, her best tennis has been played after she reached the age of 29—an age at which many female tennis players have been retired. In 2010, she won the **French Open singles** championship, three weeks prior to her 30th birthday. In 2011, she was ranked number four in the world, and again reached the finals at **Roland Garros** where she was defeated by Li Na. She played **Fed Cup** tennis from 2002 to 2011 with a record of 21–16 in singles and 4–0 in **doubles** in 20 **ties** through May 2011 and helped Italy win the Cup in 2006, 2009, and 2010. She played both singles and doubles in the 2004 and 2008 Olympic Games and was a singles quarter-finalist in 2004 and doubles quarter-finalist in 2008. In singles, she has reached the quarter-finals of the U.S. Open in 2003 and 2010, Wimbledon in 2009 and the **Australian Open** in 2011. In doubles, she and partner Casey Dellacqua were losing French Open women's doubles finalists in 2008 and Australian Open semi-finalists in 2009. In 2006, Francesca and Kveta Peschke were quarter-finalists at Wimbledon and semi-finalists at the U.S. Open. Through May 2011, the 5'5" Schiavone has won four singles and eight doubles titles and was a singles runner-up 11 times.

SCORING. The scoring system used in **lawn tennis** is quaint and has its origins with the game's predecessor, **court tennis**. When a player has successfully hit the **ball** in the opponent's **court** and the opponent has not satisfactorily returned it, the player wins a **point**. The first point won gives a player a score of 15. The second point won results in a score of 30. The third point won, however, results in a score of 40. The fourth point won results in a **game** won. To win a game, a player must have a two-point **advantage**. If the score is tied at 40, it is referred to as "**deuce**." At deuce, after a player wins the next point, the score is referred to as "**advantage** in" if the **server** is ahead or "advantage out" if the server is behind. A score of zero is referred to as "**love**." The first player to win six games (with a margin of two) wins a "**set**." Since the early 1970s, if the score is tied at six games for each side, a "**tiebreaker**" is played to decide the set. In the tiebreaker, the first player to win seven points (with a margin of two) wins the set. Most **matches** are played best of three sets—the first player to win two sets wins the match. In major men's **tournaments**, matches are generally played best of five sets. There have been attempts at changing the scoring system, such as the **Van Alen** Simplified Scoring System, in which sets are played to 31 points and each point is counted sequentially, and as in **World Team Tennis**, in which points are also counted sequentially and the first side to reach four points wins a game, but nearly all tennis matches still use the traditional scoring method.

SEARS, RICHARD DUDLEY "DICK." B. 26 October 1861, Boston, Massachusetts. D. 8 April 1943, Boston, Massachusetts. Dick Sears won the first **United States National Singles** Championships in 1881, at the age of 19, while a student at Harvard University. As defending champion, he was not required to play in the preliminary rounds the following year, and he defended his title successfully in the **challenge round**. The five-foot nine-inch right-hander repeated this performance each year through 1887, losing only three of the 21 sets in that time. He also was the men's **doubles** champion each year from 1882 to 1887, with partner Joseph Clark in 1885 and **James Dwight** the other five years. He retired from the sport in 1888 and did not defend his titles. He was the president of the **United States National Lawn Tennis Association** from 1887 to 1888. He switched to **court tennis** and won the United States Court Tennis Championship in 1892. His tennis career was over by 1900 when the first **Davis Cup** match was played, and he never competed in that event. He was among the first seven players inducted into the **International Tennis Hall of Fame** in 1955. His younger cousin Eleonora Sears was also a champion tennis player and is also in the International Tennis Hall of Fame.

SEDGMAN, FRANK ALLAN. B. 29 October 1927, Mont Albert, Victoria, **Australia**. Frank Sedgman began playing top-level **amateur** tennis in 1946. From 1947 to 1952, he reached the finals of 33 **Grand Slam** events, winning 22 of them. The only males to win more Grand Slam championships than Sedgman were **John Newcombe** (28) and **Todd Woodbridge** (25), and they both required many more years to do so. **Bill Tilden** also won 22 over a much longer time span. Sedgman won eight consecutive Slam men's **doubles**—the 1950 **United States Nationals** (with **John Bromwich**), all four 1951 Slam events, and the first three in 1952 (with Ken McGregor), losing the United States Nationals to **Merv Rose** and **Vic Seixas**, 8–6, in the fifth **set**. In 1952, Sedgman won 8 of the 12 Grand slam events and was runner-up in three others. At the **Australian Championships**, he was men's **singles** champion in 1949 and 1950 and runner-up in 1952. He was men's **doubles** runner-up there in 1947 and 1948 and champion in 1951 and 1952. In 1949 and 1950, he was Australian **mixed doubles** champion. At **Wimbledon**, he was singles runner-up in 1950 and champion in 1952. He was men's doubles champion there in 1948, 1951, and 1952, mixed doubles runner-up in 1948, and mixed doubles champion in 1951 and 1952. At **Roland Garros**, he lost in the finals of the men's singles in 1952 and lost in the men's doubles final in 1948 but won the men's doubles in 1951 and 1952. In mixed doubles there, he lost in 1948 but won in 1951 and 1952. He won the United States singles title in 1951 and 1952, reached the men's doubles each year from 1949 to 1952, winning in 1950 and 1951, and was mixed doubles finalist from 1950 to 1952, winning in 1951 and 1952. **Doris Hart** was Sedgman's partner for all his Grand Slam triumphs.

He played on the Australian **Davis Cup** team from 1949 to 1952. In those four years, he played in 10 **ties** and had a record of 16–3 in singles and 9–0 in doubles. He helped Australia reach the **challenge round** in 1949, where the team lost to the **United States**. The next three years, Sedgman played on the Cup winning side in the challenge round. He became a **professional** in 1953. He played against **Jack Kramer** on the pro tour that year and was defeated by Kramer, 54–41. He continued as a touring pro through the early 1960s and won the U.S. Pro doubles with **Andrés Gimeno** as partner in 1961. In retirement from the pro tour, he owned a stable of thoroughbred race horses and continued playing in **seniors** tournaments. He was inducted into the **International Tennis Hall of Fame** in 1979.

SEEDING. Seeding is a method of placing players in the **draw** so that they will not meet until the later rounds of a **tournament**. In major tournaments, the top 16 or 32 players are **ranked** and then placed in the draw so that the first and second highest ranked will not meet before the finals, the third and fourth highest ranked will not meet a higher-ranked player before the semifinals, and so forth. An unseeded player is one who is not seeded and will generally be required to play better opponents during a tournament's early rounds.

SEGURA CANO, FRANCISCO OLEGARIO "PANCHO," "SEGOO." B. 20 June 1921, Guayaquil, **Ecuador**. Francisco "Pancho" Segura was a sickly child. Born prematurely, he suffered from hernias, malaria, and rickets, which left him with bowed legs. Only five feet six inches tall, he, nonetheless, was extremely fast and developed a powerful two-handed **forehand**, one of the first successful players with a two-handed forehand. He received a tennis scholarship to the University of Miami in Florida in the **United States**. While there, he won the **National Collegiate Athletic Association (NCAA)**

National Tennis Championship three consecutive years, from 1943 to 1945, the second man ever to win three consecutive national collegiate tennis championships. In 1946, he reached the finals of the **French National Doubles** Championships and, in 1944, the **United States National** doubles finals. In the United States Nationals, he was a **mixed doubles** finalist in 1943 and 1947. He was a **singles** semifinalist at the U.S. Nationals in 1942, 1943, 1944, and 1945 and a quarterfinalist in 1946 and 1947. Segura's best years as an **amateur** occurred during World War II, when **Davis Cup** competition was suspended. As a result, he never competed in a Davis Cup match.

In 1947, he became a **professional** tennis player and ineligible for Davis Cup play. As a professional, most of his matches were in a series of one-night stands, although the pro tour culminated in a **U.S. Pro Championship** tournament, which he won in 1950, 1951, and 1952 and was runner-up in 1955, 1956, 1957, and 1962. Although past his prime at the age of 47, he competed in the first **open Wimbledon** tournament in 1968 with partner **Alex Olmedo** and in the second round won the longest doubles **set**, 32–30, in one of the longest matches in Wimbledon history. After retiring from competitive play, he was based in Southern California and became one of the most respected tennis **coaches**. He was **Jimmy Connors's** coach and mentor. Segura was inducted into the **International Tennis Hall of Fame** in 1984.

SEIXAS, ELIAS VICTOR "VIC" JR. B. 30 August 1923, Overbrook, Pennsylvania. Vic Seixas had a long career in **amateur** tennis. He first played in the **United States National tournament** in 1940 and competed in that tournament nearly every year through 1967, missing a few during the war years when he served in the U.S. Army Air Force as a pilot. He graduated from the University of North Carolina in 1949. His best years were the 1950s, when he was twice a losing finalist at **Forest Hills** (losing in 1951 to Frank Sedgman and 1953 to **Tony Trabert**) and was the U.S. champion in 1954, when he defeated Rex Hartwig. In 1953, he was the **Wimbledon singles** champion, **French National** singles finalist, and **Australian** semifinalist. The 6-foot 1-inch, 180-pound right-hander concluded the year **ranked** number three in the world. An excellent **doubles** player, he won the 1955 Australian Championships with Tony Trabert, was a losing finalist in Wimbledon men's doubles in 1952 and 1954, and won the Wimbledon **mixed doubles** four consecutive years, from 1953 to 1956, with **Doris Hart** the first three years and **Shirley Fry** the fourth. At **Roland Garros**, Seixas and Trabert were men's doubles champions in 1954 and 1955, and Seixas and Hart won the mixed doubles in 1953. Teaming with **Merv Rose**, Seixas won the United States men's doubles in 1952, and he won again with Trabert in 1954. Seixas also was a losing men's doubles finalist in 1956 with partner Ham Richardson. In 1953, 1954, and 1955, Seixas and Hart were U.S. mixed doubles champions. At the age of 42, he played one of the longest singles matches in history in a tournament in Pennsylvania in 1966, losing the first set to Bill Bowrey, 32–34, and then winning the match, 6–4, 10–8. Seixas was also an excellent **squash** player and, from 1964 to 1966, won the American **senior** squash championship.

Seixas was a member of the **United States Davis Cup** team each year from 1951 to 1957, playing and losing to Australia in the **challenge round** each of those years except 1954, when the United States won the Cup. Seixas's Davis Cup record was 24–12 in singles and 14–5 in doubles in 23 **ties** during those seven years. He was inducted into the **International Tennis Hall of Fame** in 1971. Seixas worked as a stockbroker from the late 1950s until the early 1970s, was a director of tennis at a resort in West Virginia and later in New Orleans, and moved to California in 1989.

SELES, MONICA. B. 2 December 1973, Novi Sad, **Serbia, Yugoslavia**. Monica Seles began playing tennis at the age of five, **coached** by her father Károly Szeles, a Hungarian cartoonist. In 1985, aged 11, she won the **Orange Bowl tournament**. The following year, her family moved to the **United States**, and she enrolled in the **Nick Bollettieri** Tennis Academy. By 1989, she was playing **professional** tennis. In her first **Grand Slam** tournament, the 1989 **French Open**, she reached the semifinals. In 1990, at age 16, she won it, becoming the youngest ever winner of that tournament. In 1991, she won three of the four Grand Slam **singles** championships, bypassing **Wimbledon** due to injuries, and reached the world number-one **ranking**. In 1992, she again won the **Australian Open**, French Open, and **United States Open** and was a finalist at Wimbledon, losing to **Steffi Graf**. Monica began 1993 by winning the Australian Open for the third consecutive year. In eight consecutive Grand Slam events in which she competed, she reached the finals in all, winning seven of them.

In a tournament in Hamburg, **Germany**, on 30 April in a quarterfinal match with **Magdalena Maleeva**, a crazed fan ran out onto the **court** and stabbed Monica in the back with a nine-inch-long knife. The fan claimed that he stabbed her so that Steffi Graf would be able to regain her number-one ranking. The fan, Günter Parche, was not jailed as he was found to be "psychologically abnormal" and was allowed to go free sentenced to two years probation and psychological treatment. In 1994, Monica became a **United States** citizen. She returned to tennis in August 1995 and won the **Canadian Open** in her first comeback tournament. She won her final Grand Slam title in January 1996 when she won the Australian Open for the fourth time. She continued playing on the women's tour through 2002 and reached the 1996 U.S. Open finals and 1998 French Open finals. A foot injury sidelined her in 2003, and she never again competed in a **Women's Tennis Association** match, although she played a few **exhibition** tournaments in subsequent years. She officially announced her retirement on 14 February 2008.

In her career, the 5-foot 10-inch, 155-pound **left-hander** won 53 singles and 6 **doubles** titles. She competed in the singles event in the 1996 **Olympic Games**, reaching the quarterfinal round as a representative of the United States. In 2000, she was the bronze medalist. She played on the United States **Fed Cup** team in 1996, 1998 to 2000, and 2002. In 10 **ties**, her record was 15–2 in singles and 2–0 in doubles, and she was on the Cup-winning team in 1996 and 2000. She won the **Hopman Cup** in 1991 with partner Goran Prpić. She was inducted into the **International Tennis Hall of Fame** in 2009.

SENIOR TENNIS. The sport of **lawn tennis** provides for competition at all ages. The **United States Tennis Association** has **tournaments** for people aged 35 and over in 5-year increments (40 and over, 45 and over, etc.). A supersenior category has tournaments for players from 60 to 80, again in 5-year increments. The major events also have invitational tournaments for players no longer on the tour aged 35 and over. *See also* CHAMPIONS SERIES.

SERBIA. The Serbian Tennis Federation (Teniski Savez Srbije) administers the sport in Serbia. Prior to 2004, Serbians competed for **Yugoslavia** and, from 2004 to 2006, for Serbia and Montenegro. From 1927 through May 2011, Serbia has competed in 77 **Davis Cup tournaments** with a record of 100–71 in 171 **ties**. The team has competed 13 times in the World Group since its formation in 1981. In 2010, Serbia defeated France in the Cup final to be Cup champions for the first time. As Yugoslavia, the team reached the semifinals in 1988, 1989, and 1991. Top Davis Cup players have been **Novak Djoković**, Boro Jovanović, Josip Palada, **Niki Pilić**, Franjo Punčec, Dušan Vemić, and Nenad Zimonjić. The first year that Serbia competed as a separate nation was 2008. Novak Djoković won the silver medal in men's **singles**, and **Jelena Janković** reached the quarterfinals in women's singles. In **Federation Cup** competition, from 2004 to 2006, as Serbia and Montenegro, the team competed 3 years, none in World Group, played 11 ties with a record of 7–4. In the four and a half years from 2007 to May 2011, as Serbia, twice in World Group, in 15 ties, with a record of 11–4. In 2010, Serbia reached the World Group finals. Among the best Serbian male tennis players not mentioned above are Ilija Bozoljac, Janko Tipsarević, and Viktor Troicki. The best female tennis players include Ana Ivanović, Jelena Janković, and Bojana Jovanovski. *See also* CROATIA.

SERVE. The start of each **point** begins with one player serving. The player must stand behind the **baseline** and hit the **ball** diagonally over the **net** so that it lands in the opponent's service **court**. In modern play, the serve is always made with an **overhead** stroke; an underhand or sidearm serve is permissible but no longer used. *See also* ACE.

SERVE AND VOLLEY. Serve and **volley** is a method of play in which the server immediately runs to the **net** after serving in order to catch the return of serve with a volley stroke and possibly hit a **winner** to end the **point**. Serve and volley was a common playing style during the 1950s and 1960s, but in recent years, due to changing equipment capabilities, most players seldom use this method.

SERVICE. *See* SERVE.

SET. In **lawn tennis**, a set is a unit of scoring. A player winning six **games** wins a set. If the score reaches five games **all**, a player must have a two-game advantage to win the set. In recent years, when the score reaches six games all, a **tiebreaker** game is played to decide the set. **Matches** generally are best two of three sets, and in major **tournaments**, men usually play best three of five set matches. *See also* SCORING.

SET POINT. Set point is reached when the winner of the **point** about to be played would win the set.

SHARAPOVA, MARIA YURYEVNA. B. 19 April 1987, Nyagan, **Russia,** Union of Soviet Socialist Republics. Although born in Western Siberia, Maria Sharapova spent her early years in Sochi, Russia. She began playing tennis at the age of four and, when she was just seven years old, was spotted by **Martina Navratilova** at a tennis clinic in Moscow. Navratilova recommended sending her to the **Nick Bollettieri** Tennis Academy in the **United States**. Maria traveled there with her father, Yuri, in 1994 and, at the age of nine, was sponsored by the International Management Group (IMG) and enrolled in the school. By 2001, she was a **professional** tennis player. In 2002, she was a finalist at both the **Australian Open junior girls' singles** and **Wimbledon** girls' singles. In 2003, she entered the **main draw** at all four **Grand Slam** tournaments and reached the fourth round at Wimbledon. The following year, at the age of 17, she won the Wimbledon ladies' singles championship by defeating defending champion **Serena Williams** in the final **match**. In 2005, Maria reached the quarterfinals of the **French Open** and semifinals of the other three Grand Slam singles events. She won the **United States Open** women's singles in 2006. In 2007, she lost to Serena Williams in the finals of the Australian Open but won that event in 2008. A shoulder injury and subsequent surgery hampered her play in 2008 and 2009.

At six feet two inches, she is one of the tallest players on the women's tour. She has a powerful game and mental toughness, never giving up until the match is over. She is also known for her loud grunts or shrieks each time she makes contact with the **ball**. She has done a considerable amount of modeling and has been featured in quite a few commercial advertisements, both on television and in print. Although she has lived in the United States for most of her life (and speaks accentless English), she still considers herself to be a Russian and represents that country in international competition. Due to a variety of reasons, she has only played two **ties** for Russia in **Fed Cup** competition won two singles matches in 2008, losing only six **games** in four **sets** but was defeated in her only singles match in 2011. Through May 2011, she has won 27 singles and 3 doubles titles and first reached the world number-one **ranking** in 2005. In October 2010, she became engaged to professional basketball player, Sasha Vujačić.

SHIELDS, FRANCIS XAVIER "FRANK." B. 18 November 1909, New York, New York. D. 19 August 1975, New York, New York. Frank Shields was one of the best tennis players in the **United States** in the early 1930s, although he never won one of the major **Grand Slam** events. He was the **singles** finalist and **mixed doubles** finalist at the 1930 **United States National Championships**, and was the men's **doubles** losing finalist there in 1933. In 1931, he reached the men's singles finals at **Wimbledon** but had to default due to an injured ankle suffered in his semifinal victory over **Jean Borotra**. In 1933, the six-foot three-inch Shields was the number-one–**ranked** United States male player. He played on the United States **Davis Cup** team in 1931, 1932, and 1934. In 13 **ties** in those three years, his record was 16–6 in singles and 3–0 in doubles. In 1951, he was the nonplaying Davis Cup captain. In 1934, he played on the losing side in the **challenge round**.

A handsome, flamboyant man, he moved to Los Angeles during the 1930s and appeared in seven films. A heavy drinker, he was married and divorced three times and is the grandfather of actress Brooke Shields. He was inducted into the **International Tennis Hall of Fame** in 1964. He died in a taxicab in New York after his third heart attack.

SHRIVER, PAMELA HOWARD "PAM." B. 4 July 1962, Baltimore, Maryland. Pam Shriver is a graduate of the McDonogh School in Maryland. In her first appearance at the **United States Open** in 1978, the 16-year-old defeated **Martina Navratilova** in the semifinals and reached the women's finals but was defeated by **Chris Evert**. Although she would be a finalist in 29 **Grand Slam** events throughout her career, this was the only time she reached a Grand Slam **singles** final. She would play Navratilova 40 times in her career and only won 3 of those 40 **matches**. Shriver did reach the semifinals at the

Australian Open three times, three times at **Wimbledon**, and twice at the U.S. Open. She won 21 Grand Slam women's **doubles** championships and one **mixed doubles** championship.

The 6-foot tall, 160-pound right-hander won all but one of her women's doubles titles with Navratilova as her partner. They had the unusual distinction of winning one Grand Slam championship in 1981, two in 1982, three in 1983, and four in 1984. From 1983 to 1985, they won a record 109 consecutive matches and were finalists in 11 consecutive Grand Slam events. They won the Australian Open each year from 1982 to 1989 and were runners-up in 1981; the **French Open** in 1984, 1985, 1987, and 1988; Wimbledon in 1981 to 1984 and 1986 and were runners-up in 1985; and the United States Open in 1983, 1984, 1986, and 1987 and were runners-up in 1985. Shriver and **Natalia Zvereva** also won the U.S. Open in 1991. Shriver and **Betty Stove** in 1981 and Shriver and **Mary Joe Fernández** in 1989 were runners-up at the U.S. Open. In 1987, Shriver and Emilio Sánchez won the French Open mixed doubles title.

Shriver entered the 1988 **Olympic Games** singles and doubles events, reached the quarterfinals of the singles, and won the doubles with partner **Zina Garrison**. She played on the United States **Federation Cup** team in 1986, 1987, 1989, and 1992. She lost only 1 of 20 matches in 17 **ties** and was 5–0 in singles and 14–1 in doubles. She was on the Cup championship team in 1986 and 1989 and runner-up team in 1987. She played on the **United States Wightman Cup** team for five years from 1978 to 1987 and had a record of 6–1 in singles and 3–1 in doubles. In her career, from 1978 to 1997, she won 21 singles and 112 doubles titles and was first ranked number three in singles in 1984 and number one in doubles in 1985. She was inducted into the International Tennis Hall of Fame in 2002.

She married Los Angeles law professor Joe Shapiro, a lawyer formerly with the Walt Disney Company on 5 December 1998. He died of cancer in 1999. In 2002, she married actor George Lazenby. They have three children and were divorced in 2008. She has had a successful career as a tennis announcer for several networks.

SINGLES. The game of **lawn tennis** can be played by one player on each side, called singles, or two players a side, called **doubles**. *See also* MIXED DOUBLES.

SLICE. A slice is a tennis shot made by hitting under the **ball**, which causes the ball to spin and bounce low.

SLOVAKIA. Tennis in Slovakia is administered by the Slovak Tennis Federation located in Bratislava. It was founded in 1968 while Slovakia was still a part of the country of **Czechoslovakia**. Prior to 1993, Slovakia competed as Czechoslovakia. From 1994 through May 2011, the Slovak Republic has competed in all 18 **Davis Cup tournaments** with a record of 25–16 in 41 **ties**. The country has competed seven times in the World Group. In 2005, it was the tournament runner-up, losing to **Croatia** in the final. Top Davis Cup players have been Dominik Hrbatý, Jan Kroslak, Karol Kučera, and Branislav Stanković. As an independent country, Slovakia competed in **Olympic** tennis from 1996 to 2008. Its best performance was in 2000, when Dominik Hrbatý and Karol Kučera reached the quarterfinals of the men's **doubles**.

Among the best male tennis players have been Karol Beck, Pavol Červenák, and Michal Mertiňák, in addition to the players named above. The best female tennis players include Karina Habšudová, Daniela Hantuchová, Janette Husárová, Ľubomíra Kurhajcová, Henrietta Nagyová, and Martina Suchá. In **Federation Cup** competition, from 1994 to May 2011, Slovakia has competed 18 years, seven in World Group, played 46 ties with a record of 28–18. *See also* CZECH REPUBLIC.

SMASH. A smash is an **overhead** shot hit with a hard stroke to cause the **ball** to bounce high. It will normally result in a **winner** if correctly struck.

SMITH, ANNE. B. 1 July 1959, Dallas, Texas. Anne Smith is one of only 19 women who have won women's **doubles** championships at all four major events. As a **junior** player, she won the **French Open** Junior Championship in 1977. She attended Trinity University in San Antonio, Texas, majoring in psychology, and played **professional** tennis from 1978 to 1992. In that time, she reached her highest **ranking** of 12 in **singles** in 1982 and 1 in doubles in 1981. She won the French Open doubles in 1980 and 1982, was runner-up in 1983, and won the **mixed doubles** there in 1980 and 1984. She won **Wimbledon** doubles in 1980 and was runner-up in 1981, 1982, and 1984. She also won Wimbledon mixed doubles in 1982, with partner Kevin Curren, by playing and winning four **matches** on the final day of the **tournament**. She won the **United States Open** doubles in 1981 and mixed doubles in 1981 and 1982 and **Australian Open** doubles in 1981. Kathy Jordan was her partner for all major women's doubles titles except 1982 at Wimbledon, when **Martina Navratilova** was her partner. In mixed doubles, Billy Martin, Dick Stockton, and Kevin Curren were her partners.

A five-foot five-inch, right-handed player, she reached the singles quarterfinals in three of the four majors, the exception being the French Open, where her best was the fourth round. In 1984, she and Kathy Jordan played the doubles match in each of four **ties** for the **United States Federation Cup** team and had a record of 3–1. She was a member of the United States **Wight-**

man Cup team in 1980 and 1982 and won one singles match and split two doubles matches. She also played **World Team Tennis (WTT)** and was a member of three WTT championship teams.

After retiring from active play, she returned to Trinity University, earned her undergraduate degree in psychology and continued her education with a PhD in psychology from the University of Texas. She also competed in **senior** events and won the 35-and-over doubles championship at the United States Open in 1996 and at Wimbledon in 1996 and 1997. She **coached** the Harvard University women's tennis team in 2005 and 2006 and the World Team Tennis Boston Lobsters from 2005 to 2007. In 2005, at the age of 46, she returned to the **Women's Tennis Association (WTA)** tour and won her 39th WTA doubles title in June 2005. She is the author of two books on the mental aspects of tennis, is a licensed psychologist in three states, and was enshrined in the Texas Sports Hall of Fame in 1993 and Trinity University Athletics Hall of Fame in 1999.

SMITH, STANLEY ROGER "STAN." B. 14 December 1946, Pasadena, California. Stan Smith attended the University of Southern California (USC) and was the 1968 **National Collegiate Athletic Association (NCAA) singles** champion and 1967 and 1968 NCAA **doubles** champion with **Bob Lutz** as partner. They also helped lead USC to the NCAA team title in 1967 and 1968. Smith and Lutz continued their successful partnership after college and won five **Grand Slam** doubles titles (**Australian Open** in 1970 and **United States Open** in 1968, 1974, 1978, 1980) and were Grand Slam runners-up five other times (1974 **French Open**, 1979 U.S. Open, and 1974, 1980, 1981 **Wimbledon**). Smith was also runner-up at the 1971 French Open with Tom Gorman and the 1971 U.S. Open and 1972 Wimbledon with Erik Van Dillen. In singles play, Smith was the 1971 U.S. Open and 1972 Wimbledon champion and was runner-up at Wimbledon in 1971. Smith and **Rosie Casals** were also U.S. National **mixed doubles** runners-up in 1967.

Smith was a member of the **United States Davis Cup** team from 1968 to 1981, playing each year except 1974 and 1980. His record in 24 **ties** over 12 years was 15–4 in singles and 20–3 in doubles. He helped the United States win the Cup five consecutive years (from 1968 to 1973, by winning 10 of his 11 **rubbers** in the final round), reach the final in 1974 but lose to **Australia**, and win again in 1978 and 1979. He concluded his Davis Cup activity by playing and winning a doubles match in the 1981 quarterfinal round for the team that would win the Cup later that year. The 6-foot 4-inch, 180-pound right-hander retired from active play in 1985 with 36 singles and 54 doubles titles to his credit and reached a world ranking of number one in 1972.

After retiring, he became a **coach** for the **United States Tennis Association** and later opened the Smith Stearns Tennis Academy in Hilton Head,

South Carolina, with partner Billy Stearns. Smith is also the director of the Sea Pines Resort in Hilton Head. In 2000, Smith was the **coach** of the United States men's Olympic tennis team. He still competes in **senior** events and, in 2004, won the 55-and-over U.S. Open title. In 1972, the Adidas Shoe Company began producing a Stan Smith model tennis shoe that has become the best-selling tennis shoe of all time. Smith was inducted into the **International Tennis Hall of Fame** in 1987.

SMITH COURT, MARGARET. B. 16 July 1942, Albury, New South Wales, **Australia**. Margaret Smith has one of the most remarkable records of tennis players in the history of the sport. She played from 1960 to 1977 and reached the finals of 87 **Grand Slam tournaments**, winning 64 of them, the most of any player. **Martina Navratilova** is second with 85 tournaments and 59 wins. Smith Court's career **singles** won-loss record was 1,177–106, a .914 percentage, with more than 100 wins in each of four years—1965, 1968, 1970, and 1973. What makes these numbers more remarkable is that she retired after the **Wimbledon** tournament in 1966 and did not resume until 1968. She also took time out from tennis to give birth to children in 1972, 1974, and 1976. She retired in 1977 when she was pregnant with her fourth child. She won 24 Grand Slam singles titles—11 in Australia, 3 at Wimbledon, and 5 each at **Roland Garros** and **Forest Hills** and was a losing singles finalist once at each of the four venues and twice at Wimbledon. She was a Grand Slam women's **doubles** finalist 33 times, winning 19. She was a Grand Slam **mixed doubles** finalist 25 times, winning 21. She is one of only five players to win all four Grand Slam singles events in the same year, which she did in 1970. In 1963, she and **Ken Fletcher** also won all four Grand Slam mixed doubles events, and in 1965, she did it again with three different partners—**John Newcombe** in Australia, Fletcher at Roland Garros and Wimbledon, and **Fred Stolle** at the United States championships. She played on the **Federation Cup** team for Australia from 1963 to 1965 and 1968 to 1970. In 20 **ties** over the six years, she was undefeated in singles play with a perfect 20–0 record. In doubles, her record was 15–5. In those 20 ties, the Australian team won 55 **rubbers**, while losing only 5. She was on the Cup championship team in 1964, 1965, 1968, and 1970 and the runner-up team in 1963 and 1969.

In 1973, **Bobby Riggs**, then 55 years old, challenged the 30-year-old Smith Court (who had won 89 of her last 92 matches on the women's tour) to a "battle of the sexes" match played on 13 May (Mother's Day) in Romana, California. Ironically, Riggs, at five feet eight inches tall, was two inches shorter than Smith Court and played a **baseline** game more typical of women's tennis. Smith Court, known for her powerful **serve**, lost a battle of nerves and played poorly. The nationally-televised **match** was won easily by

Riggs, 6–2, 6–1, in 57 minutes. Riggs then challenged **Billie Jean King** with drastically different results.

Margaret Smith married Barrymore Court in 1967 and, from then on, used both surnames in competition. She was inducted into the **International Tennis Hall of Fame** in 1979. In retirement, she has become active in the Pentecostal church and, in 1991, became a minister and later founded the Margaret Court Ministries.

SÖDERLING, ROBIN BO CARL. B. 14 August 1984, Tibro, **Sweden.** Robin Söderling began playing **professional** tennis in 2001. As a **junior**, he won the prestigious **Orange Bowl** tournament that year as well. His career was relatively unspectacular until 2008, when he helped lead Sweden to the **World Team Cup** championship. The highlight of his career occurred in 2009, when he defeated **Rafael Nadal** in the fourth round of the **French Open** and ended Nadal's 31-**match** winning streak at **Roland Garros**. Söderling then defeated **Nikolay Davydenko** in the quarterfinals and Fernando González in the semifinals but lost to **Roger Federer** in the finals. In 2010, he again did exceptionally well at the French Open. He defeated Roger Federer in the quarterfinals and ended Federer's streak of 23 consecutive **Grand Slam** semifinals. Söderling defeated Tomáš Berdych in five sets in the semifinals but, once again, lost in the finals—this time to Nadal. His best performance at **Wimbledon** was the quarterfinals in 2010 and at the **United States Open** he reached the quarterfinals in 2009 and 2010. Soderling reached a career-high ranking of four in the world in November 2010. He has never gone past the second round at the **Australian Open**. He played both **singles** and **doubles** in the 2004 and 2008 **Olympic Games** but lost in the first round of all four events. He was a member of the Swedish **Davis Cup** team in 2004 and 2006 to May 2011. His record in 10 **ties** over seven years was 13–3 in singles and 1–1 in doubles. Through May 2011, the 6-foot 4-inch, 190-pound, right-handed Söderling has won nine singles and one doubles title.

SOLOMON, HAROLD CHARLES. B. 17 September 1952, Washington DC. Harold Solomon attended Rice University and was an All-American there. In 1972, he became a **professional** tennis player. He played **singles** for the **United States Davis Cup** team in 1972, 1973, 1974, and 1978 and helped the team win the Cup in 1972 and 1973, although he did not play in the final round. His Davis Cup record for four years and seven **ties** was 9–4. In 1976, he reached his only **Grand Slam** final but lost to **Adriano Panatta** at the **French Open**. In 1977, he was a semifinalist at the United States Open. He only played four times at **Wimbledon** and did not win a **match** there. The 5-foot 6-inch, 130-pound right-hander was known for his ability to keep the ball in play, often using **lobs** to do so. When he played **Eddie Dibbs**, another player who excelled in returning the **ball**, **rallies** occasionally exceeded 50 strokes. His best year was 1980, when he reached a ranking of fifth in the world and had a 64–23 match record. From 1980 to 1983, he was the president of the **Association of Tennis Professionals (ATP)**. He retired from the ATP tour in 1986 with a career record of 22 singles titles and 16 runner-up finishes. He has since **coached** several top tennis players including **Mary Joe Fernández, Jennifer Capriati, Jim Courier, Monica Seles**, and **Anna Kournikova**. He founded and runs the Harold Solomon Tennis Institute in Fort Lauderdale, Florida.

SOUTH AFRICA. South Africa has a long tradition as a sports-loving nation. Tennis there is administered by the South Africa Tennis Association. From 1913 through May 2011, South Africa has competed in 53 **Davis Cup** tournaments with a record of 79–50 in 129 **ties**. The country has competed four times in the World Group since its formation in 1981. In 1974, the team won the Cup when **India** refused to play South Africa in the finals and forfeited. South Africa's top Davis Cup players have been **Wayne Ferreira, Cliff Drysdale, Frew McMillan,** and **Bob Hewitt**.

South Africa first competed in **Olympic** tennis in 1908. John P. Richardson was fourth in men's **singles** that year, and the team of Victor Gauntlett and Harry Kitson also finished fourth in **doubles**. In 1912, Kitson finished second in singles to countryman Charles Winslow, and the pair also won the doubles. In 1920, Winslow was third in singles and Louis Raymond, another South African, won the gold medal. Both South African men's doubles teams reached the quarterfinals that year as well. In 1924, the team of Ivie Richardson and Jack Condon were fourth in men's doubles. In 1992, South Africa won the silver medal in men's doubles with Wayne Ferreira and Piet Norval, and in 2000, John-Laffnie de Jager and David Adams finished fourth in doubles.

In addition to the players named above, the best South African male tennis players include Pieter Aldrich, Kevin Anderson, Jeff Coetzee, Kevin Curren, Rik de Voest, Eustace Fannin, Norman Farquharson, Ellis Ferreira, Gordon Forbes, Robbie Koenig, **Johan Kriek**, Robert Maud, Wesley Moodie, Brian Norton, Abe Segal, Patrick Spence, Eric Sturgess, Lionel Tapscott, Christo van Rensburg, Ian Vermaak, and Danie Visser. The best female tennis players include Beryl Bartlett, Delina Ann "Linky" Boshoff, Irene Bowder, Amanda Coetzer, Mariaan de Swardt, Rosalyn Fairbank, Tanya Harford, Liezel Horn Huber, Ilana Kloss, Alida Neave, Sheila Piercey Summers, Hazel Redick, Sandra Reynolds, Chanelle Scheepers, Renee Schuurman, Greer Stevens, Annette Van Zyl, Patricia Walkden, and Julia Wipplinger. In **Federation Cup** competition from 1963 to May 2011, South Africa has competed 35 years, 20 years in World Group, and played 116 ties with a record of 71–45. South Africa was the champion in 1972 and runner-up in 1973.

SPAIN. In Spain, the Real Federación Española de Tenis (Royal Spanish Tennis Federation) administers the sport. Spain first had contestants in **Olympic** tennis in 1920. Although its best results were only quarterfinals in 1920 and 1924, since that time Spain has had medalists in tennis in nearly every Olympic Games. In the demonstration events in 1968, **Manuel Santana** defeated his countryman **Manuel Orantes** in men's **singles** and Santana and Juan Gisbert were second in men's **doubles**. In demonstration tennis in 1984, Spain entered but did not medal. In 1988, Emilio Sánchez and Sergio Casal won the silver medal in men's doubles. In 1992, Jordi Arrese won the silver medal in men's singles, **Arantxa Sánchez Vicario** (Emilio's sister) won the bronze medal in women's singles, and Arantxa and Conchita Martínez won the silver medal in women's doubles. In 1996, Sergei Bruguera won the silver medal in men's singles, Arantxa Sánchez Vicario won the silver medal in women's singles, and she and Martínez were bronze medalists in women's doubles. In 2000, Álex Corretja and Albert Costa were bronze medalists in men's doubles. In 2004, Martínez and **Virginia Ruano Pascual** won the silver in women's doubles. In 2008, **Rafael Nadal** won the gold medal in men's singles, and Ruano Pascual and Anabel Medina Garrigues won the silver medal in women's doubles.

From 1921 through May 2011, Spain has competed in 76 **Davis Cup** tournaments with a record of 115–70 in 76 **ties**. The country has competed 27 times in the World Group since its formation in 1981, won the Cup in 2000, 2004, 2008, and 2009, and was runner-up in 1965, 1967, and 2003. Top Davis Cup players have been Manuel Santana, José-Luis Arilla, Sergio Casal, and Manuel Orantes. Among the best Spanish male tennis players not mentioned above have been Nicolás Almagro, José Maria Alonso, Manuel Alonso, Alberto Berasategui, Tomás Carbonell, Manuel de Gomar, David Ferrer, Juan Carlos Ferrero, **Andrés Gimeno**, **José Higueras**, Feliciano López, **Carlos Moyá**, Tommy Robredo, and Fernando Verdasco.

The best female tennis players include Lili Alvarez, Lourdes Dominguez Lino, Beatriz Garcia Vidagany, Gala León Garcia, Nuria Llagostera-Vives, María José Martínez Sánchez, Arantxa Parra Santonja, and Cristina Torrens Valero, in addition to those mentioned above. In **Federation Cup** competition, from 1972 to May 2011, Spain has competed 40 years, 38 years in World Group, and played 118 ties with a record of 73–45. Spain won the championship five times—in 1991, 1993, 1994, 1995, and 1998—and was runner-up six times. From 1991 to 1996, the Spanish team has reached the finals six consecutive years. Arantxa Sánchez Vicario holds the Fed Cup records for most total matches won (72), most singles matches won (50), and, with partner **Conchita Martínez**, best doubles partnership with 18 victories.

SPHAIRISTIKE. *Sphairistike* (pronounced sfair-RIST-ik-ee) is the name given by Major **Walter Clopton Wingfield** to his patented game that is now known as **lawn tennis**. It is a shortened form of the ancient Greek phrase *sphairistike techne* meaning the art of playing with a **ball**.

SQUASH. Squash (or squash racquets) is an indoor **racket** sport played by two or four players using rackets, a small hollow rubber **ball**, and a four-walled **court**. Its origins are in common with **lawn tennis** in that both originated from games played in 16th-century Europe. *See also* SEIXAS, ELIAS VICTOR "VIC," JR.

STATISTICS. For most of the history of **lawn tennis**, very few statistics were kept. Researchers wishing to know details of important matches are unable to find much besides the game scores and possibly a brief narrative of the **match**. Tennis reporting has notoriously been unappreciative of precise statistics. A case in point—in 1987, during a **Davis Cup** relegation playoff match, **Boris Becker** defeated **John McEnroe** in a marathon match. The *New York Times* reported the match duration as 6 hours and 38 minutes and "believed it to be the longest in duration involving an American team." The *Bud Collins Tennis Encyclopedia*, 1997 edition, lists the match as 6 hours and 20 minutes, "12 minutes shy of the Cup singles record set . . . in 1982." *Bud Collins Total Tennis*, published in 2003, has "six hours, 21 minutes for Boris' 1987 Cup relegation victory." In recent years, with the advent of computers and televised tennis, detailed statistics, such as total **points** won, first **serve** percentage, number of **aces**, number of **double faults**, **unforced errors**, number of **winners**, fastest serve speed, average first and second serve speed, receiving points won, **break point** conversions, and **net** approaches, are now being tracked. Unlike other sports, such as baseball, basketball, football, and cricket, that have long traditions of statistical tracking, tennis is still in its infancy as far as the compilation and comparison of historical match details.

STICH, MICHAEL DETLEF. B. 18 October 1968, Pinneberg, **Germany**. Michael Stich began his **professional** tennis career in 1988. In 1991, he won the **Wimbledon singles** championship by defeating countryman **Boris Becker** in straight **sets**. In Stich's semifinal match, he defeated the world number-one player, **Stefan Edberg**, without breaking Edberg's **serve**, 4–6, 7–6, 7–6, 7–6, on 3 July 1991—the day that the inventor of the tiebreak, **James Van Alen**, died. After the match, Edberg was quoted as saying, "If he (Van Alen) had not lived, Michael and I would still be out there playing."

In 1992, at Wimbledon, Stich with partner **John McEnroe**, won the men's **doubles** over Jim Grubb and Richey Reneberg in a five-hour final that was played over two days, 5–7, 7–6, 3–6, 7–6, 19–17. (The fifth set at Wimbledon is not played with a **tiebreaker**). He competed in the 1992 **Olympic Games** and won the men's doubles gold medal with partner Boris Becker but lost in the second round of the men's singles event. In 1993, Stich won the year-end **Association of Tennis Professionals** World Championships. That year, he also won the **Hopman Cup** with partner **Steffi Graf**. In 1994, Stich reached the finals of the **United States Open** but was defeated by **Andre Agassi**.

The 6-foot 4-inch, 175-pound, right-handed Stich was a member of the German **World Team Cup** championship team in 1994. In 1996, he reached the finals of the **French Open** but was defeated by **Yevgeny Kafelnikov** in straight sets, although two of them were tiebreak sets. Stich played **Davis Cup** tennis for Germany from 1990 to 1996, leading the team to the championship in 1993 as he won all three of his matches. His overall Cup record was 21–9 in singles and 14–2 in doubles in 17 **ties** during those seven years. He retired after the Wimbledon **tournament** in 1997. In his nine-year career, he won 18 singles and 10 doubles titles and reached a high world **ranking** of two in singles in 1993 and nine in doubles in 1991. He and Boris Becker are the only players to win Wimbledon, the Olympic Games, the Davis Cup, the Hopman Cup, and the World Team Cup. In retirement, he has done television work for the British Broadcasting Corporation.

STOLLE, FREDERICK SYDNEY "FRED." B. 8 October 1938, Hornsby, New South Wales, **Australia**. Fred Stolle reached 36 finals of **Grand Slam** events. **Roy Emerson** is the only male player who has done this more times than Stolle. (**Ken Rosewall** and **John Bromwich** also have 36.) Despite this, Stolle is not known quite as well as some of his contemporaries, such as **Arthur Ashe**, Rosewall, **Rod Laver**, **Tony Roche**, **John Newcombe**, and **Ilie Năstase**. Stolle, a 6-foot 3-inch, 205-pound right-hander, was ranked second in the world in 1964 and won the **French National singles** title in 1966 and the **United States Nationals** in 1966. He reached the men's singles final six other times in Grand Slam events but was defeated by Roy Emerson five of those times—Australia and **Wimbledon** in 1964 and 1965 and **Forest Hills** in 1964. He also lost to **Chuck McKinley** in the 1963 Wimbledon final.

Stolle was more successful in **doubles** and won men's doubles titles at all four major venues. He was **Australian** men's doubles finalist from 1962 to 1966 and 1969, winning in 1963 and 1964 with **Bob Hewitt** and 1966 with Emerson. He won Wimbledon men's doubles in 1963 and 1964 with Hewitt and was a losing finalist in 1961, 1968, and 1970. He won men's doubles at Roland Garros in 1965 and 1968 and at the United States Nationals in 1965, 1966, and 1969. Stolle was also a **mixed doubles** finalist three times in

Australia, winning in 1962, losing in 1963, and being named cochampion in 1969, when the final **match** was not played. He was three-time Wimbledon mixed doubles champion—1961, 1964, and 1969. At **Roland Garros**, he and **Lesley Turner** were runners-up in 1962, 1963, and 1964. At the United States Nationals, he won in 1962 and 1965 and was runner-up in 1975 with **Billie Jean King**. She and Stolle, as player-**coach**, played on the New York Apples of the **World Team Tennis** league during the 1970s. He played on the 1964, 1965, and 1966 **Davis Cup** champion Australian teams and had a record of 10–2 in singles and 3–1 in doubles in six **ties**. He was inducted into the **International Tennis Hall of Fame** in 1985. In retirement from tennis, he has worked as a television commentator for Australian television and as the director of tennis at Turnberry Isle Resort in Florida. His son, Sandon Stolle, is also a **professional** tennis player and has played Davis Cup tennis for Australia.

STOSUR, SAMANTHA JANE "SAM." B. 30 March 1984, Brisbane, Queensland, **Australia**. Samantha Stosur, although born in Brisbane, was raised in Adelaide. She attended Helensville State High School in Queensland, the Queensland Academy of Sport, and the Australian Institute of Sport. In 1999, she became a **professional** tennis player. The 5-foot 8-inch, 140-pound right-hander is best known as a **doubles** player and achieved a **ranking** of number one in the world in doubles in 2006. Known for her powerful **serve**, which has been measured at nearly 120 miles per hour, she has reached the doubles finals in all four **Grand Slam** events, winning the **Australian Open mixed doubles** in 2005 and being runner-up in women's doubles in 2006 with partner **Lisa Raymond**. She won **Wimbledon** mixed doubles in 2008 and was runner-up in women's doubles in both 2008 (with Raymond) and 2009 (with Rennae Stubbs). In 2006, she and Raymond won the **French Open** women's doubles, and at **Flushing Meadows**, they won the 2005 women's doubles and were runners-up in 2008. In both 2005 and 2006, Stosur and Raymond were named the **Women's Tennis Association** Doubles Team of the Year.

Sam competed for Australia in the 2004 and 2008 **Olympic Games** in both **singles** and doubles but lost both first round matches in 2004 and only reached the second round in 2008. She was a member of the Australian **Fed Cup** team each year from 2003 to 2011 except 2008. In 20 **ties** over seven years, her record was 19–9 in singles and 6–0 in doubles. In 2010, she improved her singles performance and defeated Justine Henin at the French Open, enabling her to reach the finals where she lost to **Francesca Schiavone**. As a result of her improved singles play, her world singles ranking reached a high of five in 2010. Through May 2011, she has won 34 doubles and 6 singles titles.

STOVE, BETTY. B. 24 June 1945, Rotterdam, **the Netherlands**. The 5-foot 11-inch right-handed Betty Stove towered over most opponents in her era and used her height to good advantage as an excellent **doubles** player. She was **ranked** number one in the world in doubles. In **singles**, she reached the **Wimbledon** ladies' finals in 1977 but, after winning the first **set**, lost to **Virginia Wade**, 4–6, 6–3, 6–1. Stove also reached the **United States Open** women's semifinals that year, losing to eventual champion **Chris Evert**. Stove was a finalist in 28 **Grand Slam** doubles events, winning just 10 of them. She and **Billie Jean King** won the Wimbledon ladies' doubles in 1972. Stove was a runner-up in women's doubles in 1973, 1975, 1976, 1977, and 1979 with partners **Françoise Durr** (twice), King, **Martina Navratilova**, and **Wendy Turnbull**. Stove won the **French Open** women's doubles in 1972 with King and again in 1979 with Turnbull and was runner-up in 1973 with Durr. Stove was also a five-time United States Open women's doubles finalist, winning in 1972 with Durr, 1977 with Navratilova, and 1979 with Turnbull, and she was runner-up in 1974 with Durr and 1980 with six-foot tall Pam Shriver. In **mixed doubles**, Stove and **Frew McMillan** won Wimbledon in 1978 and 1981, and she was a runner-up in 1975 with Allan Stone and 1977 and 1979 with McMillan. At the French Open, she was a mixed doubles runner-up in 1973 and 1981. Her best mixed doubles success came at the U.S. Open, where she and McMillan reached the finals five consecutive years, 1976 through 1980, winning in 1977 and 1978. She was also runner-up there in 1971 with Rob Maud as partner. She was a member of the **Federation Cup** team of the Netherlands from 1964 to 1983. In 33 **ties** over 11 years, her record was 22–5 in singles and 23–10 in doubles. After retiring from active play, with a career total of 75 doubles victories, she became the **coach** of **Hana Mandlíková** from 1980 to 1990, was the first female member of the **International Tennis Federation** Committee of Management, and wrote an instructional book with Mandlíková, *Total Tennis: A Guide to the Fundamentals of the Game*, published in 1990.

STRINGER. Tennis **rackets** are generally sold without **strings**. The job of the stringer is to affix the strings to the racket with a specific tension. Players often use multiple rackets with different string tension depending upon the **match** conditions.

STRINGS. Tennis strings are woven through the face of the **racket**. Various materials are used for tennis strings. Natural gut (generally made from cow or sheep intestines), synthetic gut (made from nylon), multifilament (made from nylon and other synthetic materials, such as polyurethane), Kevlar, Vectran, and Zyex are some of the more popular strings. Strings are measured in gauge—the higher the gauge, the thinner the string. *See also* STRINGER.

SUKOVÁ, HELENA. B. 23 February 1965, Prague, **Czechoslovakia**. Helena Suková's parents were both prominent in the tennis world. Her mother, Vera Puzejova Suková, was a **Wimbledon singles** finalist in 1962 and a 1957 **French National mixed doubles** champion. Her father, Cyril Suk II, was the president of the Czech Tennis Federation. Helena became a **professional** tennis player in 1981, just one year before her mother passed away. In her professional career, she reached the finals of 25 **Grand Slam** events, 21 in **doubles**, and she won 14 women's doubles and mixed doubles titles. She was the losing singles finalist at the **Australian Open** in 1984 and 1989 and at the **United States Open** in 1986 and 1993. The exceptionally tall (six feet two inches) right-hander excelled in doubles and won women's doubles titles at all four Grand Slam tournaments and mixed doubles titles at all but the Australian Open. Her doubles score sheet shows:

Australian Open

- 1984 and 1985 women's doubles runner-up
- 1990 and 1992 women's doubles champion
- 1994 and 1998 mixed doubles runner-up (in 1998 with her brother Cyril Suk III as partner)

French Open

- 1985 and 1988 women's doubles runner-up
- 1990 women's doubles champion
- 1991 mixed doubles champion (with her brother as partner)

Wimbledon

- 1987, 1989, 1990, and 1996 women's doubles champion
- 1994, 1996, and 1997 mixed doubles champion (1994 with **Todd Woodbridge**, the other two years with her brother)

U.S. Open

- 1985 and 1993 women's doubles champion
- 1990 women's doubles runner-up
- 1993 mixed doubles champion
- 1992 mixed doubles runner-up

She competed in the 1988, 1992, and 1996 **Olympic Games**. She did not advance past the second round in three attempts at the singles but won two silver medals in the doubles—in 1988 and 1996, both with partner **Jana No-**

votná. She played **Federation Cup** tennis for Czechoslovakia from 1981 to 1989 and 1992 and for the Czech Republic in 1993, 1995, and 1996. In 54 **ties** over 13 years, her record was 45–11 in singles and 12–5 in doubles. She was a member of the Federation Cup championship team in 1983, 1984, 1985, and 1988 and the runner-up team in 1986. She won the inaugural **Hopman Cup** in 1989 with partner Miloslav Mečíř. When she retired in 1998, she had won 10 singles and 69 doubles titles in her career and had reached a world **ranking** of four in singles in 1985 and one in doubles in 1990. In 1999, she became the president of the International **Lawn Tennis** Club of the Czech Republic.

SURFACES. The sport of **lawn tennis**, originally intended to be played on **grass**, is now played on several different surfaces. **Clay** (red or green), grass, **hard courts**, and carpet courts are the most popular. The **French Open** has been played on red clay since 1928. **Wimbledon** has always been played on grass. The **Australian Championships** were played on grass until 1987. Since 1988, a **hard-court** surface has been used. The **United States Open** has also been on a hard-court surface since 1978. It was played on grass until 1974 and from 1975 to 1977 on clay.

SWEDEN. Tennis in Sweden is administered by the Svenska Tenisförbundet (Swedish Tennis Federation) founded in 1906. For a country with less than 10 million population, Sweden has done exceptionally well in international tennis. In fact, a member of Swedish royalty, King Gustav V, was an avid tennis player and supporter of the game and has been enshrined in the **International Tennis Hall of Fame** for his efforts. Four other Swedish men have also been enshrined there: **Björn Borg**, Sven Davidson, **Stefan Edberg**, and **Mats Wilander**. From 1925 through May 2011, Sweden has competed in 78 **Davis Cup tournaments** with a record of 146–70 in 216 **ties**. Sweden has competed 30 times in the World Group since its formation in 1981. From 1975 to 1998, the team won the Cup seven times and was runner-up five times. Sweden was a finalist each year from 1983 to 1989. Top Davis Cup players have been **Jonas Björkman**, Sven Davidson, Jan-Erik Lundqvist, and Ulf Schmidt.

The year 1908 marked Sweden's first appearance in **Olympic** tennis. Gunnar Settarwall and Wollmar Boström both reached the quarterfinal round of the men's indoor **singles**, and the pair won the bronze medal in the men's indoor **doubles**. Märtha Adlerstråhle won the bronze in women's indoor singles, and Elsa Wallenberg was fourth in that event. In 1912, the Olympic Games were held in Stockholm, and 10 Swedish men and 6 Swedish women were entered in tennis events. Settarwall and Carl Kempe won the silver medal in indoor men's doubles, Settarwall and Sigrid Fick won bronze in the indoor mixed doubles and silver in the outdoor mixed doubles, and Fick and Edith Arnheim Lasch finished fourth in women' singles—Fick in the indoor event and Arnheim Lasch in the outdoor. Both fourth-place teams in **mixed doubles** were also Swedes—Margareta Cederschiöld and Carl Kempe in indoor and Annie Holmström and Torsten Grönfors in outdoor. In 1920, Fick was again fourth in women's singles. Stefan Edberg won the demonstration men's singles in 1984 and, in 1988, won the bronze medal in singles and, with partner Anders Järryd, the bronze in doubles. In 2008, Thomas Johansson and Simon Aspelin won the silver medal in men's doubles. Their semifinal match lasted 4 hours and 46 minutes and included a third and final set of 19–17.

In addition to those players cited above, the best Swedish male tennis players include Thomas Enqvist, Joachim Johansson, Magnus Larsson, **Robin Söderling**, **Magnus Norman**, and Joakim Nyström. The best female tennis players include Sofia Arvidsson, Ingrid Bentzer, Johanna Larsson, Catarina Lindqvist-Ryan, Christina Sandberg, and Asa Svensson. In **Federation Cup** competition, from 1964 to May 2011, Sweden has competed 44 years, 29 years in World Group, and played 124 ties with a record of 63–61. Sweden was a quarterfinalists four times—in 1970, 1977, 1980, and 1988.

SWITZERLAND. Swiss Tennis, founded in 1896, is the organization that administers tennis in Switzerland. From 1923 through May 2011, Switzerland has competed in 81 **Davis Cup tournaments** with a record of 68–82 in 150 **ties**. Switzerland has competed 20 times in the World Group since its formation in 1981. In 1992, the country was runner-up to the **United States**. Top Davis Cup players have been **Roger Federer**, Heinz Günthardt, Markus Günthardt, Jakob Hlasek, and Marc Rosset.

Switzerland first entered **Olympic** tennis in 1920 with three competitors in men's **singles** and one men's **doubles** team. They had entrants in 1924, 1968, and 1984 demonstration events and in 1988 also. Switzerland's first Olympic tennis medal was in 1992, when Marc Rosset won the gold medal in men's singles in an upset. Among the losers in 1992 were more accomplished players, such as **Stefan Edberg**, **Michael Chang**, **Pete Sampras**, **Boris Becker**, and **Jim Courier**, although in Rosset's path to the championship, he faced only Courier. The most famous Swiss tennis player, Roger Federer, finished fourth in men's singles in 2000, lost to **Czech** Tomáš Berdych in the second round in 2004 and to **James Blake** in the 2008 quarterfinals, and won the 2008 men's doubles with Stanislas Wawrinka.

Switzerland's best tennis player by far has been Federer, who is arguably the greatest player of all time. In addition to the players named above, other accomplished Swiss males include Yves Allegro, Marco Chiudinelli, and Michael Lammer. The best female tennis player is **Martina Hingis**. Other top Swiss female players include Patty Schnyder, Timea Bacsinszky, Emmanuelle Gagliardi, and Lolette Payot. In **Federation Cup** competition, from 1963 to May 2011, Switzerland has competed 47 years, 35 years in World Group, played 126 ties with a record of 70–56, and was runner-up in 1998.

T

TABLE TENNIS. Table tennis, also known as wiff-waff or ping-pong, originated in England in the 19th century. It is played on a table 9 feet long by 5 feet wide and 30 inches high with a 6 inch high **net** placed across the middle of the table. Small paddles and a lightweight celluloid **ball** are used. The object of the game, as in **lawn tennis**, is to win a **point** by hitting the ball over the net so that the opponent cannot satisfactorily retrieve it. Eleven points wins a game (with a two-point lead), and matches are usually best of five or best of seven games. Table tennis was added to the **Olympic Games** as a medal sport in 1988. There have been several lawn tennis players who were also proficient at table tennis, including **Fred Perry**, who won the World Table Tennis Championship in 1929, five years before he won the **Wimbledon** Lawn Tennis Championship. *See also* HAYDON-JONES, ADRIENNE SHIRLEY "ANN."

TALBERT, WILLIAM FRANKLIN "BILL," III. B. 4 September 1918, Cincinnati, Ohio. D. 28 February 1999, New York, New York. Bill Talbert won the Ohio State Singles Tennis Championship in 1936 while a student at Hughes High School in Cincinnati. He also played tennis while attending the University of Cincinnati. Although he was a diabetic, it did not stop him from playing world class tennis. His two **Grand Slam** finals appearances occurred at the **United States Nationals** in 1944 and 1945, but he was defeated by **Frank Parker** each time. Talbert did much better as a **doubles** player and was the U.S. National doubles champion in 1942, 1945, 1946, and 1948 and runner-up in 1950 and 1953 with partner **Gardnar Mulloy**. Their 1946 championship was memorable in that it required saving seven **match points** and a fifth **set** score of 20–18. Talbert was also the U.S. National doubles runner-up in 1943, 1944, and 1947 when his partner was not Mulloy. (It was David Freeman in 1943, Pancho Segura in 1944, and Bill Sidwell in 1947.) In **mixed doubles**, the team of Talbert and **Margaret Osborne** won four consecutive United States National titles from 1943 to 1946. She married William duPont Jr. in 1947, and the team of Talbert and Osborne duPont was

U.S. National mixed doubles losing finalists in 1948 and 1949. Talbert competed at **Roland Garros** only once, in 1950. That year, he reached the **singles** semifinals, won the men's doubles with fellow Cincinnatian **Tony Trabert**, and was the runner-up in the mixed doubles with Pat Canning Todd. He played **Davis Cup** tennis for the **United States** from 1946 to 1953. In eight **ties** in six years, his record was 2–0 in singles and 7–1 in doubles. Although the United States reached the **challenge round** each year from 1946 to 1953 and won the Cup from 1946 to 1949, Talbert only played in the challenge round in 1948 and 1949.

After retiring from competitive play in 1955, he worked for the United States Banknote Corporation (becoming its executive vice president), captained the Davis Cup team from 1952 to 1957, wrote several books (instructional, historical, and autobiographical), did television commentary, and was tournament director of the **United States Open** from 1971 to 1975 and 1978 to 1987. He was inducted into the **International Tennis Hall of Fame** in 1967. Since 1987, the **United States Tennis Association** has presented the Bill Talbert Junior Sportsmanship Award to four **junior** players, "who exemplify the finest qualities of sportsmanship in tournament play and the finest traditions of the great sportspersons of tennis past and present."

TANNER, LEONARD ROSCOE. B. 15 October 1951, Chattanooga, Tennessee. Roscoe Tanner, a resident of Lookout Mountain, Tennessee, was treated by sportswriters as a tennis-playing hillbilly, but he was anything but. Lookout Mountain is actually a wealthy suburb of Chattanooga, and he had an upper middle class upbringing. He attended the Baylor School, a private prep school near Chattanooga, and Stanford University. He won the **United States Amateur** Championships in 1970 and helped Stanford reach the **National Collegiate Athletic Association** National Championship in 1973. He won the **Australian Open Singles** Championship played in January 1977 and was runner-up to **Björn Borg** at **Wimbledon** in five **sets** in 1979. He twice reached the semifinals at the **United States Open** and once reached the fourth round of the **French Open**. In 1979, he achieved his highest world singles **ranking** of four. Although he is only 6 feet tall and 170 pounds, he had a powerful **left-handed serve** that was measured at 153 miles per hour in 1978—the fastest until **Andy Roddick** surpassed that with a 155 miles per hour serve in 2004. Tanner played singles for the **United States Davis Cup** team from 1975 to 1977 and again in 1981. He was a member of the 1981 Cup championship team. His overall record in Cup play was 9–4 in seven **ties**. He retired in 1984 with 17 singles titles to his credit.

After he retired, he incurred a number of problems with the law from 1997 to 2010. He was arrested in the United States for failure to pay child support and was arrested in **Germany** as a fugitive for fleeing from Florida from charges of passing bad checks. Although his initial sentence was only probation, he violated the probation and was sentenced to two years imprisonment in Florida. After being released for good behavior after serving just one year, he was again arrested for passing bad checks. That felony was dismissed after he made restitution, but in 2010, he was again a wanted man. A 23 July 2010 television broadcast stated that Tanner was in contempt of court for failing to appear in another child support case and was being sought as a fugitive from justice.

TEGART DALTON, JUDITH ANNE MARSHALL "JUDY." B. 12 December 1937, Melbourne, Victoria, **Australia**. Judy Tegart was a **doubles** specialist. She reached the finals of 20 **Grand Slam** events—19 in doubles. She was also the finalist in ladies' **singles** at **Wimbledon** in 1968, where she was defeated by **Billie Jean King**. Tegart is one of only 19 players to have won the women's doubles at each of the four Grand Slam events. (Only 21 men have won the men's doubles at each of the four Grand Slam events.) She won the **Australian** Championships in 1964 and 1967 with partner **Lesley Turner**. After reaching the finals and losing with Turner in 1968, Tegart switched to **Margaret Smith Court** as partner and won again in 1969 and 1970. Tegart and **Tony Roche** won the Australian **mixed doubles** in 1966 and were losing finalists in 1967. At **Wimbledon**, Tegart and Smith Court lost in 1966 and won in 1969. Tegart reached the finals with **Françoise Durr** in 1972 but lost. She and Roche also were mixed doubles finalists there in 1965 and 1969. Tegart's lone **French National** women's doubles finals was in 1966, when she and Margaret Smith Court won. At the **United States Open**, Tegart won women's doubles in 1970 and 1971—1970 with Smith Court and 1971 with **Rosie Casals**. Tegart also reached the finals of the mixed doubles there in 1963, 1964, 1965, and 1970 with three different partners but lost each time.

She played for Australia in **Federation Cup** competition from 1965 to 1967 and 1969 to 1970. In five years and 15 **ties**, her record was 6–1 in singles and 12–3 in doubles. She was a member of the Cup championship team in 1965 and 1970 and runner-up team in 1969. She married Dr. David Dalton on 18 November 1969. In 1971, she was one of the original nine players to join the **Virginia Slims professional** tour. In Grand Slam singles during her career, which lasted from 1957 to 1977, her best results were: semifinals at the Australian in 1968, fourth round at the French four times, finals at Wimbledon in 1968, and quarterfinals twice at the United States Open.

TENNIS ATTIRE. Since **lawn tennis** originated as a gentile game for ladies and gentlemen, certain standards have been maintained as far as proper decor.

At some tennis clubs, such as the **All-England Lawn Tennis and Croquet Club** or the **Newport Casino** Lawn Tennis Club, players are requested to wear all white outfits. In recent years, rules have been relaxed somewhat. In the early years of tennis history, men would wear long-sleeved shirts and long trousers, and women wore floor-length skirts, but in the 1930s standards changed, and shorts or short skirts became acceptable. Ironically, at some private clubs today, men are not allowed to wear long trousers but must wear shorts. Many clubs still require certain standards of dress, and for example, men may not wear sleeveless shirts, and women may not wear midriff-baring tops.

TENNIS BALL. A **lawn tennis** ball is approximately 2.7 inches in diameter and weighs between 56 and 59 grams (about 2 ounces). It was originally all white, but in the 1970s, it was found that yellow tennis balls were easier to see, especially on television, and today's tennis balls are generally a fluorescent yellow. The ball is covered with a felt material that modifies the aerodynamic properties. Balls are usually kept in a pressurized can until used since once the can is opened, the balls generally lose some of their bounce. *See also* NEW BALLS.

TENNIS CHANNEL. The Tennis Channel is a cable and satellite television network that broadcasts tennis 24 hours a day, 7 days a week. It is based in Santa Monica, California, and began operation in 2003. As its viewership has grown, the station has expanded its coverage and now has telecast rights to the four major **Grand Slam tournaments** as well as **Davis Cup**, **Fed Cup**, **Association of Tennis Professionals** tournaments, and **Women's Tennis Association** tournaments. It has many features on tennis players, past and present, and from 2006 to 2008 sponsored its own **Association of Tennis Professionals** tennis tournament in Las Vegas, Nevada.

TIE. In some **lawn tennis** team competitions, such as **Davis Cup** or **Fed Cup**, individual matches are referred to as **rubbers**, and the series of matches (or rubbers) are referred to as a tie. To win a Davis Cup tie, a team must win three of five rubbers. Fed Cup ties prior to 2002 were best of three rubbers but are now also best of five.

TIEBREAKER. Beginning in the late 1960s, a system was employed to shorten the length of **matches**. Prior to the tiebreaker system, a player needed to have a two-**game** advantage to win a **set**, and sets often lasted for more than 20 games. With the advent of the tiebreaker, once the set was tied at six games all, a special tiebreaker game was played in which the first player to win seven **points** (with a two-point margin) wins the set. **James Van Alen** introduced the concept of the tiebreaker system as part of his Van Alen Simplified Scoring System. *See also* LONGEST MATCH IN TENNIS HISTORY.

TILDEN, WILLIAM TATEM "BILL," "BIG BILL." B. 10 February 1893, Philadelphia, Pennsylvania. D. 5 June 1953, Hollywood, California. Bill Tilden is among those players who can be included in a discussion of the greatest **lawn tennis** player of all time. In 1950, he was named the Greatest Player of the First Half Century by the Associated Press. Yet his story is one of the tragic ones in sports history. He was one of the world's most talented athletes but was also arrogant, narcissistic, popular yet unpopular, wealthy yet died virtually penniless. But, in **Ted Tinling's** words "Tilden remains one of the great legends of American sport."

Born of a wealthy Philadelphia family, Tilden was educated at the Germantown Academy and the University of Pennsylvania. His mother was an invalid, and at the age of 15, he was sent to live with his aunt and her sister. His father died when Bill was only 19, and Bill's brother, Herbert, himself an accomplished tennis player, died when Bill was 22. Bill was not a particularly good tennis player at school. He partnered **Mary K. Browne** and won the **United States National mixed doubles** in 1913 and 1914. In 1916, 1917, and 1919, Tilden and Florence Ballin reached the U.S. National finals each year but were defeated each time. He did better with **Molla Bjurstedt Mallory**, losing in the 1921 final but winning in 1922 and 1923 and losing in 1924. He did not do well in **singles** during his early years and lost in the first round in 1912 and 1916. In 1918, he reached the finals but was defeated. After he again lost in the finals in 1919, he spent the winter working on his game and, in 1920, began a stretch in which he was virtually undefeated for seven years. From 1920 to 1925, he won the United States National men's singles each year. He also won the **Wimbledon** men's singles in 1920 and defended his title in 1921—the only two years in that span in which he played that tournament. He won the men's **doubles** in 1918 with his then 15-year-old protégé **Vinnie Richards**, lost in the finals in 1919, but then won again with Richards in 1921 and 1922. In 1923, Tilden again won the doubles with Brian "Babe" Norton.

After suffering a decline in the late 1920s during the height of the **French Four Musketeers** eminence, Tilden reemerged and won the Wimbledon doubles in 1927 and singles in 1930. At the **French Nationals**, Tilden was defeated by **René Lacoste** in 1927 and **Henri Cochet** in 1930 in the finals. He lost in the French mixed doubles finals in 1927 but won in 1930 with Cilly Aussem as partner. At the U.S. Nationals, after his dominance in the early 1920s, he was defeated in the singles by Lacoste in 1927 but came back to win in 1929 against American Frank Hunter. In U.S. National doubles, Tilden lost in the finals with another of his protégés, Al Chapin, in 1926, but won with established professional Frank Hunter in 1927. A 6-foot 2-inch, 155-pounder, "Big Bill" had a complete mastery of all the shots. In tennis expert **Bud Collins's** words: "Nobody had a more devastating **service** than Tilden's cannonball, or a more challenging second serve than his kicking American twist. No player had a stronger combination of **forehand** and **backhand** drives, supplemented by a forehand chop and backhand slice."

Tilden thought of himself as a writer, and he was the author of several juvenile moralistic novels in the Horatio Alger tradition. He also wrote and produced a dramatic play that was not well-received by critics. His instructional tennis books, on the other hand, were critically acclaimed, and his *Match Play and the Spin of the Ball* is considered a classic in instructional tennis literature.

His penchant for writing caused problems with the **United States Lawn Tennis Association (USLTA)**. During the 1920s, he had a running feud with **USLTA** executives who attempted to ban him from playing because he was also writing newspaper columns, and they considered that as a "**professional**" activity. On more than one occasion, the president of the **United States** was required to intervene to enable Tilden to represent the United States in **Davis Cup** play. He was a member of the United States Davis Cup team each year from 1920 to 1930. In those 11 years, he played in 17 **ties** and had a record of 25–5 in singles and 9–2 in doubles. The United States reached the **challenge round** in each of those years, winning the Cup each year from 1920 to 1926 and finishing second to France each year from 1927 to 1930. From 1920 to 1926, Tilden won 16 consecutive singles **matches** in Cup play, losing his final match in 1926 to **René Lacoste** in a **dead rubber**. In doubles during those years, he won five of six matches. Tilden became a good friend of Baron **Gottfried von Cramm** and was made a paid advisor to the **German** Davis Cup team. During the famous **Don Budge**–Gottfried von Cramm 1937 Davis Cup match, Tilden was sitting in the stands rooting for Germany. In 1931, Tilden became a professional player, and even though, at the age of 38, he was past his prime, he continued playing on various pro tours into the 1940s. In 1945, the then 52-year-old Tilden and Vinnie Richards won the U.S. Pro Doubles Championship.

In 1946, Tilden was arrested for "contributing to the delinquency of a minor" and served seven and one-half months of a one-year prison sentence. In 1949, he was again arrested and again imprisoned—this time on a parole violation—and served 10 months. His imprisonments were in part due to his failure to hire a lawyer to defend himself, feeling that the great Bill Tilden would be excused. His last few years were spent in a small apartment in Hol-

The charismatic Big Bill Tilden was in a class by himself during the 1920s—the golden age of sport. (courtesy of the International Tennis Hall of Fame and Museum)

lywood, shunned by most, and he died of a stroke, virtually penniless. His tragic story should be the basis of a Hollywood film, but as of 2010, none has yet been made. Frank Deford's biography of Tilden, *Big Bill Tilden: The Triumphs and the Tragedy* is must reading to gain a better appreciation of one of the most unique personalities in the world of sports. Despite the ostracism he was subjected to in his later life, Tilden was inducted into the **International Tennis Hall of Fame** in 1959.

TINLING, CUTHBERT COLLINGWOOD "TED." B. 23 June 1910, Eastbourne, England. D. 23 May 1990, Cambridge, England. The six-foot five-inch Ted Tinling was around the game of tennis for more than 60 years and contributed to the sport in many ways. As a youth, he suffered from asthma and was told by doctors to spend time at the French Riviera to improve his health. While there, he began playing tennis at the Nice Tennis Club, a facility that was also used by **Suzanne Lenglen**. Although still a teenager, he was asked to **umpire** one of her **matches**. She became fond of him and requested that he become her personal match umpire. This connection led him to **Wimbledon**, where he became player liaison. He served in the British Intelligence during World War II, with the rank of lieutenant colonel. He was a dress designer by trade and designed tennis outfits for most of the top female tennis players of his era.

In 1949, he designed one outfit, lace panties for **Gussie Moran**, that shocked the conservative people at Wimbledon, and he was dismissed from his position there and not reinstated until 1982. He designed for the **Virginia Slims** circuit and became its minister of protocol and emcee. He was friendly with **Billie Jean King** and designed her outfit for the famous "battle of the sexes" match with **Bobby Riggs** in 1973. From 1978 until his death in 1990, he was the **International Tennis Federation**'s Chief of Protocol. His 1979 book, cowritten with Rod Humphries, *Love and Faults: Personalities Who Have Changed the History of Tennis,* provides insights on a half-century of tennis. He was inducted into the **International Tennis Hall of Fame** in 1986 as a contributor.

ȚIRIAC, ION. B. 9 May 1939, Brașov, **Romania**. Ion Țiriac is one of the world's wealthiest men. In addition to playing world-class tennis, he played ice hockey in the 1964 **Olympic Games** for Romania, which finished 12th of 16 teams in the **tournament**. He was on the Romanian **Davis Cup** team from 1959 to 1977 and from 1966 to 1977; he and **Ilie Năstase** played virtually all of the important Cup matches for their country. They reached the **challenge round** in 1969, 1971, and 1972 but lost to the **United States** each year. Țiriac's overall Cup record was 40–28 in **singles** and 30–11 in **doubles** in 43 **ties** over 15 years. In 1966, he and Năstase reached the men's doubles finals at the **French National** Championships but lost to Americans **Clark Graebner** and **Dennis Ralston**. In 1970, he and Năstase were **French Open** doubles champions with their victory over Charlie Pasarell and **Arthur Ashe**. Țiriac also twice was runner-up for the French **mixed doubles** title—in 1967 with **Ann Haydon Jones** and in 1979 with **Virginia Ruzici**. After retiring from tennis, he managed the career of **Boris Becker** from 1984 to 1993.

Țiriac also became an entrepreneur in **Germany** with various interests. When communism fell in Romania in 1990, he returned there and became involved in multiple business interests, including founding Bank Țiriac, the first private bank in post-Communist Romania. His Țiriac Holdings Ltd., of which he is the primary owner, employs 200 people, and its businesses include Țiriac Auto (an auto dealership), Allianz Țiriac (an insurance firm), Țiriac Air (a charter airline company), Tir Travel (a travel agency), and real estate, among others. In 2010, he was ranked number 937 on Forbes's annual list of the world's billionaires, with an estimated net worth of one billion dollars. He was president of the Romanian National Olympic Committee from 1998 to 2004. He also organizes **Association of Tennis Professionals** tennis tournaments in Romania, Germany, and **Spain**.

TOPSPIN. By striking the **ball** in a certain manner, a player can impart topspin, which causes the ball to spin forward as it travels and bounce higher once it lands, making its return more difficult to hit.

TOUCH. Touch in **lawn tennis** has two meanings. If a player contacts the **net** with any part of his or her body or **racket** while the **ball** is in play, that is a touch, and he or she loses the **point**. Touch also refers to a player's ability to strike the ball with varying degrees of speed.

TOURNAMENT. Most **lawn tennis** contests take place in a tournament format. A **draw** of all entrants is conducted and matches held with the loser of a match being eliminated from the tournament. Often, several of the better entrants are **seeded** so that they do not face each other in the early rounds of the tournament. Some tournaments have pretournament **qualifying** rounds in which players who are not eligible for the tournament based on their past performance get a chance to qualify for the main tournament. *See also* WILD CARD.

TRABERT, MARION ANTHONY "TONY." B. 16 August 1930, Cincinnati, Ohio. Tony Trabert attended Walnut Hills High School in Cincinnati and the University of Cincinnati. He was a standout scholastic athlete in both tennis and basketball. In high school, he was a three-time state singles tennis champion and a member of the 1948 district basketball championship team. In 1951, he was the **National Collegiate Athletic Association** national **singles** champion. In his relatively brief **amateur** career, he reached 11 **Grand Slam** finals and won 10 of them. In 1950, he won the **French National Doubles** Championships with **Bill Talbert**. In 1953, he won the **United**

States National Singles Championships. In 1954, he won the French singles title and, with partner **Vic Seixas**, the French and United States doubles titles and was runner-up for the **Wimbledon** doubles title. In 1955, he had one of the best years that any player ever had in the long history of **lawn tennis**. He won 30 titles, including 18 of 23 singles titles, had **a match** record of 106–7, including 36 consecutive match victories, and won the French, Wimbledon, and United States singles and was a semifinalist at the **Australian National** singles and won the Australian and French doubles. He was also **ranked** number one in the world.

Trabert played on the **United States Davis Cup** team each year from 1951 to 1955. The United States reached the **challenge round** each of those years but could only win the Cup in 1954. Trabert's Cup record for 14 **ties** in five years was 16–5 in singles and 11–3 in doubles. He became team captain in 1976 and helped lead the United States to the Cup in 1978 and 1979. Following his outstanding amateur year in 1955, he became a **professional** tennis player. He was defeated by **Pancho Gonzáles** in the 1955–56 tour, 74–27. Trabert did win the French Pro Championship in 1956 and 1959. After retiring from active play, he became a teaching professional and television tennis analyst. He was inducted into the **International Tennis Hall of Fame** in 1970.

TSONGA, JO-WILFRIED. B. 17 April 1985, LeMans, **France**. Jo-Wilfried Tsonga is the son of a Congolese handball player, Didier Tsonga, and a French mother. He facially resembles the famed boxer Muhammad Ali, and reputedly, he and Ali are distant cousins. The 6-foot 2-inch, 200-pound, right-handed Tsonga also physically resembles Ali. Tsonga had an exceptional **junior tennis** career and won the 2003 **United States Open** Junior **Singles** Championship and reached the semifinals of the other three major junior singles championships. He became a **professional** tennis player in 2004, but his career since then has been plagued by injuries. His greatest victories occurred in 2008, when playing as an **unseeded** player, he reached the finals of the **Australian Open** but was defeated in four **sets** by **Novak Djoković**. To reach the finals, he defeated **Andy Murray**, Richard Gasquet, Mikhail Youzhny, and **Rafael Nadal**. In 2010, he reached the semifinals of the Australian Open and defeated Djoković in the quarterfinals. He also had his best showing at **Wimbledon** in 2010, when he reached the quarterfinals. He played on the French **Davis Cup** team from 2008 to 2010. His Cup record was 6–1 in singles and 1–0 in **doubles** in four **ties** in those three years. In Tsonga's career, through May 2011, he has won five singles titles and four doubles titles and has been ranked 6th in singles in 2008 and 33rd in doubles in 2009. Tsonga's younger brother, Enzo, is a member of the French national junior basketball team.

TURNBULL, WENDY MAY "RABBIT." B. 26 November 1952, Brisbane, Queensland, **Australia**. Wendy Turnbull began playing in major **tournaments** in 1970 and continued until 1989. In her career, the 5-foot 4-inch, 120-pound, right-hander reached the finals of 24 **Grand Slam** events, winning 9 of them. In 1985, she reached a world **singles ranking** of three. Nicknamed "Rabbit" for her speed on the **court**, she was a singles finalist at the **United States Open** in 1977, the **French Open** in 1979, and the **Australian Open** in 1980. Her best effort in **Wimbledon** singles was the quarterfinals, which she reached in 1979, 1980, and 1981. She was a good **doubles** player and reached 15 Grand Slam finals in women's doubles (although she won only four) and 6 Grand Slam finals in **mixed doubles**. She reached the women's doubles finals at all four major tournaments and won Wimbledon in 1978 with Kerry Melville Reid, the French Open and United States Open in 1979 with **Betty Stove**, and the United States Open in 1982 with **Rosie Casals**. She won the mixed doubles at the 1979 French Open with **Bob Hewitt**, 1980 United States Open and 1982 French Open with Marty Riessen, and 1983 and 1984 Wimbledon with **John Lloyd**. She competed in the 1988 **Olympic Games** in both singles and doubles. She lost in the second round of the singles but won the bronze medal in the doubles with partner Elizabeth Smylie. She was a member of the Australian **Federation Cup** team each year from 1977 to 1988, captain from 1985 to 1988, and **coach** from 1989 to 1993. In 45 **ties** over 12 years, her record was 17–8 in singles and 29–8 in doubles. She played for the runner-up team in 1977, 1978, 1979, 1980, and 1984. In her career, she won 10 singles and 54 doubles titles. In 1991, she was the only player appointed to the **International Tennis Federation**'s Olympic Committee.

TURNER BOWREY, LESLEY ROSEMARY. B. 16 August 1942, Trangie, New South Wales, **Australia**. Although Lesley Turner made her mark in tennis as a **doubles** player, she also won the **French National** women's **singles** twice. In 1963, she defeated **Ann Haydon-Jones**, and in 1965, she defeated **Margaret Smith Court**. The petite (5 feet 4 inches, 117 pounds) right-hander also twice was a losing finalist at Roland Garros (in 1962 and 1967) and twice at the **Australian Championships** (1964 and 1967). She reached the finals of 22 **Grand Slam** doubles championships and won 11 of them. She won the women's doubles championship at all four major Slam events and the **mixed doubles** twice each at the Australian and **Wimbledon**. She played on the Australian **Federation Cup** team from 1963 to 1965 and 1967. In 13 **ties** over four years, her record was 7–3 in singles and 6–3 in doubles. She played in the first Federation Cup in 1963 and was on the runner-up team. She was a member of the Cup championship team in 1964 and 1965. She married tennis player Bill Bowrey in 1968. She retired from active competition in 1978. She was inducted into the **International Tennis Hall of Fame** in 1997. In 2009, she was awarded membership into the Order of Australia for her accomplishments.

TWEENER. One of the more recent tennis shots is the tweener. This shot is rarely taken but when it is successful it is a definite crowd-pleaser. It occurs when a player runs after a **lob** and does not have time to turn but hits the ball between his legs with his back to his opponent. **Roger Federer** has executed this for a **winner** on occasion, including a notable one during the 2009 **U.S. Open** semi-final against **Novak Djokovic**.

TWINS. Throughout the long history of **lawn tennis**, there have been a few instances of twins performing at a high level. The first notable occurrence was the **Renshaw twins**. They were the greatest players of their era. **Willie Renshaw** was the **Wimbledon singles** champion seven times between 1881 and 1889. His brother **Ernest** won Wimbledon in 1888 and was runner-up to his brother in 1882, 1883, and 1889. The brothers won the Wimbledon **doubles** championship in 1884, 1885, 1886, 1888, and 1889. Shortly after the Renshaws retired from tennis came the Baddeley twins—Wilfred and Herbert. Wilfred was Wimbledon champion three times during the 1890s and, with twin brother Herbert, won the Wimbledon doubles titles four times during that decade. After their retirement, they both became London solicitors. The Gullikson twins, Tom and Tim, were top-ranked players in the 1980s. In 1983, they were the Wimbledon runners-up in men's doubles to **John McEnroe** and Peter Fleming. Tom won the **United States Open mixed doubles** in 1984 with **Manuela Maleeva**, and Tim was the **Australian Open** mixed doubles runner-up with **Martina Navratilova** in 1988. After retiring from competition, Tom became a **coach** for the **United States Tennis Association** player development program, was coach of the 1996 **United States** men's **Olympic** tennis team, and was **Davis Cup** captain from 1994 to 1999. Tim was also a tennis coach but was stricken with a brain tumor and died on 3 May 1996. In the 21st century, the **Bryan twins—Mike** and **Bob**—have had one of the most illustrious doubles careers. In February 2010, they won their 600th match and, in July 2010, passed **the Woodies'** record for most career doubles victories when they won their 62nd doubles championship.

Other twins of note: Thai professionals Sanchai and Sonchat Ratawatana; **Czech** professionals Karolina and Krystina Plistova; high school stars Abigail and Vanessa Madrigal of Highland, Indiana; Millennium High School's Hunter and Yates Johnson (Goodyear, Arizona); East Grand Rapids High School's Amanda and Molly Wickman (Michigan); Gordon and Heather Hayward of Indiana (Gordon later played professional basketball); college players Angelina and Angelika Jogasuria of Indonesia, who played for the University of Akron; Scott (Loyola University Maryland) and Glenn (Fairfield University) Gannon; **Women's Tennis Association** professionals Rachel and Melody Snelen of Texas; and Austrian **International Tennis Federation** professionals Daniela and Sandra Klemenschits. **Roger Federer's** wife, Mirka, gave birth to twin girls, Myla Riva and Charlene Rose on 23 July 2009. London bookmakers immediately began giving odds on the girls' future tennis success with a 25–1 quote on one of the twins winning a **Grand Slam** event.

U

ULRICH, TORBEN. B. 4 October 1928, Frederiksberg, Denmark. Torben Ulrich is one of tennis's most intriguing personalities. As a youth, he competed in many sports, including soccer, **table tennis**, speed skating, and team handball, in addition to tennis. The 5-foot 11-inch, bearded, **left-handed**, free spirit competed in **Wimbledon**, the **French Nationals**, and the **United States Nationals** in **singles, doubles,** and **mixed doubles** in most years from the late 1940s through the 1970s and reached the men's doubles semifinals at Wimbledon in 1959 and mixed doubles semifinals at the **U.S. Open** in 1969. In that year, aged 41, he lost in the third round in a five-**set** match to **Pancho Gonzáles**, also 41. In 1966, Ulrich and partner Cliff Richey set the Wimbledon record (broken in 2007) for longest doubles match at 98 games.

After competing in **amateur** tennis for 25 years, he was one of the founding members of the **Association of Tennis Professionals (ATP)** in 1972. During the 1970s, he played on both the ATP tour and the Tennis Grand Masters tour for players over 45 years of age at the same time. In 1976, he was the number-one–ranked **seniors** player. He was still playing top-level tennis in his 60s and won the **United States Tennis Association's** Men's 60s Indoor Championships in 1989 and 1990 and men's 65s in 1993. He competed in the 1968 **Olympic** demonstration tennis tournament in Mexico at the age of 40 and reached the quarterfinals of the men's singles but lost in the first round of the doubles. He played **Davis Cup** tennis for Denmark from 1948 to 1977. His final Cup match was a singles match on 18 September 1977, when he was 49 years old. His overall Cup record for 40 **ties** in 20 years was 31–35 in singles and 15–21 in doubles.

Throughout his life, in addition to his tennis activities, he has been a painter with gallery exhibits, radio announcer with his own jazz show, author, actor, director, musician (clarinet, saxophone, and flute, with several records and co-owner of a jazz club), and filmmaker. His website (www.torbenulrich.com) gives a much more complete list of his accomplishments. His son, Lars Ulrich, is a drummer with the heavy metal band Metallica, and Torben's brother, Jørgen, was a member of the Danish Davis Cup team from 1955 to

1971. Torben's father, Einer, was also a member of the Danish Davis Cup team from 1924 to 1938.

UMPIRE. *See* CHAIR UMPIRE.

UNFORCED ERROR. An unforced error is an errant shot that a player makes that is the result of poor judgment or execution and was not caused by his or her opponent's good shot. *See also* WINNER.

UNION OF SOVIET SOCIALIST REPUBLICS. *See* RUSSIA.

UNITED KINGDOM. *See* GREAT BRITAIN.

UNITED STATES LAWN TENNIS ASSOCIATION (USLTA). *See* UNITED STATES TENNIS ASSOCIATION (USTA).

UNITED STATES NATIONAL CHAMPIONSHIPS. *See* UNITED STATES OPEN.

UNITED STATES OF AMERICA. The **United States Tennis Association** administers tennis in the United States of America. One of the four major **lawn tennis tournaments** is the **United States Open**, played in late August and early September. The United States first entered **Olympic** tennis in 1900. That year, Spalding de Garmendia teamed with Frenchman Max Decugis to finish second in men's **doubles**. Marion Jones was third in women's **singles** and, with **Englishman Hugh Doherty**, was third in **mixed doubles**. The 1904 Olympic Games in St. Louis was a nearly exclusive American tournament with only one non-American entrant, Hugo Hardy of **Germany**. Only men's singles and doubles were held. Beals Wright won the singles, and he and Edgar Leonard won the doubles. In 1906, the United States sent only two competitors to Athens for Olympic tennis, and they reached the quarterfinals of the men's doubles. There were no Americans entered in the 1908 Olympic tennis events. Two Americans did compete in the 1908 *jeu de paume* (real tennis) event, and Jay Gould was the champion. Olympic tennis in 1912 at Stockholm had only one American entrant, Roosevelt Pell. He had a **bye** in the first round, a **walkover** in the second round, won his third round match, and was defeated in the fourth round. In 1920, the **United States National Championships** took place at the same time as the Olympic Games, and consequently, no Americans entered the Olympic tennis events. The 1924 Olympic Games were the first not held in the United States in which a sizeable American contingent entered the tennis events. Four men and five women entered, and the United States won the gold medal in each of the five events. **Vincent Richards** won men's singles, doubles (with Frank Hunter), and silver medal in mixed doubles (with Marion Jessup). **Dick Williams** and **Hazel Wightman** won the gold medal in mixed doubles. **Helen Wills** won women's singles, and Wightman and Wills the women's doubles.

In the 1968 demonstration and **exhibition** tennis tournaments in **Mexico**, Herb Fitzgibbon and **Julie Heldman** won demonstration mixed doubles and Jane "Peaches" Bartkowicz defeated Julie Heldman in exhibition women's singles. Bartkowicz also finished second in demonstration women's singles and Heldman was third in that event. James Osborne and Bartkowicz were third in demonstration mixed doubles. Heldman and Frenchwoman Rosa Marie Darmon won exhibition women's doubles over Bartkowicz and Valerie Ziegenfuss. Bartkowicz also finished second in exhibition mixed doubles with German partner Ingo Buding. In the 1984 tennis demonstration in Los Angeles, **Jimmy Arias** reached the semifinals. The year 1988 saw a successful Olympic tennis tournament for the United States—**Tim Mayotte** won silver in men's singles, the team of Ken Flach and Robert Seguso won the gold in men's doubles, **Zina Garrison** won the bronze medal in women's singles, and she and **Pam Shriver** won the gold in women's doubles. In 1992, **Jennifer Capriati** won the gold in women's singles, and the unrelated team of **Mary Joe Fernández** and **Gigi Fernández** won the gold in women's doubles. Mary Joe also won the bronze medal in women's singles. In Atlanta in 1996, **Andre Agassi** won the men's singles tournament, **Lindsay Davenport** won the women's singles, and the two Fernándezes repeated a victory in doubles. In 2000, **Venus Williams** won women's singles, and she and sister **Serena** won the doubles. **Monica Seles**, former Yugoslavian but now naturalized American citizen, was third in women's singles. In 2004, there was only one American tennis medalist—Mardy Fish, who won the silver medal in men's singles. **Martina Navratilova**, at age 47, entered the doubles with **Lisa Raymond** and reached the quarterfinals. In 2008, the Williams sisters again won the women's doubles, and the **Bryan twins** won the men's doubles bronze medal. **James Blake**, who defeated Roger Federer en route to the semifinals, finished in fourth place.

From 1900 through May 2011, the United States has competed in 97 **Davis Cup** tournaments with a record of 210–64 in 274 **ties**. The team has competed 30 times in the World Group since its formation in 1981. The United States won the Cup 32 times and was runner-up 29 times—more championships and more second-place finishes than any other team. Top Davis Cup players have been **John McEnroe**, John Van Ryn, and the Bryan twins, Mike and Bob. Among the best male tennis players not mentioned above have been **Arthur Ashe**, **Don Budge**, **Michael Chang**, **Jimmy Connors**, **Jim**

Courier, Richard "Pancho" Gonzáles, Bill Johnston, Jack Kramer, Rick Leach, John McEnroe, Gardnar Mulloy, Vinnie Richards, Marty Riessen, Bobby Riggs, Pete Sampras, Richard Sears, Vic Seixas, Stan Smith, Bill Talbert, Bill Tilden, Tony Trabert, Ellsworth Vines, and Richard Norris Williams. The best female tennis players include **Pauline Betz Addie, Louise Brough, Rosie Casals, Maureen Connolly,** Lindsay Davenport, **Chris Evert,** Gigi **Fernández,** Mary Joe Fernández, **Shirley Fry, Althea Gibson, Darlene Hard, Doris Hart, Helen Jacobs, Billie Jean King, Alice Marble,** Czech-born American citizen Martina Navratilova, **Margaret Osborne DuPont, Sarah Palfrey, Lisa Raymond,** Pam Shriver, Hazel Wightman, sisters Serena and Venus Williams, and Helen Wills Moody. The United States dominated play in the **Wightman Cup** in most years, and by 1990, when the series was discontinued, the United States had won 51 of the 61 events. In **Federation Cup** competition from 1963 to May 2011, the United States has competed 48 years, all 48 in World Group, and played 172 ties with a record of 140–32 and is the most successful nation in that tournament with 17 championships and 11 runner-up finishes. The United States won seven consecutive championships from 1976 to 1982. After being defeated by Belgium and Germany in 2011, the United States was relegated to World Group II for the first time in its Fed Cup history.

UNITED STATES OPEN. In 1881, the **United States National Lawn Tennis Association** sponsored its first national championship **tournament** and held it at the **Newport Casino** in Newport, Rhode Island. As was the custom of the times, the tournament was open to Caucasian male **amateur** contestants only, and **singles** and **doubles** events were held. **Richard Sears** won the first men's singles tournament and proceeded to defend his title for the next six years, although in 1884, a **challenge-round** system was adopted whereby the incumbent champion did not have to compete in the preliminary rounds but only had to play the preliminary-round winner for the championship. That system lasted until 1912, when the challenge round was abolished. The tournament was moved to the **West Side Tennis Club** in **Forest Hills,** New York, in 1915, remaining there for most years until the venue was changed to its present one at **Flushing Meadows.** In 1917, the men's doubles championship was moved to the **Longwood Cricket Club** near Boston and remained there (with the exception of a few years) until 1967, when it returned to Forest Hills. A women's national championship tournament was adopted in 1887 and played at the **Philadelphia Cricket Club.** Ellen Hansell was the first women's champion. In 1889, women's doubles were added, and in 1892, **mixed doubles** were also added. In 1935, the women's singles moved to Forest Hills.

In 1968, the United States National Championships became an **open** tournament, and **professionals** were allowed to compete along with the amateurs. Also that year, all five events—men's and women's singles and doubles and mixed doubles—were all contested at Forest Hills. In 1978, the new United States Tennis Association facility at **Flushing Meadows** was opened, and the event moved there. The U.S. Open is the fourth of the major Grand Slam tennis tournaments and is held over a two-week period, usually beginning at the end of August and continuing through the second Sunday in September. In recent years, both day and night matches are held most days of the tournament. *See also* APPENDIX C (for a list of champions).

UNITED STATES TENNIS ASSOCIATION (USTA). The United States Tennis Association was founded in 1881 as the United States National **Lawn Tennis** Association. In 1920, the word "national" was dropped from its name, and in 1975, the name was officially changed to the present one. Its first president was R. S. Oliver. It is the world's largest tennis association with over 700,000 individual and 7,000 organizational members. It promotes tennis throughout the United States and administers tour events, including the United States Open. It oversees the operations of the **Billie Jean King National Tennis Cente**r at Flushing Meadows and runs the USTA Pro Circuit, which holds Futures- and **Challenger**-level development **tournaments** throughout the world. In its Player Development program, it maintains USTA training centers in Boca Raton, Florida; Carson, California; and New York, New York. It also presents various annual awards to individuals and organizations to recognize exceptional performance. The five award categories are adult service, adult competition, **junior**, organization, and **umpire**.

UNSEEDED. *See* SEEDING.

U.S. PRO CHAMPIONSHIPS. The U.S. Pro Championships was an annual men's **tournament** that began in 1927 and lasted until 1999. Until the start of the **open** era in 1968, this was one of the only major tournaments that **professional** tennis players could enter. After open tennis began, the tournament was held under the auspices of the Grand Prix and later the **Association of Tennis Professionals**. The tournament was held at various venues in the eastern United States from 1927 to 1963 (with the exception of the 1939 tournament, which was held at the Beverly Hills Country Club in Los Angeles, California.) From 1964 to 1999, it was held at the **Longwood Cricket Club** in Chestnut Hill, Massachusetts. The event was not held in 1944 and 1996 and not completed due to rain in 1995. During the 1950s, the event was billed as the World Pro Championships. **Pancho Gonzáles** holds the record for most consecutive championships won with seven from 1953 to 1959. He also won it in 1961 and was runner-up in 1951, 1952, and 1964.

USTA BILLIE JEAN KING NATIONAL TENNIS CENTER. The tennis facility at **Flushing Meadows,** New York, site of the **United States Open tournament** since 1978, was rededicated as the USTA Billie Jean King National Tennis Center on 28 August 2006. There are 3 stadiums within the facility and an additional 22 **courts** on the grounds. The **Arthur Ashe Stadium** has a capacity of 23,200 and is the largest tennis-only stadium in the world. The **Louis Armstrong Stadium** is a 10,000-seat arena, and its adjoining Grandstand Stadium seats another 6,000 people. When the United States Open is not in session, the courts on the grounds are available for public use.

V

VAN ALEN, JAMES HENRY "JIMMY." B. 19 September 1902, Newport, Rhode Island. D. 3 July 1991, Newport, Rhode Island. James Van Alen was educated at Cambridge University, graduating in 1924. He was a good **lawn tennis** player and competed on the university tennis team. He also played in the Championships at **Wimbledon** as well as the **French** and **United States National Championships**. As a **court tennis** player, he won the **United States Singles** Championship in 1933, 1938, and 1940. He served in the U.S. Navy during World War II. Van Alen is best known for his nonplaying accomplishments.

He was a leader in the preservation of the **Newport Casino**, he founded the **International Tennis Hall of Fame** there in 1954, and he was elected its president in 1957. He was the inventor of the Van Alen Streamlined Scoring System (VASSS) in 1965. That system provided for single-**point** scoring and 21- or 31-point **matches**, **no-ad** scoring, and **games** scored 1, 2, 3, 4, with a sudden-death point if the game was tied 3–3. Although that system did not catch on, it did lead to a best of nine-point **tiebreaker** and today's version (first player to seven points with a two-point margin). At tennis matches at the Newport Casino, he also introduced electric scoreboards and night tennis. He was inducted into the International Tennis Hall of Fame in 1965. He was the vice president of Farrar Straus publishers and owned a chain of weekly newspapers on Long Island. He died at the age of 88 as a result of a fall at his home.

VERGEER, ESTHER. B. 18 July 1981, Woerden, **the Netherlands**. Esther Vergeer became a paraplegic at the age of eight following surgery. In rehabilitation, she participated in wheelchair basketball, wheelchair volleyball, and **wheelchair tennis**. In 1997, she was a member of the Dutch wheelchair basketball team that won the European championship. Her achievements in wheelchair tennis have been nothing short of amazing, and she has become the world's best wheelchair tennis player in history. Through 4 June 2011, her record is 634–25 in **singles** (418 consecutive) and 415–32 in **doubles**. From August 2004 to October 2006, she won 250 consecutive **sets**. She has won 149 singles and 127 doubles championships, including 18 **Grand Slam** singles and 19 Grand Slam doubles titles. She won the women's singles gold medal in the 2000, 2004, and 2008 Paralympic Games. She also won the women's doubles gold medal in 2000 and 2004 with partner Maaike Smit and the silver medal in 2008 with partner Jiske Griffioen. In 2002 and again in 2008, she was named the Laureus Sportsperson of the Year with a Disability. To put her accomplishments in perspective, though, she was asked during an interview if she could trade all of her titles and world travel for an ordinary life with complete physical ability. Her poignant answer was "yes."

VILAS, GUILLERMO APOLINARIO. B. 17 August 1952, Buenos Aires, **Argentina**. Guillermo Vilas was one of the world's best tennis players during the 1970s. Although better on **clay courts**, he won on all **surfaces**. He won the **French Open** and the **United States Open** in 1977 and the **Australian Open** in 1978 and 1979. He was also runner-up in the Australian Open in 1977 and the French Open in 1975, 1978, and 1982. He had a remarkable year in 1977. In addition to winning the two **Grand Slam tournaments**, he won 17 of 33 tournaments that he entered and had a **match** won-lost record of 145–14 for the year. Despite that accomplishment, he was only **ranked** number two worldwide, equaling his best ranking achieved earlier in 1975. The 5-foot 11-inch, 175-pound **left-hander** played **Davis Cup** tennis for Argentina from 1970 to 1974 and 1976 to 1984. In 1981, he helped lead Argentina to the final round for the first time, where the team was defeated by the **United States**. Vilas's overall Cup record was 45–10 in singles and 12–14 in doubles in 29 **ties** in 14 years. He was inducted into the **International Tennis Hall of Fame** in 1991. He retired in 1992 with a career record of 68 **singles** and 15 **doubles** titles.

VINES, HENRY ELLSWORTH, JR. B. 28 September 1911, Los Angeles, California. D. 17 March 1994, La Quinta, California. Ellsworth Vines attended the University of Southern California. From 1930 to 1933, the 6-foot 2-inch, 145-pound right-hander was one of the world's best **amateur** tennis players and achieved a world number-one **ranking** in 1932. In those four years, he won the **Wimbledon** men's **singles** in 1932 and was runner-up in 1933, the **United States National** men's singles in 1931 and 1932, the United States National men's **doubles** in 1932, the U.S. National **mixed doubles** in 1933 and runner-up in 1932, and the **Australian** men's doubles in 1933 and runner-up in **mixed doubles** that year as well. In 1932 and 1933, he played singles as a member of the **United States Davis Cup** team. In eight **ties** in two years, his record was 13–3. In 1932, the United States reached the **challenge round** but was defeated by **France**, 3–2.

He became a **professional** tennis player in 1934 and toured in a series of **matches** with **Bill Tilden**. The 23-year-old Vines defeated the 40-year-old Tilden, 47 matches to 26. Each year from 1934 to 1936, he won the World Professional Championships at Wembley. In 1940, at the age of 28, he gave up tennis for golf. He became successful enough in that sport to become a teaching golf professional and semifinalist at the 1951 Professional Golf Association Championship, one of golf's four major tournaments. He also won the 1946 Massachusetts Open and 1955 Utah Open golf tournaments. He was inducted into the **International Tennis Hall of Fame** in 1962. In 1994, at the age of 82, Vines died at his home in La Quinta, California, from complications of kidney disease.

VIRGINIA SLIMS. Virginia Slims is a brand of cigarettes manufactured by Philip Morris that was introduced in 1968 with advertising aimed at women. In 1970, a **professional** women's tennis tour was begun with the Virginia Slims brand as the primary sponsor. The tour, the forerunner of today's **Women's Tennis Association**, was begun by nine players, led by **Billie Jean King**, with the backing of Gladys Heldman and Joe Cullman, chief executive officer of Philip Morris. The initial players were: Billie Jean King, Jane "Peaches" Bartkowicz, **Rosie Casals**, **Julie Heldman** (Gladys's daughter), Kerry Melville Reid, Kristy Pigeon, **Nancy Richey**, **Judy Tegart Dalton**, and Valerie Ziegenfuss. The inaugural series of 19 **tournaments** was known as the Virginia Slims Circuit.

VOLLEY. A volley is a return shot made before the **ball** bounces. **Doubles** play often features many volleys as players position themselves near the **net**. *See also* HALF-VOLLEY; SERVE AND VOLLEY.

VON CRAMM, GOTTFRIED ALEXANDER MAXIMILIAN WALTER KURT FREIHERR (BARON). B. 7 July 1909, Nettlingen, **Germany**. D. 8 November 1976, Cairo, Egypt. Baron Gottfried von Cramm was Germany's best tennis player during the Adolf Hitler regime. A six-foot tall, handsome, blonde, blue-eyed man, he was the epitome of Hitler's Aryan ideal, although von Cramm was not a Nazi supporter and refused to join the Nazi party. In 1933, he and Hilde Krahwinkel won the **mixed doubles** at **Wimbledon**. He won the **French National** Championships in 1934 and 1936 and was runner-up in 1935. He was the runner-up at Wimbledon three straight years, 1935 to 1937, and at the **United States National Championships** in 1937. In 1937, he and Henner Henkel won the French and United States Men's **Doubles** Championship. In 1938, they reached the finals of the **Australian** Men's Doubles Championship. Von Cramm played on the German **Davis Cup** team from 1932 to 1937 and again from 1951 to 1953. His record in 37 **ties** during those nine years was 58–10 in **singles** and 24–9 in doubles. His fifth **rubber match** with American **Don Budge** on 20 July 1937 in the Davis Cup Inter-Zonal Finals has been called "the greatest tennis match ever played." Had von Cramm, a homosexual, won that match, his life might have been different, for Germany would have won that tie and most likely have defeated England and won the 1937 Davis Cup. Because he did not, he was arrested by the Nazi government in 1938 and sentenced to a one-year prison sentence. He was released after serving six months.

After his release, he attempted to resume his tennis activity but was refused a visa to the **United States** based on his morals conviction and was also banned from playing in Wimbledon, although he did compete in lesser tournaments in England. He was drafted into the German military service in 1940 and served two years until he was dismissed for his prior morals conviction. After the war, he continued playing Davis Cup tennis for Germany and had a successful cotton importing business. He died while on a business trip to Cairo in 1976, when the driver of his car collided with a truck. Von Cramm was inducted into the **International Tennis Hall of Fame** in 1977. An excellent account of von Cramm's life appears in Marshall Jon Fisher's book, *A Terrible Splendor*.

WADE, SARAH VIRGINIA. B. 10 July 1945, Bournemouth, England. Virginia Wade was born in England but raised in **South Africa** as her father, a vicar, was transferred there to be the Archdeacon of Durban when she was just one year old. The family returned to England when she was 15, and she attended Tunbridge Wells Girls' Grammar School, Talbot Heath School, and the University of Sussex, graduating in 1966. She first played at **Wimbledon** in 1962 and competed there each year through 1985. Her 24 consecutive appearances in the ladies' **singles** is the Wimbledon all-time record. In her lengthy career, she won **Grand Slam** championships at each of the four venues, winning singles at the inaugural **United States Open** in 1968, at the **Australian Open** in 1972, and **Wimbledon** in 1977—the last British player to win there as of 2010. Her best singles performances at **Roland Garros** were the quarterfinals in 1970 and 1972. The 5-foot 7-inch, 135-pound right-hander also won the Australian Open, **French Open**, and United States Open women's **doubles** in 1973 with **Margaret Smith Court**. The pair won the U.S. again in 1975. Wade was also four-time runner-up at the U.S. Open—1969 and 1972 with Court, 1970 with **Rosie Casals**, and 1976 with Olga Morozova. Wade and **Françoise Durr** were runners-up at Wimbledon in 1970 and in 1979 at Roland Garros.

She played on the **Great Britain Fed Cup** team each year from 1967 to 1983. Her record in 17 years and 57 **ties** is 36–20 in singles and 30–13 in doubles. She was a member of the runner-up team in 1967, 1971 (December 1970), 1972, and 1981. She played more **Wightman Cup** matches than anyone and was a member of the British team each year from 1965 to 1985. Her record for those events was 12–23 in singles and 7–14 in doubles. She retired from competitive play in 1986 with 55 singles titles to her credit and was honored as an Officer of the Order of the British Empire (OBE) that year. She was inducted into the **International Tennis Hall of Fame** in 1989. She has worked as a television announcer in both Britain and the **United States**.

WALKOVER. A "walkover" is the term used to denote an unopposed victory in a **lawn tennis match** when one of the participants fails to appear and the match does not take place. When a match has begun and a player is unable or unwilling to continue prior to its conclusion, that result is termed a "default" or "retirement."

WASHINGTON, ORA MAE. B. 23 January 1898, Caroline County, Virginia. D. 21 December 1971, Philadelphia, Pennsylvania. Ora Mae Washington, although born in Virginia, was raised in the Germantown section of Philadelphia, Pennsylvania. She never achieved the fame during her lifetime that she probably would have had she been an athlete 50 years later. She was the best black tennis player in the **United States** and won the **American Tennis Association's** National Women's **Singles** Championship eight times in nine years from 1929 to 1937. She also won 12 straight **doubles** championships from 1925 to 1936 and **mixed doubles** titles in 1939, 1946, and 1947 (at the age of 49). **Helen Wills Moody**, the white woman's champion, refused to play Washington. Washington was also an outstanding basketball player and played center for the Germantown Hornets team and later for the Philadelphia Tribunes. The Tribunes won 11 straight Women's Colored World's Basketball Championships. During the 18 years that she played for the Tribunes, the team only lost six games—and all of them were to men's teams. She was inducted into the Black Athletes Hall of Fame in 1976 and was enshrined in the Women's Basketball Hall of Fame in 2009.

WEST SIDE TENNIS CLUB. The West Side Tennis Club was founded in 1892 and was originally located on the west side of Manhattan in New York City at Central Park West. It relocated further uptown in 1902 and again in 1908. In 1911, it hosted the **International Lawn Tennis Challenge** (now known as the **Davis Cup**.) In 1913, the club moved to a new site in **Forest Hills**, in the Borough of Queens, still within the borders of New York City. The **United States Lawn Tennis Association** National Championship was first held there in 1915. In 1923, a 14,000-seat stadium was built to house the event. The **tournament** continued to be played at that site through 1977, when it was moved to its present site in **Flushing Meadows**. The club is still in existence today and has 38 tennis **court**s of four different **surface**s, including **grass** and **clay**, over 14 acres.

WHEELCHAIR TENNIS. Wheelchair tennis is a variant of tennis played by people with limited mobility. The rules of **lawn tennis** are used with two exceptions—players are seated in wheelchairs, and the **ball** may bounce twice before being returned. The sport is contested internationally and is included in the Paralympic Games as well as at major international tournaments, such as the **United States Open**. Both men's and women's **singles**

and **doubles** events are held. A category for players with limited upper body ability, called "quads," is also contested. Quads players use electric-powered wheelchairs and have the **rackets** taped to their hands. Brad Parks, in 1976, created the sport that was added to the Paralympic Games in 1992. He was inducted in the **International Tennis Hall of Fame** in 2010. Several of the best wheelchair tennis players have been Dutch, including **Esther Vergeer**, Korie Homans, and Robin Ammerlaan. American David Wagner is among the best quads players.

WIGHTMAN, HAZEL. *See* HOTCHKISS WIGHTMAN, HAZEL VIRGINIA.

WIGHTMAN CUP. The Wightman Cup was a women's **tournament** held annually from 1923 to 1989 between teams from the **United States** and **Great Britain**. It was not held from 1940 to 1945 because of World War II. The tournament was originated by **Hazel Hotchkiss Wightman**, an American tennis player of world renown who donated a sterling vase as the prize for the event, more formally known as the "Ladies International Tennis Challenge." The 1923 tournament was played at the **West Side Tennis Club** in **Forest Hills**, New York, and at **Wimbledon** the following year. The site was alternated between the two countries. From 1923 to 1949, it was played at Forest Hills in odd-numbered years, but after that, when the United States hosted the tournament, it was held at various venues. It remained at Wimbledon in even-numbered years through 1972 before other sites were used in the United Kingdom. The format consisted of five **singles matches** and two **doubles** matches. The United States dominated play in most years, and by 1990, when the series was discontinued, the United States had won 51 of the 61 events. **Virginia Wade** played the most years, 21, and had the most matches, 56. **Chris Evert** won the most matches, 34, and was undefeated in 26 singles matches. **Louise Brough** had an unsurpassed record of 12–0 in singles and 10–0 in doubles, and **Margaret Osborne duPont** was also undefeated at 10–0 in singles and 9–0 in doubles. *See also* APPENDIX G (for a list of champions).

WILANDER, MATS ARNE OLOF. B. 22 August 1964, Växjö, **Sweden**. The six-foot tall Mats Wilander became a **professional** tennis player in 1980. **Ranked** 283rd at the end of his first year, by 1988, he improved to the number-one ranking. He played 255 **tournaments** from 1988 until his retirement in 1996 and had a **match** record of 571–222 in that time, winning 33 tournaments and reaching the final round in 26 others. His best year was 1988, when he won the **Australian Open**, **French Open**, and **Wimbledon**

and reached the quarterfinal round of the **United States Open** and was ranked number one. His record in major tournaments that year was 25–1. In his career, he was a three-time winner of the Australian Open, three-time winner of the French Open, won Wimbledon once, but could never advance past the quarterfinal round of the United States Open. In **Davis Cup** competition for Sweden, from 1981 to 1990 and again in 1995, he had a record of 36–16 in singles and 7–2 in doubles in 27 **ties** and helped Sweden reach the final round each year from 1983 to 1989 and win the Cup in 1984, 1985, and 1987. He holds the Davis Cup record for the longest and third-longest matches. In 1982, he and **John McEnroe** played a 6-hour 32-minute Davis Cup match, and in 1989, he and Horst Skoff of Austria went 6 hours and 4 minutes. In retirement, he moved to Idaho in the **United States**. He still plays on the **seniors' Champions Tour** and has been a Davis Cup captain and **coach** of **Marat Safin**. Wilander was elected to the **International Tennis Hall of Fame** in 2002. *See also* LONGEST MATCH IN TENNIS HISTORY.

WILD CARD. In most tournaments, the organizers reserve one or more places for players who might not otherwise qualify to compete. These players are known as wild-card entries. Usually, wild cards are given to local players, established players returning from injury, or others whom the **tournament** promoters feel would draw additional spectators. A wild card is usually not **seeded** and, consequently, may have to face some of the better players during the early rounds of the event.

WILDING, ANTHONY FREDERICK "TONY." B. 31 October 1883, Christchurch, New Zealand. D. 9 May 1915, Neuve Chapelle, France. Tony Wilding is arguably the greatest New Zealand tennis player in history. The son of a wealthy lawyer in Christchurch, he was educated at Mr. Wilson's school and Canterbury University College in New Zealand and Cambridge University in England. In 1909, he became a barrister and solicitor at the Supreme Court of New Zealand. He was the bronze medalist in the indoor **singles** tennis event at the 1912 **Olympic Games** in Stockholm. From 1910 to 1913, he was the **Wimbledon** singles champion and was finally defeated in 1914 by his **doubles** partner **Norman Brookes**. He and Brookes were Wimbledon doubles champions in 1907 and 1914. In 1908 and 1910, Wilding and Josiah Ritchie were Wimbledon doubles champions and in 1911 were runners-up. Wilding also reached the Wimbledon **mixed doubles** finals in 1914. At the **Australasian** Championships, Wilding won the singles title in 1906 and 1909 and the doubles in 1906 and was a losing doubles finalist in 1908 and 1909. In **Davis Cup** play, he was a member of the Australasian team from 1905 to 1909 and again in 1914 and played in the **challenge round** for the Cup championship team in 1907, 1908, 1909, and 1914. His record was 15–6 in singles and 6–3 in doubles in 11 **ties** during those six years. When the First World War began, he enlisted in the Royal Marines and had a rank of captain. He was killed in action at the battle of Aubers Ridge in France. In 1912, he wrote a book entitled *On the Court and Off*. His biographers credit him with more than 112 career **tournament** victories. He was inducted into the **International Tennis Hall of Fame** in 1978.

WILLIAMS, RICHARD NORRIS "DICK," II. B. 29 January 1891, Geneva, Switzerland. D. 2 June 1968, Bryn Mawr, Pennsylvania. R. Norris Williams was a **United States National singles**, **doubles**, and **mixed doubles** champion and **Wimbledon** men's doubles titleholder but would not have achieved any of those feats had he not accomplished an even greater one in 1912. He was a survivor of the sinking of the Titanic. After he was rescued, the rescuing ship's doctor wanted to amputate Williams' frozen legs, but Williams convinced him not to do so. Williams recovered and was able to resume his tennis activities. Later that year, he won his first United States National title—the mixed doubles with **Mary K. Browne**. In 1913, he was United States National singles runner-up to **Maurice McLoughlin** and, in 1914, defeated McLoughlin for the title. Williams won it again in 1916.

He volunteered for the American Expeditionary Forces in 1917 and served with the rank of captain as an artillery officer during World War I and was awarded the Croix de Guerre and Chevalier de la Legion d'Honneur. He was a graduate of Harvard University. A decade later, he was a five-time U.S. National men's doubles finalist, winning in 1925 and 1926 with partner **Vinnie Richards** and losing in 1921 and 1923 with Watson Washburn and in 1927 with **Bill Johnston**. He also won the Wimbledon men's doubles in 1920 and was runner-up in 1924 with Washburn. The 5-foot 11-inch, right-handed Williams competed in all three events at the 1924 **Olympic Games** in Paris and won the mixed doubles with **Hazel Hotchkiss Wightman** and was a quarterfinalist in both men's singles and doubles. He played on the **United States Davis Cup** team in 1913, 1914, 1921, 1923, 1925, and 1926 and was team captain from 1921 to 1926 and 1934. In nine **ties** during those six years, his record was 6–3 in singles and 4–0 in doubles. He appeared in the **challenge round** in each of the six years and was on the Cup-winning team in all except 1914.

He was a successful investment banker in Philadelphia. His love of history (president of the Pennsylvania Historical Society for 22 years) and his involvement in significant historical events enabled him to save many documents that were later donated to the University of Pennsylvania library. His extensive collection of World War I books, documents, and ephemera was donated to the library by Williams's widow in 1987. He was elected to the **International Tennis Hall of Fame** in 1957. *See also* BEHR, KARL HOWELL.

WILLIAMS, SERENA JAMEKA. B. 26 September 1981, Saginaw, Michigan. Serena and **Venus Williams** are the most successful pair of tennis-playing sisters in history and are the most accomplished **African American** tennis players of all time with a combined total of 48 **Grand Slam** victories and 13 Grand Slam runner-up finishes. Eight of those thirteen finals losses were to each other. Serena was born in Michigan but raised in Compton, California. Her parents, Oracene Price and Richard Williams, moved the family to Florida when Serena was nine so that she and her older sister, Venus, could attend tennis school. After several years, their father removed the sisters from the school and became their full-time **coach**. Serena became a **professional** player in 1995. Since then, through 2010, she has reached the finals of 32 Grand Slam events, winning 27 of them and losing to her sister in two others. Serena won the women's **singles** five times at the **Australian Open** (2003, 2005, 2007, 2009, and 2010), once at the **French Open** (2002), four times at **Wimbledon** (2002, 2003, 2009, and 2010), and three times at the **United States Open** (1999, 2002, and 2008). In six of those victories, she defeated her sister, Venus, in the championship match. Serena is also an accomplished **doubles** player and, with big sister Venus as partner, has won 12 Grand Slam women's doubles titles—the Australian Open in 2001, 2003, 2009, and 2010; the French Open in 1999 and 2010; Wimbledon in 2000, 2002, 2008, and 2009; and the U.S. Open in 1999 and 2009. They have never lost a Grand Slam women's doubles final. In addition, Serena and Max Mirnyi won the 1998 Wimbledon and U.S. Open **mixed doubles** and were runners-up at the 1999 Australian Open. Serena and Luis Lobo were 1998 mixed doubles runners-up at the French Open. Serena is not quite as tall (five feet nine inches) as her six-foot one-inch sister but is just as powerful and has the second-fastest **serve** in women's tennis.

Serena entered the 2000 and 2008 **Olympic** tennis **tournaments** and won the women's doubles both years with his sister as partner. She also entered the singles competition in 2008 and reached the quarterfinal round. She played on the United States **Fed Cup** team in 1999, 2003, and 2007. In four **ties**, she has an undefeated record of 4–0 in singles and 3–0 in doubles (with sister Venus as partner). She was a member of the Fed Cup championship team in 1999. She won the **Hopman Cup** in 2003 with partner **James Blake** and again in 2008 with partner Mardy Fish. Serena and Venus became minority owners of the Miami Dolphins National Football League team in 2009. Serena has also donated much time and effort to charities and has helped to build a school in Kenya. On 7 July 2010, Serena stepped on broken glass in a restaurant cutting her foot and requiring 18 stitches. The cut later required surgery. On 28 February 2011, she was rushed to a hospital for treatment of a pulmonary embolism.

WILLIAMS, VENUS EBONY STARR. B. 17 June 1980, Lynwood, California. Venus Williams was raised in Compton, California, until age 10, when her parents, Oracene Price and Richard Williams, moved the family to Florida so that Venus and her younger sister **Serena Williams** could attend tennis school there. After several years, their father removed the sisters from the school and became their full-time **coach**. Venus became a **professional** player in October 1994, at age 14. The sisters are the most accomplished **African American** tennis players of all time with a combined total of 48 **Grand Slam** victories and 13 Grand Slam runner-up finishes. Eight of those thirteen finals losses were to each other. In 1997, Venus entered the Grand Slam tournaments for the first time—losing in the second round at the **French Open** and first round at **Wimbledon**. The **United States Open** was a different story, and Venus, aged 17, reached the finals in her first appearance in that tournament. After being a semifinalist there in both 1998 and 1999, she won her first Grand Slam **singles** championship in 2000 at Wimbledon and then followed it up with the U.S. Open singles title. In 2001, she again won Wimbledon and the U.S. Open singles, defeating sister Serena in the final at **Flushing Meadows**. Venus repeated at Wimbledon in 2005, 2007, and 2008, again defeating sister Serena in the 2008 final. In her career, through May 2011, she has won a total of seven Grand Slam singles titles and was runner-up seven additional times. She has also won 10 Grand Slam women's **doubles** and two **mixed doubles**. She has reached the finals in 29 Grand Slam events, winning 21 and losing to sister Serena 6 times and other players only twice. Serena defeated Venus in the finals of the 2003 **Australian Open**; 2002 French Open; 2002, 2003, and 2009 Wimbledon; and 2002 U.S. Open. In 2002 and 2003, they met in four consecutive Grand Slam finals.

The sisters are also excellent doubles players and have won 12 Grand Slam women's doubles titles—the Australian Open in 2001, 2003, 2009, and 2010; the French Open in 1999 and 2010; Wimbledon in 2000, 2002, 2008, and 2009; and the U.S. Open in 1999 and 2009. They have never lost a Grand Slam women's doubles final. Venus has also won mixed doubles titles in 1998 at the Australian Open and French Open with **Justin Gimelstob** and lost in the finals at Wimbledon in 2006 with **Bob Bryan**. Venus, at six feet one inch, is one of the tallest players on the women's tour and has the most powerful **serve** and **ground strokes**. Her serve has been measured at a record 130 miles per hour. She entered both singles and doubles in three **Olympic Games**—from 2000 to 2008. She won the singles in 2000, reached the third round in 2004, and reached the quarterfinal round in 2008. In the doubles event, she won the gold medal in 2000 and 2008 with her sister, Serena, as partner. In 2004, Serena was injured and did not compete in the Olympic Games, and with partner Chanda Rubin, Venus lost in the first round of the doubles event. Venus's three Olympic tennis gold medals are more than any other female in history, and only **Arantxa Sánchez Vicario**, with four, has won more total Olympic tennis medals. Venus played for the **United States** in the **Fed Cup** of 1999, 2003 to 2005, and 2007. In eight **ties** over five years, her record was 14–2 in singles and 3–2 in doubles. She was a member of the Fed Cup championship team in 1999. Venus is a fashion designer who has her own fashion line and who often designs her own tennis outfits. In 2007, she was a cum laude graduate of the Art Institute of Fort Lauderdale with a degree in fashion design.

WILLS MOODY ROARK, HELEN NEWINGTON "LITTLE MISS POKER FACE." B. 6 October 1905, Centerville, California. D. 1 January 1998, Carmel, California. Helen Wills was one of the dominant figures in women's tennis during the 1920s and 1930s. She was a graduate of the Head-Royce School, a private school in Oakland, California, and a 1925 Phi Beta Kappa graduate of the University of California, Berkeley, with a degree in fine arts. Some of her records border on the unbelievable. She had a **match** record of 398–35, won 158 consecutive matches, did not lose a **set** in **singles** from 1927 to 1932, was a finalist in every one of the 22 Grand Slam singles events she played in (excluding defaults at **Wimbledon** and the **French Nationals** in 1926 due to an emergency appendectomy), and had a **Grand Slam** match record of 126–3. Ironically, **Suzanne Lenglen**, who also won nearly every match she played, was a contemporary of Helen, but the two only played once, in 1926, when the 27-year-old Lenglen, then at the top of her game, defeated the up-and-coming 20-year-old Wills, 6–3, 8–6. In her career, from 1919 to 1938, Wills reached the finals of 39 Grand Slam events, winning 31 of them. She is tied with **Chris Evert** for eighth place in total Grand Slam finals and seventh for most Grand Slams won. Helen won the French Nationals in 1928, 1929, 1930, and 1932; Wimbledon in 1927 to 1930, 1932 to 1935, and 1938; and the **United States Nationals** in 1923 to 1925 and 1927 to 1931. Her three Grand Slam losses were to **Kitty McKane** in three sets at Wimbledon in 1924, **Molla Mallory** in straight sets at the 1922 U.S. Nationals, and **Helen Jacobs** in that tournament in 1933, when she retired in the third set due to back pain. She also did well in Grand Slam doubles events, winning the Wimbledon ladies' doubles in 1924 with **Hazel Hotchkiss Wightman** and in 1927 and 1930 with **Elizabeth "Bunny" Ryan**. Wills also won the Wimbledon **mixed doubles** in 1929 with Frank Hunter. At **Roland Garros**, she and Ryan won in 1930 and 1932, and Wills and Hunter were mixed doubles runners-up in 1928 and 1929. Wills and Sidney Wood were also runners-up there in 1932. She won four United States National women's doubles titles (1922 with Marion Zinderstein Jessup, 1924 and 1928 with Hazel Hotchkiss Wightman, and 1925 with **Mary K. Browne**) and was runner-up in 1933 with Ryan. She was also the U.S. National mixed doubles runner-up in 1922 with Howard Kinsey and champion in 1924 with **Vinnie Richards** and in 1928 with Jack Hawkes.

Due to her introverted personality and stoic demeanor on the **court**, she was given the nickname "Little Miss Poker Face" by sportswriter Grantland Rice. Her typical **tennis attire** was a white sailor suit, pleated knee-length skirt, white stockings, white shoes, and a white visor. She won both the women's singles and women's doubles events in the 1924 **Olympic Games**—the latter with partner Hazel Hotchkiss Wightman. She married stockbroker Frederick Moody in December 1929 and was known as Helen Wills Moody until their divorce in 1937. In October 1939, she married Aidan Roark, a film writer and noted polo player. They divorced about 30 years later. She had no children. She played on the **United States Wightman Cup** team 10 years from 1923 to 1938. Her record for those matches was 18–2 in singles and 3–7 in doubles. She was elected to the **International Tennis Hall of Fame** in 1969. In retirement, she continued to play recreationally until she was 82, and was an avid painter with **exhibitions** in New York galleries. She also was the author of several books, including an instructional manual, autobiography, and mystery novel, and wrote articles for leading magazines. Upon her death, she bequeathed $10 million to the University of California, Berkeley, to establish a neuroscience institute.

WILSON EQUIPMENT. The Wilson Sporting Goods Company is one of the largest manufacturers of tennis equipment. Based in Chicago, Illinois, it was founded in 1913 as the Ashland Manufacturing Company and began by manufacturing products using animal by-products. It first made tennis **racket strings**, violin strings, and surgical sutures but soon expanded to the manufacture of tennis rackets and athletic uniforms. After World War II, Wilson signed **Jack Kramer** and began producing Jack Kramer-model tennis rackets. By 1979, Wilson **tennis balls** became the official ball of the **United States Open**. Wilson also is one of the leading manufacturers for baseball, football, golf, and volleyball equipment.

WIMBLEDON. Wimbledon is both a place and the popular name for the most important **tournament** in **lawn tennis**. It is a district of South London in England and has a current population of slightly less than 50,000 inhabitants. Located in Wimbledon are the grounds of the **All-England Lawn Tennis and Croquet Club**, the administrators of the annual tournament called simply the Championships. The first tournament was held in 1877 and was limited to gentlemen's **singles**. It drew 22 entrants, and Spencer Gore was the first champion. In 1884, ladies' singles and gentlemen's **doubles** championships were added. In 1913, ladies' doubles and **mixed doubles** were added. In 1968, the Championships were made an **Open** tournament and **professionals** as well as **amateurs** were allowed to enter. The Championships are presently held annually during two weeks at the end of June and beginning of July with 128 men and 128 women entered in the tournament's **main draw** for singles competition. The tournament is one of the highlights of the social scene, and royalty usually is invited to present the winners' trophies. Among tennis professionals, Wimbledon is considered to be the most prestigious tournament and is the only major still contested on **grass surfaces**. *See also* APPENDIX B (for a list of champions).

WINGFIELD, WALTER CLOPTON. B. 16 October 1833, Ruabon Vicarage, Wales. D. 18 April 1912, London, England. Major Walter Wingfield was educated at Rossall School in Lancashire, England, and was a member of the Royal Guard and a captain in the 1st Dragoon Guards. In 1874, he patented a new game to be played outdoors on lawns to which he gave the Greek name *sphairistike*. He packaged the equipment for the game and sold more than 1,000 sets in 1874 and 1875. The game caught on among the upper class, although its name was quickly changed to **lawn tennis**. He also published two books on the new game, *The Book of the Game* and *The Major's Game of Lawn Tennis*. He probably is not the inventor of the game since it had been played for about a decade previously. Major Thomas Henry "Harry" Gem and Augurio Perera are generally credited as the inventors of **lawn tennis**, but Wingfield is usually acknowledged for the development of interest in the game. For his contributions to the sport, he was inducted into the **International Tennis Hall of Fame** in 1997.

WINNER. A "winner" in tennis terminology is a shot that cannot be returned successfully by the opponent and wins the **point**. An **ace** is a **serve** that is untouched by the opponent. A **service** winner is a serve that is reached by the opponent but not returned successfully. *See also* UNFORCED ERROR.

WOMEN'S TENNIS ASSOCIATION (WTA). The Women's Tennis Association was formed in 1973 and is the organization that controls women's **professional** tennis. Based in St. Petersburg, Florida, with international offices in London and Beijing, it coordinates **tournaments** and provides a system for **ranking** players based on points earned within the tournaments. Points earned range from one for winning a tournament **qualifying** round to 2,000 for winning one of the four major **Grand Slam** tournaments. Since

2005, its annual series of tournaments has been sponsored and, in 2010, is known as the Sony Ericsson WTA Tour.

WOODBRIDGE, TODD ANDREW. *See* WOODIES, THE.

WOODFORDE, MARK RAYMOND. *See* WOODIES, THE.

WOODIES, THE. The **Australian doubles** team of Todd Andrew Woodbridge, born 2 April 1971 in Sydney, and Mark Raymond Woodforde, born 23 September 1965 in Adelaide, were one of the best doubles teams from 1990 to 2000. In their careers, they won 11 **Grand Slam** doubles as a team, including five consecutive years at **Wimbledon** from 1993 to 1997, and 61 total **Association of Tennis Professionals** doubles titles. They each won doubles and **mixed doubles** in all four of the Slam tournaments. The six-foot two-inch **left-handed** Woodforde began his **professional** tennis career in 1984 and played through 2000. He won 17 Grand Slam doubles and mixed doubles titles and was runner-up six times. In addition to the 11 doubles titles with Woodbridge, he also won in 1989 with **John McEnroe** as partner and five mixed doubles with partners Nicole Provis (twice), **Larisa Savchenko** (twice), and **Martina Navratilova**.

The right-handed Woodbridge, five and one-half years younger and four inches shorter, played from 1988 through 2005. He won 22 Grand Slam doubles and mixed doubles titles and was runner-up 12 times. He won five doubles with **Jonas Björkman** as partner after Woodforde had retired and six mixed doubles with partners Rennae Stubbs, Elizabeth Smylie, **Helena Suková** (twice), and **Arantxa Sánchez Vicario** (twice). Todd Woodbridge entered four **Olympic** tennis tournaments from 1992 to 2004—both **singles** and doubles in 1992 and 1996 and doubles only in 2000 and 2004. In 1996, he and partner Mark Woodforde won the doubles gold medal, and in 2000, they won the silver medal. Those were Woodforde's only two Olympic appearances. In **Davis Cup** play, Woodforde played for Australia from 1988 to 1989 and 1993 to 2000 and had a record of 4–10 in singles and 17–5 in doubles in 24 **ties** in 10 years. Woodbridge played on the Australian Davis Cup team from 1991 to 1999 and 2001 to 2005. His record in 32 ties was 5–4 in singles and 25–7 in doubles. As a team, the Woodies helped Australia win the Cup in 1999. Woodbridge, with Wayne Arthurs as doubles partner, was also on the 2003 Cup-winning team. After retiring as an active player, Woodforde was named **coach** of the Australian **Fed Cup** team in 2003. In 2009, Woodbridge was named coach of the Australian Davis Cup team. The pair was elected to both the Australian Tennis Hall of Fame and the **International Tennis Hall of Fame** in 2010.

WOOSNAM, MAXWELL "MAX." B. 6 September 1892, Liverpool, England. D. 14 July 1965 Westminster, England. Max Woosnam, the son of a clergyman, was one of England's greatest all-around athletes, although in the words of his biographer, Mick Collins, "Woosnam's name has been largely forgotten today, his modesty when alive helping to ensure his anonymity when dead." He was raised in Aberhafesp, Wales. At Winchester College, he starred in **lawn tennis, court tennis, racquets**, football (soccer), golf, and cricket. He competed in both the 1920 and 1924 **Olympic Games** and won the 1920 men's **doubles** event with partner Noel Turnbull and was the silver medalist in the 1920 **mixed doubles** with partner **Kathleen "Kitty" McKane**. At school in Winchester, he was team captain in both cricket and golf and played on the racquets and soccer teams as well. After graduation from Winchester, he enrolled in 1912 at Trinity College at Cambridge University, where he played soccer, golf, lawn tennis, real tennis, and cricket. In 1914, as a member of the Corinthians Football Club, he went on a tour of South America, but as soon as they arrived in Rio de Janeiro, Brazil, they learned that war had broken out in Europe, and they immediately returned home. The entire team joined the military service, and Woosnam became a member of Montgomeryshire Yeomanry and later was a member of the Royal Welch Fusiliers. During World War I, he served at Gallipoli. After the war, he returned to Cambridge and continued his sporting activities.

He was selected as a member of the British soccer team for the 1920 Olympic Games but withdrew to concentrate on lawn tennis. In 1921, with partner Randolph Lycett, he won the **Wimbledon** men's doubles championship. He and partner Phyllis Howkins finished second at Wimbledon that year to Lycett and partner **Elizabeth "Bunny" Ryan** in the mixed doubles championship. In Davis Cup competition in 1921 and 1924, he had a record of 4–4 (1–1 in singles and 3–3 in doubles) in six **ties**. As a center-half for the Manchester soccer team, he played in 89 matches from 1919 to 1925, leading the team to the runner-up position in the First Division in 1920 and 1921. In 1919, after graduation from Cambridge, he became a member of the staff of Imperial Chemical Industries in Manchester and remained with that company until his retirement in 1954.

WORLD CHAMPIONSHIP TENNIS (WCT). World Championship Tennis was an organization that was the predecessor of the **Association of Tennis Professionals**. It organized and coordinated a series of tennis **tournaments** for male **professionals** from 1968 to 1990. It was founded by Lamar Hunt and David Dixon. Players were ranked based on their performance in WCT events, and a season-ending WCT Finals tournament was held. A rival organization, the Grand Prix circuit, existed from 1970 to 1978. The WCT merged with the Grand Prix circuit in 1978, but the WCT withdrew from 1982 to 1984, while suing the Men's Tennis Council, the organizers of the Grand Prix circuit. The suit was settled in 1985, and the WCT once again was incorporated into the Grand Prix circuit.

WORLD GROUP. *See* DAVIS CUP; FEDERATION CUP.

WORLD TEAM CUP. The World Team Cup is an annual international men's team tennis **tournament** contested on **clay courts** in Düsseldorf, Germany. It began in 1978 and was played each year through 2010. In the first 24 years of the tournament, through 2011, **Germany** has won it five times and the **United States**, **Argentina**, **Spain**, and **Sweden** have each won the event four times. The eight nations whose top two men's players have the highest year-end **Association of Tennis Professionals rankings** are selected for the event. The eight nations are divided into two groups of four, and each team within the group plays the other three teams once. The leading teams of the two groups then play for the championship. Each **tie** consists of two singles and one doubles match.

WORLD TEAM TENNIS (WTT). World Team Tennis was created in 1973 by Larry King, Dennis Murphy, Fred Barman, and Jordan Kaiser. The league built upon a concept created by **Billie Jean** and Larry **King**. It is a unique format with several innovations to promote fan interest. Teams of two men and two women (with substitutes) play contests that consist of five one-**set matches**—one each of men's and women's **singles** and **doubles** and **mixed doubles**. Sets are played to five **games**, and each game won counts in the overall scoring. The team winning the most games wins the contest. **No-ad** scoring is used, and fans are encouraged to cheer for their favorites—unlike traditional tennis that insists on silence for much of the match. A 16-team league began in 1974, playing a 44-game schedule in 16 cities throughout the United States. Because of the uniqueness of the league and the influence of Billie Jean King, most of the top **professionals** have played World Team Tennis at one time or another. The league flourished from 1974 to 1978, was suspended until 1981, and then resumed with a shorter schedule. It is currently played only in the month of July, following the **Wimbledon** tournament, with a 10-team league. The concept has been expanded to include recreational leagues as well as the professional one.

WYNNE BOLTON, NANCYE HAZEL MEREDITH. B. 10 June 1916, Melbourne, Victoria, **Australia**. D. 9 November 2001, Melbourne, Victoria, Australia. At 5 feet 11 inches, Nancye Wynne Bolton was exceptionally tall for a woman in her generation. In 1933, she won her first tennis title—the Victorian Schoolgirls Championship. In 1936, she joined the St. Kilda Tennis Club and began competing in more important events. She had her greatest success in her homeland of Australia. Only **Margaret Smith Court**, with 23 total Australian titles, won more than Nancye's 20 **Australian Championships**—6 **singles**, 10 **doubles**, and 4 **mixed doubles** from 1937 to 1951. She was also twice runner-up in singles, twice in doubles, and once in mixed doubles. She was twice a mixed doubles finalist at **Wimbledon** and once at **Roland Garros** and was a singles finalist at **Forest Hills**. Had World War II not intervened and caused the major tournaments to be cancelled, she most likely would have won several more titles. She and partner **Thelma Coyne Long** won the Australian doubles each year from 1936 to 1940. The championships were not held in 1941 to 1945, and she and Long were runners-up in 1946; champions in 1947, 1948, and 1949; runners-up in 1950; and champions again in 1951 and 1952. In 1947 and 1948, she was ranked number four in the world.

She married Peter Bolton, an Air Force Sergeant who was killed in action in Cologne, Germany, in 1942, leaving Nancye with a four-month-old daughter. After retiring from tennis in 1952, she turned to golf and lawn bowls, and was club champion at the Kew Golf Club 17 times. She was inducted into the Australian Tennis Hall of Fame in 2000 and the **International Tennis Hall of Fame** in 2006. Her daughter, Pam Stockley, wrote a biography of her mother, entitled *Nancye Wynne Bolton: An Australian Tennis Champion*, published in 2009.

YUGOSLAVIA. In 1922, the Yugoslav Tennis Association (Teniski Savez Jugoslavije) was formed in Zagreb. In the 1924 **Olympic Games**, Yugoslavia had one entrant in the tennis competition, Aleksander Đurđenski, who lost his first round **singles** match. Among the best Yugoslavian male tennis players have been Željko Franulović, **Goran Ivanišević**, Boro Jovanović, Franjo Kukuljević, Dragutin Mitić, Sima Nikolić, Bruno Orešar, **Nikki Pilić**, and Slobodan Živojinović. The best female tennis players include Alice Florian, Sabrina Goleš, Mima Jaušovec, Hella Kovac, Renata Sasak, and **Monica Seles**. In **Federation Cup** competition, from 1969 to 2003, Yugoslavia competed 28 years and played 87 **ties** with a record of 44–43 and was a quarterfinalist in 1970, 1983, and 1984.

From 1927 through 2003, Yugoslavia competed in 69 **Davis Cup** tournaments with a record of 85–67 in 152 ties. The country competed nine times in the World Group since its formation in 1981 and reached the semifinals in 1988, 1989, and 1991. Top Davis Cup players have been Boro Jovanović, Dragutin Mitic, Josip Palada, Nikki Pilić, and Franjo Punčec. In 1984, Goleš won the women's singles in the Olympic demonstration tennis event in Los Angeles. The men's doubles team of Živojinović and Ivanišević reached the quarterfinals of the 1988 Olympic tournament. In 1992, Yugoslavia was broken up into several independent countries. One of these new nations, known as the Federal Republic of Yugoslavia, consisted mainly of the former republics of Serbia and Montenegro and competed as Yugoslavia until 2003. In the 1992 Olympic Games, former Yugoslavian athletes from **Serbia**, such as Srđan Muškatirović, competed as independent Olympic participants while those from **Croatia** and Slovenia competed for their new countries. From 2003 to 2006, Yugoslavia competed as Serbia and Montenegro and since 2007 as just Serbia.

Z

ŽEMLA, LADISLAV "RAZNY." B. 6 November 1887, Kladruby, Bohemia. D. 18 June 1955, Prague, **Czechoslovakia**. Ladislav Žemla was a member of the Ceska **Lawn Tennis** Club in Prague and is one of only four people to compete in tennis in five different **Olympic Games**. From 1906 to 1924, he entered 10 Olympic events—as a representative of Bohemia from 1906 to 1912 and the new republic of Czechoslovakia in 1920 and 1924. He won the bronze medal in men's **doubles** in 1906 with his brother Zdeněk as partner, finished fourth in both men's **singles** and doubles in 1912, and won the bronze medal in **mixed doubles** in 1920 with Milada Skrbkova, whom he later married. Razny's overall Olympic tennis record in 29 matches was 16 victories (including 3 **walkovers**), 12 losses, and 1 **bye**. He played **Davis Cup** tennis for Czechoslovakia in 1921 and 1923 to 1927. His record in 12 **ties** was 6–5 in singles and 7–5 in doubles during those six years.

ZVEREVA, NATALIA "NATASHA." B. 16 April 1971, Minsk, Byelorussian Soviet Socialist Republic, Union of Soviet Socialist Republics (now Belarus). The five-foot eight-inch, right-handed Natalia Zvereva won the **Wimbledon girls' singles** championship in 1986 and the **United States Open** girls' title in 1987. She became a **professional** tennis player in 1988 and reached the final of the **French Open** singles that year, where she was defeated by **Steffi Graf**, 6–0, 6–0, in just 32 minutes. By May 1989, Zvereva had attained a ranking of number five in singles. Her best singles performances in the other **Grand Slam** events were the quarterfinals of the United States Open in 1993, quarterfinals of the **Australian Open** in 1995, and the semifinals at Wimbledon in 1998. Zvereva won only four **World Tennis Association (WTA)** singles titles and was best known for her **doubles** play, with 20 Slam doubles championships and 80 other WTA doubles titles. In 1991, she reached a world ranking of number-one doubles player. She won the French Open Doubles Championship six times (including four consecutive from 1992 to 1995), Wimbledon doubles championship five times (1991–94 and 1997), the United States Open doubles title four times, and the Australian Open doubles title three times. She also won the Australian Open mixed doubles title twice. Her Slam championship partners were **Beatrix "Gigi" Fernández**, **Martina Hingis**, Jim Pugh, and Rick Leach in Australia; **Larisa Savchenko** and Fernández in France; **Pam Shriver** at Wimbledon; and Fernández in the United States. In addition to her 20 Slam titles, she was also runner-up 16 times. In each year from 1992 to 1994 and in 1997, she won three of the four Slam doubles titles.

Natasha competed in four **Olympic Games** tennis tournaments from 1988 to 2000, won the doubles bronze medal in 1992 with partner Leila Meshki, and finished fourth in 2000 with partner Olga Barabanschikova. Zvereva played in the **Federation Cup** for the Soviet Union from 1986 to 1991 and for Belarus from 1994 to 1999 and 2002. Her record in Fed Cup play is 35–16 in singles and 24–5 in doubles in 54 **ties** over 13 years. In 1988 and 1990, she played in the finals for the runner-up team. She retired from active competition in 2002, with career won-lost records of 434–252 in singles and 714–170 in doubles. She was the nonplaying captain of the Belarus Fed Cup team in 2009. In 2010, she was elected to the **International Tennis Hall of Fame** along with her doubles partner Gigi Fernández.

Appendix A:
International Tennis Hall of Fame Inductees

Table 1. International Tennis Hall of Fame Inductees

Year	Inducted Players
2011	Andre Agassi
1961	Fred Alexander
1963	Wilmer Allison
1977	Manuel Alonso
2000	Malcolm Anderson
1985	Arthur Ashe
1974	Juliette Paxton Atkinson
1997	Henry "Bunny" Austin
1992	Tracy Austin
1958	Maud Barger-Wallach
2003	Boris Becker
1969	Karl Behr
1965	Pauline Betz Addie
2006	Nancye Wynne Bolton
1987	Björn Borg
1976	Jean Borotra
1984	John Bromwich
1977	Norman Brookes
1967	A. Louise Brough (Clapp)
1957	Mary Kendall Browne
1976	Jacques "Toto" Brugnon
1964	J. Donald Budge
1978	Maria Bueno
1976	Mabel Esmonde Cahill
1955	Oliver Campbell
1996	Rosemary Casals
1961	Malcolm Chace
2008	Michael Chang
2004	Dorothy Bundy Cheney
1983	Clarence Clark
1955	Joseph Clark
1956	William Clothier
1976	Henri Cochet
1968	Maureen Connolly Brinker
1998	Jimmy Connors
1991	Ashley Cooper
2005	Jim Courier
1979	Margaret Smith Court

Year	Inducted Players
1979	Jack Crawford
2010	Owen Davidson
2007	Sven Davidson
1957	Dwight Davis
1983	Charlotte "Lottie" Dod
1962	John Doeg
1980	Laurence Doherty
1980	Reginald Doherty
1981	Dorothea Douglass Lambert Chambers
1983	Jaroslav Drobný
1967	Margaret Osborne duPont
2003	Françoise Durr
1955	James Dwight
2004	Stefan Edberg
1982	Roy Emerson
1978	Pierre Etchebaster
1995	Christine Evert
1974	Robert Falkenburg
2006	Marion Jones Farquhar
2010	Beatriz "Gigi" Fernández
1984	Neale Fraser
1970	Shirley Fry-Irvin
1969	Charles Garland
1971	Althea Gibson
2009	Andrés Gimeno
1968	Richardo "Pancho" González
1988	Evonne Goolagong Cawley
2006	Arthur Gore
2004	Steffi Graf
1972	Bryan "Bitsy" Grant
1961	Harold Hackett
1965	Ellen Hansell Allderdice
1973	Darlene Hard
1969	Doris Hart
1985	Ann Haydon-Jones
1992	Bob Hewitt
1980	Lew Hoad
1978	Harry Hopman
1957	Hazel Hotchkiss Wightman
1974	Frederick Hovey
1966	Joe Hunt
1961	Frank Hunter
1962	Helen Hull Jacobs
1958	William Johnston
1987	Billie Jean Moffitt King
1990	Jan Kodeš
2006	Karel Koželuh
1968	Jack Kramer

Year	Inducted Players
1976	Jean Lacoste
1956	William Larned
1969	Arthur Larsen
1981	Rod Laver
2006	Herbert Lawford
2001	Ivan Lendl
1978	Suzanne Lenglen
1964	George Lott
1973	Gene Mako
1958	Molla Bjurstedt Mallory
1994	Hana Mandlíková
1964	Alice Marble
2006	Simone Mathieu
1999	John McEnroe
1999	Ken McGregor
1978	Kathleen McKane Godfree
1986	Chuck McKinley
1957	Maurice McLoughlin
1992	Frew McMillan
1965	Don McNeill
1971	Elisabeth Moore
1993	F Angela Mortimer Barrett
1972	Gardnar Mulloy
1958	R. Lindley Murray
1991	Ilie Năstase
2000	Martina Navratilova
1986	John Newcombe
2005	Yannick Noah
2005	Jana Novotná
2006	Hans Nüsslein
1977	Betty Nuthall Shoemaker
1987	Alex Olmedo
1979	Rafael Osuna
1963	Sarah Palfrey Fabyan Cooke Danzig
1966	Frank Parker
1989	Gerald Patterson
1977	John "Budge" Patty
1966	Theodore Pell
1975	Frederick Perry
1982	Thomas Pettitt
1986	Nicola Pietrangeli
1984	Adrian Quist
2006	Patrick Rafter
1987	R. Dennis Ralston
1983	J. Ernest Renshaw
1983	William Renshaw
1961	Vincent Richards
2003	Nancy Richey

Year	Inducted Players
1967	Bobby Riggs
1986	Tony Roche
1975	Ellen Roosevelt
2001	Mervyn Rose
1980	Ken Rosewall
1986	Dorothy Round Little
1972	Elizabeth "Bunny" Ryan
2006	Gabriela Sabatini
2007	Pete Sampras
2007	Arantxa Sánchez Vicario
1984	Manuel Santana
1976	Dick Savitt
1966	Frederick "Ted" Schroeder
1968	Eleonora Sears
1955	Richard Sears
1979	Frank Sedgman
1984	Francisco "Pancho" Segura
1971	E. Victor Seixas
2009	Monica Seles
1964	Frank Shields
2002	Pam Shriver
1955	Henry Slocum
1987	Stan Smith
1985	Fred Stolle
1956	May Sutton Bundy
1967	Bill Talbert
1959	Bill Tilden
1974	Bertha Townsend Toulmin
1970	Tony Trabert
1997	Lesley Turner Bowrey
1963	John Van Ryn
1991	Guillermo Vilas
1962	H. Ellsworth Vines
1977	Gottfried von Cramm
1989	S. Virginia Wade
1969	Marie Wagner
1956	Holcombe Ward
1965	Watson Washburn
1955	Malcolm Whitman
2002	Mats Wilander
1978	Anthony Wilding
1957	Richard Norris Williams
1959	Helen Wills Moody Roark
1964	Sidney Wood
2010	Todd Woodbridge
2010	Mark Woodforde
1955	Robert Wrenn
1956	Beals Wright
2010	Natalia Zvereva

Year	Inducted Players
Contributors	
2007	Russ Adams
1964	George Adee
1975	Lawrence Baker
2005	Earl "Butch" Buchholz, Jr.
1992	Philippe Chatrier
2006	Gianni Clerici
1994	Arthur "Bud" Collins
1990	Joseph Cullman, III
1968	Allison Danzig
1998	Herman David
2009	Donald Dell
1985	David Gray
1970	Clarence "Peck" Griffin
1980	King Gustav V of Sweden
2010	Derek Hardwick
1979	Gladys Medalie Heldman
1981	William "Slew" Hester
1993	Lamar Hunt
2009	Robert Johnson
1970	Perry Jones
2000	Robert Kelleher
2011	Fern Lee "Peachy" Kellmeyer
1979	Albert Laney
1974	Alastair Martin
1982	William Martin
1996	Dan Maskell
2008	Mark McCormack
1963	Julian Myrick
1971	Arthur Nielsen
1981	Mary Ewing Outerbridge
2010	Brad Parks
2008	Eugene Scott
1982	Lance Tingay
1986	Cuthbert "Teddy" Tinling
2003	Brian Tobin
1965	James Van Alen
1997	Walter Wingfield

Appendix B: Wimbledon Champions

Table 2. Singles

Year	Gentlemen	Ladies
1877	Spencer Gore, GBR	not held
1878	Frank Hadow, GBR	not held
1879	John Hartley, GBR	not held
1880	John Hartley, GBR	not held
1881	William Renshaw, GBR	not held
1882	William Renshaw, GBR	not held
1883	William Renshaw, GBR	not held
1884	William Renshaw, GBR	Maud Watson, GBR
1885	William Renshaw, GBR	Maud Watson, GBR
1886	William Renshaw, GBR	Blanche Bingley, GBR
1887	Herbert Lawford, GBR	Charlotte Dod, GBR
1888	Ernest Renshaw, GBR	Charlotte Dod, GBR
1889	William Renshaw, GBR	Blanche Bingley Hillyard, GBR
1890	Willoughby Hamilton, GBR	Helena Rice, GBR
1891	Wilfred Baddeley, GBR	Charlotte Dod, GBR
1892	Wilfred Baddeley, GBR	Charlotte Dod, GBR
1893	Joshua Pim, IRL	Charlotte Dod, GBR
1894	Joshua Pim, IRL	Blanche Bingley Hillyard, GBR
1895	Wilfred Baddeley, GBR	Charlotte Cooper, GBR
1896	Harold Mahony, GBR	Charlotte Cooper, GBR
1897	Reginald Doherty, GBR	Blanche Bingley Hillyard, GBR
1898	Reginald Doherty, GBR	Charlotte Cooper, GBR
1899	Reginald Doherty, GBR	Blanche Bingley Hillyard, GBR
1900	Reginald Doherty, GBR	Blanche Bingley Hillyard, GBR
1901	Arthur Gore, GBR	Charlotte Cooper Storry, GBR
1902	Lawrence Doherty, GBR	Muriel Robb, GBR
1903	Lawrence Doherty, GBR	Dorothea Douglass, GBR
1904	Lawrence Doherty, GBR	Dorothea Douglass, GBR
1905	Lawrence Doherty, GBR	May Sutton, USA
1906	Lawrence Doherty, GBR	Dorothea Douglass, GBR
1907	Norman Brookes, AUS	May Sutton, USA
1908	Arthur Gore, GBR	Charlotte Cooper Storry, GBR
1909	Arthur Gore, GBR	Dora Boothby, GBR
1910	Anthony Wilding, NZL	Dorothea Douglass Chambers, GBR
1911	Anthony Wilding, NZL	Dorothea Douglass Chambers, GBR
1912	Anthony Wilding, NZL	Ethel Thomson Larcombe, GBR
1913	Anthony Wilding, NZL	Dorothea Douglass Chambers, GBR

Year	Gentlemen	Ladies
1914	Norman Brookes, AUS	Dorothea Douglass Chambers, GBR
1915–18	not held	not held
1919	Gerald Patterson, AUS	Suzanne Lenglen, FRA
1920	Bill Tilden, USA	Suzanne Lenglen, FRA
1921	Bill Tilden, USA	Suzanne Lenglen, FRA
1922	Gerald Patterson, AUS	Suzanne Lenglen, FRA
1923	Bill Johnston, USA	Suzanne Lenglen, FRA
1924	Jean Borotra, FRA	Kitty McKane, GBR
1925	René Lacoste, FRA	Suzanne Lenglen, FRA
1926	Jean Borotra, FRA	Kitty McKane Godfree, GBR
1927	Henri Cochet, FRA	Helen Wills, USA
1928	René Lacoste, FRA	Helen Wills, USA
1929	Henri Cochet, FRA	Helen Wills, USA
1930	Bill Tilden, USA	Helen Wills Moody, USA
1931	Sidney Wood, USA	Cilly Aussem, GER
1932	Ellsworth Vines, USA	Helen Wills Moody, USA
1933	Jack Crawford, AUS	Helen Wills Moody, USA
1934	Fred Perry, GBR	Dorothy Round, GBR
1935	Fred Perry, GBR	Helen Wills Moody, USA
1936	Fred Perry, GBR	Helen Jacobs, USA
1937	Don Budge, USA	Dorothy Round, GBR
1938	Don Budge, USA	Helen Wills Moody, USA
1939	Bobby Riggs, USA	Alice Marble, USA
1940–45	not held	not held
1946	Yvon Petra, FRA	Pauline Betz, USA
1947	Jack Kramer, USA	Margaret Osborne, USA
1948	Bob Falkenburg, USA	Louise Brough, USA
1949	Ted Schroeder, USA	Louise Brough, USA
1950	Budge Patty, USA	Louise Brough, USA
1951	Dick Savitt, USA	Doris Hart, USA
1952	Frank Sedgman, AUS	Maureen Connolly, USA
1953	Vic Seixas, USA	Maureen Connolly, USA
1954	Jaroslav Drobný, EGY	Maureen Connolly, USA
1955	Tony Trabert, USA	Louise Brough, USA
1956	Lew Hoad, AUS	Shirley Fry, USA
1957	Lew Hoad, AUS	Althea Gibson, USA
1958	Ashley Cooper, AUS	Althea Gibson, USA
1959	Alex Olmedo, USA	Maria Bueno, BRA
1960	Neale Fraser, AUS	Maria Bueno, BRA
1961	Rod Laver, AUS	Angela Mortimer, GBR
1962	Rod Laver, AUS	Karen Hantze Susman, USA
1963	Chuck McKinley, USA	Margaret Smith, AUS
1964	Roy Emerson, AUS	Maria Bueno, BRA
1965	Roy Emerson, AUS	Margaret Smith, AUS
1966	Manuel Santana, ESP	Billie Jean King, USA
1967	John Newcombe, AUS	Billie Jean King, USA
1968	Rod Laver, AUS	Billie Jean King, USA
1969	Rod Laver, AUS	Ann Haydon-Jones, GBR
1970	John Newcombe, AUS	Margaret Smith Court, AUS

Year	Gentlemen	Ladies
1971	John Newcombe, AUS	Evonne Goolagong, AUS
1972	Stan Smith, USA	Billie Jean King, USA
1973	Jan Kodeš, TCH	Billie Jean King, USA
1974	Jimmy Connors, USA	Chris Evert, USA
1975	Arthur Ashe, USA	Billie Jean King, USA
1976	Björn Borg, SWE	Chris Evert, USA
1977	Björn Borg, SWE	Virginia Wade, GBR
1978	Björn Borg, SWE	Martina Navratilova, USA
1979	Björn Borg, SWE	Martina Navratilova, USA
1980	Björn Borg, SWE	Evonne Goolagong Cawley, AUS
1981	John McEnroe, USA	Chris Evert Lloyd, USA
1982	Jimmy Connors, USA	Martina Navratilova, USA
1983	John McEnroe, USA	Martina Navratilova, USA
1984	John McEnroe, USA	Martina Navratilova, USA
1985	Boris Becker, FRG	Martina Navratilova, USA
1986	Boris Becker, FRG	Martina Navratilova, USA
1987	Pat Cash, AUS	Martina Navratilova, USA
1988	Stefan Edberg, SWE	Steffi Graf, FRG
1989	Boris Becker, FRG	Steffi Graf, FRG
1990	Stefan Edberg, SWE	Martina Navratilova, USA
1991	Michael Stich, GER	Steffi Graf, GER
1992	Andre Agassi, USA	Steffi Graf, GER
1993	Pete Sampras, USA	Steffi Graf, GER
1994	Pete Sampras, USA	Conchita Martínez, ESP
1995	Pete Sampras, USA	Steffi Graf, GER
1996	Richard Krajicek, NED	Steffi Graf, GER
1997	Pete Sampras, USA	Martina Hingis, SUI
1998	Pete Sampras, USA	Jana Novotná, CZE
1999	Pete Sampras, USA	Lindsay Davenport, USA
2000	Pete Sampras, USA	Venus Williams, USA
2001	Goran Ivanišević, CRO	Venus Williams, USA
2002	Lleyton Hewitt, AUS	Serena Williams, USA
2003	Roger Federer, SUI	Serena Williams, USA
2004	Roger Federer, SUI	Maria Sharapova, RUS
2005	Roger Federer, SUI	Venus Williams, USA
2006	Roger Federer, SUI	Amélie Mauresmo, FRA
2007	Roger Federer, SUI	Venus Williams, USA
2008	Rafael Nadal, ESP	Venus Williams, USA
2009	Roger Federer, SUI	Serena Williams, USA
2010	Rafael Nadal, ESP	Serena Williams, USA
2011	Novak Djoković, SRB	Petra Kvitová, TCH

Table 3. Doubles

Year	Gentlemen	Ladies
1884	William Renshaw, GBR Ernest Renshaw, GBR	not held
1885	William Renshaw, GBR Ernest Renshaw, GBR	not held
1886	William Renshaw, GBR Ernest Renshaw, GBR	not held
1887	Herbert Wilberforce, GBR Patrick Bowes-Lyon, GBR	not held
1888	William Renshaw, GBR Ernest Renshaw, GBR	not held
1889	William Renshaw, GBR Ernest Renshaw, GBR	not held
1890	Joshua Pim, IRL Frank Stoker, IRL	not held
1891	Wilfred Baddeley, GBR Herbert Baddeley, GBR	not held
1892	Harry Barlow, GBR Ernest Lewis, GBR	not held
1893	Joshua Pim, IRL Frank Stoker, IRL	not held
1894	Wilfred Baddeley, GBR Herbert Baddeley, GBR	not held
1895	Wilfred Baddeley, GBR Herbert Baddeley, GBR	not held
1896	Wilfred Baddeley, GBR Herbert Baddeley, GBR	not held
1897	Lawrence Doherty, GBR Reginald Doherty, GBR	not held
1898	Lawrence Doherty, GBR Reginald Doherty, GBR	not held
1899	Lawrence Doherty, GBR Reginald Doherty, GBR	not held
1900	Lawrence Doherty, GBR Reginald Doherty, GBR	not held
1901	Lawrence Doherty, GBR Reginald Doherty, GBR	not held
1902	Frank Riseley, GBR Sydney Smith, GBR	not held
1903	Lawrence Doherty, GBR Reginald Doherty, GBR	not held
1904	Lawrence Doherty, GBR Reginald Doherty, GBR	not held
1905	Lawrence Doherty, GBR Reginald Doherty, GBR	not held
1906	Frank Riseley, GBR Sydney Smith, GBR	not held
1907	Norman Brookes, AUS Tony Wilding, NZL	not held

Year	Gentlemen	Ladies
1908	Josiah Ritchie, GBR Tony Wilding, NZL	not held
1909	Arthur Gore, GBR Herbert Roper Barrett, GBR	not held
1910	Josiah Ritchie, GBR Tony Wilding, NZL	not held
1911	Max Decugis, FRA Andre Gobert, FRA	not held
1912	Herbert Roper Barrett, GBR Charles Dixon, GBR	not held
1913	Herbert Roper Barrett, GBR Charles Dixon, GBR	Winifred Slocock McNair, GBR Dora Boothby, GBR
1914	Norman Brookes, AUS Tony Wilding, NZL	Agnes Morton, GBR Elizabeth Ryan, GBR
1915–18	not held	not held
1919	Ronald Thomas, AUS Pat O'Hare Wood, AUS	Suzanne Lenglen, FRA Elizabeth Ryan, USA
1920	Chuck Garland, USA R. Norris Williams, USA	Suzanne Lenglen, FRA Elizabeth Ryan, USA
1921	Randolph Lycett, GBR Max Woosnam, GBR	Suzanne Lenglen, FRA Elizabeth Ryan, USA
1922	James Anderson, GBR Randolph Lycett, GBR	Suzanne Lenglen, FRA Elizabeth Ryan, USA
1923	Randolph Lycett, GBR Leslie Godfree, GBR	Suzanne Lenglen, FRA Elizabeth Ryan, USA
1924	Francis Hunter, USA Vincent Richards, USA	Hazel Hotchkiss Wightman, USA Helen Wills, USA
1925	Jean Borotra, FRA René Lacoste, FRA	Suzanne Lenglen, FRA Elizabeth Ryan, USA
1926	Jacques Brugnon, FRA Henri Cochet, FRA	Mary K. Browne, USA Elizabeth Ryan, USA
1927	Francis Hunter, USA Bill Tilden, USA	Helen Wills, USA Elizabeth Ryan, USA
1928	Jacques Brugnon, FRA Henri Cochet, FRA	Peggy Saunders, GBR Phoebe Holcroft Watson, GBR
1929	Wilmer Allison, USA John Van Ryn, USA	Peggy Saunders, GBR Phoebe Holcroft Watson, GBR
1930	Wilmer Allison, USA John Van Ryn, USA	Helen Wills Moody, USA Elizabeth Ryan, USA
1931	George Lott, USA John Van Ryn, USA	Dorothy Shepherd Barron, GBR Phyllis Mudford, GBR
1932	Jean Borotra, FRA Jacques Brugnon, FRA	Doris Metaxa, FRA Josane Sigart, BEL
1933	Jean Borotra, FRA Jacques Brugnon, FRA	Simone P. Mathieu, FRA Elizabeth Ryan, USA
1934	George Lott, USA Lester Stoefen, USA	Simone P. Mathieu, FRA Elizabeth Ryan, USA
1935	Jack Crawford, AUS Adrian Quist, AUS	Freda James, GBR Kay Stammers, GBR

Year	Gentlemen	Ladies
1936	Pat Hughes, GBR	Freda James, GBR
	Raymond Tuckey, GBR	Kay Stammers, GBR
1937	Don Budge, USA	Simone P. Mathieu, FRA
	Gene Mako, USA	Billie Yorke, GBR
1938	Don Budge, USA	Sarah Palfrey Fabyan, USA
	Gene Mako, USA	Alice Marble, USA
1939	Elwood Cooke, USA	Sarah Palfrey Fabyan, USA
	Bobby Riggs, USA	Alice Marble, USA
1940–45	not held	not held
1946	Thomas Brown, USA	Louise Brough, USA
	Jack Kramer, USA	Margaret Osborne, USA
1947	Bob Falkenburg, USA	Doris Hart, USA
	Jack Kramer, USA	Pat Canning Todd, USA
1948	John Bromwich, AUS	Louise Brough, USA
	Frank Sedgman, AUS	Margaret Osborne duPont, USA
1949	Pancho Gonzáles, USA	Louise Brough, USA
	Frank Parker, USA	Margaret Osborne duPont, USA
1950	John Bromwich, AUS	Louise Brough, USA
	Adrian Quist, AUS	Margaret Osborne duPont, USA
1951	Ken McGregor, AUS	Shirley Fry, USA
	Frank Sedgman, AUS	Doris Hart, USA
1952	Ken McGregor, AUS	Shirley Fry, USA
	Frank Sedgman, AUS	Doris Hart, USA
1953	Lew Hoad, AUS	Shirley Fry, USA
	Ken Rosewall, AUS	Doris Hart, USA
1954	Rex Hartwig, AUS	Louise Brough, USA
	Mervyn Rose, AUS	Margaret Osborne duPont, USA
1955	Rex Hartwig, AUS	Angela Mortimer, GBR
	Lew Hoad, AUS	Ann Shilcock, GBR
1956	Lew Hoad, AUS	Angela Buxton, GBR
	Ken Rosewall, AUS	Althea Gibson, USA
1957	Gardnar Mulloy, USA	Darlene Hard, USA
	Budge Patty, USA	Althea Gibson, USA
1958	Sven Davidson, SWE	Maria Bueno, BRA
	Ulf Schmidt, SWE	Althea Gibson, USA
1959	Roy Emerson, AUS	Jeanne Arth, USA
	Neale Fraser, AUS	Darlene Hard, USA
1960	Rafael Osuna, MEX	Maria Bueno, BRA
	Dennis Ralston, USA	Darlene Hard, USA
1961	Roy Emerson, AUS	Karen Hantze, USA
	Neale Fraser, AUS	Billie Jean Moffitt, USA
1962	Bob Hewitt, AUS	Karen Hantze Susman, USA
	Fred Stolle, AUS	Billie Jean Moffitt, USA
1963	Rafael Osuna, MEX	Maria Bueno, BRA
	Antonio Palafox, MEX	Darlene Hard, USA
1964	Bob Hewitt, AUS	Margaret Smith, AUS
	Fred Stolle, AUS	Lesley Turner, AUS
1965	John Newcombe, AUS	Maria Bueno, BRA
	Tony Roche, AUS	Billie Jean Moffitt, USA

Year	Gentlemen	Ladies
1966	Ken Fletcher, AUS	Maria Bueno, BRA
	John Newcombe, AUS	Nancy Richey, USA
1967	Bob Hewitt, RSA	Rosie Casals, USA
	Frew McMillan, RSA	Billie Jean King, USA
1968	John Newcombe, AUS	Rosie Casals, USA
	Tony Roche, AUS	Billie Jean King, USA
1969	John Newcombe, AUS	Margaret Smith Court, AUS
	Tony Roche, AUS	Judy Tegart, AUS
1970	John Newcombe, AUS	Rosie Casals, USA
	Tony Roche, AUS	Billie Jean King, USA
1971	Roy Emerson, AUS	Rosie Casals, USA
	Rod Laver, AUS	Billie Jean King, USA
1972	Bob Hewitt, RSA	Betty Stove, NED
	Frew McMillan, RSA	Billie Jean King, USA
1973	Jimmy Connors, USA	Rosie Casals, USA
	Ilie Năstase, ROM	Billie Jean King, USA
1974	John Newcombe, AUS	Evonne Goolagong, AUS
	Tony Roche, AUS	Peggy Michel, USA
1975	Vitas Gerulaitis, USA	Ann Kiyomura, JPN
	Gene Mayer, USA	Kazuku Sawamatsu, JPN
1976	Brian Gottfried, USA	Chris Evert, USA
	Raúl Ramírez, MEX	Martina Navratilova, TCH
1977	Ross Case, AUS	Helen Gourlay Cawley, AUS
	Geoff Masters, AUS	JoAnne Russell, USA
1978	Bob Hewitt, RSA	Kerry Melville Reid, AUS
	Frew McMillan, RSA	Wendy Turnbull, AUS
1979	Peter Fleming, USA	Billie Jean King, USA
	John McEnroe, USA	Martina Navratilova, TCH
1980	Peter McNamara, AUS	Kathy Jordan, USA
	Paul McNamee, AUS	Anne Smith, USA
1981	Peter Fleming, USA	Martina Navratilova, USA
	John McEnroe, USA	Pam Shriver, USA
1982	Peter McNamara, AUS	Martina Navratilova, USA
	Paul McNamee, AUS	Pam Shriver, USA
1983	Peter Fleming, USA	Martina Navratilova, USA
	John McEnroe, USA	Pam Shriver, USA
1984	Peter Fleming, USA	Martina Navratilova, USA
	John McEnroe, USA	Pam Shriver, USA
1985	Heinz Günthardt, SUI	Kathy Jordan, USA
	Balázs Taróczy, HUN	Elizabeth Sayers Smylie, AUS
1986	Joakim Nystrom, SWE	Martina Navratilova, USA
	Mats Wilander, SWE	Pam Shriver, USA
1987	Ken Flach, USA	Claudia Kohde Kilsch, FRG
	Robert Seguso, USA	Helena Suková, TCH
1988	Ken Flach, USA	Steffi Graf, FRG
	Robert Seguso, USA	Gabriela Sabatini, ARG
1989	John Fitzgerald, AUS	Jana Novotná, TCH
	Anders Järryd, SWE	Helena Suková, TCH

Year	Gentlemen	Ladies
1990	Rick Leach, USA Jim Pugh, USA	Jana Novotná, TCH Helena Suková, TCH
1991	John Fitzgerald, AUS Anders Järryd, SWE	Larisa Savchenko, LAT Natalia Zvereva, URS
1992	John McEnroe, USA Michael Stich, GER	Gigi Fernández, USA Natalia Zvereva, BLR
1993	Todd Woodbridge, AUS Mark Woodforde, AUS	Gigi Fernández, USA Natalia Zvereva, BLR
1994	Todd Woodbridge, AUS Mark Woodforde, AUS	Gigi Fernández, USA Natalia Zvereva, BLR
1995	Todd Woodbridge, AUS Mark Woodforde, AUS	Jana Novotná, CZE Arantxa Sánchez Vicario, ESP
1996	Todd Woodbridge, AUS Mark Woodforde, AUS	Martina Hingis, SUI Helena Suková, CZE
1997	Todd Woodbridge, AUS Mark Woodforde, AUS	Gigi Fernández, USA Natalia Zvereva, BLR
1998	Jacco Eltingh, NED Paul Haarhuis, NED	Jana Novotná, CZE Martina Hingis, SUI
1999	Mahesh Bhupathi, IND Leander Paes, IND	Lindsay Davenport, USA Corina Morariu, USA
2000	Todd Woodbridge, AUS Mark Woodforde, AUS	Venus Williams, USA Serena Williams, USA
2001	Donald Johnson, USA Jared Palmer, USA	Lisa Raymond, USA Rennae Stubbs AUS
2002	Jonas Björkman, SWE Todd Woodbridge, AUS	Venus Williams, USA Serena Williams, USA
2003	Jonas Björkman, SWE Todd Woodbridge, AUS	Kim Clijsters, BEL Ai Sugiyama, JPN
2004	Jonas Björkman, SWE Todd Woodbridge, AUS	Cara Black, ZIM Rennae Stubbs, AUS
2005	Stephen Huss, AUS Wesley Moodie, RSA	Cara Black, ZIM Liezel Huber, RSA
2006	Bob Bryan, USA Mike Bryan, USA	Yan Zi, CHN Zheng Jie, CHN
2007	Arnaud Clément, FRA Michaël Llodra, FRA	Cara Black, ZIM Liezel Huber, RSA
2008	Daniel Nestor, CAN Nenad Zimonjić, SRB	Venus Williams, USA Serena Williams, USA
2009	Daniel Nestor, CAN Nenad Zimonjić, SRB	Venus Williams, USA Serena Williams, USA
2010	Jürgen Melzer, AUT Philipp Petzschner, GER	Vania King, USA Yaroslava Shvedova, KAZ
2011	Bob Bryan, USA Mike Bryan, USA	Kvéta Peschke, TCH Katarina Srebotnik, SVK

Table 4. Mixed Doubles

Year	Winner
1913	Agnes Daniell Tuckey, GBR / Hope Crisp, GBR
1914	E. Thomson Larcombe, GBR / Jim Parke, IRL
1915–18	not held
1919	Elizabeth Ryan, USA / Randolph Lycett, GBR
1920	Suzanne Lenglen, FRA / Gerald Patterson, AUS
1921	Elizabeth Ryan, USA / Randolph Lycett, GBR
1922	Suzanne Lenglen, FRA / Pat O'Hara Wood, AUS
1923	Elizabeth Ryan, USA / Randolph Lycett, GBR
1924	Kitty McKane, GBR / Brian Gilbert, GBR
1925	Suzanne Lenglen, FRA / Jean Borotra, FRA
1926	Kitty McKane Godfree, GBR / Leslie Godfree, GBR
1927	Elizabeth Ryan, USA / Frank Hunter, USA
1928	Elizabeth Ryan, USA / Pat Spence, RSA
1929	Helen Wills, USA / Frank Hunter, USA
1930	Elizabeth Ryan, USA / Jack Crawford, AUS
1931	Anna McCune Harper, USA / George Lott, USA
1932	Elizabeth Ryan, USA / Enrique Maier, ESP
1933	Hilde Krahwinkel, GER / Gottfried von Cramm, GER
1934	Dorothy Round, GBR / Ryuki Miki, JPN
1935	Dorothy Round, GBR / Ryuki Miki, JPN
1936	Dorothy Round, GBR / Fred Perry, GBR
1937	Alice Marble, USA / Don Budge, USA
1938	Alice Marble, USA / Don Budge, USA
1939	Alice Marble, USA / Bobby Riggs, USA

Year	Winner
1940–45	not held
1946	Louise Brough, USA
	Tom Brown, USA
1947	Louise Brough, USA
	John Bromwich, AUS
1948	Louise Brough, USA
	John Bromwich, AUS
1949	Sheila PierceySummers, RSA
	Eric Sturgess, RSA
1950	Louise Brough, USA
	Eric Sturgess, RSA
1951	Doris Hart, USA
	Frank Sedgman, AUS
1952	Doris Hart, USA
	Frank Sedgman, AUS
1053	Doris Hart, USA
	Vic Seixas, USA
1954	Doris Hart, USA
	Vic Seixas, USA
1955	Doris Hart, USA
	Vic Seixas, USA
1956	Shirley Fry, USA
	Vic Seixas, USA
1957	Darlene Hard, USA
	Merv Rose, AUS
1958	Lorraine Coghlan, AUS
	Bob Howe, AUS
1959	Darlene Hard, USA
	Rod Laver, AUS
1960	Darlene Hard, USA
	Rod Laver, AUS
1961	Lesley Turner, AUS
	Fred Stolle, AUS
1962	Margaret Osborne duPont, USA
	Neale Fraser, AUS
1963	Margaret Smith, AUS
	Ken Fletcher, AUS
1964	Lesley Turner, AUS
	Fred Stolle, AUS
1965	Margaret Smith, AUS
	Ken Fletcher, AUS
1966	Margaret Smith, AUS
	Ken Fletcher, AUS
1967	Billie Jean King, USA
	Owen Davidson, AUS
1968	Margaret Smith Court, AUS
	Ken Fletcher, AUS
1969	Ann Haydon-Jones, GBR
	Fred Stolle, AUS

Year	Winner
1970	Rosie Casals, USA
	Ilie Năstase, ROM
1971	Billie Jean King, USA
	Owen Davidson, AUS
1972	Rosie Casals, USA
	Ilie Năstase, ROM
1973	Billie Jean King, USA
	Owen Davidson, AUS
1974	Billie Jean King, USA
	Owen Davidson, AUS
1975	Margaret Smith Court, AUS
	Marty Riessen, USA
1976	Françoise Durr, FRA
	Tony Roche, AUS
1977	Greer Stevens, RSA
	Bob Hewitt, RSA
1978	Betty Stove, NED
	Frew McMillan, RSA
1979	Greer Stevens, RSA
	Bob Hewitt, RSA
1980	Tracy Austin, USA
	John Austin, USA
1981	Betty Stove, NED
	Frew McMillan, RSA
1982	Anne Smith, USA
	Kevin Curren, RSA
1983	Wendy Turnbull, AUS
	John Lloyd, GBR
1984	Wendy Turnbull, AUS
	John Lloyd, GBR
1985	Martina Navratilova, USA
	Paul McNamee, AUS
1986	Kathy Jordan, USA
	Ken Flach, USA
1987	Jo Durie, GBR
	Jeremy Bates, GBR
1988	Zina Garrison, USA
	Sherwood Stewart, USA
1989	Jana Novotná, TCH
	Jim Pugh, USA
1990	Zina Garrison, USA
	Rick Leach, USA
1991	Elizabeth Sayers Smylie, AUS
	John Fitzgerald, AUS
1992	Larisa Savchenko Neiland, LAT
	Cyril Suk, TCH
1993	Martina Navratilova, USA
	Mark Woodforde, AUS

Year	Winner
1994	Helena Suková, CZE
	Todd Woodbridge, AUS
1995	Martina Navratilova, USA
	Jonathan Stark, USA
1996	Helena Suková, CZE
	Cyril Suk, CZE
1997	Helena Suková, CZE
	Cyril Suk, CZE
1998	Serena Williams, USA
	Max Mirnyi, BLR
1999	Lisa Raymond, USA
	Leander Paes, IND
2000	Kimberly Po, USA
	Donald Johnson, USA
2001	Daniela Hantuchová, SVK
	Leos Friedl, CZE
2002	Elena Likhovtseva, RUS
	Mahesh Bhupathi, IND
2003	Martina Navratilova, USA
	Leander Paes, IND
2004	Cara Black, ZIM
	Wayne Black, ZIM
2005	Mary Pierce, FRA
	Mahesh Bhupathi, IND
2006	Vera Zvonareva, RUS
	Andy Ram, ISR
2007	Jelena Janković, SRB
	Jamie Murray, GBR
2008	Samantha Stosur, AUS
	Bob Bryan, USA
2009	Anna-Lena Grönefeld, GER
	Mark Knowles, BAH
2010	Cara Black, ZIM
	Leander Paes, IND

Appendix C:
United States National/Open Champions

Table 5. Singles

Year	Men	Women
1881	Richard Sears, USA	not held
1882	Richard Sears, USA	not held
1883	Richard Sears, USA	not held
1884	Richard Sears, USA	not held
1885	Richard Sears, USA	not held
1886	Richard Sears, USA	not held
1887	Richard Sears, USA	Ellen Hansell, USA
1888	Henry Slocum, USA	Bertha Townsend, USA
1889	Henry Slocum, USA	Bertha Townsend, USA
1890	Oliver Campbell, USA	Ellen Roosevelt, USA
1891	Oliver Campbell, USA	Mabel Cahill, USA
1892	Oliver Campbell, USA	Mabel Cahill, USA
1893	Robert Wrenn, USA	Aline Terry, USA
1894	Robert Wrenn, USA	Helen Hellwig, USA
1895	Frederick Hovey, USA	Juliette Atkinson, USA
1896	Robert Wrenn, USA	Elisabeth Moore, USA
1897	Robert Wrenn, USA	Juliette Atkinson, USA
1898	Malcolm Whitman, USA	Juliette Atkinson, USA
1899	Malcolm Whitman, USA	Marion Jones, USA
1900	Malcolm Whitman, USA	Myrtle McAteer, USA
1901	William Larned, USA	Elisabeth Moore, USA
1902	William Larned, USA	Marion Jones, USA
1903	Lawrence Doherty, GBR	Elisabeth Moore, USA
1904	Holcombe Ward, USA	May Sutton, USA
1905	Beals Wright, USA	Elisabeth Moore, USA
1906	William Clothier, USA	Helen Homans, USA
1907	William Larned, USA	Evelyn Sears, USA
1908	William Larned, USA	Maud Barger Wallach, USA
1909	William Larned, USA	Hazel Hotchkiss, USA
1910	William Larned, USA	Hazel Hotchkiss, USA
1911	William Larned, USA	Hazel Hotchkiss, USA
1912	Maurice McLoughlin, USA	Mary K. Browne, USA
1913	Maurice McLoughlin, USA	Mary K. Browne, USA
1914	R. Norris Williams, USA	Mary K. Browne, USA
1915	Bill Johnston, USA	Molla Bjurstedt, NOR
1916	R. Norris Williams, USA	Molla Bjurstedt, NOR
1917	Lindley Murray, USA	Molla Bjurstedt, NOR

Year	Men	Women
1918	Lindley Murray, USA	Molla Bjurstedt, NOR
1919	Bill Johnston, USA	Hazel Hotchkiss Wightman, USA
1920	Bill Tilden, USA	Molla Bjurstedt Mallory, USA
1921	Bill Tilden, USA	Molla Bjurstedt Mallory, USA
1922	Bill Tilden, USA	Molla Bjurstedt Mallory, USA
1923	Bill Tilden, USA	Helen Wills, USA
1924	Bill Tilden, USA	Helen Wills, USA
1925	Bill Tilden, USA	Helen Wills, USA
1926	René Lacoste, FRA	Molla Bjurstedt Mallory, USA
1927	René Lacoste, FRA	Helen Wills, USA
1928	Henri Cochet, FRA	Helen Wills, USA
1929	Bill Tilden, USA	Helen Wills Moody, USA
1930	John Doeg, USA	Betty Nuthall, GBR
1931	Ellsworth Vines, USA	Helen Wills Moody, USA
1932	Ellsworth Vines, USA	Helen Jacobs, USA
1933	Fred Perry, GBR	Helen Jacobs, USA
1934	Fred Perry, GBR	Helen Jacobs, USA
1935	Wilmer Allison, USA	Helen Jacobs, USA
1936	Fred Perry, GBR	Alice Marble, USA
1937	Don Budge, USA	Anita Lizana, CHI
1938	Don Budge, USA	Alice Marble, USA
1939	Bobby Riggs, USA	Alice Marble, USA
1940	Don McNeill, USA	Alice Marble, USA
1941	Bobby Riggs, USA	Sarah Palfrey Cooke, USA
1942	Ted Schroeder, USA	Pauline Betz, USA
1943	Joseph Hunt, USA	Pauline Betz, USA
1944	Frank Parker, USA	Pauline Betz, USA
1945	Frank Parker, USA	Sarah Palfrey Cooke, USA
1946	Jack Kramer, USA	Pauline Betz, USA
1947	Jack Kramer, USA	Louise Brough, USA
1948	Pancho Gonzáles, USA	Margaret Osborne duPont, USA
1949	Pancho Gonzáles, USA	Margaret Osborne duPont, USA
1950	Arthur Larsen, USA	Margaret Osborne duPont, USA
1951	Frank Sedgman, AUS	Maureen Connolly, USA
1952	Frank Sedgman, AUS	Maureen Connolly, USA
1953	Tony Trabert, USA	Maureen Connolly, USA
1954	Vic Seixas, USA	Doris Hart, USA
1955	Tony Trabert, USA	Doris Hart, USA
1956	Ken Rosewall, AUS	Shirley Fry, USA
1957	Malcolm Anderson, AUS	Althea Gibson, USA
1958	Ashley Cooper, AUS	Althea Gibson, USA
1959	Neale Fraser, AUS	Maria Bueno, BRA
1960	Neale Fraser, AUS	Darlene Hard, USA
1961	Roy Emerson, AUS	Darlene Hard, USA
1962	Rod Laver, AUS	Margaret Smith, AUS
1963	Rafael Osuna, MEX	Maria Bueno, BRA
1964	Roy Emerson, AUS	Maria Bueno, BRA
1965	Manuel Santana, ESP	Margaret Smith, AUS
1966	Fred Stolle, AUS	Maria Bueno, BRA

Year	Men	Women
1967	John Newcombe, AUS	Billie Jean King, USA
1968	Arthur Ashe, USA	Virginia Wade, GBR
1969	Rod Laver, AUS	Margaret Smith Court, AUS
1970	Ken Rosewall, AUS	Margaret Smith Court, AUS
1971	Stan Smith, USA	Billie Jean King, USA
1972	Ilie Năstase, ROM	Billie Jean King, USA
1973	John Newcombe, AUS	Margaret Smith Court, AUS
1974	Jimmy Connors, USA	Billie Jean King, USA
1975	Manuel Orantes, ESP	Chris Evert, USA
1976	Jimmy Connors, USA	Chris Evert, USA
1977	Guillermo Vilas, ARG	Chris Evert, USA
1978	Jimmy Connors, USA	Chris Evert, USA
1979	John McEnroe, USA	Tracy Austin, USA
1980	John McEnroe, USA	Chris Evert, USA
1981	John McEnroe, USA	Tracy Austin, USA
1982	Jimmy Connors, USA	Chris Evert Lloyd, USA
1983	Jimmy Connors, USA	Martina Navratilova, USA
1984	John McEnroe, USA	Martina Navratilova, USA
1985	Ivan Lendl, TCH	Hana Mandlíková, TCH
1986	Ivan Lendl, TCH	Martina Navratilova, USA
1987	Ivan Lendl, TCH	Martina Navratilova, USA
1988	Mats Wilander, SWE	Steffi Graf, FRG
1989	Boris Becker, FRG	Steffi Graf, FRG
1990	Pete Sampras, USA	Gabriela Sabatini, ARG
1991	Stefan Edberg, SWE	Monica Seles, YUG
1992	Stefan Edberg, SWE	Monica Seles, YUG
1993	Pete Sampras, USA	Steffi Graf, GER
1994	Andre Agassi, USA	Arantxa Sánchez Vicario, ESP
1995	Pete Sampras, USA	Steffi Graf, GER
1996	Pete Sampras, USA	Steffi Graf, GER
1997	Patrick Rafter, AUS	Martina Hingis, SUI
1998	Patrick Rafter, AUS	Lindsay Davenport, USA
1999	Andre Agassi, USA	Serena Williams, USA
2000	Marat Safin, RUS	Venus Williams, USA
2001	Lleyton Hewitt, AUS	Venus Williams, USA
2002	Pete Sampras, USA	Serena Williams, USA
2003	Andy Roddick, USA	Justine Henin-Hardenne, BEL
2004	Roger Federer, SUI	Svetlana Kuznetsova, RUS
2005	Roger Federer, SUI	Kim Clijsters, BEL
2006	Roger Federer, SUI	Maria Sharapova, RUS
2007	Roger Federer, SUI	Justine Henin-Hardenne, BEL
2008	Roger Federer, SUI	Serena Williams, USA
2009	Juan Martín Del Potro, ARG	Kim Clijsters, BEL
2010	Rafael Nadal, ESP	Kim Clijsters, BEL

Table 6   Doubles

Year	Men	Women
1881	Clarence Clark, USA Fred Taylor, USA	not held
1882	Richard Sears, USA James Dwight, USA	not held
1883	Richard Sears, USA James Dwight, USA	not held
1884	Richard Sears, USA James Dwight, USA	not held
1885	Richard Sears, USA James Dwight, USA	not held
1886	Richard Sears, USA James Dwight, USA	not held
1887	Richard Sears, USA James Dwight, USA	not held
1888	Oliver Campbell, USA Valentine Hall, USA	not held
1889	Henry Slocum, USA Howard Taylor, USA	Margarette Ballard, USA Bertha Townsend, USA
1890	Valentine Hall, USA Clarence Hobart, USA	Ellen Roosevelt, USA Grace Roosevelt, USA
1891	Oliver Campbell, USA Bob Huntington, USA	Mabel Cahill, USA Emma Levitt Morgan, USA
1892	Oliver Campbell, USA Bob Huntington, USA	Mabel Cahill, USA Adeline McKinlay, USA
1893	Clarence Hobart, USA Fred Hovey, USA	Aline Terry, USA Harriet Butler, USA
1894	Clarence Hobart, USA Fred Hovey, USA	Helen Hellwig, USA Juliette Atkinson, USA
1895	Malcolm Chace, USA Robert Wrenn, USA	Helen Hellwig, USA Juliette Atkinson, USA
1896	Carr Neel, USA Sam Neel, USA	Elisabeth Moore, USA Juliette Atkinson, USA
1897	Leo Ware, USA George Sheldon, USA	Juliette Atkinson, USA Kathleen Atkinson, USA
1898	Leo Ware, USA George Sheldon, USA	Juliette Atkinson, USA Kathleen Atkinson, USA
1899	Holcombe Ward, USA Dwight Davis, USA	Jane Craven, USA Myrtle McAteer, USA
1900	Holcombe Ward, USA Dwight Davis, USA	Edith Parker, USA Hallie Champlin, USA
1901	Holcombe Ward, USA Dwight Davis, USA	Juliette Atkinson, USA Myrtle McAteer, USA
1902	Reggie Doherty, GBR Laurie Doherty, GBR	Juliette Atkinson, USA Marion Jones, USA
1903	Reggie Doherty, GBR Laurie Doherty, GBR	Elisabeth Moore, USA Carrie Neely, USA
1904	Holcombe Ward, USA Beals Wright, USA	May Sutton, USA Miriam Hall, USA

Year	Men	Women
1905	Holcombe Ward, USA Beals Wright, USA	Helen Homans, USA Carrie Neely, USA
1906	Holcombe Ward, USA Beals Wright, USA	Ann Burdette Coe, USA Ethel Bliss Platt, USA
1907	Fred Alexander, USA Harold Hackett, USA	Marie Wimer, USA Carrie Neely, USA
1908	Fred Alexander, USA Harold Hackett, USA	Evelyn Sears, USA Margaret Curtis, USA
1909	Fred Alexander, USA Harold Hackett, USA	Hazel Hotchkiss, USA Edith Rotch, USA
1910	Fred Alexander, USA Harold Hackett, USA	Hazel Hotchkiss, USA Edith Rotch, USA
1911	Ray Little, USA Gus Touchard, USA	Hazel Hotchkiss, USA Eleonora Sears, USA
1912	Maurice McLoughlin, USA Tom Bundy, USA	Dorothy Green, USA Mary K. Browne, USA
1913	Maurice McLoughlin, USA Tom Bundy, USA	Louise Riddell Williams, USA Mary K. Browne, USA
1914	Maurice McLoughlin, USA Tom Bundy, USA	Louise Riddell Williams, USA Mary K. Browne, USA
1915	Bill Johnston, USA Clarence Griffith, USA	Hazel Hotchkiss Wightman, USA Eleonora Sears, USA
1916	Bill Johnston, USA Clarence Griffith, USA	Molla Bjurstedt, NOR Eleonora Sears, USA
1917	Fred Alexander, USA Harold Throckmorton, USA	Molla Bjurstedt, NOR Eleonora Sears, USA
1918	Bill Tilden, USA Vinnie Richards, USA	Marion Zinderstein, USA Eleanor Goss, USA
1919	Norman Brookes, AUS Gerald Patterson, AUS	Marion Zinderstein, USA Eleanor Goss, USA
1920	Bill Johnston, USA Clarence Griffith, USA	Marion Zinderstein, USA Eleanor Goss, USA
1921	Bill Tilden, USA Vinnie Richards, USA	Mary K. Browne, USA Louise Riddell Williams, USA
1922	Bill Tilden, USA Vinnie Richards, USA	Marion Zinderstein Jessup, USA Helen Wills, USA
1923	Bill Tilden, USA Brian Norton, RSA	Kitty McKane, GBR Phyllis Howkins Covell, GBR
1924	Howard Kinsey, USA Robert Kinsey, USA	Hazel Hotchkiss Wightman, USA Helen Wills, USA
1925	Dick Williams, USA Vinnie Richards, USA	Mary K. Browne, USA Helen Wills, USA
1926	Dick Williams, USA Vinnie Richards, USA	Elizabeth Ryan, USA Eleanor Goss, USA
1927	Bill Tilden, USA Frank Hunter, USA	Kitty McKane Godfree, GBR Ermyntrude Harvey, GBR
1928	George Lott, USA John Hennessey, USA	Helen Wills, USA Hazel Hotchkiss Wightman, USA

Year	Men	Women
1929	George Lott, USA	Phoebe Holcroft Watson, GBR
	Johnny Doeg, USA	Peggy Michell, USA
1930	George Lott, USA	Betty Nuthall, GBR
	Johnny Doeg, USA	Sarah Palfrey, USA
1931	Wilmer Allison, USA	Betty Nuthall, GBR
	John Van Ryn, USA	E. Bennett Whittingstall, GBR
1932	Ellsworth Vines, USA	Sarah Palfrey, USA
	Keith Gledhill, USA	Helen Jacobs, USA
1933	George Lott, USA	Betty Nuthall, GBR
	Lester Stoefen, USA	Freda James, GBR
1934	George Lott, USA	Helen Jacobs, USA
	Lester Stoefen, USA	Sarah Palfrey, USA
1935	Wilmer Allison, USA	Helen Jacobs, USA
	John Van Ryn, USA	Sarah Palfrey Fabyan, USA
1936	Don Budge, USA	Marjorie Gladman Van Ryn, USA
	Gene Mako, USA	Carolin Babcock, USA
1937	Gottfried von Cramm, GER	Alice Marble, USA
	Henner Henkel, GER	Sarah Palfrey Fabyan, USA
1938	Don Budge, USA	Alice Marble, USA
	Gene Mako, USA	Sarah Palfrey Fabyan, USA
1939	Adrian Quist, AUS	Alice Marble, USA
	John Bromwich, AUS	Sarah Palfrey Fabyan, USA
1940	Jack Kramer, USA	Alice Marble, USA
	Ted Schroeder, USA	Sarah Palfrey Fabyan, USA
1941	Jack Kramer, USA	Sarah P. Fabyan Cooke, USA
	Ted Schroeder, USA	Margaret Osborne, USA
1942	Gardnar Mulloy, USA	Louise Brough, USA
	Bill Talbert, USA	Margaret Osborne, USA
1943	Jack Kramer, USA	Louise Brough, USA
	Frank Parker, USA	Margaret Osborne, USA
1944	Don McNeill, USA	Louise Brough, USA
	Bob Falkenburg, USA	Margaret Osborne, USA
1945	Gardnar Mulloy, USA	Louise Brough, USA
	Bill Talbert, USA	Margaret Osborne, USA
1946	Gardnar Mulloy, USA	Louise Brough, USA
	Bill Talbert, USA	Margaret Osborne, USA
1947	Jack Kramer, USA	Louise Brough, USA
	Ted Schroeder, USA	Margaret Osborne, USA
1948	Gardnar Mulloy, USA	Louise Brough, USA
	Bill Talbert, USA	Margaret Osborne, USA
1949	John Bromwich, AUS	Louise Brough, USA
	Bill Sidwell, AUS	Margaret Osborne duPont, USA
1950	John Bromwich, AUS	Louise Brough, USA
	Frank Sedgman, AUS	Margaret Osborne duPont, USA
1951	Ken McGregor, AUS	Shirley Fry, USA
	Frank Sedgman, AUS	Doris Hart, USA
1952	Merv Rose, AUS	Shirley Fry, USA
	Vic Seixas, USA	Doris Hart, USA

Year	Men	Women
1953	Rex Hartwig, AUS	Shirley Fry, USA
	Merv Rose, AUS	Doris Hart, USA
1954	Vic Seixas, USA	Shirley Fry, USA
	Tony Trabert, USA	Doris Hart, USA
1955	Kosei Kamo, JPN	Louise Brough, USA
	Atsushi Miyagi, JPN	Margaret Osborne duPont, USA
1956	Lew Hoad, AUS	Louise Brough, USA
	Ken Rosewall, AUS	Margaret Osborne duPont, USA
1957	Ashley Cooper, AUS	Louise Brough, USA
	Neale Fraser, AUS	Margaret Osborne duPont, USA
1958	Alex Olmedo, USA	Jeanne Arth, USA
	Hamilton Richardson, USA	Darlene Hard, USA
1959	Neale Fraser, AUS	Jeanne Arth, USA
	Roy Emerson, AUS	Darlene Hard, USA
1960	Neale Fraser, AUS	Maria Bueno, BRA
	Roy Emerson, AUS	Darlene Hard, USA
1961	Chuck McKinley, USA	Lesley Turner, AUS
	Dennis Ralston, USA	Darlene Hard, USA
1962	Rafael Osuna, MEX	Maria Bueno, BRA
	Antonio Palafox, MEX	Darlene Hard, USA
1963	Chuck McKinley, USA	Robyn Ebbern, AUS
	Dennis Ralston, USA	Margaret Smith, AUS
1964	Chuck McKinley, USA	Billie Jean Moffitt, USA
	Dennis Ralston, USA	Karen Hantze Susman, USA
1965	Roy Emerson, AUS	Carol Caldwell Graebner, USA
	Fred Stolle, AUS	Nancy Richey, USA
1966	Roy Emerson, AUS	Maria Bueno, BRA
	Fred Stolle, AUS	Nancy Richey, USA
1967	John Newcombe, AUS	Rosie Casals, USA
	Tony Roche, AUS	Billie Jean King, USA
1968	Bob Lutz, USA	Maria Bueno, BRA
	Stan Smith, USA	Margaret Smith Court, AUS
1969	Ken Rosewall, AUS	Françoise Durr, FRA
	Fred Stolle, AUS	Darlene Hard, USA
1970	Pierre Barthès, FRA	Margaret Smith Court, AUS
	Niki Pilić, YUG	Judy Tegart Dalton, AUS
1971	John Newcombe, AUS	Rosie Casals, USA
	Roger Taylor, GBR	Judy Tegart Dalton, AUS
1972	Cliff Drysdale, RSA	Françoise Durr, FRA
	Roger Taylor, GBR	Betty Stove, NED
1973	Owen Davidson, AUS	Margaret Smith Court, AUS
	John Newcombe, AUS	Virginia Wade, GBR
1974	Bob Lutz, USA	Rosie Casals, USA
	Stan Smith, USA	Billie Jean King, USA
1975	Jimmy Connors, USA	Margaret Smith Court, AUS
	Ilie Năstase, ROM	Virginia Wade, GBR
1976	Tom Okker, NED	Delina Boshoff, RSA
	Marty Riessen, USA	Ilana Kloss, RSA

Year	Men	Women
1977	Bob Hewitt, RSA Frew McMillan, RSA	Martina Navratilova, TCH Betty Stove, NED
1978	Bob Lutz, USA Stan Smith, USA	Martina Navratilova, TCH Billie Jean King, USA
1979	John McEnroe, USA Peter Fleming, USA	Betty Stove, NED Wendy Turnbull, AUS
1980	Bob Lutz, USA Stan Smith, USA	Martina Navratilova, TCH Billie Jean King, USA
1981	John McEnroe, USA Peter Fleming, USA	Anne Smith, USA Kathy Jordan, USA
1982	Kevin Curren, RSA Steve Denton, USA	Rosie Casals, USA Wendy Turnbull, AUS
1983	John McEnroe, USA Peter Fleming, USA	Pam Shriver, USA Martina Navratilova, USA
1984	John Fitzgerald, AUS Tomáš Šmíd, TCH	Pam Shriver, USA Martina Navratilova, USA
1985	Ken Flach, USA Robert Seguso, USA	Claudia Kohde Kilsch, FRG Helena Suková, TCH
1986	Andrés Gómez, ECU Slobodan Živojinović, YUG	Pam Shriver, USA Martina Navratilova, USA
1987	Stefan Edberg, SWE Anders Järryd, SWE	Pam Shriver, USA Martina Navratilova, USA
1988	Sergio Casal, ESP Emilio Sánchez, ESP	Gigi Fernández, USA Robin White, USA
1989	John McEnroe, USA Mark Woodforde, AUS	Hana Mandlíková, AUS Martina Navratilova, USA
1990	Pieter Aldrich, RSA Danie Visser, RSA	Gigi Fernández, USA Martina Navratilova, USA
1991	John Fitzgerald, AUS Anders Järryd, SWE	Pam Shriver, USA Natalia Zvereva, URS
1992	Jim Grabb, USA Richey Reneberg, USA	Gigi Fernández, USA Natalia Zvereva, BLR
1993	Ken Flach, USA Rick Leach, USA	Arantxa Sánchez Vicario, ESP Helena Suková, CZE
1994	Jacco Eltingh, NED Paul Haarhuis, NED	Arantxa Sánchez Vicario, ESP Jana Novotná, CZE
1995	Todd Woodbridge, AUS Mark Woodforde, AUS	Gigi Fernández, USA Natalia Zvereva, URS
1996	Todd Woodbridge, AUS Mark Woodforde, AUS	Gigi Fernández, USA Natalia Zvereva, URS
1997	Yevgeny Kafelnikov, RUS Daniel Vacek, CZE	Jana Novotná, CZE Lindsay Davenport, USA
1998	Sandon Stolle, AUS Cyril Suk, CZE	Martina Hingis, SUI Jana Novotná, CZE
1999	Sebastian Lareau, CAN Alex O'Brien, USA	Serena Williams, USA Venus Williams, USA
2000	Lleyton Hewitt, AUS Max Mirnyi, BLR	Julie Halard-Decugis, FRA Ai Sugiyama, JPN

Year	Men	Women
2001	Wayne Black, ZIM Kevin Ullyett, ZIM	Rennae Stubbs, AUS Lisa Raymond, USA
2002	Max Mirnyi, BLR Mahesh Bhupathi, IND	Paola Suárez, ARG Virginia Ruano Pascual, ESP
2003	Jonas Björkman, SWE Todd Woodbridge, AUS	Paola Suárez, ARG Virginia Ruano Pascual, ESP
2004	Mark Knowles, BAH Daniel Nestor, CAN	Paola Suárez, ARG Virginia Ruano Pascual, ESP
2005	Mike Bryan, USA Bob Bryan, USA	Lisa Raymond, USA Samantha Stosur, AUS
2006	Martin Damm, CZE Leander Paes, IND	Nathalie Dechy, FRA Vera Zvonareva, RUS
2007	Simon Aspelin, SWE Julian Knowle, AUT	Nathalie Dechy, FRA Dinara Safina, RUS
2008	Mike Bryan, USA Bob Bryan, USA	Cara Black, ZIM Liezel Huber, USA
2009	Lukáš Dlouhý, CZE Leander Paes, IND	Serena Williams, USA Venus Williams, USA
2010	Mike Bryan, USA Bob Bryan, USA	Vania King, USA Yaroslava Shvedova, KAZ

Table 7. Mixed Doubles

Year	Winner
1892	Mabel Cahill, USA Clarence Hobart, USA
1893	Ellen Roosevelt, USA Clarence Hobart, USA
1894	Juliette Atkinson, USA Edwin Fischer, USA
1895	Juliette Atkinson, USA Edwin Fischer, USA
1896	Juliette Atkinson, USA Edwin Fischer, USA
1897	Laura Henson, USA D. L. Magruder, USA
1898	Carrie Neely, USA Edwin Fischer, USA
1899	Elizabeth Rastall, USA Albert Hoskins, USA
1900	Margaret Hunnewell, USA Alfred Codman, USA
1901	Marion Jones, USA Ray Little, USA
1902	Elisabeth Moore, USA Wylie Grant, USA

Year	Winner
1903	Helen Chapman, USA
	Harry Allen, USA
1904	Elisabeth Moore, USA
	Wylie Grant, USA
1905	Augusta Schultz Hobart, USA
	Clarence Hobart, USA
1906	Sarah Coffin, USA
	Edward Dewhurst, USA
1907	May Sayers, USA
	Wallace Johnson, USA
1908	Edith Rotch, USA
	Nathaniel Niles, USA
1909	Hazel Hotchkiss, USA
	Wallace Johnson, USA
1910	Hazel Hotchkiss, USA
	Joseph Carpenter Jr., USA
1911	Hazel Hotchkiss, USA
	Wallace Johnson, USA
1912	Mary K. Browne, USA
	Dick Williams, USA
1913	Mary K. Browne, USA
	Bill Tilden, USA
1914	Mary K. Browne, USA
	Bill Tilden, USA
1915	H. Hotchkiss Wightman, USA
	Harry Johnson, USA
1916	Eleonora Sears, USA
	Willis Davis, USA
1917	Molla Bjurstedt, NOR
	Irving Wright, USA
1918	H. Hotchkiss Wightman, USA
	Irving Wright, USA
1919	Marion Zinderstein, USA
	Vinnie Richards, USA
1920	H. Hotchkiss Wightman, USA
	Wallace Johnson, USA
1921	Mary K. Browne, USA
	Bill Johnston, USA
1922	M. Bjurstedt Mallory, USA
	Bill Tilden, USA
1923	M. Bjurstedt Mallory, USA
	Bill Tilden, USA
1924	Helen Wills, USA
	Vinnie Richards, USA
1925	Kitty McKane, GBR
	Jack Hawkes, AUS
1926	Elizabeth Ryan, USA
	Jean Borotra, FRA

Year	Winner
1927	Eileen Bennett, USA
	Henri Cochet, FRA
1928	Helen Wills, USA
	Jack Hawkes, AUS
1929	Betty Nuthall, GBR
	George Lott, USA
1930	Edith Cross, USA
	Wilmer Allison, USA
1931	Betty Nuthall, GBR
	George Lott, USA
1932	Sarah Palfrey, USA
	Fred Perry, GBR
1933	Elizabeth Ryan, USA
	Ellsworth Vines, USA
1934	Helen Jacobs, USA
	George Lott, USA
1935	Sarah Palfrey Fabyan, USA
	Enrique Maier, ESP
1936	Alice Marble, USA
	Gene Mako, USA
1937	Sarah Palfrey Fabyan, USA
	Don Budge, USA
1938	Alice Marble, USA
	Don Budge, USA
1939	Alice Marble, USA
	Harry Hopman, AUS
1940	Alice Marble, USA
	Bobby Riggs, USA
1941	Sarah P. Fabyan Cooke, USA
	Jack Kramer, USA
1942	Louise Brough, USA
	Ted Schroeder, USA
1943	Margaret Osborne, USA
	Bill Talbert, USA
1944	Margaret Osborne, USA
	Bill Talbert, USA
1945	Margaret Osborne, USA
	Bill Talbert, USA
1946	Margaret Osborne, USA
	Bill Talbert, USA
1947	Louise Brough, USA
	John Bromwich, AUS
1948	Louise Brough, USA
	Tom Brown, USA
1949	Louise Brough, USA
	Eric Sturgess, USA
1950	M. Osborne duPont, USA
	Ken McGregor, AUS

Year	Winner
1951	Doris Hart, USA
	Frank Sedgman, AUS
1952	Doris Hart, USA
	Frank Sedgman, AUS
1953	Doris Hart, USA
	Vic Seixas, USA
1954	Doris Hart, USA
	Vic Seixas, USA
1955	Doris Hart, USA
	Vic Seixas, USA
1956	Margaret Osborne duPont, USA
	Ken Rosewall, AUS
1957	Althea Gibson, USA
	Kurt Nielsen, DEN
1958	Margaret Osborne duPont, USA
	Neale Fraser, AUS
1959	Margaret Osborne duPont, USA
	Neale Fraser, AUS
1960	Margaret Osborne duPont, USA
	Neale Fraser, AUS
1961	Margaret Smith, AUS
	Bob Mark, AUS
1962	Margaret Smith, AUS
	Fred Stolle, AUS
1963	Margaret Smith, AUS
	Ken Fletcher, AUS
1964	Margaret Smith, AUS
	John Newcombe, AUS
1965	Margaret Smith, AUS
	Fred Stolle, AUS
1966	Donna Floyd Fales, USA
	Owen Davidson, AUS
1967	Billie Jean King, USA
	Owen Davidson, AUS
1968	Mary Ann Eisel, USA
	Peter Curtis, GBR
1969	Margaret Smith Court, AUS
	Marty Riessen, USA
1970	Margaret Smith Court, AUS
	Marty Riessen, USA
1971	Billie Jean King, USA
	Owen Davidson, AUS
1972	Margaret Smith Court, AUS
	Marty Riessen, USA
1973	Billie Jean King, USA
	Owen Davidson, AUS
1974	Pam Teeguarden, USA
	Geoff Masters, AUS

Year	Winner
1975	Rosie Casals, USA
	Dick Stockton, USA
1976	Billie Jean King, USA
	Phil Dent, AUS
1977	Betty Stove, NED
	Frew McMillan, RSA
1978	Betty Stove, NED
	Frew McMillan, RSA
1979	Greer Stevens, RSA
	Bob Hewitt, RSA
1980	Wendy Turnbull, AUS
	Marty Riessen, USA
1981	Anne Smith, USA
	Kevin Curren, RSA
1982	Anne Smith, USA
	Kevin Curren, RSA
1983	Elizabeth Sayers, AUS
	John Fitzgerald, AUS
1984	Manuela Maleeva, BUL
	Tom Gullickson, USA
1985	Martina Navratilova, USA
	Heinz Günthardt, SUI
1986	Rafaella Reggi, ITA
	Sergio Casal, ESP
1987	Martina Navratilova, USA
	Emilio Sánchez, ESP
1988	Jana Novotná, TCH
	Jim Pugh, USA
1989	Robin White, USA
	Shelby Cannon, USA
1990	Elizabeth Sayers Smylie, AUS
	Todd Woodbridge, AUS
1991	Manon Bollegraf, NED
	Tom Nijssen, NED
1992	Nicole Provis, AUS
	Mark Woodforde, AUS
1993	Helena Suková, CZE
	Todd Woodbridge, AUS
1994	Elna Reinach, RSA
	Patrick Galbraith, USA
1995	Meredith McGrath, USA
	Matt Lucena, USA
1996	Lisa Raymond, USA
	Patrick Galbraith, USA
1997	Manon Bollegraf, NED
	Rick Leach, USA
1998	Serena Williams, USA
	Max Mirnyi, BLR

Year	Winner
1999	Ai Sugiyama, JPN
	Mahesh Bhupathi, IND
2000	Arantxa Sánchez Vicario, ESP
	Jared Palmer, USA
2001	Rennae Stubbs, AUS
	Todd Woodbridge, AUS
2002	Lisa Raymond, USA
	Mike Bryan, USA
2003	Katarina Srebotnik, SLV
	Bob Bryan, USA
2004	Vera Zvonareva, RUS
	Bob Bryan, USA
2005	Daniela Hantuchová, SVK
	Mahesh Bhupathi, IND
2006	Martina Navratilova, USA
	Bob Bryan, USA
2007	Victoria Azarenka, BLR
	Max Mirnyi, BLR
2008	Cara Black, ZIM
	Leander Paes, IND
2009	Carly Gullickson, USA
	Travis Parrott, USA
2010	Liezel Huber, USA
	Bob Bryan, USA

Appendix D: French National/Open Champions

The tournament was known as Les Championnats de France (the French Championships) from 1891 to 1924, Les Championnats Internationaux de France (the French International Championships) from 1925 to 1967, and Les Internationaux de France de Roland Garros (the French Open) from 1968 to date. Entries were restricted to French amateurs from 1891 to 1924 and international amateurs from 1925 to 1967, and since 1968, both professionals and amateurs may enter.

Table 8. Singles

Year	Men	Women
1891	H. Briggs, GBR	not held
1892	Jean Schopfer, FRA	not held
1893	Laurent Riboulet, FRA	not held
1894	André Vacherot, FRA	not held
1895	André Vacherot, FRA	not held
1896	André Vacherot, FRA	not held
1897	Paul Aymé, FRA	Adine Masson, FRA
1898	Paul Aymé, FRA	Adine Masson, FRA
1899	Paul Aymé, FRA	Adine Masson, FRA
1900	Paul Aymé, FRA	Hélène Prévost, FRA
1901	André Vacherot, FRA	P. Girod, FRA
1902	Michel Vacherot, FRA	Adine Masson, FRA
1903	Max Decugis, FRA	Adine Masson, FRA
1904	André Vacherot, FRA	Kate Gillou, FRA
1905	Maurice Germot, FRA	Kate Gillou, FRA
1906	Maurice Germot, FRA	Kate Gillou-Fenwick, FRA
1907	Max Decugis, FRA	Comtesse de Kermel, FRA
1908	Max Decugis, FRA	Kate Gillou-Fenwick, FRA
1909	Max Decugis, FRA	Jeanne Mathey, FRA
1910	Maurice Germot, FRA	Jeanne Mathey, FRA
1911	André Gobert, FRA	Jeanne Mathey, FRA
1912	Max Decugis, FRA	Jeanne Mathey, FRA
1913	Max Decugis, FRA	Marguerite Broquedis, FRA
1914	Max Decugis, FRA	Marguerite Broquedis, FRA
1915–19	not held	not held
1920	André Gobert, FRA	Suzanne Lenglen, FRA
1921	Jean Samazeuilh, FRA	Suzanne Lenglen, FRA

Year	Men	Women
1922	Henri Cochet, FRA	Suzanne Lenglen, FRA
1923	François Blanchy, FRA	Suzanne Lenglen, FRA
1924	Jean Borotra, FRA	Emilienne "Didi" Vlasto, FRA
1925	René Lacoste, FRA	Suzanne Lenglen, FRA
1926	Henri Cochet, FRA	Suzanne Lenglen, FRA
1927	René Lacoste, FRA	Kea Bouman, NED
1928	Henri Cochet, FRA	Helen Wills Moody, USA
1929	René Lacoste, FRA	Helen Wills Moody, USA
1930	Henri Cochet, FRA	Helen Wills Moody, USA
1931	Jean Borotra, FRA	Cilly Aussem, GER
1932	Henri Cochet, FRA	Helen Wills Moody, USA
1933	Jack Crawford, AUS	Margaret Scriven, USA
1934	Gottfried von Cramm, GER	Margaret Scriven, USA
1935	Fred Perry, GBR	Hilde Krahwinkel Sperling, DEN
1936	Gottfried von Cramm, GER	Hilde Krahwinkel Sperling, DEN
1937	Henner Henkel, GER	Hilde Krahwinkel Sperling, DEN
1938	Don Budge, USA	Simone P. Mathieu, FRA
1939	Don McNeill, USA	Simone P. Mathieu, FRA
1940–45	not held	not held
1946	Marcel Bernard, FRA	Margaret Osborne, USA
1947	József Asbóth, HUN	Pat Canning Todd, USA
1948	Frank Parker, USA	Nelly Adamson Landry, FRA
1949	Frank Parker, USA	Margaret Osborne duPont, USA
1950	Budge Patty, USA	Doris Hart, USA
1951	Jaroslav Drobný, EGY	Shirley Fry, USA
1952	Jaroslav Drobný, EGY	Doris Hart, USA
1953	Ken Rosewall, AUS	Maureen Connolly, USA
1954	Tony Trabert, USA	Maureen Connolly, USA
1955	Tony Trabert, USA	Angela Mortimer, GBR
1956	Lew Hoad, AUS	Althea Gibson, USA
1957	Sven Davidson, SWE	Shirley Bloomer, GBR
1958	Mervyn Rose, AUS	Suzi Körmöczi, HUN
1959	Nicola Pietrangeli, ITA	Christine Truman, GBR
1960	Nicola Pietrangeli, ITA	Darlene Hard, USA
1961	Manuel Santana, ESP	Ann Haydon, GBR
1962	Rod Laver, AUS	Margaret Smith, AUS
1963	Roy Emerson, AUS	Lesley Turner, AUS
1964	Manuel Santana, ESP	Margaret Smith, AUS
1965	Fred Stolle, AUS	Lesley Turner, AUS
1966	Tony Roche, AUS	Ann Haydon-Jones, GBR
1967	Roy Emerson, AUS	Françoise Durr, FRA
1968	Ken Rosewall, AUS	Nancy Richey, USA
1969	Rod Laver, AUS	Margaret Smith Court, AUS
1970	Jan Kodeš, TCH	Margaret Smith Court, AUS
1971	Jan Kodeš, TCH	Evonne Goolagong, AUS
1972	Andrés Gimeno, ESP	Billie Jean King, USA
1973	Ilie Năstase, ROM	Margaret Smith Court, AUS
1974	Björn Borg, SWE	Chris Evert, USA
1975	Björn Borg, SWE	Chris Evert, USA

Year	Men	Women
1976	Adriano Panatta, ITA	Sue Barker, GBR
1977	Guillermo Vilas, ARG	Mima Jaušovec, YUG
1978	Björn Borg, SWE	Virginia Ruzici, ROM
1979	Björn Borg, SWE	Chris Evert Lloyd, USA
1980	Björn Borg, SWE	Chris Evert Lloyd, USA
1981	Björn Borg, SWE	Hana Mandlíková, TCH
1982	Mats Wilander, SWE	Martina Navratilova, USA
1983	Yannick Noah, FRA	Chris Evert Lloyd, USA
1984	Ivan Lendl, TCH	Martina Navratilova, USA
1985	Mats Wilander, SWE	Chris Evert Lloyd, USA
1986	Ivan Lendl, TCH	Chris Evert Lloyd, USA
1987	Ivan Lendl, TCH	Steffi Graf, FRG
1988	Mats Wilander, SWE	Steffi Graf, FRG
1989	Michael Chang, USA	Arantxa Sánchez Vicario, ESP
1990	Andrés Gómez, ECU	Monica Seles, YUG
1991	Jim Courier, USA	Monica Seles, YUG
1992	Jim Courier, USA	Monica Seles, YUG
1993	Sergi Bruguera, ESP	Steffi Graf, GER
1994	Sergi Bruguera, ESP	Arantxa Sánchez Vicario, ESP
1995	Thomas Muster, AUT	Steffi Graf, GER
1996	Yevgeny Kafelnikov, RUS	Steffi Graf, GER
1997	Gustavo Kuerten, BRA	Iva Majoli, CRO
1998	Carlos Moyá, ESP	Arantxa Sánchez Vicario, ESP
1999	Andre Agassi, USA	Steffi Graf, GER
2000	Gustavo Kuerten, BRA	Mary Pierce, FRA
2001	Gustavo Kuerten, BRA	Jennifer Capriati, USA
2002	Albert Costa, ESP	Serena Williams, USA
2003	Juan Carlos Ferrero, ESP	Justine Henin-Hardenne, BEL
2004	Gastón Gaudio, ARG	Anastasia Myskina, RUS
2005	Rafael Nadal, ESP	Justine Henin-Hardenne, BEL
2006	Rafael Nadal, ESP	Justine Henin-Hardenne, BEL
2007	Rafael Nadal, ESP	Justine Henin-Hardenne, BEL
2008	Rafael Nadal, ESP	Ana Ivanović, SRB
2009	Roger Federer, SUI	Svetlana Kuznetsova, RUS
2010	Rafael Nadal, ESP	Francesca Sciavone, ITA
2011	Rafael Nadal, ESP	Li Na, CHN

Table 9. Doubles

Year	Men	Women
1925	Jean Borotra, FRA René Lacoste, FRA	Suzanne Lenglen, FRA Didi Vlasto, FRA
1926	Didi Vlasto, FRA Howard Kinsey, USA	Suzanne Lenglen, FRA Didi Vlasto, FRA
1927	Henri Cochet, FRA Jacques Brugnon, FRA	Irene Bowder Peacock, RSA Bobbie Heine, AUS
1928	Jean Borotra, FRA Jacques Brugnon, FRA	Phoebe Holcroft Watson, GBR Eileen Bennett, GBR
1929	René Lacoste, FRA Jean Borotra, FRA	Lili de Alvarez, ESP Kea Bouman, NED
1930	Henri Cochet, FRA Jacques Brugnon, FRA	Helen Wills Moody, USA Elizabeth Ryan, USA
1931	George Lott, USA John Van Ryn, USA	E. Bennett Whittingstall, GBR Betty Nuthall, GBR
1932	Henri Cochet, FRA Jacques Brugnon, FRA	Helen Wills Moody, USA Elizabeth Ryan, USA
1933	Pat Hughes, GBR Fred Perry, GBR	Simone P. Mathieu, FRA Elizabeth Ryan, USA
1934	Jean Borotra, FRA Jacques Brugnon, FRA	Simone P. Mathieu, FRA Elizabeth Ryan, USA
1935	Jack Crawford, AUS Adrian Quist, AUS	Margaret Scriven, GBR Kay Stammers, GBR
1936	Jean Borotra, FRA Marcel Bernard, FRA	Simone P. Mathieu, FRA Billie Yorke, GBR
1937	Gottfired von Cramm, GER Henner Henkel, GER	Simone P. Mathieu, FRA Billie Yorke, GBR
1938	Bernard Destremau, FRA Yvon Petra, FRA	Simone P. Mathieu, FRA Billie Yorke, GBR
1939	Don McNeill, USA Charles Harris, USA	Simone P. Mathieu, FRA Jadwiga Jędrzejowska, POL
1940–45	not held	not held
1946	Marcel Bernard, FRA Yvan Petra, FRA	Louise Brough, USA Margaret Osborne, USA
1947	Eustace Fannin, RSA Eric Sturgess, RSA	Louise Brough, USA Margaret Osborne, USA
1948	Lennart Bergelin, SWE Jaroslav Drobný, TCH	Doris Hart, USA Pat Canning Todd, USA
1949	Pancho González, USA Frank Parker, USA	Louise Brough, USA Margaret Osborne duPont, USA
1950	Bill Talbert, USA Tony Trabert, USA	Doris Hart, USA Shirley Fry, USA
1951	Ken McGregor, AUS Frank Sedgman, AUS	Doris Hart, USA Shirley Fry, USA
1952	Ken McGregor, AUS Frank Sedgman, AUS	Doris Hart, USA Shirley Fry, USA
1953	Lew Hoad, AUS Ken Rosewall, AUS	Doris Hart, USA Shirley Fry, USA

Year	Men	Women
1954	Vic Seixas, USA	Maureen Connolly, USA
	Tony Trabert, USA	Nell Hall Hopman, AUS
1955	Vic Seixas, USA	Beverly Baker Fleitz, USA
	Tony Trabert, USA	Darlene Hard, USA
1956	Don Candy, AUS	Angela Buxton, GBR
	Bob Perry, USA	Althea Gibson, USA
1957	Mal Anderson, AUS	Darlene Hard, USA
	Ashley Cooper, AUS	Shirley Bloomer, GBR
1958	Ashley Cooper, AUS	Rosie Reyes, MEX
	Neale Fraser, AUS	Yola Ramírez, MEX
1959	Nicola Pietrangeli, ITA	Sandra Reynolds, RSA
	Orlando Sirola, ITA	Renee Schuurman, RSA
1960	Roy Emerson, AUS	Darlene Hard, USA
	Neale Fraser, AUS	Maria Bueno, BRA
1961	Roy Emerson, AUS	Sandra Reynolds, RSA
	Rod Laver, AUS	Renee Schuurman, RSA
1962	Roy Emerson, AUS	Sandra Reynolds Price, RSA
	Neale Fraser, AUS	Renee Schuurman, RSA
1963	Roy Emerson, AUS	Ann Haydon-Jones, GBR
	Manuel Santana, ESP	Renee Schuurman, RSA
1964	Roy Emerson, AUS	Margaret Smith, AUS
	Ken Fletcher, AUS	Lesley Turner, AUS
1965	Roy Emerson, AUS	Margaret Smith, AUS
	Fred Stolle, AUS	Lesley Turner, AUS
1966	Clark Graebner, USA	Margaret Smith, AUS
	Dennis Ralston, USA	Judy Tegart, AUS
1967	John Newcombe, AUS	Françoise Durr, FRA
	Tony Roche, AUS	Gail Sherriff, AUS
1968	Ken Rosewall, AUS	Françoise Durr, FRA
	Fred Stolle, AUS	Ann Haydon-Jones, GBR
1969	John Newcombe, AUS	Françoise Durr, FRA
	Tony Roche, AUS	Ann Haydon-Jones, GBR
1970	Ilie Năstase, ROM	Françoise Durr, FRA
	Ion Țiriac, ROM	Gail Sherriff Chanfreau, FRA
1971	Arthur Ashe, USA	Françoise Durr, FRA
	Marty Riessen, USA	Gail Sherriff Chanfreau, FRA
1972	Bob Hewitt, RSA	Billie Jean King, USA
	Frew McMillan, RSA	Betty Stove, NED
1973	John Newcombe, AUS	Margaret Smith Court, AUS
	Tom Okker, NED	Virginia Wade, GBR
1974	Dick Crealy, AUS	Chris Evert, USA
	Onny Parun, NZL	Olga Morozova, URS
1975	Brian Gottfried, USA	Chris Evert, USA
	Raúl Ramírez, MEX	Martina Navratilova, TCH
1976	Fred McNair, USA	Fiorella Bonicelli, URU
	Sherwood Stewart, USA	Gail Sherriff Lovera, FRA
1977	Brian Gottfried, USA	Regina Maršíková, TCH
	Raúl Ramírez, MEX	Pam Teeguarden, USA

Year	Men	Women
1978	Gene Mayer, USA Hank Pfister, USA	Mima Jaušovec, YUG Virginia Ruzici, ROM
1979	Gene Mayer, USA Sandy Mayer, USA	Betty Stove, NED Wendy Turnbull, AUS
1980	Victor Amaya, USA Hank Pfister, USA	Kathy Jordan, USA Anne Smith, USA
1981	Heinz Günthart, SUI Balázs Taróczy, HUN	Rosalyn Fairbank, RSA Tayna Harford, RSA
1982	Sherwood Stewart, USA Ferdi Taygan, USA	Martina Navratilova, USA Anne Smith, USA
1983	Anders Järryd, SWE Hans Simonsson, SWE	Rosalyn Fairbank, RSA Candy Reynolds, USA
1984	Henri Leconte, FRA Yannick Noah, FRA	Martina Navratilova, USA Pam Shriver, USA
1985	Mark Edmondson, AUS Kim Warwick, AUS	Martina Navratilova, USA Pam Shriver, USA
1986	John Fitzgerald, AUS Tomáš Šmíd, TCH	Martina Navratilova, USA Andrea Temesvári, HUN
1987	Anders Järryd, SWE Robert Seguso, USA	Martina Navratilova, USA Pam Shriver, USA
1988	Andrés Gómez, ECU Emilio Sánchez, ESP	Martina Navratilova, USA Pam Shriver, USA
1989	Jim Grabb, USA Patrick McEnroe, USA	Larisa Savchenko, URS Natalia Zvereva, URS
1990	Sergio Casal, ESP Emilio Sánchez, ESP	Jana Novotná, TCH Helena Suková, TCH
1991	John Fitzgerald, AUS Anders Järryd, SWE	Gigi Fernández, USA Jana Novotná, TCH
1992	Jakob Hlasek, SUI Marc Rosset, SUI	Gigi Fernández, USA Natalia Zvereva, BLR
1993	Luke Jensen, USA Murphy Jensen, USA	Gigi Fernández, USA Natalia Zvereva, BLR
1994	Byron Black, ZIM Jonathan Stark, USA	Gigi Fernández, USA Natalia Zvereva, BLR
1995	Jacco Eltingh, NED Paul Haarhuis, NED	Gigi Fernández, USA Natalia Zvereva, BLR
1996	Yevgeny Kafelnikov, RUS Daniel Vacek, CZE	Lindsay Davenport, USA Mary Joe Fernández, USA
1997	Yevgeny Kafelnikov, RUS Daniel Vacek, CZE	Gigi Fernández, USA Natalia Zvereva, BLR
1998	Jacco Eltingh, NED Paul Haarhuis, NED	Martina Hingis, SUI Jana Novotná, CZE
1999	Mahesh Bhupathi, IND Leander Paes, IND	Venus Williams, USA Serena Williams, USA
2000	Todd Woodbridge, AUS Mark Woodforde, AUS	Martina Hingis, SUI Mary Pierce, FRA
2001	Mahesh Bhupathi, IND Leander Paes, IND	Paola Suárez, ARG Virgina Ruano Pascual, ESP

Year	Men	Women
2002	Paul Haarhuis, NED Yevgeny Kafelnikov, RUS	Paola Suárez, ARG Virgina Ruano Pascual, ESP
2003	Bob Bryan, USA Mike Bryan, USA	Kim Clijsters, BEL Ai Sugiyama, JPN
2004	Xavier Malisse, BEL Olivier Rochus, BEL	Paola Suárez, ARG Virgina Ruano Pascual, ESP
2005	Jonas Björkman, SWE Max Mirnyi, BLR	Paola Suárez, ARG Virgina Ruano Pascual, ESP
2006	Jonas Björkman, SWE Max Mirnyi, BLR	Lisa Raymond, USA Samantha Stosur, AUS
2007	Mark Knowles, BAH Daniel Nestor, CAN	Alicia Molik, AUS Mara Santangelo, ITA
2008	Pablo Cuevas, ARG Luis Horna, PER	Anabel Medina Garrigues, ESP Virgina Ruano Pascual, ESP
2009	Lukáš Dlouhý, CZE Leander Paes, IND	Anabel Medina Garrigues, ESP Virgina Ruano Pascual, ESP
2010	Daniel Nestor, CAN Nenad Zimonjić, SRB	Venus Williams, USA Serena Williams, USA
201	Max Mirnyi, BLR Daniel Nestor, CAN	Andrea Hlavackova, CZE Lucie Hradecka, CZE

Table 10. Mixed Doubles

Year	Winner
1925	Suzanne Lenglen, FRA Jacques Brugnon, FRA
1926	Suzanne Lenglen, FRA Jacques Brugnon, FRA
1927	M. Broquedis Bordes, FRA Jean Borotra, FRA
1928	Eileen Bennett, GBR Henri Cochet, FRA
1929	Eileen Bennett, GBR Henri Cochet, FRA
1930	Cilly Aussem, GER Bill Tilden, USA
1931	Betty Nuthall, GBR Pat Spence, RSA
1932	Betty Nuthall, GBR Fred Perry, GBR
1933	Margaret Scriven, GBR Jack Crawford, AUS
1934	Colette Rosambert, FRA Jean Borotra, FRA
1935	Lolette Payot, FRA Marcel Bernard, FRA
1936	Billie Yorke, GBR Marcel Bernard, FRA

Year	Winner
1937	Simone P. Mathieu, FRA
	Yvon Petra, FRA
1938	Simone P. Mathieu, FRA
	Dragutin Mitić, YUG
1939	Sarah Palfrey Fabyan, USA
	Elwood Cooke, USA
1940–45	not held
1946	Pauline Betz, USA
	Budge Patty, USA
1947	Sheila Piercey Summers, RSA
	Eric Sturgess, RSA
1948	Pat Canning Todd, USA
	Jaroslav Drobný, TCH
1949	Sheila Piercey Summers, RSA
	Eric Sturgess, RSA
1950	Barbara Scofield, USA
	Enrique Morea, ARG
1951	Doris Hart, USA
	Frank Sedgman, AUS
1952	Doris Hart, USA
	Frank Sedgman, AUS
1953	Doris Hart, USA
	Vic Seixas, USA
1954	Maureen Connolly, USA
	Lew Hoad, AUS
1955	Darlene Hard, USA
	Gordon Forbes, RSA
1956	Thelma Coyne Long, AUS
	Luis Ayala, CHI
1957	Vera Puzejova, TCH
	Jiri Javorsky, TCH
1958	Shirley Bloomer, GBR
	Nicola Pietrangeli, ITA
1959	Yola Ramírez, MEX
	Billy Knight, GBR
1960	Maria Bueno, BRA
	Bob Howe, AUS
1961	Darlene Hard, USA
	Rod Laver, AUS
1962	Renee Schuurman, RSA
	Bob Howe, AUS
1963	Margaret Smith, AUS
	Ken Fletcher, AUS
1964	Margaret Smith, AUS
	Ken Fletcher, AUS
1965	Margaret Smith, AUS
	Ken Fletcher, AUS
1966	Annette Van Zyl, RSA
	Frew McMillan, RSA

Year	Winner
1967	Billie Jean King, USA
	Owen Davidson, AUS
1968	Françoise Durr, FRA
	Jean Claude Barclay, FRA
1969	Margaret Smith Court, AUS
	Marty Riessen, USA
1970	Billie Jean King, USA
	Bob Hewitt, RSA
1971	Françoise Durr, FRA
	Jean Claude Barclay, FRA
1972	Evonne Goolagong, AUS
	Kim Warwick, AUS
1973	Françoise Durr, FRA
	Jean Claude Barclay, FRA
1974	Martina Navratilova, TCH
	Ivan Molina, COL
1975	Fiorella Bonicelli, URU
	Thomaz Koch, BRA
1976	Ilana Kloss, RSA
	Kim Warwick, AUS
1977	Mary Carillo, USA
	John McEnroe, USA
1978	Renata Tomanova, TCH
	Pavel Slozil, TCH
1979	Wendy Turnbull, AUS
	Bob Hewitt, RSA
1980	Anne Smith, USA
	Billy Martin, USA
1981	Andrea Jaeger, USA
	Jimmy Arias, USA
1982	Wendy Turnbull, AUS
	John Lloyd, GBR
1983	Barbara Jordan, USA
	Eliot Teltscher, USA
1984	Anne Smith, USA
	Dick Stockton, USA
1985	Martina Navratilova, USA
	Heinz Günthardt, SUI
1986	Kathy Jordan, USA
	Ken Flach, USA
1987	Pam Shriver, USA
	Emilio Sánchez, ESP
1988	Lori McNeil, USA
	Jorge Lozano, MEX
1989	Manon Bollegraf, NED
	Tom Nijssen, NED
1990	Arantxa Sánchez Vicario, ESP
	Jorge Lozano, MEX

Year	Winner
1991	Helena Suková, TCH
	Cyril Suk, TCH
1992	Arantxa Sánchez Vicario, ESP
	Todd Woodbridge, AUS
1993	Eugenia Maniokova, RUS
	Andrei Olkhovskiy, RUS
1994	Kristie Boogert, NED
	Menno Oosting, NED
1995	Larisa Savchenko Neiland, LAT
	Mark Woodforde, AUS
1996	Patricia Tarabini, ARG
	Javier Frana, ARG
1997	Rika Hiraki, JPN
	Manesh Bhupathi, IND
1998	Venus Williams, USA
	Justin Gimelstob, USA
1999	Katarina Srebotnik, SLV
	Piet Norval, RSA
2000	Mariaan de Swardt, RSA
	David Adams, RSA
2001	Virginia Ruano Pascual, ESP
	Tomás Carbonell, ESP
2002	Cara Black, ZIM
	Wayne Black, ZIM
2003	Lisa Raymond, USA
	Mike Bryan, USA
2004	Tatiana Golovin, FRA
	Richard Gasquet, FRA
2005	Daniela Hantuchová, SVK
	Fabrice Santoro, FRA
2006	Katarina Srebotnik, SLV
	Nenad Zimonjić, SRB
2007	Nathalie Dechy, FRA
	Andy Ram, ISR
2008	Victoria Azarenka, BLR
	Bob Bryan, USA
2009	Liezel Huber, USA
	Bob Bryan, USA
2010	Katarina Srebotnik, SVK
	Nenad Zimonjić, SRB
2011	Casey Dellacqua, AUS
	Scott Lipsky, USA

Appendix E: Australian Championships/Open Champions

The tournament was known as the Australasian Championships from 1905 to 1926, the Australian Championships from 1927 to 1968, and the Australian Open from 1969 to date.

Table 11. Singles

Year	Men	Women
1905	Rodney Heath, AUS	not held
1906	Anthony Wilding, NZL	not held
1907	Horace Rice, AUS	not held
1908	Fred Alexander, USA	not held
1909	Anthony Wilding, NZL	not held
1910	Rodney Heath, AUS	not held
1911	Norman Brookes, AUS	not held
1912	James Cecil Parke, IRL	not held
1913	Ernie Parker, AUS	not held
1914	Arthur O'Hara Wood, AUS	not held
1915	Gordon Lowe, GBR	not held
1916–18	not held	not held
1919	Algernon Kingscote, GBR	not held
1920	Pat O'Hara Wood, AUS	not held
1921	Rhys Gemmell, AUS	not held
1922	James Anderson, AUS	Margaret Molesworth, AUS
1923	Pat O'Hara Wood, AUS	Margaret Molesworth, AUS
1924	James Anderson, AUS	Sylvia Lance, AUS
1925	James Anderson, AUS	Daphne Akhurst, AUS
1926	John Hawkes, AUS	Daphne Akhurst, AUS
1927	Gerald Patterson, AUS	Esna Boyd, AUS
1928	Jean Borotra, FRA	Daphne Akhurst, AUS
1929	John Colin Gregory, GBR	Daphne Akhurst, AUS
1930	Edgar Moon, AUS	Daphne Akhurst, AUS
1931	Jack Crawford, AUS	Coral M. Buttsworth, AUS
1932	Jack Crawford, AUS	Coral M. Buttsworth, AUS
1933	Jack Crawford, AUS	Joan Hartigan, AUS
1934	Fred Perry, GBR	Joan Hartigan, AUS
1935	Jack Crawford, AUS	Dorothy Round, GBR
1936	Adrian Quist, AUS	Joan Hartigan, AUS
1937	Vivian McGrath, AUS	Nancye Wynne, AUS

Year	Men	Women
1938	Don Budge, USA	Dorothy Bundy, USA
1939	John Bromwich, AUS	Emily Hood Westacott, AUS
1940	Adrian Quist, AUS	Nancye Wynne, AUS
1941–45	not held	not held
1946	John Bromwich, AUS	Nancye Wynne Bolton, AUS
1947	Dinny Pails, AUS	Nancye Wynne Bolton, AUS
1948	Adrian Quist, AUS	Nancye Wynne Bolton, AUS
1949	Frank Sedgman, AUS	Doris Hart, USA
1950	Frank Sedgman, AUS	Louise Brough, USA
1951	Richard Savitt, USA	Nancye Wynne Bolton, AUS
1952	Ken McGregor, AUS	Thelma Coyne Long, AUS
1953	Ken Rosewall, AUS	Maureen Connolly, USA
1954	Merv Rose, AUS	Thelma Coyne Long, AUS
1955	Ken Rosewall, AUS	Beryl Penrose, AUS
1956	Lew Hoad, AUS	Mary Carter, AUS
1957	Ashley Cooper, AUS	Shirley Fry, USA
1958	Ashley Cooper, AUS	Angela Mortimer, GBR
1959	Alex Olmedo, USA	Mary Carter Reitano, AUS
1960	Rod Laver, AUS	Margaret Smith, AUS
1961	Roy Emerson, AUS	Margaret Smith, AUS
1962	Rod Laver, AUS	Margaret Smith, AUS
1963	Roy Emerson, AUS	Margaret Smith, AUS
1964	Roy Emerson, AUS	Margaret Smith, AUS
1965	Roy Emerson, AUS	Margaret Smith, AUS
1966	Roy Emerson, AUS	Margaret Smith, AUS
1967	Roy Emerson, AUS	Nancy Richey, USA
1968	Bill Bowrey, AUS	Billie Jean King, USA
1969	Rod Laver, AUS	Margaret Smith Court, AUS
1970	Arthur Ashe, USA	Margaret Smith Court, AUS
1971	Ken Rosewall, AUS	Margaret Smith Court, AUS
1972	Ken Rosewall, AUS	Virginia Wade, GBR
1973	John Newcombe, AUS	Margaret Smith Court, AUS
1974	Jimmy Connors, USA	Evonne Goolagong, AUS
1975	John Newcombe, AUS	Evonne Goolagong, AUS
1976	Mark Edmondson, AUS	Evonne Goolagong Cawley, AUS
1977	Roscoe Tanner, USA	Kerry Melville Reid, AUS
1977*	Vitas Gerulaitis, USA	Evonne Goolagong Cawley, AUS
1978	Guillermo Vilas, ARG	Chris O'Neil, AUS
1979	Guillermo Vilas, ARG	Barbara Jordan, USA
1980	Brian Teacher, USA	Hana Mandlíková, TCH
1981	Johan Kriek, RSA	Martina Navratilova, USA
1982	Johan Kriek, RSA	Chris Evert Lloyd, USA
1983	Mats Wilander, SWE	Martina Navratilova, USA
1984	Mats Wilander, SWE	Chris Evert Lloyd, USA
1985	Stefan Edberg, SWE	Martina Navratilova, USA
1986*	not held	not held
1987	Stefan Edberg, SWE	Hana Mandlíková, TCH
1988	Mats Wilander, SWE	Steffi Graf, FRG
1989	Ivan Lendl, TCH	Steffi Graf, FRG

Year	Men	Women
1990	Ivan Lendl, TCH	Steffi Graf, FRG
1991	Boris Becker, GER	Monica Seles, USA
1992	Jim Courier, USA	Monica Seles, USA
1993	Jim Courier, USA	Monica Seles, USA
1994	Pete Sampras, USA	Steffi Graf, FRG
1995	Andre Agassi, USA	Mary Pierce, FRA
1996	Boris Becker, GER	Monica Seles, USA
1997	Pete Sampras, USA	Martina Hingis, SUI
1998	Petr Korda, CZE	Martina Hingis, SUI
1999	Yevgeny Kafelnikov, RUS	Martina Hingis, SUI
2000	Andre Agassi, USA	Lindsay Davenport, USA
2001	Andre Agassi, USA	Jennifer Capriati, USA
2002	Thomas Johansson, SWE	Jennifer Capriati, USA
2003	Andre Agassi, USA	Serena Williams, USA
2004	Roger Federer, SUI	Justine Henin-Hardenne, BEL
2005	Marat Safin, RUS	Serena Williams, USA
2006	Roger Federer, SUI	Amélie Mauresmo, FRA
2007	Roger Federer, SUI	Serena Williams, USA
2008	Novak Djoković, SRB	Maria Sharapova, RUS
2009	Rafael Nadal, ESP	Serena Williams, USA
2010	Roger Federer, SUI	Serena Williams, USA
2011	Novak Djoković	Kim Clijsters, BEL

Table 12. Doubles

Year	Men	Women
1905	Randolph Lycett, GBR Tom Tachell, AUS	not held
1906	Rodney Heath, AUS Anthony Wilding, NZL	not held
1907	Bill Gregg, AUS Harry Parker, AUS	not held
1908	Fred Alexander, USA Alfred Dunlop, AUS	not held
1909	J. P. Keane, AUS Ernest Parker, AUS	not held
1910	Ashley Campbell, AUS Horace Rice, AUS	not held
1911	Rodney Heath, AUS Randolph Lycett, GBR	not held
1912	James Cecil Parke, IRL Charles Dixon, GBR	not held
1913	Alf Hedeman, AUS Ernest Parker, AUS	not held
1914	Ashley Campbell AUS Gerald Patterson, AUS	not held

Year	Men	Women
1915	Horace Rice, AUS Clarrie Todd, AUS	not held
1916–18	not held	not held
1919	Pat O'Hara Wood, AUS Ronald Thomas, AUS	not held
1920	Pat O'Hara Wood, AUS Ronald Thomas, AUS	not held
1921	S. H. Eaton, AUS Rhys Gemmell, AUS	not held
1922	John Hawkes, AUS Gerald Patterson, AUS	Esna Boyd, AUS Marjorie Mountain, AUS
1923	Pat O'Hara Wood, AUS Bert St. John, AUS	Esna Boyd, AUS Sylvia Lance, AUS
1924	James Anderson, AUS Norman Brookes, AUS	Daphne Akhurst, AUS Sylvia Lance, AUS
1925	Pat O'Hara Wood, AUS Gerald Patterson, AUS	Daphne Akhurst, AUS Sylvia Lance Harper, AUS
1926	John Hawkes, AUS Gerald Patterson, AUS	Esna Boyd, AUS Meryl O'Hara Wood, AUS
1927	John Hawkes, AUS Gerald Patterson, AUS	Louie Bickerton, AUS Meryl O'Hara Wood, AUS
1928	Jean Borotra, FRA Jacques Brugnon, FRA	Daphne Akhurst, AUS Esna Boyd, AUS
1929	Jack Crawford, AUS Harry Hopman, AUS	Daphne Akhurst, AUS Louie Bickerton, AUS
1930	Jack Crawford, AUS Harry Hopman, AUS	Emily Hood, AUS Margaret Molesworth, AUS
1931	Charles Donohue, AUS Ray Dunlop, AUS	Daphne Akhurst Cozens, AUS Louie Bickerton, AUS
1932	Jack Crawford, AUS Gar Moon, AUS	Coral M. Buttsworth, AUS Marjorie Cox Crawford, AUS
1933	Keith Gledhill, USA Ellsworth Vines, USA	Emily Hood Westacott, AUS Margaret Molesworth, AUS
1934	Fred Perry, GBR Pat Hughes, GBR	Emily Hood Westacott, AUS Margaret Molesworth, AUS
1935	Jack Crawford, AUS Vivian McGrath, AUS	Evelyn Dearman, AUS Nancy Lyle, AUS
1936	Adrian Quist, AUS Don Turnbull, AUS	Thelma Coyne Long, AUS Nancye Wynne, AUS
1937	Adrian Quist, AUS Don Turnbull, AUS	Thelma Coyne Long, AUS Nancye Wynne, AUS
1938	John Bromwich, AUS Adrian Quist, AUS	Thelma Coyne Long, AUS Nancye Wynne, AUS
1939	John Bromwich, AUS Adrian Quist, AUS	Thelma Coyne Long, AUS Nancye Wynne, AUS
1940	John Bromwich, AUS Adrian Quist, AUS	Thelma Coyne Long, AUS Nancye Wynne, AUS
1941–45	not held	not held

Year	Men	Women
1946	John Bromwich, AUS Adrian Quist, AUS	Mary Bevis, AUS Joyce Fitch, AUS
1947	John Bromwich, AUS Adrian Quist, AUS	Thelma Coyne Long, AUS Nancye Wynne Bolton, AUS
1948	John Bromwich, AUS Adrian Quist, AUS	Thelma Coyne Long, AUS Nancye Wynne Bolton, AUS
1949	John Bromwich, AUS Adrian Quist, AUS	Thelma Coyne Long, AUS Nancye Wynne Bolton, AUS
1950	John Bromwich, AUS Adrian Quist, AUS	Louise Brough, USA Doris Hart, USA
1951	Ken McGregor, AUS Frank Sedgman, AUS	Thelma Coyne Long, AUS Nancye Wynne Bolton, AUS
1952	Ken McGregor, AUS Frank Sedgman, AUS	Thelma Coyne Long, AUS Nancye Wynne Bolton, AUS
1953	Lew Hoad, AUS Ken Rosewall, AUS	Maureen Connolly, AUS Julia Sampson, AUS
1954	Rex Hartwig, AUS Merv Rose, AUS	Mary Bevis Hawton, AUS Beryl Penrose, AUS
1955	Vic Seixas, USA Tony Trabert, USA	Mary Bevis Hawton, AUS Beryl Penrose, AUS
1956	Lew Hoad, AUS Ken Rosewall, AUS	Mary Bevis Hawton, AUS Thelma Coyne Long, AUS
1957	Neale Fraser, AUS Lew Hoad, AUS	Althea Gibson, AUS Shirley Fry, AUS
1958	Ashley Cooper, AUS Neale Fraser, AUS	Mary Bevis Hawton, AUS Thelma Coyne Long, AUS
1959	Rod Laver, AUS Bob Mark, AUS	Sandra Reynolds, RSA Renee Schuurman, RSA
1960	Rod Laver, AUS Bob Mark, AUS	Maria Bueno, BRA Christine Truman, GBR
1961	Rod Laver, AUS Bob Mark, AUS	Mary Carter Reitano, AUS Margaret Smith, AUS
1962	Roy Emerson, AUS Neale Fraser, AUS	Robyn Ebbern, AUS Margaret Smith, AUS
1963	Bob Hewitt, AUS Fred Stolle, AUS	Robyn Ebbern, AUS Margaret Smith, AUS
1964	Bob Hewitt, AUS Fred Stolle, AUS	Judy Tegart Dalton, AUS Lesley Turner, AUS
1965	John Newcombe, AUS Tony Roche, AUS	Margaret Smith, AUS Lesley Turner, AUS
1966	Roy Emerson, AUS Fred Stolle, AUS	Carol Caldwell Graebner, USA Nancy Richey, USA
1967	John Newcombe, AUS Tony Roche, AUS	Judy Tegart Dalton, AUS Lesley Turner, AUS
1968	Dick Crealy, AUS Allan Stone, AUS	Karen Krantzcke, AUS Kerry Melville, AUS

Year	Men	Women
1969	Roy Emerson, AUS Rod Laver, AUS	Margaret Smith Court, AUS Judy Tegart Dalton, AUS
1970	Bob Lutz, USA Stan Smith, USA	Margaret Smith Court, AUS Judy Tegart Dalton, AUS
1971	John Newcombe, AUS Tony Roche, AUS	Evonne Goolagong, AUS Margaret Smith Court, AUS
1972	Owen Davidson, AUS Ken Rosewall, AUS	Helen Gourlay, AUS Kerry Harris, AUS
1973	Mal Anderson, AUS John Newcombe, AUS	Margaret Smith Court, AUS Virginia Wade, GBR
1974	Ross Case, AUS Geoff Masters, AUS	Evonne Goolagong, AUS Peggy Michel, USA
1975	John Alexander, AUS Phil Dent, AUS	Evonne Goolagong, AUS Peggy Michel, USA
1976	John Newcombe, AUS Tony Roche, AUS	Evonne Goolagong Cawley, AUS Helen Gourlay, AUS
1977	Arthur Ashe, USA Tony Roche, AUS	Diane Fromholtz Balestrat, AUS Helen Gourlay Cawley, AUS
1977*	Ray Ruffels, AUS Allan Stone, AUS	**Evonne Goolagong Cawley, AUS Helen Gourlay Cawley, AUS Kerry Melville Reid, AUS Mona Schallau Guerrant, USA
1978	Wojtek Fibak, POL Kim Warwick, AUS	Betsy Nagelsen, USA Renáta Tomanová, TCH
1979	Peter McNamara, AUS Paul McNamee, AUS	Judy Chaloner, AUS Dianne Evers, AUS
1980	Mark Edmondson, AUS Kim Warwick, AUS	Betsy Nagelsen, USA Martina Navratilova, USA
1981	Mark Edmondson, AUS Kim Warwick, AUS	Kathy Jordan, USA Anne Smith, USA
1982	John Alexander, AUS John Fitzgerald, AUS	Martina Navratilova, USA Pam Shriver, USA
1983	Mark Edmondson, AUS Paul McNamee, AUS	Martina Navratilova, USA Pam Shriver, USA
1984	Mark Edmondson, AUS Sherwood Stewart, USA	Martina Navratilova, USA Pam Shriver, USA
1985	Paul Annacone, USA Christo van Rensburg, RSA	Martina Navratilova, USA Pam Shriver, USA
1986*	not held	not held
1987	Stefan Edberg, SWE Anders Järryd, SWE	Martina Navratilova, USA Pam Shriver, USA
1988	Rick Leach, USA Jim Pugh, USA	Martina Navratilova, USA Pam Shriver, USA
1989	Rick Leach, USA Jim Pugh, USA	Martina Navratilova, USA Pam Shriver, USA
1990	Pieter Aldrich, RSA Danie Visser, RSA	Jana Novotná, TCH Helena Suková, TCH

Year	Men	Women
1991	Scott Davis, USA David Pate, USA	Patty Fendick, USA Mary Joe Fernández, USA
1992	Todd Woodbridge, AUS Mark Woodforde, AUS	Arantxa Sánchez Vicario, ESP Helena Suková, TCH
1993	Danie Visser, RSA Laurie Warder, AUS	Gigi Fernández, USA Natalia Zvereva, BLR
1994	Jacco Eltingh, NED Paul Haarhuis, NED	Gigi Fernández, USA Natalia Zvereva, BLR
1995	Jared Palmer, USA Richey Reneberg, USA	Jana Novotná, CZE Arantxa Sánchez Vicario, ESP
1996	Stefan Edberg, SWE Petr Korda, CZE	Chanda Rubin, USA Arantxa Sánchez Vicario, ESP
1997	Todd Woodbridge, AUS Mark Woodforde, AUS	Martina Hingis, SUI Natalia Zvereva, BLR
1998	Jonas Björkman, SWE Jacco Eltingh, NED	Martina Hingis, SUI Mirjana Lučić, CRO
1999	Patrick Rafter, AUS Jonas Björkman, SWE	Martina Hingis, SUI Anna Kournakova, RUS
2000	Rick Leach, USA Ellis Ferreira, RSA	Lisa Raymond, USA Rennae Stubbs, AUS
2001	Jonas Björkman, SWE Todd Woodbridge, AUS	Serena Williams, USA Venus Williams, USA
2002	Daniel Nestor, CAN Mark Knowles, BAH	Martina Hingis, SUI Anna Kournakova, RUS
2003	Michaël Llodra, FRA Fabrice Santoro, FRA	Serena Williams, USA Venus Williams, USA
2004	Fabrice Santoro, FRA Michaël Llodra, FRA	Virginia Ruano Pascual, ESP Paola Suárez, ARG
2005	Wayne Black, ZIM Kevin Ullyett, ZIM	Svetlana Kuznetsova, RUS Alicia Molik, AUS
2006	Mike Bryan, USA Bob Bryan, USA	Yan Zi, CHN Zheng Jie, CHN
2007	Mike Bryan, USA Bob Bryan, USA	Cara Black, ZIM Liezel Huber, RSA
2008	Jonathan Ehrlich, ISR Andy Ram, ISR	Alona Bondarenko, UKR Katyryna Bondarenko, UKR
2009	Mike Bryan, USA Bob Bryan, USA	Serena Williams, USA Venus Williams, USA
2010	Mike Bryan, USA Bob Bryan, USA	Serena Williams, USA Venus Williams, USA
2011	Mike Bryan, USA Bob Bryan, USA	Gisela Dulko, ARG Flavia Pennetta, ITA

Table 13. Mixed Doubles

Year	Winner
1922	Esna Boyd, AUS
	Jack Hawkes, AUS
1923	Sylvia Lance, AUS
	Horace Rice, AUS
1924	Daphne Akhurst, AUS
	John Willard, AUS
1925	Daphne Akhurst, AUS
	John Willard, AUS
1926	Esna Boyd, AUS
	Jack Hawkes, AUS
1927	Esna Boyd, AUS
	Jack Hawkes, AUS
1928	Daphne Akhurst, AUS
	Jean Borotra, FRA
1929	Daphne Akhurst, AUS
	Gar Moon, AUS
1930	Nell Hall, AUS
	Harry Hopman, AUS
1931	Marjorie Cox Crawford, AUS
	Jack Crawford, AUS
1932	Marjorie Cox Crawford, AUS
	Jack Crawford, AUS
1933	Marjorie Cox Crawford, AUS
	Jack Crawford, AUS
1934	Joan Hartigan, AUS
	Gar Moon, AUS
1935	Louie Bickerton, AUS
	Christian Boussus, FRA
1936	Nell Hall Hopman, AUS
	Harry Hopman, AUS
1937	Nell Hall Hopman, AUS
	Harry Hopman, AUS
1938	Margaret Wilson, AUS
	John Bromwich, AUS
1939	Nell Hall Hopman, AUS
	Harry Hopman, AUS
1940	Nancye Wynne, AUS
	Colin Long, AUS
1941–45	not held
1946	Nancye Wynne Bolton, AUS
	Colin Long, AUS
1947	Nancye Wynne Bolton, AUS
	Colin Long, AUS
1948	Nancye Bolton, AUS
	Colin Long, AUS
1949	Doris Hart, USA
	Frank Sedgman, AUS

Year	Winner
1950	Doris Hart, USA
	Frank Sedgman, AUS
1951	Thelma Coyne Long, AUS
	George Worthington, AUS
1952	Thelma Coyne Long, AUS
	George Worthington, AUS
1953	Julia Sampson, AUS
	Rex Hartwig, AUS
1954	Thelma Coyne Long, AUS
	Rex Hartwig, AUS
1955	Thelma Coyne Long, AUS
	George Worthington, AUS
1956	Beryl Penrose, AUS
	Neale Fraser, AUS
1957	Fay Muller, AUS
	Mal Anderson, AUS
1958	Mary Bevis Hawton, AUS
	Bob Howe, AUS
1959	Sandra Reynolds, AUS
	Bob Mark, AUS
1960	Jan Lehane, AUS
	Trevor Fancutt, AUS
1961	Jan Lehane, AUS
	Bob Hewitt, AUS
1962	Lesley Turner, AUS
	Fred Stolle, AUS
1963	Margaret Smith, AUS
	Ken Fletcher, AUS
1964	Margaret Smith, AUS
	Ken Fletcher, AUS
1965**	Margaret Smith, AUS
	John Newcombe, AUS
	Robyn Ebbern, AUS
	Owen Davidson, AUS
1966	Judy Tegart, AUS
	Tony Roche, AUS
1967	Lesley Turner, AUS
	Owen Davidson, AUS
1968	Billie Jean King, USA
	Dick Crealy, AUS
1969**	Margaret Smith Court, AUS
	Marty Riessen, USA
	Ann Haydon-Jones, GBR
	Fred Stolle, AUS
1970–86	not held
1987	Zina Garrison, USA
	Sherwood Stewart, USA
1988	Jana Novotná, TCH
	Jim Pugh, USA

Year	Winner
1989	Jana Novotná, TCH
	Jim Pugh, USA
1990	Natalia Zvereva, BLR
	Jim Pugh, USA
1991	Jo Durie, GBR
	Jeremy Bates, GBR
1992	Nicole Provis, AUS
	Mark Woodforde, AUS
1993	Arantxa Sánchez Vicario, ESP
	Todd Woodbridge, AUS
1994	Larisa Savchenko Neiland, LAT
	Andrei Olhovskiy, RUS
1995	Natalia Zvereva, BLR
	Rick Leach, USA
1996	Larisa Savchenko Neiland, LAT
	Mark Woodforde, AUS
1997	Manon Bollegraf, NED
	Rick Leach, USA
1998	Venus Williams, USA
	Justin Gimelstob, USA
1999	Mariaan de Swardt, RSA
	David Adams, RSA
2000	Rennae Stubbs, AUS
	Jared Palmer, USA
2001	Corina Morariu, USA
	Ellis Ferreira, RSA
2002	Daniela Hantuchová, SVK
	Kevin Ulyett, ZIM
2003	Martina Navratilova, USA
	Leander Paes, IND
2004	Elena Bovina, RUS
	Nenad Zimonjić, SCG
2005	Samantha Stosur, AUS
	Scott Draper, USA
2006	Martina Hingis, SUI
	Mahesh Bhupathi, IND
2007	Elena Likhovtseva, RUS
	Daniel Nestor, CAN
2008	Sun Tiantian, CHN
	Nenad Zimonjić, SRB
2009	Sanya Mirza, IND
	Mahesh Bhupathi, IND
2010	Cara Black, ZIM
	Leander Paes, IND
2011	Katrina Srebotnik, SLV
	Daniel Nestor, CAN

* The tournament date changed from January to December in 1977. It was changed back in 1987.

* Cochampions (final match rained out)

Appendix F:
Davis Cup Champions

Table 14. Davis Cup Champions

Year	Winner	Score	Loser	Court	Site
1900	United States	3–0	British Isles	Grass	Boston, MA, USA
1901	not played				
1902	United States	3–2	British Isles	Grass	Brooklyn, NY, USA
1903	British Isles	4–1	United States	Grass	Boston, MA, USA
1904	British Isles	5–0	Belgium	Grass	London, ENG
1905	British Isles	5–0	United States	Grass	London, ENG
1906	British Isles	5–0	United States	Grass	London, ENG
1907	Australasia	3–2	British Isles	Grass	London, ENG
1908	Australasia	3–2	United States	Grass	Melbourne, AUS
1909	Australasia	5–0	United States	Grass	Melbourne, AUS
1910	not played				
1911	Australasia	4–0	United States	Grass	Christchurch, NZL
1912	British Isles	3–2	Australasia	Grass	Melbourne, AUS
1913	United States	3–2	Great Britain	Grass	London, ENG
1914	Australasia	3–2	United States	Grass	New York, NY, USA
1915	not played				
1916	not played				
1917	not played				
1918	not played				
1919	Australasia	4–1	Great Britain	Grass	Sydney, AUS
1920	United States	5–0	Australasia	Grass	Auckland, NZL
1921	United States	5–0	Japan	Grass	New York, NY, USA
1922	United States	4–1	Australasia	Grass	New York, NY, USA
1923	United States	4–1	Australia	Grass	New York, NY, USA
1924	United States	5–0	Australia	Grass	Philadelphia, PA, USA
1925	United States	5–0	France	Grass	Philadelphia, PA, USA
1926	United States	4–1	France	Grass	Philadelphia, PA, USA
1927	France	3–2	United States	Grass	Philadelphia, PA, USA
1928	France	4–1	United States	Clay	Paris, FRA
1929	France	3–2	United States	Clay	Paris, FRA
1930	France	4–1	United States	Clay	Paris, FRA
1931	France	3–2	Great Britain	Clay	Paris, FRA
1932	France	3–2	United States	Clay	Paris, FRA

Year	Winner	Score	Loser	Court	Site
1933	Great Britain	3–2	France	Clay	Paris, FRA
1934	Great Britain	4–1	United States	Grass	London, ENG
1935	Great Britain	5–0	United States	Grass	London, ENG
1936	Great Britain	3–2	Australia	Grass	London, ENG
1937	United States	4–1	Great Britain	Grass	London, ENG
1938	United States	3–2	Australia	Grass	Philadelphia, PA, USA
1939	Australia	3–2	United States	Grass	Haverford, PA, USA
1940	not played				
1941	not played				
1942	not played				
1943	not played				
1944	not played				
1945	not played				
1946	United States	5–0	Australia	Grass	Melbourne, AUS
1947	United States	4–1	Australia	Grass	New York, NY, USA
1948	United States	5–0	Australia	Grass	New York, NY, USA
1949	United States	4–1	Australia	Grass	New York, NY, USA
1950	Australia	4–1	United States	Grass	New York, NY, USA
1951	Australia	3–2	United States	Grass	Sydney, AUS
1952	Australia	4–1	United States	Grass	Adelaide, AUS
1953	Australia	3–2	United States	Grass	Melbourne, AUS
1954	United States	3–2	Australia	Grass	Sydney, AUS
1955	Australia	5–0	United States	Grass	New York, NY, USA
1956	Australia	5–0	United States	Grass	Adelaide, AUS
1957	Australia	3–2	United States	Grass	Melbourne, AUS
1958	United States	3–2	Australia	Grass	Brisbane, AUS
1959	Australia	3–2	United States	Grass	New York, NY, USA
1960	Australia	4–1	Italy	Grass	Sydney, AUS
1961	Australia	5–0	Italy	Grass	Melbourne, AUS
1962	Australia	5–0	Mexico	Grass	Brisbane, AUS
1963	United States	3–2	Australia	Grass	Adelaide, AUS
1964	Australia	3–2	United States	Clay	Cleveland, OH, USA
1965	Australia	4–1	Spain	Grass	Sydney, AUS
1966	Australia	4–1	India	Grass	Melbourne, AUS
1967	Australia	4–1	Spain	Grass	Brisbane, AUS
1968	United States	4–1	Australia	Grass	Adelaide, AUS
1969	United States	5–0	Romania	Hard	Cleveland, OH, USA
1970	United States	5–0	W. Germany	Hard	Cleveland, OH, USA
1971	United States	3–2	Romania	Clay	Charlotte, NC, USA
1972	United States	3–2	Romania	Clay	Bucharest, ROM
1973	Australia	5–0	United States	Carpet	Cleveland, OH, USA*
1974	South Africa**	w/o	India	not held	
1975	Sweden	3–2	Czech.	Carpet	Stockholm, SWE*
1976	Italy	4–1	Chile	Clay	Santiago, CHI
1977	Australia	3–1	Italy	Grass	Sydney, AUS
1978	United States	4–1	Great Britain	Hard	R. Mirage, CA, USA

Year	Winner	Score	Loser	Court	Site
1979	United States	5–0	Italy	Carpet	S. Francisco, CA, USA*
1980	Czechoslovakia	4–1	Italy	Carpet	Prague, TCH*
1981	United States	3–1	Argentina	Carpet	Cleveland, OH, USA*
1982	United States	4–1	France	Clay	Grenoble, FRA*
1983	Australia	3–2	Sweden	Grass	Melbourne, AUS
1984	Sweden	4–1	United States	Clay	Gothenburg, SWE*
1985	Sweden	3–2	W. Germany	Carpet	Munich, FRG*
1986	Australia	3–2	Sweden	Grass	Melbourne, AUS
1987	Sweden	5–0	India	Clay	Gothenburg, SWE*
1988	West Germany	4–1	Sweden	Clay	Gothenburg, SWE*
1989	West Germany	4–1	Sweden	Carpet	Stuttgart, FRG*
1990	United States	3–2	Australia	Clay	St. Petersburg, FL, USA*
1991	France	3–1	United States	Carpet	Lyon, FRA*
1992	United States	3–1	Switzerland	Hard	Fort Worth, TX, USA*
1993	Germany	4–1	Australia	Clay	Düsseldorf, GER*
1994	Sweden	4–1	Russia	Carpet	Moscow, RUS*
1995	United States	3–2	Russia	Clay	Moscow, RUS*
1996	France	3–2	Sweden	Hard	Malmö, SWE*
1997	Sweden	5–0	United States	Carpet	Gothenburg, SWE*
1998	Sweden	4–1	Italy	Clay	Milan, ITA*
1999	Australia	3–2	France	Clay	Nice, FRA*
2000	Spain	3–1	Australia	Clay	Barcelona, ESP*
2001	France	3–2	Australia	Grass	Melbourne, AUS
2002	Russia	3–2	France	Clay	Paris, FRA*
2003	Australia	3–1	Spain	Grass	Melbourne, AUS
2004	Spain	3–2	United States	Clay	Seville, ESP*
2005	Croatia	3–2	Slovakia	Hard	Bratislava, SVK*
2006	Russia	3–2	Argentina	Hard	Moscow, RUS*
2007	United States	4–1	Russia	Hard	Portland, OR, USA*
2008	Spain	3–1	Argentina	Hard	Mar del Plata, ARG*
2009	Spain	5–0	Czech Rep.	Clay	Barcelona, ESP*
2010	Serbia	3–2	France	Hard	Belgrade, SRB

Australasia was comprised of players from Australia and New Zealand.

* Matches played indoors

** India refused to play South Africa.

Table 15. All-Time Final Round Results by Country

	W–L
United States	32–29
Australia/Australasia	28–19
Great Britain/British Isles	9–8
France	9–7
Sweden	7–5
Spain	4–3
Germany/West Germany	3–2
Russia	2–3
Italy	1–6
Czechoslovakia/Czech Republic/Slovakia	1–3
South Africa	1–0
Croatia	1–0
Serbia	1–0
Argentina	0–3
India	0–3
Romania	0–3
Belgium	0–1
Japan	0–1
Mexico	0–1
Chile	0–1
Switzerland	0–1

Appendix G:
Wightman Cup Champions

Table 16. Wightman Cup Champions

Year	Winner	Score	Loser	Site
1923	United States	7–0	Great Britain	Forest Hills, NY, USA
1924	Great Britain	6–1	United States	Wimbledon, ENG
1925	Great Britain	4–3	United States	Forest Hills, NY, USA
1926	United States	4–3	Great Britain	Wimbledon, ENG
1927	United States	5–2	Great Britain	Forest Hills, NY, USA
1928	Great Britain	4–3	United States	Wimbledon, ENG
1929	United States	4–3	Great Britain	Forest Hills, NY, USA
1930	Great Britain	4–3	United States	Wimbledon, ENG
1931	United States	5–2	Great Britain	Forest Hills, NY, USA
1932	United States	4–3	Great Britain	Wimbledon, ENG
1933	United States	4–3	Great Britain	Forest Hills, NY, USA
1934	United States	5–2	Great Britain	Wimbledon, ENG
1935	United States	4–3	Great Britain	Forest Hills, NY, USA
1936	United States	4–3	Great Britain	Wimbledon, ENG
1937	United States	6–1	Great Britain	Forest Hills, NY, USA
1938	United States	5–2	Great Britain	Wimbledon, ENG
1939	United States	5–2	Great Britain	Forest Hills, NY, USA
1940	not played			
1941	not played			
1942	not played			
1943	not played			
1944	not played			
1945	not played			
1946	United States	7–0	Great Britain	Wimbledon, ENG
1947	United States	7–0	Great Britain	Forest Hills, NY, USA
1948	United States	6–1	Great Britain	Wimbledon, ENG
1949	United States	7–0	Great Britain	Haverford, PA, USA
1950	United States	7–0	Great Britain	Wimbledon, ENG
1951	United States	6–1	Great Britain	Chestnut Hill, MA, USA
1952	United States	7–0	Great Britain	Wimbledon, ENG
1953	United States	7–0	Great Britain	Rye, NY, USA
1954	United States	6–0	Great Britain	Wimbledon, ENG
1955	United States	6–1	Great Britain	Rye, NY, USA
1956	United States	5–2	Great Britain	Wimbledon, ENG
1957	United States	6–1	Great Britain	Sewickley, PA, USA
1958	Great Britain	4–3	United States	Wimbledon, ENG
1959	United States	6–1	Great Britain	Sewickley, PA, USA

Year	Winner	Score	Loser	Site
1960	Great Britain	4–3	United States	Wimbledon, ENG
1961	United States	6–1	Great Britain	Chicago, IL, USA
1962	United States	4–3	Great Britain	Wimbledon, ENG
1963	United States	6–1	Great Britain	Cleveland, OH, USA
1964	United States	5–2	Great Britain	Wimbledon, ENG
1965	United States	5–2	Great Britain	Cleveland, OH, USA
1966	United States	4–3	Great Britain	Wimbledon, ENG
1967	United States	6–1	Great Britain	Cleveland, OH, USA
1968	Great Britain	4–3	United States	Wimbledon, ENG
1969	United States	5–2	Great Britain	Cleveland, OH, USA
1970	United States	4–3	Great Britain	Wimbledon, ENG
1971	United States	4–3	Great Britain	Cleveland, OH, USA
1972	United States	3–2	Great Britain	Wimbledon, ENG
1973	United States	5–2	Great Britain	Brookline, MA, USA
1974	Great Britain	5–2	United States	Queensferry, WAL
1975	Great Britain	7–0	United States	Cleveland, OH, USA
1976	United States	4–3	Great Britain	Wimbledon, ENG
1977	United States	7–0	Great Britain	Oakland, CA, USA
1978	Great Britain	4–3	United States	London, ENG
1979	United States	7–0	Great Britain	West Palm Beach, FL, USA
1980	United States	5–2	Great Britain	London, ENG
1981	United States	7–0	Great Britain	Chicago, IL, USA
1982	United States	6–1	Great Britain	London, ENG
1983	United States	6–1	Great Britain	Williamsburg, VA, USA
1984	United States	5–2	Great Britain	London, ENG
1985	United States	7–0	Great Britain	Williamsburg, VA, USA
1986	United States	7–0	Great Britain	London, ENG
1987	United States	5–2	Great Britain	Williamsburg, VA, USA
1988	United States	7–0	Great Britain	London, ENG
1989	United States	7–0	Great Britain	Williamsburg, VA, USA

Overall totals: United States 51, Great Britain 10

Appendix H:
Federation Cup Champions

Table 17. Federation Cup Champions

Year	Winner	Score	Loser	Court	Site
1963	United States	2–1	Australia	Grass	London, ENG
1964	Australia	2–1	United States	Grass	Philadelphia, PA, USA
1965	Australia	2–1	United States	Grass	Melbourne, AUS
1966	United States	3–0	W. Germany	Clay	Turin, ITA
1967	United States	2–0	Great Britain	Clay	W. Berlin, GER
1968	Australia	3–0	Netherlands	Clay	Paris, FRA
1969	United States	2–1	Australia	Clay	Athens, GRE
1970	Australia	3–0	W. Germany	Clay	Freiburg, FRG
1971**	Australia	3–0	Great Britain	Grass	Perth, AUS
1972	South Africa	2–1	Great Britain	Hard	Johannesburg, RSA
1973	Australia	3–0	South Africa	Clay	Bad Homburg, FRG
1974	Australia	2–1	United States	Clay	Naples, ITA
1975	Czechoslovakia	3–0	Australia	Clay	Aix-en-Provence, FRA
1976	United States	2–1	Australia	Carpet	Philadelphia, PA, USA*
1977	United States	2–1	Australia	Grass	Eastbourne, ENG
1978	United States	2–1	Australia	Grass	Melbourne, AUS
1979	United States	3–0	Australia	Clay	Madrid, ESP
1980	United States	3–0	Australia	Clay	West Berlin, GER
1981	United States	3–0	Great Britain	Clay	Tokyo, JPN
1982	United States	3–0	W. Germany	Hard	Santa Clara, CA, USA
1983	Czechoslovakia	2–1	W. Germany	Clay	Zurich, SUI
1984	Czechoslovakia	2–1	Australia	Clay	São Paulo, BRA
1985	Czechoslovakia	2–1	United States	Hard	Nagoya, JPN
1986	United States	3–0	Czech	Clay	Prague, TCH
1987	West Germany	2–1	United States	Hard	Vancouver, CAN
1988	Czechoslovakia	2–1	Soviet Union	Hard	Melbourne, AUS
1989	United States	3–0	Spain	Hard	Tokyo, JPN
1990	United States	2–1	Soviet Union	Hard	Atlanta, GA, USA
1991	Spain	2–1	United States	Hard	Nottingham, ENG
1992	Germany	2–1	Spain	Clay	Frankfurt, GER
1993	Spain	3–0	Australia	Clay	Frankfurt, GER
1994	Spain	3–0	United States	Clay	Frankfurt, GER
1995	Spain	3–2	United States	Clay	Valencia, ESP

Year	Winner	Score	Loser	Court	Site
1996	United States	5–0	Spain	Carpet	Atlantic City, NJ, USA*
1997	France	4–1	Netherlands	Carpet	Den Bosch, NED*
1998	Spain	3–2	Switzerland	Hard	Geneva, SUI*
1999	United States	4–1	Russia	Hard	Stanford, CA, USA
2000	United States	5–0	Spain	Carpet	Las Vegas, NV, USA*
2001	Belgium	2–1	Russia	Clay	Madrid, ESP*
2002	Slovakia	3–1	Spain	Hard	Gran Canaria, ESP*
2003	France	4–1	United States	Carpet	Moscow, RUS
2004	Russia	3–2	France	Carpet	Moscow, RUS
2005	Russia	3–2	France	Clay	Paris, FRA
2006	Italy	3–2	Belgium	Hard	Charleroi, BEL*
2007	Russia	4–0	Italy	Hard	Moscow, RUS*
2008	Russia	4–0	Spain	Clay	Madrid, ESP
2009	Italy	4–0	United States	Clay	Reggio Calabria, ITA
2010	Italy	3–1	United States	Hard	San Diego, CA, USA

*Matches played indoors

** Matches played 27–29 December, 1970

Table 18. All-Time Final Round Results by Country

	W–L
United States	17–11
Australia/Australasia	7–10
Spain	5–6
Czechoslovakia/Slovakia	6–1
Russia/Soviet Union	4–4
Germany/West Germany	2–4
France	2–2
Italy	3–1
South Africa	1–1
Belgium	1–1
Great Britain	0–4
Netherlands	0–2
Switzerland	0–1

Appendix I:
Olympic Games Champions

1896 Athens, Greece 8–11, April
Neo Phaliron Velodrome and Athens Lawn Tennis Club at Illisus
Men's Singles: 13 entrants, 7 nations
G-John Pius Boland, GBR S-Dionysios Kasdaglis, EGY
B-Konstantinos Paspatis, GRE B-Momcsilló Tapavicza, HUN

Men's Doubles: 5 teams entered, 5 nations
G-John Pius Boland, GBR S-Dionysios Kasdaglis, EGY
Fritz Traun, GER Dimitrios Petrokokkinos, GRE
B-Edward Flack, AUS George Stuart Robinson, GBR

1900 Paris, France, 6–11 July
Ile du Puteaux Club
Men's Singles: 13 entrants, 3 nations
G-Hugh Doherty, GBR S-Harold Mahony, GBR
B-Reginald Doherty, GBR B-Arthur Norris, GBR

Men's Doubles: 8 teams entered, 3 nations
G-Hugh Doherty, GBR S-Spalding de Garmendia, USA
Reginald Doherty, GBR Max Décugis, FRA
B-Harold Mahony, GBR B-André Prévost, FRA
Arthur Norris, GBR Georges de la Chapelle, FRA

Women's Singles: 6 entrants, 4 nations
G-Charlotte Cooper, GBR S-Hélène Prévost, FRA
B-Marion Jones, USA B-Hedwiga Rosenbaumová, BOH

Mixed Doubles: 6 teams entered, 4 nations
G-Charlotte Cooper, GBR S-Harold Mahony, GBR
Reginald Doherty, GBR Hélène Prévost, FRA
B-Hugh Doherty, GBR B-Archibald Warden, GBR
Marion Jones, USA Hedwiga Rosenbaumová, BOH

1904 St. Louis, Missouri, United States, 29 August–3 September
Francis Field
Men's Singles: 27 entrants, 2 nations
G-Beals Wright, USA   S-Robert LeRoy, USA
B-Alphonzo Bell, USA   B-Edgar Leonard, USA

Men's Doubles: 15 teams entered, 2 nations
G-Beals Wright, USA   S-Robert LeRoy, USA
Edgar Leonard, USA   Alphonzo Bell, USA
B-Clarence Gamble, USA   B-Joseph Wear, USA
Arthur Wear, USA   Allen West, USA

1906 Athens, Greece, 23–26 April
Athens Lawn Tennis Club at Illisus
Men's Singles: 18 entrants, 6 nations
G-Max Decugis, FRA   S-Maurice Germot, FRA
B-August Kessler, NED   B-Zdeněk Žemla, BOH

Men's Doubles: 7 teams entered, 5 nations
G-Max Decugis, FRA   S-Ioannis Ballis, GRE
Maurice Germot, FRA   Xenofon Kasdaglis, GRE/EGY
B-Ladislav Žemla, BOH   B-Georgios Simiriotis, GRE
Zdeněk Žemla, BOH   Nikolaos Zarifis, GRE

Women's Singles: 6 entrants, 2 nations
G-Esmée Simirioti, GRE   S-Sofia Marinou, GRE
B-Aspatsia Matsa, GRE   B-Euphrosine Paspati, GRE

Mixed Doubles: 5 teams entered, 2 nations
G-Marie Decugis, FRA   S-Aspasia Matsa, GRE
Max Decugis, FRA   Xenophon Kasdaglis, GRE/EGY
B-Georgios Simiriotis, GRE   B-Nikolaos Zarifis, GRE
Sofia Marinou, GRE   Esmee Simirioti, GRE

1908 London, England, 6–9 May
Queen's Club, West Kensington, covered court tennis (indoor lawn tennis)
Men's Singles: 6 entrants, 2 nations
G-Arthur WentworthGore, GBR   S-George Caridia, GBR
B-Josiah Ritchie, GBR   4th-Wilberforce Eaves, GBR

Men's Doubles: 5 teams entered, 2 nations
G-Arthur Wentworth Gore, GBR   S-George Caridia, GBR
H. Roper Barrett, GBR   George Simond, GBR
B-Gunnar Setterwall, SWE   4th-Josiah Ritchie, GBR
Wollmar Boström, SWE   Lionel Escombe, GBR

Women's Singles: 7 entrants, 2 nations
G-Gladys Eastlake-Smith, GBR   S-Alice Greene, GBR
B-Martha Adlerstrahle, SWE   4th-Elsa Wallenberg, SWE

1908 London, England, 18–28 May
Queen's Club, West Kensington, *jeu de paume* (real tennis)
Men's Singles: 11 entrants, 2 nations
G-Jay Gould, USA   S-Eustace Miles, GBR
B-Neville Lytton, GBR   4th-Arthur Page, GBR

1908 London, England, 6–11 July
All-England Lawn Tennis and Croquet Club, Wimbledon, lawn tennis
Men's Singles: 31 entrants, 9 nations
G-Josiah Ritchie, GBR   S-Otto Froitzheim, GER
B-Wilberforce Eaves, GBR   B-John Richardson, GBR

Men's Doubles: 12 teams entered, 8 nations
G-George Hillyard, GBR   S-Josiah Ritchie, GBR
Reginald Doherty, GBR   James Parke, IRL
B-Clement Cazalet, GBR   Charles Dixon, GBR

Women's Singles: 5 entrants, 1 nation
G-D. Lambert Chambers, GBR   S-Penelope Boothby, GBR
B-Joan Winch, GBR   B-Agatha Morton, GBR

1912 Stockholm, Sweden, 5–12 May
Royal Tennis Pavilion, covered court tennis (indoor lawn tennis)
Men's Singles: 22 entrants, 6 nations
G-André Gobert, FRA   S-Charles Dixon, GBR
B-Anthony Wilding, NZL   4th-F. Gordon Lowe, GBR

Men's Doubles: 8 teams entered, 3 nations
G-André Gobert, FRA   S-Gunnar Setterwall, SWE
Maurice Germot, FRA   J. Carl Kempe, SWE
B-Charles Dixon, GBR   4th-Arthur Wentworth Gore, GBR
Alfred Beamish, GBR   H. Roper Barrett, GBR

Women's Singles: 8 entrants, 3 nations
G-Edith Hannam, GBR S-Sofie Castenschiold, DEN
B-Mabel Parton, GBR 4th-Sigrid Fick, SWE

Mixed Doubles: 8 teams entered, 3 nations
G-Edith Hannam, GBR S-Helen Aitchison, GBR
Charles Dixon, GBR H. Roper Barrett, GBR
B-Sigrid Fick, SWE 4th-Margareta Cederschiöld, SWE
Gunnar Settarwall, SWE J. Carl Kempe, SWE

1912 Stockholm, Sweden, 28 June–5 July
Östermalm Idrottsplats, lawn tennis
Men's Singles: 49 entrants, 12 nations
G-Charles Winslow, RSA S-Harry Kitson, RSA
B-Oscar Kreuzer, GER 4th-Ladislav Žemla, BOH

Men's Doubles: 22 teams entered, 10 nations
G-Charles Winslow, RSA S-F. Felix Piepes, AUT
Harry Kitson, RSA Arthur Zborzil, AUT
B-Albert Canet, FRA 4th-Ladislav Žemla, BOH
Marc Meny de Marangue, FRA Jaroslav Just, BOH

Women's Singles: 8 entrants, 4 nations
G-Marguerite Broquedis, FRA S-Dorothea "Dora" Köring, GER
B-Molla Bjurstedt, NOR 4th-Edith Arnheim Lasch, SWE

Mixed Doubles: 6 teams entered, 4 nations
G-Dorothea Köring, GER S-Sigrid Fick, SWE
Heinrich Schomburgk, GER Gunnar Setterwall, SWE
B-Marguerite Broquedis, FRA 4th-M. Rieck, GER
Albert Canet, FRA Oscar Kreuzer, GER

1916 Olympic Games not held due to World War I

1920 Antwerp, Belgium, 16–24 August
Beerschot Tennis Club
Men's Singles: 41 entrants, 14 nations
G-Louis Raymond, RSA S-Ichiya Kumagai, JPN
B-Charles Winslow, RSA 4th-Noel Turnbull, GBR

Men's Doubles: 22 teams entered, 11 nations
G-Noel Turnbull, GBR   S-Ichiya Kumagai, JPN
Max Woosnam, GBR   Seiichiro Kashio, JPN
B-Max Decugis, FRA   4th-François Blanchy, FRA
Pierre Albarran, FRA   Jacques Brugnon, FRA

Women's Singles: 18 entrants, 7 nations
G-Suzanne Lenglen, FRA   S-Dorothy Holman, GBR
B-Kitty McKane, GBR   4th-Sigrid Fick, SWE

Women's Doubles: 9 teams entered, 5 nations
G-Winifred McNair, GBR   S-Geraldine Beamish, GBR
Kitty McKane, GBR   Dorothy Holman, GBR
B-Suzanne Lenglen, FRA   4th-Marie Storms, BEL
Elisabeth d'Ayen, FRA   Fernande Arendt, BEL

Mixed Doubles: 16 teams entered, 7 nations
G-Suzanne Lenglen, FRA   S-Kitty McKane, GBR
Max Decugis, FRA   Max Woosnam, GBR
B-Milada Skrbkova, TCH   4th-Amory Hansen, DEN
Ladislav Žemla, TCH   Erik Tegner, DEN

1924 Paris, France, 14–21 July
Stade de Colombes
Men's Singles: 82 entrants, 27 nations
G-Vincent Richards, USA   S-Henri Cochet, FRA
B-Umberto de Morpurgo, ITA   4th-Jean Borotra, FRA

Men's Doubles: 39 teams entered, 24 nations
G-Vincent Richards, USA   S-Jacques Brugnon, FRA
Frank Hunter, USA   Henri Cochet, FRA
B-Jean Borotra, FRA   4th-John Condon, RSA
René Lacoste, FRA   Ivie John Richardson, RSA

Women's Singles: 31 entrants, 14 nations
G-Helen Wills, USA   S-Julie "Didi" Vlasto, FRA
B-Kitty McKane, GBR   4th-Germaine Golding, FRA

Women's Doubles: 11 teams entered, 8 nations
G-Hazel Wightman, USA   S-Phyllis Covell, GBR
Helen Wills, USA   Kathleen "Kitty" McKane, GBR

B-D. Shepherd-Barron, GBR   4th-Marguerite Billout, FRA
Evelyn Colyer, GBR   Yvonne Bourgeois, FRA

Mixed Doubles: 16 teams entered, 7 nations
G-Hazel Wightman, USA   S-Marion Jessup, USA
Richard N. Williams, USA   Vincent Richards, USA
B-Cornelia Bouman, NED   4th-Kitty McKane, GBR
Hendrik Timmer, NED   John Gilbert, GBR

1928–64, no Olympic tennis competition

1968 Mexico City, Mexico, 14–20 October
Guadaljara Country Club, demonstration tournament
Men's Singles: 32 entrants, 14 nations
G-Manuel Santana, ESP   S-Manuel Orantes, ESP
B-Pierre Darmon, FRA   B-Joaquin Loyo-Mayo, MEX

Men's Doubles: 15 teams entered, 14 nations
G-Rafael Osuna, MEX   S-Juan Gisbert, ESP
Vicente Zarazura, MEX   Manuel Santana, ESP
B-Pierre Darmon, FRA   4th-Francisco Guzman, ECU
Joaquin Loyo-Mayo, MEX   Miguel Lovera, ECU

Women's Singles: 13 entrants, 7 nations
G-Helga Niessen, FRG   S-Jane "Peaches" Bartkowicz, USA
B-Julie Heldman, USA   4th-Lourdes Gongora, MEX

Women's Doubles: 6 teams entered, 6 nations
G-Edda Buding, FRG   S-Rosa Maria Darmon, FRA
Helga Niessen, FRG   Julie Heldman, USA
B-Jane Bartkowicz, USA   4th-Patricia Montano, MEX
Valerie Ziegenfuss, USA   Lourdes Gongora, MEX

Mixed Doubles: 14 teams entered, 9 nations
G-Julie Heldman, USA   S-Jürgen Fassbender, FRG
Herbert Fitzgibbon, USA   Helga Niessen, FRG
B-Jane Bartkowicz, USA   4th-Pierre Darmon, FRA
James Osborne, USA   Rosa Darmon, FRA

1968 Mexico City, Mexico, 24–26 October
Guadalajara Sports Club, exhibition tournament
Men's Singles: 15 entrants, 7 nations
G-Rafael Osuna, MEX   S-Ingo Buding, FRG
B-Vladimir Korotkov, URS   B-Nicola Pietrangeli, ITA

Men's Doubles: 7 teams entered, 6 nations
G-Rafael Osuna, MEX   S-Pierre Darmon, FRA
Vicente Zarazura, MEX   Joaquin Loyo-Mayo, MEX
B-Francisco Guzman, ECU   B-Vladimir Korotkov, URS
Teimuraz Kakulia, URS   Anatoly Volkov, URS

Women's Singles: 9 entrants, 6 nations
G-Jane Bartkowicz, USA   S-Julie Heldman, USA
B-Maria E. Guzman, ECU   4th-Suzana Petersen, BRA

Women's Doubles: 5 teams entered, 5 nations
B-Rosa Maria Darmon, FRA   S-Jane "Peaches" Bartkowicz, USA
Julie Heldman, USA   Valerie Ziegenfuss, USA
B-Maria E. Guzman, ECU   B-Cecilia Rosado, MEX
Suzana Petersen, BRA   Zaiga Yansone, URS

Mixed Doubles: 10 teams entered, 7 nations
G-Zaiga Yansone, URS   S-Jane "Peaches" Bartkowicz, USA
Vladimir Korotkov, URS   Ingo Buding, FRG
B-Pierre Darmon, FRA   B-Teimuraz Kakulia, URS
Rosa Darmon, FRA   Suzana Petersen, BRA

1972–80, no Olympic tennis competition

1984 Los Angeles, California, United States, 6–11 August
Los Angeles Tennis Center, University of California–Los Angeles, demonstration tournament (under 21 years of age)
Men's Singles: 32 entrants, 22 nations
G-Stefan Edberg, SWE   S-Francisco Maciel, MEX
B-Jimmy Arias, USA   B-Paolo Cane, ITA

Women's Singles: 32 entrants, 24 nations
G-Steffi Graf, FRG   S-Sabrina Goleš, YUG,
B-Raffaella Reggi, ITA   B-Catherine Tanvier, FRA

1988 Seoul, Korea, 20 September–1 October
Seoul Olympic Park Tennis Center

Men's Singles: 64 entrants, 32 nations
G-Miloslav Mečíř, TCH   S-Tim Mayotte, USA
B-Stefan Edberg, SWE   B-Brad Gilbert, USA

Men's Doubles: 32 teams entered, 32 nations
G-Ken Flach, USA   S-Emilio Sánchez, ESP
Robert Seguso, USA   Sergio Casal, ESP
B-Miloslav Mečíř, TCH   B-Stefan Edberg, SWE
Milan Srejber, TCH   Anders Järryd, SWE

Women's Singles: 48 entrants, 26 nations
G-Steffi Graf, FRG   S-Gabriella Sabatini, ARG
B-Zina Garrison, USA   B-Manuella Maleeva, BUL

Women's Doubles: 14 teams entered, 14 nations
G-Pam Shriver, USA   S-Jana Novotná, TCH
Zina Garrison, USA   Helena Suková, TCH
B-Elizabeth Smylie, AUS   B-Steffi Graf, FRG
Wendy Turnbull, AUS   Claudia Kohde-Kilsch, FRG

1992 Barcelona, Spain, 28 July–9 August
Tennis de la Vall d'Hebron

Men's Singles: 64 entrants, 36 nations
G-Marc Rosset, SUI   S-Jordi Arrese, ESP
B-Goran Ivanišević, CRO   B-Andrei Cherkasov, EUN

Men's Doubles: 32 teams entered, 32 nations
G-Boris Becker, GER   S-Wayne Ferreira, RSA
Michael Stich, GER   Piet Norval, RSA
B-Javier Frana, ARG   B-Goran Ivanišević, CRO
Christian Miniussi, ARG   Goran Prpić, CRO

Women's Singles: 64 entrants, 33 nations
G-Jennifer Capriati, USA   S-Steffi Graf, GER
B-Mary Joe Fernández, USA   B-Arantxa Sánchez Vicario, ESP

Women's Doubles: 32 teams entered, 32 nations
G-Gigi Fernández, USA   S-Conchita Martínez, ESP
Mary Joe Fernández, USA   Arantxa Sánchez, ESP

B-Leila Meshki, EUN   B-Nicole Provis Bradtke, AUS
Natasha Zvereva, EUN   Rachel McQuillan, AUS

1996 Atlanta, Georgia, United States, 23 July–3 August
Stone Mountain Tennis Center
Men's Singles: 64 entrants, 36 nations
G-Andre Agassi, USA   S-Sergi Bruguera, ESP
B-Leander Paes, IND   4th-Fernando Meligeni, BRA

Men's Doubles: 32 teams entered, 32 nations
G-Todd Woodbridge, AUS   S- Neil Broad, GBR
Mark Woodforde, AUS   Tim Henman, GBR
B-Marc-Kevin Goellner, GER   4th-Jacco Elting, NED
David Prinosil, GER   Paul Haarhuis, NED

Women's Singles: 64 entrants, 34 nations
G-Lindsay Davenport, USA   S-Arantxa Sánchez Vicario, ESP
B-Jana Novotná, CZE   4th-Mary Joe Fernández, USA

Women's Doubles: 31 teams entered, 31 nations
G-Gigi Fernández, USA   S-Jana Novotná, CZE
Mary Joe Fernández, USA   Helena Suková, CZE
B-Conchita Martínez, ESP   4th-Manon Bollegraf, NED
A. Sánchez Vicario, ESP   Brenda Schultz-McCarthy, NED

2000 Sydney, Australia, 19–28 September
Sydney Tennis Centre
Men's Singles: 64 entrants, 32 nations
G-Yevgeny Kafelnikov, RUS   S-Tommy Haas, GER
B-Arnaud di Pasquale, FRA   4th-Roger Federer, SUI

Men's Doubles: 29 teams entered, 29 nations
G-Sebastian Lareau, CAN   S-Todd Woodbridge, AUS
Daniel Nestor, CAN   Mark Woodforde, AUS
B-Alex Corretja, ESP   4th-David Adams, RSA
Albert Costa, ESP   John-Laffnie de Jager, RSA

Women's Singles: 64 entrants, 33 nations
G-Venus Williams, USA   S-Elena Dementieva, RUS
B-Monica Seles, USA   4th-Jelena Dokić, AUS

Women's Doubles: 31 teams entered, 31 nations
G-Venus Williams, USA   S-Kristie Boogert, NED
Serena Williams, USA   Miriam Oremans, NED
B-Els Callens, BEL   4th-Olga Barabanschikova, BLR
Dominique Van Roost, BEL   Natasha Zvereva, BLR

2004 Athens, Greece, 15–22 August
Olympic Tennis Center
Men's Singles: 64 entrants, 32 nations
G-Nicolás Massú, CHI   S-Mardy Fish, USA
B-Fernando González, CHI   4th-Taylor Dent, USA

Men's Doubles: 32 teams entered, 26 nations
G-Fernando González, CHI   S-Nicolas Kieffer, GER
Nicolás Massú, CHI   Rainer Schüttler, GER
B-Mario Ančić, CRO   4th-Mahesh Bhupathi, IND
Ivan Ljubičić, CRO   Leander Paes, IND

Women's Singles: 64 entrants, 32 nations
G-Justine Henin-Hardenne, BEL   S-Amélie Mauresmo, FRA
B-Alicia Molik, AUS   4th-Anastasia Myskina, RUS

Women's Doubles: 32 teams entered, 21 nations
G-Li Ting, CHN   S-Conchita Martínez, ESP
Sun Tiantian, CHN   Virginia Ruana Pascual, ESP
B-Paola Suárez, ARG   4th-Shinobu Asagoe, JPN
Patricia Tarabini, ARG   Ai Sugiyama, JPN

2008 Beijing, China, 10–17 August
Olympic Green Tennis Center
Men's Singles: 64 entrants, 33 nations
G-Rafael Nadal, ESP   S-Fernando González, CHI
B-Novak Djoković, SRB   4th-James Blake, USA

Men's Doubles: 32 teams entered, 24 nations
G-Roger Federer, SUI   S-Simon Aspelin, SWE
Stanislaus Wawrinka, SUI   Thomas Johansson, SWE
B-Bob Bryan, USA   4th-Arnaud Clément, FRA
Mike Bryan, USA   Michaël Llodra, FRA

Women's Singles: 64 entrants, 33 nations
G-Elena Dementieva, RUS   S-Dinara Safina, RUS
B-Vera Zvonareva, RUS   4th-Li Na, CHN

Women's Doubles: 32 teams entered, 22 nations
G-Venus Williams, USA   S-Anabel Medina Garrigues, ESP
Serena Williams, USA   Virginia Ruana Pascual, ESP
B-Yan Zi, CHN   4th-Alona Bondarenko, UKR
Zheng Jie, CHN   Kateryna Bondarenko, UKR

2012 London, England, 27 July–12 August
All-England Lawn Tennis and Croquet Club, Wimbledon

2016 Rio de Janeiro, Brazil

G-gold medal, S-silver medal, B-bronze medal
Note: third-place match not contested in all years; both semifinal losers awarded bronze medals in some years

Bibliography

CONTENTS

Introduction	392
I. Reference	394
A. Encyclopedias	394
B. Annuals and Yearbooks	395
C. Bibliography	395
D. Other	395
II. History	395
A. General	395
B. Davis Cup	396
C. United States Open	396
D. Wimbledon	397
E. Single Match	397
F. Black Players	397
G. Professional	397
III. Biography	397
A. Collections	397
B. Single Individual	398
1. Players	398
2. Others	403
C. Photographic Essay	403
IV. Women's Tennis	403
A. History	403
B. Biography	404
1. Collections	404
2. Two Players	404
3. Individual Players	404
C. Instructional	408
D. Photographic Essay	409
E. Other	409
V. Instructional	409
A. Rules and Officiating	409
B. Coaching	409
C. Playing	409

	1. General	409
	2. Specialized	412
	D. Combination Instructional and History	413
VI.	Other Books	413
	A. Anthology	413
	B. Fiction	413
	1. Tennis	413
	2. Other Fiction by Tennis Players	414
	C. Humor	414
	D. Nontennis Books by Tennis Players	414
	E. Other Racket Sports	415
	1. Badminton	415
	2. Court Tennis	415
	3. Squash Racquets	415
	4. General	415
	F. Miscellaneous	415
	G. Foreign Language	416
	1. Czech	416
	2. Dutch	416
	3. French	416
	4. German	416
	5. Italian	416
	6. Portuguese	416
	7. Spanish	416
	8. Swedish	417
VII.	Periodicals	417
	A. English Language	417
	B. Foreign Language	417
VIII.	Websites of Interest	417

INTRODUCTION

Although there are not nearly as many books on tennis as there are on other sports such as baseball, basketball, football, golf, or boxing, there is a considerable collection. They have been published since shortly after the game was invented. Many of the early ones had limited printing editions and, consequently, today are hard to find and quite expensive. There are booksellers, especially in England, who specialize in tennis and are able to locate most of these, although, at a price. The copyright on some of the oldest books has expired, and a few may be found in their entirety on the Internet through such resources as Project Gutenberg.

In the early years, the A. G. Spalding and Bros. Company, after purchasing the Wright and Ditson sporting goods company in 1871, published annual compilations of the previous year's activity, rules, and instructions on how to play the game. Although published by Spalding, they retained the name Wright and Ditson and are excellent sources for early results. Various other instructional books were also published by Spalding. Although tennis books are not nearly as numerous as books on other sports, such as baseball, in recent years, there has been a growing number published each year.

Nearly every major language contains tennis publications. A brief selection of books in other languages is included in the section on other books, and several non-English periodicals are listed in the foreign language section. The following list contains most of the more useful resources. Many of the titles listed below are in the author's own library and have been consulted in the preparation of this book.

The *Bud Collins' Encyclopedia of Tennis* and its updated editions (with various titles) is the most comprehensive history of the sport. But, the reader should be wary since there are quite a few factual typos throughout. Other histories that focus on a particular tournament, such as Alan Trengove's *The Story of the Davis Cup*, provide many more details not included in the more general encyclopedias. An interesting collection is *The Complete Book of Tennis*, edited by Gene Brown. It consists of articles from the *New York Times* covering tennis' history from the 19th century to the late 1970s. Other books such as John Feinstein's *Hard Courts: Real Life on the Professional Tennis Tours* or Michael Mewshaw's *Short Circuit: Six Months on the Men's Professional Tennis Tour* detail the authors' perspectives while they followed the professional tennis tour for a complete season. Feinstein emphasizes the greed involved while Mewshaw looks at the inconsistencies of the tour organizers.

Three books that focus on individual matches are among the best tennis books. John McPhee's critically acclaimed book, *Levels of the Game*, about a 1968 Arthur Ashe–Clark Graebner U.S. Open match, L. Jon Wertheim's *Strokes of Genius: Federer, Nadal, and the Greatest Match Ever Played*, and Marshall Jon Fisher's *A Terrible Splendor*, about the Don Budge–Gottfried von Cramm 1937 Davis Cup match, are all essential reading.

As with all sports, many books are biographies, usually written in the first person, with an established author as coauthor. Virtually every top player has a published biography. Among the most interesting are Frank Deford's story of the tragic life of Bill Tilden, *Big Bill Tilden: The Triumphs and the Tragedy*; Bruce Schoenfeld's *The Match: Althea Gibson and Angela Buxton*; and Corina Morariu's story of comeback from leukemia, detailed in *Living through the Racket*. Alice Marble's story, *Courting Danger*, contains some elements that are nearly unbelievable as she details her posttennis life as a spy for the United States government. There are also many tennis biographies written for juniors—in quite a few cases, these are the only books written about some players.

There are probably more tennis books that are instructional than any other category. The older ones are interesting from a historical perspective, since equipment and conditions have changed significantly, but some of the strategic elements contained in them may still apply. Among the most useful instructional books are Bill Tilden's classic *Match Play and the Spin of the Ball* and Brad Gilbert's *Winning Ugly*.

Tilden also wrote quite a bit of tennis fiction that, while not qualifying as classic literature, nonetheless, shows an aspect of his personality. Some other champion tennis players, including Helen Jacobs, Helen Wills, Ilie Năstase, and Martina Navratilova, have attempted to write novels.

The *Fireside Book of Tennis* is an excellent anthology that includes many short pieces written by the best tennis writers, among them many former players, such as Helen Hull Jacobs, Helen Wills, and George Lott. Arthur Ashe's three-volume *A Hard Road to Glory* is a comprehensive history of African American achievement in all sports, not just tennis. This is another book that is essential for the serious sports researcher.

Gianni Clerici is the best-known Italian tennis writer and has been inducted into the International Tennis Hall of Fame. His major work is *500 Anni di Tennis*, which has been translated into English (*The Ultimate Tennis Book: 500 Years of the Sport*), French, German, Japanese, and Spanish.

Tennis websites of interest include the ones for the four major tournaments (www.australianopen.com, www.rolandgarros.com, www.wimbledon.org, and www.usopen.org). For information on rankings and other tournaments, the ATP World Tour website (www.atpworldtour.com) and the Sony Ericsson WTA Tour website (www.sonyericssonwtatour.com) are the two sources. Historical and current information are found on the websites for the Davis Cup (www.daviscup.com) and the Fed Cup (www.fedcup.com). The International Tennis Hall of Fame's website (www.tennisfame.com) has brief biographies of all inductees as well as information about the museum.

The Information Research Center at the International Tennis Hall of Fame in Newport, Rhode Island, is one of the largest devoted to tennis publications and may be consulted by the researcher by appointment. It contains more than 5,000 books and has a photograph and document collection and an audio, film and video collection.

I. REFERENCE

A. Encyclopedias

Brady, Maurice. *The Lawn Tennis Encyclopedia*. New York: A. S. Barnes, 1969.

Collins, Bud. *Bud Collins' Tennis Encyclopedia*. Detroit: Visible Ink, 1997.

———, ed. *Total Tennis: The Ultimate Tennis Encyclopedia*. Toronto: Sport Media, 2003.

Collins, Bud, and Zander Hollander, eds. *Bud Collins' Modern Encyclopedia of Tennis*. Garden City, NY: Doubleday, 1980.

Hedges, Martin. *The Concise Dictionary of Tennis*. New York: Mayflower Books, 1978.

Porter, David L., ed. *Biographical Dictionary of American Sports*. Vol. 3, *Outdoor Sports*. New York: Greenwood, 1989.

Robertson, Max. *The Encyclopedia of Tennis*. New York: Viking, 1974.

United States Lawn Tennis Association. *Official Encyclopedia of Tennis*. New York: Harper and Row, 1981.

B. Annuals and Yearbooks

Hughes, G. P., ed. *The Lawn Tennis Almanack*. Surrey, UK: E. J. Burrow for Dunlop Sports, 1939, 1946–58.
Spalding's Lawn Tennis Annual. New York: American Sports, c. 1900–50.
Wright and Ditson's Official Lawn Tennis Guide. Boston: Wright and Ditson, c. 1890–1940.
United States Lawn Tennis Association. *The Official Yearbook and Tennis Guide with the Official Rules 1972*. Lynn, MA: H. O. Zimman, 1972.
United States Tennis Association. *1994 USTA Tennis Yearbook*. Lynn, MA: H. O. Zimman, 1994.

C. Bibliography

Lumpkin, Angela. *A Guide to the Literature of Tennis*. Westport, CT: Greenwood, 1985.
Phillips, Dennis J. *The Tennis Sourcebook*. Lanham, MD: Scarecrow, 1995.

D. Other

Brown, Gene, ed. *The New York Times Encyclopedia of Sports*. Vol. 6, *Tennis*. New York: Arno, 1979.
Wallechinsky, David, and Jaime Loucky. *The Complete Book of the Olympics: 2008 Edition*. London: Aurum, 2008.

II. HISTORY

A. General

Baltzell, E. Digby. *Sporting Gentlemen: Men's Tennis from the Age of Honor to the Cult of the Superstar*. New York: Simon and Schuster, 1995.
Berry, Eliot. *Topspin: Ups and Downs in Bigtime Tennis*. New York: Henry Holt, 1996.
———. *Tough Draw: The Path to Tennis Glory*. New York: Henry Holt, 1992.
Clerici, Gianni. *The Ultimate Tennis Book: 500 Years of the Sport*. Chicago: Follett, 1975.
Cummings, Parke. *American Tennis: The Story of a Game and its People*. Boston: Little, Brown, 1957.
Eggman, Jack. *The Roots of Tennis: Blue Bloods to Blue Collars*. Hazleton, MO: Tennis History, 2008.
Feinstein, John. *Hard Courts: Real Life on the Professional Tennis Tours*. New York: Villard, 1991.
Flink, Steve. *The Greatest Tennis Matches of the Twentieth Century*. Danbury, CT: Rutledge, 1999.

Gillmeister, Heiner. *Tennis: A Cultural History*. London: Leicester University Press, 1997.
Grimsley, Will. *Tennis: Its History, People and Events*. Englewood Cliffs, NJ: Prentice-Hall, 1971.
Hawk, Philip B. *Off the Racket: Tennis Highlights and Lowdowns*. New York: American Lawn Tennis, 1937.
Metzler, Paul. *Tennis Styles and Stylists*. Sydney: Angus and Robertson, 1969.
Mewshaw, Michael. *Short Circuit: Six Months on the Men's Professional Tennis Tour*. New York: Atheneum, 1983.
Potter, Edward C. *Kings of the Court: The Story of Lawn Tennis*. New York: A. S. Barnes, 1963.
Riessen, Marty, and Richard Evans. *Match Point: A Candid View of Life on the International Tennis Circuit*. Englewood Cliffs, NJ: Prentice-Hall, 1973.
Schickel, Richard. *The World of Tennis*. New York: Random House, 1975.
Scott, Eugene. *Tennis: Game of Motion*. New York: Crown, 1973.
Sharnik, John. *Remembrance of Games Past: On Tour with the Tennis Grand Masters*. New York: Macmillan, 1986.
Slocum, Henry W., Jr. *Lawn Tennis in Our Own Country*. New York: A. G. Spalding, 1890.
Smyth, Brigadier J. G. *Lawn Tennis*. London: Phoenix House, 1954.
Voss, Arthur. *Tilden and Tennis in the Twenties*. Troy, NY: Whitston, 1985.
United States Lawn Tennis Association. *Fifty Years of Lawn Tennis in the United States*. New York: United States Lawn Tennis Association, 1931.
Walker, Randy. *On This Day in Tennis History: A Day-by-Day Anthology of Anecdotes and Historical Happenings*. New York: New Chapter, 2008.
Whitman, Malcolm D. *Tennis Origins and Mysteries*. 1932. Reprint, Mineola, NY: Dover, 2004.
Wind, Herbert Warren. *Game, Set, and Match: The Tennis Boom of the 1960's and 70's*. New York: E. P. Dutton, 1979.

B. Davis Cup

Merrihew, S. Wallis. *The Quest of the Davis Cup*. New York: American Lawn Tennis, 1928.
Potter, Edward C. *The Davis Cup*. Cranbury, NJ: A. S. Barnes, 1969.
Trengove, Alan. *The Story of the Davis Cup*. London: Stanley Paul, 1985.

C. United States Open

Bell, Marty. *Carnival at Forest Hills*. New York: Random House, 1975.
Kent, Richard. *Inside the U.S. Open*. Charleston, SC: Booksurge, 2008.
Talbert, William F. *Tennis Observed: The USLTA Men's Singles Champions, 1881–1966*. With Pete Axthelm. Barre, VT: Barre, 1967.
United States Tennis Association. *The Open Book: Celebrating 40 Years of America's Grand Slam*. Edited by Rick Rennert. Chicago: Triumph Books, 2008.

D. Wimbledon

Brady, Maurice. *The Centre Court Story—Wimbledon*. London: W. Foulsham, 1954.
McPhee, John. *Wimbledon: A Celebration*. New York: Viking, 1972.
Revie, Alastair. *Wonderful Wimbledon*. London: Pelham, 1972.
Robertson, Max. *Wimbledon 1877–1977*. London: A. Barker, 1977.
Robyns, Gwen. *Wimbledon: The Hidden Drama*. New York: Drake, 1974.

E. Single Match

Fisher, Marshall Jon. *A Terrible Splendor: Three Extraordinary Men, a World Poised for War, and the Greatest Tennis Match Ever Played*. New York: Three Rivers, 2009.
Folley, Malcolm. *Borg Versus McEnroe*. London: Headline, 2005.
McPhee, John. *Levels of the Game*. New York: Farrar, Straus and Giroux, 1969.
Roberts, Selena. *A Necessary Spectacle: Billie Jean King, Bobby Riggs, and the Tennis Match that Leveled the Game*. New York: Crown, 2005.
Wertheim, L. Jon. *Strokes of Genius: Federer, Nadal, and the Greatest Match Ever Played*. New York: Houghton Mifflin Harcourt, 2009.

F. Black Players

Djata, Sundiata. *Blacks at the Net: Black Achievement in the History of Tennis*. Vol. 1. Syracuse, NY: Syracuse University Press, 2005.
———. *Blacks at the Net: Black Achievement in the History of Tennis*. Vol. 2. Syracuse, NY: Syracuse University Press, 2008.
———. *Blacks in Tennis: A Global History of "White Sport" and Its Colorful Players*. Princeton, NJ: Markus Wiener, 2002.
Harris, Cecil, and Larryette Kyle-DeBose. *Charging the Net: A History of Blacks in Tennis from Althea Gibson and Arthur Ashe to the Williams Sisters*. Chicago: Ivan R. Dee, 2007.

G. Professional

McCauley, Joe. *The History of Professional Tennis*. London: self-published, 2003.

III. BIOGRAPHY

A. Collections

Bellamy, Rex. *Love Thirty: Three Decades of Champions*. London: Simon and Schuster, 1990.
Cooke, Jane, ed. *International Who's Who in Tennis*. Dallas: World Championship Tennis, 1983.

Davidson, Owen. *Lawn Tennis: The Great Ones*. London: Pelham, 1970.
Glickman, William G. *Winners on the Tennis Court*. New York: Franklin Watts, 1978. [juvenile].
Hart, Stan. *Once a Champion: Legendary Tennis Stars Revisited*. New York: Dodd, Mead, 1985.

B. Single Individual

1. Players

Andre Agassi
Agassi, Andre. *Open: An Autobiography*. New York: Alfred A. Knopf, 2009.
Bauman, Paul. *Agassi and Ecstasy: The Turbulent Life of Andre Agassi*. Chicago: Bonus Books, 1997.
Christopher, Matt. *On the Court with Andre Agassi*. Athlete Biographies. New York: Little, Brown, 1997. [juvenile].
Cobello, Dominic. *The Agassi Story*. With Mike Agassi and Kate Shoup Welsh. Toronto: ECW, 2004.
Knapp, Ron. *Andre Agassi: Star Tennis Player*. Sports Reports. Berkeley Heights, NJ.: Enslow, 1997. [juvenile].
Philip, Robert. *Agassi: The Fall and Rise of the Enfant Terrible of Tennis*. London: Bloomsbury, 1993.

Vijay Amritraj
Evans, Richard. *Vijay from Madras to Hollywood Via Wimbledon*. London: Libri Mundi, 1990.

Arthur Ashe
Ashe, Arthur. *Advantage Ashe*. As told to Clifford George Gewecke Jr. New York: Coward McCann, 1967.
———. *Arthur Ashe: Portrait in Motion*. With Frank Deford. Boston: Houghton Mifflin, 1975.
———. *Off the Court*. With Neil Amdur. New York: New American Library, 1981.
Ashe, Arthur, and Arnold Rampersad. *Days of Grace: A Memoir*. New York: Alfred A. Knopf, 1993.
Collins, David R. *Arthur Ashe: Against the Wind*. New York: Dillon, 1994. [juvenile].
Jacobs Altman, Linda. *Arthur Ashe: Alone in the Crowd*. Black American Athletes. St. Paul, MN: EMC, 1976. [juvenile].
Towle, Mike. *I Remember Arthur Ashe: Memories of a True Tennis Pioneer and Champion of Social Causes by the People Who Knew Him*. Nashville, TN: Cumberland House, 2001.

Henry "Bunny" Austin
Austin, Henry Wilfred. *Lawn Tennis Bits and Pieces*. London: Sampson Low, Marston, 1930.

Austin, Henry Wilfred, and Phyllis Konstam. *A Mixed Double*. London: Chatto and Windus, 1969.

Marcos Baghdatis
Baghdatis, Marcos. *Marcos Baghdatis*. Cyprus: self-published, 2007.

Boris Becker
Becker, Boris. *The Player: The Autobiography*. With Robert Lubenoff and Helmut Sorge. London: Transworld, 2005.
Waller, Johnny, and Marianne Lassen. *Boris Becker: Wunderkind*. London: Virgin Books, 1986.

James Blake
Blake, James. *Breaking Back: How I Lost Everything and Won Back My Life*. With Andrew Friedman. New York: HarperCollins, 2007.

Björn Borg
Audette, Larry. *Björn Borg*. Cape Town: Quick Fox, 1979.
Borg, Björn. *Borg by Borg*. London: Octopus, 1980.
———. *Björn Borg: My Life and Game*. As told to Eugene L. Scott. New York: Simon and Schuster, 1980.
Borg, Björn. *The Björn Borg Story*. London: Pelham, 1975.
Borg, Mariana. *Love Match: My Life with Björn*. London: Sidgwick and Jackson, 1981.
Skarke, Lars. *Björn Borg*. Philadelphia: Blake, 1993.

Jean Borotra
Smyth, John George. *Jean Borotra, the Bounding Basque: His Life of Work and Play*. London: Stanley Paul, 1974.

Norman Brookes
Brookes, Dame Mabel Balcombe. *Crowded Galleries*. With chapters on tennis by Sir Norman Brookes. London: Heinemann, 1956.

Don Budge
Budge, Don, and Frank Deford. *Don Budge: A Tennis Memoir*. New York: Viking, 1969.

Pat Cash
Cash, Pat. *Uncovered: The Autobiography of Pat Cash*. Exeter, UK: Greenwater, 2002.
Matthews, Bruce. *Pat Cash: My Story*. Ringwood, Victoria, Australia: Penguin, 1987.

Michael Chang
Chang, Michael. *Holding Serve: Persevering On and Off the Court*. With Mike Yorkey. London: Hodder and Stoughton, 2002.

Dell, Pamela. *Michael Chang: Tennis Champion*. Picture-Story Biographies. Danbury, CT: Childrens, 1992. [juvenile].

Jimmy Connors
Batson, Larry. *Jimmy Connors*. Superstars. Mankato, MN: Creative Education, 1975. [juvenile].
Burchard, Marshall. *Sports Hero, Jimmy Connors*. New York: Putnam, 1976. [juvenile].
Drucker, Joel. *Jimmy Connors Saved My Life: A Personal Biography*. Toronto: Sport Classic, 2005.
Sabin, Francene. *Jimmy Connors: King of the Courts*. New York: Putnam, 1978. [juvenile].

Dwight Davis
Kriplen, Nancy. *Dwight Davis: The Man and the Cup*. London: Ebury, 1999.

Jaroslav Drobný
Drobný, Jaroslav. *Jaroslav Drobný: Champion in Exile*. London: Hodder and Stoughton, 1955.

Cliff Drysdale
Drysdale, Andrew. *Beyond Match Point: The Cliff Drysdale Story*. London: Purnell, 1968.

Roger Federer
Bowers, Chris. *Fantastic Federer: The Biography of the World's Greatest Tennis Player*. London: John Blake, 2007.
Stauffer, Rene. *The Roger Federer Story: Quest for Perfection*. New York: New Chapter, 2006.

Ken Fletcher
Lunn, Hugh. *The Great Fletch: The Dazzling Life of Wimbledon Aussie Larrikin Ken Fletcher*. Sydney: ABC Books, 2008.
———. *Over the Top with Jim. 1991*. Brisbane: University of Queensland Press, 1991.

Gordon Forbes
Forbes, Gordon. *A Handful of Summers*. London: HarperCollins, 1978.
———. *Too Soon to Panic*. New York: Lyons and Burford, 1996.

Richard "Pancho" Gonzáles
Gonzáles, Pancho. *Man with a Racket: The Autobiography of Pancho Gonzáles*. As told to Cy Rice. New York: A. S. Barnes, 1959.

Tim Henman
Felstein, Simon. *Tim Henman: England's Finest*. London: John Blake, 2005.

Bob Hewitt
Hewitt, Bob, and Rory Brown. *The Bad Boy of Tennis*. Greenville, South Africa: Don Nelson, 1974.

Lleyton Hewitt
Sheppard, Barrie. *Lleyton Hewitt*. London: Heinemann, 2003. [juvenile].

Lew Hoad
Hoad, Jenny, and Jack Pollack. *My Life with Lew*. Pymble, New South Wales, Australia: HarperSports, 2002.
Hoad, Lew. *The Lew Hoad Story*. With Jack Pollack. Englewood Cliffs, NJ: Prentice-Hall, 1958.
Hodgson, Larry, and Dudley Jones. *Golden Boy: The Life and Times of Lew Hoad, A Tennis Legend*. Denton, UK: DSM, 2001.

Jan Kodeš
Kolar, Peter. *A Journey to Glory from Behind the Iron Curtain*. With Jan Kodeš. New York: New Chapter, 2010.

Jack Kramer
Kramer, Jack. *The Game: My 40 Years in Tennis*. With Frank Deford New York: Putnam, 1979.

Ramanathan Krishnan
Krishnan, Ramanathan. *A Touch of Tennis: A Story of a Tennis Family*. With Ramesh Krishnan and Nirmal Shekar. New Delhi, India: Penguin, 2003.

Rod Laver
Laver, Betty. *Rod Laver: The Red-Headed Rocket from Rockhampton*. Gladstone, Queensland, Australia: self-published, 2001.
Laver, Rod. *The Education of a Tennis Player*. With Bud Collins. New York: Simon and Schuster, 1973.

John Lucas
Simmons, Alex. *John Lucas*. Contemporary African Americans. Austin, TX: Raintree Steck-Vaughn, 1996. [juvenile].

John McEnroe
Cross, Tania. *McEnroe: The Man with the Rage to Win*. London: Arrow, 1982.
Evans, Richard. *McEnroe: A Rage for Perfection*. New York: Simon and Schuster, 1982.
McEnroe, John. *You Cannot Be Serious*. With James Kaplan. New York: G.P. Putnam's Sons, 2002.

Patrick McEnroe
McEnroe, Patrick. *Hardcourt Confidential: Tales from Twenty Years in the Pro Tennis Trenches.* With Peter Bodo. New York: HarperCollins, 2010.

Gardnar Mulloy
Mulloy, Gardnar P. *As It Was: Reminisences from a Man for All Seasons.* Breinigsville, PA: Flexigroup, 2010.
———. *The Will to Win.* New York: A. S. Barnes, 1960.

Ilie Năstase
Evans, Richard. *Nasty: Ilie Năstase vs. Tennis.* New York: Stein and Day, 1979.
Năstase, Ilie. *Mr. Năstase.* New York: HarperCollins, 2006.

John Newcombe
Newcombe, John. *Newk: Life On and Off the Court.* Sydney, Australia: Pan McMillan, 2002.

Bobby Riggs
Riggs, Bobby. *Court Hustler.* With George McGann. Philadelphia, PA: J. B. Lippincott, 1973.

Pete Sampras
Sampras, Pete. *A Champion's Mind: Lessons from a Life in Tennis.* With Peter Bodo. New York: Crown, 2008.

Pancho Segura
Seebohm, Caroline. *Little Pancho: The Life of Tennis Legend Pancho Segura.* Lincoln, NE: University of Nebraska Press, 2009.

Stan Smith
Hasegawa, Sam. *Stan Smith.* Creative Education Sports Superstars. Mankato, MN: Childrens, 1975. [juvenile].

Bill Talbert
Talbert, William F. *Playing for Life: Billy Talbert's Story.* With John Sharnik. Boston: Little, Brown, 1958.

Roscoe Tanner
Tanner, Roscoe. *Double Fault: My Rise and Fall and My Road Back.* With Mike Yorkey. Chicago: Triumph Books, 2005.

Bill Tilden
Deford, Frank. *Big Bill Tilden: The Triumphs and the Tragedy.* Toronto: Sport Media, 2004.
Tilden, William T. *Aces, Places and Faults.* London: Robert Hale, 1938.

———. *Me—The Handicap*. London: Methuen, 1929.
———. *My Story: A Champion's Memoirs*. New York: Hellman Williams, 1948.

Anthony Wilding
Myers, A. Wallis. *Captain Anthony Wilding*. London: Hodder and Stoughton, 1916.
Richardson, Len, and Shelley Richardson. *Anthony Wilding: A Sporting Life*. Christchurch, New Zealand: University of Canterbury Press, 2005.
Wilding, Anthony Frederick. *On the Court and Off*. London: Methuen, 1912.

Max Woosnam
Collins, Mick. *All-Round Genius: The Unknown Story of Britain's Greatest Sportsman*. London: Aurum, 2006.

2. Others

Nick Bollettieri
Bollettieri, Nick, and Dick Schaap. *My Aces, My Faults*. New York: Avon, 1996.

Bud Collins
Collins, Bud. *My Life with the Pros*. New York: E. P. Dutton, 1989.

Donald Dell
Dell, Donald. *Never Make the First Offer (Except When You Should): Wisdom from a Master Dealmaker*. New York: Penguin, 2009.

Dr. Robert Walter Johnson
Smith, Doug. *Whirlwind: the Godfather of Black Tennis; The Life and Times of Dr. Robert Walter Johnson*. Washington DC: Blue Eagle, 2004.

Ted Tinling
Tinling, Ted. *Love and Faults: Personalities Who Have Changed the History of Tennis in My Lifetime*. With Rod Humphries. New York: Crown, 1979.

C. Photographic Essay

Gould, Roger. *Pat Cash*. Port Melbourne, Australia: Lothian, 1987.
Moussatamy-Ashe, Jeanne. *Daddy and Me: A Photo Story of Arthur Ashe and His Daughter, Camera*. New York: Alfred A. Knopf, 1993.

IV. WOMEN'S TENNIS

A. History

King, Billie Jean, and Cynthia Starr. *We Have Come a Long Way: The Story of Women's Tennis*. New York: McGraw Hill, 1988.

Lichtenstein, Grace. *A Long Way, Baby: Behind the Scenes in Women's Pro Tennis.* New York: William Morrow, 1974.

Lumpkin, Angela. *Women's Tennis: A Historical Documentary of the Players and Their Game.* Albany, NY: Whitston, 1981.

Mewshaw, Michael. *Ladies of the Court: Grace and Disgrace on the Women's Tennis Tour.* New York: Crown, 1993.

Wade, Virginia. *Ladies of the Court: A Century of Women at Wimbledon.* With Jean Rafferty. New York: Atheneum, 1984.

Wertheim, L. Jon. *Venus Envy: A Sensational Season Inside the Women's Tennis Tour.* New York: HarperCollins, 2001.

B. Biography

1. Collections

Davidson, Owen, and C. M. Jones. *Great Women Tennis Players.* London: Pelham, 1971.

Jacobs, Helen Hull. *Famous American Women Athletes.* New York: Dodd, Mead, 1964. [juvenile].

———. *Famous Modern American Women Athletes.* Famous Biographies for Young People. New York: Dodd, Mead, 1975. [juvenile].

———. *Gallery of Champions.* New York: A. S. Barnes, 1949.

Phillips, Dennis J. *Women Tennis Stars: Biographies and Records of Champions, 1800s to Today.* Jefferson, NC: McFarland, 2009.

2. Two Players

Davidson, Sue. *Changing the Game: The Story of Tennis Champions Alice Marble and Althea Gibson.* Berkeley, CA: Seal, 1989.

Engelmann, Larry. *The Goddess and the American Girl: The Story of Suzanne Lenglen and Helen Wills.* New York: Oxford, 1988.

Howard, Johnette. *The Rivals: Chris Evert vs. Martina Navratilova; Their Epic Duels and Extraordinary Friendship.* New York: Broadway Books, 2006.

Schoenfeld, Bruce. *The Match: Althea Gibson and Angela Buxton.* New York: HarperCollins, 2004.

Williams, Venus, and Serena Williams. *Venus and Serena: Serving from the Hip, Ten Rules for Living, Loving and Winning.* With Hilary Beard. Boston, MA: Houghton Mifflin, 2005. [juvenile].

3. Individual Players

Tracy Austin

Austin, Tracy. *Beyond Center Court: My Story.* With Christine Brennan. New York: William Morrow, 1992.

Burchard, Sue H. *Tracy Austin*. Sports Star. New York: Harcourt, Brace, Jovanovich, 1982. [juvenile].
Hahn, James. *Tracy Austin: Powerhouse in Pinafore*. St. Paul, MN: EMC, 1978. [juvenile].

Pauline Betz Addie
Betz Addie, Pauline. *Wings on My Tennis Shoes*. London: Sampson Low, Marston, 1949.

Rosie Casals
Thacher, Alida M. *Raising a Racket, Rosie Casals*. Milwaukee, WI: Childrens, 1976.

Lottie Dod
Pearson, Jeffrey. *Lottie Dod: Champion of Champions; Story of an Athlete*. Wallasey, UK: Wirral, 1988.

Chris Evert
Burchard, S. H. *Chris Evert*. Sports Star. New York: Harcourt, Brace, Jovanovich, 1976. [juvenile].
Evert-Lloyd, Chris. *Chrissie: My Own Story*. With Neil Amdur. New York: Simon and Schuster, 1982.
Lloyd, Chris, and John Lloyd. *Lloyd on Lloyd*. With Carol Thatcher. New York: Beaufort, 1985.
Schmitz, Dorothy Childers. *Chris Evert, Women's Tennis Champion*. The Pros. Mankato, MN: Crestwood, 1977. [juvenile].

Mary Joe Fernández
Cole, Melanie. *Mary Joe Fernández*. Real-Life Reader Biography. Hockessin, DE: Mitchell Lane, 1998. [juvenile].

Zina Garrison
Porter, A. P. *Zina Garrison: Ace*. Achievers. Minneapolis, MN: Lerner, 1992. [juvenile].

Althea Gibson
Biracree, Tom. *Althea Gibson*. New York: Chelsea House, 1989.
Gibson, Althea. *I Always Wanted to be Somebody*. Edited by Ed Fitzgerald. New York: HarperCollins, 1958.
Gibson, Althea. *So Much to Live For*. With Richard Curtis. New York: Putnam, 1968.

Evonne Goolagong
Goolagong, Evonne. *Evonne! On the Move*. With Bud Collins. New York: E. P. Dutton, 1975.
Goolagong Cawley, Evonne. *Home! The Evonne Goolagong Story*. With Phil Jarrett. East Roseville, New South Wales, Australia: Simon and Schuster, 1993.

Steffi Graf
Brooks, Philip. *Steffi Graf: Sports Champ*. Sports Stars. Danbury, CT: Children's, 1996. [juvenile].

Knapp, Ron. *Sports Great Steffi Graf*. Sports Great Books. Berkeley Heights, NJ: Enslow, 1995. [juvenile].

Doris Hart
Hart, Doris. *Tennis with Hart*. Philadelphia, PA: J. P. Lippincott, 1955.

Justine Henin
Ryan, Mark. *Justine Henin: From Tragedy to Triumph*. New York: St. Martin's, 2008.

Martina Hingis
Rambeck, Richard. *Martina Hingis*. Sports Superstars. Mankato, MN: Child's World, 1998. [juvenile].

Spencer, Bev. *Martina Hingis*. Champion Sport Biographies. Lynchburg, VA: Warwick House, 1999. [juvenile].

Hazel Hotchkiss Wightman
Carter, Tom. *First Lady of Tennis: Hazel Hotchkiss Wightman*. Berkeley, CA: Creative Arts, 2001.

Helen Hull Jacobs
Jacobs, Helen Hull. *Beyond the Game: An Autobiography*. Philadelphia, PA: J. B. Lippincott, 1936.

———. *"By Your Leave, Sir": The Story of a WAVE*. New York: Dodd, Mead, 1944.

Andrea Jaeger
Jaeger, Andrea. *First Service: Following God's Calling and Finding Life's Purpose*. Deerfield Beach, FL: Health Communications, 2004.

Pierson, Don. *Andrea Jaeger: Pro in Ponytails*. Sports Stars. Danbury, CT: Childrens Press, 1981. [juvenile].

Billie Jean King
Hahn, James, Lynn Hahn, and Howard Schroeder. *King: The Sports Career of Billie Jean King*. Sports Legends. New York: Crestwood House, 1981. [juvenile].

King, Billie Jean. *Billie Jean*. With Kim Chapin. New York: Harper and Row, 1974.

King, Billie Jean. *Billie Jean*. With Frank Deford. New York: Viking, 1982.

Anna Kournikova
Berman, Connie. *Anna Kournikova*. Women Who Win. New York: Chelsea House, 2001. [juvenile].

Suzanne Lenglen
Little, Alan. *Suzanne Lenglen: Tennis Idol of the Twenties*. London: Wimbledon Lawn Tennis Museum, 1988.

Hana Mandlíková
Mandlíková, Hana. *Hana: An Autobiography*. With Michael Folley. London: Arthur Baker, 1989.

Alice Marble
Marble, Alice. *Courting Danger*. With Dale Leatherman. New York: St. Martin's, 1991.
——. *The Road to Wimbledon*. New York: C. Scribner's Sons, 1946.

Kitty McKane Godfree
Green, Geoffrey. *Kitty Godfree: Lady of a Golden Age*. Kingswood, UK: Kingswood, 1987.

Corina Morariu
Morariu, Corina. *Living through the Racket: How I Survived Leukemia . . . and Rediscovered My Self*. With Allen Rucker. Carlsbad, CA: Hay House, 2010.

Martina Navratilova
Faulkner, Sandra. *Love Match: Nelson vs. Navratilova*. With Judy Nelson. New York: Carol, 1993.
Navratilova, Martina. *Martina*. With George Vecsey. New York: Alfred A. Knopf, 1985.

Renée Richards
Richards, Renée. *Second Serve: The Renée Richards Story*. With John Ames. New York: Stein and Day, 1983.

Arantxa Sánchez Vicario
Burnet, Caroline, and Caroline Harding. *Arantxa Sánchez-Vicario: Fighter, Survivor, Champion*. Bloomington, IN: IUniverse, 2000.

Monica Seles
Seles, Monica. *Monica: From Fear to Victory*. With Nancy Ann Richardson. New York: HarperCollins, 1996.

Maria Sharapova
Glaser, Jason. *Maria Sharapova*. Sports Idols. New York: PowerKids, 2007. [juvenile].
Stewart, Mark. *Maria Sharapova*. Today's Superstars. Pleasantville, NY: Gareth Stevens, 2010. [juvenile].

Pam Shriver

Shriver, Pam, Frank Deford, and Susan Adams. *Passing Shots: Pam Shriver on Tour.* New York: McGraw Hill, 1987.

Margaret Smith Court

Court, Margaret Smith. *Court on Court: A Life in Tennis.* With George McGann. New York: Dodd, Mead, 1975.

Oldfield, Barbara. *Winning Faith: The Margaret Court Story.* Tunbridge, UK: Sovereign World, 1993.

Christine Truman

Truman, Christine. *Tennis Today.* Edited by Kenneth Wheeler. London: Arthur Barker, 1961.

Virginia Wade

Wade, Virginia. *Courting Triumph.* With Mary Lou Mellace. New York: Mayflower Books, 1978.

Serena Williams

Williams, Serena. *On the Line.* With Daniel Paisner. New York: Grand Central, 2009.

Helen Wills

Wills, Heen. *Fifteen–Tthirty: The Story of a Tennis Player.* New York: Scribner, 1937.

Nancye Wynne Bolton

Hill, Warren, and Pam Stockley. *Nancye Wynne Bolton: An Australian Tennis Champion.* Burwood East, Victoria, Australia: Memoirs Foundation, 2009.

C. Instructional

Bjurstedt, Molla, and Samuel Crowther. *Tennis for Women.* New York: Doubleday, Page, 1916.

Davis, Dorothy, ed. *Selected Tennis and Badminton Articles.* Washington, DC: American Association for Health, Physical Education, and Recreation, 1963.

Jacobs, Helen Hull. *Modern Tennis.* Indianapolis, IN: Bobbs Merrill, 1933.

———. *Tennis.* New York: A. S. Barnes, 1941.

King, Billie Jean, and Reginald Brace. *Play Better Tennis.* London: Octopus, 1981.

Lambert Chambers, Dorothea Douglass. *Tennis for Ladies.* London: 1910. [book now in public domain available on Project Gutenberg].

Lenglen, Suzanne. *Lawn Tennis for Girls.* New York: American Sports, 1920.

Navratilova, Martina. *Tennis My Way.* With Mary Carillo. New York: Charles Scribner's Sons, 1983.

Overton, Wendy, et al. *Tennis for Women.* New York: Doubleday, 1973.

Palfrey Cooke, Sarah. *Winning Tennis and How to Play It*. Garden City, NY: Doubleday, 1946.
Round, Dorothy. *Tennis for Girls*. Hitchin, UK: James Nisbet, 1938.

D. Photographic Essay

Bolofo, Koto. *Venus Williams*. London: Steidl, 2008.

E. Other

King, Billie Jean. *Pressure Is a Privilege: Lessons I've Learned from Life and the Battle of the Sexes*. With Christine Brennan. New York: LifeTime Media, 2008.

V. INSTRUCTIONAL

A. Rules and Officiating

Barrett, John, ed. *The Original Rules of Tennis*. Oxford: University of Oxford Press, 2010.
Wingfield, Walter. *The Game of Sphairistike or Lawn Tennis: A Facsimile of the Original (1874) Rules of Tennis*. London: Artists and Photographers', 2008.

B. Coaching

Anderson, Kirk. *Coaching Tennis Technical and Tactical Skills*. Champaign, IL: Human Kinetics, 2009.
King, Billie Jean, and Greg Hoffman. *Tennis Love: A Parents' Guide to the Sport*. New York: MacMillan, 1978.

C. Playing

1. General

Allen, James. *Learn to Play Tennis*. Chicago: Rand McNally, 1968.
Ashe, Arthur. *Arthur Ashe on Tennis*. With Alexander McNab. New York: Alfred A. Knopf, 1995.
———. *Arthur Ashe's Tennis Clinic*. New York: Simon and Schuster, 1981.
Barnaby, John M. *Racket Work: The Key to Tennis*. Boston: Allyn and Bacon, 1969.
Beasley, Mercer. *How to Play Tennis: The Beasley System of Tennis Instruction*. Garden City, NY: Garden City, 1937.
Betz Addie, Pauline. *Tennis for Everyone, with Official USLTA Rules*. Washington DC: Acropolis Books, 1973.

——. *Tennis for Teenagers, with Official USLTA Rules and Leighton Tennis Tests.* New York: Pond, 1966.
Braden, Vic, and Bill Bruns. *Vic Braden's Tennis for the Future.* Boston: Little, Brown, 1977.
Bradlee, Dick. *Instant Tennis.* New York: Simon and Schuster, 1974.
Browne, Mary K. *Design for Tennis.* New York: A. S. Barnes, 1949.
——. *Streamline Tennis.* New York: American Sports, 1940.
——. *Top-Flite Tennis.* New York: American Sports, 1928.
Buchholz, Earl. *Tennis Tips.* St. Louis, MO: Rawlings, 1967.
Budge, J. Donald, and Allison Danzig. *Budge on Tennis.* New York: Prentice-Hall, 1939.
Budge, Lloyd. *Tennis Made Easy.* New York: A. S. Barnes, 1945.
Campbell, Oliver Samuel. *The Game of Lawn Tennis and How to Play It.* New York: American Sports, 1893.
Clark, Rolf. *Breakthrough Tennis.* Washington DC: Farragut, 1991.
Connolly, Maureen. *Power Tennis.* New York: A. S. Barnes, 1954.
Creek, F. N. S. *Teach Yourself Lawn Tennis.* London: English Universities Press, 1958.
Cutler, Merritt. *The Tennis Book.* New York: McGraw Hill, 1967.
Doherty, Hugh Lawrence, and Reginald Frank. *R. F. and H. L. Doherty on Lawn Tennis.* New York: Baker and Taylor, 1903.
Dwight, James. *Practical Lawn-Tennis.* New York: Harper and Brothers, 1893.
Fiske, Loring. *How to Beat Better Tennis Players.* Garden City, NY: Doubleday, 1970.
Fraser, Neale. *Power Tennis.* As told to Ian McDonald. London: Stanley Paul, 1962.
——. *Successful Tennis.* London: Pitman, 1974.
Gallwey, W. Timothy. *The Inner Game of Tennis.* New York: Random House, 1974.
Gensemer, Robert E. *Tennis.* Philadelphia, PA: Saunders, 1969.
Gonzáles, Pancho, and Dick Hawk. *Tennis.* New York: Fleet, 1962.
Gould, Dick. *Tennis, Anyone?* Palo Alto, CA: National, 1971.
Harman, Bob, and Keith Monroe. *Use Your Head in Tennis.* London: Phoenix House, 1951.
Hopman, Harry. *Better Tennis for Boys and Girls.* New York: Dodd, Mead, 1972.
Hotchkiss Wightman, Hazel. *Better Tennis.* New York: Houghton Mifflin, 1933.
Houston, Graham J. *Lawn Tennis.* Liverpool, UK: W. Foulsham, 1964.
Jacobs, Helen Hull. *Young Sportsmen's Guide to Tennis.* New York: Thomas Nelson, 1961.
Johnson, Joan, and Paul Xanthos. *Tennis.* Dubuque, IA: W. C. Brown, 1967.
Jones, Clarence. *How to Play Tennis.* Secaucus, NJ: Chartwell Books, 1979.
Kraft, Virginia. *Tennis Instruction for Fun and Competition.* New York: Grosset and Dunlap, 1976.
King, Billie Jean. *Tennis to Win.* With Kim Chapin. New York: Cornerstone, 1973.
King, Billie Jean, and Reginald Brace. *Play Better Tennis.* London: Octopus, 1981.
King, Billie Jean, and Joe Hyams. *Billie Jean King's Secrets of Winning Tennis.* New York: Holt, Rinehart and Winston, 1974.

Lardner, Rex. *The Complete Beginner's Guide to Tennis.* Garden City, NY: Doubleday, 1967.

———. *Finding and Exploiting Your Opponent's Weaknesses.* Garden City, NY: Doubleday, 1978.

Leighton, Harry "Cap." *Tennis.* New York: Sterling, 1964.

Lendl, Ivan, and George Mendoza. *Hitting Hot: Ivan Lendl's 14-Day Tennis Clinic.* New York: Random House, 1986.

Lendl, Ivan, and Eugene L. Scott. *Ivan Lendl's Power Tennis.* New York: Simon and Schuster, 1986.

Lenglen, Suzanne. *Lawn Tennis: The Game of Nations.* New York: Dodd, Mead, 1925.

Lenglen, Suzanne, and Margaret Morris. *Tennis by Simple Exercises.* London: W. Heinemann, 1937.

Littleford, John. *Tennis Strokes and Tactics: Improve Your Game.* With Andrew Magrath. Buffalo, NY: Firefly Books, 2009.

Loehr, James E. *The Mental Game: Winning at Pressure Tennis.* New York: Penguin, 1991.

Mace, Wynn. *Tennis Techniques Illustrated.* New York: Ronald, 1952.

McEnroe, Patrick. *Tennis for Dummies.* With Peter Bodo. New York: Hungry Minds, 1998.

McLoughlin, Maurice. *Tennis as I Play It.* New York: George H. Doran, 1915.

Metzler, Paul. *Advanced Tennis.* New York: Sterling, 1973.

Morton, Jason, and Russell Seymour. *Winning Tennis after Forty.* With Clyde Burleson. Englewood Cliffs, NJ: Prentice-Hall, 1980.

Mottram, Tony. *Play Better Tennis with Tony Mottram.* London: Stanley Paul, 1971.

Murphy, Bill, and Chet Murphy. *Lifetime Treasury of Tested Tennis Tips: Secrets of Winning Play.* West Nyack, NY: Parker, 1978.

Murray, H. A. *Tennis for Beginners.* North Hollywood, CA: Wilshire, 1974.

Myers, A. Wallis. *Lawn Tennis Its Principles and Practice.* London: Seeley, Service, 1930.

Palfrey, Sarah. *Tennis for Anyone!* New York: Hawthorn Books, 1966.

Paret, Jahial Parmly. *How to Play Lawn Tennis.* New York: American Sports, 1903.

———. *Lawn Tennis Lessons for Beginners.* New York: Macmillan, 1916.

———. *Mechanics of the Game of Lawn Tennis.* New York: American Lawn Tennis, 1926.

———. *Methods and Players of Modern Lawn Tennis.* New York: American Lawn Tennis, 1915.

Patty, John Edward. *Tennis My Way.* New York: Hutchinson, 1951.

Peile, S. C. F. *Lawn Tennis as a Game of Skill.* London: William Blackwood and Sons, 1884.

Ralston, Dennis. *Dennis Ralston's Tennis Workbook.* With Steve Flink and Bud Freeman. Englewood Cliffs, NJ: Prentice-Hall, 1987.

Ramo, Simon. *Extraordinary Tennis for the Ordinary Player.* New York: Crown, 1970.

Rosewall, Ken. *Ken Rosewall on Tennis.* New York: Frederick Fell, 1978.

Round, Dorothy. *Modern Lawn Tennis*. London: G. Newnes, 1935.
Sánchez Vicario, Arantxa. *The Young Tennis Player*. Young Enthusiast. New York: Dorling Kindersley, 1996. [juvenile].
Segura, Pancho. *Pancho Segura's Championship Strategy: How to Play Winning Tennis*. With Gladys Heldman. New York: McGraw Hill, 1976.
Seixas, Vic. *Prime Time Tennis*. With Joel H. Cohen. New York: Scribner, 1983.
Smith, Stan. *Stan Smith's Guide to Better Tennis*. New York: Grosset and Dunlap, 1975.
———. *Stan Smith's Six Tennis Basics*. New York: Atheneum, 1974.
Sports Illustrated. *Sports Illustrated Book of Tennis*. Philadelphia, PA: J. B. Lippincott, 1961.
Summerfield, Sidney C. *Tennis: Learn to Volley First*. New York: Vantage, 1970.
Talbert, William F. *Weekend Tennis*. With Gordon Greer. North Hollywood, CA: Wilshire Book Co., 1974.
Talbert, William F., and Bruce S. Old. *Tennis Tactics: Singles and Doubles*. New York: Harper and Row, 1983.
Tennis Magazine. *Tennis Strokes and Strategies*. New York: Simon and Schuster, 1975.
Tilden, William T. *The Art of Lawn Tennis*. New York: G. H. Doran, 1922.
———. *The Common Sense of Lawn Tennis*. New York: Simon and Schuster, 1924.
———. *The Expert*. New York: American Sports, 1923.
———. *How to Play Better Tennis*. New York: Simon and Schuster, 1969.
———. *Match Play and the Spin of the Ball*. New York: American Lawn Tennis, 1925.
———. *Singles and Doubles*. New York: G. H. Doran, 1923.
———. *Tennis for the Junior Player, the Club Player, the Expert*. New York: American Sports, 1927.
Trabert, Tony. *Trabert on Tennis: The View from Center Court*. Lincolnwood, IL: Contemporary Books, 1988.
Vasquez, Jr., Reggie. *Kids' Book of Tennis*. Secaucus, NJ: Carol, 1997.
Wills, Helen. *Tennis*. New York: C. Scribner's Sons, 1928.

2. Specialized

Connors, Jimmy. *Don't Count Yourself Out! Staying Fit after 35 with Jimmy Connors*. With Neil Gordon and Catherine McEvily Harris. New York: Hyperion Books, 1992.
Gilbert, Brad, and Steve Jamison. *Winning Ugly: Mental Warfare in Tennis—Tales from the Tour and Lessons from a Master*. New York: Simon and Schuster, 1993.
Graebner, Clark, and Carole Graebner. *Mixed Doubles Tennis*. With Kim Prince. New York: McGraw Hill, 1973.
King, Billie Jean, and Fred Stolle. *How to Play Mixed Doubles*. With Greg Hoffman. New York: Simon and Schuster, 1980.
Lott, George, and Jeffrey Bairstow. *How to Play Winning Doubles*. New York: Simon and Schuster, 1979.

Richmond, M. Barrie. *Total Tennis: The Mind-Body Method*. New York: MacMillan, 1980.
Schwed, Peter. *Quality Tennis after 50 . . . or 60 . . . or 70 . . . or . . . .* New York: St. Martin's, 1990.
———. *Sinister Tennis: How to Play against and with Left-Handers*. Garden City, NY: Doubleday, 1975.
Smith, Stan. *Stan Smith's Winning Doubles*. Champaign, IL: Human Kinetics, 2002.
Talbert, William F., and Bruce S. Old. *The Game of Doubles in Tennis*. Philadelphia, PA: J. B. Lippincott, 1968.
———. *The Game of Singles in Tennis*. Philadelphia, PA: J. B. Lippincott, 1962.
Trabert, Tony, and Jim Hook. *The Serve: Key to Winning Tennis*. New York: Dodd, Mead, 1984.

D. Combination Instructional and History

Paret, Jahial Parmley. *Lawn Tennis: It's Past, Present, and Future*. New York: Macmillan, 1904.
Pollard, Jack, ed. *Lawn Tennis: The Australian Way*. New York: Drake, 1973.
Teeman, Lawrence, ed. *Consumer Guide Magazine Complete Guide to Tennis*. Skokie, IL: Consumer Guide, 1975.
Vines, Ellsworth, and Gene Vier. *Tennis: Myth and Method*. New York: Viking, 1978.

VI. OTHER BOOKS

A. Anthology

Bartlett, Michael, and Bob Gillen. *The Tennis Book*. New York: Arbor House, 1981.
Danzig, Allison, and Peter Schwed, eds. *The Fireside Book of Tennis*. New York: Simon and Schuster, 1972.

B. Fiction

1. Tennis

Bredes, Don. *Muldoon*. New York: Holt, Rinehart, Winston, 1982.
Goodchild, George. *Death on the Center Court*. New York: Green Circle, 1936.
Jacobs, Helen Hull. *Center Court*. New York: A. S. Barnes, 1950.
———. *Judy, Tennis Ace*. New York: Dodd, Mead, 1951. [juvenile].
———. *Proudly She Serves!* New York: Dodd, Mead, 1953.
———. *Storm against the Wind*. New York: Dodd, Mead, 1944.
———. *The Tennis Machine*. New York: Scribner, 1972. [juvenile].
Jennings, Jay, ed. *Tennis and the Meaning of Life: A Literary Anthology of the Game*. New York: Harcourt, Brace, 1995.

Marx, Arthur. *Set to Kill.* Fort Lee, NJ: Barricade Books, 1993.
Năstase, Ilie. *Break Point.* New York: St. Martin's, 1986.
Navratilova, Martina. *The Total Zone.* With Liz Nickles. New York: Villard, 1994.
Tilden, William T., II. *Glory's Net.* Garden City, NY: Doubleday, 1930.
———. *It's All in the Game, and Other Tennis Tales.* Garden City, NY: Doubleday, Page, 1922. [juvenile].
———. *The Phantom Drive, and Other Tennis Stories.* New York: American Lawn Tennis, 1924. [juvenile].
———. *The Pinch Quitter, and Other Tennis Stories for Junior Players.* New York: American Lawn Tennis, 1924. [juvenile].
Wills, Helen, and Robert W. Murphy. *Death Serves an Ace.* New York: Scribner's, 1939.

2. Other Fiction by Tennis Players

Cahill, Mabel Esmonde. *Carved in Marble.* New York: Worthington, 1892.
———. *Her Playthings, Men: A Novel.* New York, Worthington, 1891.
———. *Purple Sparkling.* New York: Worthington, 1892.
Jacobs, Helen Hull. *Adventure in Bluejeans.* New York: Dodd, Mead, 1947. [juvenile].
———. *Courage to Conquer.* New York: Dodd, Mead, 1967. [juvenile].

C. Humor

Fein, Paul. *You Can Quote Me on That: Greatest Tennis Quips, Insights, and Zingers.* Washington: Potomac Books, 2005.
Lardner, Rex. *The Fine Art of Tennis Hustling.* New York: Hawthorn Books, 1975.
———. *The Underhanded Serve; or, How to Play Dirty Tennis.* New York: Hawthorn Books, 1968.
Liebman, Glenn. *Tennis Shorts: 1,001 of the Game's Funniest One-Liners.* Lincolnwood, IL: Contemporary Books, 1997.
Wiltse, David, ed. *It Only Hurts When I Serve.* Norwalk, CT: Golf Digest/Tennis, 1980.

D. Nontennis Books by Tennis Players

Ashe, Arthur. *A Hard Road to Glory.* 3 vols. New York: Amistad, 1993.
Jacobs, Helen Hull. *Better Physical Fitness for Girls.* New York: Dodd, Mead, 1964.
Paret, Jahial Parmly. *The Women's Book of Sports.* New York: D. Appleton, 1901.
Wooden, John. *Inch and Miles: The Journey to Success.* With Steve Jamison and Peanut Louie Harper. Logan, IA: Perfection Learning, 2003. [juvenile].

E. Other Racquet Sports

1. Badminton

Jackson, Carl H., and Lester A. Swan. *Better Badminton.* New York: A. S. Barnes, 1939.

Pelton, Barry C. *Badminton.* Englewood Cliffs, NJ: Prentice-Hall, 1971.

2. Court Tennis

Danzig, Allison. *The Winning Gallery.* New York: United States Court Tennis Association, 1987.

Etchebaster, Pierre. *Pierre's Book.* Barre, MA: Barre, 1971.

Ronaldson, Chris. *Tennis: A Cut above the Rest.* Oxford: Ronaldson, 1985.

3. Squash Racquets

Potter, Arthur M. *Squash Racquets.* Annapolis, MD: United States Naval Institute, 1966.

4. General

Aberdare, Clarence Napier Bruce, ed. *Rackets, Squash Rackets, Tennis, Fives and Badminton.* Philadelphia, PA: J. P. Lippincott, 1933.

Danzig, Allison. *The Racquet Game.* New York: MacMillan, 1930.

Squires, Dick. *The Other Racquet Sports.* New York: McGraw Hill, 1978.

F. Miscellaneous

Casewit, Curtis. *America's Tennis Book.* New York: Charles Scribner's Sons, 1975.

Cox, Roger. *The World's Best Tennis Vacations.* New York: Penguin, 1990.

Frazier, Claude A., ed. *The Doctors' Guide to Better Tennis and Health.* New York: Funk and Wagnalls, 1974.

Gordon, Dee, De Lora Maurus, and Shirley Gorospe. *Celebrities Serve: A Celebrity Tennis Cookbook.* Newport, RI: Chefs to the Court, 1991.

Hess, Kenneth G. *The Tennis Alphabet: A Celebration of Tennis from A to Z.* New York: Simon and Schuster, 1991.

Scott, Eugene. *The Tennis Experience.* New York: Larousse, 1979.

Tennis Magazine. *Tennis Player's Handbook: A Buyer's Guide and Service Directory.* Norwalk, CT: Tennis Magazine, 1980.

Tingay, Lance. *The Guinness Book of Tennis Facts and Feats.* Enfield, UK: Sterling, 1983.

G. Foreign Language

1. Czech

Janousek, Jiri, and Pavel Vitous. *Ivan Lendl*. Prague: Lidove Nakladatelstvi, 1990.

2. Dutch

de Bie, Eric. *De Missie van Richard Krajicek*. Amsterdam: L. J. Veen, 1997.
Krajicek, Richard. *Harde Ballen*. Baarn, the Netherlands: Tirion, 2005.
———. *Honger Naar de Bal*. Baarn, the Netherlands: Tirion, 2006.
Nienaber, L. J. *Tennis Sport en Spel*. Amsterdam: C. A. J. van Dishoeck, 1962.

3. French

Lambert, Gilles. *La Legende des Mousquetaires*. Paris: Presses de la Cité, 1982.
Noah, Yannick. *T'as Pas Deux Balles?* Paris: Stock, 1984.
Tillier, Jean, René Lacoste, and Henri Darsonval. *La Méthode d'initiation au Tennis de Suzanne Lenglen*. Paris: Gallimard, 1942.

4. German

Bosch, Günther. *Boris*. Berlin: Ullstein-Verlag, 1986.
Steinkamp, Egon W. *Gottfried von Cramm, der Tennisbaron: Eine Biographie*. Munich, Germany: Herbig, 1990.

5. Italian

Clerici, Gianni. *500 Anni di Tennis*. Segrate, Italy: Mondadori, 1975.
———. *Divina: Suzanne Lenglen—La Più Grande Tennista del Mondo*. Milan, Italy: Fandango Tascabili, 2010.
———. *Gianni Clerici agli Internazionali d'Italia. Cronache dello scriba, 1930–2110*. Milan, Italy: Rizzoli, 2010.
———. *Postumo in Vita*. Milan, Italy: Writers/Sartorio, 2005.
Lombardi, Roberto. *100 Anni di Tennis in Italia*. Rome: Federazione Italiana Tennis, 2010.

6. Portuguese

Cleto, Paulo. *Gustavo Kuerten e Roland Garros: Uma História de Amor*. São Paulo, Brazil: Instituto Takano, 2002.

7. Spanish

Murray, John F. *Tenis Inteligente*. Barcelona, Spain: Editorial Paidotribo, 2001.

8. Swedish

Wilander, Mats, and Per Yng. *Mats Wilander och Spelet Bakom Rubrikerna.* Stockholm: Wahlstrom, 1990.

VII. PERIODICALS

A. English Language

Ace Tennis Magazine, London, bimonthly.
American Lawn Tennis, New York, monthly.
Australian Tennis Magazine, Melbourne: Tennis Australia, Ltd., monthly (1976–2010).
Black Tennis. (1977–).
British Lawn Tennis and Squash
Eastern Tennis Magazine. (1960–64).
Inside Tennis
International Tennis Weekly. Association of Tennis Professionals (1987–).
ITF World
Racquet Quarterly. New York: Heather and Pine (1981–).
Racquet Sports Industry
Tennis. Des Moines, IA. (1965–).
Tennis Annual. Norwalk, CT: Tennis Features (1978–).
Tennis Industry
Tennis USA. New York: United States Tennis Association (1966–).
Tennis Week. (1987–).
World Tennis. Boulder, CO. (1953–).

B. Foreign Language

French: *Tennis de France*
German: *Tennis Magazin*
Italian: *Tennis Italiano*
Spanish: *Tennis Espanol*

VIII. WEBSITES OF INTEREST

Davis Cup, extremely comprehensive site: www.daviscup.com
International Tennis Hall of Fame and Museum: www.tennisfame.com
Federation Cup site with historical records: www.fedcup.com
Tennis Collectables, excellent store specializing in tennis books: www.tenniscollectables.com
Australian Open, tournament details (current and historical): www.australianopen.com

Roland Garros, tournament details (current and historical): www.rolandgarros.com
Wimbledon, tournament details (current and historical): www.wimbledon.org
U.S. Open, tournament details (current and historical): www.usopen.org
Australian Dictionary of Biography, excellent source for biographical information on early Australian players and administrators who died prior to 1980. Subsequent editions will contain players who died after 1980: adbonline.anu.edu.au/adbonline.htm
Association of Tennis Professionals: www.atpworldtour.com
Women's Tennis Association: www.sonyericssonwtatour.com
International Tennis Federation: www.itftennis.com
United States Tennis Association: www.usta.com

In addition, many tennis professionals maintain their own websites with varying degrees of skill and information.

About the Author

John Grasso has written on boxing and basketball and has traveled extensively—visiting more than 40 countries and attending 7 Olympic Games. An amateur tennis player, he has seen Olympic tennis in Korea, Greece, and the United States; the U.S. Open and World Team Tennis in New York and Chicago; and Challenger-level tennis in Binghamton, New York.

He is an Olympic historian and has been the treasurer of the International Society of Olympic Historians (ISOH) since 2004 and is a member of Association for Professional Basketball Research and the North American Society for Sport History (NASSH) and was the founder of the International Boxing Research Organization (IBRO) in 1982.

His published boxing work includes *505 Boxing Questions Your Friends Can't Answer* with Bert R. Sugar, *The 100 Greatest Boxers of All Time* with Bert R. Sugar, *The Olympic Games Boxing Record Book*, and *1984 Ring Record Book and Boxing Encyclopedia*. He also contributed boxing essays to the *Biographical Dictionary of American Sports* and to *American National Biography* as well as several columns to *Ring Magazine* and *Boxing and Wrestling Magazine*.

His basketball work includes: the *Historical Dictionary of Basketball*, the section on early professional basketball with Robert Bradley in *Total Basketball*, and two monographs—*The Absurd "Official" Statistics of the 1954–55 NBA Season* and *Olympic Games Basketball Records*.

This is his first book on tennis, but in preparation for it, he has become a member of the International Tennis Hall of Fame and Museum, made three trips to its museum at the Newport Casino in Newport, Rhode Island, played tennis on the grass courts there, watched Mardy Fish win the Hall of Fame tennis tournament, watched the Binghamton Challenger USTA Pro Tournament event, and expanded his tennis library ten-fold, from about two dozen books to over two hundred books and magazines.